CLASSICS IN LOGIC

CLASSICS IN LOGIC

Readings in Epistemology, Theory of Knowledge and Dialectics

Edited by Dagobert D. Runes

Philosophical Library   -   New York

Type set at The Polyglot Press, New York

Printed in the United States of America

PREFACE

THIS Preface is, like most others, written at the end of the book and not at its beginning. After my work of compilation, assembly as well as elimination is done and I have finished jotting down a few notes about each of the scholars quoted, so as to refresh the reader about the tide and time of the respective logician, I feel hesitant to engage in the customary practice of summarizing and recapitulating the writings of these outstanding personalities.

Let them speak for themselves, and let me say only as little as I had to.

However, if it so pleases the reader, I would like to make known in the following some of my personal ideas on the subject of man's mind and motivations.

Man's principles of logic, the fundamental categories of his thinking processes, are universal and identical, not only in today's world, from nation to nation, race to race, group to group, and sex to sex, but also historically. The structure of civilized man's thinking apparatus of the past and of tomorrow, as far as we can analyze documents and actions, is the same. We could not live together with our fellow citizens for a single day without confusing or even destroying each other were this not the case.

The most ancient proverbs, as well as codes going back almost ten thousand years, seem to have been based upon processes quite similar to ours, indeed, identical with ours. If twentieth century *anthropos* could be placed in the city of Jericho seven thousand years ago, provided he knew the language, he would quickly fall in line with what the citizens of that city considered the way of life and the way of work, the way of sin and the way of strife. Even their gods would appear to him quite familiar; perhaps more so than, let us say, the familiars of present-day witchcraft devotees in California. By the same token, if an aborigine, pulled out of the Congolese or Australian bushlands, could be placed directly in the heart of a modern metropolis, how very quickly he would merge with its activity!

Man's treasury of accumulated facts (and sometimes, fancies) has grown considerably since what we choose to call the dawn of civilization, but that is only the dawn of the finding of documents of civilization such as writings and artifacts. Man may have lived for a million years on the level of an African jungle creature, leaving not a single trace of what we refer to as cultural objects, yet this very jungle creature thinks today and undoubtedly did then in the very same manner we do.

Man's thinking processes are universal in time and space.

However, man's thinking differs not only in time and space, but even from person to person, from sex to sex, from group to group, in accordance with the differences in the respective emotional grounds in which that thinking is rooted.

I should like to point out that large segments of applied thought are hardly, if at all, affected by this emotional grounding. I am referring to such general faculties as mathematics, physics, mechanics, technology, and other subjects of similar character that frequently in the past led philosophers, especially in the days of Descartes, to profess that such forms of mechanical and mathematical thinking were the only manner by which truth could be found.

Be this as it may, such mathematical and mechanical subjects do not disturb the peace of mind of man nor the peace or order of nations. Their pursuit is limited by the natural limitations of human understanding. Where there are differences, added information will in time doubtless resolve them to everybody's satisfaction, and if unresolved, no one will be very much perturbed by it excepting the few that to begin with were interested in the problem.

What concerns us strongly, very strongly indeed, is the thought

processes governing the rest of man's preoccupation, going beyond the mere technological issues of daily living, beyond the
mathematical queries in mechanics and other sciences. Excluding the above, all man's thinking is motivated. And it differs
from that of his fellow creatures only to the extent that his
motives differ. These motives are often hidden; hidden from the
observer, but also from the participant. *Tell me your motives,
and I will tell you your thoughts.* Or, if you prefer, tell me your
thoughts and I will tell you your motives.

Although the above is axiomatic, man's inner motivations are
quite intricate and complicated; more often than not, there is
a combination of motives that shapes the resolves of man, and
not a single affection. Underneath all this remains man's sub-
liminal emotional drive for self-preservation that differs in intensity and orientation, but never in direction. Motives are
sometimes uncouth and blatant, like those of the Southern White
Council member who thinks the Negro is savage, but who
actually is in fear of the black man's competition. Motives are
sometimes mere ambitious greed, like those of the Southern
rabble-rouser who, knowing differently, pursues a line of Negro
slander in order to gain an election. Motives may be subtle,
like those of a physiologically weak white specimen threatening
or assaulting a helpless black man in order to impress his friends
or a sexual companion with his prowess. Motives may lie in
traditional hatred, inculcated in Southern persons by their elders.

I could go on and enumerate scores of variations in motivation
that may, and do, lead to anti-Negro thinking. This method may
be applied to similar though slightly different relations between
any dominant and minority group. It should not be difficult at
all to analyze the thinking of the Germans of the Hitler era or
the Ukrainians of the present era in their relationship to the
Jewish minority; these two large nations have developed, from
a whole set of ugly envy motivations, a Mephistophelian thought-
pattern about the Jews which exists nowhere but in their de-
cadent minds.

What has driven their minds into a frightful, morbid corner

Preface

is not a variation in thinking, but rather a variation in their emotional grounding.

It is interesting to note that persons beset with superiority pretensions are indeed people suffering from severe feelings of inferiority who try to attach their own blemishes to a helpless minority group. For instance, the Russians, and especially the Ukrainians, professing to an international solidarity, but in fact imbued by strong national pride, accuse their Jewish fellow citizens of Zionistic nationalism; the Communists, who relentlessly pursue a policy of world conquest while pretending to sponsor self-determination of the little nations, accuse the Jews of desiring to control the world; the Communists, who run their government by a self-perpetuating clique in the Kremlin, under a system by which the people are never given even the semblance of a choice, accuse the government of Israel of dictatorship, a government which has the most democratic election procedure in all of Asia. We will often find that persons attack those they deride mainly on points in which they themselves are most vulnerable. Perhaps the intensity of their dislike is fanned by the guilt feelings over their own inadequacy.

Every man in every nation likes to sail under the unfurling banner of some glorious slogan even if he carries a cargo of destruction and pestilence in his pirate hold.

D. D. R.

viii

Contents

x

xii

PETER ABAILARD
(1079-1142)

One of the most eminent representatives of early Scholasticism. He studied logic with the nominalist Roscellinus and with William of Champeaux. His religious views were censored by the Church. He taught dialectics and metaphysics at Notre Dame in Paris and other French schools of theology and philosophy. His work on the methodology of doubt, *Sic et non*, frequently attacked by the patristic authorities, was a major contribution to medieval dialectics and found many epigones. His tragic love interlude with Héloise obtained for him early and undesired popularity. He died at Cluny, having made his peace with the Church.

Main Works:

Theologia "Summi Boni" (Tract. de unitate et trinitate divina); Theologia christiana; Theologia "scholarium" (Introd. ad theologiam); Comm. in epistolam ad Romanos; Sic et non; Historia calamitatum; Scito Te ipsum; Logica ingredientibus.

Obscurity as Sources of Error

Since in the vast outpouring of words many sayings of the Saints seem not only contradictory, but self-contradictory, it should not be considered unreasonable to pass judgment on those through whom the universe itself must be judged, as it is written: The Saints shall judge the nations. And again: You shall sit in judgment. Nor should we presume to accuse them of mendacity, or spurn them for their errors, to whom it was said by the Lord:

From: *Sic et Non.*

1

Who hearkens to you, hearkens to me: who scorns you, scorns me. Acknowledging therefore our defectiveness let us believe rather that it is we who lack grace in understanding them than they did in writing, for it was said to them by the Gospel itself: For it is not you who speak, but the spirit of your father who speaks to you.

What then is so strange if, lacking the spirit itself through which those words were written and said, we also lack the understanding inherent in those writers, in the attainment of which their unusual style of expression is a very great hindrance, as well as the contradictory meanings of the same terms, since the same word involves different connotations at different times. In fact, each writer is as prolific in meanings as in their expression. And since, according to Cicero, identity in all things is the mother of satiety, that is, it produces disgust, words themselves too ought to be varied in the same subject; nor is it necessary to refrain from the ordinary and common terminology in all instances. For, as St. Augustine declares, those words are hidden to prevent them from deteriorating and so they are all the more acceptable, the more eagerly they are searched for and the greater the difficulty in finding them. Often, too, as a diversion for those to whom we are speaking, it is necessary to change words: since it frequently happens that the proper meaning of a word is unknown or rather rare to many. If we wish to speak to them in regard to doctrine, we must emulate their usage of terminology rather than the exactitude of their speech, as that master of grammar and guide in idiom Priscian advocates. That most learned father of the Church, St. Augustine, when in his treatise on Christian Doctrine he was instructing a father of the Church, advised him to disregard all those things that obstructed the intelligence of those to whom he spoke, and to shun both the ornate style and exactitude of phraseology, if he could secure understanding more readily without them: the teacher, he adds, not being concerned how eloquently he teaches, but how lucidly. *An eager appetite at times disregards the more polished words.* Hence a certain scholar declared, when discussing such a style of expression, that it had a kind of careful negligence. Likewise: Good scholars show such didactic concern that a word which, unless obscure or ambiguous, cannot be Latin, is pronounced in the so-called popular manner to avoid ambiguity and obscurity, not as it is usually pronounced by the learned, but rather by the masses. For if our interpreters were not ashamed to speak of blood offerings, since they felt it pertinent, in the context, to pronounce this word in the plural, which in the Latin tongue is expressed in the singular only, why should a doctor of divinity addressing the illiterate be ashamed to say *ossum* rather than *os*, to prevent confusion between *ossa* and *ora?* For what avails correct speech that is not understood by the hearer, when there is no reason whatever for speaking, if what we say is not understood by those to whose understanding we are appealing. The teacher, then, will shun all words that do not inform. It is a mark of a noble character to love the truth in words, not the words. For what is the purpose of a golden key, if it cannot open what we want? Or what objection is there to a wooden key, if it is effective, since we seek only to reveal what is concealed?

Who also could not see how unreasonable it is for one man to judge the intent and understanding of another? Since our hearts and thoughts are open to God alone, who recalls us from this presumption too, saying: Do not judge and ye shall not be judged. And the apostle says: Do not judge before the time, until there will come he who will illuminate what is hidden in darkness and reveal the counsels of the heart. As if he were openly declaring: Entrust your judgment in such things to him who alone knows all and discerns thoughts themselves, in respect of which and of his secret mysteries it is figuratively written about the Paschal Lamb: If anything is left, let it be burned by fire: that is, if there is anything in the divine mysteries that we cannot understand, let us reserve it for enlightenment to the spirit, through which they have been written, rather than define it unreasonably.

It behooves us also to take careful precautions, when confronted with some of the sayings of the Saints as being contradictory or at variance with the truth, to prevent our being misled by a wrong ascription of title or a corrupt reading. For many apocryphal passages, to give them authority, are attributed to the Saints. And many passages, even in the Holy Scriptures, have been corrupted through the fault of the copyists. Hence Jerome, that most scrupulous writer and most veracious interpreter, writing to Laeta on the training of her daughter, warned us, with these words: Let her beware of all Apocrypha; and if at any time she desires to read them not for the truth of their dogmas but through respect for the names, she should know that they are not the work of those with whose names they are identified, and that it is a mark of great prudence to seek gold in the mud. So with Psalm 77, in respect of the title, which means this: Asaph said: It is written according to St. Matthew. When the Lord had spoken in parables and they did not understand, etc.. These things are done, he said, to fulfil what was written through the prophet Isaiah: I sall open my mouth in parables. The Gospels have it so to this day. This is not what Isaiah says, but Asaph.

Similarly, then, let us simply say, as it is written in Matthew and John, that at the sixth hour the Lord was crucified, and in Mark, at the third hour. This was a copyist's error, and in Mark it was written, at the sixth hour. But many took the gamma for a Greek monogram, so there was a copyist's mistake, writing Isaiah for Asaph. For we know that many congregations consisted of ignorant gentiles. Since then they read in the Gospel: *To fulfil what was written in Asaph the prophet*, the first copyist of the Gospel began by saying: Who is this Asaph the prophet? He was not known among the people. And what did he do? To correct the mistake, he made another one. Let us say something like this in another passage in Matthew: He brought thirty pieces of silver, the price of him that was valued, as it was written in Jeremiah the prophet. In Jeremiah we cannot find this at all, but in Zachariah. You see therefore that this mistake was like the other one. What is so strange then if, in the Gospels, too, many passages were corrupted through the ignorance of the copyists, as frequently occurs in the writings of the later Fathers, who are of far lesser authority? So if something in the writings of the Saints happens to appear inconsistent with the truth, it is a pious and charitable act, a mark of humility, that believes everything, hopes for everything, and suffers everything, and does not readily suspect the weaknesses of those whom it embraces, for us to believe that a passage in the Scriptures was not faithfully interpreted or was corrupted, or to admit that we do not understand it.

Nor do I think that less consideration should be given to the question whether such passages are those that are taken from the writings of the Saints, or that have elsewhere been retracted by them, and, after discovering the truth later on, have been emended, as St. Augustine did in many instances. Or they gave their views in accordance with the opinion of others rather than their own just as in many passages Ecclesiastes introduces the contrary views of various authorities, and even confusedly interprets them, according to the testimony of Saint Gregory, in his fourth Dialogue. Or they rather left in question those passages in their search for a convincing definition, as the aforesaid venerable learned Augustine declares he did in his edition of Genesis. Mentioning first of all his retractions in this work, he says: In this book more things have been sought than found, and of those found, fewer have been confirmed, while the rest are such as still require further search.

With the testimony too of Saint Jerome, we know that the procedure of the Catholic doctors was such that in their commentaries they even included, along with their own views, the worst opinions of the heretics, while, in their zeal for perfection, rejoicing that they omitted nothing of the ancients.

Poetry and philosophical writings also express many opinions as if they are completely at variance with truth. Hence Ovid:

> The grass is always greener in the other field
> And neighbors' cattle give a greater yield.

When Boethius too in the Fourth Topic said that accident and substance are the first two genera, he considered opinion rather than truth. The philosophers as well made many assertions based on the opinions of others rather than on their own. Cicero, in Book 2 of *De Officiis,* clearly admits it in these words: Since justice has sufficient authority without wisdom, wisdom without justice is of no avail in inspiring faith. For the more shrewd and clever a man is, the more he is an object of jealousy and suspicion, his reputation for honesty being destroyed. Therefore justice added to intelligence will have all the power it wants to inspire faith. Justice without wisdom will avail to a large extent: without justice wisdom will be of no avail. But let no one wonder why, since it is accepted by all philosophers and has often been disputed by me that the man who has one virtue has all the virtues, I now separate them as if anyone could be just without being wise. There is a difference between truth that is investigated carefully in disputation, and truth in a speech suited to all listeners. For this reason, we talk like the people, saying some men are brave, others are good, others are wise. In short, in ordinary conversation many statements, based on the physical senses, are made contrary to the actual facts. For although there is no place in the whole world that is completely empty, without being filled with either air or some body, yet we say that a box is quite empty, in which we perceive nothing visible. The man who judges things according to his sight sometimes says that the heavens are studded with stars, and sometimes not: that at times the sun is hot, and again very cold, or that at one time the moon shines more or less, at another time it does not shine at all, although these things always remain the same in fact, yet do not always appear so to us. Then what is so surprising, if many passages have sometimes been put forward or even written by the Holy Fathers too from opinion rather than truth? There should be a thorough examination, when different statements are made about the same thing, of this point too: What is intended as a summation of a precept, what as a remission of indulgence, what as an exhortation to perfection, so that we may seek a solution for the diversity according to the diversity of intentions. If it is a precept, whether general or particular, that is, whether it is directed to all men in general or to some specially. The occasion too must be distinguished and the reasons for dispensations, because what is often granted at one moment is found to be prohibitive at another time; and what is often prescribed as a rigorous measure is sometimes tempered by a dispensation. In the institutions of the ecclesiastical decrees or canons these points must be carefully distinguished. Generally an easy solution for the controversies will be found, if we can defend the same expressions used in different connotations by different writers.

By all these methods previously described the diligent reader will attempt to resolve the contradictions in the writings of the Saints. But if the contradiction happens to be so flagrant that it can be resolved in no manner whatever, authorities must be compared, and the one that carries greater testimony and more convincing confirmation should be preferably retained. Hence Isidore's note to Bishop Massio: At the end of the letter I thought that this should be added, that whenever in the Acts of the Councils a divergent opinion is found, his opinion should be held of greater import whose authority is older or more dominating. It is agreed that the prophets themselves sometimes lacked the grace of prophecy and that from their practice of prophesying, believing that they had the spirit of prophesying, they uttered many false prophecies through their spirit: and this must be granted them for the protection of their humility, that they thus discovered more truly what kind of men lived by the spirit of God, and what kind by their own spirit, and that when they had the spirit that cannot lie or deceive, it was a gift. Just as this spirit does not confer all gifts on one man, so it does not illuminate the mind of the man that it fills on all subjects, but reveals only occasional secrets, and when it discloses one, it conceals another.

This St. Gregory in his first homily on Ezekiel illustrates with illuminating examples, that the chief of the Apostles, who shone with so many gifts and miracles of divine grace, after that special emanation of the holy spirit promised by the Lord, that teaches his disciples the whole truth, lapsed into error in regard to the observance of circumcision and certain ancient rites, when he was gravely and properly publicly corrected by his co-apostle Paul. What is so strange, when it is known that even the prophets themselves and the apostles were not utterly free from error, if in such a voluminous mass of writings of the Holy Fathers some seem to have been produced and written erroneously for the reason given above? But it is not right for the Saints to be accused of mendacity, if, thinking that some passages are contrary to the true facts, they so declare, not through duplicity, but through ignorance. Nor should whatever is said charitably for edification be imputed as sinful presumption, since with the Lord it is fitting for everything to be viewed for the intention, as it is written: If your eye is simple, your entire body will be clear.

With these introductory remarks, my plan is, as I resolved, to collect various writings of the Holy Fathers that occur to my memory: some of them, in their apparent disagreement, provoking investigation and challenging young readers to the fullest exercise in tracking down the truth and making them all the more keen as a result.

This is defined as the first key to wisdom, namely, constant or frequent inquiry. Aristotle, the most discerning of all philosophers, exhorting students to grasp that key ardently, in the category *aliquid*: It is perhaps difficult to speak confidently of such matters, unless they have been subject to frequent investigation. To doubt particular things will not be useless.

For by doubt we come to inquiry. By inquiry we perceive the truth. In this regard the Gospel itself says: Seek, and ye shall find. Knock, and it will be opened to you.

Instructing us morally by his own example, the Lord, in the twelfth year of his age, preferred to be found sitting and questioning in the midst of the learned men, displaying to us rather the appearance of a pupil questioning than a master preaching, although the total and perfect wisdom of God was in him.

Now when certain sayings in the Scriptures are brought forward, they arouse and entice the reader to an investigation of the truth in proportion to the authority attached to the writing itself.

Peter Abailard

Hence we resolved to prescribe for this work of ours, compiled in one volume from the sayings of the Saints, the decree of Pope Gelasius on the authentic books, to prove that we have included nothing from the Apocrypha. We have also added excerpts from the retractions of St. Augustine, from which it is evident that none of his corrections by retractions have been included herein.

ALBERTUS MAGNUS
(1193-1280)

Born in Bavaria as Albert, Count of Bollstaedt; studied at Padua and Bologna; entered the Dominican Order in 1223 and served for a while as Bishop of Regensburg. He taught theology in several German cities as well as Cologne and Paris. Albertus, referred to as Magnus, and Doctor Universalis, was a considerable student of the natural sciences as well as an outstanding philosopher and theologian. In his efforts toward a synthesis of Greek, Arabic and Hebrew writings his numerous papers constitute a veritable library of metaphysical and scientific literature of the thirteenth century.

Main Works:

Summa theologiae; Summa de Creaturis; De Causis; De Intellectu et Intelligibili.

On the Nature of the Intellect

I.

As we said at the beginning of this work, the science of the soul is not complete enough in that which, in the book *on the Soul,* has been determined concerning the soul in respect to itself alone. For in addition to that it is necessary to know about the objects which occasion the passion proper to the parts of the soul. Of these objects of which the soul has passive qualities for parts or powers, some occasion passions peculiar to the soul. Of these objects of which the soul has passive qualities for

---

From: *Parva Naturalia, De Intellectu et Intelligibili.*

parts or powers, some occasion passions peculiar to the soul, and some arouse passions common to soul and body. For passions are common which are such that the soul uses a corporeal instrument in operating with them, such as the passions which have to do with the vegetative and the sensitive soul. Because of that circumstance, moreover, the ancient peripatetics said that the sciences of such common passions were sciences of the soul and the body. We have already treated in part, in our small measure, of these passions in the books *on Nutriment and the Nutrible* and *on Sense and the Sensed.* There remain still however the books *on Sleep and Waking, on Youth and Old Age, on Inspiration and Expiration,* and *on the Motions* which are called *Animal, on Life and Death,* which are all concerning the common operations of soul and body.

But since the interpretation and nature of sleep can not be determined definitely, unless one have knowledge first of the intellect and the intelligible, it is necessary that we interpose here the science of the intellect and the intelligible, even though understanding [*intelligere*] is proper to the human soul apart from the body. For we consider, as we have often insisted, principally the facility of doctrine: because of this we follow in the translation of the books of natural sciences the order by which the auditor is more easily taught, rather than the order of natural things. And for this reason we did not hold, in the sequence of these books, to the order which we set forth in our introduction where we stated the division of the books of natural sciences.

In treating of the intellect and the intelligible, moreover, we shall take for granted any principles which have been determined appropriately in the third book of our work *on the Soul.* But whatsoever it seems necessary to inquire into here, we shall treat, so far as we shall be able to investigate, by demonstration and reason, following in the footsteps of our prince, for although we have not seen his book on this science, we have examined a great many books and letters of many of his disciples which treat of this matter very well. Moreover we shall bear in mind the position of Plato too in these doctrines of the peripatetics.

Since, moreover, according to a great many of the sounder philosophers, the intellect makes the intelligible in the form of intelligibility, it is necessary that we speak first of the nature of the intellect with respect to what the intellect is, and then of the intelligible with respect to what it is in relation to the intellect, and then of the unity and diversity of the intellect with respect to intelligibles: for when these points are known, one has a sufficiently perfect knowledge of the intellect and the intelligible. The value of the investigation moreover is this, that when the above things are known, man knows properly what he himself properly is, since he is intellect alone, as Aristotle says in Book X of the *Ethics*, and he knows moreover the principle of those actions which make for contemplative felicity in him. Therefore in beginning the investigation of the nature of the intellect, we shall state first the things which are prior in nature.

II.

Let us say then that every nature which has the power of knowing any thing either has the power of knowledge from itself or from some other nature which is anterior to it. But it is known that it does not have it from itself, for then it would itself be the principle of cognition in all other things, and its own cognitive power would not be imperfect, but perfect, not passive but active; all of these conclusions are not in accordance with the souls of animals, as is clear from what was stated in the book *on the Soul*.

If, however, any one should say that the soul of animals has its cognitive power from itself, in that its cognitive power is in its own nature, just as the triangle must from its own nature have three angles, etc., and because of this there is no principle causing any thing in other things, we shall say that a thing may be said to have a property from itself in two ways. In one way according to the formal cause. We however are inquiring here concerning that which is cognitive through itself according to both causes, just as in physics the first mover is moved by itself as well because it does not have an efficient cause of its motion anterior to itself as because it is by its nature and its essence a mover: because of it, furthermore, all that it moves has motive power from it, and its motive power influences like a fountain all motive powers in all other moving things. For in inquiring thus whether the soul of animals is cognitive by itself, the things which have been determined before follow. For since everything which is created by that which is nobler falls away necessarily from the first cause, the defect of cognition which is in the cognitive power of the soul of animals shows not only that it has its cognitive power from something other than itself, but also that it is far removed from that which is the first cause and fountain of cognition. What it has from some certain thing other than itself, which is first and perfectly cognitive of all things, must therefore be stated. For if the soul be said to have it from something else which is not first and perfectly, there would be the same question concerning that, and the process would go on *in infinitum,* or else the soul will be in the first and perfect cognitive.

Moreover, every cognitive element of mortal animals, is the same in genus with every cognitive element of mortals; or if one were said to be prior or posterior, it is with respect to some one thing. But everything which has such an agreement and unity of genus or nature, proceeds from some one thing which is the cause of agreement of that genus in all its members. It is necessary therefore that that which is cognitive of animals be caused by some one first cognitive with respect to efficient cause as well as formal cause.

If, however, some one should say that this conclusion holds only for things caused univocally, as man generates man, but cognitive things do not have a univocal but an equivocal cause in genus, we shall convince our adversary of the truth by the fact that every equivocal is reduced to some thing univocal, which is anterior to it. Here the generating therefore will be equivocal, which, as he says, has something univocal before it, which is its first cause; and thus the conclusion will be the same as that arrived at above.

Moreover, we see that it is thus in all things, because whenever some powers and forms are found in many things, and are imperfect in certain of them but perfect in others, the imperfect are caused by the perfect, and the imperfection comes from the diversity and imperfection of the matter. Thus therefore it is necessary that this be the case too in cognitive natures. The nature therefore by which other animal natures are cognitive, will be from some cognitive and perfect first nature.

This entire discussion however is derived from a certain letter of Aristotle which he wrote *on the beginning of the universe,* which Avicenna mentions in his *Metaphysics.* Eustratius says in his commentary on the sixth book of the *Ethics* of Aristotle that all cognition of animals flows from a first cognitive cause.

III.

Let us inquire then what that first nature is. For since the first in the order of nature flows into the second, and not conversely; and since living is prior in order of nature to perceiving, and perceiving to understanding, it seems to some perhaps that the first fountain, of all knowledge would be only living, and not sentient and intelligent; especially since the first in the order of nature is by the mode of one, and the second by the mode of two, one of which is added to another, the third by the mode of three following each other in the order of the nature of added units, if perceiving is added to living, and understanding to perceiving, because as we said in the book *on the Soul,* the constitution[*ratio*] of soul is the same as the constitution of figure. For just as in figures the triangle is in the tetragon, so the vegetative is in the sensible and the sensible in the intellective.

14

This opinion is proved to be erroneous by the fact that according to nature the imperfect is never the univocal cause of the perfect: but living separated in being from sensible and intelligible is the most imperfect in the genus of living things, nor does it have any nobility of life by which it could be a principle.

Still it is true in all things caused univocally with respect to nature, that whatsoever is present essentially in the thing caused, that is present more powerfully and more nobly and more clearly and prior and more perfectly in cause of that which is caused. In all things cognoscitive there is present essentially a cognoscitive principle; that therefore is present more powerfully, more nobly, prior and more perfectly in the cause of those things which are cognitive. Therefore the nature by which they are sometimes cognitive does not flow from some one living thing, the living of which is separate from the cognitive.

Moreover, among things which are caused the more noble is nearer to the first principle which is the cause because it approaches with more nobilities and goodnesses; but the intellective approaches with more nobilities and goodnesses to the first and perfectly cognitive: and it is intellective rather than living only or only perceiving and living; it is necessary therefore that the fountain and origin of the knowledge of life be some intellectual nature.

Moreover, we see that all things which are perfective of sight are caused by that which is visible through itself and perfectly. For every diversity of colors is caused by light, and the diversity of colors comes from the multiform permixture of an opaque and determined body with a diaphanous body, of which the actuality in itself is illumination. Similarly therefore all cognition flows from that which is most perfectly cognitive, and the diversity of cognitions comes from the multiform overshadowing of the cognitive light radiating over those things which are cognitive in the diversity of creatures with souls [*animalium*].

From all these considerations, moreover, very excellently grounded reasons have determined that every intelligible and sensible cognition of animal flows from an intellectual nature perfectly and intellectually cognitive. For since it may be said that the first cause influences more than the second, the peripatetics held that this is true of the cause. The living, however, separated from the cognitive, is not the cause of the cognitive, and therefore has no influence. But although the first cause pours all its goodnesses on that which is caused, and goodnesses have no distinction and order in it, because the first cause itself has all simply before that which is caused, still in the effects those things which are poured, are poured from the first cause under an order and distinction: and thus that influences first which according to the order of understanding is more general and prior, because if the causality of the first is removed, none of the second has influence, but on the other hand if the causality of the second is removed, the first still influences. In the same way in the cause which is the fountain of life and knowledge, the living does not add something above the others, for its living is its understanding, but in the effects in which living has its distinctness, the living is in some other thing as if the foundation of it. With respect however to attributed nobilities, nothing is as multiplex as the first cause, because it has all these nobilities simply and in unity anterior to that which is caused, and therefore the Philosopher says very well that the first cause is pre-named for all its effects and that it is rich in itself in respect in which it is given to none and dispensed to none of its effects, and it is rich in other things which it communicates proportionally to its effects.

IV.

Now that these things have been stated, it is necessary to investigate further what that nature is which like a fountain pours forth every cognition and life. And it seems that Plato holds that intellectuality in man and sensibility in brutes, as well as the principle of life in vegetables and brutes, flow from the movers of the orbs and the stars, for he argues in the *Timalus* from the greatest of the gods to the movers of the heavenly bodies, remarking and saying, *I shall make a sowing of these, and I shall bestow them on you: and it is proper that you follow after.* Moreover platonists seem to agree in the same thing, however many souls of animals they derive, drawn from and caused by the intelligences.

They confirm their statements very cogently with three reasons, of which one is that every last effect in order of things caused does not derive from the first cause except by way of the causes which are intermediate. The last effects, however, are forms of generable and corruptible things. The intermediate causes are the movers of the celestial orbs, which the Philosophers called the celestial intelligences. The nearest of these, pouring forth souls, is the intelligence moving the last orb. The second reason is that the intelligence impresses on the soul, as the soul on the nature of the animate body. Therefore as we say that the soul is the cause of the animate body and of the movements and passions of it according to which it is animated, so we must say that the lowest intelligence is the cause of the cognitive soul according to which it is cognitive, because the cognition of the soul is a certain result of the light of the intelligence. The third reason is that, just as the body is animated under a celestial body, and is caused, and ruled by it, so the soul of the body is under an intelligence and ruled by it.

The contrary of this, however, appears. For if the cognitive element of mortals should flow from and be ruled by the intelligence of the lowest orb or of some one of the other orbs or of all, then it would itself necessarily be subordinated in its own movements and operations of knowledge and emotion to the motions of the stars, because all that flows from any thing is contained and restrained by it in powers of operations. However, that the soul is especially restrained under the motions of the stars is contrary to all the peripatetics and contrary to Ptolemy. For it itself apprehends the higher movements in the spheres, and turns freely from those things toward which the motion of the stars inclines, and directs itself toward other things by wisdom in understanding, as Ptolemy says.

Moreover, the order in nature is of the first to the intermediate and of the intermediate to the last, because something which is not perfected by the first cause may be caused in the last by the intermediate. I speak of these effects, which carry some nobility in their name, for otherwise there would be no recourse from the last to the intermediate to the first; and this can not be, since everything which is, desires some goodness of the first cause, and because of that it does whatever it does. Therefore whether or not we say that the intermediate contributes something in the production of the last, the goodnesses of the last are always principally and efficaciously from the first cause, and those which are intermediate operate as instruments if they do anything with reference to the last.

Once again, we see in the light which is the universal cause of colors that although it constitutes the last colors by a commixture of the prior, still every constitution of color is by the nature of the perspicuous preservation of light as the first hypostasis of colors; and whatever any color has of the nature of color, it has from light, and if there is anything else in it, it is rather from the privation of the nature of color than from that which deserves to be called the essence of color.

In quite the same way, therefore, when the first cause pours its goodnesses upon the intermediate and last, if something should flow from the intermediate into the last, the constitution of the last will still be only from the participation of the goodnesses of the first, and if something else is in the last, it is something of privation; and this was the opinion of the best wise men of Greece, of Theophrastus and Dionysius and other philosophers. Moreover they used the simile of the light of the sun which pours itself out in the limpid air and in different earthly clouds: and although it is in the cloud by way of the air, and it is in the earth by way of the cloud, still because the intermediates give only what they have received from the sun, that which is in the last is entirely from the sun; and if the light in the intermediate and the last terms is far from the limpidity of the sun, that is rather because of the privation of matter than the result of any efficient cause.

Since we hold these opinions, therefore we say that when Plato says that the property of celestial bodies is to follow after the goodnesses of the first cause, the sowings of cognitive substances follow in the manner that instruments lead to the things which are in the art of the artist who moves those instruments, and it is clear that these instruments of the mover do not make the things from any influx proper to themselves. For there is in all intelligences an order of practical form, which descends through the forms themselves into the matter of generable things, and the forms are the same in all, but in inferior things they are more and more determined, just as the form of light[*lux*] is the same in the sun and in the air and in the cloud and in a determined body, although the illumination [*lumen*] in the degree that it descends further from the sun is more and more constricted and determined to the nature of color. It is moreover the same in the case of the form of the art in the mind of the artist, which the hand follows through and which falls under the instrument, and which the iron assumes, which is proportionally the same in all, and yet it is more determined to matter in the hand than in the mind of the artist, and more in the hammer than in the hand, but it is determined most in the iron, because the iron assumes it materially. And in the case of the many intelligences this simile would apply both to the first cause and the matter of the generables, if the hand and the hammer had an intellect by which they might make explicit and follow through the form conceived by the mind of the artist. Wherefore, just as notwithstanding the existence of such an hypothesis, in art, all things will be from the mind of the artist, so all things are in potentiality from the first cause, although the intelligences make explicit certain goodnesses, and they are introduced by the celestial motion into matter. The first Philosopher however treats of these questions more fully. What has been inferred indeed is sufficient for the question; but however many of the later philosophers have treated of the souls caused by and poured forth by the intelligences, they have understood this manner of flux which has been spoken of: and for this reason they have asserted that the soul is first from the intelligence and that it is the offshoot of the intelligence and subject to the illuminations of the intelligence, in this undoubtedly speaking the truth, as the divinations of dreams show and many other phenomena concerning which we shall treat in other books. Because of this the soul is said likewise, in the book *on the Motion of the Heart,* to be perceptive by a second revolution of illuminations which are from the first cause.

Likewise, from what has been said, it is sufficiently clear how the movers of the lower spheres pour forth and how they do not: for the first and complete fusion of soul and all nature is from the first cause. But the lower orbs operate organically by determining and inclining natures to matter. Because of this Plato says that in every orb the soul takes on something, memory in the orb of Saturn, and other functions in other orbs, as we have stated in the first book *on the Soul.* And in this manner the essence of the soul is wholly and solely from the first cause, but the application and determination to the body is by other things instrumentally subject to the first cause; and in this respect it is subjected to the intelligences of the other orbs to be ruled in illuminations and to be moved in temporal motions: and since the whole harmony of the heaven is referred thus to the first cause, therefore the philosophers who understood this thing best have said that the whole has a single mover, and they have said that the lower movers to the spheres are powers and members of the first heaven and of its mover.

V.

The consequence of these doctrines moreover is that we determine a manner of descent of souls. For since the first cause, illumining souls in its light, is a single simple intellectual nature, it will seem strange how many genera of souls there are, namely, vegetative, sensitive and intellectual. For this can not come about from intermediate motors, for all these are said by the philosophers to be intellectual. Nor is what Pythagoras said true, that all souls are intellectual, and all bodies are animate; and he says that the motion of sense or intellect cannot follow the soul into certain bodies because of the gravity of matter. For the stone, as he says, is animate; but the soul in it is oppressed because of terrestrialness, so that it does not display the motion of vegetation, or understanding, or sense. In plants, however, because of a slighter terrestrialness, the soul displays and performs vegetation, but not sense. In less terrestrial brutes, further, it operates one or two or all senses, but not understanding. Finally, in the human body which is least terrestrial of all and which recedes most in incomplexity from the excellence of contraries, the soul has all operations completely.

This indeed can not be, since nature is never lacking in that which is necessary. For if the sensitive and intellective soul were perfect in the stone or the plant, nature would certainly have given to the stone and the plant the organs by which sensible things could make explicit the operations of the sensitive and intellectual soul.

Yet, all diversity of matter is because of diversity of form, as has often been stated before in the books which have been completed. How therefore can it be said that the genus of the soul is the same in all bodies, which are obviously different in figures and in quantity and in nature?

Nor is the reason of Plato cogent when he says that the forms are infused according to the worth of the matter, because according to this the material diversity would be the cause of the diversity of forms, although this is not true, for the diversity of matters is not the cause but the sign of the diversity of forms. For if it were said to be the cause, then it would be necessary that the matter be before the form according to nature and understanding, and it would be the cause of the form; but whosoever is well instructed with respect to those things which have been proved in the books on Physics does not doubt that all this is absurd.

There remains therefore the question, whence arises the diversity of genera of the soul, vegetative, sensitive and intelligible? For that which is derived from one in the same manner can not be other than one according to what all philosophers have commonly held.

But this question is solved more readily, if one consider subtly by what manner of bestowing of natures souls proceed from the first cause. For all forms are bestowed by the first cause on the nature of the whole universe; but the further they are removed from it, the more they are deprived of its nobilities and goodnesses; and the less they recede from it, the more they are noble and the more forces and powers of goodnesses they have; and as we said in the *Physics,* those things which are undistinguished in it, when they proceed from it, are distinguished with respect to being and essences and diverse species, just as the rays, coming from the sun into air and clear glass and colored glass, take on a different being and different species. And in this manner diversity arises, for it flows single from a single source through things informed by it, as was determined in part in the eighth book of the *Physics* too. And there are grades of dissimilitude in this descent, since the descending principle of life, which is the soul, possessed of a noble operation, divine and intellectual and animal, remains even down to the organic body composed of contraries, the combination of which is proportioned by celestial equality, for it is formative; otherwise it would be generative of the things which are reformed in these things; for nothing generates something else, except by something divine which is in it; moreover, the soul is intellectual because it operates without using the body and animal because it uses the organic body; but nevertheless its intellectual aspect is overshadowed in that it is inquisitive, not certain like the intellectual aspect of the celestial intellects which are not overshadowed by the disturbances of bodies. Receding further however in the region of dissimilitude it is more overshadowed, so that it loses the intellectual entirely, retaining only knowledge of sensible things. Still further removed moreover it retains only the lowest power of the soul, which is to vegetate, and functions of this sort. There is an example of this in the light receding from the sun into the limpid air and the subtle cloud and the body colored with a white color or a black or a red; for this light little by little is closed in and loses the strength of its power more and more, until it comes to privation; in all things in which it proceeds it has a different being and species. Nor is it one except by procession from one first fountain of light, and since the procession of forms from the first cause is similar in all respects to this, Plato says that the first form is unique, and from it alone all things are made. But Democritus and Leucippus also said that all things are one, and the same is made diversity by order and composition.

Both sects however were in error, for that which is one by procession from one simple being and many with respect to being and figure, is still one with respect to its relation to the first unique efficient cause; and if the natures of souls and of forms were considered with respect to that diverse being, then they are the proper natures of souls and forms, and the diversity of matter is because of them and not conversely, and they give being to matters; and this consideration is properly of them, and they are defined and known according to that which Isaac says in his book of *Definitions,* namely, that the rational soul is produced in the shadow of the intelligence, and the sensible soul in the shadow of the rational, and the vegetative soul in the shadow of the sensible, and the nature of the heavens in the shadow of the vegetative, since essence which gives being proceeds from the first cause, and so, since it is far removed and is taken by similitude, it will be the most simple in being and the most powerful and the most noble and the most universal nature with respect to abstraction; but according to what we say, that the more universal nature causes and influences more, for that reason, this essence is vegetative, intellectual, causative, motive, and possessed of many other powers of goodnesses; and with respect to all these, it is given in the first effect, which is the intellectual being causative of the motion of the orb. This essence, however, descending is deprived of simplicity and power more and more, as we say, even to the final being which receives a minimum difference of being and power; and this privation is called its overshadowing by philosophers. From this the true understanding of the matter is clear, because all things are from the idea itself of one; and it is clear also how the idea is unique in the first cause, possessed of no plurality except by procession and by the vicinity of things caused. For it is not true that life in the first cause is separated from being, but it is a simple emanation of essence from the simple first being. And as the cognitive and motive faculties of the first being are one, so too is the essence emanating in the same powers, so long as it is not overshadowed by the distance of dissimilitude.

From this, three corollaries follow. One, that where there is intellective and sensitive and vegetative and motive being, there is a single essence there and simple substance, but it is multiple in power, and both these characteristics it has from the propinquity of its procession to the first being from which it proceeds. The second is that if any substantial form is motive of its subject with respect to place, it has that power from agreement with the first being which, existing immobile, moves with respect to place, and it does not have it from the fact that it is composite, as certain of the latins asserted. Third, that when it does not recede necessarily far from the first being by privation of nobilities, as intellectual it remains separate and perpetual; but when it recedes far, it is mixed and it is made mortal and corporeal.

From these statements it is known how animals (i.e., creatures with souls) move themselves, and not other beings, and how the intellectual soul is not the actuality of the body, and is not corrupted when the body is corrupted, as Alexander mistakenly said.

AL-FARABI
(about 870-950)

Leading Muslim philosopher. Born in Turkestan, he was educated by a Christian physician at Baghdad. Taught there and at Damascus where he died. A versatile man, he was a noted musician whose compositions are still chanted in the East. As a philosopher he was perhaps more important as expounder and commentator of Greek philosophy than as an original thinker. He was one of the first Arabs to deal seriously with Aristotle, writing a commentary on his logical treatises. However, his own thinking was influenced by Plato and Plotinus, dealing with various aspects of the soul with an idealism that bordered upon mysticism.

Main Works:

Alpharabii vetustissimi Aristotelis interpretis opera omnia; De Intellectu; De Divisione Scientiarum.

On Concepts

I. *Knowledge* is divided into (a) generally accepted concepts (concepts of the sun, moon, intellect, and the soul), and (b) those concepts that require verification (such as making certain that the heaven consists of spheres, one in the other; or that the world has been created in time).

It is necessary for every concept to have a prior concept. The concluding concept may be established without connecting it to a concept preceding it. This is true of being: the necessary and the possible. These concepts do not require one to previ-

---

From: *The Main Problems of Abu Nasr Al-Farabi.*

ously perceive that something comprises them. These three are rather distinct, correct concepts, innate to understanding. If someone desires to verbally clarify these concepts, then this is only a stimulus to understanding; but they cannot be clarified beyond the clarity of the concepts themselves.

II. It is impossible for us to understand the verifications of concepts without previously having understood other things. For instance, if we wish to know that the world has been created in time, then we must have the prior certainty that the world is composite. However, all that is composite has also been originated in time; consequently we know also that the world has been originated in time. Without doubt, this verification ultimately ends in another which then does not require another to precede it for confirmation.

These, then, are the basic principles that are clearly present in the intellect: of two sides of an opposite, one must always be true, the other false; the whole is greater than any part of it. Logic is the science by which we get acquainted with these methods so that they assist us in our concepts of things and guide us to their verification. The two methods mentioned here aid us in distinguishing between complete and deficient concepts, between the certain and those only approximately certain; as well as the preponderant opinion and the doubtful one. By doing this we become aware of all the aspects of the complete concept as well as the certain verification of those that do not contain any doubt.

III. Thus we maintain: All that there is is divided into two categories. In the first category it is unnecessary to cogitate the nature of the things, since they are of a possible existence. If we reflect on the nature of the second category of things, we find that their being is a necessary one and we say accordingly, it is of necessary existence. It is not absurd to postulate that some things of possible existence are not present; for in order for a thing to exist, it must have a cause; however, if it becomes a necessary being, then it attains necessary existence through something other than that which it itself is. From this it follows that it is necessary for it to belong to that which naturally always has a possible existence and became a necessary being only by virtue of something else. This possibility either never ceases or it takes place at a particular time. The possibility cannot move forever as cause and effect, as it were, in a circle; instead it must end in something necessary to itself. The latter would be that which would be present at first.

IV. However, if we postulate that which is necessary as not present, then we state an absurdity. For its being has no cause, and furthermore, it cannot have its being by virtue of something else. It is the first cause of the being of things, and its being must of necessity be the prime being. We are compelled to imagine the same in every way free of want. Its being is thus complete. Moreover, its being must of necessity be the most perfect one, free from causes, i.e., matter, form, creation, and the final goal.

ANSELM OF CANTERBURY
(1033-1109)

The real father of Scholasticism who, in opposition to Abailard, taught that cognition must rise out of faith (credo ut intelligam). He was born in Aosta, Italy, and educated by the Benedictines, whose Order he entered in 1060. He was strongly under the influence of Augustinus. His interest in dialectics was purely religious. In his Platonic idealism he considered Christianity as the highest truth. He became renowned for his ontological argument for the existence of God. An Italian by birth, he spent most of his life in France and England.

Main Works:
> Cur Deus Homo; Monologium; Proslogium; De Veritate.

Dialogue on Truth

I have, at various times in the past, written three treatises pertaining to the study of the sacred Scriptures, which have this similarity, that they are presented by question and answer, the person questioning designated by the name of disciple, the person answering by the name of master. I do not wish to number with these (since it pertains to a different study than the other three) a fourth which I published in the same manner, not without its use, I think, as an introduction to dialectic, which begins with the words: *Concerning the Grammarian.* One of these three is *On Truth,* namely, what truth is, and of what things it is ordinarily predicated, and what justice is. Another

-----

From: *Dialogus de Veritate.*

of the treatises is *On the Freedom of the Will*, what it is, and whether man always has it, and how many diversities of it there are in either having or not having rightness of will, to preserve which is the prerogative of the rational creature. In this treatise I showed only the natural strength of the will for preserving the rightness which was received, and not how necessary it is that grace should follow to that end. The third treatise is on the question in which it is asked in what way the devil sinned by not standing firm in truth: for God did not give him the perseverance, which he could not have unless God gave it to him: and if God had given it to him he would have had it, just as the good angels had it because God gave it to them. I entitled this treatise, although I spoke in it of the confirmation of the good angels, *On the Fall of the Devil*, since what I said of the good angels followed from the statement of the question. Although these treatises obviously do not hang together by any sequence of presentation, nevertheless their material and the similarity of the investigation demand that they be brought together in the order in which I have presented them. Consequently, although they have been copied in another order by certain persons in haste, before they had been perfected, nevertheless I wish them ordered as I have here set down.

CHAPTER I.

That truth does not have a beginning or an end.

Disciple. Since we believe that God is truth, and since we say truth is in many other things, I would like to know whether we ought to affirm that wherever truth is spoken of, God is that truth. For in your *Monologium* you prove by the truth of discourse that the supreme truth does not have a beginning or an end, saying,

> Let him who can, think of a time when the following began to be true, or when it was not true, namely, that something was in the future to be: or let him think of

a time when the following will cease to be true, and when it will not be true, namely, that something will have been in the past. But if neither of these two suppositions can be conceived, and if they can not be true without truth, it is impossible even to think that truth have a beginning or an end. Moreover, if truth had a beginning, or if it will have an end, it was then true before truth began that there was no truth; and after truth will have ceased to be, it will be true that there will be no truth. But nothing can be true without truth: consequently, there was truth before there was truth; and there will be truth after truth will have ceased to be; which is utterly inconsistent. Whether, then, truth be said to have, or whether it be understood not to have, beginning or end, truth can be limited by no beginning or end.

This you said in your *Monologium*. Wherefore I expect to learn a definition of truth from you.

Master. I do not remember to have found a definition of truth, but if you wish, let us inquire what truth is in the diversities of things in which we say truth is.

Disc. If I can do nothing else, I shall help by listening.

Chapter II.

On the truth of signification and on the two truths of statement.

Mast. Let us inquire first, then, what is truth in statement, since we most frequently call a statement true or false.

Disc. You inquire, and whatever you find, I shall observe.

Mast. When is a statement true?

Disc. When that is which it states, whether by affirming or denying; for I say that what the proposition states is, even when it denies that that which is not, is, since it states thus in what manner the thing is.

Mast. Does it seem to you then that the thing declared is

the truth of the statement?

Disc. No.

Mast. Why not?

Disc. Because nothing is true except by participating in truth, and therefore the truth of what is true is in that which is true; but the thing stated is not in the true statement and therefore it must be called, not the truth of it, but the cause of its truth. Wherefore it seems to me that its truth must be sought only in discourse itself.

Mast. Consider then whether discourse itself or its signification or any of those things which are in the definition [*diffinitione*] of the statement, is what you seek?

Disc. I think not.

Mast. Why not?

Disc. Because if that were the case, it would always be true, since all things which are involved in the definition of a statement remain the same; and whether that which is stated is or is not, the sentence is the same, and the signification is the same, and the others similarly.

Mast. What then does truth in statement seem to you to be?

Disc. I know nothing other than that when it signifies that that which is is, then truth is in it, and it is true.

Mast. To what end is an affirmation made?

Disc. To signify that that which is is.

Mast. Then it should do that?

Disc. Certainly.

Mast. Then when it signifies that that which is is, it signifies as it should.

Disc. That is clear.

Mast. But when it signifies as it should it signifies rightly?

Disc. That is so.

Mast. However, when it signifies rightly, the signification is right?

Disc. There is no doubt of that.

Mast. Therefore, when it signifies that that which is is, the signification is right?

Disc. That follows.

Mast. Likewise when it signifies that that which is is, the signification is true?

Disc. Yes, it is both right and true, when it signifies that that which is is.

Mast. It is the same, therefore, for the affirmation to be right and true, that is, to signify that that which is is?

Disc. Yes, it is the same.

Mast. Consequently, truth, for it, is not other than rightness.

Disc. I see clearly now that truth is this rightness.

Mast. It is the same when the statement signifies that that which is not, is not.

Disc. I understand what you say, but tell me what I can answer if some one should say that likewise when reason signifies that that which is not, is, it signifies as it should. For reason has the power to signify equally that that which is and that which is not, is. For if it had not the power to signify that that which is not, is, it would not signify it. Wherefore, too, since it signifies that that which is not, is, it signifies as it should. But if by signifying what it should, it is true and right, as you have shown, then discourse is true even when it states that that which is not, is.

Mast. It is not ordinarily said to be true when it signifies that that which is not, is. But it has truth and rightness in that it does that which it should. But when it signifies that that which is, is, it does doubly what it should, since it signifies both what it has the power to signify and what has happened. But according to this latter rightness and truth, by which it signifies that that which is, is, a statement is called by usage right and true, and not according to the former by which it signifies that that which is not, is. For more is required of it because it undertook signification than because it did not undertake it. [It has more rightness, its *ought* is greater, in fulfilling a positive than only a negative task.] For it took on the power of signifying that a thing is when it is not or that it is not when it is, only because it could not be made to signify only at the moment when the thing is that it is or that it is not only when it is not. Consequently, the one is rightness and truth of statement, in that it signifies that which it was made to signify; the other in that it signifies that which it undertook to signify. So, the latter is the immutable possession of speech itself, but the former is mutable; for speech always has the latter, it does not always have the former; for it has the latter naturally, but it has the former accidently and according to use. For when I say, It is day, I use the meaning of this sentence rightly to signify that that which is, is, because it was made for this, and therefore it is said to signify rightly. But when I signify by the same sentence that that which is not, is, I do not use it rightly, for it was not made for that, and on that account the signification of it is then said not to be right: although in certain statements these two rightnesses or truths are inseparable, as when we say, Man is an animal, or, Man is not a stone. For the affirmation in this case always signifies that that which is, is, and the negation always signifies that that which is not, is not. Nor can the former be used to signify that that which is not, is, for man is always an animal. Nor can the latter be used to signify that that which is, is not, for man is never a stone. We began therefore to inquire concerning the truth which discourse has according as one uses it rightly, since the common use of speech judges a statement to be true according to that. We shall speak later of the truth which it can not but have.

Disc. Go back then to that with which you began, since you have made sufficiently clear to me the distinction between the two truths of discourse, if you showed it to have some measure of truth none the less even when it lies, as you say.

Mast. Let that suffice for the time for the truth of signification with which we began. For the same principle [*ratio*] and relation of truth which we examined in the proposition of the spoken word, must be taken up in all signs which are used for signifying that something is or is not, among which are written characters and the language of fingers.

Disc. Proceed then to the other.

CHAPTER III.

On the truth of opinion.

Mast. We call thought true when that is which we think is, whether by reason or in some other way, and we call thought false when that is not.

Disc. Usage has it thus.

Mast. What then does truth in thought seem to you to be?

Disc. According to the principle which we saw in the case of proposition, nothing is more properly called the truth of thought than its rightness. For the power has been given us to think that something is or is not, to the end that we think that that which is, is, and that that which is not, is not. Wherefore whoever thinks that that which is, is, thinks as he should, and consequently the thought is right. If therefore the thought is true and right for no other reason than that we think that that which is, is, or that that which is not, is not, then there is no other truth of thought than rightness.

CHAPTER IV.

On the truth of will.

Mast. You take the matter up rightly. But Truth himself says that truth is in the will when he says that the devil did not stand in truth.[2] For the devil was not in truth nor did he abandon truth except in will.

Disc. I believe that is so. For if he had always wished what he should have wished, he would never have sinned, since he did not abandon the truth except by sinning.

Mast. Tell me then what you understand by truth here?

Disc. Nothing except rightness. For if he was in rightness and truth as long as he wished that which he should, that, namely, for which he was given will, and if he abandoned rightness and truth, when he wished that which he should not have,

34

then truth can not here be understood to be other than rightness, for truth or rightness was nothing other in his will than to wish that which he should.

CHAPTER V.

On the truth of natural action and of action which is not natural.

Mast. You understand it well. But we must believe truth to be in action, too, as the Lord said. For *he that doeth evil hateth the light* and *he that doeth the truth cometh to the light.*[3]

Disc. I follow what you say.

Mast. Consider then, if you can, what truth is here.

Disc. Unless I am mistaken, truth in action must also be considered according to the same principle by which we investigated truth above in the others.

Mast. So it is. For if to do evil and to do the truth are opposed, as the Lord shows when he says: *he that doeth evil hateth the light,* and *he that doeth the truth cometh to the light,* it is the same to do the *truth* as to do good. For doing good is the contrary of doing evil. Wherefore if to do the truth and to do good are identical because they are opposite to the same thing, they are not diverse in signification; but the opinion of all is that he who does as he should, does good and does rightness. Wherefore it follows that to do rightness is to do the truth. For it is clear that to do the truth is to do good and to do good is to do rightness. Wherefore nothing is more apparent than that the truth of action is rightness.

Disc. I see nothing faltering in your consideration.

Mast. Consider then whether every action which does what it should, may properly be said to do the truth. Obviously there is rational action, as alms-giving; and there is irrational action, as the action of fire which warms. Consider then whether we may properly say that the fire does the truth?

Disc. If the fire, when it warms, is determined for warming by that from which it has its being, it does that which it should when it warms. Therefore I do not see what impropriety there is that the fire should do the truth and rightness when it does that which it should.

Mast. It appears no differently to me. Therefore we can observe that there are two rightnesses or truths of action, a necessary one and one which is not necessary. For fire does the truth and rightness of necessity when it warms, and man does the truth and rightness out of no necessity when he does good: but the Lord wanted *to do* to be understood not only for that which *to do* properly means, but for every verb, when he said that *he that doeth the truth cometh to the light.*[4] For he does not exclude from this truth or light him who suffers persecution because of justice, or him who is where he should be and at the time he should be, or him who stands or sits when he should, or anything of this sort. For no one says that such persons do not act well. And when the Apostle says that *each one shall receive according as he has done*[5] that must be understood to mean whatever we ordinarily call doing good or doing evil.

Disc. The common usage of the word is to call suffering and many other things which are not *doing, doing.* Consequently, unless I am mistaken, we can number among right actions the right will too, to the truth of which we had turned our attention above before taking up the truth of action.

Mast. You are not mistaken. For whoever wishes what he should, is said to do rightly and good, nor is he excluded from the number of those who do the truth. But since we speak of truth in investigating that [the right will], and since the Lord seems to speak especially of that truth which is in the will when he says of the devil that he has not stood in truth,[6] for that reason I wanted to take up separately what truth is in the will.

Disc. I am content that it was so done.

Mast. Since therefore it is clear that the truth of action is in one fashion natural and in another not natural, that truth of discourse which we saw above[7] can not be separated from it, must be classed under the natural. For, just as fire, when it warms, does the truth since it was determined by that from which it has its being, so also this sentence, *it is day,* does the truth when it signifies that it is day, whether it is day or not, since it was determined naturally to do that.

Disc. I see truth now for the first time in false discourse.

CHAPTER VI.

On the truth of the senses, and that the falsity which is thought to be in sense is in opinion.

Mast. Do you think that we have discovered all the places of truth other than the supreme truth?

Disc. I remember now a certain truth which I do not find among these which you have treated.

Mast. What is that?

Disc. Truth is certainly in the senses of the body, but not always, for they sometimes deceive us. For sometimes when I see something through the medium of glass my sight deceives me, in that my body sometimes reports to me that what I see beyond the glass is of the same color as the glass, when it is of another color; and sometimes it makes me think that the glass has the color of the thing which I see beyond it, when it does not have that color. There are many other ways in which sight and the other senses deceive us.

Mast. It does not seem to me that this truth or falsity is in the senses but in opinion. For the interior sense deceives itself; the exterior sense does not lie to it. Sometimes we recognize this easily, sometimes with difficulty. For when a child fears a sculptured dragon with a gaping mouth, it is easy to perceive that it is not sight which brings this about, since it reports nothing more to the child than to adults, but rather it is the childish interior sense which does not yet know how to distinguish clearly between a thing and the likeness of a thing. So it is when, seeing one man like another, we think he is the man he is like, or when some one, hearing what is not the voice of a man, thinks it to be the voice of a man. For the interior sense does this too. What you say of the glass, moreover, is for the following reason, that when sight passes through a body of the color of air it is prevented from taking on the likeness of the color of that which it sees beyond no otherwise than when it passes through air, except in so far as that body through which it passes is thicker and more obscure than air; this is the case when it passes through glass of its own color, that is, a glass to which no other color is added, or when it passes through very pure water, or through crystal, or through something having a like color. But when the same sight passes through another color, as through a glass not of its own color but to which another color is added, it takes on the very color which first it happens on. Wherefore since after it has taken on one color, in so far as it has been affected by it, it takes on any other which may appear either not at all or less completely: for that reason it reports the color which it took on first either alone or with that which appeared later. For if sight, in so far as it is susceptible of color, is affected very much by the first color, it can not perceive another color at the same time: but if it is affected by the first color to a degree less than it is able to perceive color, then it can perceive another. So, if sight pass through some body such as glass which is so perfectly red that sight itself is wholly affected by its redness, it can not at the same time be affected by a different color; but if it finds a redness not so perfect which comes first, it will be able still, so far as it is capable of color, to assume, as if not yet full, another color as far as its capacity is not satiated by the first color. Any one therefore who is ignorant of this, imagines that sight reports that all things, which it perceives after the first color is taken on, are either wholly or at least in part of the same color. Whence it happens that the interior sense imputes its error to the exterior sense. In the same way, when a whole staff, of which part is submerged in water and part is out of water, is thought to be broken, or when we think that our sight discovers our own faces in a mirror, and when sight and the other senses seem to report to us many other things otherwise than they are, it is not the fault of the senses, which report what they are able to, since they were given just this potency; but it must be imputed to the judgment of the mind, which does not distinguish clearly what they can or what they ought to do. But since to demonstrate this is rather more laborious than fruitful to the inquiry which concerns us here, I do not think time should be devoted to it. Let it suffice to say only, that whatsoever the senses seem to report, whether they do it because of their own nature or because of some other cause, they do that which they should, and therefore they do rightness and the truth, and this truth is contained under the truth which is in action.

Disc. You have satisfied me with your reply, and I do not wish to detain you longer in this question of the senses.

Chapter VII.

On the truth of the essence of things

Mast. Consider now whether, apart from the supreme truth, truth is to be understood in anything besides these things which have been investigated above.

Disc. What could that be?

Mast. Do you think that anything could be at any time or in any place which was not in the supreme truth, and which did not receive from it that which it is, in so far as it is, or which could be other than what it is in the truth?

Disc. That is not to be thought.

Mast. Whatsoever is, therefore, is truly, in so far as it is that which it is in the supreme truth.

Disc. You can conclude absolutely that everything which is, is truly, since it is not other than it is in the truth.

Mast. Truth is therefore in the essence of all things which are, because they are that which they are in the supreme truth.

Disc. I see that truth is there in such fashion that no falsity can be there, for that which is falsely is not.

Mast. You express it well. But tell me whether any thing should be other than that which it is in the supreme truth?

Disc. No.

Mast. If therefore all things are what they are there, they are without doubt what they should be.

Disc. Truly they are what they should be.

Mast. But whatever is that which it should be, is rightly.

Disc. It can not be otherwise.

Mast. Therefore everything that is, is rightly.

Disc. Nothing could follow more cogently.

Mast. If therefore truth and rightness are in the essence of things, in that the things are that which in the supreme truth they are, it is certain that the truth of things is rightness.

SAINT THOMAS AQUINAS
(1225-1274)

The undisputed head of Christian scholasticism. Like his master, Albertus Magnus, whose synthesis he completed, Thomas was a Dominican. His codification of Catholic theology and philosophy is still authoritative. Son of the Count of Aquino, he was a relative of Emperor Frederick II. St. Thomas achieved an encyclopedically worked out reconciliation between faith and reason. The Angelic Doctor had taken the middle way of Aristotle to reach his goal. He taught philosophy at Paris, at the Papal Curia in Rome, and at Naples. His popular works show a dominant influence by Augustinus; his later works by Aristotle, whom he referred to as *the philosopher*. He made a direct division between philosophy which is based on natural data and theology which is grounded on the supernatural.

Main Works:

> Summa Contra Gentiles; Summa Theologica; De Trinitate Quaestiones Disputatae; De Divinis Nominibus.

On Knowledge

ARTICLE I

The Problem under Discussion Is Truth, and in the First Article We Ask: WHAT IS TRUTH?

Difficulties:

It seems that the true is exactly the same as being, for

1. Augustine says: "The true is that which is." But that which is, is simply being. The true, therefore, means exactly the same as being.

From: *Quaestiones disputatae de veritate.*

2. It was said in reply that the true and being are the same materially but differ formally.—On the contrary the nature of a thing is signified by its definition; and the definition of the true, according to Augustine, is "that which is." He rejects all other definitions. Now, since the true and being are materially the same, it seems that they are also formally the same.

3. Things which differ conceptually are so related to each other that one of them can be understood without the other. For this reason, Boethius says that the existence of God can be understood if for a moment we mentally separate His goodness from His existence. Being, however, can in no way be understood apart from the true, for being is known only in so far as it is true. Therefore, the true and being do not differ conceptually.

4. If the true is not the same as being, it must be a state of being. But it cannot be a state of being. It is not a state that entirely corrupts—otherwise, this would follow: "It is true. Therefore, it is non-being"—as it follows when we say: "This man is dead. Therefore, this is not a man."

Similarly, the true is not a state that limits. If it were, one could not say: "It is true. Therefore it is." For one cannot say that a thing is white simply because it has white teeth. Finally, the true is not a state which contracts or specifies being, for it is convertible with being. It follows therefore that the true and being are entirely the same.

5. Things in the same state are the same. But the true and being are in the same state. Therefore, they are the same. For Aristotle writes: "The state of a thing in its act of existence is the same as its state in truth." Therefore, the true and being are entirely the same.

6. Things not the same differ in some respect. But the true and being differ in no respect. They do not differ essentially, for every being is true by its very essence. And they do not differ in any other ways, for they must belong to some common genus. Therefore, they are entirely the same.

7. If they were not entirely the same, the true would add

something to being. But the true adds nothing to being, even though it has greater extension than being. This is borne out by the statement of the Philosopher that we define the true as: "That which affirms the existence of what is, and denies the existence of what is not." Consequently, the true includes both being and non-being; since it does not add anything to being, it seems to be entirely the same as being.

To the Contrary:

1'. Useless repetition of the same thing is meaningless: so, if the true were the same as being, it would be meaningless to say: "Being is true." This, however, is hardly correct. Therefore, they are not the same.

2'. Being and the good are convertible. The true and the good, however, are not interchangeable, for some things, such as fornication, are true but not good. The true, therefore, and being are not interchangeable. And so they are not the same.

3'. In all creatures, as Boethius has pointed out, "to be is other than that which is." Now, the true signifies the existence of things. Consequently, in creatures it is different from that which is. But that which is, is the same as being. Therefore, in creatures the true is different from being.

4'. Things related as before and after must differ. But the true and being are related in the aforesaid manner; for, as is said in *The Causes:* "The first of all created things is the act of existence." In a study of this work, a commentator writes as follows: "Everything else is predicated as a specification of being." Consequently, everything else comes after being. Therefore, the true and being are not the same.

5'. What are predicated of a cause and of the effects of the cause are more united in the cause than in its effects—and more so in God than in creatures. But in God four predicates—being, the one, the true, and the good—are appropriated as follows: being, to the essence; the one, to the Father; the true, to the Son; and the good, to the Holy Spirit.

Since the divine Persons are really and not merely conceptually distinct, these notions cannot be predicated of each other; if really distinct when verified of the Divine Persons, the four notions in question are much more so when verified of creatures.

REPLY:

When investigating the nature of anything, one should make the same kind of analysis as he makes when he reduces a proposition to certain self-evident principles. Otherwise, both types of knowledge will become involved in an infinite regress, and science and our knowledge of things will perish.

Now, as Avicenna says, that which the intellect first conceives as, in a way, the most evident, and to which it reduces all its concepts, is being. Consequently, all the other conceptions of the intellect are had by additions to being. But nothing can be added to being as though it were something not included in being—in the way that a difference is added to a genus or an accident to a subject—for every reality is essentially a being. The Philosopher has shown this by proving that being cannot be a genus. Yet, in this sense, some predicates may be said to add to being inasmuch as they express a mode of being not expressed by the term *being*. This happens in two ways.

First, the mode expressed is a certain special manner of being; for there are different grades of being according to which we speak when we speak of different levels of existence, and according to these grades different things are classified. Consequently, *substance* does not add a difference to being by signifying some reality added to it, but *substance* simply expresses a special manner of existing, namely, as a being in itself. The same is true of the other classes of existents.

Second, some are said to add to being because the mode they express is one that is common, and consequent upon every being. This mode can be taken in two ways; first, in so far as it follows upon every being considered in relation to another. In the first, the term is used in two ways because it expresses something in the being either affirmatively or negatively. We can, however, find nothing that can be predicated of every being affirmatively and, at the same time, absolutely, with the exception of its essence by which the being is said to be. To express this, the term *thing* is used; for, according to Avicenna, thing differs from being because being gets its name from to-be, but thing expresses the quiddity or essence of the being. There is, however, a negation consequent upon every being considered absolutely: its undividedness, and this is expressed by *one*. For the *one* is simply undivided being.

If the mode of being is taken in the second way—according to the relation of one being to another—we find a twofold use. The first is based on the distinction of one being from another, and this distinctness is expressed by the word *something*, which implies, as it were, *some other thing*. For, just as a being is said to be *one* in so far as it is without division in itself, so it is said to be *something* in so far as it is divided from other. The second division is based on the correspondence one being has with another. This is possible only if there is something which is such that it agrees with every being. Such a being is the soul, which, as is said in *The Soul*, "in some way is all things." The soul, however, has both knowing and appetitive powers. *Good* expresses the correspondence of being to the appetitive power, for, and so we note in the *Ethics*, the good is "that which all desire." *True* expresses the correspondence of being to the knowing power, for all knowing is produced by an assimilation of the knower to the thing known, so that assimilation is said to be the cause of knowledge. Similarly, the sense of sight knows a color by being informed with a species of the color.

The first reference of being to the intellect, therefore, consists in its agreement with the intellect. This agreement is called "the conformity of thing and intellect." In this conformity is fulfilled the formal constituent of the true, and this is what *the true* adds to being, namely the conformity or equation of thing and intellect. As we said, the knowledge of a thing is a consequence of this conformity; therefore, it is an effect of truth, even though the fact that the thing is a being is prior to its truth.

Consequently, truth or the true has been defined in three ways. First of all, it is defined according to that which precedes truth and is the basis of truth. This is why Augustine writes: "The true is that which is"; and Avicenna: "The truth of each thing is a property of the act of being which has been established for it." Still others say: "The true is undividedness of the act of existence from that which is."

Truth is also defined in another way—according to that in which its intelligible determination is formally completed. Thus, Isaac writes: "Truth is the conformity of thing and intellect"; and Anselm: "Truth is a rectitude perceptible only by the mind." This rectitude, of course, is said to be based on some conformity. The Philosopher says that in defining truth we say that truth is had when one affirms that "to be which is, and that not to be which is not."

The third way of defining truth is according to the effect following upon it. Thus, Hilary says that the true is that which manifests and proclaims existence. And Augustine says: "Truth is that by which that which is, is shown"; and also: "Truth is according to which we judge about inferior things."

Answers to Difficulties:

1. That definition of Augustine is given for the true as it has its foundation in reality and not as its formal nature is given complete expression by conformity of thing and intellect. An alternative answer would be that in the statement, "The true is that which is," the word *is* is not here understood as referring to the act of existing, but rather as the mark of the intellectual act of judging, signifying, that is, the affirmation of a proposition. The meaning would then be this: "The true is that which is—it is had when the existence of what is, is affirmed." If this is its meaning, then Augustine's definition agrees with that of the Philosopher mentioned above.

2. The answer is clear from what has been said.

3. "Something can be understood without another" can be

taken in two ways. It can mean that something can be known while another remains unknown. Taken in this way, it is true that things which differ conceptually are such that one can be understood without another: when it is known even though the other does not exist. Taken in this sense, being cannot be known without the true, for it cannot be known unless it agrees with or conforms to intellect. It is not necessary, however, that everyone who understands the formal notion of being should also understand the formal notion of the true—just as not everyone who understands being understands the agent intellect, even though nothing can be known without the agent intellect.

4. The true is a state of being even though it does not add any reality to being or express any special mode of existence. It is rather something that is generally found in every being, although it is not expressed by the word *being*. Consequently, it is not a state that corrupts, limits, or contracts.

5. In this objection, *condition* should not be understood as belonging to the genus of quality. It implies, rather, a certain order; for those which are the cause of the existence of other things are themselves beings most completely, and those which are the cause of the truth of other things are themselves true most completely. It is for this reason that the Philosopher concludes that the rank of a thing in its existence corresponds to its rank in truth, so that when one finds that which is most fully being, he finds there also that which is most fully true. It means simply that in the degree in which a thing has being, in that degree it is capable of being proportioned to intellect. Consequently, the true is dependent upon the formal character of being.

6. There is a conceptual difference between the true and being since there is something in the notion of the true that is not in the concept of the existing—not in such a way, however, that there is something in the concept of being which is not in the concept of the true. They do not differ essentially nor are they distinguished from one another by opposing differences.

7. The true does not have a wider extension than being. Being

is, in some way, predicated of non-being in so far as non-being is apprehended by the intellect. For, as the Philosopher says, the negation or the privation of being may, in a sense, be called being. Avicenna supports this by pointing out that one can form propositions only of beings, for that about which a proposition is formed must be apprehended by the intellect. Consequently, it is clear that everything true is being in some way.

Answers to Contrary Difficulties:

1'. The reason why it is not tautological to call a being true is that something is expressed by the word *true* that is not expressed by the word *being,* and not that the two differ in reality.

2'. Although fornication is evil, it possesses some being and can conform to intellect. So it is clear that *true* is coextensive with *being.*

3'. In the statement, "To be is other than that which is," the act of being is distinguished from that to which that act belongs. But the name of being is taken from the act of existence, not from that whose act it is. Hence, the argument does not follow.

4'. The true comes after being in this respect, that the notion of the true differs from that of being in the manner we have described.

5'. This argument has three flaws. First, although the Persons are really distinct, the things appropriated to each Person are only conceptually, and not really distinct. Secondly, although the Persons are really distinct from each other, they are not really distinct from the essence; so, truth appropriated to the Person of the Son is not distinct from the act of existence He possesses through the divine essence. Thirdly, although being, the true, the one, and the good are more united in God than they are in created things, it does not follow from the fact that they are conceptually distinct in God that they are really distinct in created beings. This line of argumuent is valid only when it is applied to things which are not by their very nature one in reality, as wisdom and power, which, although one in God, are distinct in creatures. But being, the true, the one, and the good are such that by their very nature they are one in reality. Therefore, no matter where they are found, they are really one. Their unity in God, however, is more perfect than their unity in creatures.

In the Second Article We Ask: Is Truth Found Principally in the Intellect or in Things?

Difficulties:

It seems that it is found principally in things, for

1. It was pointed out that the true is convertible with being. But being is found more principally in things than in the soul. The true, therefore, is principally outside the soul.

2. Things are not in the soul through their essences but, as pointed out by the Philosopher, through species. If, therefore, truth is found principally in the soul, truth will not be the essence of a thing but merely its likeness or species; and the true will be the species of a being existing outside the soul. But the species of a thing existing in the soul is not predicated of a thing outside the soul and is not convertible with it; for, if this were so, the true could not be converted with being—which is false.

3. That which is in something is based upon that in which it is. If truth, then, is principally in the soul, judgments about truth will have as their criterion the soul's estimation. This would revive that error of the ancient philosophers who said that any opinion a person has in his intellect is true and that two contradictories can be true at the same time. This, of course, is absurd.

4. If truth is principally in the intellect, anything which pertains to the intellect should be included in the definition of truth. Augustine, however, sharply criticizes such definitions, as, for example, "The true is that which is as it is seen." For, according

to this definition, something would not be true if it were not seen. This is clearly false of rocks hidden deep in the earth. Augustine similarly criticizes the following definition: "The true is that which is as it appears to the knower, provided he is willing and able to know." For, according to this definition, something would not be true unless the knower wished and were able to know. The same criticism can be leveled against other definitions that include any reference to intellect. Truth, therefore, is not principally in the intellect.

To the Contrary:

1'. The Philosopher says: "The true and the false are not in things but in the mind."

2'. Truth is "the conformity of thing and intellect." But since this conformity can be only in the intellect, truth is only in the intellect.

REPLY:

When a predicate is used primarily and secondarily of many things, it is not necessary that that which is the cause of the others receive the primary predication of the common term, but rather that in which the meaning of the common term is first fully verified. For example, *healthy* is primarily predicated of an animal, for it is in an animal that the nature of health is first found in its fullest sense. But inasmuch as medicine causes health, it is also said to be healthy. Therefore, since truth is predicated of many things in a primary and a secondary sense, it ought to be primarily predicated of that in which its full meaning is primarily found.

Now, the fulfillment of any motion is found in the term of the motion; and, since the term of the motion of a cognitive power is the soul, the known must be in the knower after the manner of the knower. But the motion of an appetitive power terminates in things. For this reason the Philosopher speaks of a sort of circle formed by the acts of the soul: for a thing outside

50

the soul moves the intellect, and the thing known moves the appetite, which tends to reach the things from which the motion originally started. Since good, as mentioned previously, expresses a relation to appetite, and true, a relation to the intellect, the Philosopher says that good and evil are in things, but true and false are in the mind. A thing is not called true, however, unless it conforms to an intellect. The true, therefore, is found secondarily in things and primarily in intellect.

Note, however, that a thing is referred differently to the practical intellect than it is to the speculative intellect. Since the practical intellect causes things, it is a measure of what it causes. But, since the speculative intellect is receptive in regard to things, it is, in a certain sense, moved by things and consequently measured by them. It is clear, therefore, that, as is said in the *Metaphysics,* natural things from which our intellect gets its scientific knowledge measure our intellect. Yet these things are themselves measured by the divine intellect, in which are all created things—just as all works of art find their origin in the intellect of an artist. The divine intellect, therefore, measures and is not measured; a natural thing both measures and is measured; but our intellect is measured, and measures only artifacts, not natural things.

A natural thing, therefore, being placed between two intellects is called *true* in so far as it conforms to either. It is said to be true with respect to its conformity with the divine intellect in so far as it fulfills the end to which it was ordained by the divine intellect. This is clear from the writings of Anselm and Augustine, as well as from the definition of Avicenna, previously cited: "The truth of anything is a property of the act of being which has been established for it." With respect to its conformity with a human intellect, a thing is said to be true in so far as it is such as to cause a true estimate about itself; and a thing is said to be false if, as Aristotle says, "by nature it is such that it seems to be what it is not, or seems to possess qualities which it does not possess."

In a natural thing, truth is found especially in the first, rather than in the second, sense; for its reference to the divine intellect comes before its reference to a human intellect. Even if there were no human intellects, things could be said to be true because of their relation to the divine intellect. But if, by an impossible supposition, intellect did not exist and things did continue to exist, then the essentials of truth would in no way remain.

Answers to Difficulties:

1. As is clear from the discussion, *true* is predicated primarily of a true intellect and secondarily of a thing conformed with intellect. *True* taken in either sense, however, is interchangeable with being, but in different ways. Used of things, it can be interchanged with being through a judgment asserting merely material identity, for every being is conformed with the divine intellect and can be conformed with a human intellect. The converse of this is also true.

But if *true* is understood as used of the intellect, then it can be converted with being outside the soul—not as denominating the same subject, but as expressing conformity. For every true act of understanding is referred to a being, and every being corresponds to a true act of understanding.

2. The solution of the second argument is clear from the solution of the first.

3. What is in another does not depend on that other unless it is caused by the principles of that other. For example, even though light is in the air, it is caused by something extrinsic, the sun; and it is based on the motion of the sun rather than on air. In the same way, truth which is in the soul but caused by things does not depend on what one thinks but on the existence of things. For from the fact that a thing is or is not, a statement or an intellect is said to be true or false.

4. Augustine is speaking of a thing's being seen by the human intellect. Truth, of course, does not depend on this, for many things exist that are not known by our intellects. There is nothing, however, that the divine intellect does not actually know,

and nothing that the human intellect does know potentially, for the agent intellect is said to be that "by which we make all things knowable," and the possible intellect, as that "by which we become all things." For this reason, one can place in the definition of a true thing its actually being seen by the divine intellect, but not its being seen by a human intellect—except potentially, as is clear from our earlier discussion.

In the Third Article We Ask: Is Truth Only in the Intellect Joining and Separating?

Difficulties:

It seems not, for

1. The true is predicated from the relation of being to intellect. But the first operation by which an intellect is related to things is that in which the intellect forms the quiddities of things by conceiving their definitions. Truth, therefore, is principally and more properly found in that operation of the intellect.

2. The true is a "conformity of thing and intellect." Now, although the intellect in joining and separating, can be conformed with things, it can also be conformed with things in understanding their quiddities. Truth, therefore, is not merely in the intellect joining and separating.

To the Contrary:

1'. In the *Metaphysics* we read: "The true and the false are not in things but in the mind. In regard to simple natures and quiddities, however, it is not in the mind."

2'. In *The Soul* the statement is made that the true and the false are not to be found in simple apprehension.

REPLY:

Just as the true is found primarily in the intellect rather than in things, so also is it found primarily in an act of the intellect joining and separating, rather than in an act by which it forms the quiddities of things. For the nature of the true consists in a conformity of thing and intellect. Nothing becomes conformed with itself, but conformity requires distinct terms. Consequently, the nature of truth is first found in the intellect when the intellect begins to possess something proper to itself, not possessed by the thing outside the soul, yet corresponding to it, so that between the two—intellect and thing—a conformity may be found. In forming the quiddities of things, the intellect merely has a likeness of a thing existing outside the soul, as a sense has a likeness when it perceives the species of a sensible thing. But when the intellect begins to judge about the thing it has apprehended, then its judgment is something found outside in the thing. And the judgment is said to be true when it conforms to the external reality. Moreover, the intellect judges about the thing it has apprehended at the moment when it says that something is or is not. This is the role of "the intellect composing and dividing."

For these reasons, the Philosopher says that composition and division are in the intellect, and not in things. Moreover, this is why truth is found primarily in the joining and separating by the intellect, and only secondarily in its formation of the quiddities of things or definitions, for a definition is called true or false because of a true or false combination. For it may happen that a definition will be applied to something to which it does not belong, when the definition of a circle is assigned to a triangle. Sometimes, too, the parts of a definition cannot be reconciled, as happens when one defines a thing as "an animal entirely without the power of sensing." The judgment implied in such a definition—"some animal is incapable of sensing"— is false. Consequently, a definition is said to be true or false only because of its relation to a judgment, as a thing is said to be true because of its relation to intellect.

From our discussion, then, it is clear that the true is predicated, first of all, of joining and separating by the intellect;

54

second, of the definitions of things in so far as they imply a true or a false judgment. Third, the true may be predicated of things in so far as they are conformed with the divine intellect or in so far as, by their very nature, they can be conformed with human intellects. Fourth, true or false may be predicated of man in so far as he chooses to express truth, or in so far as he gives a true or false impression of himself or of others by his words and actions; for truth can be predicated of words in the same way as it can be predicated of the ideas which they convey.

Answers to Difficulties:

1. Although the formation of a quiddity is the first operation of the intellect, by it the intellect does not yet possess anything that, properly speaking, is its own and can be conformed to the thing. Truth, accordingly, is not found in it.

2. From this the solution of the second difficulty is clear.

ARTICLE IV

In the Fourth Article We Ask: Is There Only One Truth by Which All Things Are True?

Difficulties:

It seems that this is so, for

1. Anselm says that the relation of truth to all true things is like that of time to all temporal things. But there is only one time to which all temporal things are related. Therefore, there will be only one truth to which all true things are related.

2. But it was said that truth is used in two ways. In one, it means the entity of a thing, as when Augustine says: "The true is that which is." If truth be understood in this sense, then there should be as many truths as there are essences of things. In the second way in which truth is used, it signifies truth as it is expressed in the intellect. Consequently, Hilary writes: "The true affirms existence." But since nothing can manifest anything

to the intellect except in virtue of the first divine truth, all truths are, in some sense, one, inasmuch as they all move the intellect —just as colors are one in moving the sense of sight, since they all move it because of one thing: light.

On the contrary, however, time, the measure of all temporal things, is numerically one; and if truth is related to true things as time is related to temporal things, the truth of all true things must also be numerically one. It will not be sufficient for all truths to be one in their action of moving the intellect or to be one in their exemplary cause.

3. Anselm argues as follows: If there are as many truths as there are true things, then truths should change as true things change. But truths do not change with the changes of true things, for, even when true and correct things are destroyed, the truth and correctness by which they are true and correct remain. There is, therefore, only one truth. He proves the minor from this: When a sign is destroyed, the correctness of the signification remains, for it remains correct that the sign should signify that which it did signify. For the same reason, rectitude or truth remains even when a true or correct thing has been destroyed.

4. With regard to created things, nothing is identical with that whose truth it is. The truth of a man is not the man; the truth of flesh is not the flesh. But every created thing is true. No created thing, therefore, is truth. Consequently, every truth is uncreated, and so there is only one truth.

5. As Augustine says, only God is greater than the human mind. But, as he proves elsewhere, truth is greater than the human mind, for truth certainly cannot be said to be less than the human mind. If this were so, it would be within the competence of the mind to pass judgment on truth. This, of course, is false, for the mind does not judge truth but judges according to the truth, like a magistrate who does not pass judgment upon the law but, as Augustine himself says, judges according to the

law. Similarly, the mind of man cannot be said to be equal to truth, for it judges everything according to truth. It does not judge everything to itself. Truth, therefore, must be God alone, and so there is only one truth.

6. Augustine has proved that truth is not perceived by any bodily sense. His proof is that nothing is perceived by sense unless it is changeable. But truth is unchangeable. Truth, therefore, is not perceived by sense.

One could similarly argue that everything created is changeable. But truth is not changeable. Therefore, it is not a creature but is something uncreated. Consequently, there is only one truth.

7. Augustine offers another proof in the same place: "There is no sensible thing that does not have some similarity to what is false, and as a result, the two cannot be distinguished. To mention only one example: all that we sense through the body. Even these objects are not present to the senses, we experience their images as though they were present, as when we are asleep or become delirious." Truth, however, has no resemblance to what is false. Therefore, truth is not perceived by a sense.

One could similarly argue that every created thing has some similarity to what is false in so far as it has some defect. Nothing created therefore, is truth, and so there is only one truth.

To the Contrary:

1'. Augustine writes: "As likeness is the form of like things, so truth is the form of true things." But for many like things there are many likenesses. Therefore, for many true things there are many truths.

2'. Just as every created truth is derived from the uncreated as its model, and has its truth from it, so all intelligible light is derived from the first uncreated light as from its exemplary cause, and from it possesses its power of making things known. But we say that there are many intelligible lights, as is clear from the writings of Dionysius. Therefore, following this analogy, it seems we must likewise simply concede that there are many truths.

3'. Although all colors are able to affect the sense of sight in virtue of light, nevertheless, in themselves colors are distinct and different, and cannot be said to be one, except from a particular point of view. Consequently, even though all created truths manifest themselves in the intellect by virtue of the first truth, we cannot for this reason say that there is one truth, unless considered under this one aspect.

4'. Just as a created truth can manifest itself to the intellect only by virtue of the uncreated truth, so no power in a creature can act except by virtue of the uncreated power. Yet we do not say that somehow or other there is one power for all powers; so, in the same manner, we should not say that in some way there is one truth for all truths.

5'. God as a cause is related to things in three ways: as an efficient, an exemplary, and as a final cause. Consequently, by a kind of appropriation, the entity of things is referred to God as efficient cause, their truth to Him as an exemplary cause, their goodness to Him as a final cause—even though, properly speaking, each single one could be referred to each single cause. But in no manner of speaking do we say that there is one goodness for all things, or one entity for all beings. Therefore, we should not say that there is one truth for all true things.

6.' Although there is one uncreated truth from which all created truths take their model, these truths are not modeled on it in the same way. For while it is true that the uncreated truth has the same relation to all, all do not have the same relation to it—as pointed out in *The Causes*. Necessary and contingent truths are modeled on the uncreated truth in quite different ways. But different ways of imitating the divine model cause diversity among created things. Consequently, there are many created truths.

7'. Truth is "the conformity of thing and intellect." But since things differ specifically, there cannot be a single conformity to the intellect. So, since true things are specifically different, there cannot be one truth for all true things.

8'. Augustine writes as follows: "One must believe that the nature of the human mind is so connected with intelligible things that it gazes upon all it knows by means of a unique light." Now, the light by whose means the soul knows all things is truth. Truth, therefore, belongs to the same genus as the soul and must be a created thing. Consequently, in different creatures there are different truths.

REPLY:

From our previous discussion it is clear that truth is properly found in the human or divine intellect, as health is found in an animal. In things, however, truth is found because of some relation to intellect just as health is said to be in things other than animals in so far as they bring about or preserve animal health. Truth, therefore, is properly and primarily in the divine intellect. In the human intellect, it exists properly but secondarily, for it exists there only because of a relation to either one of the two truths just mentioned.

In his gloss on these words of Psalm 11 (v. 2), "Truths are decayed from among the children of men," Augustine writes that the truth of the divine intellect is one, and from it are drawn the many truths that are in the human intellect—"just as from one man's face many likenesses are reflected in a mirror." Now, there are many truths in things, just as there are many entities of things. But truth predicated of things because of their relation to the human intellect is, as it were, accidental to those things; for, supposing that the human intellect did not or could not exist, things would still remain essentially the same. But truth predicated of things because of their relation to the divine intellect is inseparably attendant on them, for they cannot exist except by reason of the divine intellect which keeps bringing them into being. Again, truth is primarily in a thing because of its relation to the divine intellect, not to human intellect, because it is related to the divine intellect as to its cause, but to the human intellect as to its effect in the sense that the latter receives its knowledge from things. For this reason, a thing is said to be true principally because of its order to the truth of the divine intellect rather than because of its relation to the truth of a human intellect.

So, if truth in its proper sense be taken as that by which all things are primarily true, then all things are true by means of one truth, the truth of the divine intellect. This is the truth which Anselm writes about. But if truth in its proper sense be taken as that by which things are said to be true secondarily, then there are many truths about many true things, and even many truths in different minds about one true thing. Finally if truth in its improper sense be taken as that by which all things are said to be true, then there are many truths for many true things, but only one truth for one true thing.

Things are called true from the truth in the divine or human intellect, just as food is called healthy, not because of any inherent form, but because of the health which is in an animal. If, however, a thing is called true because of the truth in the thing, which is simply its entity conformed with intellect, then it is so called because of something inhering in it after the manner of a form, as food is said to be healthy because of a quality of its own—which is the reason for its being said to be healthy.

Answers to Difficulties:

1. Time is related to temporal things as a measure is related to the measured. It is clear, therefore, that Anselm is referring to that truth which is only the measure of all true things. There is only one such truth numerically, just as there is only one time

—as the second argument concludes. However, the truth in the human intellect or in things themselves is not related to things as an extrinsic or common measure is related to those it measures. It is related as a measured thing is related to a measure, for such is the relation of truth in a human intellect to things, and it must as a consequence, vary as things vary. Or, it is related as an intrinsic measure to the thing itself, as is the case with the truth that is in things themselves. Intrinsic measures must be multiplied as the number of things measured is multiplied—just as dimensions must be multiplied with the multiplicity of bodies.

2. We concede the second argument.

3. The truth which remains after things are destroyed is the truth of the divine intellect, and this is numerically one. However, the truth which is in things or in the soul is diversified according to the diversity of things.

4. The proposition "Nothing is its own truth" is understood of things having a complete act of existence in reality. It is likewise said that "Nothing is its own act of existence," yet the act of existence of a thing is, in a sense, something created. In the same way, the truth of a thing is something created.

5. The truth by which the soul passes judgment on all things is the first truth; for, just as from the truth of the divine intellect there flow into the angelic intellects those intelligible species by which angels know all things, so does the truth of the divine intellect as from its exemplary cause. Since we can judge by means of the truth of these first principles only in so far as this truth is a likeness of the first truth, we are said to judge everything according to the first truth.

6. That immutable truth is the first truth, which is neither perceptible by sense nor something created.

7. Although every creature has some similarity to what is false, created truth itself does not have this similarity. For a creature has some similarity to what is false in so far as it is

deficient. Truth, however, does not depend on a creature in so far as it rises above its deficiency by being conformed to the first truth.

Answers to Contrary Difficulties:

1'. Properly speaking, when two things are similar, likeness is found in both. Truth, however, being a certain agreement of intellect and thing, is not, properly speaking, found in both, but only in intellect; and since all things are true and said to be true in so far as they are in conformity with one intellect, the divine intellect, everything must be true according to one truth, even though in many like things there are many different likenesses.

2'. Although intelligible light has the divine light for its exemplary cause, light is nevertheless predicated in the proper sense of created intelligible lights. Truth, however, is not predicated in the proper sense of things having the divine intellect as their exemplary cause. Consequently, we do not say that there is one light in the same way that we say that there is one truth.

3'. Our reply given immediately above will answer the argument taken from colors, for visible is properly predicated of colors, also, even though they are not seen except by means of light.

4'-5'. Our answer to the fourth argument (from the nature of power) and to the fifth (from the nature of being) is the same.

6'. Even though things are modeled in different ways upon the divine truth, this does not keep things from being true in the proper sense of the term by a single truth—not by many truths. For that which is received in different ways in the things modeled upon the exemplar is not properly called truth with the same propriety as truth is said to be in the exemplar itself.

7'. Although things differing specifically are not on their own part conformed with the divine intellect by one conformity, the divine intellect to which all things are conformed is one, and on its part there is one conformity with all things—even though all things are not conformed to it in the same way. The truth of all things, therefore, is one in the manner described.

8'. Augustine is speaking of truth in our mind as it is modeled upon the divine mind as the likeness of a face is reflected in a mirror; and, as we said, there are many reflections of the first truth in our souls. Or one can say that the first truth belongs to the genus of the soul if *genus* be taken in a broad sense, namely, in so far as everything intelligible or incorporeal is said to belong to one genus. *Genus* is used in this way in the Acts of the Apostles (17:28) where we read: "For we are also his offspring [*genus*]."

ARISTOTLE
(384-322 B.C.)

The great eclectic and synthesizer of Greek philosophy left behind him a system that dominated Western thought for almost two thousand years. His influence is still tremendous, especially in the field of epistemology. Much of philosophical writings, even in our days, reads, as it has been said, like annotations to Aristotle. Born in Stagira, he went to Athens, where he studied under Plato, the master against whom he was later to rebel. After serving as tutor to the Macedonian prince who was to become Alexander the Great, he returned to Athens where he opened a school. Aristotle's mind embraced all areas of human knowledge; he produced in each area an encyclopedic synthesis based on his belief that the mean is preferable to the extremes.

Main Works:

> Organon, Rhetoric, Topics, Metaphysics, Physics, On the Soul, Ethics, Politics, Poetics.

ON METAPHYSICS

1. [*The advance from sensation, through memory, experience, and art, to theoretical knowledge.*] All men by nature desire to know. An indication of this is the delight we take in our senses; for even apart from their usefulness they are loved for themselves; and above all others the sense of sight. For not only with a view to action, but even when we are not going to do anything, we prefer seeing (one might say) to everything else. The rea-

---

From: *Metaphysics* (translated by W. D. Ross).

son is that this, most of all the senses, makes us know and brings to light many differences between things.

By nature animals are born with the faculty of sensation, and from sensation memory is produced in some of them, though not in others. And therefore the former are more intelligent and apt at learning than those which cannot remember; those which are incapable of hearing sounds are intelligent though they cannot be taught, e. g., the bee, and any other race of animals that may be like it; and those which besides memory have this sense of hearing can be taught.

The animals other than man live by appearances and memories, and have but little of connected experience; but the human race lives also by art and reasonings. Now from memory experience is produced in men; for the several memories of the same thing produce finally the capacity for a single experience. And experience seems pretty much like science and art, but really science and art come to men *through* experience; for "experience made art," as Polus says, "but inexperience luck." Now art arises when from many notions gained by experience one universal judgment about a class of objects is produced. For to have a judgement that when Callias was ill of this disease this did him good, and similarly in the case of Socrates and in many individual cases, is a matter of experience; but to judge that it has done good to all persons of a certain constitution, marked off in one class, when they were ill of this disease, e. g., to phlegmatic or bilious people when burning with fever—this is a matter of art.

With a view to action experience seems in no respect inferior to art, and men of experience succeed even better than those who have theory without experience. (The reason is that experience is knowledge of individuals, art of universals, and actions and productions are all concerned with the individual; for the physician does not cure *man*, except in an incidental way, but Callias or Socrates or some other called by some such individual name, who happens to be a man. If, then, a man has the theory without the experience, and recognizes the universal but does not know the individual included in this, he will often fail to cure; for it is the individual that is to be cured). But yet we think that *knowledge* and *understanding* belong to art rather than to experience, and we suppose artists to be wiser than men of experience (which implies that Wisdom depends in all cases rather on knowledge); and this because the former know the cause, but the latter do not. For men of experience know that the thing is so, but do not know why, while the others know the "why" and the cause. Hence we think also that the master workers in each craft are more honorable and know in a truer sense and are wiser than the manual workers, because they know the causes of the things that are done (we think the manual workers are like certain lifeless things which act indeed, but act without knowing what they do, as fire burns—but while the lifeless things perform each of their functions by a natural tendency, the laborers perform them through habit); thus we view them as being wiser not in virtue of being able to act, but of having the theory for themselves and knowing the causes. And in general it is a sign of the man who knows and of the man who does not know, that the former can teach, and therefore we think art more truly knowledge than experience is; for artists can teach, and men of mere experience cannot.

Again, we do not regard any of the senses as Wisdom; yet surely these give the most authoritative knowledge of particulars. But they do not tell us the "why" of anything—e. g., why fire is hot; they only say *that* it is hot.

At first he who invented any art whatever that went beyond the common perceptions of man was naturally admired by men, not only because there was something useful in the inventions, but because he was thought wise and superior to the rest. But as more arts were invented, and some were directed to the necessities of life, others to recreation, the inventors of the latter were naturally always regarded as wiser than the inventors of the former, because their branches of knowledge did not aim at utility. Hence when all such inventions were already established, the sciences which do not aim at giving pleasure or at the necessities of life were discovered, and first in the places where men first began to have leisure. This is why the mathematical arts were founded in Egypt; for there the priestly caste was allowed to be at leisure.

We have said in the *Ethics* what the difference is between art and science and the other kindred faculties; but the point of our present discussion is this, that all men suppose what is called Wisdom to deal with first causes and the principles of things; so that, as has been said before, the man of experience is thought to be wiser than the possessors of any sense perception whatever, the artist wiser than the men of experience, the master worker than the mechanic, and the theoretical kinds of knowledge to be more of the nature of Wisdom than the productive. Clearly then Wisdom is knowledge about certain principles and causes.

2. [*Characteristics of "Wisdom" (philosophy)*] Since we are seeking this knowledge, we must inquire of what kind are the causes and the principles, the knowledge of which is Wisdom. If one were to take the notions we have about the wise man, this might perhaps make the answer more evident. We suppose first, then, that the wise man knows all things, as far as possible, although he has not knowledge of each of them in detail; secondly, that he who can learn things that are difficult, and not easy for man to know, is wise (sense perception is common to all, and therefore easy and no mark of Wisdom); again, that he who is more exact and more capable of teaching the causes is wiser, in every branch of knowledge; and that of the sciences, also, that which is desirable on its own account and for the sake of knowing it is more of the nature of Wisdom than that which is desirable on account of its results, and the superior science is more of the nature of Wisdom than the ancillary; for the wise man must not be ordered but must order, and he must not obey another, but the less wise must obey *him*.

Such and so many are the notions, then, which we have about Wisdom and the wise. Now of these characteristics that of knowing all things must belong to him who has in the highest degree universal knowledge; for he knows in a sense all the instances that fall under the universal. And these things, the most universal, are on the whole the hardest for men to know; for they are farthest from the senses. And the most exact of the sciences are those which deal most with first principles; for those which involve fewer principles are more exact than those which involve additional principles, e. g., arithmetic than geometry. But the science which investigates causes is also *instructive,* in a higher degree, for the people who instruct us are those who tell the causes of each thing. And understanding and knowledge pursued for their own sake are found most in the knowledge of that which is most knowable (for he who chooses to know for the sake of knowing will choose most readily that which is most truly knowledge, and such is the knowledge of that which is most knowable); and the first principles and the causes are most knowable; for by reason of these, and from these, all other things come to be known, and not these by means of the things subordinate to them. And the science which knows to what end each thing must be done is the most authoritative of the sciences, and more authoritative than any ancillary science; and this end is the good of that thing, and in general the supreme good in the whole of nature. Judged by all the tests we have mentioned, then, the name in question falls to the same science; this must be a science that investigates the first principles and causes; for the good, i.e., the end, is one of the causes.

That it is not a science of production is clear even from the history of the earliest philosophers. For it is owing to their wonder that men both now begin and at first began to philosophize; they wondered originally at the obvious difficulties, then advanced little by little and stated difficulties about the greater matters, e. g., about the phenomena of the moon and those of the sun and of the stars, and about the genesis of the universe. And a man who is puzzled and wonders thinks himself ignorant (whence even the lover of myth is in a sense a lover of Wisdom, for the myth is composed of wonders); therefore since they philosophized in order to escape from ignorance, evidently they were pursuing science in order to know, and not for any utilitarian end. And this is confirmed by the facts; for it was when almost all the necessities of life and the things that make for comfort and recreation had been secured, that such knowledge began to be sought. Evidently then we do not seek it for the sake of any other advantage; but as the man is free, we say, who exists for his own sake and not for another's, so we pursue this as the only free science, for it alone exists for its own sake.

Hence also the possession of it might be justly regarded as beyond human power; for in many ways human nature is in bondage, so that, according to Simonides, "God alone can have this privilege," and it is unfitting that man should not be content to seek the knowledge that is suited to him. If, then, there is something in what the poets say, and jealousy is natural to the divine power, it would probably occur in this case above all, and all who excelled in this knowledge would be unfortunate. But the divine power cannot be jealous (nay, according to the proverb, "bards tell many a lie"), nor should any other science be thought more honorable than one of this sort. For the most divine science is also most honorable; and this science alone must be, in two ways, most divine. For the science which it would be most meet for God to have is a divine science, and so is any science that deals with divine objects; and this science alone has both these qualities; for (1) God is thought to be among the causes of all things and to be a first principle, and (2) such a science either God alone can have, or God above all others. All the sciences, indeed, are more necessary than this, but none is better.

Yet the acquisition of it must in a sense end in something which is the opposite of our original inquiries. For all men begin, as we said, by wondering that things are as they are, as they do about self-moving marionettes, or about the solstices or the incommensurability of the diagonal of a square with the side; for it seems wonderful to all who have not yet seen the reason, that there is a thing which cannot be measured even by the smallest unit. But we must end in the contrary and, according to the proverb, the better state, as is the case in these instances too when men learn the cause; for there is nothing which would surprise a geometer so much as if the diagonal turned out to be commensurable.

We have stated, then, what is the nature of the science we are searching for, and what is the mark which our search and our whole investigation must reach.

3. [*The successive recognition by earlier philosophers of the material, efficient, and final causes.*] Evidently we have to acquire knowledge of the original causes (for we say we know each thing only when we think we recognize its first cause), and causes are spoken of in four senses. In one of these we mean the substance, i.e., the essence (for the "why" is reducible finally to the definition, and the ultimate "why" is a cause and principle); in another the matter or substratum, in a third the source of the change, and in a fourth cause opposed to this, the purpose and the good (for this is the end of all generation and change). We have studied these causes sufficiently in our work on nature, but yet let us call to our aid those who have attacked the investigation of being and philosophized about reality before us. For obviously they too speak of certain principles and causes; to go over their views, then, will be of profit to the present inquiry, for we shall either find another kind of cause, or be convinced of the correctness of those which we now maintain.

Of the first philosophers, then, most thought the principles which were of the nature of matter were the only principles of all things. That of which all things that are consist, the first from which they come to be, the last into which they are resolved (the substance remaining, but changing in its modifications), this they say is the element and this the principle of things, and therefore they think nothing is either generated or destroyed, since this sort of entity is always conserved, as we say Socrates neither comes to be absolutely when he comes to be beautiful or musical, nor ceases to be when he loses these characteristics, because the substratum, Socrates himself, remains. Just so they say nothing else comes to be or ceases to be;

for there must be some entity—either one or more than one—from which all other things come to be, it being conserved.

Yet they do not all agree as to the number and the nature of these principles. Thales, the founder of this type of philosophy, says the principle is water (for which reason he declared that the earth rests on water), getting the notion perhaps from seeing that the nutriment of all things is moist, and that heat itself is generated from the moist and kept alive by it (and that from which they come to be is a principle of all things). He got his notion from this fact, and from the fact that the seeds of all things have a moist nature, and that water is the origin of the nature of moist things.

Some think that even the ancients who lived long before the present generation, and first framed accounts of the gods, had a similar view of nature; for they made Ocean and Tethys the parents of creation, and described the oath of the gods as being by water, to which they give the name of Styx; for what is oldest is most honorable, and the most honorable thing is that by which one swears. It may perhaps be uncertain whether this opinion about nature is primitive and ancient, but Thales at any rate is said to have declared himself thus about the first cause. Hippo no one would think fit to include among these thinkers, because of the paltriness of his thought.

Anaximenes and Diogenes make air prior to water and the most primary of the simple bodies, while Hippasus of Metapontium and Heraclitus of Ephesus say this of fire, and Empedocles says it of the four elements (adding a fourth—earth—to those which have been named); for these, he says, always remain and do not come to be, except that they come to be more or fewer, being aggregated into one and segregated out of one.

Anaxagoras of Clazomenae, who, though older than Empedocles, was later in his philosophical activity, says the principles are infinite in number; for he says almost all the things that are made of parts like themselves, in the manner of water or fire, are generated and destroyed in this way, only by aggregation and segregation, and are not in any other sense generated or destroyed, but remain eternally.

From these facts one might think that the only cause is the so-called material cause; but as men thus advanced, the very facts opened the way for them and joined in forcing them to investigate the subject. However true it may be that all generation and destruction proceed from some one or (for that matter) from more elements, why does this happen and what is the cause? For at least the substratum itself does not make itself change; e.g., neither the wood nor the bronze causes the change of either of them, nor does the wood manufacture a bed and the bronze a statue, but something else is the cause of the change. And to seek this is to seek the second cause, as *we* should say—that from which comes the beginning of the movement. Now those who at the very beginning set themselves to this kind of inquiry, and said the substratum was one, were not at all dissatisfied with themselves; but some at least of those who maintain it to be one—as though defeated by this search for the second cause— say the one and nature as a whole is unchangeable not only in respect of generation and destruction (for this is a primitive belief, and all agreed in it), but also of all other change; and this view is peculiar to them. Of those who said the universe was one, then, none succeeded in discovering a cause of this sort, except perhaps Parmenides, and he only inasmuch as he supposes that there is not only one but also in some sense two causes. But for those who make more elements it is more possible to state the second cause, e.g., for those who make hot and cold, or fire and earth, the elements; for they treat fire as having a nature which fits it to move things, and water and earth and such things they treat in the contrary way.

When these men and the principles of this kind had had their day, as the latter were found inadequate to generate the nature of things men were again forced by the truth itself, as we said, to inquire into the next kind of cause. For it is not likely either that fire or earth or any such element should be the reason why things manifest goodness and beauty both in their being and in their coming to be, or that those thinkers should have supposed it was; nor again could it be right to entrust so great a matter to spontaneity and chance. When one man said, then, that reason was present—as in animals, so throughout nature— as the cause of order and of all arrangement, he seemed like a sober man in contrast with the random talk of his predecessors. We know that Anaxagoras certainly adopted these views, but Hermotimus of Clazomenae is credited with expressing them earlier. Those who thought thus stated that there is a principle of things which is at the same time the cause of beauty, and that sort of cause from which things acquire movement.

4. [*Inadequacy of the treatment of these causes.*] One might suspect that Hesiod was the first to look for such a thing—or some one else who put love or desire among existing things as a principle, as Parmenides, too, does; for he, in constructing the genesis of the universe, says:

> Love first of all the Gods she planned.

And Hesiod says:

> First of all things was chaos made, and then
> Broad-breasted earth, . . .
> And love, 'mid all the gods pre-eminent,

which implies that among existing things there must be from the first a cause which will move things and bring them together. How these thinkers should be arranged with regard to priority of discovery let us be allowed to decide later; but since the contraries of the various forms of good were also perceived to be present in nature—not only order and the beautiful, but also disorder and the ugly, and bad things in greater number than good, and ignoble things than beautiful—therefore another thinker introduced friendship and strife, each of the two the cause of one of these two sets of qualities. For if we were to follow out the view of Empedocles, and interpret it according to its meaning and not to its lisping expression, we should find that friendship is the cause of good things, and strife of bad. Therefore, if we said that Empedocles in a sense both mentions, and is the first to mention, the bad and the good as principles, we should perhaps be right, since the cause of all goods is the good itself.

These thinkers, as we say, evidently grasped, and to this extent, two of the causes which we distinguished in our work on nature—the matter and the source of the movement—vaguely, however, and with no clearness, but as untrained men behave in fights; for they go round their opponents and often strike fine blows, but they do not fight on scientific principles, and so too these thinkers do not seem to know what they say; for it is evident that, as a rule, they make no use of their causes except to a small extent. For Anaxagoras uses reason as a *deus ex machina* for the making of the world, and when he is at a loss to tell from what cause something necessarily is, then he drags reason in, but in all other cases ascribes events to anything rather than to reason. And Empedocles, though he uses the causes to a greater extent than this, neither does so sufficiently nor attains consistency in their use. At least, in many cases he makes love segregate things, and strife aggregate them. For whenever the universe is dissolved into its elements by strife, fire is aggregated into one, and so is each of the other elements; but whenever again under the influence of love they come together into one, the parts must again be segregated out of each element.

Empedocles, then, in contrast with his predecessors, was the first to introduce the dividing of this cause, not positing one source of movement, but different and contrary sources. Again, he was the first to speak of four material elements; yet he does not *use* four, but treats them as two only; he treats fire by itself, and its opposites—earth, air, and water—as one kind of thing. We may learn this by study of his verses.

This philosopher then, as we say, has spoken of the principles in this way, and made them of this number. Leucippus and his associate Democritus say that the full and the empty are the elements, calling the one being and the other non-being—the full and solid being being, the empty non-being (whence they say being no more is than non-being, because the solid no more is than the empty); and they make these the material causes of things. And as those who make the underlying substance one generate all other things by its modifications, supposing the rare and the dense to be the sources of the modifications, in the same way these philosophers say the differences in the elements are the causes of all other qualities. These differences, they say, are three—shape and order and position. For they say the real is differentiated only by "rhythm" and "inter-contact" and "turning"; and of these rhythm is shape, inter-contact is order, and turning is position; for A differs from N in shape, AN from NA in order, ⊢ from H in position. The question of movement—whence or how it is to belong to things—these thinkers, like the others, lazily neglected.

Regarding the two causes, then, as we say, the inquiry seems to have been pushed thus far by the early philosophers.

5. [*The Pythagorean and Eleatic schools.*] Contemporaneously with these philosophers and before them, the so-called Pythagoreans, who were the first to take up mathematics, not only advanced this study, but also having been brought up in it they thought its principles were the principles of all things. Since of these principles numbers are by nature the first, and in numbers they seemed to see many resemblances to the things that exist and come into being—more than in fire and earth and water (such and such a modification of numbers being justice, another being soul and reason, another being opportunity—and similarly almost all other things being numerically expressible); since, again, they saw that the modifications and the ratios of the musical scales were expressible in numbers; since, then, all other things seemed in their whole nature to be modelled on numbers, and numbers seemed to be the first things in the whole of nature, they supposed the elements of numbers to be the elements of all things, and the whole heaven to be a musical scale and a number. And all the properties of numbers and scales which they could show to agree with the attributes and parts and the whole arrangement of the heavens, they collected and fitted into their

scheme; and if there was a gap anywhere, they readily made additions so as to make their whole theory coherent. E.g., as the number 10 is thought to be perfect and to comprise the whole nature of numbers, they say that the bodies which move through the heavens are ten, but as the visible bodies are only nine, to meet this they invent a tenth—the "counter-earth." We have discussed these matters more exactly elsewhere.

But the object of our review is that we may learn from these philosophers also what they suppose to be the principles and how these fall under the causes we have named. Evidently, then, these thinkers also consider that number is the principle both as matter for things and as forming both their modifications and their permanent states, and hold that the elements of number are the even and the odd, and that of these the latter is limited, and the former unlimited; and that the One proceeds from both of these (for it is both even and odd), and number from the One; and that the whole heaven, as has been said, is numbers.

Other members of this same school say there are ten principles, which they arrange in two columns of cognates—limit and unlimited, odd and even, one and plurality, right and left, male and female, resting and moving, straight and curved, light and darkness, good and bad, square and oblong. In this way Alcmaeon of Croton seems also to have conceived the matter, and either he got this view from them or they got it from him; for he expressed himself similarly to them. For he says most human affairs go in pairs, meaning not definite contrarieties such as Pythagoreans speak of, but any chance contrarieties, e. g., white and black, sweet and bitter, good and bad, great and small. He threw out indefinite suggestions about the other contrarieties, but the Pythagoreans declared both how many and which their contrarieties are.

From both these schools, then, we can learn this much, that the contraries are the principles of things; and how many these principles are and which they are, we can learn from one of the two schools. But how these principles can be brought together under the causes we have named has not been clearly and articulately stated by them; they seem, however, to range the elements under the head of matter; for out of these as immanent parts they say substance is composed and molded.

From these facts we may sufficiently perceive the meaning of the ancients who said the elements of nature were more than one; but there are some who spoke of the universe as if it were one entity, though they were not all alike either in the excellence of their statement or in its conformity to the facts of nature. The discussion of them is in no way appropriate to our present investigation of causes, for they do not, like some of the natural philosophers, assume being to be one and yet generate it out of the one as out of matter, but they speak in another way; those others add change, since they generate the universe, but these thinkers say the universe is unchangeable. Yet *this* much is germane to the present inquiry: Parmenides seems to fasten on that which is one in definition, Melissus on that which is one in matter, for which reason the former says that it is limited, the latter that it is unlimited; while Xenophanes, the first of these partisans of the One (for Parmenides is said to have been his pupil), gave no clear statement, nor does he seem to have grasped the nature of either of these causes, but with reference to the whole material universe he says the One is God. Now these thinkers, as we said, must be neglected for the purposes of the present inquiry—two of them entirely, as being a little too naive, viz., Xenophanes and Melissus; but Parmenides seems in places to speak with more insight. For, claiming that, besides the existent, nothing nonexistent exists, he thinks that of necessity one thing exists, viz., the existent and nothing else (on this we have spoken more clearly in our work on nature), but being forced to follow the observed facts, and supposing the existence of that which is one in definition, but more than one according to our sensations, he now posits two causes and two principles, calling them hot and cold, i. e., fire and earth; and of these he ranges the hot with the existent, and the other with nonexistent.

From what has been said, then, and from the wise men who have now sat in council with us, we have got thus much—on the one hand from the earliest philosophers, who regard the first principle as corporeal (for water and fire and such things are bodies), and of whom some suppose that there is one corporeal principle, others that there are more than one, but both put these under the head of matter; and on the other hand from some who posit both this cause and besides this the source of movement, which we have got from some as single and from others as two-fold.

Down to the Italian school, then, and apart from it, philosophers have treated these subjects rather obscurely, except that, as we said, they have in fact used two kinds of cause, and one of these—the source of movement—some treat as one and others as two. But the Pythagoreans have said in the same way that there are two principles, but added this much, which is peculiar to them, that they thought that finitude and infinity were not attributes of certain other things, e.g., of fire or earth or anything else of this kind, but that infinity itself and unity itself were the substance of all things. On this subject, then, they expressed themselves thus; and regarding the question of essence they began to make statements and definitions, but treated the matter too simply. For they both defined superficially and thought that the first subject of which a given definition was predicable was the substance of the thing defined, as if one supposed that "double" and "2" were the same, because 2 is the first thing of which "double" is predicable. But surely to be double and to be 2 are not the same; if they are, one thing will be many—a consequence which they actually drew. From the earlier philosophers, then, and from their successors we can learn thus much.

ANTOINE ARNAULD
(1612-1694)

Leading French Jansenist at the Abbey of Port-Royal. Taught at the Sorbonne in Paris until his expulsion in 1656. He was an ardent follower of Descartes.

Main Works:
L'art de penser (with Pierre Nicole); De la fréquente communion.

Mental Confusion

In the preceding chapter we mentioned various instances of confused ideas, that may also be termed false, for the reason stated. But since the examples have all been taken from physics, it will not be without value to add others derived from ethics: the false ideas that are formed with respect to good and evil being infinitely more dangerous.

Whether a man has a false or a true idea, clear or obscure, of weight, of the sensible qualities, and of sensible actions, does not make him any more happy or unhappy. If he is thereby somewhat more or less knowledgeable, he is not on that account either more upright or more wicked. Whatever be our opinion on all these matters, they will not change for us. Their being is independent of our knowledge, and the conduct of our life is independent of a knowledge of their being. Thus, everyone can refer it to what we shall know in the next life, and in general

---

From: *Logique de Port Royal.*

rely for the universal order on the bounty and wisdom of him who governs it.

But no one can dispense with forming judgments on good and evil, since it is by these judgments that we must conduct our lives, regulate our actions, and bring everlasting happiness or unhappiness upon oneself: and as the false ideas that we have of all these things are the source of our bad judgments, it would be infinitely more important to apply ourselves to discover and correct them, than not to change those that our hasty judgments or the prejudices of our childhood make us conceive of the things in nature that are nothing but the object of a barren speculation.

To discover them all, we should have to construct an entire system of ethics: but here the only intention is to present some examples of the manner of forming them, by assembling together various ideas that are not united with truth, of which we thus compose vain phantoms that men run after and on which they nourish themselves wretchedly all their life.

Man finds within himself the idea of happiness and unhappiness, and this idea is neither false nor confused while it remains general. He has also ideas of pettiness and grandeur, of baseness and excellence: he craves happiness, he shuns unhappiness: he admires excellence, and scorns baseness.

But the corruption of sin, that separates him from God, in whom alone he could find his true happiness, and to whom alone consequently he should refer the concept of happiness, makes him attach it to an infinity of things into the lust for which he has flung himself in his desire to find the happiness that he had lost: and it is thus on this account that he has formed an infinity of false and obscure ideas, by imagining all the objects of his passion as being capable of making him happy and those that deprive him of it as making him miserable. He has likewise lost through sin true greatness and true excellence, and so he is constrained, in order to feel love for himself, to imagine that it is in fact otherwise: to conceal his wretchedness and poverty, and to enclose in his idea a great number of things that are entirely separated from it: finally, to heighten and magnify it: and here follows the ordinary course of those false ideas.

The primary and principal descent of concupiscence is toward the pleasure of the senses, that arises from certain external objects: and as the soul perceives that this pleasure that he loves comes from those objects, it straightway attaches thereto the concept of good, and the concept of evil to the deprivation thereof. Next, seeing that wealth and human power are the ordinary means of mastering these objects of concupiscence, it begins to regard them as great advantages and consequently it considers the rich and the great who possess them, as happy, and as unfortunate the poor who are deprived thereof.

Now, as there is a certain excellence in happiness, the soul never separates those two ideas, and it always regards as great all those whom it considers happy, and as petty those that it judges poor and unfortunate. And that is the reason for the contempt that we have for the poor, and the esteem that we have for the wealthy. These judgments are so unjust and so false, that Saint Thomas Aquinas believes it is this regard of esteem and admiration for the rich that is condemned so severely by the apostle St. James, when he refuses to grant a higher seat to the rich than to the poor in ecclesiastical assemblies. For this passage cannot be taken literally as a prohibition against giving certain external duties rather to the rich than to the poor, since secular society, untroubled by religion, permits such preferences, and since the saints too have practiced them. It seems then that one must understand it of that inner preference that makes the poor regarded as beneath the feet of the wealthy, and the wealthy as being infinitely above the poor.

But although those ideas and the judgments that arise therefrom are false and irrational, they are nevertheless common to all men who have not corrected them, because they are produced by the concupiscence that has affected all of them. Hence it is that we not only form those ideas of the wealthy, but we know that others have for them the same feelings of esteem and admiration: with the result that we consider their condition surrounded not only by all the pomp and comfort associated therewith, but also by all those advantageous judgments that we form of the wealthy, and that we recognize by the ordinary talk among men and by our own experience.

It is really this phantom, composed of all the admirers of the rich and the great, that is conceived as surrounding their throne and regarding them with inner feelings of dread, respect, and abasement, that becomes the idol of the ambitious, for which they labor all their life and expose themselves to so many perils.

To prove that this is what they seek and cherish, it is necessary merely to consider that if there were in the world one contemplative man only, and that all the others with human faces nothing but automata; and that moreover the solitary rational man, knowing perfectly well that all these statues that resembled him externally were entirely deprived of reason and thought, knew nevertheless the secret of manipulating them by means of springs and thereby securing all the services that we secure from human beings, we can quite well believe that he would occasionally amuse himself with the various manipulations that he would contrive in those statues: but he would certainly never equate his pleasure and glory with the external respect that he would extract from them: he would never be flattered by their reverence and he would even tire of it as quickly as one tires of puppets; so that he would normally be satisfied with securing from them the necessary services without worrying about collecting a greater number of them than he would require for his use.

It is not then the simple, external effects of men's obedience, separated from the view of their thoughts, that are the object of passion among the ambitious: they want to dominate men, not automata, and their pleasure consists in the sight of the movements of fear, esteem, and admiration that they arouse in others.

This reveals that the idea with which they are obsessed is as vain and as unsubstantial as that entertained by those that one properly calls vain men, who are such as feed on praise, acclamation, eulogy, titles and other things of this nature. The only thing that distinguishes them is the difference in the notions and judgments that they like to provoke: for instead of vain men having as their object the provocation of feelings of love and esteem for their knowledge, their eloquence, their wit, their suavity, their kindness, the ambitious want to arouse feelings of terror, respect, and abasement under their greatness, and ideas conforming to those judgments whereby they are regarded as awesome, distinguished, powerful. Thus, both types place their happiness in the thoughts of others: but one group selects certain thoughts, and the other, different ones.

There is nothing more common than to see these hollow phantoms, composed of false judgments of men, setting in motion the greatest enterprises and serving as the chief goal to all conduct in the life of man.

This value, so highly esteemed in society, that makes the seemingly brave plunge without fear into the greatest dangers, is often nothing but the effect of the application of their spirit to those empty and hollow thoughts that fill it. Few men seriously disdain life: and those who seem to confront death with such hardihood in a breach or in battle, tremble like the others, and often more so, when death attacks them in their bed. But what produces the great-heartedness that they manage to display in some encounters, is that they envisage on the one hand the mockery that we make of cowards, and on the other hand the praise given to gallant men: and this double phantom haunts them and turns them away from a consideration of danger and death.

It is for this reason that those who have cause to believe that men are watching them, being more inspired with these judgments, are more courageous and more generous. Thus captains are usually braver than soldiers, and nobler than those who are not, because, having more honor to lose or to acquire, they are also more intimately affected thereby. The same task, said a great captain, is not equally painful to an army general and to a private soldier, because a general is sustained by the judgments of an entire army that has its eyes on him, while a soldier has nothing to sustain him except the hopes of a slight reward and a humble reputation as a good soldier, that frequently does not extend beyond the particular campaign.

What is the aim of those people who build magnificent houses far above their position and their fortune? It is not simple comfort that they seek: this excessive magnificence is more harmful than serviceable, and it is evident too that if they were alone in the world, they would never take such trouble, any more than if they thought that all those who saw their homes would have nothing but feelings of contempt for them. It is then for men that they labor, and for men who acclaim them. They imagine that all those who see their palaces will conceive feelings of respect and admiration for the man who is the owner of the edifice: and thus they picture themselves among their palaces, surrounded by a retinue of men who survey them and consider them great, powerful, magnificent. And it is for this idea that overwhelms them, that they contract all these lavish expenses and take all these pains.

Why do we think the carriages of this vast throng of lackeys is loaded? It is not for the service that is secured thereby: they are more inconvenient than helpful. It is to arouse in passing, in those who see them, the idea that a personage of great importance is passing by: and the sight of this idea, that they picture is being formed on seeing these carriages, satisfies the vanity of those to whom they belong.

If one examines likewise all the conditions, all the employments, all the professions that are esteemed in society, it will be found that what makes them pleasant and allays the trouble and exhaustion that accompany them, is that they often present to the mind feelings of respect, esteem, fear, and admiration that others have for us.

On the other hand, what makes solitude irksome to most people is that, excluding them from the sight of men, it also excludes them from the sight of their judgments and thoughts. Thus, their heart remains hungry and empty, being deprived of this ordinary nourishment, and not finding within itself wherewith to fill it. And that is why the pagan philosophers judged the solitary life so unbearable that they dared to say that their Sage would not want to have all the physical and spiritual blessings if he had always to live alone without communicating his happiness to anyone. Only the Christian religion has been able to make the solitary life pleasant, because, leading men to scorn these vain ideas, it gives them at the same time other objectives more capable of occupying the mind and more worthy to fill their heart, for which they have no need whatever of the sight and commerce of men.

But we must observe that the love of men does not end immediately with knowing the thoughts and the sentiments of others; but that they use them only to magnify and heighten the notion that they have of themselves, adding and incorporating therein all these alien ideas and imagining by a coarse illusion that they are actually greater, because they are in a larger house and there are more people to admire them, although all these things that are external to them and all these thoughts of other men contribute nothing and leave them as poor and as unhappy as before.

It can be discovered from this what makes men like many things that seem to have nothing by themselves that is capable of amusing or pleasing these men: for the reason for their pleasure in such things is that the idea of themselves is presented to them as greater than normal through some vain circumstance that they attach thereto.

We take pleasure in speaking of the dangers that we have incurred, because we base on these accidents an idea that presents us to our own selves either as wise or as favored particularly by God. We like to talk of the sickness of which we have been cured, because we picture ourselves as having great strength in resisting serious misfortunes.

We want to secure an advantage in all circumstances, and

even in games of chance, where there is no skill, even when we do not play for money, because we add to our idea the concept of happiness: it seems that fortune has chosen us, and has favored us in view of our merits. We even conceive such putative happiness as a permanent quality that gives us the right to hope for like success in the future. That is why there are some men whom the players select and with whom they prefer to associate rather than with others. An entirely ridiculous situation: for it is quite reasonable to say that a man has been happy up to a certain moment: but as for the next moment, there is no greater probability that he will be so, any more than there is for those who have been most unfortunate.

Thus, the spirit of those that love mundane things only has, in fact, as its goal, nothing but vain phantoms to offer it wretched amusement and occupation; and those who pass for being very wise nourish themselves, like the others, solely on illusions and fantasies. Only those whose life and actions are associated with the eternals can be said to have a steadfast goal, real and subsistent; for it is true in respect of all the others that they love empty vanity, and that they pursue lies and falsehood.

We have already said that the necessity that compels us to employ external signs for mutual understanding makes us attach our ideas to words to such a degree that we often give more consideration to the words than to the things. Now, that is one of the most common causes of confusion in our thoughts and our talks.

For it should be observed that, although men often have different ideas about the same things, they nonetheless use the same words to express them. For example: A pagan philosopher's concept of virtue is not the same as a theologian's, and yet each expresses his idea by the same term *virtue*.

Further, the same men in different ages have considered the same things in very different ways, and yet they have always gathered all these ideas under the same name: which makes the pronunciation of this expression, or hearing it pronounced, a cause for easy confusion, as one man takes it in reference to one concept, and another to another concept. For example: A man who realized that there was in him something, whatever it might be, that gave him nourishment and growth, called it *soul,* and extended this idea to whatever was similar, not only in animals, but even in plants. And, having observed that he also thought, he still called by the name of *soul* that which was in him the principle of thinking: whence it happened that, through this resemblance of name, he took for the same thing that which thought and that which gave the body nourishment and growth. Similarly, the word *life* has equally been extended to that which is the cause of operations among animals, and to that which makes us think, two things absolutely different.

There is similarly much ambiguity in the words *sense* and *feelings,* even when these words are merely taken for one of the five corporeal senses. For normally three things occur in us when we use our senses, as when we observe something. The first thing is that certain notions take place in the physical organs, as in the eye and in the brain. The second, that these notions give reason to our soul to conceive something, as, when following the movement that occurs in our eye by the reflection of the light in raindrops opposed to the sun, it has ideas of red, blue, and orange. The third, the judgment that we form of what we see, as the rainbow, to which we attribute these colors and which we conceive to be of a certain grandeur, a certain shape, and at a certain distance. The first of these three things is solely in our body: the other two are only in our soul, although only at the time when something occurs in our body: and yet we include all three, although so different, under the same name of *sense* and *feeling,* or of *sight, hearing,* and so on. For when we say that the eye sees, that the ear hears, this can be understood only according to the motion of the corporeal organ, as it is quite clear that the eye has no perception of the objects that strike it, and that it is not the eye that forms a judgment. We say on the other hand that we have not seen a person who presented himself before us and who caught our eyes, when we have not reflected on the incident. And then the word *see* is taken for the thought that is formed in our mind, following what occurs in our eye and our brain: and according to this denotation of the word *see*, it is the mind that sees and not the body, as Plato maintains, and Cicero after him in these words: We do not even now see with our eyes that which we see, nor is there any feeling in the body. There are, as it were, certain hollowed-out channels leading from the seat of the mind to the eyes, ears, nostrils. Thus we are frequently prevented either by thought or some condition due to sickness, and, although our eyes and ears are open and unimpaired, we neither see nor hear: so that it can be readily understood that the mind both sees and hears, not those parts that are, so to speak, the windows of the soul. Finally, the words *sense, sight, hearing,* etc. are taken for the last of these three things, that is, for the judgments that our own mind forms subsequently of the perceptions that it has experienced at the incidence of what happened in the corporeal organs, when we say that the senses are mistaken, as when they see in the water a broken stick, and when the sun seems to us only two feet in diameter. For it is certain that there cannot be any error or falsity either in all that occurs in the corporeal organ, or in the mere perception of our mind, which is only a simple apprehension: but that the entire error comes solely from our bad judgment in concluding, for example, that the sun is only two feet in diameter, because its vast remoteness makes the image formed deep in the eye almost of the same size as that formed by an object two feet distant, which is more in accord with our usual way of seeing. But because we have formed this judgment since childhood and are so accustomed to it that it occurs at the very moment of seeing the sun, without almost any reflection, we attribute it to sight and say that we see the objects as small or large, as they are nearer and farther from us, although it is our mind and not our eye that judges their small and large size.

Every language is full of an infinite number of such words,

that have the same sound, but are nevertheless signs of entirely different ideas.

But it should be observed that when an ambiguous word signifies two things that have no relation to each other, and that people have never confused in their thought, it is almost impossible in that case for a mistake to be made and for the word to be the cause of any error: just as we are not confused, provided we have a little common sense, by the ambiguity of the word *ram*, that denotes an animal, and a sign of the zodiac. Although the ambiguity came from man's own mistake, erroneously confusing different ideas, as in the word *mind*, it is difficult to rid oneself of the misconception, because we assume that those who first used those words understood them quite well: and thus we are often satisfied to pronounce them, without ever investigating whether the idea that we form of these words is clear and distinct: and we even attribute to that which we call by the same name what applies to incompatible things only, without perceiving that this occurs merely from our having confused two different things under the same name.

The best way to avoid confusion of words that occur in ordinary languages is to create a new language and new words that are not associated only with the concepts that we want them to represent: but, for that purpose, it is not necessary to create new sounds, because we can use those that are already in use, treating them as if they had no denotation, in order to give them the denotation that we want them to have, and to designate by other simple words, completely unambiguous, the idea to which we want to apply them: as when I want to prove that our soul is immortal, the word *soul*, being ambiguous, as we have shown, will readily create confusion in what I have to say: so that, to avoid this situation, I shall consider the word *soul* as if it were a sound that had not yet any meaning, and I shall apply it solely to that which is in us the principle of thought, and say: I call *soul* that which is in us the principle of thought.

This is what is called the definition of the word, *definitio nominis*, that geometricians employ so usefully, and which must be distinguished from the definition of the thing, *definitio rei*.

For in the definition of the thing, as, perhaps, thus: Man is a rational animal, Time is the measure of motion, we let the defined term, as *man* or *time*, retain its usual idea, in which we claim that other ideas are contained, as *rational animal* or *measure of motion*, instead of in the definition of the word, as we have already said, we consider only the sound, and then we determine this sound as being a sign of an idea that we designate by other words.

We must also take care not to confuse the definition of names of which we are speaking here with that of which some philosophers speak, who understand thereby the explanation of what a word signifies according to the ordinary usage of a language, or according to its etymology, a topic we shall be able to discuss elsewhere: but here, on the contrary, we consider only the particular use in which the person who defines the word wants it to be taken for his thought to be clearly understood, without troubling whether others take it in the same sense.

And hence it follows in the first place that the definitions of names are arbitrary, and that the definitions of things are not: for each sound being different, of itself and by its nature, in signifying all sorts of ideas, I may, for my own particular use, and provided that I warn others, determine a sound to signify precisely a certain thing, without intrusion of any other thing: but it is quite otherwise with the definition of things: for it does not in the least depend on men's wishes that ideas should include what they want them to include: so that if, when we want to define them, we attribute to these ideas something that they do not contain, we necessarily fall into error.

Thus, as an example of each: If I strip the word *parallelogram* of all meaning, and apply it to signify a triangle, I may do so, and I am guilty of no error thereby, provided that I take it only in this way: and I shall be able to say then that the parallelogram has three angles equal to two right angles.

But if, letting this now retain its meaning and its usual concept, which is to signify a figure whose sides are parallel, I had just stated that the parallelogram is a figure with three sides, because that would then be a definition of things, it would be quite false, since it is impossible for a figure with three sides to have parallel sides.

It follows secondly that the definitions of names are incontrovertible, by the very fact that they are arbitrary. For you cannot deny that a man has given to a sound the meaning that he says he has given, nor that it has this meaning in the way that this person uses it, after warning us about it. But as for the definition of things, we are often right in questioning them, since they may be false, as we have shown.

It follows, thirdly, that every definition of a name, being incontrovertible, can be taken as a principle, while the definitions of things can in no sense be taken as principles and are true propositions that can be refuted by those who find any obscurity therein: and consequently these propositions require proof like other propositions, and must not be assumed, unless they are as evident as axioms.

Nevertheless, what I have just stated, that the definition of a name can be taken as a principle, requires explanation. For this is not true except that we need not question the idea that we have formed being able to be called by the name we have given it. But we must not draw any conclusion from this in favor of this idea, or think that, just because we have given it a name, it signifies something real. For example: I can define the word *chimera* by saying: I understand by *chimera* that which implies a contradiction: and yet it will not follow from this that the chimera is something. Similarly, if a philosopher says to me: I understand by *weight* the inner principle that makes a stone fall without being pushed, I shall not question this definition. On the contrary, I shall accept it willingly, because it helps me to understand what he means. But I shall deny that what he means by the word *weight* is something real, because there is no such principle in stones.

My intention has been to make this rather long explanation, because there are two great abuses committed on this subject in philosophy in general. The first is to confuse the definition of the thing with the definition of the name, and to attribute to the former what is appropriate only to the latter. For, after forming, as their fancy suggested, hundreds of definitions, not of name, but of things, that are totally false, and that in no sense explain the entire nature of the things nor the ideas that we have of them naturally, these philosophers then want these definitions to be considered as incontrovertible principles: and, if there is any refutation of these definitions, for they are very open to refutation, they claim that their opponents are unworthy of dispute.

The second abuse is that, scarcely ever using any definition of names in order to remove obscurity and attach them to certain ideas clearly denoted, they leave them thus in their confused state. Whence it happens that most of their disputes are merely wordy disputes: and, what is more, that they use whatever is clear and true in the confused ideas, to establish whatever obscurity and falsity these ideas have. This could easily be recognized if the names had been defined. Thus, the philosophers usually believe that the most evident thing in the world is that fire is hot, and that a stone has weight and that it would be foolish to deny it, and, in fact, they would like to persuade everyone of it, so long as there is no definition of names: but, by defining them, we shall easily discover whether what is denied of these names under this topic is clear or obscure: for we must ask these philosophers what they mean by the word *hot* and the word *weight*. If they reply that by *hot* they understand only that which is apt to cause in us the feeling of heat, and by *weight,* that which falls, having no support, they are right in saying that one must be irrational to deny that fire is hot and that a stone has weight. But, if they understand by *hot* that which has in itself a quality similar to that which we imagine when we think of heat, and by *weight* that which has in itself an inner principle that makes it move toward the center, without being pushed by anything whatever, then it will be easy to point out to them that it is not a denial of an evident fact, but a very obscure, not to say very false one, when we deny that in this sense fire is hot and that a stone has weight: because it is quite evident that fire produces in us the feeling of heat through the impression that it makes on our body: but it is by no means evident that fire has anything in it similar to that which we feel when we are near the fire: and it is likewise very evident that a stone falls when we release it: but it is by no means evident that it falls of its own accord, without being pushed by something.

Herein then lies the great usefulness of definition of names, in explaining clearly what the subject is about, in order to avoid useless discussion of words, that are taken in one sense or another, as is so often the case, even in ordinary conversations.

But, apart from this usefulness, there is still another one: that is, that we can often have no distinct idea of a thing except by using many words to denote it. Now, it would be irksome, especially in books on science, to repeat constantly this vast sequence of words. That is why, after explaining the thing by means of all these words, we attach to one single word the idea that we have conceived, and this word takes the place of all the others. Thus, understanding that there are numbers that are equally divisible in two, to avoid the frequent repetition of all these terms, we give a name to this property and say: I call every number that is equally divisible in two, an even number. That shows that whenever we use a word that we have defined, we must mentally substitute the definition in place of the thing defined, and keep this definition so present that, as soon as we name, for example, the even number, we understand precisely that it is the one which is equally divisible in two, and that these two things are so united and inseparable in thought, that the moment our talk expresses one of them, the mind immediately attaches the other thereto. For those who define terms, we geometricians do, with the greatest care, do so only to curtail the talk, that would become boring with such frequent circumlocutions. Let us not create delays by constant circumlocutions, as St. Augustine says. But they do not do this to curtail the ideas of the things that they discuss, because they claim that the mind will furnish the short terms with the entire definitions that are employed merely to avoid the embarrassment that a multitude of words would cause.

SIR FRANCIS BACON
(1561-1626)

Bacon was raised to the peerage as Baron Verulam. Educated at Cambridge, he became a lawyer and, through his uncle Lord Burghley obtained a seat in the House of Commons. His real rise in politics started only after Elizabeth was succeeded by James I, who made Bacon Solicitor-General, Attorney-General, Lord Keeper of the Seal and Lord Chancellor. He retired in disgrace after a technical conviction for bribery. Bacon represents the finest flowering of the Elizabethan era as far as science is concerned. His empirical mode of philosophy was long dominant in Anglo-Saxon countries and has not even now been really superseded. He forms a link between the Renaissance and the Age of Science. In revolt against Aristotelianism and scholastic logic he suggested the inductive method of discovering truth based upon empirical observation and verification by experiment. He considered prejudgment as the real impediment of truth which he classifies as the four idols: Idols of the Tribe, or presuming; Idols of the Cave, or personal prejudice; Idols of the Market-Place, or lack of proper definition; Idols of the Theatre, or uncritical acceptance of tradition.

Main Works:

> De dignitate et augmentis scientiarum; Novum Organum; Historia Naturalis et Experimentalis; Essays.

Induction

But by far the greatest obstacle to the progress of science and to the undertaking of new tasks and provinces therein, is found in this—that men despair and think things impossible. For wise

---

From: *Novum Organum.*

and serious men are wont in these matters to be altogether distrustful; considering with themselves the obscurity of nature, the shortness of life, the deceitfulness of the senses, the weakness of the judgment, the difficulty of experiment and the like; and so supposing that in the revolution of time and of the ages of the world the sciences have their ebbs and flows: that at one season they grow and flourish, at another wither and decay, yet in such sort that when they have reached a certain point and condition they can advance no further. If therefore any one believes or promises more, they think this comes of an ungoverned and unripened mind, and that such attempts have prosperous beginnings, become difficult as they go on, and end in confusion. Now since these are thoughts which naturally present themselves to grave men and of great judgment, we must take good heed that we be not led away by our love for a most fair and excellent object to relax or diminish the severity of our judgment; we must observe diligently what encouragement dawns upon us and from what quarter; and, putting aside the lighter breezes of hope, we must thoroughly sift and examine those which promise greater steadiness and constancy. Nay, and we must take state-prudence too into our counsels, whose rule is to distrust, and to take the less favourable view of human affairs. I am now therefore to speak touching Hope; especially as I am not a dealer in promises, and wish neither to force nor to ensnare men's judgments, but to lead them by the hand with their good will. And though the strongest means of inspiring hope will be to bring men to particulars; especially to particulars digested and arranged in my Tables of Discovery (the subject partly of the second, but much more of the fourth part of my Instauration), since this is not merely the promise of the thing itself; nevertheless that everything may be done with gentleness, I will proceed with my plan of preparing men's minds: of which preparation to give hope is no unimportant part. For without it the rest tends rather to make men sad (by giving them a worse and meaner opinion of things as they are than they now have, and making them more fully to feel and know the unhappiness of their own condition) than to induce any alacrity or to whet their industry in making trial. And therefore it is fit that I publish and set forth those conjectures of mine which make hope in this matter reasonable; just as Columbus did, before that wonderful voyage of his across the Atlantic, when he gave the reasons for his conviction that new lands and continents might be discovered besides those which were known before; which reasons, though rejected at first, were afterwards made good by experience, and were the causes and beginnings of great events.

The beginning is from God; for the business which is in hand, having the character of good so strongly impressed upon it, appears manifestly to proceed from God, who is the author of good, and the Father of Lights. Now in divine operations even the smallest beginnings lead of a certainty to their end. And as it was said of spiritual things, "The kingdom of God cometh not with observation," so is it in all the greater works of Divine Providence; everything glides on smoothly and noiselessly, and the work is fairly going on before men are aware that it has begun. Nor should the prophecy of Daniel be forgotten, touching the last ages of the world: "Many shall go to and fro, and knowledge shall be increased;" clearly intimating that the thorough passage of the world (which now by so many distant voyages seems to be accomplished, or in course of accomplishment), and the advancement of the sciences, are destined by fate, that is, by Divine Providence, to meet in the same age.

Next comes a consideration of the greatest importance as an argument of hope; I mean that drawn from the errors of past time, and of the ways hitherto trodden. For most excellent was the censure once passed upon a Government that had been unwisely administered. "That which is the worst thing in reference to the past, ought to be regarded as best for the future. For if you had done all that your duty demanded, and yet your affairs were no better, you would not have even a hope left you that further improvement is possible. But now, when your misfortunes are owing, not to the force of circumstances, but to your own errors, you may hope that by dismissing or correcting these errors, a great change may be made for the better." In like manner, if during so long a course of years men had kept the true road for discovering and cultivating sciences, and had yet been unable to make further progress therein, bold doubtless and rash would be the opinion that further progress is possible. But if the road itself has been mistaken, and men's labour spent on unfit objects, it follows that the difficulty has its rise not in things themselves, which are not in our power, but in the human understanding, and the use and application thereof, which admits of remedy and medicine. It will be of great use therefore to set forth what these errors are; for as many impediments as there have been in times past from this cause, so many arguments are there of hope for the time to come. And although they have been partly touched before, I think fit here also, in plain and simple words to represent them.

Those who have handled sciences have been either men of experiment or men of dogmas. The men of experiment are like the ant; they only collect and use: the reasoners resemble spiders, who make cobwebs out of their own substance. But the bee takes a middle course; it gathers its material from the flowers of the garden and of the field, but transforms and digests it by a power of its own. Not unlike this is the true business of philosophy; for it neither relies solely or chiefly on the powers of the mind, nor does it take the matter which it gathers from natural history and mechanical experiments and lay it up in the memory whole, as it finds it; but lays it up in the understanding altered and digested. Therefore from a closer and purer league between these two faculties, the experimental and the rational (such as has never yet been made), much may be hoped.

We have as yet no natural philosophy that is pure; all is

tainted and corrupted; in Aristotle's school by logic; in Plato's by natural theology; in the second school of Platonists, such as Proclus and others, by mathematics, which ought only to give definiteness to natural philosophy, not to generate or give it birth. For a natural philosophy pure and unmixed, better things are to be expected.

No one has yet been found so firm of mind and purpose as resolutely to compel himself to sweep away all theories and common notions, and to apply the understanding, thus made fair and even, to a fresh examination of particulars. Thus it happens that human knowledge, as we have it, is a mere medley and ill-digested mass, made up of much credulity and much accident, and also of the childish notions which we at first imbibed.

Now if any one of ripe age, unimpaired sense, and well-purged mind, apply himself anew to experience and particulars, better hopes may be entertained of that man. In which point I promise to myself a like fortune to that of Alexander the Great; and let no man tax me with vanity till he have heard the end; for the thing which I mean tends to the putting off of all vanity. For of Alexander and his deeds Aeschines spake thus: "Assuredly we do not live the life of mortal men; but to this end were we born, that in after ages wonders might be told of us;" as if what Alexander had done seemed to him miraculous. But in the next age Titus Livius took a better and a deeper view of the matter, saying in effect, that Alexander "had done no more than take courage to despise vain apprehensions." And a like judgment I suppose may be passed on myself in future ages: that I did no great things, but simply made less account of things that were accounted great. In the meanwhile, as I have already said, there is no hope except in a new birth of science; that is, in raising it regularly up from experience and building it afresh; which no one (I think) will say has yet been done or thought of.

Now for grounds of experience—since to experience we must

come—we have as yet had either none or very weak ones; no search has been made to collect a store of particular observations sufficient either in number, or in kind, or in certainty, to inform the understanding, or in any way adequate. On the contrary, men of learning, but easy withal and idle, have taken for the construction or for the confirmation of their philosophy certain rumours and vague fames or airs of experience, and allowed to these the weight of lawful evidence. And just as if some kingdom or state were to direct its counsels and affairs, not by letters and reports from ambassadors and trustworthy messengers, but by the gossip of the streets; such exactly is the system of management introduced into philosophy with relation to experience. Nothing duly investigated, nothing verified, nothing counted, weighed, or measured, is to be found in natural history: and what in observation is loose and vague, is in information deceptive and treacherous. And if any one thinks that this is a strange thing to say, and something like an unjust complaint, seeing that Aristotle, himself so great a man, and supported by the wealth of so great a king, has composed so accurate a history of animals; and that others with greater diligence, though less pretence, have made many additions; while others, again, have compiled copious histories and descriptions of metals, plants, and fossils; it seems that he does not rightly apprehend what it is that we are now about. For a natural history which is composed for its own sake is not like one that is collected to supply the understanding with information for the building up of philosophy. They differ in many ways, but especially in this; that the former contains the variety of natural species only, and not experiment of the mechanical arts. For even as in the business of life a man's disposition and the secret workings of his mind and affections are better discovered when he is in trouble than at other times; so likewise the secrets of Nature reveal themselves more readily under the vexations of art than when they go their own way. Good hopes may therefore be conceived of natural philosophy, when natural history, which is the basis and foundation of it, has been drawn up on a better plan; but not till then.

Again, even in the great plenty of mechanical experiments, there is yet a great scarcity of those which are of most use for the information of the understanding. For the mechanic, not troubling himself with the investigation of truth, confines his attention to those things which bear upon his particular work, and will not either raise his mind or stretch out his hand for anything else. But then only will there be good ground of hope for the further advance of knowledge, when there shall be received and gathered together into natural history a variety of experiments, which are of no use in themselves, but simply serve to discover causes and axioms; which I call *"Experimenta lucifera,"* experiments of *light*, to distinguish them from those which I call *"fructifera,"* experiments of *fruit*.

Now experiments of this kind have one admirable property and condition; they never miss or fail. For since they are applied, not for the purpose of producing any particular effect, but only of discovering the natural cause of some effect, they answer the end equally well which ever way they turn out; for they settle the question.

But not only is a greater abundance of experiments to be sought for and procured, and that too of a different kind from those hitherto tried; an entirely different method, order, and process for carrying on and advancing experience must also be introduced. For experience, when it wanders in its own track, is, as I have already remarked, mere groping in the dark, and confounds men rather than instructs them. But when it shall proceed in accordance with a fixed law, in regular order, and without interruption, then may better things be hoped of knowledge.

But even after such a store of natural history and experience as is required for the work of the understanding, or of philosophy, shall be ready to hand, still the understanding is by no means competent to deal with it off-hand and by memory alone; no more than if a man should hope by force of memory to retain and make himself master of the computation of an ephemeris. And yet hitherto more has been done in matter of invention by thinking than by writing; and experience has not yet learned her letters. Now no course of invention can be satisfactory unless it be carried on in writing. But when this is brought into use, and experience has been taught to read and write, better things may be hoped.

Moreover, since there is so great a number and army of particulars, and that army so scattered and dispersed as to distract and confound the understanding, little is to be hoped for from the skirmishings and slight attacks and desultory movements of the intellect, unless all the particulars which pertain to the subject of inquiry shall, by means of Tables of Discovery, apt, well arranged, and as it were animate, be drawn up and marshalled; and the mind be set to work upon the helps duly prepared and digested which these tables supply.

But after this store of particulars has been set out duly and in order before our eyes, we are not to pass at once to the investigation and discovery of new particulars or works; or at any rate if we do so we must not stop there. For although I do not deny that when all the experiments of all the arts shall have been collected and digested, and brought within one man's knowledge and judgment, the mere transferring of the experiments of one art to others may lead, by means of that experience which I term *literate,* to the discovery of many new things of service to the life and state of man, yet it is no great matter that can be hoped from that; but from the new light of axioms, which having been educed from those particulars by a certain method and rule, shall in their turn point out the way again to new particulars, greater things may be looked for. For our road does not lie on a level, but ascends and descends; first ascending to axioms, then descending to works.

The understanding must not however be allowed to jump and fly from particulars to remote axioms and of almost the highest generality (such as the first principles, as they are called, of arts and things), and taking stand upon them as truths that cannot be shaken, proceed to prove and frame the middle axioms by reference to them; which has been the practice hitherto; the understanding being not only carried that way by a natural impulse, but also by the use of syllogistic demonstration trained and inured to it. But then, and then only, may we hope well of the sciences, when in a just scale of ascent, and by successive steps not interrupted or broken, we rise from particulars to lesser axioms; and then to middle axioms, one above the other; and last of all to the most general. For the lowest axioms differ but slightly from bare experience, while the highest and most general (which we now have) are notional and abstract and without solidity. But the middle are the true and solid and living axioms, on which depend the affairs and fortunes of men; and above them again, last of all, those which are indeed the most general; such I mean as are not abstract, but of which those intermediate axioms are really limitations.

The understanding must not therefore be supplied with wings, but rather hung with weights, to keep it from leaping and flying. Now this has never yet been done; when it is done, we may entertain better hopes of the sciences.

HENRI BERGSON
(1859-1941)

Taught philosophy at Clermont-Ferrand and later at the Collège de France in Paris, where his courses became immensely popular. Being of Jewish origin, he was subject to the racial laws passed in France under the Nazi occupation; one of his last and most dignified acts was to reject the Vichy government's offer of exemption. Bergson's philosophy was that of "creative evolution". It was part of the anti-rationalist and anti-mechanist reaction of the late 19th century and emphasized intuition and the "life-force". Bergson had a great influence in the cultural life of France and the West generally.

Main Works:

> Essai sur les données immédiates de la conscience; Matière et Mémoire; Introduction à la métaphysique; Le Rire; L'Evolution Créatrice; Les deux sources de la morale et de la religion; Les données immédiates de l'expérience.

Defining Metaphysics

1

If we compare the various ways of defining metaphysics and of conceiving the absolute, we shall find, despite apparent discrepancies, that philosophers agree in making a deep distinction between two ways of knowing a thing. The first implies going all around it, the second entering into it. The first depends on the viewpoint chosen and the symbols employed, while the

From: *Introduction à la Métaphysique.*

second is taken from no viewpoint and rests on no symbol. Of the first kind of knowledge we shall say that it stops at the *relative;* of the second that, wherever possible, it attains the *absolute.*

Take, for example, the movement of an object in space. I perceive it differently according to the point of view from which I look at it, whether from that of mobility or of immobility. I express it differently, furthermore as I relate it to the system of axes or reference points, that is to say, according to the symbols by which I translate it. And I call it *relative* for this double reason: in either case, I place myself outside the object itself. When I speak of an absolute movement, it means that I attribute to the mobile an inner being and, as it were, states of soul; it also means that I am in harmony with these states and enter into them by an effort of imagination. Therefore, according to whether the object is mobile or immobile, whether it adopts one movement or another, I shall not have the same feeling about it. And what I feel will depend neither on the point of view I adopt toward the object, since I am in the object itself, nor on the symbols by which I translate it, since I have renounced all translation in order to possess the original. In short, the movement will not be grasped from without and, as it were, from where I am, but from within, inside it, in what it is in itself. I shall have hold of an absolute.

Or again, take a character whose adventures make up the subject of a novel. The novelist may multiply traits of character, make his hero speak and act as much as he likes: all this has not the same value as the simple and indivisible feeling I should experience if I were to coincide for a single moment with the personage himself. The actions, gestures and words would then appear to flow naturally, as though from their source. They would no longer be accidents making up the idea I had of the character, constantly enriching this idea without ever succeeding in completing it. The character would be given to me all at once in its entirety, and the thousand and one incidents which make it manifest, instead of adding to the idea and enriching it,

105

would, on the contrary, seem to me to fall away from it without in any way exhausting or impoverishing its essence. I get a different point of view regarding the person with every added detail I am given. All the traits which describe it to me, yet which can only enable me to know it by comparisons with persons or things I already know, are signs by which it is more or less symbolically expressed. Symbols and points of view then place me outside it; they give me only what it has in common with others and what does not belong properly to it. But what is properly itself, what constitutes its essence, cannot be perceived from without, being internal by definition, nor be expressed by symbols, being incommensurable with everything else. Description, history and analysis in this case leave me in the relative. Only by coinciding with the person itself would I possess the absolute.

It is in this sense, and in this sense alone, that *absolute* is synonymous with *perfection*. Though all the photographs of a city taken from all possible points of view indefinitely complete one another, they will never equal in value that dimensional object, the city along whose streets one walks. All the translations of a poem in all possible languages may add nuance to nuance and, by a kind of mutual retouching, by correcting one another, may give an increasingly faithful picture of the poem they translate, yet they will never give the inner meaning of the original. A representation taken from a certain point of view, a translation made with certain symbols still remain imperfect in comparison with the object whose picture has been taken or which the symbols seek to express. But the absolute is perfect in that it is perfectly what it is.

It is probably for the same reason that the *absolute* and the *infinite* are often taken as identical. If I wish to explain to someone who does not know Greek the simple impression that a line of Homer leaves upon me, I shall give the translation, then I shall develop my commentary, and from explanation to explanation I shall get closer to what I wish to express; but I shall never quite reach it. When you lift your arm you accomplish a movement the simple perception of which you have inwardly; but outwardly, for me, the person who sees it, your arm passes through one point, then through another, and between these two points there will be still other points, so that if I begin to count them, the operation will continue indefinitely. Seen from within, an absolute is then a simple thing; but considered from without, that is to say relative to something else, it becomes, with relation to those signs which express it, the piece of gold for which one can never make up the change. Now what lends itself at the same time to an indivisible apprehension and to an inexhaustible enumeration is, by definition, an infinite.

It follows that an absolute can only be given in an *intuition*, while all the rest has to do with *analysis*. We call intuition here the *sympathy* by which one is transported into the interior of an object in order to coincide with what there is unique and consequently inexpressible in it. Analysis, on the contrary, is the operation which reduces the object to elements already known, that is, common to that object and to others. Analyzing then consists in expressing a thing in terms of what is not it. All analysis is thus a translation, a development into symbols, a representation taken from successive points of view from which are noted a corresponding number of contacts between the new object under consideration and others believed to be already known. In its eternally unsatisfied desire to embrace the object around which it is condemned to turn, analysis multiplies endlessly the points of view in order to complete the ever incomplete representation, varies interminably the symbols with the hope of perfecting the always imperfect translation. It is analysis ad infinitum. But intuition, if it is possible, is a simple act.

This being granted, it would be easy to see that for positive science analysis is its habitual function. It works above all with symbols. Even the most concrete of the sciences of nature, the sciences of life, confine themselves to the visible form of living beings, their organs, their anatomical elements. They compare these forms with one another, reduce the more complex to the more simple, in fact they study the functioning of life in what is, so to speak, its visual symbol. If there exists a means of possessing a reality absolutely, instead of knowing it relatively, of placing oneself within it instead of adopting points of view toward it, of having the intuition of it instead of making the analysis of it, in short, of grasping it over and above all expression, translation or symbolical representation, metaphysics is that very means. *Metaphysics is therefore the science which claims to dispense with symbols.*

2

There is at least one reality which we all seize from within, by intuition and not by simple analysis. It is our own person in its flowing through time, the self which endures. With no other thing can we sympathize intellectually, or if you like, spiritually. But one thing is sure: we sympathize with ourselves.

When, with the inner regard of my consciousness, I examine my person in its passivity, like some superficial encrustment, first I perceive all the perceptions which come to it from the material world. These perceptions are clear-cut, distinct, juxtaposed or mutually juxtaposable; they seek to group themselves into objects. Next I perceive memories more or less adherent to these perceptions and which serve to interpret them; these memories are, so to speak, as if detached from the depth of my person and drawn to the periphery by perceptions resembling them, they are fastened on me without being absolutely myself. And finally, I become aware of tendencies, motor habits, a crowd of virtual actions more or less solidly bound to those perceptions and these memories. All these elements with their well-defined forms appear to me to be all the more distinct from myself the more they are distinct from one another. Turned outwards from within, together they constitute the surface of a sphere which tends to expand and lose itself in the external world. But if I pull myself in from the periphery toward the center, if I seek deep down within me what is the most uniformly, the most constantly and durably myself, I find something altogether different.

Henri Bergson

What I find beneath these clear-cut crystals and this superficial congelation is a continuity of flow comparable to no other flowing I have ever seen. It is a succession of states each one of which announces what follows and contains what precedes. Strictly speaking they do not constitute multiple states until I have already got beyond them, and turn around to observe their trial. While I was experiencing them they were so solidly organized, so profoundly animated with a common life, that I could never have said where any one of them finished or the next one began. In reality, none of them do begin or end; they all dovetail into one another.

It is, if you like, the unrolling of a spool, for there is no living being who does not feel himself coming little by little to the end of his span; and living consists in growing old. But it is just as much a continual winding, like that of thread into a ball, for our past follows us, becoming larger and larger with the present it picks up on its way; and consciousness means memory.

To tell the truth, it is neither a winding nor an unwinding, for these two images evoke the representation of lines or surfaces whose parts are homogeneous to and superposable on one another. Now, no two moments are identical in a conscious being. Take for example the simplest feeling, suppose it to be constant, absorb the whole personality in it: the consciousness which will accompany this feeling will not be able to remain identical with itself for two consecutive moments, since the following moment always contains, over and above the preceding one, the memory the latter has left it. A consciousness which had two identical moments would be a consciousness without memory. It would therefore die and be re-born continually. How otherwise can unconsciousness be described?

We must therefore evoke a spectrum of a thousand shades, with imperceptible graduations leading from one shade to another. A current of feeling running through the spectrum, becoming tinted with each of these shades in turn, would suffer gradual changes, each of which would announce the following and sum up within itself the preceding ones. Even then the successive shades of the spectrum will always remain external to each other. They are juxtaposed. They occupy space. On the contrary, what is pure duration excludes all idea of juxtaposition, reciprocal exteriority and extension.

Instead, let us imagine an infinitely small piece of elastic, contracted, if that were possible, to a mathematical point. Let us draw it out gradually in such a way as to bring out of the point a line which will grow progressively longer. Let us fix our attention not on the line as line, but on the action which traces it. Let us consider that this action, in spite of its duration, is indivisible if one supposes that it goes on without stopping; that, if we intercalate a stop in it, we make two actions of it instead of one and that each of these actions will then be the indivisible of which we speak; that it is not the moving act itself which is never indivisible, but the motionless line it lays down beneath it like a track in space. Let us take our mind off the space subtending the movement and concentrate solely on the movement itself, on the act of tension or extension, in short, on pure mobility. This time we shall have a more exact image of our development in duration.

And yet that image will still be incomplete, and all comparison furthermore will be inadequate, because the unrolling of our duration in certain aspects resembles the unity of a movement which progresses, in others, a multiplicity of states spreading out, and because no metaphor can express one of the two aspects without sacrificing the other. If I evoke a spectrum of a thousand shades, I have before me a complete thing, whereas duration is the state of completing itself. If I think of an elastic being stretched, of a spring being wound or unwound, I forget the wealth of coloring characteristic of duration as something lived and see only the simple movement by which consciousness goes from one shade to the other. The inner life is all that at once, variety of qualities, continuity of progress, unity of direction. It cannot be represented by images.

But still less could it be represented by *concepts,* that is, by abstract ideas, whether general or simple. Doubtless no image

110

will quite answer to the original feeling I have of the flowing of myself. But neither is it necessary for me to try to express it. To him who is not capable of giving himself the intuition of the duration constitutive of his being, nothing will ever give it, neither concepts nor images. In this regard, the philosopher's sole aim should be to start up a certain effort which the utilitarian habits of mind of everyday life tend, in most men, to discourage. Now the image has at least the advantage of keeping us in the concrete. No image will replace the intuition of duration, but many different images, taken from quite different orders of things, will be able, through the convergence of their action, to direct the consciousness to the precise point where there is a certain intuition to seize on. By choosing images as dissimilar as possible, any one of them will be prevented from usurping the place of the intuition it is instructed to call forth, since it would then be driven out immediately by its rivals. By seeing that in spite of their differences in aspect they all demand of our mind the same kind of attention and, as it were, the same degree of tension, one will gradually accustom the consciousness to a particular and definitely determined disposition, precisely the one it will have to adopt in order to appear unveiled to itself. But even then the consciousness must acquiesce in this effort; for we shall have shown it nothing. We shall simply have placed it in the attitude it must take to produce the desired effort and, by itself, to arrive at the intuition. On the other hand the disadvantage of too simple concepts is that they are really symbols which take the place of the object they symbolize and which do not demand any effort on our part. Upon close examination one would see that each of them retains of the object only what is common to that object and to others. Each of them is seen to express, even more than does the image, a *comparison* between the object and those objects resembling it. But as the comparison has brought out a resemblance, and as the resemblance is a property of the object, and as a property seems very much as though it were a *part* of the object possessing it, we are easily persuaded that by juxtaposing concepts to concepts we shall recompose the

111

whole of the object with its parts and obtain from it, so to speak, an intellectual equivalent. We shall in this way think we are forming a faithful representation of duration by lining up the concepts of unity, multiplicity, continuity, finite or infinite divisibility, etc. That is precisely the illusion. And that, also, is the danger. In so far as abstract ideas can render service to analysis, that is, to a scientific study of the object in its relations with all others, to that very extent are they incapable of replacing intuition, that is to say, the metaphysical investigation of the object in what essentially belongs to it. On the one hand, indeed, these concepts placed end to end will never give us anything more than an artificial recomposition of the object of which they can symbolize only certain general and, as it were, impersonal aspects: therefore it is vain to believe that through them one can grasp a reality when all they present is its shadow. But on the other hand, alongside the illusion, there is also a very grave danger. For the concept generalizes at the same time that it abstracts. The concept can symbolize a particular property only by making it common to an infinity of things. Therefore it always more or less distorts this property by the extension it gives to it. A property put back into the metaphysical object to which it belongs coincides with the object, at least moulds itself on it, adopting the same contours. Extracted from the metaphysical object and represented in a concept, it extends itself indefinitely, surpassing the object since it must henceforth contain it along with others. The various concepts we form of the properties of a thing are so many much larger circles drawn round it, not one of which fits it exactly. And yet, in the thing itself, the properties coincided with it and therefore with each other. We have no alternative then but to resort to some artifice in order to reestablish the coincidence. We shall take any one of these concepts and with it try to rejoin the others. But the junction will be brought about in a different way, depending upon the concept we start from. According to whether we start, for example, from unity or from multiplicity, we shall form a different conception of the multiple unity of duration. Everything will depend on the weight we assign to this or that concept, and this weight will always be arbitrary, since the concept, extracted from the object, has no weight, being nothing more than the shadow of a body. Thus a multiplicity of different *systems* will arise, as many systems as there are external viewpoints on the reality one is examining or as there are larger circles in which to enclose it. The simple concepts, therefore, not only have the disadvantage of dividing the concrete unity of the object into so many symbolical expressions; they also divide philosophy into distinct schools, each of which reserves its place, chooses its chips, and begins with the others a game that will never end. Either metaphysics is only this game of ideas, or else, if it is a serious occupation of the mind, it must transcend concepts to arrive at intuition. To be sure, concepts are indispensable to it, for all the other sciences ordinarily work with concepts, and metaphysics cannot get along without the other sciences. But it is strictly itself only when it goes beyond the concept, or at least when it frees itself of the inflexible and ready-made concepts and creates others very different from those we usually handle, I mean flexible, mobile, almost fluid representations, always ready to mould themselves on the fleeting forms of intuition. I shall come back to this important point a little later. It is enough for us to have shown that our duration can be presented to us directly in an intuition, that it can be suggested indirectly to us by images, but that it cannot—if we give the word *concept* its proper meaning—be enclosed in a conceptual representation.

GEORGE BERKELEY
(1685-1753)

Of a prominent Anglo-Irish family, studied at Kilkenny and Trinity College, Dublin. Ordained a Protestant clergyman in 1707, he rose to be bishop of Cloyne in 1734. He spent some time in America. Berkeley was a champion of idealism, or rather of a theological immaterialism. His main purpose was to make evident the existence of God and to prove that God is the true cause of all things. He stressed the distinction between the ideas and mind itself in a manner that made him a precursor of Kant. To Berkeley, nothing can be said to exist excepting spirits and ideas (*esse est percipii*).

Main Works:

A New Theory of Vision; Treatise concerning the Principles of Human Knowledge; Three Dialogues Between Hylas and Philonous; Alciphron; De Motu; Siris.

Of Human Knowledge

1. It is evident to any one who takes a survey of the *objects of human knowledge,* that they are either *ideas* actually imprinted on sense; or else such as are perceived by attending to the passions and operations of the mind; or lastly, *ideas* formed by help of memory and imagination—either compounding, dividing, or barely representing those originally perceived in the aforesaid ways. By sight I have the ideas of light and colours,, with their several degrees and variations. By touch I perceive hard and not soft, heat and cold, motion and resistance; and

---

From: *Principles of Human Knowledge.*

of all these more and less either as to quantity or degree. Smelling furnishes me with odours; the palate with tastes; and hearing conveys sounds to the mind in all their variety of tone and composition.

And as several of these are observed to accompany each other, they come to be marked by one name, and so to be reputed as one *thing*. Thus, for example, a certain colour, taste, smell, figure and consistence having been observed to go together, are accounted one distinct thing, signified by the name apple; other collections of ideas constitute a stone, a tree, a book, and the like sensible things; which as they are pleasing or disagreeable excite the passions of love, hatred, joy, grief, and so forth.

2. But, besides all that endless variety of ideas or objects of knowledge, there is likewise Something which knows or perceives them; and exercises diverse operations, as willing, imagining, remembering, about them. This perceiving, active being is what I call *mind, spirit, soul,* or *myself.* By which words I do not denote any one of my ideas, but a thing entirely distinct from them, wherein they exist, or, which is the same thing, whereby they are perceived; for the existence of an idea consists in being perceived.

3. That neither our thoughts, nor passions, nor ideas formed by the imagination, exist without the mind is what everybody will allow. And to me it seems no less evident that the various sensations or ideas imprinted on the Sense, however blended or combined together (that is, whatever objects they compose), cannot exist otherwise than in a mind perceiving them. I think an intuitive knowledge may be obtained of this, by any one that shall attend to what is meant by the term *exist* when applied to sensible things. The table I write on I say exists; that is, I see and feel it: and if I were out of my study I should say it existed; meaning thereby that if I was in my study I might perceive it, or that some other spirit actually does perceive it. There was an odour, that is, it was smelt; there was a sound, that is, it was

heard; a colour or figure, and it was perceived by sight or touch. This is all that I can understand by these and like expressions. For as to what is said of the *absolute* existence of unthinking things, without any relation to their being perceived, that is to me perfectly unintelligible. Their *esse* is *percipi;* nor is it possible they should have any existence out of the minds or thinking things which perceive them.

4. It is indeed an opinion strangely prevailing amongst men, that houses, mountains, rivers, and in a word all sensible objects, have an existence, natural or real, distinct from their being perceived by the understanding. But with how great an assurance and acquiescence soever this Principle may be entertained in the world, yet whoever shall find in his heart to call it in question may, if I mistake not, perceive it to involve a manifest contradiction. For, what are the forementioned objects but the things we perceive by sense? and what do we perceive besides our own ideas or sensations? and is it not plainly repugnant that any one of these, or any combination of them, should exist unperceived? . . .

6. Some truths there are so near and obvious to the mind that a man need only open his eyes to see them. Such I take this important one to be, viz. that all the choir of heaven and furniture of the earth, in a word all those bodies which compose the mighty frame of the world, have not any subsistence without a mind; that the *being* is to be perceived or known; that consequently so long as they are not actually perceived by me, or do not exist in my mind, or that of any other created spirit, they must either have no existence at all, or else subsist in the mind of some Eternal Spirit: it being perfectly unintelligible, and involving all the absurdity of abstraction, to attribute to any single part of them an existence independent of spirit. [To be convinced of which, the reader need only reflect, and try to

separate in his own thoughts the *being* of a sensible thing from its *being perceived.*]

7. From what has been said it is evident there is not any other Substance than *Spirit,* or that which perceives. But, for the fuller proof of this point, let it be considered the sensible qualities are colour, figure, motion, smell, taste, and such like, that is, the ideas perceived by sense. Now, for an idea to exist in an unperceiving thing is manifest contradiction; for to have an idea is all one as to perceive: that therefore wherein colour, figure, and the like qualities exist must perceive them. Hence it is clear there can be no unthinking substance or *substratum* of those ideas.

8. But, say you, though the ideas themselves do not exist without the mind, yet there may be things like them, whereof they are copies or resemblances; which things exist without the mind, in an unthinking substance. I answer, an idea can be like nothing but an idea; a colour or figure can be like nothing but another colour or figure. If we look but ever so little into our thought, we shall find it impossible for us to conceive a likeness except only between our ideas. Again, I ask whether those supposed *originals,* or external things, of which our ideas are the pictures or representations, be themselves perceivable or no? If they are, then *they* are ideas, and we have gained our point: but if you say they are not, I appeal to any one whether it be sense to assert a colour is like something which is invisible; hard or soft, like something which is intangible; and so of the rest.

9. Some there are who make a distinction *betwixt primary* and *secondary* qualities. By the former they mean extension, figure, motion, rest, solidity or impenetrability, and number; by the latter they denote all other sensible qualities, as colours, sounds, tastes, and so forth. The ideas we have of these last they acknowledge not to be the resemblances of anything

existing without the mind, or unperceived; but they will have our ideas of the *primary qualities* to be patterns or images of things which exist without the mind, in an unthinking substance which they call Matter. By Matter, therefore, we are to understand an inert, senseless substance, in which extension, figure, and motion do actually subsist. But it is evident, from what we have already shewn, that extension, figure and motion are only ideas existing in the mind, and that an idea can be like nothing but another idea; and that consequently neither they nor their archetypes can exist in an unperceiving substance. Hence, it is plain that the very notion of what is called *Matter* or *corporeal substance,* involves a contradiction in it. [Insomuch that I should not think it necessary to spend more time in exposing its absurdity. But, because the tenet of the existence of Matter seems to have taken so deep a root in the minds of philosophers, and draw after it so many ill consequences, I choose rather to be thought prolix and tedious than omit anything that might conduce to the full discovery and extirpation of that prejudice.]

10. They who assert that figure, motion, and the rest of the primary or original qualities do exist without the mind, in unthinking substances, do at the same time acknowledge that colours, sounds, heat, cold, and such-like secondary qualities, do not; which they tell us are sensations, existing in the mind alone, that depend on and are occasioned by the different size, texture, and motion of the minute particles of matter. This they take for an undoubted truth, which they can demonstrate beyond all exception. Now, if it be certain that those *original* qualities are inseparably united with the other sensible qualities, and not, even in thought, capable of being abstracted from them, it plainly follows that *they* exist only in the mind. But I desire any one to reflect, and try whether he can, by any abstraction of thought, conceive the extension and motion of a body without all other sensible qualities. For my own part, I see evidently that it is not in my power to frame an idea of a body extended and moving, but I must withal give it

some colour or other sensible quality, which is acknowledged to exist only in the mind. In short, extension, figure, and motion, abstracted from all other qualities, are inconceivable. Where therefore the other sensible qualities are, there must these be also, to wit, in the mind and nowhere else . . .

14. I shall farther add, that after the same manner as modern philosophers prove certain sensible qualities to have no existence in Matter, or without the mind, the same thing may be likewise proved of all other sensible qualities whatsoever. Thus, for instance, it is said that heat and cold are affections only of the mind, and not at all patterns of real beings, existing in the corporeal substances which excite them; in that the same body which appears cold to one hand seems warm to another. Now, why may we not as well argue that figure and extension are not patterns or resemblances of qualities existing in Matter; because to the same eye at different stations, or eyes of a different texture at the same station, they appear various, and cannot therefore be the images of anything settled and determinate without the mind? Again, it is proved that sweetness is not really in the sapid thing; because the thing remaining unaltered the sweetness is changed into bitter, as in case of a fever or otherwise vitiated palate. Is it not as reasonable to say that motion is not without the mind; since if the succession of ideas in the mind become swifter, the motion, it is acknowledged, shall appear slower, without any alteration in any external object?

15. In short, let any one consider those arguments which are thought manifestly to prove that colours and tastes exist only in the mind, and he shall find they may with equal force be brought to prove the same thing of extension, figure, and motion. Though it must be confessed this method of arguing does not so much prove that there is no extension or colour

in an outward object, as that we do not know by sense which is the true extension or colour of the object. But the arguments foregoing plainly shew it to be impossible that any colour or extension at all, or other sensible quality whatsoever, should exist in an unthinking subject without the mind, or in truth that there should be any such thing as an outward object . . .

18. But, though it were possible that solid, figured, moveable substances may exist without the mind, corresponding to the ideas we have of bodies, yet how is it possible for us to know this? Either we must know it by Sense or by Reason. As for our senses, by them we have the knowledge only of our sensations, ideas, or those things that are immediately perceived by sense, call them what you will: but they do not inform us that things exist without the mind, or unperceived, like to those which are perceived. This the materialists themselves acknowledge.—It remains therefore that if we have any knowledge at all of external things, it must be by reason inferring their existence from what is immediately perceived by sense. But [I do not see] what reason can induce us to believe the existence of bodies without the mind, from what we perceive, since the very patrons of Matter themselves do not pretend there is any necessary connexion betwixt them and our ideas? I say it is granted on all hands (and what happens in dreams, frenzies, and the like, puts it beyond dispute) that it is possible we might be affected with all the ideas we have now, though no bodies existed without resembling them. Hence it is evident the supposition of external bodies is not necessary for the producing our ideas; since it is granted they are produced sometimes, and might possibly be produced always, in the same order we see them in at present, without their concurrence.

19. But, though we might possibly have all our sensations without them, yet perhaps it may be thought easier to conceive

and explain the manner of their production, by supposing external bodies in their likeness rather than otherwise; and so it might be at least probable there are such things as bodies that excite their ideas in our minds. But neither can this be said. For, though we give the materialists their external bodies, they by their own confession are never the nearer knowing how our ideas are produced; since they own themselves unable to comprehend in what manner body can act upon spirit, or how it is possible it should imprint any idea in the mind. Hence it is evident the production of ideas or sensations in our minds, can be no reason why we should suppose Matter or corporeal substances; since that is acknowledged to remain equally inexplicable with or without this supposition. If therefore it were possible for bodies to exist without the mind, yet to hold they do so must needs be a very precarious opinion; since it is to suppose, without any reason at all, that God has created innumerable beings that are entirely useless, and serve to no manner of purpose.

20. In short, if there were external bodies, it is impossible we should ever come to know it; and if there were not, we might have the very same reasons to think there were that we have now. Suppose—what no one can deny possible—an intelligence, without the help of external bodies, to be affected with the same train of sensations or ideas that you are, imprinted in the same order and with like vividness in his mind. I ask whether that intelligence hath not all the reason to believe the existence of Corporeal Substances, represented by his ideas, and exciting them in his mind, that you can possibly have for believing the same thing? Of this there can be no question. Which one consideration were enough to make any reasonable person suspect the strength of whatever arguments he may think himself to have, for the existence of bodies without the mind . . .

22. I am afraid I have given cause to think I am needlessly prolix in handling this subject. For, to what purpose is it to dilate on that which may be demonstrated with the utmost evidence in a line or two, to any one that is capable of the least reflexion? It is but looking into your own thoughts, and so trying whether you can conceive it possible for a sound, or figure, or motion, or colour to exist without the mind or unperceived. This easy trial may perhaps make you see that what you contend for is a downright contradiction. Insomuch that I am content to put the whole upon this issue:—If you can but conceive it possible for one extended moveable substance, or in general for any one idea, or anything like an idea, to exist otherwise than in a mind perceiving it, I shall readily give up the cause. And, as for all that compages of external bodies you contend for, I shall grant you its existence, though you cannot either give me any reason why you believe it exists, or assign any use to it when it is supposed to exist. I say, the bare possibility of your opinions being true shall pass for an argument that it is so.

23. But, say you, surely there is nothing easier than for me to imagine trees, for instance, in a park, or books existing in a closet, and nobody by to perceive them. I answer, you may so, there is no difficulty in it. But what is all this, I beseech you, more than framing in your mind certain ideas which you call *books* and *trees*, and at the same time omitting to frame the idea of any one that may perceive them? But do not you yourself perceive or think of them all the while? This therefore is nothing to the purpose: it only shews you have the power of imagining, or forming ideas in your mind; but it does not shew that you can conceive it possible the objects of your thought may exist without the mind. To make out this, it is necessary that you conceive them existing unconceived or unthought of; which is a manifest repugnancy. When we do our utmost to conceive the existence of external bodies, we

are all the while only contemplating our own ideas. But the mind, taking no notice of itself, is deluded to think it can and does conceive bodies existing unthought of, or without the mind, though at the same time they are apprehended by, or exist in, itself. A little attention will discover to any one the truth and evidence of what is here said, and make it unnecessary to insist on any other proofs against the existence of *material substance*.

24. [Could men but forbear to amuse themselves with words, we should, I believe, soon come to an agreement in this point.] It is very obvious, upon the least inquiry into our own thoughts, to know whether it be possible for us to understand what is meant by the *absolute existence of sensible objects in themselves*, or *without the mind*. To me it is evident those words mark out either a direct contradiction, or else nothing at all. And to convince others of this, I know no readier or fairer way than to entreat they would calmly attend to their own thoughts: and if by this attention the emptiness or repugnancy of those expressions does appear, surely nothing more is requisite for their conviction. It is on this therefore that I insist, to wit, that the *absolute existence of unthinking things* are words without a meaning, or which includes a contradiction. This is what I repeat and inculcate, and earnestly recommend to the attentive thoughts of the reader.

25. All our ideas, sensations, notions, or the things which we perceive, by whatsoever names they may be distinguished, are visibly inactive: there is nothing of power or agency included in them. So that one idea or object of thought cannot produce or make any alteration in another. To be satisfied of the truth of this, there is nothing else requisite but a bare observation of our ideas. For, since they and every part of them exist only in the mind, it follows that there is nothing in them but what is perceived: but whoever shall attend to his ideas, whether of sense or reflexion, will not perceive in them

any power or activity; there is, therefore, no such thing contained in them. A little attention will discover to us that the very being of an idea implies passiveness and inertness in it; insomuch that it is impossible for an idea to do anything, or, strictly speaking, to be the cause of anything: neither can it be the resemblance or pattern of any active being, as is evident from Section 8. Whence it plainly follows that extension, figure, and motion cannot be the cause of our sensation. To say, therefore, that these are the effects of powers resulting from the configuration, number, motion, and size of corpuscles, must certainly be false.

26. We perceive a continual succession of ideas; some are anew excited, others are changed or totally disappear. There is therefore, *some* cause of these ideas, whereon they depend, and which produces and changes them. That this cause cannot be any quality or idea or combination of *ideas,* is clear. It must therefore be a *substance;* but it has been shewn that there is no corporeal or material substance: it remains therefore that the cause of ideas is an incorporeal active substance or Spirit . . .

JACOB BERNOUILLI
(1654-1705)

Jacob, or Jacques, or James Bernouilli was Professor of mathematics at Basel. He had a distinguished career as a mathematical analyst after considerable experiment and travel. Among his many discoveries is the equiangular spiral. He wrote the first textbook of the calculus of probability, based on the ideas of Pascal, Fermat and Huyghens. In his old age the curve appeared to him a symbol of his life and faith and by his wish the spiral was engraved on his tombstone.

Main Work:
  Ars Conjectandi.

Probabilities

Although in games governed by pure chance the results are usually uncertain, it can nevertheless always be determined with certainty how much nearer a player is to win than to lose. For example, if some one wagers that he will take a six at the first throw of the dice, it is uncertain whether he will win: but the probability that he has of winning or losing has nothing doubtful in it, and can be submitted to calculation. Similarly, too, if I play with someone a game in three sets, and have already won one, it is still uncertain which of us two will be the first to win three sets. But we can determine by very accurate reasoning the validity of my expectation and his too, and consequently determine in what proportion the bet or the

---

From: *Ars Conjectandi.*

common stake should be shared between us, if we agreed to leave the game unfinished at this point: or at what price I could equitably sell my chance to someone who wanted to take my place. Hence an endless number of questions can arise between two, three, or more players. But since this type of calculation is quite uncommon, and there is frequent occasion for employing it, I shall here succinctly expound its principle or method and then explain what is particularly pertinent to dice.

The basic principle of my method is this: In games of hazard, the chance or the expectation of each player in gaining any point must be estimated in the degree to which he can ultimately realize that same chance or expectation when playing with equal stakes. For example: If someone without my knowledge hides three cents in one hand and seven cents in the other, and he lets me choose from either hand, I assert that this advantage is for me the same as if he gave me five cents: for, with five cents, I can find myself in the situation of having an equal expectation of three cents or seven cents, and that while playing with equal stakes.

PROPOSITION I

If I expect a or b and one may happen as easily as the other, my expectation may be said to have the value of $\dfrac{a+b}{2}$.

Here is how we can not only demonstrate but actually formulate this rule.

Let x be the value of my expectation. Having x, I am bound, playing with equal stakes, to find myself in the position of having a similar chance. Suppose then that I play with another man on the following conditions: first, that each one stakes x and that the winner hands over a to the loser. This condition is valid and it is clear that, by this procedure, I have an equal chance to gain a, if I lose the game, or $2x-a$, if I win. For, in the latter case, I have $2x$, that was staked, of which I must give a to my opponent. Now if $2x-a$ has the same value as b, I have

an equal chance for *a* and for *b*. Therefore I make 2x—a=b, and I have x=a+b for the value of my expectation. The proof
$$\overline{2}$$
of this is simple. For, having a+b, I can play with another
$$\overline{2}$$
person, who will also stake a+b, on condition that the winner
$$\overline{2}$$
hands over *a* to the loser. In this fashion, my chance is equal for *a* if I lose, and for *b*, if I win: since, in the latter case, I win the stake a+b, of which I give *a* to my opponent.

In Numbers. If my chance is to have 3 or 7, with equal probability, my expectation has the value of 5 according to the previous proposition: and it is certain that having 5 I can still attain the same expectation: for having 5 I can play with someone 5 against 5, on condition that the winner gives 3 to the other. The law of playing will be perfectly fair, and it is evident that my chance will be equal for 3, if I lose, and for 7, if I win: since, in the latter case, I have 10, of which I give my opponent 3.

NOTES

The author of this treatise, at the end of his introduction, expounds in general in this proposition, and more particularly in the two following propositions, the fundamental principle of the entire art of conjecture. Since it is most important that this principle should be thoroughly understood, I shall attempt to demonstrate it by a more popular method of reasoning, adapted to everyone's capacity, and starting only by postulating this axiom or definition: That everyone should expect, or should be assumed to expect, what he will infallibly obtain. Consider the first proposition. Let us conceive that a person has hidden in one hand three cents or *a,* and in the other hand seven cents or *b*: and we agree that one of us takes what is in one hand, and the other what is in the other hand: in this way it is bound to happen that we shall infallibly and conjointly have, and accordingly ought to expect, what is hidden in the two hands, namely, ten cents, or $a+b$. But it must also be conceded that each of us has an equal right to what we expect: hence it follows that the total expectation must be divided into two equal parts, and that we must each receive half of the total expectation, namely, five cents, or $\dfrac{a+b}{2}$.

COROLLARY

Hence it is evident that, if something or a is hidden in one hand, and nothing in the other, the expectation of each player separately is half of that something, or ½ a.

SCHOLIUM

From what has been said it can be deduced that the term *expectation* is not used here in its popular sense, according to which we are generally said to expect or hope for the most favorable occurrence; although a less favorable one may happen to us. But here we understand the hope that we have of obtaining the best, tempered and diminished by fear of the worst: so that the value of the expectation always signifies something intermediary between the best that we hope and the worst that we fear. This is the interpretation that must be understood here and in what follows.

PROPOSITION II

If I expect a, b, or c, any one of which may turn up for me with equal facility, my expectation can be estimated as $\dfrac{a+b+c}{3}$.

To formulate this rule, let x, as before, be the value of my expectation. It is therefore necessary, having x, for me to be able to reach the same expectation with equal stakes. Let the game be played with two other players on this condition, that each one of us stakes x, and I start with one of us. If he wins, he will give me a, and I will give him b, if I win. I make the same condition with the other player, so that if he wins he will give me c, or I will give him c, if I win. It is evident that this game is fair. Now in this way I shall have the chance of obtaining b, if the first player wins, or c, if the second player wins, or even $3x-b-c$, if I win. For I then have $3x$, that was staked, of which I give b to one player and c to the other. But if $3x-b-c$ had the value of a, I should have the same expectation of obtaining a, b, or c. I therefore make $3x-b-c=c$, and let $x=\dfrac{a+b+c}{3}$ for the value of my expectation. In the same way it is found that if my chance is equal for a, b, c, or d, its value is $\dfrac{a+b+c+d}{4}$: and so on.

NOTES

Another method of demonstrating this proposition: Let us suppose that there are three boxes, in one of which a has been hidden, b in another, and c in the third. Let three of us be given the opportunity of receiving a box each and of keeping what he finds in it. Thus all of us conjointly receive the boxes and have what is contained in them, namely: $a+b+c$. Hence, since it cannot be stated that any one of us has a greater hope or expectation than the other, it follows that the expectation of each of us is equivalent to a third of this total, namely: $\dfrac{a+b+c}{3}$.

Similarly, if there are four boxes, in which a, b, c, and d have been hidden, and I have the chance of securing one of them, my expectation will be reckoned as equal to a fourth of the total sum, or $\dfrac{a+b+c+d}{4}$. Thus if there are five boxes, my expectation

will be $\dfrac{a+b+c+d+e}{5}$: and so on.

COROLLARY

It is evident also, if in one or several boxes there is nothing hidden, that my expectation will similarly be a third of what is contained in the other boxes: or a fourth, if there are four, or a fifth, if there are five: and so on.

PROPOSITION III

If the number of chances in which a turns up for me is p; and the number of chances in which b turns up is q: assuming all the chances can occur with equal facility, my expectation will have the value of $\dfrac{pa+qb}{p+q}$.

To formulate this rule, let x again be the value of my expectation. It is necessary, having x, for me to be able to attain the same expectation as before, with the stakes being equal. For this purpose, I shall take with me as many players as will complete the number $p+q$. Let each of us put down x, so that the stakes are $px+qx$: and each of us would have the same expectation of winning. Further, I shall arrange with as many of the players as the number indicates, that if one of them wins he will give me b, or I shall give the same b to him, if I win. Similarly, I shall make this condition individually with the other players, totaling $p-1$, that if one of them wins, he will give me a, and I shall give him a if I win. It is evident that on this condition it is a fair game, since none of the players is at a disadvantage. It is also clear that I now have q expectations for b, and $p-1$ for a, and one expectation, if I win, for $px+qx-bq-ap+a$: for then I have px+qx, that was staked, from which I am obliged to give *b* to each of the players and *a* to each of the p−1 players: making a total of bq+ap−a. If then px+qx−bq−ap+a were equal to *a*, I should have *p* expectations for *a* (since I already had p−1) and *q* expectations for *b* and so I should again have my first chance. Therefore I make px+qx−bq−ap+a=*a*, and $x=\dfrac{ap+bq}{p+q}$ for the value of my expectation, as was stated at the beginning.

In Numbers:

If I had three chances for 13, and two for 8, I should have according to this rule eleven chances. And it is easy to show that, if I have eleven, I can still have the same expectation. For, playing against four others, and each of us staking eleven, I shall again agree with two of the other players that if one of us wins he will give me eight, or I will give eight to each of them, if I win. Similarly, I shall arrange with the other two that whichever one wins will give me thirteen, or I shall give each one thirteen, if I win. This is an equitable arrangement. And it is evident that in this way I have two chances for 8, if either of the two players, who promised me 8, wins; and three chances for 13, if either of the two who must give me thirteen wins, or if I myself win the game. For if I win I have the stakes, that is, 55, of which I must give 13 to each of the two players, and 8 to each of the two others, so that 13 remains for me.

NOTES

Another proof, as follows: Let us assume that there are as many players with me as there are chances in general, that is, p+q, and that there is a chance for each player. Conceive that there are p+q boxes and that in each one there is placed as much as is gained by one throw each, namely, *a* in each of the boxes numbering *p*, and *b* in each of the boxes numbering *q*.

Let each of the players receive one box each; altogether they will receive the sum of the boxes and they will infallibly obtain whatever was contained in the boxes, namely pa+qb. Therefore since they all have an equal chance, it will be necessary to divide what they receive conjointly by the number of players or throws, so that the expectation of each has the value of $\frac{pa+qb}{p+q}$. In the same manner it can be demonstrated that, if I have p throws for a, q throws for b, and r throws for c, my chance will be $\frac{pa+qb+rc}{p+q+r}$.

COROLLARY 1: Hence it follows: first, that if I have p throws to obtain a, and q throws to obtain o, my expectation will be $\frac{pa}{p+q}$.

2. It follows then, if the numbers of the throws have a common divisor, that the value of the expectation can be reduced to smaller terms. For example, if a turns up for me in mp cases, and b in mq cases, my expectation will have the value, according to the rule, of $\frac{mpa+mqb}{mp+mq}$, which, by division by m, has the value of $\frac{pa+qb}{p+q}$.

3. If I have p chances for a, q for b, and r for c, my expectation has the same value as if, by joining p and q, I had p+q chances for $\frac{pa+qb}{p+q}$ and r chances for c: for, on the basis of either hypothesis, according to the rule, the value of my chance is $\frac{pa+qb+rc}{p+q+r}$.

4. If I have p chances for a, q for b, and r chances for remain-

ing in the position in which I am, that is, for retaining my previous chance, this chance will be $\dfrac{pa+qb}{p+q}$, exactly the same as if I did not have any of the chances with the number r. For let x be the value of my chance; then I have by hypothesis p chances for a, q for b, and r for x: which, according to the rule, makes my chance $\dfrac{pa+qb+rx}{p+q+r}$; and since this chance of mine is called x, x will equal $\dfrac{pa+qb+rx}{p+q+r}$; that is, by multiplying, $px+qx+rx=pa+qb+rx$, and, cancelling rx, $px+qx=pa+qb$, or finally $x=\dfrac{pa+qb}{p+q}$.

5. If I have p chances of obtaining a (of which I have contributed a half), and q chances for o, my expectation, $\dfrac{pa}{p+q}$ which is found according to corollary 1, refers to the entire stakes, and signifies the share that is due to me, and not merely how much I gain or lose: for, if it is a question only of gain or loss, I consider that in obtaining the stake a, I gain only ½a: and if I obtain nothing, I lose ½a, that is, I acquire $-½a$: my chance, in this sense, becomes $\dfrac{p.½a+q-½a}{p+q}=\dfrac{(p-q)½a}{p+q}$. This signifies the gain, if p is greater than q: and the loss, if q is greater than p.

6. If I have p chances for acquiring a, and q chances for obtaining b, without having contributed anything, and yet my throw of the dice must cost me n, then my expectation $\dfrac{pa+qb}{p+q}$, must not be reckoned entirely as gain, but must first be diminished by the value of n. For when I give n to the other player and he in turn gives me a or b, it is the same as if I gave

133

nothing, and received only a—n, or b—n: which restricts my expectation to $\dfrac{\text{p.a}-\text{n}+\text{q.b}-\text{n}}{\text{p}+\text{q}} = \dfrac{\text{pa}+\text{qb}-\text{n}}{\text{p}+\text{q}}$: an expression that again signifies the gain or loss, according as the affirmative part defeats the negative part, or the negative the affirmative.

SCHOLIUM

From a consideration of this calculation it is quite clear that it has a great affinity with the arithmetical rule known as the Rule of Mixtures, whereby the price of a mixture is found, composed of given quantities of things of different price; or rather, the calculation is absolutely the same on both sides. For as the sum of the products of the quantities of the things mixed, by their respective prices, divided by the sum of all the mixed quantities, gives the required price, that is always between the greatest and the smallest price: so the sum of the products of the number of different chances, by the chances that each one offers, divided by the number of all the chances, gives the value of the expectation, which accordingly will always be intermediary between the maximum and the minimum that can be obtained. Hence, if the same numbers are taken, on the one hand, for the quantity of things mixed and their prices: and on the other hand, for the chances and what they each give, the same number will denote in one case the price of the thing mixed and in the other case the expectation. For example: If three pints of wine are mixed at thirteen cents with two pints at eight cents, multiplying three by thirteen and two by eight, you have 55 as the price of all the pints. Dividing by five the number of pints, you have eleven cents as the price of one pint mixed. This is also, according to the rule, the value of the expectation of anyone who has three chances for thirteen, and two chances for eight.

Jacob Bernouilli

PROPOSITION IV

Assuming that I am playing with someone, on this condition that the player who is the first to win three times takes the stakes, and that I have already won twice, and my opponent once: I want to know, if we do not wish to continue the game, but to share the money in the stakes in the right proportion, how much should come to me.

To come then to the question that was first raised, namely, the distribution to be made among the various players, whose shares are unequal, we must begin with the easier points.

First of all, we must consider the games that each player still has to play. For it is certain that, if it is agreed between us, for example, that the stakes will be his who is the first to win twenty times, and I win nineteen times, and my opponent eighteen times, my chance will thereby be as much greater as it is now, when I have won two out of three games and my opponent only one: for, in each case, I lack one game only, while he lacks two.

Furthermore, to find out how large a share is due to each, we must examine what would happen if we finished the game. For it is certain that, if I won the first game, I would complete the prescribed number and I would have the entire stakes which may be called a. But if my opponent won the first game, then his chance would be equal to mine, since one game would still be lacking to each of us, and each would have ½a. Now it is evident that I have the same chance of winning the first game or losing it, so that my expectation is now equal for a or for ½a: which, according to the first proposition, is as if I had half of each chance, that is, ¾a: and there is left for my opponent ¼a, which is his share and which could have been found direct from the beginning in the same way. It is thus clear that if anyone wanted to take my place in the game, he would have to give me ¾a for it; and that accordingly anyone who wants to win one game, before the other wins two games, must always wager three against one.

NOTES

We must first of all consider the games that each player has to play. So, in computing the chances, consideration must not be given to the preceding games, but only to the games that follow: since for each of the games that follow there is no greater probability that fortune should favor the same persons whom it favored before than those who have been the most unfortunate of all: this must be observed contrary to the ridiculous opinion of many people who regard fortune as a kind of habit that dwells in man for some time and gives him, in some fashion, the right of hoping for similar fortune in the future.

Which may be called a:

By the letter *a* we may understand not only, with the author, the money staked, that can be shared among the players as the chances dictate, but also all that which, though undivided in itself, can nevertheless be conceived as divisible, according to the number of chances whereby there can be acquisition or loss, action or lack of action, as will be shown in greater detail in the last part of this book. For example: Any prize whatever, a wreath, a victory, the status or condition of a person or a thing, a certain public office, some work undertaken, life or death, and so on. Thus, if by the special grace of the Prince two malefactors draw for their life by lot, with equal chances, each of them is reckoned to have ½ of life, and ½ of death, according to Proposition 1, so that a person in this state can, strictly speaking, be called half alive and half dead.

There remains ¼a for my opponent:

That is, the rest of the stakes *a;* because at the end of the game both of us will infallibly have the entire *a*: but if it can happen by some chance that two players claim conjointly more or less of *a*, it is evident that in that case the expectation of the one cannot be the complement of the expectation of the other in regard to *a*. For example: If two men, deserving the utmost punishment, are compelled to play dice on condition that the one who throws fewer points will be hanged, while the other remains alive, and that if they throw the same number they will both be spared: we find for the expectation of one $\frac{7}{12}$a, or, $\frac{7}{12}$ of life, as will be clear in the proper place. However, it does not follow that the expectation of the other will be only $\frac{5}{12}$ of life: for, since here the chances are manifestly equal, the other player also may expect $\frac{7}{12}$ of life, and accordingly each one has $\frac{7}{6}$ of life, that is, more than the totality of life. This situation occurs because there is no chance where, after the dice are cast, at least one of the players does not remain alive; and in some cases both may remain alive.

Which is his share and which could have been found direct:
This is the method: If my fellow player wins the next game, his chance and mine will be equal, and accordingly we shall each have ½ a: but if I win, he will receive nothing. Therefore, since he can, with equal facility, have ½ a or *o*, the value of his expectation is ¼ a, by corollary 1 of Proposition III.

And accordingly wager three against one:
It must be demonstrated that the one who has three chances to win, and one to lose, or who expects three quarters of the stakes, can wager three against one. For this purpose he need only be assumed to take the place of three players. For if there are four players, playing with equal chances, and each staking one, each player will expect what he himself staked, that is, a quarter of the entire stakes, by corollary II of Proposition III: and hence any three players among them can expect three quarters of the stakes, and the fourth only ¼. But as these three players have also staked three, while the fourth has staked one only, it is evidently quite equitable that the one who wishes to replace the three players, that is, to expect three times as much as the other player, should also stake three times as much. Another method of demonstration, as follows: The player who

has three chances to win, and one to lose, can win three times as often as the other player can win only once. Accordingly, if the game is to be equitable, it is necessary that in three chances the first player wins as much as the other in one chance. This cannot happen, unless he stakes three to one. And so it is proved in general that the greater the expectation of winning that a player has over his opponent, the more he should, in all justice, stake, if they want to play with equal chances.

PROPOSITION V

Let us assume that one play is due to me, and three to my opponent. What will the share be?

Let us examine again in what state we should be, if one of us won the next game. If I won, I should have the stakes, that is, a: but if he won the next game, two games would be coming to him and one to me: and accordingly we should be in the same position that was postulated in the preceding proposition, and I would receive ¾ a, as was indicated there. Thus with equal facility I could have a or ¾ a, which has the value of $\frac{7}{8}$a, by the first proposition, and $\frac{1}{8}$ remains for my opponent, so that my chance in relation to his is as seven is to one.

As this calculation is derived from the preceding one, the following one is derived from this one. If we assume that I have one throw to make, and my opponent four throws, it is found, in the same way, that $\frac{15}{16}$ of the stakes are due to me, and $\frac{1}{16}$ to him.

NOTES

From the sequence of these fractions, $\frac{3}{4}$a, $\frac{7}{8}$a, $\frac{15}{16}$a, that have been found by this proposition and the preceding one, it is deduced that if five throws are due to my opponent, my chance will be $^{31}/_{32}$a: if six are due to him, my chance will be $\frac{63}{64}$a: if seven are due to him, my chance will be $^{127}/_{128}$a: and in general, if one throw is due to me, and any number whatever to my opponent, my chance will be to his in relation of the power of the number 2 multiplied by the number of games due to my opponent, diminished from unity, to one.

PROPOSITION VI

Let us assume that I have two plays to make, and my opponent three.

In the first play this is what will happen: either I shall have one play to make and my opponent three (hence by the preceding proposition I shall have $\frac{7}{8}$a): or each of us will still have two plays to make, and then $\frac{1}{2}$a will be due to me, since our chance will thus be equal. Now I have an equal facility for winning or losing the first play: so that I have an equal expectation of gaining $\frac{7}{8}$a or $\frac{1}{2}$a, which has the value for me of $\frac{11}{16}$a, by the first proposition. And there are due to me eleven parts of the stakes, and five parts to my opponent.

PROPOSITION VII

Let us assume that I have two plays to make and my opponent has four.

This is what will occur. If I win the first game, I should win one play and my opponent four: or, if I lose, I should win two plays and my opponent three. Thus I have the same probability for $\frac{15}{16}$a or $\frac{11}{16}$a, which has the value of $\frac{13}{16}$ by the first proposition. It clearly follows from this that the player who must win two plays while his opponent wins four, has a better chance than the player who has to win one play against his opponent's two. For in this latter case between one and two, my share, by the fourth proposition, is $\frac{3}{4}$a, which is smaller than $\frac{13}{16}$a.

NOTES

It clearly follows from this etc.:

So, the player who has to win three points while his opponent wins six has a better chance: for his share will be found to be $^{219}/_{256}$a, which is greater than $1\frac{3}{16}$a. Similarly, too, the player who is to win one point while the other wins four, does not have the same chance as the one who is to win two points while the other wins eight: but his chance is the same as if he is bound to win two points while the other wins six: and yet there is perhaps no one who is not convinced that the chances must be the same, when the number of plays coming to each one also maintains the same proportion, if our calculation had not taught us otherwise. We are accordingly warned by this fact to be circumspect in our judgment and not to base our reasoning on the first analogy that presents itself: and yet this is usually done all too frequently by those who appear to be among the very wise.

In conclusion, I should like to add here a table for two players, such as the author gives for three players, following Proposition IX:

This table may be extended very easily as far as may be necessary: in the first transversal series, according to the notes on Proposition V: in the first perpendicular series by the continuous division of $\frac{1}{2}$ by 2; in the intermediary places by half of the sum of the two squares immediately preceding in the same perpendicular and transversal series. The reason for this construction is sufficiently evident from what has been said.

PROPOSITION VIII

Now let us assume that there are three players, and that the first one has one play to make, the second player one, but the third player two.

TABLE FOR TWO PLAYERS

Plays to be made by	Player B	1.	2.	3.	4.	5.	6.	7.
1		1 : 2	3 : 4	7 : 8	15 : 16	31 : 32	63 : 64	127 : 128
2		1 : 4	4 : 8	11 : 16	26 : 32	57 : 64	120 : 128	247 : 256
Player A 3	Chances	1 : 8	5 : 16	16 : 32	42 : 64	99 : 128	219 : 256	466 : 512
4	of Player A	1 : 16	6 : 32	22 : 64	64 : 128	163 : 256	382 : 512	848 : 1024
5		1 : 32	7 : 64	29 : 128	93 : 256	256 : 512	638 : 1024	1486 : 2048
6		1 : 64	8 : 128	37 : 256	130 : 512	385 : 1024	1024 : 2048	2510 : 4096
7		1 : 128	9 : 256	46 : 512	176 : 1024	562 : 2048	1586 : 4096	4096 : 8192
8		1 : 256	10 : 512	56 : 1024	232 : 2048	794 : 4096	2380 : 8192	6476 : 16384
9		1 : 512	11 : 1024	67 : 2048	299 : 4096	1093 : 8192	3473 : 16384	9949 : 32768

To find then the chance of the first player, we must again examine what would be due to him, if he or one of the other two players won the next throw. If he won, he would have the stakes, call it a. But if the second player won, the first would have nothing, since the second would have brought the game to an end. But if the third player won, then there would still be lacking one throw to each of the three players, and hence $\frac{1}{3}a$ would be due both to the first player and to each of the other two. And the first would have one chance for a, one for o, and one for $\frac{1}{3}a$, which has the value for him of $\frac{4}{9}a$, by the second proposition (since each of the three with equal facility can win the next game). Similarly the second player would have $\frac{4}{9}a$, and $\frac{1}{9}a$ would remain for the third. His share could also have been found separately, and the shares of the others could thereby have been determined.

NOTE

His share could also have been found separately:

This is the method: If he won the next game, his expectation would be $\frac{1}{3}a$: but if the winner of the next game turned out to be the first or the second player, the third would have nothing: therefore he has one chance for $\frac{1}{3}a$, and two chances for o, which amounts to $\frac{1}{9}a$, by the corollary of Proposition III.

PROPOSITION IX

To find the share of any one of as many players as you like, who each have to play a different number of throws, we must consider what would be due to the one whose share we want to find, if either he or any of the others won the next game. If these shares are added together and the total is divided by the number of players, the quotient will give the required share of one player.

Let us assume that there are three players A, B, and C, and

TABLE FOR THREE PLAYERS

Plays to be made	1. 1. 2	1. 2. 2	1. 1. 3	1. 2. 3
Players' shares	4. 4. 1.	17. 5. 5.	18. 13. 1.	19. 6. 2
	9.	27.	27.	27.

Plays to be made	1. 1. 4	1. 1. 5	1. 2. 4	1. 2. 5
Players' shares	40. 40. 1.	121. 121. 1.	178. 58. 7.	542. 179. 8.
	81.	243.	243.	729.

Plays to be made	1. 3. 3	1. 3. 4	1. 3. 5
Players' shares	65. 8. 8.	616. 82. 31.	629. 87. 13.
	81.	729.	729.

Plays to be made	2. 2. 3	2. 2. 4	2. 2. 5	2. 3. 3	2. 3. 4	2. 3. 5
Players' shares	34. 34. 13.	338. 338. 53.	353. 353. 23.	133. 55. 55.	451. 195. 83.	1493. 635. 119.
	81.	729.	729.	243.	729.	2187.

143

that A has one throw to make, B two, and C likewise two. The problem is to find what share of the stakes, call it q, is due to B.

We must first of all examine what B's expectation would be, if he, or A, or C won the first of the plays to follow.

If A won, he would bring the game to an end, and consequently B's expectation would be o. If B won, he would still have one play to make, so A would have one, and C would have two. Hence in this game there would be due to B $\frac{4}{9}q$, by the eighth proposition.

Finally, if C won the first of the games to follow, then both A and C would each have one throw to make, and consequently $\frac{1}{9}q$ would be due to B, by the same eighth proposition. Now we collect into one sum what was due to B in these three chances, that is, o, $\frac{4}{9}q$, $\frac{1}{9}q$, the total of which is $\frac{5}{9}q$. This, divided by three, the number of players, gives $^5/_{27}q$. This is the share required by B. The proof of this is evident from the second proposition. For, since B has the same chance to win o, $\frac{4}{9}q$, or $\frac{1}{9}q$, he has by the second proposition $o+\frac{4}{9}q+\frac{1}{9}q$, that is, $^5/_{27}q$. And it is certain that this divisor three is the number of players.

Now, to find out the expectation of any one of the players in each game, that is, assuming that he or some one of the other players wins the next throw, it is necessary to investigate first of all the simpler chances, and, by means of them, the remaining chances. For just as this last chance could not have been solved before submitting to calculation the chance of the eighth proposition, where the plays to be made were 1, 1, 2, so too the share of each player cannot be computed in a case where the plays to be made are 1, 2, 3 without first submitting to calculation the chance of the plays 1, 2, 2, as we have already done, besides, the chance where the plays to be made are 1, 1, 3: which similarly could have been computed by the eighth proposition. And in this manner we can compute successively all the chances that are included in the following table, and an infinite number of others.

BOËTHIUS
(about 470/480-about 524 A.D.)

Boethius, whose full name was Anicius Manlius Torquatus Severinus Boethius, was a Roman patrician who gained the confidence of the Ostrogothic ruler of Italy, Theodoric the Great. Their joint purpose was to civilize the Goths through the heritage of classical antiquity. All went well until Theodoric lent his ears to intriguers and had Boethius jailed and finally executed. It was while in prison that Boethius wrote his masterpiece, *On the Consolation of Philosophy*. Boethius himself was an eclectic, with some bias towards Neoplatonism and Augustinianism.

Main Works:
> De Consolatione Philosophiae; De Musica; De Sancta Trinitate.

The Hypothetical Syllogism

Since I consider that the greatest consolation in life lies in instruction and training in the disciplines of philosophy, I apply myself all the more cheerfully, and, as it were, with a kind of benefit gained from the task, to those studies that I compose for our common edification. For though speculation on truth should be followed within its own sphere, so to speak, it becomes still more agreeable when it is pursued in common. For there is no good that does not become more beautifully lucid when approved by the recognition of many. For what has been stifled in silence and otherwise is on the point of dying in extinction,

---

From: *De Syllogismo Hypothetico.*

blooms more expansively, and is protected from destruction and oblivion by the participation of scholars, and also becomes a more pleasurable discipline when it demands a philosopher among the associates of the same philosophy. If, in addition (as our relationship is at this moment) factors that are of their own accord pleasant are made contributory to our friendly participation, the pleasure of study should be spiced as it were by the sweet flavor of affection. Although you acquired a very profound knowledge of categorical syllogisms, you often asked about hypothetical syllogisms, of which there is nothing written by Aristotle. Theophrastus, a philosopher who embraced every discipline, presents only a cursory survey. Eudemus enters more extensively into his teaching procedure but in such a manner that he appears to have scattered seeds as it were without however deriving any fruitful result. Therefore, in so far as we could with whatever talent we possess and in the interests of your friendship, we have undertaken to elucidate carefully and to pursue in detail what was either mentioned by them briefly or altogether omitted: and in this respect I am rewarded for overcoming the difficulty, if I appear to you to have fulfilled a friendly service, although I do not seem to have fulfilled the demands of learning.

Every syllogism is contained within certain conveniently arranged propositions. Now every proposition is either categorical, called also predicative, or hypothetical, also known as conditional. The predicative is a proposition in which something is predicated about something else, as: Man is an animal. Here animal is predicated of man. A hypothetical proposition is one that, with a particular condition, asserts that something is if something else is, as when we say: If it is day, it is light. Hypothetical propositions consist of categorical propositions, as will shortly be evident: hence a syllogism that is composed of categorical propositions is called categorical, that is, predicative; a proposition consisting of hypothetical propositions is called hypothetical, that is, conditional. To perceive the difference between these two kinds of syllogism, we must first examine the differences between them in the nature of propositions. For it is clear that in some propositions there is no difference between the predicative proposition and the conditional proposition, except in the mere form of the expression. For example: If someone states that man is an animal, and if he restates it thus: If he is a man, he is an animal: then these propositions are different in expression, but their significance does not appear to have been different. First of all then we should say that a predicative proposition asserts its force not in a condition, but solely in its declarativeness; while in the conditional proposition, the conclusion depends on the condition. Again, the predicative is a simple proposition, while the condition cannot be so, unless it is linked with predicative propositions, as when we say: If it is day, it is light. It is day, and there is light. These are two predicative propositions, that is, simple propositions. In addition, the peculiarity of each type of proposition is particularly clarified by the fact that the predicative proposition has one subject term, the other has a predicate. And what is the subject in a predicative proposition seems to take the name of that which is predicated in the same proposition, as when we say: Man is an animal. Man is the subject, animal is the predicate, and man assumes the name of animal, since man himself is taken to be an animal. But in those propositions that are termed conditional the same kind of predication is not made. For something is not completely predicated of something, but one thing is said to be, only if something else is, as when we say: If she gives birth, she has slept with a man. For it is not said that giving birth is sleeping with a man, but only that there could never have been a birth without cohabitation with a man. But if the peculiarity occurs in one and the same proposition, then according to the manner of stating the proposition the form of interpretation will vary in this manner. For when we say: Man is an animal, we make a predicative proposition: and if we assert it thus: If there is a man, there is living spirit, the proposition becomes a declarative condition. In the predicative proposition then we envisage the fact that man is an animal, that is: he is in himself animal. But in the conditional proposition we understand that if there were something that man is said to be, it would be necessary for this something to be what is called man. So the predicative proposition shows that the thing that is the subject of the predicative takes its name. The meaning of a conditional proposition is that only then is something so, if another thing is, even if neither has the name of the other. Thus then, from the distinction of propositions, syllogisms too have taken their names from the peculiarities of the assertion, some being called predicative, others conditional. For we call predicative syllogisms those in which the propositions are predicative. But those syllogisms in which the major premise is a hypothetical proposition (for both the hypothesis and the conclusion may be predicative), are called hypothetical and conditional merely by the character of one hypothetical proposition. In regard to simple syllogisms, that is, predicative syllogisms, we expounded in the two sections that we wrote of their constitution.

But after the discussion of the simple syllogisms we should treat the non-simple ones as well. The non-simple syllogisms are those that are called hypothetical, which we designate by the Latin name as conditional. Now the non-simple syllogisms are so called, since they are composed of simple syllogisms and are resolved into the same syllogisms finally, especially since their first propositions acquire the force of their own conclusion from the categorical, that is, the simple syllogisms: for the first proposition of a hypothetical syllogism, if there is any doubt as to its validity, will be proved by the predicative conclusion. But the hypothesis in many modes of such syllogisms seems to be predicative; and likewise the conclusion. For example, we say: If it is day, there is light. But there is day—this hypothesis is predicative. If there is a question about it, it will be proved by the predicative syllogism: there is light. Therefore once again the predicative conclusion follows. Every conditional proposition from predicatives, as has been said, is associated with them. But if they acquire reliability and derive the sequence of their parts from them, it is necessary for the categorical syllogisms to lend the force of the conclusion to the hypothetical syllogisms. But since we are speaking about hypothetical syllogisms, we must first explain the meaning of hypothesis. Hypothesis, from which hypothetical syllogisms derive their name, is said to be of two modes, according to Eudemus. Either something is assumed that must be united in its essence under a certain condition the validity of which cannot be drawn to its logical conclusion. Or in a posited condition the conclusion is shown by the force of a conjunction or a disjunction. An example of the first proposition: When we prove that all corporeal things subsist in the union of matter and form. For when we assume what is impossible in the nature of things, we separate the entire nature of form from the subject matter, if not actually, at least in thought: and since nothing is left of the corporeal things, we assume that the substance of corporeal things is composed of the same things uniting, by which it is disintegrated when they are separated and withdrawn from it. Thus in this example a condition of union is posited such that what is impossible is gradually understood to be the case, that forms are separated from matter; and we imply the conclusion, namely, that bodies die, thus accepting the principle that the same things consist of the same things. For since the disintegration of corporeal things follows, we rightly say that all corporeal things consist of form and matter. But propositions of this type that derive from the condition of harmonizing things, differ in no respect from those propositions that, according to Book 1, are simple categorical propositions: but they differ from simple propositions, when something is said to be or not be, if something else was or was not. They are always expressed conjointly, as we say: If he is a man, he is an animal. If it is a third, it is odd: and other examples of this kind. These propositions are propounded in such a fashion that if one thing is, something else follows. For example: If he is a man, he is not a horse. Again, the negative is propounded in the same way as the affirmative stated above. For here it is asserted: If this is, that is not: and similarly with other examples. Sometimes the propositions may also be stated thus: When this is, that is. For example: When it is a man, it is an animal. Or: When it is a man, it is not a horse. This proposition is equivalent to a proposition stated thus: If he is a man, he is an animal. If he is a man, he is not a horse. Hypothetical propositions are also made by disjunction, thus: Either this is, or that is. This should not seem the same proposition as was previously stated thus: If this is, that is not. For this is a proposition not by disjunction, but by negation. Every negation is undefined, and hence may be both in contraries and in the intermediaries of contraries, and disparates. I call those terms disparates that are diverse only in themselves, having no contrary, as: clothes, fire, and so on. For if it is white, it is not black. If it is white, it is not red. If it is a discipline, it is not a man. But in the proposition that is made by disjunction, one of two must always be posited, thus: Either day, or night. But if we transfer to disjunction all those propositions that are properly stated by negation, the reasoning does not follow. For what if one should say: It is either white or black? Or: It is either white or red? Or: It is a discipline or a man? For none of these propositions may be true. Therefore, since a proposition by disjunction is posited in certain cases only in which one of two things must necessarily occur, separation by negation can also be posited in all those things that mutually destroy their own nature too: this is abundantly proved by reason. Every hypothetical proposition then occurs either through conjunction (I mean by conjunction the mode that is made by negation also), or by disjunction: for each mode is constituted of simple propositions. Now simple propositions are those that we called predicative in Book 1 of the categorical propositions. These propositions occur when something is predicated of something, either by affirmation or by denial, as: It is day, it is light. But if a middle condition intervenes, it will become: If it is day, it is light. And one hypothetical proposition is made by the conjunction of two categorical propositions. But since every simple proposition is either affirmative or negative, hypothetical propositions can be constructed in four modes by conjunction: either from two affirmatives, or from two negatives, or from an affirmative and a negative, or from a negative and an affirmative. Examples of all these types are subjoined, to clarify what we assert.

From two affirmatives: If it is day, it is light.
From two negatives: If it is not an animal, it is not a man.
From an affirmative and a negative: If it is day, it is not night.
From a negative and an affirmative: If it is not day, it is night.

But since it has been stated that the conjunctions *if* and *when* have the same meaning, when posited in hypothetical propositions, conditional propositions may be made in two modes: one according to accident, the other, to give them some natural conclusion. Thus, according to accident: When fire is hot, the sky is round. The sky is not round because fire is hot: but this proposition indicates this: at the time that fire is hot, at that same time too the sky is round. There are other propositions that have in them a natural conclusion. They too have a two-fold mode: one, when it must necessarily follow, yet the conclusion itself does not occur through the position of the terms: the other, when a conclusion occurs through the position of the terms. Now an example of the first mode: When there is a man, there is an animal. This conclusion is dependent on an unassailable truth. But he is not an animal because he is a man, for the genus does occur because there is a species, but possibly a beginning stems from the genus, and more essence can be derived from the universals, so that he is a man for the reason that he is an animal. For the cause of species is genus. But if one says: Since he is a man, he is an animal, he is making a correct and necessary conclusion. But such a conclusion does not proceed through the position of the terms. There are other hypothetical propositions in which both a necessary condition is found, and the position of the terms is the source of the cause of the conclusion, as follows: If there is an opposition of the earth, an eclipse of the moon follows. The conclusion is rare, and hence an eclipse of the moon follows because an opposition of the earth occurs. Such propositions then are valid and useful for demonstration.

Now we make a division of hypothetical propositions into two, simple propositions: the first, introduced by a conjunction, we call the protasis: the second, the conclusion. For example: If it is day, it is light. We call the protasis that which states: if it is day: the conclusion: it is light. In the disjunctive propositions the assertion can begin with the protasis or the conclusion, as: Either it is day, or it is night. For what comes first is called the protasis, and what follows is called the conclusion. This will suffice for the parts of hypothetical propositions. Now it seems proper to explain what Aristotle also said. Since the same thing is and is not, it is not necessary for it to be the same. For example: Since it is a, it is necessary for it to be b: if it is not a, it is not necessary for it to be b, since it is not a. To demonstrate this, the definition of impossibility must be presented, thus: That is impossible when, the impossibility being posited, something false and impossible is performed on the ground that it was anteriorly considered impossible. Let it therefore be postulated that b is, since a is, that is, there is this conclusion between a and b, that if it is granted that a is, it must necessarily be granted that b is. So let it be assumed if a is, b is, because if a is not, it is not necessary for b to be. And first let us consider what the conclusion of propositions is. If there is such a conjunction that if a is, b must also necessarily be: if b is not, a too must necessarily not be. From this demonstration it is evident that if a is, b must necessarily be, because, as I assert, if b is not, a will not be. For it is posited that b is not and if it were possible it would be a. But it was stated: If a is, b must necessarily be granted. Since therefore b is, there will not be b. For as we postulated that b is not, there will not be b, because we postulate that if a is, b will be. B therefore will be and will not be, which is impossible. It is therefore impossible for b not to be and for a to be. Thus we produce a convincing proof. An example

152

will make this clearer: If he is a man, he is an animal; if he is not an animal, he is not a man. Not: If he is not a man, he is not an animal. For there are many animals that are not men. Thus in the conclusion of a conjoined proposition, if there is a first, there must be a second: if there is no second, there is no first: but if there is no first, it is not necessary for a second not to be. The proof of this has already been given by us. Let there be *a*, and since this is so, *b* must be, because if *a* is not, it is not necessary for *b* to be: nor is it necessary for *b* not to be if *a* is not, but only for *b* not to be. For, as has already been proved, if *b* is not, *a* is necessarily not; and if *b* happens to be a term, *a* will not be. But if, though *a* is not, *b* must necessarily be, this *b* will necessarily both be and not be. For, since *b* is not a term, it will not be. Because if *a* is not, *b* must be; therefore *b* will be a term and not a term, which is impossible. From these examples then I believe that it has been proved that, in the conclusion of a hypothetical proposition, if there is a first, it follows that there is a second: if there is no second, it follows that there is no first: but if there is no first, it does not follow that there is a second or not. For it is clear that, if there is a second, it does not follow that there is a first or not, as in the proposition: If it is a man, it is an animal. If it is an animal, it does not follow that it is a man or not. But if the first is not, it does not follow that the second is necessarily or is not. For example: In the same proposition, if it is not a man, it is not necessarily either an animal or not. Therefore of all these propositions two conclusions only are stable and remain unchangeable: If there is a first, there follows a second. If the second is not, it necessarily follows that the first is not. Thus, as I have now determined these assertions, I shall add this: Although every hypothetical proposition is not simple, and is conjoined with other propositions, yet there are certain hypothetical propositions that, if a comparison is made with other conditional propositions, are considered simple. For every conditional proposition is either conjunctive or disjunctive. But since they are composed of predicative propositions, it necessarily follows that in the conjunctive propositions there should be four modes of this conjunction. For the hypothetical proposition is either composed of two simple propositions, and is called a simple hypothetical conjunction, as: If *a* is, *b* is. Or: If it is a man, it is an animal. For it is a man, and it is an animal are two simple propositions. Or it is composed of two hypothetical propositions, and is called a compound proposition. For example: When *a* is, *b* is: since *c* is, *d* is. Or we assert this proposition: When it is a man, it is an animal. Since it is a body, it is a substance. For: When it is a man, it is an animal is a hypothetical proposition; but the other—since it is a body, it is a substance—is called a compound proposition from the fact of its composition. There is conjunction either from one simple and one hypothetical proposition, as: If *a* is since *b* is, *c* is. For example: If it is a man since it is an animal, it is a substance. For: It is a man is a simple proposition, and it is evident that since it is an animal it is a substance is the conclusion of the hypothesis itself. Or the proposition is composed of an anterior hypothesis and a simple posterior. For example: Since *a* is, *b* is, and *c* is. Or: Since it is a man, it is an animal and a body. For the hypothesis is that which propounds—since it is a man, it is an animal. The simple posterior is that which follows this hypothetical proposition, that is, it is a body. Since these propositions too are not composed of simple propositions, they are said to be compound. But the former, that consist of simple propositions, and are called simple hypothetical propositions, are formed with two terms. Now I call terms the simple parts of the proposition by which they are joined. But the compound hypothetical propositions, those that consist of two hypothetical propositions, are composed of four terms. Those that are composed of a hypothesis and a simple proposition, or a simple proposition and a hypothesis, are composed of three terms.

We must therefore discuss the differences and the similarities of those propositions that are simple or compound hypothetical propositions. For if the propositions composed of simple propositions are compared with those compounded of two hypothetical propositions, the conclusion is the same, and the correlation remains the same, only the terms are doubled. For the position in these hypothetical propositions consisting of simple propositions that the simple propositions maintain, is the same in those hypothetical propositions consisting of hypotheses as those conditions maintain with which those propositions are said to be conjoined and connected. For in the proposition that states. If *a* is, *b* is, and in the one that states: Since *a* is, *b* is; since *c* is, *d* is, whatever position in that proposition composed of two simple propositions the first—if *a* is—has, that same position in —the proposition composed of two hypothetical propositions is maintained by the first proposition—when *a* is, *b* is. For here the conclusion follows from the condition of reciprocal conjunction of two propositions. Similarly, whatever power the concluding part has, namely, that which is inferred, that *b* is, of the hypothesis composed of both propositions, that same power lies in the part, in the proposition composed of hypotheses, that follows, namely, since *c* is, *d* is; and the only difference is that in the first proposition composed of simple propositions the compound proposition follows the proposition, while in the second proposition composed of hypotheses, the condition of the conclusion is a concomitant of the conclusion of the condition. For there is no distinction between: If *a* is, *b* is and the proposition in which we predicate that *a* is a concomitant of *b*. But when we state a proposition resulting from hypotheses—since *a* is, *b* is: since *c* is, we postulate that the conclusion between *a* and *b* is a concomitant of *c* and *d*, so that if it follows that *a* is *b*, it indubitably follows that *c* is *d*. But in the propositions that consist of a simple and a hypothetical proposition, the reasoning is that either the condition of the conclusion follows the proposition, or the proposition is a concomitant of the condition of the conclusion. For when we say: If *a* is since *b* is, *c* is, we imply thereby, in the proposition stating: If *a* is, the following condition: Since *b* is, *c* is: that is, if *a* is, the term *c* must necessarily be a concomitant of the term *b*. But when we assert: When *a* is, and *b* is, *c* is, we mean nothing more than that the conclusion of two conjoined propositions contains the truth of one proposition so that if they together produce a conclusion a and b, this condition must necessarily contain the truth of the concluding proposition in which we assert that c is: that is, if a is necessarily b, c also must necessarily be. Similar syllogisms then can be made of propositions that are composed of simple propositions and of propositions that are not simple. Of propositions composed of simple proposition and a hypothesis, the syllogisms are different from the others, yet they are similar to each other. And there is no difference whether the first proposition is a hypothesis and the second one simple, or conversely, the first one is simple and the second one is a hypothesis, in relation to the modes of the syllogism, unless perhaps only in relation to the change of the order. Since then the principles of the syllogism has been expounded in the case of simple propositions, it seemed fitting to describe syllogisms of propositions composed of hypotheses: and since we have examined the character of syllogisms of whatever propositions consisting of simple and hypothetical propositions, we have also examined the character of the converse order of propositions that produce syllogisms. There is also another type of propositions conjoined together, which are in a sense an intermediary between propositions composed of hypothetical and simple propositions, and propositions consisting of two hypotheses. For if one considers the number of terms, they seem to consist of three. If you observe conditional propositions, they seem to be composed of two conditionals. This intermediary character arises from the fact that in these terms one term is found to be common to both conditionals. These conditionals present themselves either in the first figure, or the second, or the third. In the first figure, as follows: If a is, b is, and if b is, c is. Therefore b is included in both propositions, and there are these three terms: a is, b is, c is, for b is common to both: and hence between the propositions composed of three terms, and those composed of four terms, there are intermediary propositions of this kind. In the second figure this is the situation: If a is, b is: if a is not, c is. In the third figure: If b is, a is: if c is, a is not. This must suffice for conjunctive propositions. Disjunctive propositions always consist of contraries. For example: Either *a* is, or *b* is. For if one is posited, the other is eliminated, and vice versa. For if *a* is, *b* is not. If *a* is not, *b* is. Similarly: If *b* is, *a* is not: if *b* is not, *a* is.

After these explanations, let us return to conjunctive propositions, for in them either one proposition follows the other, or a condition follows a condition, or a proposition follows a condition, or a condition follows a proposition. The question to be discussed then is which propositions appear to be the conclusions of which other propositions: which differ to the utmost extent from each other in the mode of their contrariety: and which are different in the contradiction of opposition. With regard to simple propositions, that is, predicative propositions, some are postulated with the mode, others without the mode. Without the mode are those that signify mere being, as: It is day. Socrates is a philosopher, and those that are similarly asserted. Those postulated with the mode are of this type: Socrates is truly a philosopher. For the term truly is the mode of the proposition. But the greatest distinctions in syllogisms occur in propositions predicated with mode, to which the force of necessity or possibility is added. Necessity: When we declare that it is necessary for fire to be hot. Possibility: It is possible for the Trojans to be defeated by the Greeks. Hence every proposition signifies an inherent quality, or a necessarily inherent quality, or that though something is not, yet it is a possible contingency. But a proposition signifying an inherent quality is simple, and cannot be changed into any other form. But a proposition that designates the necessarily inherent quality of something is postulated in three modes: one mode, when it is similar to a proposition signifying inherent quality. For example: It is necessary for Socrates to be sitting, while he sits. This proposition has the same force as the statement: Socrates sits. But another meaning of necessity is thus expressed: It is necessary for a man to have a heart while he exists and lives. This is what the statement seems to signify, not that it is necessary to have a heart while he has one, but that it is necessary to have one as long as the man who has one lives. Another meaning of necessity is universal and particular, whereby it predicates necessity absolutely, as, for example: It is necessary that God is immortal: without any contradictory condition of determination. Possible is expressed in three modes. Either what is, is said to be possible, as: It is possible for Socrates to be sitting, while he sits. Or that which can happen at any time, while this thing remains for which it is postulated that something can happen, as: It is possible for Socrates to read, for as long as Socrates is, he can read. Similarly that is possible which can happen absolutely at any time, as: A bird flies. From these instances then it is clear that there are some propositions signifying inherent quality, others necessary ones: others contingent and possible, and since there are three divisions of necessary and contingent propositions, the individual propositions of the same divisions are related to those that signify inherent quality. There remain therefore two necessary and two contingent propositions, which, included with the proposition that signifies inherent quality, make in all five different kinds of proposition. In regard to all these propositions, some are affirmative, others negative. The affirmative signifying inherent quality is that which states: Socrates is. The negative asserts: Socrates is not. Of necessary affirmative propositions two seem to be negations, one a contrary, the other an opposite. In regard to the proposition that asserts that it is necessary for a to be, in the mode that states: they are, either the proposition that declares it is necessary for a not to be, or the proposition that declares it is not necessary for a to be, is a negation. The one that says: It is necessary for a not to be, is the contrary of that which says: It is necessary for a to be. For both will be found to be false, as when we say: It is necessary for Socrates to read: it is necessary for Socrates not to read. Both propositions are false. For when he reads, he does not read from necessity, and when he does not read, he is not constrained by any necessity not to read: but either proposition is possible.

But the proposition that asserts: It is not necessary for *a* to be, is the opposite of that which postulates: It is necessary for *a* to be. For one of them is always true, the other is always found to be false. In contingent and possible propositions the situation is the same: for the proposition that asserts: *a* is contingently, appears to have an opposite that asserts: It is contingent for *a* not to be, and one that asserts: It is not contingent for *a* to be. The proposition that asserts: It is contingent for *a* not to be is called a negative contingent, and it may be true with the affirmation that declares it is contingent for *a* to be, as when we say: It is contingent for Socrates to sit: it is contingent for Socrates not to sit. These propositions are said to be contraries, since they cannot simultaneously be true. Opposites occur whenever a contingent is negated. For example: The opposite of the proposition stating that it is contingent for *a* to be is the proposition stating that it is not contingent for *a* to be: for this signifies that it cannot be contingently at all. Under these circumstances, when propositions signifying inherent quality are said to be without any mode, and when a negative adverb is joined to being, a complete negation is made. When propositions are postulated with a mode, if they are necessary and a negation is attached to being, as—it is necessary not to be—a necessary negation is made.

But if the negation precedes the term *necessary,* there occurs a negation of necessity violently opposed to affirmation. For example: It is not necessary. Similarly in the case of contingent propositions. If a negation precedes being, a contingent negation occurs, as: It is contingent for A not to be. But if a negation is attached to the contingent itself, there occurs a negation of a contingent violently opposed to an affirmative contingency, as: It is not contingent to be. But since every proposition, either universal, or particular, or indefinite, or singular, is postulated as universal, thus: Every man reads. The particular: A certain man reads. The singular: Socrates reads. The indefinite: A man reads: it is necessary, as is shown in the Principles of Categorical Syllogisms, that those propositions seem the most opposite to each other which either affirm the universal, if the negation is particular, or deny the universal, if the particular is affirmed; and which are singular, if one is affirmed and the other denied.

Since this is the case, if this reasoning is applied to contingent and necessary propositions, the same thing occurs in necessary and contingent propositions. For example: It is necessary that every *a* is a term, and the denial is: It is not necessary for every *a* to be a term. This produces an opposite negation. And if someone should say: It is contingent that every *a* is a term, and someone were to deny this, the latter makes an opposite negation. For in each case negation removes the mode and destroys the meaning of universality. This must occur in simple and categorical propositions also, the character of which we have carefully examined in the treatises that, in the second edition, we entitled *On Interpretation*. So if anyone investigates the number of all the conditional propositions, he will be able to find it from the categorical propositions. First we must investigate propositions conjoined from two simple propositions, as follows. Since a simple hypothetical is composed of two propositions, one of them will signify either inherent quality, or simply contingent being, or doubly necessary being.

But if they are affirmative propositions, they will be postulated five times affirmatively. But since every affirmation has an opposite negative, the negative proposition again will be stated five times. In the first proposition, therefore, which is one part of the hypothetical proposition, and in the negative and affirmative there will be ten modes of proposition.

The second proposition, that is part of the hypothetical proposition, can be stated in ten ways too, by affirmation and negation. There will therefore be ten propositions of this too. But since the first proposition is joined to the second proposition by a kind of conclusion, making one hypothesis, all ten affirmative and negative propositions will be added to all ten affirmative and negative propositions. Thus the propositions composed of simple propositions make in all one hundred propositions. According to this method the number of propositions can be determined even in the case of propositions that are formed from a categorical and a hypothetical proposition, or that are made from two conditional propositions. For in the case of propositions consisting of a conditional and a categorical proposition, or of three categorical propositions, if their conjunction is by affirmation or negation of two predicative propositions, or is necessarily so, it makes five modes and one hundred conjunctions, since the third proposition will be affirmative or negative, and if affirmative in five modes, signifying either being, or necessary being twice, or contingent being twice. Similarly at the same time negation will be made in as many modes, not more, as the propositions are asserted ten times. Hence it is that the third proposition joined and combined with the two previous propositions, connected and linked together in one hundred modes, makes altogether one thousand conjunctions. For one hundred modes of two propositions combined with ten modes of the third proposition make one thousand. For ten times one hundred are one thousand. Again, since a conditional proposition formed from two hypothetical propositions is combined with four categorical propositions, and the first two categorical propositions were combined by one hundred conjunctions, it necessarily follows that the second two propositions also are connected by one hundred conjunctions. But if the hundred modes of the first categorical propositions are combined with the hundred modes of the following categorical propositions, there will be 10,000 conjunctions. Now in the propositions involving three figures, if the middle term is predicated similarly both in the first and second hypothetical proposition, there will be one hundred conjunctions, as in the case of those that are composed of three categorical propositions. For then one and the same term will make in each case three, and not more propositions. Similarly in each case the proposition is as follows: If *a* is, *b* is, *c* is: for here the term *b* is used with the term *a*, and the term *c*, signifying that it belongs in both propositions.

The same relationship must be understood in the case of necessary and contingent propositions. But if the proposition is: If *a* is, *b* is, and if *b* must necessarily be, and *c* is or not, then two conditional propositions, that is, four predicatives are formed. Hence it is that according to the propositions composed of four predicatives, they produce ten thousand conjunctions. These numbers should be examined both in the first and in the second or third figure. Now, although we have determined the possible total number of propositions, yet the middle term is never predicated differently. For the middle term, joining the two extremes, prevents a conclusion of the extremes. But if the middle term is postulated in different modes, the extremes are not connected, and hence no syllogism whatever can be formed, especially since no proposition can be posited in which the middle term is differently postulated. There would be a great multiplicity in the number of propositions, if we varied the necessary and contingent affirmative and negative propositions signifying being with universal and particular, or opposite or subordinate propositions. But this is not feasible, because the terms of conditional propositions are predicated in infinite modes. And I considered it unnecessary to search for a multiplicity of propositions determined according to quantity, since conditional propositions are not usually predicated determinatively: as a rule hypothetical propositions are postulated neither through necessity nor contingency, but those particularly that signify being are used in lectures. All of them tend to have a necessary conclusion, both those that signify inherent being and those to which necessity is added, and those to which the category of possibility is applied, for the term is added.

Now the necessity of the hypothetical proposition and the character of the propositions of which the combinations are composed require a conclusion. For example: If Socrates is sitting and is alive, it is not necessary for him either to be sitting or to be alive. But if he is sitting, it is necessary for him to be alive. Similarly, we say: The sun moves, it necessarily sets in

the west. Which means the same as: If the sun moves, it sets
in the west. For the necessity of a proposition consists in the
unchangeable character of conclusion. Similarly we say: If it is
possible for a book to be read, it is possible to read the third
line. Again, the necessity of the conclusion is maintained. For
if it is possible for a book to be read it is necessary that it
should be possible to read the third line. Opposed to hypothetical propositions are those only that destroy their substance.
The substance of hypothetical proposition lies in this, that the
necessity of their conclusion is capable of permanence. If then
anyone rightly refutes a conditional proposition, he will destroy
the conclusion. For instance: If *a* is, *b* is. There will be no
opposition to this if it is shown either that *a* is not, or *b* is not,
but assuming *a* is, it is apparent that it does not immediately
follow that *b* is, but that *a* may be, even if the term *b* is not.
But if there is negation, the conditional proposition will be
destroyed by the same mode, thus: If *a* is, *b* is not. It must
now be demonstrated either that *a* is not, or that *b* is: but since *a*
is, the term *b* may be. There are hypothetical propositions,
some of which are affirmative, others negative: but I am now
speaking of those that are said to be present in the conclusion
in conjunction. The affirmative, for instance: If *a* is, *b* is: if *a*
is not, *b* is not. Negative: If *a* is, *b* is not: if *a* is not, *b* is not.
For we must examine the concluding proposition, to observe
whether it is an affirmative or a negative proposition. Similarly
we must know the compound conditional propositions.

Now in regard to the propositions that appear in disjunction,
since I am going to treat their syllogisms, I shall speak in more
ample and fuller detail. Some authorities, whose views I shall
presently refute after first showing by what names the parts
of those syllogisms are called, believe that hypothetical syllogisms, known in Latin as conditionals, consist of five parts,
while others think they consist of four, and still others of five.
For since every syllogism is composed of propositions, the
first is called the proposition, or the major: the second is the
minor: what is inferred from these is known as the conclusion.

For example: If he is a man, he is an animal. Now, he is a man: therefore he is an animal. The proposition in which we assert: If he is a man, he is an animal, is called the proposition or the major.

The proposition which we added to this—he is a man—is called the minor: the third is called the conclusion, whereby we show that he who is a man is an animal. But since it frequently happens that the conclusion of a stated proposition is not plausible, there is often attached to the proposition an approval whereby that which was postulated is shown to be true. The minor also often does not seem credible in itself, and to it too is added supporting approval to give it verisimilitude.

Hence it arises that hypothetical syllogisms often have five parts, or four, and occasionally three. The syllogism will consist of five parts if both the proposition and the minor need confirmation: but if either the proposition or the minor needs confirmation, the syllogism consists of four parts; but if neither part requires confirmation, it remains in three parts. In this view Cicero too is confirmed. For in the *De Oratore* he asserts that some syllogisms have five parts, and others four. Those authorities who object to such syllogisms having more than three parts do not think that the confirmation of the majors and the minors should be considered as parts of the syllogism. For it is not the major proposition about which there can be a syllogism that the listener does not believe. But if the confirmation which is added to a dubious proposition is itself dubious, lending credibility to the same proposition to which it is attached, it becomes acceptable to the syllogism, and thereby begins to be the major of a syllogism when it is so confirmed as to make another deduction from it possible. Then some deduction can be made from it, when with the aid of the confirmation it can be granted by the listener.

On this account it seems to be a kind of member, and, so to speak, a support for a dubious proposition or a confirmation of a minor, and not a part of a syllogism. But our opinion coincides rather with those who assert that it consists of three parts. For any confirmation that is added either to confirmation or to a minor premise is said to be the confirmation of the proposition or the minor. Since therefore that proposition whose confirmation it is refers not to the syllogism but to the proposition or the minor, it is not necessary for it to seem a proper part of the syllogism. For the argument can be that everyone knows that parts of parts are said to be also parts of the whole. But it is of the greatest importance whether these are in the first place parts of the whole, or whether they are placed at the end of the second parts. Moreover, if the proposition is in itself known to be subject to proof, the entire syllogism does not need confirmation.

But if there is no credibility in the proposition itself, it is necessary for such a proposition to need a certain kind of testimony of confirmation. A syllogism therefore does not need confirmation from the fact of its being a syllogism, but a proposition does need it, if its own credibility is destroyed. The same assertion can be made of the minor proposition as well. It is therefore evident that we should prefer their view, that declares that a syllogism is composed of three parts only. Besides, if any proposition requires confirmation to lend it real credibility, it will be demonstrated by some syllogism. Therefore how is it possible for a syllogism properly to be called a part of a simple syllogism? For it is necessary for the confirmation itself of the proposition to be a syllogism or from a syllogism.

These facts having been determined, I believe I should forthwith explain the syllogisms whose propositions in conjunction consist of two terms. They have a double form: for there are four, by the affirmation of the preceding proposition, that are the first and perfect hypotheses, and four by the negation of the following proposition, that do not seem perfect when needing proof. No syllogism whatever is produced by the negation of the first proposition and the position of the second. Let the number of all such propositions therefore now be first explained, to ensure ready recognition of the syllogisms which are made from them.

Now there are four: If *a* is, *b* is. If *a* is, *b* is not. If *a* is not, *b* is. If *a* is not, *b* is not. And this must be stated in the first place with reference to the first and perfect syllogisms. Their first mode is the one that comes from the first proposition: If *a* is, *b* is. But *a* is, therefore *b* is: for since the first proposition predicates only the condition — if *a* is — it is necessary for the term *b* to follow this being — the proposition assumes and posits what precedes and states: But *a* is: it therefore follows that *b* is, for this occurred from the conclusion of the first proposition. But if we admit and assume that which follows, no syllogism is produced. For let the conclusion be of this type: that if *a* is, *b* is, and let what follows be thus assumed: But *b* is: it does not follow that *a* should either be or not be. This will be clarified by an example. Let the proposition be: If he is a man, he is an animal, as the conclusion states: then it will not be necessary for him either to be or not to be a man.

The second mode is that of syllogisms in which the first part of the proposition is repeated in the minor, and it comes from the second proposition previously discussed, as follows: If *a* is, *b* is not: but *a* is, therefore *b* is not. For the proposition had been stated: If *a* is, *b* is not. Assuming therefore the first proposition, the conclusion of the following proposition is complete. But if one assures the conclusion, it seems that no syllogism occurs, because no necessity ensues: If *a* is, *b* is not: but *b* is not; it is not necessary then for *a* to be or not to be. Let the proposition be as follows: If it is black, it is not white. And let what follows be assumed. But it is not white: then it will not be necessary for it to be black or not, because, since it is not white, it can be something intermediary. The third mode of such syllogisms comes from the third proposition, and in the minor of these syllogisms the first proposition is posited thus: If *a* is not, *b* is. But *a* is not: therefore *b* is: therefore this conclusion again arises from the condition of the proposition, for the proposition had been: If *a* were not, *b* would not be: but if you convert and assume that *b* is, that is, the conclusion, it will not be necessary that the first proposition should either be or not be. But an example of this cannot be found because if such a proposition is stated as: Since *a* is not, *b* is, there would seem to be no intermediary between *a* and *b*. But if there is not one thing in them, it is immediately necessary of another thing to be, and if one thing is, it is immediately necessary for the other thing not to be. Therefore it seems that syllogisms are made in these cases in a kind of manner arising from the posited conclusion.

But it is of little consequence how far this is so in relation to the nature of the thing, and how far this refers to the condition of the propositions itself. This is evident from what has been already said: for in the first two modes, when the conclusion was posited, nothing was deduced from necessity: But this third mode, in so far as it refers to the conjunction of the propositions, if what follows is assumed, does not produce any syllogism. In regard to the nature of the things in which alone these propositions can be postulated, the conclusion appears to be necessary, thus: If it is not day, it is night. If it is night, it is not day: as a necessary conclusion: and these syllogisms are similar to those that are produced in disjunction, of which I shall speak a little later and show their differences and similarities in relation to the disjunctive syllogisms.

The fourth mode is from the fourth proposition, when it is postulated thus: If *a* is not, *b* is not: but *a* is not, therefore *b* is not. Again, it is shown that this can be the conclusion also from a proposition that postulated: *b* will not be, if the first term *a* has not been. But if we assume what follows, it seems that there can be no necessity, as if we said: *b* is not: it will not be necessary for *a* to be or not to be. For let this be postulated: If it is not an animal, it is not a man. And let it be assumed: But it is not a man: then it is not necessary for it to be an animal or not. It has therefore been demonstrated in syllogisms of this kind that if the first proposition is assumed, perfect and necessary syllogisms are made that can be proved from the propositions themselves. But if the conclusion is assumed, no necessity ensues except in the third mode, which, being similar to the syllogisms that are made by disjunction of postulated propositions, seems in the case of things about which propositions can be made, to preserve its necessity, since it does not preserve it in conjunction, as is proved from the other three modes, the first, second, and fourth, in which, assuming the concluding part of the proposition to be postulated, nothing occurs from necessity.

Now in regard to these syllogisms, that are formed by two terms, the first part of whose proposition is assumed, our exposition, in so far as it affects the survey, has been adequate.

BERNARD BOLZANO

(1781-1848)

A Catholic priest from Prague whose independent ideas drew the wrath of his superiors and forced him to live in retirement for the last thirty years of his life. He taught at the University of Prague. Bolzano was a mathematician and philosopher who anticipated the modern theory of transfinite numbers and whose distinction between logic and psychology was of great importance to Husserl and his disciples.

Main Works:

Zur Mathematik; Paradoxien des Unendlichen; Wissenschaftslehre.

Paradoxes of the Infinite

§1

Certainly most of the paradoxical statements encountered in the mathematical domain—though not, as *Kästner* would have it, all of them—are propositions which either immediately contain the idea of the *infinite,* or at least in some way or other depend upon that idea for their attempted proof. Still less is it open to dispute that this category of mathematical paradoxes includes precisely those which merit our closest scrutiny, inasmuch as a satisfactory refutation of their apparent contradictions is requisite for the solution of very important problems in such other sciences as physics and metaphysics.

This, then is the reason why I address myself in the present

From: *Paradoxien des Unendlichen.*

treatise exclusively to the consideration of the paradoxes of the infinite. As is readily understood, however, it would be impossible to recognise the appearance of contradiction in these paradoxes for what it is, namely a mere appearance, unless we first of all became quite clear what precise notion we attached to the term infinite. Consequently, this point shall be taken first.

§2

The very word infinite shows that we put the *infinite* into contrast with the merely *finite*. Again, the derivation of the former *name* from the latter betrays the additional fact that we consider the *idea* of the infinite to arise from the idea of the finite by, and only by, the adjunction of a new element; for such in fact is the abstract idea of *negation*. And finally: it is already one reason against denying the application of both ideas to *sets* (more precisely, to *multitudes,* that is, sets of unities) and hence to *quantities* as well, that *mathematics,* the doctrine of quantity, be the very place where we most often speak of the infinite; for we there select as matter for consideration and even for computation both finite and infinite multitudes, as also both *finite* and infinite magnitudes, the latter including not only the *infinitely great* but also the *infinitely small*. Quite independently of the hypothesis that these two ideas, of the finite and of the infinite, are applicable only to objects which in some respect or other exhibit *quantuplicity* or *quotuplicity,* we are already entitled to hope that a rigorous investigation of the circumstances in which we pronounce a set to be finite or to be infinite will also afford us information about the nature of the *infinite as such.*

§3

For this purpose, however, we must go back to one of the simplest conceptions in our minds and seek agreement on the meaning of the word by which we propose to designate it. It is the conception underlying the conjunction *And,* whose most appropriate expression, enabling it to come to the forefront as clearly as the aims both of philosophy and of mathematics demand in numberless cases, is found to my best belief in the words: 'An aggregate of well-defined objects' (ein Inbegriff gewisser Dinge) or : 'A whole composed of well-defined members.' We intend these words to be interpreted so widely that, whenever the conjunction *And* is customarily employed, for example in the sentences:

'*The sun, the earth and the moon act upon one another,*'
'*The rose, and the conception of a rose, are a couple of entirely distinct entities,*'
'The names *Socrates* and *son of Sophroniscus* designate one and the same person,'

we can say that the subject of these sentences is an *aggregate of well-defined objects,* or *a whole composed of well-defined members;* and say in the first example, that it is the whole composed of the sun, the earth and the moon as members which we pronounce to be a whole whose members act upon one another; in the second example, that it is the aggregate composed of the object 'the rose' and the object 'the conception of a rose' as members which we pronounce to be an aggregate whose members are entirely distinct entities; and so forth. These few remarks will presumably be quite sufficient for a common understanding of the conception here dealt with, at least if we add this statement: that every arbitrary object A whatever can be united with any other arbitrary objects B, C, D . . . whatever to form an aggregate, or to speak still more rigorously, that these objects already form an aggregate without our intervention (an sich selbst schon) and one about which numerous truths of different degrees of importance can be enunciated— provided only that A, B, C, D . . . really represent, each and every one of them, a *distinct* object that is, provided only that none of the propositions 'A is identical with B,' 'A is identical with C,' 'B is identical with C' and so forth be true. For if A were identical with B, it would of course be absurd to speak of an aggregate composed of the objects A and B.

§4

There exist aggregates which agree in containing the selfsame members, and nevertheless present themselves as *different* when seen under different aspects (Gesichtspunkte) or under different conceptions (Begriffe), and this kind of difference we call 'essential' (wesentlich). For example: an unbroken tumbler and a tumbler broken in pieces, considered as a drinking vessel. We call the ground of distinction between two such aggregates their *mode of combination (Art der Verbindung)* or their *arrangement* (Anordnung). An aggregate whose basic conception renders the arrangement of its members a matter of indifference, and whose permutation therefore produces no essential change from the current point of view, I shall call a *set* (Menge), and a set whose members are considered as *individuals* (*Einheiten*) of a stated species A (that is, as objects subsumable under the concept A) is called a *multitude* (Vielheit) of A.

§5

Some aggregates, it is well known, have members which are themselves composite, themselves aggregates in turn. Among these again, some are regarded from a viewpoint which renders it indifferent whether or no we take the members of the sub-aggregates as members of the main aggregate (die Teile der Teile als Teile des Ganzen selbst auffassen). I borrow a term from mathematics, and call such aggregates *sums*. For it is the essential nature of a sum that $A+(B+C)=A+B+C$.

§6

If we regard an object as belonging to a category of entities such that each two of them, say M and N, can stand in no other mutual relation than that either they are *equal,* or else one of them can be represented as a sum whose augend is equal to the other of them (in other words, either $M=N$, or else $M=N+\nu$ or $N=M+\mu$, where ν and μ must again be either equal or such that one can be considered as a part contained in the other), then we regard that object as a *quantity*.

§7

The name *series* (Reihe) shall be given to a proposed aggregate of objects . . . $A,B,C,D,E,F, \ldots , L,M,N, \ldots$ when it is possible to assign to any one member M exactly one other member N by a *law applying uniformly* to all members and *determining*, either N through its relation to M, or M through its relation to N. The members shall be called the *terms* (Glieder). The law whereby M determines N or conversely shall be called the *principle of construction* (Bildungsgesetz) of the series. One of the two terms (whichever you like, but without wishing to imply any temporal or spatial sequence) shall be called the *antecedent* (vorderes Glied) and the other the *consequent* (hinteres Glied). Every term M which has both an antecedent and a consequent (and which therefore both takes its rise by the principle of construction from another member, and in turn gives rise to a third) shall be called an *inner term* (inneres Glied) of the series. Hence, finally, it will be plain which terms (if any of the kind exist) shall be called *outer*, which *first*, and which last.

§8

Let us imagine a *series* whose *first* term is an *individual* of the species A, *and* whose every subsequent term is derived from its predecessor by adjoining a fresh individual of the species A to form a sum with that predecessor or its equal. Then clearly will all the terms of this series, with the exception of the first, which was a *mere individual* of the species A, be *multitudes of the species A*. Such multitudes I call *finite* (endlich) or *countable* (zählbar) *multitudes*, or quite boldly: *numbers*; and more specifically: *whole* numbers—under which the first term shall also be comprised.

§9

When we vary the nature of the concept here denoted by *A*, we shall find that the objects subsumed under it, the individuals of the species *A*, form now a more numerous and now a less numerous set; and the series under consideration will contain now a more numerous and now a less numerous set of terms. In particular, the series may contain so many terms that it cannot, compatibly with taking in and exhausting *all* the individuals of that species, be conceded to have a *last term;* a point which we shall handle in greater detail in the sequel. Assuming it for the present, I propose the name *infinite multitude* for one so constituted that every single finite multitude represents only a part of it.

§10

I hope it will be conceded that this definition of a *finite* and an *infinite* multitude will distinguish between them exactly in the sense intended by those who have used these terms rigorously. It will also be granted that no vicious circle lurks in the definitions. It only remains to ask, therefore, whether a definition merely of what is to be called an infinite *multitude* can put us in a position to determine what the *infinite* be in itself. That would be the case if it came to light that multitudes were the only things to which the idea of the infinite could be applied in its strict sense—in other words, if it came to light that infinitude were, strictly speaking, a property only of multitudes; or again in other words, if everything we judge *infinite* is so judged solely because, and solely in so far as, we find it possessing a property which can be considered as infinite multitude. Now to my thinking, this really is the case. Mathematicians use the word plainly in no other meaning: for what they are occupied in determining is hardly ever anything else than quantity, and they do so by first choosing one object of the species as *unit,* and then employing the idea of number. If they find a quantity

174

greater than any finite number of the assumed units, they call it *infinitely great;* if they find one so small that its every finite multiple is smaller than the unit, they call it *infinitely small;* nor do they recognise any other kind of infinitude than these two, together with the quantities derived from them as being infinite to a higher order of greatness or smallness, and thus based after all on the same idea.

§11

Some philosophers, however, and notably in our day, such as *Hegel* and his followers, are not satisfied with this mathematically familiar infinitude. They contemptuously dub it the 'bad infinity,' and claim knowledge of a true, a vastly superior, a *qualitative infinity,* to be found in *God* particularly, and speaking generally only in the *absolute.* Now I agree for my part with *Hegel, Erdmann* and others so long as they are thinking of the mathematically infinite only as a *variable* quantity knowing no limit to its growth (a definition adopted, as we shall soon see, even by many mathematicians) and so long as they are finding fault with this notion of a quantity which is always *growing* into the infinite but never *reaching* it. In fact, a *truly infinite* quantity (for example, the length of a straight line unbounded in either direction, meaning: the magnitude of the spatial entity containing all the points determined solely by their abstractly conceivable relation to two fixed points) does not by any means need to be variable, and in the adduced example it is in fact not variable. Conversely, it is quite possible for a quantity merely capable of being taken greater than we have already taken it, and of becoming larger than any one pre-assigned (finite) quantity, nevertheless to remain at all times merely finite: which holds in particular of every numerical quantity 1, 2, 3, 4, . . . ; what I refuse to admit is only this: that the philosopher knows any object to which he is entitled to attach the predicate of infinitude without having first established that in some respect or other that object exhibits infinite quantity, or at least infinite multitude. Now if I can once show that in God Himself, the Being whom we regard as the most perfectly one, aspects can be found under which we see even in Him an infinite multitude, and if I can show that we attribute infinitude to Him under those aspects alone, then it will scarcely be necessary to go on and show that similar considerations lie at the bottom of all the other cases where the idea of the infinite holds good. I say then: we call God infinite because we are compelled to admit in Him more than one kind of force possessing infinite magnitude. Thus, we must attribute to Him a power of knowledge which is true omniscience, and which therefore comprises an infinite set of truths, to wit, all truths—and so forth. And what idea of the truly infinite would people impose upon us other than the one here set up? They say it is that All which comprises every Something whatever, the absolute All outside of which there exists nothing more. Yet even on this formulation it would still be an infinite which according to our definition included an infinite multitude. It would be an aggregate not alone of all actual entities, but also of all things having no actuality, of all 'absolute propositions and truths.' Consequently, there appear to be no grounds for departing from our conception of the infinite and embracing theirs—to say nothing of all the other errors they have woven into this doctrine of the All.

GEORGE BOOLE

(1815-1864)

The Englishman who laid the foundations of modern mathematical or symbolic logic, was a teacher and school principal who did not specialize in mathematics until he was thirty. He then developed a new and efficient method of formal logic designed to avoid the ambiguities of ordinary language and commonly referred to as an algebra of logic.

Main Works:
> The Mathematical Analysis of Logic; An Investigation of the Laws of Thought.

Of Syllogisms

A Syllogism consists of three Propositions, the last of which, called the conclusion, is a logical consequence of the two former, called the premises; e.g.

<blockquote>

Premises, $\begin{cases} \text{All Ys are Xs.} \\ \text{All Zs are Ys.} \end{cases}$

Conclusion, All Zs are Xs.

</blockquote>

Every syllogism has three and only three terms, whereof that which is the subject of the conclusion is called the *minor* term, the predicate of the conclusion, the *major* term, and the remain-

---

From: *The Mathematical Analysis of Logic.*

ing term common to both premises, the middle term. Thus, in the above formula, Z is the minor term, X the major term, Y the middle term.

The figure of a syllogism consists in the situation of the middle term with respect to the terms of the conclusion. The varieties of figure are exhibited in the annexed scheme.

1st Fig.	2nd Fig.	3rd Fig.	4th Fig.
YX	XY	YZ	XY
ZY	ZY	YZ	YZ
ZX	ZX	ZX	ZX

When we designate the three propositions of a syllogism by their usual symbols (A, E, I, O), and in their actual order, we are said to determine the mood of the syllogism. Thus the syllogism given above, by way of illustration, belongs to the mood AAA in the first figure.

The moods of all syllogisms commonly received as valid, are represented by the vowels in the following mnemonic verses.

Fig. 1.—bArbArA, cElArEnt, dArII, fErIO que prioris.

Fig. 2.—cEsArE, cAmEstrEs, fEstInO, bArOkO, secundæ.

Fig. 3.—Tertia dArAptI, dIsAmIs, dAtIsI, fElAptOn,
bOkArdO, fErIsO, habet: quarta insuper addit.

Fig. 4.—brAmAntIp, cAmEnEs, dImArIs, fEsApO, frEsIsOn.

The equation by which we express any Proposition concerning the classes X and Y, is an equation between the symbols x and y, and the equation by which we express any Proposition concerning the classes Y and Z, is an equation between the symbols y and z. If from two such equations we eliminate y, the result, if it do not vanish, will be an equation between x and z, and will be interpretable into a Proposition concerning the classes X and Z. And it will then constitute the third member, or Conclusion, of a Syllogism, of which the two given Propositions are the premises.

The result of the elimination of y from the equations

$$ay+b=0,$$
$$a'y+b'=0, \quad (14),$$

is the equation $\quad ab'-a'b=0, \quad (15).$

Now the equations of Propositions being of the first order with reference to each of the variables involved, all the cases of elimination which we shall have to consider, will be reducible to the above case, the constants a, b, a', b', being replaced by functions of x, z, and the auxiliary symbol v.

As to the choice of equations for the expression of our premises, the only restriction is, that the equations must not *both* be of the form $ay=0$, for in such cases elimination would be impossible. When both equations are of this form, it is necessary to solve one of them, and it is indifferent which we choose for this purpose. If that which we select is of the form $xy=0$, its solution is

$$y=v(1-x), \quad (16),$$

if of the form $(1-x)y=0$, the solution will be

$$y=vx, \quad (17),$$

and these are the only cases which can arise. The reason of this exception will appear in the sequel.

For the sake of uniformity we shall, in the expression of particular propositions, confine ourselves to the forms

$$vx=vy, \qquad \text{Some Xs are Ys,}$$
$$vx=v(1-y), \qquad \text{Some Xs are not Ys,}$$

These have a closer analogy with (16) and (17), than the other forms which might be used.

Between the forms about to be developed, and the Aristotelian canons, some points of difference will occasionally be observed, of which it may be proper to forewarn the reader.

To the right understanding of these it is proper to remark, that the essential structure of a Syllogism is, in some measure, arbitrary. Supposing the order of the premises to be fixed, and the distinction of the major and the minor term to be thereby determined, it is purely a matter of choice which of the two shall have precedence in the Conclusion. Logicians have settled this question in favour of the minor term, but it is clear, that this is a convention. Had it been agreed that the major term should have the first place in the conclusion, a logical scheme might have been constructed, less convenient in some cases than the existing one, but superior in others. What it lost in *barbara,* it would gain in *bramantip.* Convenience is *perhaps* in favour of the adopted arrangement, but it is to be remembered that it is *merely* an arrangement.

Now the method we shall exhibit, not having reference to one scheme of arrangement more than to another, will always give the more general conclusion, regard being paid only to its abstract lawfulness, considered as a result of pure reasoning. And therefore we shall sometimes have presented to us the spectacle of conclusions, which a logician would pronounce informal, but never of such as a reasoning being would account false.

The Aristotelian canons, however, besides restricting the *ordei* of the terms of a conclusion, limit their nature also;—and this limitation is of more consequence than the former. We may, by a change of figure, replace the particular conclusion of *bramantip,* by the general conclusion of *barbara;* but we cannot thus reduce to rule such inferences, as

Some not-Xs are not Ys.

Yet there are cases in which such inferences may lawfully be drawn, and in unrestricted argument they are of frequent occur-

180

rence. Now if an inference of this, or of any other kind, is lawful in itself, it will be exhibited in the results of our method.

We may by restricting the canon of interpretation confine our expressed results within the limits of the scholastic logic; but this would only be to restrict ourselves to the use of a part of the conclusions to which our analysis entitles us.

The classification we shall adopt will be purely mathematical, and we shall afterwards consider the logical arrangement to which it corresponds. It will be sufficient, for reference, to name the premises and the Figure in which they are found.

CLASS 1st.—Forms in which v does not enter.

Those which admit of an inference are AA, EA, Fig. 1; AE; EA, Fig. 2; AA, AE, Fig. 4.

Ex. AA, Fig. 1, and, by mutation of premises (change of order), AA, Fig. 4.

All Ys are Xs,	$y(1-x)=0,$	or $(1-x)y=0,$
All Zs are Ys,	$z(1-y)=0,$	or $zy-z=0.$

Eliminating y by (15) we have

$$z(1-x)=0,$$
$$\therefore \text{ All Zs are Xs.}$$

A convenient mode of effecting the elimination, is to write the equation of the premises, so that y shall appear only as a factor of one member in the first equation, and only as a factor of the opposite member in the second equation, and then to multiply the equations, omitting the y. This method we shall adopt.

Ex. AE, Fig. 2, and, by mutation of premises, EA, Fig. 2.

$$
\begin{array}{llll}
\text{All Xs are Ys,} & x(1-y)=0, & \text{or } & x=xy \\
\text{No Zs are Ys,} & zy=0, & & \underline{zy=0} \\
& & & xx=0 \\
\end{array}
$$

$\therefore$ No Zs are Xs.

The only case in which there is no inference is AA, Fig. 2,

$$
\begin{array}{lll}
\text{All Xs are Ys,} & x(1-y)=0, & x=xy \\
\text{All Zs are Ys,} & z(1-y)=0, & \underline{zy=z} \\
& & xx=xx \\
\end{array}
$$

$\therefore 0=0.$

CLASS 2nd.—When v is introduced by the solution of an equation.

The lawful cases directly or indirectly determinable by the Aristotelian Rules are AE, Fig. 1; AA, AE, EA, Fig. 3; EA, Fig. 4.

The lawful cases not so determinable, are EE, Fig. 1; EE, Fig. 2; EE, Fig. 3; EE, Fig. 4.

Ex. AE, Fig. 1, and, by mutation of premises, EA, Fig. 4.

$$
\begin{array}{llll}
\text{All Ys are Xs,} & y(1-x)=0, & y=vx & (a) \\
\text{No Zs are Ys,} & zy \;\;=0, & \underline{0=xy} & \\
& & 0=vxx & \\
\end{array}
$$

$\therefore$ Some Xs are not Zs.

The reason why we cannot interpret $vxx=0$ into Some Zs are not-Xs, is that by the very terms of the first equation (a) the interpretation of vx is fixed, as Some Xs; v is regarded as the representative of Some, only with reference to the class X.

For the reason of our employing a solution of one of the primitive equations, see the remarks on (16) and (17). Had we solved the second equation instead of the first, we should have had

$$(1-x)y=0,$$
$$v(1-z)=y, \quad (a),$$
$$v(1-z)\ (1-x)=0, \quad (b),$$
$$\therefore \text{ Some not-Zs are Xs.}$$

Here it is to be observed, that the second equation (a) fixes the meaning of $v(1-z)$, as Some not-Zs. The full meaning of the result (b) is, that all the not-Zs which are found in the class Y are found in the class X, and it is evident that this could not have been expressed in any other way.

Ex. 2. AA, Fig. 3.

All Ys are Xs,	$y(1-x)=0,$	$y=vx$
All Ys are Zs,	$y(1-z)=0,$	$0=y(1-z)$

$$0=vx(1-z)$$
$$\therefore \text{ Some Xs are Zs.}$$

Had we solved the second equation, we should have had as our result, Some Zs are Xs. The form of the final equation particularizes what Xs or what Zs are referred to, and this remark is general.

The following, EE, Fig. 1, and, by mutation, EE, Fig. 4, is an example of a lawful case not determinable by the Aristotelian Rules.

No Ys are Xs,	$xy=0,$	$0=xy$
No Zs are Ys,	$zy=0,$	$y=v(1-z)$

$$0=v(1-z)x$$
$$\therefore \text{ Some not-Zs are not Xs.}$$

CLASS 3rd.—When v is met with in one of the equations, but not introduced by solution.

The lawful cases determinable *directly* or *indirectly* by the Aristotelian Rules, are AI, EI, Fig. 1; AO, EI, OA, IE, Fig. 2; AI, AO, EI, EO, IA, IE, OA, OE, Fig. 3; IA, IE, Fig. 4.

Those not so determinable are OE, Fig. 1; EO, Fig. 4.

The cases in which no reference is possible, are AO, EO, IA, IE, OA, Fig. 1; AI, EO, IA, OE, Fig. 2; OA, OE, AI, EI, AO, Fig. 4.

Ex. 1. AI, Fig. 1, and, by mutation, IA, Fig. 4.

$$\begin{array}{ll}
\text{All Ys are Xs,} & y(1-x) = 0 \\
\text{Some Zs are Ys,} & vz = vy \\
\hline
& vz(1-x) = 0
\end{array}$$

$\therefore$ Some Zs are Xs.

Ex. 2. AO, Fig. 2, and, by mutation, OA, Fig. 2.

$$\begin{array}{llll}
\text{All Xs are Ys,} & x(1-y)=0, & x=xy \\
\text{Some Zs are not Ys,} & vz=v(1-y), & vy=v(1-z) \\
\hline
& & vx=vx(1-z) \\
& & vxz=0
\end{array}$$

$\therefore$ Some Zs are not Xs.

The interpretation of vz as Some Zs, is implied, it will be observed, in the equation $vz=v(1-y)$ considered as representing the proposition Some Zs are not Ys.

The cases not determinable by the Aristotelian Rules are OE, Fig. 1, and, by mutation, EO, Fig. 4.

$$\begin{array}{ll}
\text{Some Ys are not Xs,} & vy=v(1-x) \\
\text{No Zs are Ys,} & 0=zy \\
\hline
& 0=v(1-x)z
\end{array}$$

$\therefore$ Some not-Xs are not Zs.

184

The equation of the first premiss here permits us to interpret $v(1-x)$, but it does not enable us to interpret vz.

Of cases in which no reference is possible, we take as examples—

AO, Fig. 1, and by mutation, OA, Fig. 4,

All Ys are Xs,	$y(1-x)=0,$		$y(1-x)=0$
Some Zs are not Ys,	$vz=v(1-y)$	(a)	$v(1-z)=vy$

$$v(1-z)\ (1-x)=0$$
$$0=0$$

since the auxiliary equation in this case is $v(1-z)=0$.

Practically it is not necessary to perform this reduction, but it is satisfactory to do so. The equation (a), it is seen, defines vz as Some Zs, but it does not define $v(1-z)$, so that we might stop at the result of elimination (b), and content ourselves with saying, that it is not interpretable into a relation between the classes X and Z.

Take as a second example AI, Fig. 2, and, by mutation, IA, Fig. 2,

All Xs are Ys,	$x(1-y)=0,$	$x=xy$
Some Zs are Ys,	$vz=vy,$	$vy=vz$

$$vx=vxz$$
$$v(1-z)x=0$$
$$0=0,$$

the auxiliary equation in this case being $v(1-z)=0$.

Indeed in every case in this class, in which no inference is possible, the result of elimination is reducible to the form $0=0$. Examples therefore need not be multiplied.

CLASS 4th.—When v enters into both equations.

No inference is possible in any case, but there exists a distinction among the unlawful cases which is peculiar to this class. The two divisions are,

1st. When the result of elimination is reducible by the auxiliary equations to the form $0=0$. The cases are II, OI, Fig. 1; II, OO, Fig. 2; II, IO, OI, OO, Fig. 3; II, IO, Fig. 4.

2nd. When the result of elimination is not reducible by the auxiliary equations to the form $0=0$.

The cases are IO, OO, Fig. 1; IO, OI, Fig. 2; OI, OO, Fig. 4.

Let us take as an example of the former case, II, Fig. 3.

$$\begin{array}{lll} \text{Some Xs are Ys,} & vx=vy, & vx=vy \\ \text{Some Zs are Ys,} & v'z=v'y, & \dfrac{v'y=v'z}{vv'x=vv'z} \end{array}$$

Now the auxiliary equations $v(1-x)=0$, $v'(1-z)=0$,

$$\text{give} \quad vx=v, \quad v'z=v'.$$

Substituting we have

$$vv'=vv',$$
$$\therefore 0=0.$$

As an example of the latter case, let us take IO, Fig. 1,

$$\begin{array}{lll} \text{Some Ys are Xs,} & vy=vx, & vy=vx \\ \text{Some Zs are not Ys,} & v'z=v'(1-y), & \dfrac{v'(1-z)=v'y}{vv'(1-z)=vv'x} \end{array}$$

Now the auxiliary equations being $v(1-x)=0$, $v'(1-z)=0$, the above reduces to $vv'=0$. It is to this form that all similar cases are reducible. Its interpretation is, that the classes v and v' have no common member, as is indeed evident.

186

The above classification is purely founded on mathematical distinctions. We shall now inquire what is the logical division to which it corresponds.

The lawful cases of the first class comprehend all those in which, from two universal premises, a universal conclusion may be drawn. We see that they include the premises of *barbara* and *celarent* in the first figure, of *cesare* and *camestres* in the second, and of *bramantip* and *camenes* in the fourth. The premises of *bramantip* are included, because they admit of an universal conclusion, although not in the same figure.

The lawful cases of the second class are those in which a particular conclusion only is deducible from two universal premises.

The lawful cases of the third class are those in which a conclusion is deducible from two premises, one of which is universal and the other particular.

The fourth class has no lawful cases.

Among the cases in which no inference of any kind is possible, we find six in the fourth class distinguishable from the others by the circumstance, that the result of elimination does not assume the form 0=0. The cases are

$$\left\{\begin{matrix}\text{Some Ys are Xs,} \\ \text{Some Zs are not Ys,}\end{matrix}\right. \left\{\begin{matrix}\text{Some Ys are not Xs,} \\ \text{Some Zs are not Ys,}\end{matrix}\right. \left\{\begin{matrix}\text{Some Xs are Ys,} \\ \text{Some Zs are not Ys,}\end{matrix}\right.$$

and the three others which are obtained by mutation of premises.

It might be presumed that some logical peculiarity would be found to answer to the mathematical peculiarity which we have noticed, and in fact there exists a very remarkable one. If we examine each pair of premises in the above scheme, we shall find that there *is virtually* no middle term, i.e. *no medium of comparison,* in any of them. Thus, in the first example, the individuals spoken of in the first premiss are asserted to belong to the class Y, but those spoken of in the second premiss are *virtually* asserted to belong to the class not-Y: nor can we by any lawful transformation or conversion alter this state of things. The comparison will still be made with the class Y in one premiss, and with the class not-Y in the other.

Now in every case beside the above six, there will be found a middle term, either expressed or implied. I select two of the most difficult cases.

In AO, Fig. 1, viz.

> All Ys are Xs,
> Some Zs are not Ys,

we have, by *negative conversion* of the first premiss,

> All not-Xs are not-Ys,
> Some Zs are not Ys,

and the middle term is now seen to be not-Y.

Again, in EO, Fig. 1,

> No Ys are Xs,
> Some Zs are not Ys,

a proved conversion of the first premiss (see *Conversion of Propositions*), gives

> All Xs are not-Ys,
> Some Zs are not-Ys,

and the middle term, the true medium of comparison, is plainly not-Y, although as the not-Ys in the one premiss *may be* different from those in the other, no conclusion can be drawn.

The mathematical condition in question, therefore,—the irreducibility of the final equation to the form 0=0,—adequately represents the logical condition of there being no middle term, or common medium of comparison, in the given premises.

I am not aware that the distinction occasioned by the presence or absence of a middle term, in the strict sense here understood, has been noticed by logicians before. The distinction, though real and deserving attention, is indeed by no means an obvious one, and it would have been unnoticed in the present instance but for the peculiarity of its mathematical expression.

What appears to be novel in the above case is the proof of the existence of combinations of premises in which there is absolutely no medium of comparison. When such a medium of comparison, or true middle term, does exist, the condition that its quantification in both premises together shall exceed its quantification as a single whole, has been ably and clearly shown by Professor De Morgan to be necessary to lawful inference (*Cambridge Memoirs*, Vol. VIII. Part 3). And this is undoubtedly the true principle of the Syllogism, viewed from the standpoint of Arithmetic.

I have said that it would be possible to impose conditions of interpretation which should restrict the results of this calculus to the Aristotelian forms. Those conditions would be,

1st. That we should agree not to interpret the forms $v(1-x)$, $v(1-z)$.

2ndly. That we should agree to reject every interpretation in which the order of the terms should violate the Aristotelian rule.

Or, instead of the second condition, it might be agreed that, the conclusion being determined, the order of the premises should, if necessary, be changed, so as to make the syllogism formal.

From the *general* character of the system it is indeed plain, that it may be made to represent any conceivable scheme of logic, by imposing the conditions proper to the case contemplated.

We have found it, in a certain class of cases, to be necessary to replace the two equations expressive of universal Propositions, by their solutions; and it may be proper to remark, that it would have been allowable in all instances to have done this, so that every case of the Syllogism, without exception, might have been treated by equations comprised in the general forms

$$y = vx,$$ or $$y - vx = 0 \dots A,$$
$$y = v(1-x),$$ or $$y + vx - v = 0 \dots E,$$
$$vy = v.x,$$ $$vy - vx = 0 \dots I,$$
$$vy = v(1-x),$$ $$vy + vx - v = 0 \dots O.$$

Perhaps the system we have actually employed is better, as distinguishing the cases in which v only *may* be employed, from those in which it *must*. But for the demonstration of certain general properties of the Syllogism, the above system is, from its simplicity, and from the mutual analogy of its forms, very convenient.

Given the three propositions of a Syllogism, prove that there is but one order in which they can be legitimately arranged, and determine that order.

All the forms above given for the expression of propositions, are particular cases of the general form,

$$a + bx + cy = 0.$$

Assume then for the premises of the given syllogism, the equations

$$a + bx + cy = 0, \quad (18),$$
$$a' + b'z + c'y = 0, \quad (19),$$

then, eliminating y, we shall have for the conclusion

$$ac' - a'c + bc'x - b'cz = 0, \quad (20).$$

Now taking this as one of our premises, and either of the original equations, suppose (18), as the other, if by elimination of a common term x, between them, we can obtain a result equivalent to the remaining premiss (19), it will appear that there are more than one order in which the Propositions may be lawfully written; but if otherwise, one arrangement only is lawful.

Effecting then the elimination, we have

$$bc(a' + b'z + c'y) = 0, \quad (21),$$

which is equivalent to (19) multiplied by a factor bc. Now on examining the value of this factor in the equations A, E, I, O, we find it in each case to be v or $-v$. But it is evident, that if an equation expressing a given Proposition be multiplied by an extraneous factor, derived from another equation, its interpretation will either be limited or rendered impossible. Thus there will either be no result at all, or the result will be a *limitation* of the remaining Proposition.

If, however, one of the original equations were

$$x=y, \qquad \text{or } x-y=0.$$

the factor bc would be -1, and would *not* limit the interpretation of the other premiss. Hence if the first member of a syllogism should be understood to represent the double proposition All Xs are Ys, and All Ys are Xs, it would be indifferent in what order the remaining Propositions were written.

A more general form of the above investigation would be, to express the premises by the equations

$$a+bx+cy+dxy=0, \quad (22),$$
$$a'+b'z+c'y+d'zy=0, \quad (23).$$

After the double elimination of y and x we should find

$$(bc-ad)\,(a'+b'z+c'y+d'zy)=0;$$

and it would be seen that the factor $bc-ad$ must in every case either vanish or express a limitation of meaning.

The determination of the order of the Propositions is sufficiently obvious.

BERNARD BOSANQUET
(1848-1923)

The British idealist philosopher, was descended from an old Huguenot family. He taught at Oxford and was a leading English Neo-Hegelian. His emphasis was on the importance of the individual.

Main Works:

Knowledge and Reality; A History of Aesthetic; The Essentials of Logic; The Psychology of the Moral Self; The Philosophical Theory of the State; The Value and Destiny of the Individual.

Scientific Induction

Hypothesis and Postulate

1. HYPOTHESIS is a name that may be applied to any conception by which the mind establishes relations between data of testimony, of perception, or of sense, so long as that conception is one among alternative possibilities, and is not referred to reality as a fact.

Hypothesis falls outside Postulate

i. From Aristotle onward, indeed, logicians have been anxious to consider a hypothesis as the suggestion of a real agent —a thing or occurrence in a thing—related to the data as 'cause' to 'effect'; and to distinguish such a suggested 'agent' from a mere suggested 'reading' of the phenomena—a principle, law, or definition. Of course there is a primary difference between a material agent and an ideal law or principle, but the distinction is not ultimate in theory and appears to be, for this reason, incapable of being sustained in scientific practice. A 'working hypothesis'—and most of the great unifying conceptions of modern

---

From: *Logic.*

science are working hypotheses—is the suggestion of a real agent taken as equivalent to the suggestion of a mere law or principle. It is worth while for the sake of clearness to look at the distinction between law and real agent in a form recently given to it by Lotze, viz. as the distinction between Postulate and Hypothesis.

In the account to which I refer[1] the name of *Postulate* is given to the conditions which are absolutely and essentially involved in a given set of appearances, and apart from which 'the content of the observation with which we are dealing would contradict the laws of our thought.' These conditions, it must be observed, need not be abstract, except in the sense of being definite and precise. They might therefore, I infer, exhaust or define the nature of a real agent, in so far as a real agent is capable of being determinately known. But it is plain that as a rule they will not suffice to do so. The concrete nature of a material thing will contain much that is indifferent to the conditions precisely involved in any determinate effect.

By *hypothesis,* therefore, in this same account, is meant a conjecture which specifies the natural agents taken to be at work in a phenomenon and to be the means of fulfilling the postulate involved in it, in the case under investigation. In other cases, it is implied, the same postulate might be satisfied by means of other agents. And, it should be added, by a *fiction* is meant the reference of an effect to a cause or principle which we know to be incapable of producing it, but from the real effects of which it only differs by an error which is capable of being determinately assigned. Omitting the case of a confessed fiction, and including a fiction, not confessed to be such, under the title of a hypothesis, we may throw the remainder of our discussion into the form of an enquiry into the distinction between Hypothesis and Postulate.

The Postulate sets an abstract problem which Hypothesis has to solve in the concrete. The distinction *prima facie* coincides

---

[1] Lotze, Logik, sect. 273.

with that upon which Mill lays stress in his treatment of hypothesis, between a quantitative law of action, and the thing which acts according to that law. But it would certainly seem that every hypothesis in order to be established must be passed over into the content of the postulate, in the sense that, without the matter suggested in the *hypothesis* also, 'the content of the observations with which we are dealing would contradict the laws of our thought.' For this is ultimately the ground on which we affirm of Reality everything that we do so affirm. When the postulate is shown to contain the hypothesis, by a concrete proof that the suggested thing or fact is necessary to prevent self-contradiction in our thought, then we have a hypothesis with a *vera causa* (see ii. below). When the hypothesis is moulded into the postulate, not or not exclusively by proof of the concrete supposition, but in a great degree by attenuating its content into a 'law of action,' then we have a 'working hypothesis,' i.e. materially an abstract postulate, but formally a supposition of a real agent. Such a hypothesis is a fiction which may or may not be a confessed fiction. In Mill's notes on Whewell [2] we see the process of attenuation at work, reducing hypotheses to fictions which are confessed by Mill and not confessed by Whewell. Modern science seems to the outsider more and more tending to substitute explanation by laws of action for causation by unknown real agents. But, in theory, a determinate agent may be involved in the postulate just as much as an abstract law, supposing that the agent is operative in the content in modes sufficiently many-sided to assign it a determinate nature. For logic, law and agent are alike conceptions by which thought constitutes the content into an organised whole; both may be 'within' the content, if we include in the content what is needed

---

[2] Mill's Logic, i. p. 335, and ii. p. 24; e.g. "Can an agency undulate? Can there be alternate motion backwards and forwards of the particles of an agency?" Mill is maintaining in effect that Whewell's view of the imponderable agents reduces them to laws of action. He is distinguishing an *agency* from an *agent* (the ether). And cf. Clifford on Causation, Lectures, etc., vol. i. p. 153.

to constitute it rightly; neither can be within the content if we separate it, by an unreal and indeed impossible distinction, from the work of thought in determining it. Every object of perception is such a conception, by which data of sense are determined in a way necessary to make them intelligible.

The real distinction which Lotze should have drawn is not between the law of action and the concrete real agent, but between the concrete real agent as known to be necessary for the explanation of the observations, and such an agent as not so known, but arbitrarily imagined, or identified with something known from other sources. If we assume a thing thus arbitrarily, or on the ground of extraneous knowledge, then (considering the thing in the latter case apart from the extraneous knowledge on the ground of which it is assumed) we have the relation 'If *a*, then *a*,' but not the reciprocal 'If *a*, then *a*'; *i.e.* in other cases other agents than *a* might satisfy the same postulate, or minimum of conditions, involved in *a*. But this unnecessary element in a hypothesis cannot of course be acquiesced in. The supposed real agent must either be elevated into the content of a postulate, or depressed into that of a fiction. Obviously, however, before deciding that the latter course is the only one open to us, we must concentrate *all* available knowledge upon the supposed real agent in order to test its right to become a postulate. One science e.g. may need one aspect of it, and another another.

Hypothesis with Vera Causa

ii. Thus to meet the difficulty that many characteristics of a *thing assumed* hypothetically to account for certain data are likely to fall outside what those data demand and justify, it is usual to require of a hypothesis that *a* the supposed agent shall be a *vera causa*. This can ultimately have but one meaning. It must come to this, that *a*, though containing elements which are superfluous for the explanation of *the data from which we happen to have started*, yet contains no elements which are not necessary to the explanation of *some other data or other*. It is commonly said that a *vera causa* is one independently known to exist, or accessible to direct perception. Of course we do not restrict our conviction of reality to matters accessible to direct perception—the centre of the earth, the inside of a block of marble, the other side of the moon, are cases in point. And if we did attempt this restriction, what is direct perception? All perception is inferential, and proceeds by furnishing conceptions which bring data of sense into intelligible relation. And if we require that the cause shall be independently known to exist, this is a mere question of the range of observations which it is to explain. A *vera causa* then is a thing, or occurrence in a thing, whose reality we are thoroughly convinced of from the necessity of reconciling observed data,[3] and there is no reason in the nature of things why a single science or a single range of reality should not suffice to produce such conviction. 'Direct perception' is a mere popular phrase without logical meaning. The question is simply whether our data are determinate enough to guide us to the nature of a real thing as explaining them. What is *really* demanded in the *vera causa* is probably *independent* evidence of the thing's reality, with an eye to the doctrine of chances. A single coherent set of errors may vitiate a whole coherent system of appearances, but the chances against errors in *independent* sets of observations are the same as the rapidly increasing chances against coincidences of independent events.[4] This is a parody (as the doctrine of chances is always a formal parody of some material truth) of the operation of multiform data in moulding a concrete hypothesis, which will be illustrated directly.

---

[3] The most thorough and simple way of classifying matters known from testimony or history is to include them under the head of conceptions which are necessary to determine observed data, the observed data being the books, speech, etc. which bring the facts to our individual notice. As to ranking agents under the head of conceptions, I may say that this is not reducing agents to mere conceptions. As known and established to us, they *are* conceptions, though they may be more.

[4] If the chance of error in one set of data is $\frac{1}{2}$, the chance of independent error in two sets (of the same but independent liability to error) is $\frac{1}{4}$, in three $\frac{1}{8}$, and so on.

Thus in a 'working hypothesis' we have postulate and hypothesis tending to indentification by attenuation[5] of the hypothesis, in a hypothesis with *vera causa* we obtain the same result by extension of the postulate to cover the alleged cause and turn it into a *vera causa*.

Phases of Hypothesis

2. In an ultimate sense, there is no knowledge without Hypothesis.

Rudimentary Hypothesis

i. All science may be rightly described as progressive "colligation of facts" through superinduction of conceptions[6] if it is understood that, though such conceptions are present in the real facts and are not mere additions out of our heads, yet in the progress of our knowledge such colligation does not operate upon the real facts themselves, but only on the facts as imperfectly understood by us. Thus the whole course of the present work has been an attempt to trace the progressive determination of feelings, or of facts imperfectly understood, by conceptions which may be regarded as hypotheses in course of development and proof. The continued identity of an individual, for example, which is the soul of the individual judgment, may be regarded as a conception or hypothesis which is superinduced (though without conscious reflection) upon the successive appearances which we observe, and 'colligates' these facts. And as we have seen in speaking of Induction, hypothesis in a genuine sense, as a conscious activity, begins to operate where the individual judgment begins to be employed in explaining the conjunction of attributes, in conjunctive or enumerative Induction. From this point, at which Hypothesis is represented by the content of a generic or specific name, we have watched its de-

---

[5] A working hypothesis often, and perhaps usually, partakes of the character of a fiction, being in fact suggested as a *vera causa*, and subsequently attenuated till it is clearly not a *vera causa*, though retaining its original claim to be so.

[6] Green, Philosophical Works, ii. p. 288.

velopment through analogy and through scientific analysis, till in the experiment of the Siren we found ourselves testing by determinate perceptive comparison a relation which can only be completely explained by a complex mathematical theorem.[7]

Mediate Hypothesis

ii. Procedure by Hypothesis proper is mediate.

Hypothetical Nature of Induction

a. It is clear from what has been said that we must assent in substance to the view of Jevons and Sigwart which is in the main that of Whewell[8] and De Morgan,[9] so far as it asserts the essential identity of Induction with procedure by Hypothesis. And indeed Mill himself might almost be reckoned on this side. He shows[10] triumphantly that the Method of Difference will test the premises of a Deduction, and the fact that the 'instances' on which it operates are in that case obtained by Deduction, he sets down as of no consequence, i.e. as not interfering with its Inductive character. But it is not so clear that this method, which unquestionably will test the consequences of a precise deduction and therefore the truth of its premises, will perform any other function that could be called Inductive. Mill's objection[11] against Whewell's hypothetical method, on the ground of insufficient provision for excluding unproved or unproveable elements of hypothesis, is an objection which arises from the impossible demand for *merely* negative and exhaustive determination. It is very probable that Whewell makes too little of the necessity for showing or for its being possible to show that *nothing but* α could produce *a*; but what Whewell seems to have rightly felt is that this is after all in its essence a material

---

[7] The theory of wave-propagation, which explains among other things the discordant beats produced by sonorous impulses which have not certain definite ratios of rapidity.

[8] See Mill's Logic, ii. 24.

[9] Budget of Paradoxes, p. 49.

[10] Logic, ii. 12.

[11] See Mill's Logic, ii. p. 24.

and positive question, depending on the degree and mode of connection between α and a, and being for logic the same as the question whether α *as such* produces a. The possibility of proof or disproof, which is claimed as essential to the 'legitimacy' of a hypothesis, must be a material or real possibility, and reduces itself to specific presumptions that proof may be had, which are in themselves grades of proof. But while accepting the general view to which I have alluded of the importance of hypothesis in Inductive Inference, I am unable to agree with some important results which have been held to follow upon such a view.

Example of fusion between hypothesis and data

β. I shall begin by endeavouring to lay the true doctrine very briefly before the reader, in the sense in which I understand it and in which it seems to me to follow from our previous discussions. It will then be necessary to speak of the relation between Induction in the scientific sense and the work of generalisation which is popularly ascribed to it, and I shall conclude the present chapter with some observations on the above-mentioned misapprehensions, and on the true relation of Induction to Inference as such.

The purpose of the example which I propose to analyse is to exhibit the mediate identification of a hypothetical cause, at first sight somewhat remote, with a given effect. I intentionally select an instance in which the identification is not quite perfect, in order to display the full nature of the difficulty to be overcome.

As a datum to be explained, we will take the curious fact, long known to scholars, that the Greek god Apollo, especially the Apollo of the Troad, is associated with the mouse, both in his appellation Smintheus and in recorded usages—there were sacred mice and figures of mice in his temple, and so forth.[12]

The conjunction of aspects which excites surprise in this fact

---

[12] My example and my arguments are all drawn from Mr. Lang's Custom

is the association of an insignificant animal with the worship and the temples of a comparatively pure religion. A large choice of analogies lies open to us, any one of which might furnish some sort of mediation between these two extremes, and of these that which is at first sight the most remote may perhaps on a consideration of all the phenomena be considered the most hopeful.

It seems that in the Peruvian religion we find this same conjunction of aspects, the association of insignificant animals with the worship and the temples of a comparatively pure creed. And in that instance, it further appears, we have a definite and complete mediation or explanation of the two terms or 'extremes.' Before the establishment of Sun-worship by the Incas as the creed of the state, the Indians of the various tribes worshipped tribal animal gods, including all sorts of insignificant animals, the Indians of each tribe believing themselves to be descended from one of these animals. 'After the establishment of the purer religion, the Incas had the good policy to collect all the tribal animal gods into their temples in and around Cuzco, in which the two leading gods were the Master of Life, and the Sun.' This toleration of an older and cruder in subordination to a purer faith is a very common phenomenon, as Mr. Lang truly observes, in religious evolution. And he cites an example of a festival described by Theocritus which still continues in a Catholic country.

Here then we have a content the whole of which is given (I assume) in perception or in the *proximate* interpretation of perception, viz. in history. Analogy or Induction would not commonly be held to apply within the limits of this content; but nevertheless in as far as within the single 'instance' or range of reality—which is really the life of a whole nation—a *principle* is detected by our thought, there is operative what constitutes the essence of inductive as of all other inference. But no details have to be referred to reality solely on the strength of the prin-

---

and Myth, p. 103 ff. My purpose however only permits the most meagre reproduction of some points out of this interesting study.

ciple, because it happens that they are all warranted by testimony.[13]

Now if the content which perplexed us in Greek religious history fell *bona fide* within the lines of the content thus warranted and interpreted in Peruvian religion, no inference would be necessary, or rather, the purely formal inference which recognized the identification would suffice to include the Greek problem under the same solution as that which supplies itself for the Peruvian problem. But the very slight and superficial abstraction which is all that we have thus far formulated of the Greek problem can warrant no such material identification —so far as we have yet stated the point, almost any hypothesis might explain it; the misunderstanding of a name, or the caprice of a priest or a king. What we must now do is to look in the Greek problem for the facts and relations of which we have seen the significance in the Peruvian problem. But as historical data such facts and relations are wanting; and here we have the essential difference between Induction by analysis of Perception, and Induction by mediate Hypothesis. Our hypothesis is *prima facie* a conjectural matter of fact falling wholly outside the content which has to be explained. The view which I wish to illustrate is that our proof of the hypothesis must ultimately depend upon the characteristic positive connection between the hypothesis and its consequences. This connection is as we have seen elucidated and purged of irrelevancy by the establishment of limiting negations, but is not otherwise dependent on the disproof of an indefinite number of alternative hypotheses, and is no more restricted to mere probability than is the determination of any perceived data by any conception which makes them intelligible.[14]

---

[13] It is probable, and appears I think from Mr. Lang's account, that the interpretation even of the known succession in Peru into an intelligible evolution would involve, as almost every interpretation does, some remodeling and supplementation of details. So far we have inference in the popular sense.

[14] Contrast with this the mechanical views of Jevons, Principles of

We have before us, as a datum of fact, a surprising conjunction between Apollo and the mouse, especially in Apollo's temple. We have as a suggested fact which might explain this conjunction, a previous state of Greek or neighbouring tribes in which they worshipped animals such as the mouse, together with a religious evolution in which the earlier cult survived by the side of the later and purer worship. According to the ordinary process of Induction as inverse Deduction, we proceed to 'deduce the consequences which might be inferred from the hypothesis.'

In drawing consequences from a hypothetical state of facts we have to apply that state of facts to the reality on the basis of which it is supposed, and to examine in detail the results of the combination. This analysis of the content of the hypothesis is not a contrivance of demonstration, but an inevitable necessity of knowledge. In working out, for example, the hypothesis now before us, we must take into account the customs relating to marriage and to names which belong to that phase of savage life which we are conjecturally imputing to the Greek race in the past. Among savages named after tribal animals which they worship and bear as name or emblem, and from which they trace their descent, the members of one family do not intermarry with people bearing the same name or emblem, and the children of every marriage take the mother's name or emblem (totem). These names consequently tend to become scattered throughout a large region, and are associated with the well-known phenomenon, for which in very early society there are obvious grounds, of counting kinship through the mother and not through the father. On the other hand, when this state of society passes away, as in European nations it has passed away, it is plain that a powerful family will crush out the names

---

Science, p. 152, and Sigwart, Logik, ii. p. 357. Jevons thinks that no proof by Imperfect Induction (Induction falling short of complete enumeration) can be more than probable. Sigwart thinks that a hypothesis is refuted by its consequences, but not proved by establishing them, though it grows in probability as its consequences agree with the facts.

of the other families in a district, and form a local tribe called by an animal name. From this hypothesis thus analyzed, if applied to 'mouse families,' there follow primarily four results which briefly stated amount to this:—

(1) There would be places named from mice, and mice will be held sacred in those places. This was so in the Troad.

(2) The mouse-name would be given locally to the god who superseded the mouse. This was so in the places called after the mouse.

(3) The figure of the mouse would be associated with the god in his temple, and used as a badge or local mark in places where the mouse had been venerated. The former usage was found, and the latter was not uncommon, in Greece.

(4) Stories would be told in the district in question to explain the worship of the mouse. This was so in the Troad.

I do not say that these four points, thus baldly stated, carry us very far. But in so far as they support the hypothesis at all, they do so not merely as an arrangement of coincidences due more probably, in a calculable degree, to a single cause than to independent unknown causes; but, like an arrangement of results *which some person has the power and a strong motive to produce,* they support the conjectural cause by the material connection of the data with it, or a material extension of the data towards including it. One of the above points for example is the appearance of the figure of a mouse as a badge or city emblem in Greece. This, when referred to an actual race of men exceedingly conservative in its customs, is a point, though a trifling one, actually in common between hypothesis and data. The badge or crest of a city is not the same thing as the totem of a family, but the connection of parts of cities with local tribes is too well made out in Greece and elsewhere to give us pause. And the veneration of an animal by the people of a city in ways strikingly analogous to totem worship is made out in the case of Egyptian cities. Of course this point *may* be otherwise explained than by the suggested hypothesis, and so may all the others; but they all, as referred to the life of a race, demand some explanation, and the only difficulty is to model that explanation rightly. It is this idea, that of moulding a hypothesis, that should be substituted for the idea of gauging its probability as something attaching to its definite and irrevocable form. To meet paradox by paradox, rather than admit that a hypothesis can only be established by the refutation of infinite others[15] and the non-refutation of itself, I would maintain that of *every set of data some positive hypothesis* (viz. that 'something or other' conditions these data) *is within our knowledge demonstrably true,* and that the problem of induction by the inverse method or by hypothesis is merely to further determine this 'something or other.' In this work of definition, as we have abundantly seen, negation is all-important; but it must be motivated and relevant negation, 'not *this,* because *that,* which has a determinate relation to this.'

I should weary the reader by further discussion of the mouse hypothesis, which moreover space forbids me to treat in its interesting details. But I must point out that by considering the peculiar marriage customs (e.g. maternal kinship), sacrificial and festival rites, and animistic beliefs, which are traceable throughout Greek life, and which are characteristic of the primitive phase that forms the content of our hypothesis, we can remodel hypothesis and data once more, and this time into a really intimate approximation to each other. Hypothesis and data approach amalgamation in the conception of a finely gifted race still bearing in its prime the traces of a natural though characteristic evolution out of a savage past. We might almost claim that a savage phase of life is a *vera causa, apart from the proof of our special hypothesis,*[16] not only in the Peruvian but in the Greek race. Is not the conception of a past and natural evolution, in the case of *any* race of men which we may be consider-

---

[15] This is the root of the idea that no results of hypothetical Induction can be certain. The idea is ridiculous when it is once seen that hypothetical Induction is identical in principle with common perception and with all Inference whatever.

[16] Every hypothesis *when proved* is a hypothesis with *vera causa.*

ing, a conception 'apart from which the content of the observation with which we are dealing would contradict the laws of our thought'? But if so, then, according to the distinction accepted above, the conception, *although* that of a real agent or event, is a postulate and not a mere hypothesis, and therefore is the conception of a *vera causa*; and the work of induction is, as said above, to assign to the postulate in detail its actual content or law of action.

Other hypotheses, independent of that which the author advocates, are carefully dealt with in the chapter from which I have been quoting. And I think that any one who considers the matter in the light of this or any equally genuine piece of research must feel that just in so far as the adverse hypotheses are independent, their refutation, although a *sine qua non* of the establishment of the hypothesis advocated, can never genuinely contribute to that establishment. In other words, the refutation of other hypotheses is a genuine assistance to one hypothesis only when it elicits positive content which goes to model this latter hypothesis.

BURIDANUS
(JEAN BURIDAN, 14th century)

Buridanus was the Latinized name of Jean Buridan, a 14th century French philosopher and natural scientist who was an adherent of Ockham and commented extensively on Aristotle. The fable attributed to Buridan (of an ass that died of starvation and thirst because he couldn't make up his mind between water and food placed at equal distances from him) became a highly popular evidence for the impossibility of freedom of will. He was Rector of the University of Paris and made some remarkably advanced statements in physics.

Main Works:

> Compendium Logicae; Quaestiones in decem libros Ethicorum Aristotelis.

Dialectic Elements

Dialectics is the art of arts, offering a means to the principles of all methods.

This text on logic contains nine sections. The first part deals with propositions, their parts, passivity, and properties. The second, with predicables. The third, with categories. The fourth, with suppositions. The fifth, with syllogisms. The sixth, with dialectic topics. The seventh, with fallacies. The eighth, with divisions, definitions, and demonstrations. The ninth, with solutions of certain sophisms.

At the beginning of this chapter stands the definition of

From: *Summula de Dialectica.*

dialectics. In this regard it should be noted that dialectics is taken in a two-fold sense. In one sense, rigidly: thus it is a certain part of logic as transmitted by Aristotle in his treatise on *Topics*. In another way it is taken in a broad dialectical sense.

In the second place it should be observed that logic is two-fold. One type is instructive logic: this is the logic that teaches division, definition, disputation, and the distinction between truth and falsity.

This logic is true knowledge or art. The other is practical logic. We use its acquisition in the division of other sciences: in defining and debating: in distinguishing truth from falsity. Thus practical logic is a true science. And it is evident that logic is both instructive and practical.

If such logic is acquired through the practice of dialectic argumentation, it is called practical dialectics. If it is acquired through sophistic practice, it is called practical sophistic logic. And if it is acquired through the practice of demonstrative argumentation, it is termed practical demonstrative logic and it is not necessary for all logic to be a science.

In the third place it should be noted that all expository logic contains two major divisions: one of which is called the new logic: the other, the old logic. Hence the new logic is that which treats of total arguments. It is discussed by Aristotle in Book I of the *Posterior Analytics,* in the *Topics,* and the *Elenchi.* But the old logic is that which treats the parts, both immediate and remote, of an argument and of the propositions and terms. This is discussed in Porphyry's treatise on predicables and in the books of the categories and in the *Interpretation* of Aristotle and in certain old monographs.

Next it should be observed that logic treating of the parts of argumentation is not old, and logic treating of the entirety of argumentation is not new: for logic that is concerned with the parts was invented first, while logic treating of the entirety of argumentation was invented later. But logic that deals with the parts is termed old, because it considers that the parts that are naturally anterior are said to be old with respect to the posterior. Another point to be considered is the term art. Art is defined thus: The proper principle of things that are achieved by us: that is, art is an intellective habit governed by a valid principle that instructs in the operation of external things.

Another observation: Of the six ethical principles five are intellective habits that are not of a nature to utter falsehood or to agree to falsehood. These are: Art, prudence, knowledge, understanding, and wisdom. Their sufficiency may be considered thus: Every intellective habit is concerned with necessity or contingency. If with necessity, either with conclusions or principles. If in the first way, it is a science. If in the second way: it is concerned either with the principles of entities or with demonstrations. If in the first way, it is wisdom, that deals with God and intelligence. If in the second way, it is understanding. If it is concerned with contingency, this is two-fold: either it is concerned with practical things, and this is an art: or with matters for discussion and this is a science.

In regard to definitions of dialectics, it has been questioned whether it is an art: a liberal art, or a slavish or technical art. On this question note that a technical or slavish art is an art established for aiding material necessities. But a liberal art is one that is established for the purpose of intellectual elegance and perfection.

Dialectics alone disputes with probability on the principles of all the other arts. Here it should be noted that this statement may be understood in two ways: That logic, from the principles of any science, teaches the construction of dialectic argument generative of opinion. In the strict acceptance of the term, dialectics thus coincides with one part of logic as distinct from others. In the second way dialectics debates on the principles of the other sciences, because it teaches, from the principles of the other sciences, how to construct arguments, whether dialectical or demonstrative or sophistic.

And thus in the acquisition of the other sciences dialectics must be prior. For logic by reason of its application is most general, as was previously stated. What is prior in doctrine must be more common. Similarly the intermediary that directs the end must precede this end. Now logic is the intermediary established in the acquisition of all the sciences. Therefore logic must be anterior by way of doctrine.

The usual argument in regard to grammar should be observed. Grammar is two-fold. One kind teaches the significations and impositions of terms. This grammar by way of doctrine must be prior to logic. But it is not a science since it is merely voluntary. The other grammar is that which by true rules teaches the construction of congruent speech and the distinction between congruent and incongruous, and this is a science. Such a grammar is posterior to logic in respect of doctrine.

To continue, however. Logic itself presupposes the congruent from grammar: therefore grammar must precede. The conclusion is that the presupposed science must precede the other. The antecedent is evident: logic considers the true and the false. It teaches the distinction between truth and falsity.

THE VERB

The verb is a significative word in accordance with a temporal relation no part of which is significative separately, or finite, or correct. When the tense of a verb is posited in regard to a noun that signifies without tense, the remaining parts are posited in the same way as if by a definition of the noun. And it should be understood that the logician posits two parts of speech only, namely: the noun and the verb. All the other parts of speech are called syncategorematic: that is, significative with other words.

The signification of words is either compound or simple. Compound, as: speech. Simple, as: a noun or a verb. A noun is a significative word with no temporal implication, in which no part is significative, finite or correct separately. A word is postulated in the definition of a noun in a genus. It is significative in regard to the differentia of a word not denoted: and is posited with regard to the differentia of a word that is naturally denotative.

Propositions are either categorical or hypothetical. The proposition is a statement denoting truth or falsity. One kind of proposition is perfect: the other, imperfect. A perfect statement is one that produces perfect sense in the mind of the listener, as: The man runs. Of perfect propositions, one kind is indicative, as: The man runs. Another kind is imperative, as: Peter, make a fire. Another is optative, as: I wish I were a good logician. Another is conjunctive, as: if you come to me, I shall give you a horse.

Of all these statements, only the indicative is said to be a proposition.

SOUND AND VOICE

Sound is a quality sensible to hearing: it is properly first perceptible through itself.

In respect of sounds, one kind is the voice; the others, not. The sound of the voice is a sound uttered by the mouth, formed by the instruments of nature. Every sound that is not voice is a not-voice sound.

One kind of sound is significative: another is not significative. A significative sound is one that represents something to the hearing, as: A man shouting, sick men groaning, a dog barking, anger, or joy. A sound that is not significative is one that represents nothing to the hearing, as: bufbaff.

In respect of significative sounds, one kind is naturally significative: the other, at discretion. A sound naturally significative is that which represents the same thing for all men, as: The groaning of the sick, the barking of dogs, rage, or joy.

A sound significative at discretion is one whereby a man denotes something to another man according to the first man's wish.

MARTIANUS CAPELLA
(4th century)

An African self-educated farmer of the late 4th century A.D. His philosophy was neoplatonist in tendency; but more important was his educational work. His literary work became a medieval textbook, and was also responsible for transmitting the standard medieval curriculum of higher education: the "seven liberal arts" of grammar, dialectics, rhetoric, geometry, arithmetic, astronomy and music, grouped in the *trivium* and *quadrivium*.

Main Work:
> De Nuptiis Philologiae et Mercurii.

On Dialectics

Genus is an assemblage of many forms under one name, as, animal: and of a particular species, as: man, horse, lion, and so on. But sometimes some species are so subordinate to the genus that they too, having other species subordinate to them, can be a genus, as the genus of man, that is a species in regard to animals, and a genus in respect of foreigners and Romans. The genus may extend to the point where, after division of its species, an indivisible point is reached: as, the division of men into male and female, and the males into boys, youth, and old men: and the boys into infants and those able to talk. And if one wants a division of boys into catamites and some

---

From: *De Nuptiis Philologiae et Mercurii.*

211

other type of boy, that is not a genus, because the indivisible has now been reached. We must use the term genus, that is relevant to our present purpose, so that if the question of man arises, we may assume that his genus is animal, which is closest to him. For if we say substance, this is true, in respect of reason, but superfluous in respect of necessity.

We call species also forms. Forms are those things that, subordinate to the genus, have its name and definition, as: man, horse, lion: since they are forms of animal: and man, horse, and lion can be called animal, and a body participating in life. The term and the definition of genus are thus determined.

Difference is the sufficient distinction in regard to what has been in question. For example: If it is asked what the difference is between a man and a horse, it is sufficient to say that the man is a biped, and a horse a quadruped. Now we must observe that as there are many differences in every single thing, we can divide each thing dissimilarly whenever we find some differences in one thing and other differences in another thing. For if we want to divide animal, we can make the division in respect of sex, as some are masculine and others are feminine: or into age groups, for some are just born, others young, and still others old: or in regard to size, for some are small, others large, others medium: or in respect of their various motions, for some walk, some crawl, some swim, some fly: or in reference to the variety of their habitation, for some live in water, some on land, some in the air, others, according to many authorities, in fire: or in respect of lingual variety, for some are articulate, some groan, some bark, some howl. Yet we should know that there must be single divisions too and that all divisions are found in single things. For male animals can be just born, and small, and able to walk, and land animals, and bipeds and articulate. Therefore though you may employ any division, you still ought to use the one that is suitable for the present undertaking. For if one has to discuss human glory it will be necessary to divide the subject into rational and obtuse divisions, to facilitate comprehension of nature's estimate of human beings, among all animals, to whom exclusively it gave the faculty of reasoning for the purpose of self-knowledge.

Accident is that which occurs to the same species only, but not invariably, as rhetoric occurs to many only, although it may not too: so that, though he may be a man, he may not be an orator.

A property is that which both occurs to the same species and invariably, making a distinction between each thing and all other things in general, as laughter in man. For man alone has the faculty of laughter, nor can man, when he so wishes, refrain from laughter, which is inherent in him. Difference is distinct from property, because difference distinguishes anything whatever from it: hence the question: Does property distinguish from all other things? For when we want to distinguish from a lion through difference, and we say that the lion is wild, and man is gentle, we merely seem to distinguish that which refers to the question under discussion. For saying that a lion is wild and man is gentle does not separate man from other gentle animals or lion from other wild beasts: but when we say that man is a 'risible animal', in that respect we distinguish him from the generality of the other animals.

Definition occurs when the complicated notion of anything is lucidly and succinctly expounded. In this matter three things are to be avoided: the meaning must not be wrong, or too exhaustive, or too restricted. A wrong definition would be: Man is an immortal irrational animal. For although it is true that man is an animal, it is still false that he is immortal or irrational. Excessive definition would be: Man is a mortal animal. For although the statement is brief, it is excessive, because it refers to all animals. An insufficient definition would be: Man is a grammatical animal. For although only man is a grammatical animal, not every man is a grammarian. A complete definition would be: Man is a rational, mortal animal. For by adding mortal, we have distinguished him from the gods, and by adding rational, we have distinguished him from the wild beasts.

The whole is that which sometimes gives its name but never

its definition to two or more parts placed in it, and this occurs in indivisible parts only. For example: When we designate a certain person and assume that the individual members are parts of him, we understand that this itself is the whole, because we designate a certain person, although the definition and the name of the whole itself fall into parts. For we cannot call either an arm or a head a man, nor do the individual limbs acquire the definition of man. But it must be observed that sometimes we can say *all* for *the whole*, but in a special sense. For *the whole* is used even in single things, and all in the case of multiple subjects. For when we say 'Cicero is a man,' being one, his entirety is thereby understood, and as man might be unskilled or a craftsman, or male or female, we preferably use the term all.

Parts are understood to be in the whole, and to compose the whole.

We have to divide until the point of indivisibility is reached, and this occurs when through differences we reduce the genera to paucity and subordinate species to them so that these species individually can become genera too for other species subordinate to them. For example: If we want to divide animal first of all briefly, we can do so through differences, because some walk, some crawl, some swim, and some fly. Hence similarly, in regard to individual species, we can make genera, as when we say that walking animals are a genus and we subordinate species to it, as: some are human, others wild beasts. And of these there can be other species, through which, if necessary, the point of indivisibility may be reached. But this assertion cannot be made in all cases, only in a particular subtle disputation. Now we can make a division in this way in a speech, when the obscurity of the case so requires: because if the case is not obscure, there must be in it a reasonable division that can be so treated, but it does not require to be very apparent.

Differences in partition do not occur frequently and so without them there can be infinite partition, if we wanted to reach the point of indivisibility. For if we designate a certain man as a whole and want to sum up his parts briefly, the differences of the parts do not suffice, and we are forced to use the names of certain parts: saying head, feet, and so on; and if we want to state them collectively and briefly, since differences are lacking, we cannot sum them up one by one: because there are many items and it would be impossible or tedious to do so.

The difference between division and partition is that in division we deal with species, and in partition with parts. Now the species are subordinate to the genus and can retain its definition and name. The parts are in the whole and can never assume the definition and only occasionally the name of the whole. However, we can take one and the same thing both as the genus and the whole, but otherwise the procedure is a violent one. For example, take man. If we want a division into youth, old man, and boy, he is a genus, and of his own species. If we want a partition into head, feet, and hands, he is the whole and his parts: because youth, old man, and boy, that we declared to be species, receive both the name of man and the definition. For example, an old person is said to be a man, and a rational, mortal animal, and a boy too, and a youth as well: but head and feet, that we said were parts, can receive neither the definition nor the name of man, because neither a head nor feet nor hands can be said to be a man and a risible animal.

Before I speak of substance, certain facts must be grasped. Whatever we say is either the subject, or about the subject, or in the subject, or about and in the subject. The subject is the first substance, because it itself occurs to nothing else inseparably, but other things are attached to it. For example: Cicero is not a name, but what is signified by that name.

About the Subject is that which is said about the subject itself and which gives it its definition and name, as: man. For Cicero is both a man and a rational mortal animal. Thus both the name and the definition, which is about the subject, are attached to the same subject. And hence what is said about the subject is found in genera or in species.

In the Subject is that which gives neither a name nor a definition to the subject, but is understood to be so contained in the subject itself as to preclude its existence without the subject. For example: rhetoric. For the subject can receive neither its name nor definition. For rhetoric is not Cicero nor is Cicero the art of effective speech: but Cicero is understood in the subject, since he himself cannot be called the subject.

About the Subject and *In the Subject* occur when it is about the subject for one thing, and in the subject for another. For example: learning. In the case of rhetoric it is about the subject and in Cicero's case it is in the subject. The first substance then is the subject: the second is that which is said about the first substance. For example: Cicero is the first substance: man and animal, the second substance. Now all resultant categories are said to be in the subject: let us then consider each singly.

Quality is that according to which we say of what kind a thing is, as: candor. From this it is reasonable to understand that the quality too is in the subject, since candor is necessarily in some thing, without which it cannot exist: and this some thing itself, in which it is, is the subject.

Quantity is that according to which we say how big a thing is, as: two feet. Quantity also must necessarily be understood in the subject.

Relative is that which is called a relation to something, as: father, brother. These are in the subject, for these nouns necessarily are related to something, and there are many nouns assertions about which will be understood conceptually. For example: Rome is relative to a place. Rome is the substance: this occurs to Rome. Relative to time: yesterday, recently, in the evening. Things by whose motion time is understood are substances, as: the sun, by whose course we understand time: and those things that give us some concept of the passage of time. Relative to place: lying, sitting. Relative to habit: booted, armed: the substance is man, and these things happen to him. Relative to action: cutting, burning. Relative to suffering: being cut, being burned.

The first substance then is that which is neither inseparably in the subject nor is predicated of any subject. The expression *inseparably* is added to the definition for the reason that every first substance, although it is in some location, can however be separated from it and move. For example: Cicero is understood to be in the senate, but from there he can speak elsewhere, and part of the first substance, although in the whole, is not so however inseparably: for actually or supposedly an arm may be separated from our body. But rhetoric is in Cicero's mind, so that even if by some chance it ceases to be, it is still not understood to depart from him, since, when it began to be, it is not assumed to have come to him from elsewhere.

The second substance is that which is predicated of the first substance, as has been said. For example: Man for Cicero, and animal for man and Cicero; and whatever the genus of the first substance is, the second substance is understood to be the same. So it is common to all substances not to be in the subject: but the first substance too is not about the subject. A substance cannot be extended or retracted, that is, receive more and less. And if nobody is more man than another man, one man will not be more man tomorrow than he was today, and in comparable instances a horse is not more a horse than a man is a man. Now we must observe in substances that there are associations, that is, a first substance is comparable to a first, and a second substance to a second. For if a second substance is compared with a first, a first substance is more substance than a second. For the first denotes a thing more, while the second has a kind of ambiguity of common relationship. For example: When I say Cicero, I clearly signify something indivisible and specific. When I say man, since we are all classified under this appellation, it is uncertain whom I mean. The consequence therefore is that a first substance is more a substance than a second substance, because it designates a thing with more certainty. Therefore more and less substance does not receive anything among its associates. Similarly, substance has no contrary: For nothing is contrary to man or horse. But if anyone asserted that Clodius was contrary to Cicero, he would mean that it was not the substances themselves that were contrary, but the qualities that were in them, as evil in goodness or vice in virtue or in justice. It seems to be a property of a substance when at one and the same time the substance is capable of contraries by a kind of self-permutation. For example: A stone, although it remains itself, can at one time be white and again black, yet it does not cease being a stone. And Cicero, at first stupid, then wise, still does not cease to be the same Cicero.

It remains for us to discuss opposites. Opposites are those things that appear to confront each other directly face to face, as it were, as contraries. However, not everything that is the opposite is contrary, but all contraries are opposites. They are opposites in such a manner that either relatives are opposites, as large to small and half to double, or contraries, as stupidity and wisdom, or possession and deprivation, vision and blindness, affirmation and negation. For example: Cicero discusses, Cicero does not discuss. These terms differ somewhat from each other: for relative is so opposed to relative that this very thing that is opposed is of the nature of that to which it is opposed, or refers to it in some manner. For half is the opposite of double and half of the same thing doubled. So that to which a thing is opposite is opposite to that of which it is a part. Small is the opposite of large so that it is part of it, as small in relation to big, to which it is the opposite, is small.

Contraries are such opposites as to belong to those things to which they are opposites, or refer to them in some manner. Stupidity is contrary to wisdom without stupidity not belonging to the same wisdom, or stupidity is related to it. It must be understood however that certain contraries have an intermediary, and certain other contraries do not. Those contraries that are such as are necessarily inherent interchangeably in the thing in which they can be, lack an intermediary. For example: Health and sickness. These two contraries are naturally inherent in the bodies of animals and are necessarily so inherent interchangeably, as we said, that, wherever there is no health in an animal's body, there is necessarily sickness, and wherever there is no sickness, there is necessarily health. But although white and black are contraries and are thus naturally found in bodies, they do not lack an intermediary, because it is not necessary for any body to be white or black: for whiteness can be lacking without the presence of black, and vice versa. Therefore some color can be found in between, as yellow or green. Possession and deprivation are opposites of such a kind that in the thing for which they can occur, one of them must necessarily be present at least from the moment when its nature permits it to be. For example: We say a person who has teeth is equipped with teeth, but we do not call a person toothless who has no teeth but whose nature is to have teeth and to have them from the time when nature permits him to have them. For we rightly do not say that a stone is toothless, since it never has teeth, nor a child: although it may sometime have teeth, nature does not permit it to have them at that age. Therefore the third kind of opposites differs in this respect from the first kind of relatives, that sight is so opposed to blindness that it is not of the same nature as blindness or is related to it in some way. It differs from the second kind, that is, the kind of contraries, in regard to those contraries that have an intermediary, because sight and blindness are understood in respect of the eyes, so that necessarily one of them is present. Therefore they differ in this respect from those contraries that have an intermediary, because one of the former must not necessarily be in the substance, while one of the latter must be so. These opposites differ from those contraries in that each has an intermediary, because the former must always necessarily and alternately occur in the thing in which they are naturally inherent. For example: Health and sickness in an animal's body: one of them is always present in an animal's body: but at some time one of them can be lacking in a thing in which they can naturally be inherent. For example: A child, while there is not yet time for it to be able to have teeth, is said to be neither possessed of teeth nor toothless, and the eyes of some animal, the time not yet being ripe for it to see, are said to be neither blind nor seeing, and they have no intermediary then. Therefore there are two species of contraries that lack an intermediary, that is, contraries that occur alternately to a thing in which they can be without the intervention of any intermediary. For example: Health and sickness, and those contraries that can at the same time be lacking in a substance, in which they cannot be at the same time and then, when they are simultaneously lacking, nothing intervenes as an intermediary: as sight and blindness, or possession and deprivation. The fourth kind of opposites is affirmation and negation, as: Cicero disputes, Cicero does not dispute. These differ from previous opposites, because the former can be stated individually, while the latter are considered only conjointly. They differ from relatives in this respect that the former opposites are stated even relatively, while the latter are not: for an argumentative person is not related to a non disputant. They differ from contraries in this respect: that the former, if they are asserted conjointly, are either false or true as long as that exists in which they can be. When this ceases to be, they are neither false nor true. For example: He is either stupid or wise while he is alive: one of these statements is true, since he has ceased to be, and the other are false, because he, who does not exist, can be neither stupid nor wise. But 'Cicero disputes' and 'Cicero does not dispute' are such opposites that while Cicero is alive one of them is necessarily so, and when he is dead it is false that he disputes, yet true that he does not dispute. In this manner these distinctions are made both from possession and from deprivation: for he who does not exist is neither blind nor seeing. Nor should one be disturbed at my having spoken about introductions, which we must discuss later. For what we did arose from the subject of opposites.

RUDOLF CARNAP
(born in 1891)

Taught philosophy at the University of Vienna and the German Uni
versity of Prague. He came to America in 1936, and taught at the
University of Chicago and the University of California in Los Angeles.
Carnap is generally acknowledged to be the leading living exponent of
logical empiricism and was a member of the *Vienna Circle* which
originated this movement.

Main Works:

Logischer Aufbau der Welt; Abriss der Logistik; Logische Syntax
der Sprache.

Elementary and Abstract Terms

We find among the concepts of physics—and likewise among
those of the whole of empirical science—differences of abstractness. Some are more elementary than others, in the sense that
we can apply them in concrete cases on the basis of observations in a more direct way than others. The others are more
abstract; in order to find out whether they hold in a certain case
we have to carry out a more complex procedure, which, however, also finally rests on observations. Between quite elementary concepts and those of high abstraction there are many intermediate levels. We shall not try to give an exact definition
for "degree of abstractness"; what is meant will become sufficiently clear by the following series of sets of concepts, pro-

---

From: *Foundations of Logic and Mathematics.*

ceeding from elementary to abstract concepts: bright, dark, red, blue, warm, cold, sour, sweet, hard, soft (all concepts of this first set are meant as properties of things, not as sense-data); coincidence; length; length of time; mass, velocity, acceleration, density, pressure; temperature, quantity of heat, electric charge, electric current, electric field; electric potential, electric resistance, coefficient of induction, frequency of oscillation; wave function.

Suppose that we intend to construct an interpreted system of physics—or of the whole of science. We shall first lay down a calculus. Then we have to state semantical rules of the kind SD for the specific signs, i.e., for the physical terms. (The SL-rules are presupposed as giving the customary interpretation of the logico-mathematical basis calculus.) Since the physical terms form a system, i.e., are connected with one another, obviously we need not state a semantical rule for each of them. For which terms, then, must we give rules, for the elementary or for the abstract ones? We can, of course, state a rule for any term, no matter what its degree of abstractness, in a form like this: "the term 'te' designates temperature," provided the meta-language used contains a corresponding expression (here the word "temperature") to specify the designatum of the term in question. But suppose we have in mind the following purpose for our syntactical and semantical description of the system of physics; the description of the system shall teach a layman to understand it, i.e., to enable him to apply it to his observations in order to arrive at explanations and predictions. A layman is meant as one who does not know physics but has normal senses and understands a language in which observable properties of things can be described (e.g., a suitable part of everyday nonscientific English). A rule like "the sign 'P' designates the property of being electrically charged" will not do. In order to fulfill the purpose, we have to give semantical rules for elementary terms only, connecting them with observable properties of things. For our further discussion we suppose the system to consist of rules of this kind, as indicated in the following diagram.

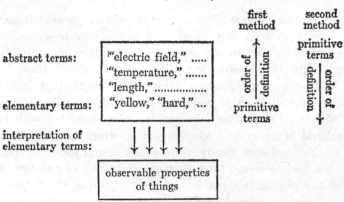

		first method	second method
abstract terms:	"electric field," ..... "temperature," .... "length,"	order of ↑ definition	primitive terms
elementary terms:	"yellow," "hard,"	primitive terms	order of definition ↓
interpretation of elementary terms:	↓ ↓ ↓ ↓		
	observable properties of things		

Now let us go back to the construction of the calculus. We have first to decide at which end of the series of terms to start the construction. Should we take elementary terms as primitive signs, or abstract terms? Our decision to lay down the semantical rules for the elementary terms does not decide this question. Either procedure is still possible and seems to have some reasons in its favor, depending on the point of view taken. The *first method* consists in taking elementary terms as primitive and then introducing on their basis further terms step by step, up to those of highest abstraction. In carrying out this procedure, we find that the introduction of further terms cannot always take the form of explicit definitions; conditional definitions must also be used (so-called reduction sentences). They describe a method of testing for a more abstract term, i.e., a procedure for finding out whether the term is applicable in particular cases, by referring to less abstract terms. The first method has the advantage of exhibiting clearly the connection between the system and observation and of making it easier to examine whether and how a given term is empirically founded. However, when we shift our attention from the terms of the system and the methods of empirical confirmation to the laws, i.e., the universal theorems of the system, we get a different perspective. Would it be possible to formulate all laws of physics in elementary terms, admitting more abstract terms only as abbreviations? If so, we would have that ideal of a science in sensationalistic form which Goethe in his polemic against Newton, as well as some positivists, seems to have had in mind. But it turns out— this is an empirical fact, not a logical necessity—that it is not possible to arrive in this way at a powerful and efficacious system of laws. To be sure, historically, science started with laws formulated in terms of a low level of abstractness. But for any law of this kind, one nearly always later found some exceptions and thus had to confine it to a narrower realm of validity. The higher the physicists went in the scale of terms, the better did they succeed in formulating laws applying to a wide range of phenomena. Hence we understand that they are inclined to choose the *second method*. This method begins at the top of the system, so to speak, and then goes down to lower and lower levels. It consists in taking a few abstract terms as primitive signs and a few fundamental laws of great generality as axioms. Then further terms, less and less abstract, and finally elementary ones, are to be introduced by definitions; and here, so it seems at present, explicit definitions will do. More special laws, containing less abstract terms, are to be proved on the basis of the axioms. At least, this is the direction in which physicists have been striving with remarkable success, especially in the past few decades. But at the present time, the method cannot yet be carried through in the pure form indicated. For many less abstract terms no definition on the basis of abstract terms alone is as yet known; hence those terms must also be taken as primitive. And many more special laws, especially in biological fields, cannot yet be proved on the basis of laws in abstract terms only; hence those laws must also be taken as axioms.

Now let us examine the result of the interpretation if the first or the second method for the construction of the calculus is chosen. In both cases the semantical rules concern the elementary signs. In the first method these signs are taken as primitive. Hence, the semantical rules give a complete interpretation for these signs and those explicitly defined on their basis. There are, however, many signs, especially on the higher levels of abstraction, which can be introduced not by an explicit definition but only by a conditional one. The interpretation which the rules give for these signs is in a certain sense incomplete. This is due not to a defect in the semantical rules but to the method by which these signs are introduced; and this method is not arbitrary but corresponds to the way in which we really obtain knowledge about physical states by our observations.

If, on the other hand, abstract terms are taken as primitive —according to the second method, the one used in scientific physics—then the semantical rules have no direct relation to the primitive terms of the system but refer to terms introduced by long chains of definitions. The calculus is first constructed floating in air, so to speak; the construction begins at the top and then adds lower and lower levels. Finally, by the semantical rules, the lowest level is anchored at the solid ground of the observable facts. The laws, whether general or special, are not directly interpreted, but only the singular sentences. For the more abstract terms, the rules determine only an *indirect interpretation*, which is—here as well as in the first method—incomplete in a certain sense. Suppose "B" is defined on the basis of "A" then, if "A" is directly interpreted, "B" is, although indirectly, also interpreted completely; if, however, "B" is directly interpreted, "A" is not necessarily also interpreted completely (but only if "A" is also definable by "B").

To give an example, let us imagine a calculus of physics constructed, according to the second method, on the basis of primitive signs like "electromagnetic field," "gravitational field," "electron," "proton," etc. The system of definitions will then lead to elementary terms, e.g., to "Fe," defined as a class of regions in which the configuration of particles fulfills certain conditions, and "Na-yellow" as a class of space-time regions in which the temporal distribution of the electromagnetic field fulfills certain conditions. Then semantical rules are laid down stating that "Fe" designates iron and "Na-yellow" designates a specified yellow color. (If "iron" is not accepted as sufficiently elementary, the rules can be stated for more elementary terms.) In this way the connection between the calculus and the realm of nature, to which it is to be applied, is made for terms of the calculus which are far remote from the primitive terms.

Let us examine, on the basis of these discussions, the example of a derivation D_2. The premises and the conclusion of D_2 are singular sentences, but most of the other sentences are not. Hence the premises and the conclusion of this as of all other derivations of the same type can be directly interpreted, understood, and confronted with the results of observations. More of an interpretation is not necessary for a practical application of a derivation. If, in confronting the interpreted premises with our observations, we find them confirmed as true, then, we accept the conclusion as a prediction and we may base a decision upon it. The sentences occurring in the derivation between premises and conclusion are also interpreted, at least indirectly. But we need not make their interpretation explicit in order to be able to construct the derivation and to apply it. All that is necessary for its construction are the formal rules of the calculus. This is the advantage of the method of formalization, i.e., of the separation of the calculus as a formal system from the interpretation. If some persons want to come to an agreement about the formal correctness of a given derivation, they may leave aside all differences of opinion on material questions of interpretation. They simply have to examine whether or not the given series of formulas fulfills the formal rules of the calculus. Here again, the function of calculi in empirical science becomes clear as instruments for transforming the expression of what we know or assume.

Against the view that for the application of a physical calculus we need an interpretation only for singular sentences, the following objection will perhaps be raised. Before we accept a derivation and believe its conclusion we must have accepted the physical calculus which furnishes the derivation; and how can we decide whether or not to accept a physical calculus for application without interpreting and understanding its axioms?

To be sure, in order to pass judgment about the applicability of a given physical calculus we have to confront it in some way or other with observation, and for this purpose an interpretation is necessary. But we need no explicit interpretation of the axioms, nor even of any theorems. The empirical examination of a physical theory given in the form of a calculus with rules of interpretation is not made by interpreting and understanding the axioms and then considering whether they are true on the basis of our factual knowledge. Rather, the examination is carried out by the same procedure as that explained before for obtaining a prediction. We construct derivations in the calculus with premises which are singular sentences describing the results of our observations, and with singular sentences which we can test by observations as conclusions. The physical theory is indirectly confirmed to a higher and higher degree if more and more of these predictions are confirmed and none of them is disconfirmed by observations. Only singular sentences with elementary terms can be directly tested; therefore, we need an explicit interpretation only for these sentences.

"UNDERSTANDING" IN PHYSICS

The development of physics in recent centuries, and especially in the past few decades, has more and more led to that method in the construction, testing, and application of physical theories which we call *formalization*, i.e., the construction of a calculus supplemented by an interpretation. It was the progress of knowledge and the particular structure of the subject matter that suggested and made practically possible this increasing formalization. In consequence it became more and more possible to forego an "intuitive understanding" of the abstract terms and axioms and theorems formulated with their help. The possibility and even necessity of abandoning the search for an understanding of that kind was not realized for a long time. When abstract, nonintuitive formulas, as, e.g., Maxwell's equations of

227

electromagnetism, were proposed as new axioms, physicists endeavored to make them "intuitive" by constructing a "model," i.e., a way of representing electromagnetic microprocesses by an analogy to known macroprocesses, e.g., movements of visible things. Many attempts have been made in this direction, but without satisfactory results. It is important to realize that the discovery of a model has not more than an aesthetic or didactic or at best a heuristic value, but is not at all essential for a successful application of the physical theory. The demand for an intuitive understanding of the axioms was less and less fulfilled when the development led to the general theory of relativity and then to quantum mechanics, involving the wave function. Many people including physicists, have a feeling of regret and disappointment about this. Some, especially philosophers, go so far as even to contend that these modern theories, since they are not intuitively understandable, are not at all theories about nature but "mere formalistic constructions," "mere calculi." But this is a fundamental misunderstanding of the function of a physical theory. It is true that a theory must not be a "mere calculus," but possess an interpretation, on the basis of which it can be applied to the facts of nature. But it is sufficient, as we have seen, to make this interpretation explicit for elementary terms; the interpretation of the other terms is then indirectly determined by the formulas of the calculus, either definitions or laws, connecting them with the elementary terms. If we demand from the modern physicist an answer to the question what he means by the symbol "Ψ" of his calculus, and are astonished that he cannot give an answer, we ought to realize that the situation was already the same in classical physics. There the physicist could not tell us what he meant by the symbol "E" in Maxwell's equations. Perhaps, in order not to refuse an answer, he would tell us that "E" designates the electric field vector. To be sure, this statement has the form of a semantical rule, but it would not help us a bit to understand the theory. It simply refers from a symbol in a symbolic calculus to a corresponding word expression in a calculus of words. We are right in demanding an interpretation for "*E*," but that will be given indirectly by semantical rules referring to elementary signs together with the formulas connecting them with "*E*." This interpretation enables us to use the laws containing "*E*" for the derivation of predictions. Thus we understand "*E*," if "understanding" of an expression, a sentence, or a theory means capability of its use for the description of known facts or the prediction of new facts. An "intuitive understanding" or a direct translation of "*E*" into terms referring to observable properties is neither necessary nor possible. The situation of the modern physicist is not essentially different. He knows how to use the symbol "ψ" in the calculus in order to derive predictions which we can test by observations. (If they have the form of probability statements, they are tested by statistical results of observations.) Thus the physicist, although he cannot give us a translation into everyday language, understands the symbol "ψ" and the laws of quantum mechanics. He possesses that kind of understanding which alone is essential in the field of knowledge and science.

LEWIS CARROLL
(CHARLES LUTWIDGE DODGSON, 1832-1898)

Lewis Carroll is the pen name of Charles Lutwidge Dodgson, who immortalized it through his authorship of the classic children's books *Alice in Wonderland* and *Through the Looking Glass.* Dodgson spent all his adult life in the cloistered surroundings of Christ Church College, Oxford. He received a college fellowship upon graduation and kept it all his life, teaching mathematics and keeping his literary activities strictly apart from his scientific work.

Main Works:

Symbolic Logic; Euclid and His Modern Rivals; The Formulae of Plane Trigonometry.

---

xy	xy'
$x'y$	$x'y'$

The Bilateral Diagram

First, let us suppose that the above Diagram is an enclosure assigned to a certain Class of Things, which we have selected as our "Universe of Discourse," or, more briefly, as our "Univ."

From: *Symbolic Logic.*

230

Lewis Carroll

[For example, we might say "Let Univ. be 'books'"; and we might imagine the Diagram to be a large table, assigned to all "books."]

[The Reader is strongly advised, in reading this Chapter, *not* to refer to the above Diagram, but to draw a large one for himself, *without any letters,* and to have it by him while he reads, and keep his finger on that particular *part* of it, about which he is reading.]

Secondly, let us suppose that we have selected a certain Adjunct, which we may call "x," and have divided the large Class, to which we have assigned the whole Diagram, into the two smaller Classes whose Differentiae are "x" and "not-x" (which we may call "x'"), and that we have assigned the *North* Half of the Diagram to the one (which we may call "the Class of x-Things," or "the x-Class"), and the *South* Half to the other (which we may call "the Class of x'-Things," or "the x'-Class").

[For example, we might say "Let x mean 'old,' so that x' will mean 'new'," and we might suppose that we had divided books into the two Classes whose Differentiae are "old" and "new," and had assigned the *North* Half of the table to "*old* books" and the *South* Half to "*new* books."]

Thirdly, let us suppose that we have selected another Adjunct, which we may call "y," and have subdivided the x-Class into the two Classes whose Differentiae are "y" and "y'," and that we have assigned the North-*West* Cell to one (which we may call the xy-Class"), and the North-*East* Cell to the other (which we may call "the xy'-Class").

[For example, we might say "Let y mean 'English,' so that y' will mean 'foreign'," and we might suppose that we had subdivided "old books" into the two Classes whose Differentiae are "English" and "foreign," and had assigned the North-*East* Cell to "old *foreign* books."]

Fourthly, let us suppose that we have subdivided the x'-Class in the same manner, and have assigned the South-*East* Cell to the $x'y'$-Class.

[For example, we might suppose that we had subdivided "new books" into the two Classes "new *English* books" and "new *foreign* books," and had assigned the South-*West* Cell to the one, and the South-*East* Cell to the other.]

It is evident that, if we had begun by dividing for y and y', and had then subdivided for x and x', we should have got the same four Classes. Hence we see that we have assigned the *West* Half to the y-Class, and the *East* Half to the y'-Class.

[Thus, in the above Example, we should find that we had assigned the *West* Half of the table to "*English* books" and the *East* Half to "*foreign* books."]

We have, in fact, assigned the four Quarters of the table to four different Classes of books, as here shown.

old English books	old foreign books
new English books	new foreign books

The Reader should carefully remember that, in such a phrase as "the x-Things," the word "Things" means that particular *kind* of Things, to which the whole Diagram has been assigned.

[Thus, if we say "Let Univ. be 'books,'" we mean that we have assigned the whole Diagram to "books." In that case, if we took "x" to mean "old," the phrase "the x-*Things*" would mean "the old books."]

The Reader should not go on to the next Chapter until he is *quite familiar* with the *blank* Diagram I have advised him to draw.

He ought to be able to name, *instantly*, the *Adjunct* assigned to any Compartment named in the right-hand column of the following Table.

Also he ought to be able to name, *instantly*, the *Compartment* assigned to any Adjunct named in the left-hand column.

To make sure of this, he had better put the book into the hands of some genial friend, while he himself has nothing but the blank Diagram, and get that genial friend to question him on this Table, *dodging* about as much as possible. The Questions and Answers should be something like this:—

TABLE I.

Adjuncts of Classes.	Compartments, or Cells, assigned to them.
x	North Half.
x' . . .	South ,,
y	West ,,
y' . . .	East ,,
xy . . .	North-West Cell.
xy' . . .	,, East ,,
$x'y$ . . .	South-West ,,
$x'y'$ . . .	,, East ,,

Q. "Adjunct for West Half?"
A. "y."
Q. "Compartment for xy'?"
A. "North-East Cell."
Q. "Adjunct for South-Cell?"
A. "$x'y$."
&c., &c.

After a little practice, he will find himself able to do without the blank Diagram, and will be able to see it *mentally* ("in my mind's eye, Horatio!") while answering the questions of his genial friend. When *this* result has been reached, he may safely go on to the next chapter.

MAGNUS AURELIUS CASSIODORUS
(about 490-575)

A Roman patrician, who like Boethius served Theodoric the Great, Ostrogothic ruler of Italy. In his old age he retired to the monastery of Vivarium established by Saint Benedict. He was much influenced by Aristotle and was, in turn, one of the main philosophical influences in the early middle ages.

Main Works:

> De Anima; De Institutione divinarum et humanarum litterarum; Variae Epistolae.

Problems in Logic

Of the two types of syllogism, one is the predicative syllogism, called categorical: the other is conditional, that we designate as hypothetical. Predicative syllogisms are those that are composed of all the predicative propositions, as, for example, the one I mentioned previously, composed of all the predicative propositions. Hypothetical syllogisms are those whose propositions depend on a condition, as: If it is day, there is light. It is day: therefore there is light. For the first proposition contains the condition that only if it is day, is there light. And hence the syllogism is known as hypothetical, that is, conditional.

Induction is a term by which progression occurs from the particular to the universal, thus: If in steering a ship a captain is chosen not by lot but for his skill: If for managing horses a

---

From *De institutione divinarum et humanarum litterarum.*

driver is assigned not through mere chance but for his warranted ability: If in the administration of the state it is not fate that elects the leader, but his capacity to govern; and so on in many other similar instances where inferences are made: and on every occasion when anyone, who proposes a leader not haphazardly but for his ability, favors intelligent guidance and administration.

You see then how an expression pervades every single thing until it reaches the universals. For when one deduced that a ship, or a carriage, or a state is controlled not by chance but by skill, as is the case in other matters, he arrived at a universal conclusion: that in all instances leadership must be specially conditioned not by chance but by ability. Often the totality of many particulars demonstrates some other particularity, as one might say: If men are not placed in charge of ships, or carriages, or fields, then they must not be considered by chance to be leaders in public affairs either. This type of argument is usually very probable, although it does not offer conviction equal to the syllogism. For the syllogism proceeds from the universal to the particular. If it is composed of true propositions, it has a firm and immutable veracity.

Induction has in fact a very great probability, but occasionally it lacks veracity, as in the following propositions: Whoever can sing is a singer: and whoever can wrestle is a wrestler: and whoever can build is a builder. By adding many more such propositions in a similar fashion, we can infer: The man therefore who knows evil is evil. Which does not follow, since the concept of evil cannot be alien to the virtuous man. For virtue esteems itself, and rejects the contrary, and vice could not be avoided unless it is known.

From these two principles and types of argument, then, two other modes of argumentation are derived: one involving the syllogism, the other induction. It would be practicable to consider, in respect of these modes, which springs from the syllogism and which from induction. However, one mode would not satisfy the syllogism and the other induction. There are the enthymeme and the example. The enthymeme is an imperfect syllogism, that is, a statement in which not all propositions have been anteriorly established and hence a premature conclusion is deduced. As if one should say: Man is an animal: therefore he is a substance. For it omits another proposition that postulates that every animal is a substance. Therefore when the enthymeme proceeds from universals to prove particulars, it is somewhat similar to a syllogism. But as it does not use all the premises that the syllogism requires, it lacks the rational character of the syllogism, and for that reason it is called an imperfect syllogism.

Example also by similar reasoning is associated with induction and is different from it. For an example is that which by a particular instance proceeds to demonstrate some particular, thus: It was right for Catiline to be killed by Cicero the consul, since Gracchus was put to death by Scipio: for it is proved that Catiline ought to be killed by Cicero, because Gracchus was killed by Scipio. The interposition of individuals indicates that these two propositions are particulars, not universals. Since therefore a part is proved, that which we call example bears a resemblance to induction: but since it does not contain more elements whereby to effect this, it differs from induction. Hence there are two principal kinds of argument: one, that is called a syllogism: the other, that is called induction. Below these, and stemming from them, appear the enthymeme and the example. All these are derived from the syllogism and acquire their strength from the syllogism. For whether it is an enthymeme, or an induction, or even an example, it receives its reliability to the greatest extent from the syllogism: as has been shown in the *Prior Analytics*, that we translated from Aristotle. So the discussion on the syllogism is sufficient, as being the principal argument containing the other types.

It remains now to explain what the topic is. The topic, as Cicero has it, is the basis of argument. I shall briefly explain what the force of this definition is. The basis of argument can be understood in one sense as the greatest proposition, and in another sense as the greatest difference in the proposition. For since there are some propositions that are known by themselves, since they have nothing more for their demonstration, and these are called the major and the principal propositions, and there are others whose reliability is furnished by the principal and major propositions, it is necessary that of all propositions that are in doubt those retain the most hieratic credibility that can so induce reliability in others that nothing can be discovered better known than themselves. For if it is the argument that produces trustworthiness in a dubious case, and it must be better known and more probable than that which is proved, it is necessary that those arguments should inspire the greatest reliability in all arguments, that are so well-known by themselves as to dispense with any other proof. But a proposition of this kind is sometimes contained within the frame of the argument: but sometimes it lies outside it, adding to and perfecting the force of the argument.

All topics then, that is, the differences of the major propositions, must either be derived from those terms that are included in the question, namely the predicate and the subject: or they are taken from extraneous sources, or they lie between these two positions. In the case of those topics that are derived from the terms that are in question, there is a two-fold mode: one, from their substance, the other from that which follows their substance. Those that are from the substance, consist of definition only. For the definition indicates the substance, and the entire demonstration of the substance is the definition. But, as we say, let us illustrate this example, so that every method of reasoning about the questions, or the arguments, or the topics may be satisfied. Let then the question be proposed: Are trees animals? And let the syllogism be of this type: An animal is an animate sensible substance. A tree is not an animate sensible substance. Therefore a tree is not an animal. Hence it is a question of genus. For the question is whether trees should be classified under the genus of animals: the topic that consists in the universal proposition is not applicable to this definition of genus.

You see then how the entire doubt in regard to the question is treated by a discussion of the syllogism through applicable and congruous propositions, that acquire their power from the first and major proposition, namely from that which denies that there is a species to which the definition of the genus does not apply. And the universal proposition itself is drawn from the substance of one of those terms that are included in the question, namely, animal, that is, from its definition, animate sensible substance. Therefore, after a brief, scrupulous mention of the differences of topics in the other question, it behooves us to perceive the property of each one with a rapid mental scrutiny.

In regard to the topic that is derived from the substance, there is a two-fold mode. For the arguments are drawn partly from the definition, and partly from the description. Now there is a difference between definition and description, because definition assumes genus and differences, while description limits the understanding, as either certain accidents produce one property, or an accumulation of essential elements beyond the proper genus. But still the definitions that arise from accidents in no way whatever appear to demonstrate substance: however since true definitions are often so presented that demonstrate substance, these propositions too that are derived from description appear to be drawn from the topic of substance. Here is an example of this. The question is: Is a white man substance? Is a white man a substance or genus? We say then: He is substance, because he can be subjected to all the accidents. But a white man is not subject to any accidents. Therefore a white man is not a substance. The topic, that is, the major proposition, is the same as before. For that of which the definition or description does not fit that which is said to be the species is not the genus of that which is said to be the species. But the description of the substance does not fit the white man: therefore the white man is not a substance.

The topic of difference derives from description, that we previously assigned to substance. There are also definitions that are derived not from the substance of a thing but from the meaning of the term, and thus they are applied to the thing under discussion: as though it were a question whether philosophy should be studied, the argument being as follows: Philosophy is the love of wisdom: nobody questions the necessity of its study: therefore philosophy should be studied. Here it was not the definition of the thing but the interpretation of the term that furnished the argument. Cicero too used this procedure in his exposition of philosophy. In Greek it is called onomatopoeia: in Latin, the definition of the term. In respect of these arguments that are derived from the substance of the terms that appear in a question, I believe I have offered illuminating examples. Now we must discuss those topics that follow the substance of the terms.

Of these there is a great variety. For many cling to single substances. From those, therefore, that accompany the substance of anything, arguments are usually derived, either from the whole, or from parts, or from efficient causes, or matter or the end. An efficient cause is that which moves and operates so that something is expressed. Matter is that from which something originates or in which it originates. The end is that on account of which it originates. Among these topics too there are those that are derived from what follows the substance, or from the effects, or from corruption, or use, or, apart from all these, accidents in common. Under these circumstances, let us first examine the topic derived from the whole.

The whole is usually described in two ways: either as the genus, or as that which consists, in its entirety, of many parts. And the whole as the genus thus often furnishes arguments for enquiries, as: If it is questioned whether justice is useful the syllogism arises: All virtue is useful. Justice is virtue. Therefore justice is useful. There is the question of accident, that is, whether useful is an accident to justice. This topic consists in the major proposition: what is present in the genus and the species. The superior topic comes from the whole, that is, from the genus, namely, virtue, that is the genus of justice. Again, the question is: Are human affairs governed by Providence?

We say: The universe is governed by Providence. Now men are part of the universe. Therefore human affairs are governed by Providence. Now a question on accident. The topic that affects the whole agrees with the part as well. The highest topic derives from the whole, that is, from the unit. That which constitutes the parts is the universe, which is the entirety of men.

From the parts also arguments arise in two ways: either from the parts of the genus, that are species: or from the parts of the unit, that is, the whole, that are called parts only by a special designation. And regarding those parts that are species, let this question be asked: Is virtue a habit of a well constituted mind? It is a question of definition, that is: Is the habit of a well constituted mind a definition of virtue? From the species we shall therefore propose the following argument: Justice, fortitude, moderation, and prudence are habits of a well constituted mind. These four qualities are subordinate to one virtue or genus. Therefore virtue is a habit of a well constituted mind. The major proposition: what subsists in the single parts must necessarily subsist in the whole. This is the argument from parts, that is, from the parts of the genus, that are called species: for justice, fortitude, moderation, and prudence are species of virtue.

Similarly, in respect of those parts that are said to be parts of the whole, let us ask the question: Is medicine useful? Medicine was established in a doubtful situation. We say then: The extermination of disease, the preservation of health, and the healing of wounds are useful. Medicine therefore is useful. Frequently any one part itself is strong enough to confirm the validity of the arguments, thus: The question is whether a certain person is a free man. If we prove that he has been set free by the census, or by a will, or by the manumission-staff, he is demonstrably a free man: and there were other forms of granting liberty too. Or again, the question is: Is that a house in the distance? The answer is no: for either the roof is missing, or the walls, or the foundation: the argument arising from one part.

Now it is necessary to examine the whole and parts not only in the substances, but in the modes too, the time, and the quantities. For when we say: sometime, that is a part. Again, if we simply assert anything, that is a whole in a mode: if we do so with some addition, it becomes a part in a mode. Similarly if we assert everything in a quantity, we postulate the whole. If we except some of the quantity, we assert a part of the quantity. Likewise in the case of the topic. What is everywhere, is the whole. What is somewhere, is a part. Let us give examples of all these together. From the whole to the part in a temporal sense: If God is always, he is now too. From the part to the whole according to mode: If the mind is moved in some way, it is moved simply as well. It moves when angry. Therefore it moves universally and simply. Again, from the whole to the parts in respect of quantity: If Apollo is a veracious prophet in all cases, it will be true that Pyrrhus is conqueror of the Romans. Again, in respect of topic: If God is everywhere, he is here too.

There follows the topic that is named from the causes. There are several causes, that is, those that produce and effect the beginning of motion: or assume as subjects the forms of the species, or something on account of them, or the form of each one.

The argument then from the efficient cause: If a person wishes to illustrate natural justice, he would say: An assemblage of men is natural. An assemblage of men produces justice. Therefore justice is natural. A question on accident. The major proposition: Those things are natural whose efficient causes are natural. A topic from efficient causes: whatever is the cause of anything, affects that thing of which it is the cause.

Again, if anyone contends that the Moors do not have weapons, he asserts that they rarely use weapons on account of the lack of iron. The major proposition: When the matter is lacking, the topic from matter is wanting, because it is derived from matter. Whether it is from the efficient causes and the matter, it is called by the same name, the topic from the cause. For that which affects and that which assumes the act of the agent are equally the causes of the thing affected.

Again, in regard to the end, the question is: Is justice good? The argument will run as follows: If being happy is good, then justice too is good. For this is the end of justice, for the man who lives according to justice to attain happiness. The major proposition: That of which the end is good, is good in itself. This is the topic from the end.

But from that topic, which is the form of anything, Daedalus could not have managed to fly, since he had no wings of natural form. The major proposition: Each man is capable only to the degree in which the form permits. This is the topic from the form.

The topic from the effects and corruptions and uses appears thus: If the construction of a house is good, the house is good. Again: If the destruction of a house is evil, a house is good, and if a house is good, the destruction of a house is evil. Likewise: If horseback riding is good, a horse is good, and if a horse is good, riding is good. The first example is drawn from generation, which can also be called from the effects. The second example is from corruption, the third from use. The major propositions of all these: That of which the effect is good, is itself good, and conversely: and that of which the corruption is bad, is itself bad, and conversely: and that of which the use is good, is itself good, and conversely.

Now arguments are derived from accidents in general, whenever such accidents are assumed as either cannot or are not accustomed to leave the subject, as if someone were to assert as follows: The wise man will have no regret, for regret accompanies an evil deed. As this is unacceptable in the case of the wise man, there is no regret. A question of accidents. The major proposition: If a thing does not have anything in it, there can be in it not even that which is its consequence. A topic from accidents in general.

After this explanation then of those topics that are taken from the terms themselves included in the proposition, we must now speak of those topics that, though placed externally, yet supply arguments to the questions. These are either from a judgment of a thing, or from similarities, or from a major, or a minor, or from proportion, or from opposites, or from transference. The topic that contains the judgment of a thing is of this type: We say a thing is so because all men consider it so, or many, and these intelligent men, or deeply learned in regard to their particular sphere. For example: The heavens revolve: so philosophers and the most learned astronomers have declared. A question on accident. The proposition, that this seems acceptable to all men, or to many or to learned men, cannot be contradicted. A topic from a judgment of a thing.

From similarities, if there is any question whether man is a biped, we similarly assert as follows: Quadrupedity is inherent in a horse, and bipedness in man. But quadrupedity is not a property of the horse: then bipedness is not the property of man. A question on property. The major proposition: If that which is similarly inherent is not a property either.

A topic from similarities. This topic is two-fold. For this similarity consists either in quality or in quantity. But in quantity it is called parity, that is, equality.

Again, from that which is greater, if the definition of something animate is that it can move of its own accord, we say it is more justifiable that the definition of animate be that it lives naturally than that it can move of its own accord. But this is not a definition of the animate, that it lives naturally, nor should even this definition that seems to be less of a definition, that it can move of itself, be considered a definition of what is animate. A question on definition. The major proposition: If that which seems to be inherent is not so, that which seems to be less inherent will not be inherent either. Topic from that which is greater.

Conversely from the smaller. For if the definition of man is that he is an animate biped that walks, and since biped seems to be less of a definition of man than an animate rational mortal being: and if the definition of man is granted that says he is an animate biped that walks, the definition of man will be that he is an animate rational mortal being. A question on definition. The major proposition: If that which seems to be inherent is inherent, that which seems to be more inherent is inherent too. There are many varieties of topics, aiding arguments from what is greater or smaller. These topics we have carefully followed in Aristotle's exposition of the *Topica*.

Similarly with proportion. For example, the question is raised: Should magistrates in the state be chosen by lot? Our reply is: Not at all. Because not even on ships is the captain chosen by lot. For this is proportion. The captain's relationship to the ship is like the magistrate's to the state. This topic is different from that which is deduced from similarities. For in the first case one thing is compared with anything else. But in proportion there is no similarity but a kind of comparative relation. A question on accidental proportion. Whatever occurs in a thing must necessarily occur in the proportional. Topic from proportion.

From opposites there is a multiple topic. For they are opposed in four modes: either as they observe contraries established from an opposite topic: or as a deprivation and position: or as a relationship: or as an affirmation and negation. The distinctions of these modes have been mentioned in the book written on the subject of the ten categories: from them arguments arise as follows.

If the question is asked of contraries whether it is a property of virtue to be praised, I shall say: No. Since it is not even the property of evil to be condemned. A question on property. The major proposition: Contraries agree with contraries. A topic from opposites, that is, from contraries.

Again, the question is asked: Is sight the property of those who have eyes? My reply is: No. For it sometimes happens that those who see are at other times blind. For whoever has possession, will also have deprivation: and what is a property cannot leave the subject. And since on the approach of blindness vision departs, it is not proved that vision is the property of those who have eyes. A question on property. The proposition: Where there may be deprivation and possession, there is no property. A topic from opposites, according to possession and deprivation.

Again, let the question be asked: Is it the property of a father to be a begetter? My reply is: It rightly appears so. Because it is the property of a son to be begotten. For the relationship of father to son is the relationship of begetter to begotten. A question of property. The major proposition: The properties of those relating to themselves are also related to each other.

Similarly, let the question be raised: Is motion the property of an animate thing? My reply is in the negative. Because not even in animate things is there the property of motion. A question on property. The major proposition: It is necessary for the opposites of opposites to be properties. A topic from opposites, according to affirmation and denial: for motion and non-motion, according to affirmation and negation, are opposed to each other.

From transference the procedure is as follows: When doubt is transferred from those terms in which a question has been set to something that is better known: and from its proof there is confirmation of those things that have raised the question. For instance, Socrates, asking about the power of justice in the case of the individual, transferred the entire argument to the magnitude of the state: and he established the power of justice from its effectiveness in the individual. This topic might possibly appear to be from the whole. But since it is not inherent in those terms that make the proposition, but is external, for the sole reason that it seems better known, it is so assumed. Therefore the topic is called transference to suit the etymological significance of the term. This transference occurs in the case of a name also, whenever an argument is transferred from an obscure term to one that is better known. For instance: If the question is asked whether the philosopher has envy and if the significance of the expression *philosopher* is unknown, my reply is, making a transference to a better known expression, that the wise man has no envy. For the expression *wise man* is better known than that of *philosopher*. We have spoken adequately of the topics that are considered external: now the discussion will proceed to middles.

MIDDLES

Middle topics are taken either from case, or from conjugations, or arise from division. Case is the principal inflexion of a word into an adverb, as: justice into justly. Case therefore is justice: what we say justly is the adverb. Conjugations are those forms that stem from the same expression and move in a different direction, as: from justice, just. These forms then are said to be conjugated among themselves and with justice, and from all of them arguments are prepared. For if that which is just is good, and that which is justly is well, and he who is just is good and justice is good: these terms then follow according to the similarity of each expression.

Topics too are called mixed: since, if the subject is justice, the arguments are drawn from the case or from the conjugations: but they happen to be derived not from justice itself, properly and conjointly speaking, nor from those topics that are external, but their own cases, that is, deduced from a kind of slight change. Rightly then these topics are called middle between those that are set by themselves and those that are external.

There remains the topic from division, that is treated as follows: Every division occurs either by negation or by partition. For example, let anyone assert: Every animal either has feet, or not. By partition, as though one were dividing, every man is well, or is sick. A universal division is either of the genus into species, or of the whole into parts, or of the word into particular meanings, or of the accident into subjects, or of the subject into accidents, or of the accident into accidents. In my book on division I have explained more fully the scheme of all these possibilities: and hence let me select appropriate examples to elucidate this. Arguments arise by division, both by the separation that occurs through negation, and by the separation through partition. But those who use these divisions either proceed by direct reasoning, or lead to something impossible and inappropriate and so again assume that which they had abandoned.

This will be better understood if attention is directed to the *Prior Analytics* for the present, however, the following examples will furnish a list. Let the question be: Has time a beginning? If anyone wants to deny this, he will be confirmative by means of the reasoning that time did not begin at all. And he will demonstrate this by direct reasoning, thus: Since the world is eternal (let this be granted for a moment for the sake of argument), the world could never be without time, and time too is eternal. But what is eternal has no beginning. Therefore time has no beginning. But if it were desired to demonstrate the same thing through impossibility, the following argument would be in order: If time has a beginning, it was not always time. It was then, when it was not time: but the significance of time is that it was. Therefore there was time when there was no time: which is impossible. Therefore there is no beginning of time. For, to start with any beginning, something awkward and impossible happens to have been time when there was no time. Now we return to the other part, that has no beginning. But this discussion that arises from negation, when arguments are concluded through it, cannot possibly be both what is divided by affirmation and by negation. Therefore, eliminating one, the other remains: and positing one, the alternate is eliminated. This is called topic by division, intermediate between those topics that are customarily derived from them, and those that are assumed externally. For when it is asked whether time has any beginning, a beginning is assumed. And from this, through the proper consequence from the thing itself that is asked, a syllogism arises that is both impossible and fallacious. This being concluded, we return to the previous point, that must necessarily be true. If there is any objection to this, it leads to something awkward and impossible. So, since a syllogism is usually formed from the thing itself that is questioned, and the topic is derived, so to speak, from themselves, and since it does not remain there but returns to its position, it is as it were assumed externally: for this reason then the topic from division is set midway between either.

But the topics that are taken from partition occur in many forms. For sometimes what is divided can exist together. For instance, a man is either well or sick. The reasoning occurs in the former mode of division, because what is asked is present in all cases, or is not: hence it is present in some instances or what is present in other cases is not present or it is not present at all.

We shall not linger any longer on these explanations, if the *Prior Analytics* or the *Topica* have given the reader adequate instruction. For if the question is raised: Is a dog a substance? this division occurs: The dog is the name either of a barking animal, or a sea creature, or a star in heaven. And it would be shown seriatim that a barking dog is a substance, and also a sea animal, and the fact that a heavenly star could be assumed for a substance showed that dog is a substance. And here it will be seen that the arguments were drawn from the topics themselves proposed in the question. But consider such syllogisms: Either he is well or sick. He is well, therefore he is not sick. But he is not well, therefore he is sick. Or: if he is sick, then he is not well. Or: If he is not sick, then he is well. The syllogism is derived from those topics that are external, that is, from opposites. Hence this entire topic from division is said to be midway between each. Because if it is formed by negation, it is in some way derived from the topics themselves, and in another sense proceeds from externals. If the arguments are drawn from partition, they supply their content at times from themselves, and at other times from externals.

Such seems to be the partition of topics as that most learned and illustrious Greek Themistius explained in his writings, referring everything to the faculty of the intelligence. Under these circumstances, I must briefly mention the division of topics so that nothing may be left out that was not proved to have been included in it. For when there is any doubt about a thing in a question, it will be confirmed by arguments. For instance, either arguments are derived from those items that are set in the question, or they are taken from external sources, or they are traced so to speak in a contiguous area. And beyond this division nothing more can be found: but if an argument is drawn from them, either it must be taken from their substance or from those that follow, or from those that occur inseparably, or are inherent to them and either cannot or are not accustomed to be separate and disjoined from their substance. Those that are drawn from their substance are either in the description or in the definition: and besides this, from the interpretation of the term. Those that follow what as it were contains the substances, are other arguments, or are present around those that are in question in the topic, or genus, or difference, or total form, or species, or parts. Similarly with causes, or ends, or effects, or corruptions, or use, or quantity, or time, or mode of subsistence. What is called properly inseparable or inherent accident will be reckoned among accidents in general. Apart from this, nothing can be discovered that can be inherent in anything.

Having thus explained these matters, let us now inquire into the topics we previously stated as being derived from external sources. For things taken from external sources are not so separated and disconnected as not to regard sometimes what is in question, from a certain kind of viewpoint. For both similarities and opposites are doubtless referred to those things to which they are similar or opposite, although properly speaking and in the right order they seem to have been brought from external sources. These are similarity, opposition, greater and smaller, judgment of a thing. In similarity both similarity of a thing and proportional ratio are contained. For all things have similarity.

Opposites appear in contraries, privations, relations, and negations. Comparison of the greater to the smaller is a kind of dissimilarity of similars: for the distinction in quantity of things similar by themselves produces the greater and the smaller. For what is disconnected in every quality and in every form of reasoning cannot be compared in any sense. Arguments that derive from the judgment of a thing offer a kind of evidence, and are inartificial topics and completely disconnected, nor do they pursue the thing rather than opinion and judgment. The topic of transference consists sometimes in equality, sometimes in the comparison of the greater or the smaller: for the reasoning and transference of arguments occur in relation either to that which is similar, or to that which is greater or smaller.

The topics that we have previously called mixed arise either from cases or from conjugations, or from division: in them all both consequences and refutations are contained. But those arguments that are drawn from definition, or genus, or difference, or causes furnish by demonstration abundant power and order to the syllogisms: the rest, by dialectic similarities. And those topics in particular that are in the substance of those about which there is any doubt in a question, refer to predicatives and simple syllogisms: the rest, to hypothetical and conditional syllogisms.

As the topics have been explained, and both definition and illustrative examples have been carefully expounded, it seems fitting to clarify briefly how these topics are the differences of the major propositions: for the subject does not require extended discussion. For all major propositions or definitions, in so far as they are major, are not different. But in so far as some come from definition, others from the genus, and still others from other topics, they are rightly said to differ, and these are said to be their differences.

TOPICS

Topics are the bases of arguments, the sources of the senses, the origins of expression. Thus it is proper to define a topic as the basis of argument and argument as the reasoning that makes a dubious matter reliable. Arguments are either in the subject itself under discussion, or are drawn from those matters that are in some manner related to the subject in question and are known to have been taken from other subjects: or they are taken from external sources. Thus the inherent topics of arguments in the subject itself are three, namely: from the whole, from the parts, and from the known.

The argument from the whole occurs when a definition is attached to that which is under discussion. For example, Cicero declares, glory is praise for good deeds and fame for great services toward the state. Since glory is a whole, by definition, he explains what glory is.

The argument from parts is as follows: Assume that the eye sees: the entire body does not on that account see.

The argument from the known, called in Greek etymology, runs thus: If the consul is the man who consults the interests of the state, what else did Cicero do when he punished the conspirators?

Now arguments are drawn from those matters that in some manner are known to have been taken from other sources: and there are thirteen topics, namely: from conjugations, from genus, from the form of the genus, that is, the species: from similarity, from difference, from the contrary, from conjunction, from antecedents, from consequences, from oppositions, from causes, from effects, from comparison of the smaller, the greater, or the equal.

First of all then let an argument be taken from the conjugations. Conjugations are so called when they are declined from a noun and a verb is formed, as: Cicero says that Verres overthrew the province: or a noun from a verb, when a robber is said to rob: or a noun from a noun, as in Terence: The beginning of madness not of love.

The argument is from the genus when it descends from a general subject to a species, as Vergil's phrase: A woman is always changeable and fickle. Dido too, who is a species, can be changeable and fickle. Or Cicero's argument, in which he descended from the genus to the species: Since you ought to show careful consideration for all the provinces and the allies, gentlemen of the jury, you ought to do so in the case of Sicily.

From the species an argument is drawn when the species makes a general question reliable, as in Vergil:

Does not the Phrygian shepherd penetrate Sparta thus? For the Phrygian shepherd is a species: and if one person acts thus, other Trojans too in general can do so.

From similarity there is an argument when similar things are drawn from things, as in Vergil:

> Give me a spear, for my right hand has hurled
> none in vain against the Rutulians, and they
> plunged into the bodies of the Greeks on the
> plains of Troy.

An argument is taken from difference, when some things are separated through difference, as in Vergil:

> You behold neither the horses of Diomedes,
> nor Achilles' chariot.

An argument is derived from contraries, when different things are contrasted with each other, as in Terence:

> For if you rebuke him who aided your life,
> what will you do to him who caused loss or harm?

The validity of an argument is secured from conjunctions. When things that are weak individually acquire the force of truth by union: for example, say a man had been poor, is a miser, and daring, whose enemy has been slain. As these individual items do not suffice, they are brought together, so that from many conjunctions something can be proved.

There is an argument from antecedents, when some of the

things previously performed are proved, as in Cicero's *Pro Milone*:

> Since he did not hesitate to reveal what he thought, can you doubt what he did?

The statement came first, where the argument is, and the act followed.

There is an argument from the consequences, when something inevitably follows that which has been posited. For example: A woman gives birth, when she has lain with her husband.

There is an argument from opposites, when that which is opposite is destroyed by some contrariety. For example, as Cicero says:

> Not only then was the man who was delivered from peril by you, but one who was given the most distinguished honor, accused of having wanted to kill you in his own house.

There is an argument from causes, when the thing under discussion is proved to have been done according to the usual custom, as in Terence:

> I was greatly afraid for a long time, Davus, that you would do what the run of slaves usually does, that is, outwit me with your tricks.

There is an argument from effects, when some act out of a number is proved, as in Vergil:

> You can arm brothers of one mind for battle.

Therefore if this is possible in the case of brothers, how much more so in others? From a comparison of the smaller: Publius Scipio, though a private citizen, put to death the high priest Tiberius Gracchus, who was only slightly undermining the condition of the state.

From a comparison of equals: Cicero, in his *In Pisonem,* says there is no difference whether the consul himself embarrasses the state with subversive assemblies and pernicious laws or whether he permits others to do so.

The arguments drawn from external sources are those that the Greeks call atechna, that is, non-technical, because the evidence is taken from some external source to inspire reliability.

From the person: not anyone at all, but that one ought to be commendable by moral uprightness, having the weight of testimony that inspires faith.

There is authority from nature, that consists in great virtue: and those arguments that produce authority derive from time: as talent, wealth, age, fortune, skill, experience, need, the accumulation of fortuitous things.

Validity is secured from the sayings and deeds of our ancestors: when the sayings and deeds of the ancients are mentioned.

Validity is proved from torture, after which no one is credited with wanting to lie.

FALLACIES

Fallacies of the first figure are made thus: from a major affirmative universal and a minor negative universal: Every man is an animal. No animal is a stone. Therefore no man is a stone. Since, changing the term, both the universal and the particular include negative and positive, the same fallacy, made from two negative universals, is proved invalid: No stone is an animal: no animal is immobile: therefore no stone is immobile.

The same fallacy, made from two particular affirmatives, thus: A certain horse is an animal. A certain animal is a biped. Therefore a certain horse is a biped.

Again, from two particular negatives, thus: A certain man is not white. A certain white thing does not move. Therefore a certain man does not move.

Then, if the major proposition is a particular affirmative, and the minor a particular negative:

A certain horse is an animal. A certain animal is not a quadruped. Therefore a certain horse is not a quadruped.

Similarly, if the major proposition is a particular negative, and the minor a particular affirmative: a certain man is not a horse. A certain horse is without motion. Therefore a certain man is without motion.

Similarly, if the major proposition is a universal affirmative, and the minor proposition a particular negative, there will be a fallacy, as follows: Every man is an animal. A certain animal is not rational. Therefore a certain man is not rational.

But if the major proposition is a universal negative, and the minor is a particular negative, there will be no syllogism: No stone is an animal. A certain animal is feathered. Therefore no stone is feathered.

Again, if the major proposition is particular, and the minor universal, and both propositions are affirmative, there will be no syllogism: A certain stone is a body. Every body is mensurable. Therefore a certain stone is mensurable.

Similarly, if the major proposition is a particular negative, and the minor a universal negative, there will be no syllogism: A certain animal is not a biped. No biped neighs. Therefore a certain animal does not neigh.

Similarly, if the major proposition is a particular affirmative, and the minor a universal negative, there is no syllogism: A certain stone is insensible. Nothing insensible lives. Therefore a certain stone does not live.

Similarly, if the major proposition is a particular negative and the minor a universal affirmative, there will be a fallacy: A certain black object is not animate. Everything animate moves. Therefore a certain black object does not move.

There is no syllogism in finite propositions, because the particulars are similar.

All propositions consist of these modes: Simple. For example: Every man is just. A certain man is just. Every man is rational. A certain man is rational. Contraries: No man is just. A certain man is not just. Contradictories: No man is rational. A certain man is not rational. From both unlimited terms: Everyone not a man is not rational. No one not a man is not rational. A certain one not a man is not rational. A certain one not a man is not not rational.

Similarly, from an unlimited subject: Every not man is rational. No not man is rational. A certain not man is rational. Therefore a certain not man is not rational.

Similarly from an unlimited predicate: Every man is not rational. No man is not rational. A certain man is not rational. A certain man is not not rational.

Similarly with things that agree: Every man is rational. No man is not rational. Every man is not rational. No man is not rational. A certain man is rational. A certain man is not not rational. A certain man is not rational. A certain man is not not rational.

Similarly: Every non animal is not a man. No non animal is not a man. A certain non animal is not a man. A certain non animal is not not a man.

Similarly with the converse from an unlimited predicate: Every non animal is a man. No non animal is a man. A certain non animal is a man. A certain non animal is not a man.

Similarly with the converse from an unlimited subject: Every animal is not a man. No animal is not a man. A certain animal is not a man. A certain animal is not not a man.

Similarly with indefinite propositions: He is a just man. He is not a just man.

Indefinite propositions with unlimited subject: A non man is just. A non man is not just.

From an unlimited predicate: He is not a just man. He is not a not just man.

From both unlimited terms: A non man is not just. A non man is not not just.

Single or individual propositions: Plato is just. Plato is not just.

From an unlimited subject: Not Plato is just. Not Plato is not just.

From an unlimited predicate: Plato is not just. Plato is not not just.

From both unlimited terms: Not Plato is not just. Not Plato is not not just.

RHETORICAL TOPICS

Rhetorical speech has six parts, the preface which is the introduction, narration, partition, confirmation, refutation, conclusion. These parts are the instruments of the rhetorical faculty, since rhetoric is present in all its species and the species will be present in it too. And they will not be more present than those things that they pervade help them. So in the legal genus of cases the preface is necessary, and the narration, and the rest of the parts: and they are necessary in the demonstrative and deliberative types. Now the function of the rhetorical faculty is to teach and persuade: nonetheless this task is assisted by almost the same six instruments, that is, the parts of an oration. The rhetorical parts, being divisions of the faculty, are themselves too faculties: so they also use the parts of an oration as materials.

And for this purpose, they will be present in the same parts. For unless there are the five previously mentioned parts of rhetoric, namely: invention, expression, arrangement, memory, delivery, the orator is helpless. Similarly too, most of the remaining parts as well are useless without all the parts of rhetoric. The effective user of this faculty is the speaker, whose duty it is to speak appropriately and persuasively. His purpose is to have spoken well, that is, appropriately and persuasively: the other faculty is persuasion. For if the speaker is in any sense prevented from persuasion, although he has performed his function, he has not attained his end: but the one who is close and intimate attains his end on completing his duty. But he who is outside often fails to attain it, without however detracting from the glory of rhetoric, that is satisfied with its own end. These elements are so mingled that rhetoric is in the species, and the species are in the causes.

The parts of the causes are said to be states: we may call them, in other terms, constitutions, and questions. They are divided in the same way as the nature of things is divided. But let us begin from the beginning with the differences of the questions, since the rhetorical questions are all involved in the circumstances, or are associated with the controversy of some piece of writing, or, apart from what is written, have drawn their preliminary contention from the facts themselves.

Those questions that are in writing can be defined in five ways. One way is when the writing defends the writer's words, and he upholds its meaning, and this is called writing and will.

Another way: If the laws, by a certain contrariety, disagree with each other, some of them defending in opposition, others creating the controversy: and this is called the state of the contrary law.

A third way: When the writing under discussion contains an ambiguous thought. This is called ambiguity, from its name.

A fourth way: When something that was not written is understood in what has been written down; since it is traced through reasoning and a kind of syllogistic consequence, it is called ratiocinative or syllogism.

A fifth way: When a speech has been written, whose force and character are not readily clear unless expounded by definition, this called the end in writing. To show that all these ways differ from each other is not our task nor that of rhetoric. We state them for examination by the learned, not as instruction for beginners: although in passing we have discussed their differences in our comments on topics.

The differences of those constitutions that, apart from writing, are included in the discussions of the subjects themselves, are separated in the same way as the nature of the things themselves is divided. For in every rhetorical question there is a doubt whether a thing is, what it is, what kind of thing it is: and, on account of this condition, whether judgment can rightly or customarily be exercised. But if the fact, or the point made by the opponent, is refuted, the question is whether there is what is called a conjectural constitution. But if the fact stands, but what was done is not known, since its significance must be demonstrated by definition, it is called a finite constitution. And if it stands, and agrees with the definition of the thing, but there is a question of what kind of thing it is, then, since there is doubt as to the genus to which it belongs, it is called a general quality. In this question lies the principle of quality, and quantity and comparison. But since it is a question of genus, according to the form of the genus the members of this constitution must be distributed in many ways.

For every general question, that is, a question on genus, quality, or quantity of an act, is divided into two parts. The quality of the proposed point is sought either in the past, or in the present, or in the future. If in the past, it is called a juridical constitution. If the question relates to the present or the future, it is known as a business constitution.

The juridical constitution, whose investigation refers to the past, is divided into two parts. For either the force of the defense lies in the act itself, and is called an absolute quality: or it is derived from external sources, and is called an extrinsic constitution.

But this is divided into four parts: either the accusation is admitted, or it is withdrawn, or it is referred, or, and this is the last course, it is compared. The accusation is admitted, when no defense of the act is brought forward, but pardon is sought. This may occur in two ways—by deprecation or purgation. Deprecation occurs, when no excuse is offered. Purgation arises, when the responsibility for the act is attributed to those who cannot be resisted or opposed and are not persons: for this falls under another constitution, namely: inadvertence, chance, and necessity.

The charge is withdrawn when it is transferred from the accused to another person. But the withdrawal of the charge may occur in two ways: If the case is referred, or the act. The case is referred when it is contended that an act was committed through the influence of another: the act, when it is shown that another person could have or must have committed it. And these procedures are particularly valid in these cases, if the action is asserted against us for not doing what ought to have been done. The charge is referred, when it is justly granted that a crime was committed against someone: since the man against whom it was committed was frequently harmful and deserved to suffer what was asserted against him.

Comparison occurs, when the defense asserts that the act which the prosecution charges was committed for a better and more useful purpose. And so much for this subject. Now invention must be treated.

INVENTION

We have already discussed dialectic topics: now we present rhetorical topics, that necessarily spring from the attributes of persons and from business. A person is one who is summoned to court and whose word or act is reprehensible. Business is an act or word of a person, on account of which he is brought to court. Thus in these two cases every topical possibility is involved: for those that offer an occasion for prosecution do not, unless tending in a pardonable direction, afford an opportunity for defense: for accusation and defense arise from the same topics.

If then a person is brought to court, without any act or word being attacked, no case is possible. Nor can an act or word be brought to court, unless the person exists. Thus in these two cases every possibility of verdict is involved both in person and in business. However, as has been said, a person is one who is brought to court: a business, is an act or word of a person, in regard to which he stands accused. A person therefore and a business cannot offer arguments, for they themselves are in question: where there is doubt, there cannot be reliance on doubt.

An argument on the other hand is a method of reasoning about a questionable matter and one that invites reliability. Those things produce reliability in business that are attributes of the person and the business. And if the person ever inspires reliability in a business, as the belief that Catiline had intentions against the state, since he is a person branded with shameful vices, then it is not because he is a person and is brought to court that he inspires confidence in the business, but because he has assumed a certain quality from the attributes of the person. But, in order to clarify the sequence of subjects still more, I believe we should discuss circumstances.

JOHANN CLAUBERG
(1622-1665)

German philosopher, philologist and psychologist. A leading German adherent of Descartes, he prepared the way for Wolff. Taught at Herborn and Duisburg.

Main Works:
> Differentia inter Cartesianam et in scholis vulgo usitatam philosophiam; Ontosophia; Logica Vetus et Nova.

On Obscure Writing

The student who has learned from the first part of this Logic the proper method of arranging his thoughts and from the second part an effective method of expounding them to others, can such a student not deservedly be considered a perfect and consummate logician?

Reply: I do not deny that the prestige of this designation can be achieved by such a person. But, for the purpose of learning how to classify our thoughts properly in relation to things that must be known in order to live honorably and happily and to expound these thoughts to others, not only must the subjects be considered in themselves, but others who discourse publicly and privately must also be listened to, and frequently sacred and secular sources must be appealed to and consulted on many points that can be learned either in no other way or with great

---

From: *Logica Vetus et Nova.*

difficulty, except through their services: and as there are things of this kind among men performed or revealed by men and God in no due sequence, as languages, antiquities, and so on, the logician must consequently be concerned in learning also about other sayings and writings and resolving them: and for this reason he is also called analytical.

In the second part of Genetic Logic was not the name of analyst given frequently not to one engaged in debate, as the logician, but to one engaged in teaching?

Reply: The analyst was there so called when he investigated the essential nature of things and from the treasury of his mind brought forth the appropriate principles of learning: but he is so called, when he probes and resolves the sayings or writings of others in his desire to discover the truth: for reading books only with the mind deserves criticism and refutation. This is a common and evil custom, and is the mark of the calumniator rather than the analyst. So there is an analysis of nature, and an analysis of writers: just as there is one interpretation of nature (and things mentally conceived) and another interpretation of writers (communicating their thoughts by means of external speech).

What ought the principal point to be in analysis, that is now being discussed?

Reply: Since it is not proper to judge what you do not perceive, it should be your primary object, unless you want to deviate at the very start, to perceive what are the thoughts of the one who addresses us, or what significance in words or writings is germane and related to the speaker's mind, and what is the true meaning of the words. Accordingly it should be repeatedly observed that, in entering, without any prejudice, upon an analysis of a writer, we should not refuse to be first of all pupils rather than critics, in order to understand primarily what is propounded, for our approval or condemnation. For anyone who brings such an attitude to the reading of men's works that, in estimating the author, he too generously thinks that he can never be crude, himself readily absorbs the mistakes that have gone unnoticed, or often uselessly exhausts himself in wresting all the statements into a more acceptable meaning. On the other hand, one who has a negative opinion of an author and girds himself to the attack (and the vain desire for fame drives many men to such a contingency), since he withdraws from considering the reasons that persuade attentive readers of the argument, in order to find other reasons to dissuade them, is rendered less capable of understanding his author. But if then you want to debate with someone, you will first of all investigate very carefully what the question involves or what is the status of the argument, or your opponent's intention, so that you do not beat the air and expose yourself to the ridicule of scholars, or injure your adversary. For it is a common fault among critics, to attribute one's own views to others and then to attack them for such views.

But is it immediately necessary, if one is to comprehend the intention of our speaker and to discover the real significance of his talk, to resort to logic and to demand therefrom precepts for such a purpose?

Reply: If our discussion were always with a speaker who was present, it would be possible to ask him personally in what sense he wanted his words to be understood. Now, when it is usually a matter of an absent or dead writer whose writings confronting our eyes or whose sayings reported by others are often not such that their meaning instantaneously becomes self-evident to our understanding, it then becomes the function of logic to prescribe the reasons and methods for the investigation of the true meaning of verbal obscurity and for differentiating it from falsity. Here in fact is a method of finding out, and so quite germane to logic, which is called a method of knowledge.

What then, in short, is required in order to discover the true meaning of speech?

Reply: Since external speech consists of words for the perception of the meaning before the significance of the words is examined: and as the significance and the meaning consist in the things designated by the talk and the words and in the author's intention, the author too must be considered and the purpose of the speaker and subject that is discussed and the other circumstances of the talk: finally, there is the necessity to understand all this in the proper way, apart from the faculty of seeing and hearing, with a ready memory, and attentive listening and reading. We shall discuss each of these points individually, in order, beginning with the end, and ending with the beginning.

I readily acknowledge, for reasons stated elsewhere, that in the analysis of writers there is need for attention, and I am quite well aware that memory is required in order to retain what contributes to our use and is conducive to an understanding and an estimate of the sequence of the author's thoughts. Now here I want to show only whether in the perusal of books there are certain special ways of strengthening attention and aids to memory.

Reply: Pertinent to this question are: 1. the annotations that occur in books when noteworthy expressions are indicated by a short line drawn beneath them or by asterisks placed in the margin. It is preferable for such underlining and asterisks to be of different, rather than the same colors. 2. a brief analysis of the author, or a condensation in the form of an epitome or summary or an outline on tablets, by means of which every expression is exposed to view at one and the same time: or, lastly, the making of an index containing the main chapters on topics and terms. 3. a description of the author, or a rendering from one language into another, by means of which we enter all the more into our author, the more we industriously translate him.

Are there other aids of this kind that promote concentration and memory in reading a great many authors?

Reply: Famous sayings should be excerpted from various sources and written down in any confused order either on tablets that are called diaries and memoranda, or in a well arranged enumeration of commonplaces.

What are these commonplaces and how may they be enumerated?

Reply: They are the headings of subjects relating to one or more disciplines, arranged in a planned sequence by your own industry or guided by others: they are placed together and grouped either alphabetically or according to the more natural series of the subjects themselves, so that whatever is heard and read that deserves to be noted can at once be recorded under one of those headings. For example, among commonplaces in Ethics you will make headings under Virtue, Vice, Fortitude, Temperance, Liberality, and so on. Such commonplaces are largely contributory in encouraging invention, aiding the memory, and forming the judgment of the mind when examining and selecting every subject.

What must be observed in general with reference to commonplaces, summaries, indexes, and similar compilations?

Reply: First of all, annotations and excerpts should be read over frequently and at every given opportunity should be added to and applied to use. Secondly, when notebooks of this kind have been filled with various apothegms of different authors, they should be used for this particular purpose: to help in recalling now and then to memory what we previously learned in the source books from which the extracts were made. For if you neglect the fountain heads and approach only the rivulets, you drink only turbid water, and do not achieve true erudition. For whatever is notable in the writings of men of distinguished talent is contained not in this or that sentence that may be excerpted: but it issues from the entire body of writing: nor do we discover this immediately on the first perusal, but gradually from frequent and repeated reading when we are inattentive, and then convert it, as it were, into our own flesh and blood. And nothing better can be imagined for discovering the true meaning and deriving the benefit therefrom than by reading our author or listening carefully to our teacher and getting acquainted with his style and manner of talking and in this way making him familiar to us. Finally, as a good interpreter should do, you must exercise every effort to comprehend the sequence and connection of the reasoning principles. Thus it is the critic's function to examine every clause, each detached from the rest of his treatment.

Is it better to read authors or to attend the lectures of scholars?

Reply: Although we derive from reading good books the same benefit as from converse with the great minds that have composed them, and possibly an even greater benefit, for you do not meet with any kind of thoughts whatever, as in familiar conversation, but only the more select thoughts they usually commit to writing: still it must be steadfastly maintained that true learning does not depend solely on books, but (apart from the fact that you require first of all private meditation, and varied practice and experience) is also compared with both private and public familiarity with the learning of notable men. And the public lecture halls should all the more eagerly be attended to ensure greater effectiveness and force of the living voice, particularly in a public academy.

I understand that there should be no separation between reading and listening: but is it possible in some way to define how many times the perusal of one and the same author should be repeated?

Reply: It is a sufficiently established fact from various sources that not all books should be read indiscriminately, but only good and useful books should be carefully read. And since the supply of books throughout the world is excessively great, not even all good books ought to or can be read with equal care, as it is generally quite sufficient to know which authors have written on various subjects: so that, when it is to our interest, they may be examined and consulted more closely and thus be able to serve us. A writer who deserves studious attention more than others should be read through at least three times. 1. Run through the entire book in one breath, as it were, get a synoptic acquaintance with subjects treated, nor let the attention flag, and do not dwell at length on any difficulties. 2. The entire book should be read through again more carefully, scrupulously attending to the causes and reasons expressed therein, and noting the passages in which difficulties occur. 3. Let the book be taken up again, to re-read once more the entire text, but somewhat more rapidly and to observe whether many difficulties have now been removed or which ones still remain. Thus by repeated readings and by making a comparison between one book and another all the difficulties will be resolved.

Why, for extracting the true meaning of obscure writing, is a knowledge of the author important, and the content, the purpose, the place and time, and similar circumstances, since all these matters appear to be extraneous to the writing?

Reply: Because only then is the effect known perfectly, when its efficient cause and everything concurring in producing the effect are understood. Moreover, an author is the efficient cause of his writing, and the other circumstances are conducive to the production of the effect.

What then is our first inquiry to be?

Reply: Who is the one that speaks, God or man: the prime author, or an aide and assistant: the teacher or the pupil: the popular dialectician or the analytical scholar, and so on. For a good interpreter should know not only the meaning of the words in the proposition or the thought, but also whose thought it is, or who thinks so. This will prevent him from attributing, as critics do, the lapses of the interpreter to the author, the mistakes of the pupil to the teacher, the opinion of one chance scholar to the entire church, the typographical errors or the publisher's carelessnesses to the writer himself. Certain inconsistencies appear, if the work is considered as propounded by a man, but they have an acceptable sense, if viewed as the words of God: and so conversely. Thus in the books of the Bible you will carefully distinguish whether Holy Scripture is speaking, or some one else is there introduced as speaking. For some things cannot be rightly understood unless considered as uttered by the impious or certainly by others than God. On the other hand, one would consider a man stupid who said to another man: I bid you to believe; since faith is a matter of persuasion, not of command, and yet you will think such an utterance, coming from the mouth of God, far from incongruous since it is only God's function to command the conscience at his will.

How is one to learn to what type an author belongs?

Reply: First of all this is indicated from the various notes printed in the work itself, whereby the author reveals himself. Thus from the divine notes refulgent in Holy Scripture the theologians prove that its author is God. Thus you will readily distinguish the dialectic writer from the analytical, if you observe on what rules of the second part of logic he has based his talk. Then the author is recognized from his own testimony, especially if he quotes another book of his. Then from the testimony of others who can know and whom one may not suspect when they want to conceal. Finally, from the heading and the title, whether it has come from the author himself or from the publisher, unless it can be proved false.

How then shall I appraise the falseness of a title, in order to distinguish spurious writings from genuine?

Reply: I. From the language and the style. For example: If an author uses a particular language or employs sentences and words that do not fit the period in which he is said to have written: thus scholars prove that the books that circulate under the name of Hermes Trismegistus are not the work of the ancient writer who introduced laws and letters to the Egyptians, because in these books, phrases and words occur that are different from the usual ancient form of the Greek tongue. 2. From a comparison with other writings of the author, because the argument of a false title in human writings is only probable, but certain in divine writings, since God cannot contradict himself, but man can. 3. If it can be shown, from history and chronology, or from any testimony whatever of a trustworthy writer, that he is not the author of the book whose name is on the title page.

What is the second consideration in regard to the author?

Reply: Whom he is addressing: that is, anyone indiscriminately, or certain persons interested in the subject on which he is speaking: superior or inferior: pupils or opponents, and so on. Thus Christ acts in one way with the Pharisees arrogant for legal justice, and in another way with others. And the sense will be discovered more easily by such an attitude, if you consider the subject, and the manner in which it is fitting for a man to speak when he addresses a particular person. Thus if you write to a person of great prestige and reverence, there is no doubt that you try to be more earnest and veracious than if you were writing a letter to someone else. Thus a person who writes to philosophers, it is thought, wants to use their language and not words in any signification different from that which is accepted among them. So we must distinguish between ways of speaking about God that are suitable for popular comprehension, and that contain the truth promulgated indiscriminately to men, that Holy Scripture is wont to use, ascribing human affections to God: and other ways expressing a more naked truth, not reported to the common populace, that must be used in metaphysics for instructing his sons in knowledge. Lastly, not infrequently during a discussion the missiles launched by an adversary rebound on his own head, and occasionally many things are said in the heat of the moment that must be returned in good measure, and that should not be accepted as though they had been didactic and enunciated absolutely.

What is the third point in considering the circumstances of a speech?

Reply: We should observe what the author is saying, that is, we must inquire into the subject under discussion, since the words, as the Hermeneutic Canon asserts, must be understood according to the subject matter. Consider then what the person should properly feel and say, who wants to treat of such and such a matter, and what method of treatment this subject requires. See whether a subject is discussed generally and in the abstract, or specifically and concretely: whether it is considered absolutely, or whether it is concerned with something else, and what this other related thing may be. Thus in Holy Scripture when few are said to be chosen, and yet elsewhere, many will come from the East and the West, you will understand *many* if you consider them by themselves, and *few* by comparison with the wicked.

What is the fourth point to be considered?

Reply: Why the author speaks, that is, what are his objective and purpose: for the words of a speaker must never be accepted apart from their purpose. Inquire, then, by what occasion he is affected, what cause urges him on, with what object and intention he has written this or that. For example: Since the purpose of Holy Scripture is to teach us that salvation is in Christ, it is not surprising that it omits many things relating to Physics and the investigation of other disciplines from the light of nature, and that Moses was much more detailed and more scrupulous in describing the creation of the world that concerned the entire universe.

But how is the author's purpose to be known?

Reply: The author's purpose, like the matter under discussion, will frequently become known to us from the title and the introduction of the book. Thus if a writer promises in the title and introduction to the books, demonstrations of God's existence, there is no reason why he should be thought to lean toward atheism, even if he reviews their arguments. Even if he records their views for the sole purpose of refuting them, he becomes an iniquitous calumniator, in attributing such opinions to the writer as his very own.

Is there not something to be noted here specially in regard to headings?

Reply: Since a title can rarely express everything, but is usually derived from the more important part of the treatise, he is a calumniator if he proposes to admit in the book what was not noted in the title. And since, on account of various subjects, or different purposes proposed by the author in the same treatise, a different title can be attached to the same book in various parts of it, the person who takes this opportunity to taunt the author for this as being hourly changeable and inconsistent, is a quibbler. Thus a person who discusses the distinction between the human soul and the body so as to reveal thereby the immortality of the soul, may inscribe one title or another on his book, as one or another topic appears to offer a greater appeal to his readers. In such cases we adjust ourselves to our readers.

What is the fifth circumstance in our inquiry?

Reply: To discover the mood and attitude of the author: whether he is speaking seriously and sincerely or not: whether

272

he is speaking according to a formulated belief or incidentally, as the occasion arises: whether he is addressing the populace and the general public, or whether he is expressing his heartfelt sentiments: whether he is speaking for another or for himself: as an exercise, or for didactic purposes: whether he has written at his own discretion, or at another's suggestion: whether he makes some proposal by means of affection or refutation, or of a reply directed against some refutation: whether he discusses realities, or things apprehended mentally in accordance with the view of his hearers: and so on. Attentive readers of this book will also note how I have occasionally explained mental attitudes by certain forms of expression, as: It is usual, it seems, it is called: commonly, commonly in the schools, and so on. Thus, distinguish in the case of philosophy what the author says hesitantly from what he says discriminatingly, what he says modestly from what as a philosopher he defines categorically, what he says in an indulgent popular sense from what he says strictly as a philosopher, what he asserts about matters he has carefully examined from subjects not investigated or at least not yet completely investigated. Thus those who read Aristotle note what must be said in his exoteric works, and where some statement must be made perfunctorily in passing, and when he usually follows the general opinion. In other great writers too similar examples occur endlessly, which critics emphasize so as to interpret what was said modestly as pronouncements made hesitantly or doubtfully and that the author himself propounded as matters for consideration requiring no assent: while they confuse with such statements what the author affirmed, what he asserted in a deliberative and inquiring spirit, what he posited with decision and assertiveness, and other matters that, as we recommended, should be differentiated by good interpreters: for they sometimes take the mistakes of hurried writing for deliberate intellectual aberrations.

What is the sixth point in evaluating the circumstances of writing?

Reply: The style and language used by the author: for he speaks either in his own vernacular or in a strange, foreign tongue: and the author's writing is one thing, the interpretation another. Furthermore, what is harsh and uncouth in one language may be in another language quite acceptable to the ear. Moreover, if you want to know whether two negatives affirm or deny, consider the language in which the author has written, and you will see that what is often an affirmation among the Romans, a fortiori is also a denial among the Greeks and the Germans.

Is there not some hermeneutic method to be observed for the other points?

Reply: To find an author's meaning, it is far better to read him in the original language than in a translation: his own autograph too should be observed rather than the transcription: and since the latter becomes gradually defective, the first transcriptions are preferable to the last. Thus the meaning of the divine word may be much more accurately perceived from the original languages, Hebrew and Greek, than from French, German, and other versions. For, among various interpretations the one that should always be judged the best is that which most closely approaches the spirit of the first speaker or writer.

How is one to find out an author's style and form of expression?

Reply: 1. One must notice to whom the talk is directed. For example: One may address slaves and inferiors in the laconic style, fathers or superiors in perhaps the Asiatic or Attic style. 2. The nationality of the author. Thus in Livy a certain *Patavinitas* was observed, and today among Germans writing in Latin Germanisms are noted, and among the French, Gallicisms. 3. The century or period in which the author lived. For example: The Germans of the time of King Ottfried, who was the first to translate the Gospel into the Teutonic tongue, spoke far

Johann Clauberg

differently in Luther's day, and in many cases differently today too. Such changes occur much more in French. Thus the ancient philosophers were wont to veil their views in enigmatic and allegorical obscurities, that some of their successors seized upon, assuming the first meaning that presented itself, and hence were frequently more slanderous than true interpreters: or at least transmitted these views less faithfully, and made them generally unappealing. 4. The purpose of the writer: for different purposes there is the historical style, or the satirical, or the pedestrian, or the sublime, the acroamatic style, or the exoteric. 5. The teachers that the author imitates most closely in the humanities and the other disciplines. Thus, the Platonist Fathers of the Church discourse in one way, and the Aristotelian Scholastics in another, and in another way our contemporaries who are ignorant of scholastic philosophy or hate it: in still a different way, the chemists when discussing medical matters, and so on.

What circumstances of speech, too, are to be appraised?

Reply: In the seventh and last place, we should observe where and when the author speaks: for the circumstances of place and time too are a quite frequent aid in discovering the true meaning, particularly when the talk centers on matters relating to geography or chronology. And here it is necessary to appeal to and consult a history contemporaneous with the writer whom it is proposed to interpret. Thus if a person wishes to understand the Fathers, he must know the history of those times: and those who criticize Aristotle for using mathematical examples and terms in his logic, forget to observe the method of training the youth that was in vogue in those days. Moreover, there is confirmation in the following statement of the theologians, derived from Augustine: Distinguish the times, and Scripture will harmonize. Thus, on account of the difference of time Christ's words (Matthew 10.5): *Go not into the way of the Gentiles* and (Matthew 28.19) *Go ye therefore and teach all the nations* do not conflict. Nor are the precepts and examples of the preceding section of logic contradictions to the statements I have postulated in the last part, since in this part I had dealt with the more advanced logician, while in the preceding parts I aimed primarily at the beginner, having in mind to teach the younger students.

So far we have explained how to examine the meaning of obscure writing by considering external factors. Now we proceed to investigate the writing itself, and since first of all words present themselves singly therein, whose denotation must be grasped before the meaning of the entire writing can be judged, one may well ask what aids are furnished for this purpose?

Reply: We must consider 1. what contributions the philological arts, grammatical, lexicographical, and rhetorical, can make in this matter. For, if not principally, at least the elementary parts of these arts are required for understanding all writers. 2. The words must be referred to everything by a consideration of which the signification of those words can be manifested in any possible way. 3. We must inquire in how many ways the significations of the words are accepted.

How useful are lexica at this stage?

Reply: They furnish definitions of words by means of synonymous terms. They list homonyms according to distinctions, then they etymologically elucidate the origin of words. Thus, if you consider the etymology of the word *idea,* you will find that it just signifies what is in Latin species (unless this latter term is more ambiguous) which comes from an old form *specio,* that is, *I see:* and since we can see mentally or apprehend with our thought a thing that is not yet in existence, but still to be made or already made, or self-existent, the term *idea* is properly distinguished as *archetype* and *model.* If you say: *Adoratio civilis,* at first glance you appear to join contradictions, but the origin of the word *adorare* removes all doubt. For *adorare* is derived from the fact that the hand is moved to the mouth, in Greek *proskynein:* from *kuo, I kiss,* whence *kuosin:* German *sie küssen.* For anciently the Greeks showed reverence by moving the hand up to the mouth, as many among us do today. To avoid mistakes, when you investigate the meaning of a word etymologically, you will observe that the original meaning often differs from the common meaning: that is, many words generally now have denotations different from their former meanings when they were first invented and attached to things: or the usage of words not infrequently differs from the original usage. Moreover, since some words are common to all men and others are peculiar to scholars in certain sciences, for such a diversity the common lexica, philological and etymological, will be serviceable on occasion: at other times theological, legal, medical, philosophical lexica, produced by experts in these disciplines, will be useful.

How does grammar help in interpretation?

Reply: Frequently only the handwriting and orthography solve the problem. Sometimes inspection of the quantity and accent removes a doubt: occasionally gender and case, inflection, and the rest of the attributes of words clarify the meaning. Thus, if with certain anatomists you consider that Cicero called the mesentery the middle of the intestines, in the genitive plural, not in the nominative singular, you will easily disentangle him from a perverse meaning. Thus the theologians try to prove the mystery of the Holy Trinity from the Gospels, whether God speaks of himself in the singular or the plural. It is also worth noting that Holy Scripture generally calls angels and the controllers of public affairs gods, in the plural: but specifically and in the singular it calls no angels or king God. Similarly, the names of the Devil and Satan are never used in the plural. Through the grammarians also are to be corrected mistakes in accent and figures of speech that sophists use by confusing words in respect of quantity, capitals, gender, declension or other accidental difference on account of some convenience in pronunciation, in writing, or an ending. For example: In the following arguments: Every man devoted to equity deserves praise. Every courtier is devoted to equines. Therefore, and so on. Those who are lords are not slaves. Christians are Lords, Therefore . . .

What aid is rhetoric in achieving the intended purpose?

Reply: It teaches one to distinguish the figurative acceptance of a word from the literal meaning. You thus learn whether a speech contains a figure, in what expression it consists, what it is, whether it belongs to some group: questions that must all be known to the interpreter, to avoid thinking that perhaps there is a figurative meaning in some expression, what is to be taken literally, not to find a figure where there is none, or to classify a figure incorrectly. A very excellent example of these three points can be found in theological discussions on the meaning of the words in the Last Supper: This is my body.

I have learned, I believe, the character and arrangement of the figures from the rhetoricians themselves. I ask this question only: When is a figure to be assumed in a word, and when not? The principles of rhetoric do not appear to help in determining this.

Reply: Since the literal meaning of a speech is naturally prior to a figure, one must persist until necessity forces one to grasp the figure. And thus St. Augustine: The literal sense of words must always be accepted unless a good reason suggests a figure of speech. This statement agrees with the legalistic view that refuses to reject literal meaning unless a proper interpretation urges this course.

What is this reason or necessity?

Reply: It is: 1. When suggested words can in no way be reconciled with other sayings of the same author, who is considered a good and intelligent writer, but a flagrant contradiction must be posited, unless a figure of speech is intended. 2. When the nature of the thing under discussion itself rejects a literal connotation, as in this proposition: Herod is a wolf. For things that are opposed cannot have the same meaning and be affirmed of each other. All the passages in Scripture, where God, who is a spirit, assigns corporeal members to himself, are of this nature. 3. When history or an event shows that words must be or must have been understood figuratively, as happens in the forecasts and prophecies of the Holy Scriptures. Necessity does not arise from a bare comparison with other passages, since the same word may be taken in different senses in different passages. Nor does this necessity occur from the fact that there are many passages by the same author, in which a particular word is taken figuratively, and a few in which it is taken literally. For in that case God would be considered corporeal, since there are more passages in Holy Scripture where a body is attributed to him than those where he is called a Spirit. Thus Scripture adapts itself to the popular understanding. And so you will note that more reliability should be placed on the multiplicity of passages when what is predicated of the subject in many passages does not conflict with the nature of the subject. In this spirit we accept Tertullian's rule: You must understand a few passages according to the large number of passages and, to prevent many other passages from being vitiated by one expression, this expression must be accepted according to all the passages rather than contrary to them.

As we have observed these points, let me now be informed what philological arts are conducive to an understanding of the meaning of words: also, what comparisons must be made to comprehend the significance of words.

Reply: First and foremost, we must consider the relation between the subject and the predicate, because the subject is described by the predicate, and the predicate in turn is specified or restricted by the subject: whence this rule is enunciated: The subject is such as it is permitted to be by the predicate and, conversely, the predicate is such as it is permitted to be by the subject. For example: If one says: The dog is the guardian of the home, the predicate does not permit the subject *dog* to denote the constellation, but an animal that barks. Whenever it happens, therefore, that many attributes are assigned to one thing by the same writer, they should all be assembled and from them it should be shown that this and not that can be understood as the subject. For every single thing is most properly known from its attributes.

What comparisons can I use, restricting myself to the same author?

Reply: A word whose meaning is obscure should be compared: 1. with the antecedent and consequent words of the same author in the same speech, and particularly with nearest ones, for adjectives appositive or opposed to substantives, adverbs to verbs, and similar expressions in apposition or opposition are capable of shedding light on each other. Thus by the expression *natural children* one thing is understood in relation to *adoptive children,* and another thing with reference to legitimate children in general. The word *man,* also, posited absolutely, denotes one thing, if we say: A man is depicted, and another thing, if we say: A dead man. And here the determination destroys its own determined thing: hence it is called a contradiction in the adjective or an opposition in the appositive, whenever one is implicitly expressed through the other, as *a wooden God, non-material money.* Sometimes there is thought to be a contradiction in the adjective, when there is none at all, as when certain letters that are all voiced are called mutes, and when certain names, by which individual things are called, are not permitted to be appellative. But if one considers that the letters are opposed by the grammarians to vowels and semi-vowels, and the names to proper names, the suspicion of a contradiction will readily disappear. 2. with parallel passages, that is, with other writings by the same author, corresponding to the treatise that we are dealing with. For example: If you ask what *the finger of God* means in Luke 21.20, compare Exodus 8.19 and you will see that God's power to create miracles is denoted, and in this interpretation you will be confirmed when you read elsewhere the *hand*, and also the *arm* of the Lord as expressing his power. Similarly, when the hand and the counsel of God are joined, as in Acts 4.28, we must understand God's powerful or efficacious plan, through the grammatical figure called Heniadys, that is, one through two.

How will the meaning of a word be classified better if one refers to matters beyond our writer?

Reply: 1. If it is compared with every usage and the common custom of good writers employing the same term, according to the argument in Logic 2.31. Thus a man who plundered the fields by night might add insult to his ravages, because a truce had been arranged for the day, not the night: on which Cicero speaks in his *De Officiis.* 2. with the definition and usage that appear in the discipline that discusses the subject represented by that expression. Thus you will best find the metaphysical terms in metaphysics: theological terms in theology: juridical terms in jurisprudence: logic terms in logic, and so with the rest. For as one discipline explains the terms of another it lacks itself, it will be useless to search therein.

Is there another special observation to be made on this last point?

Reply: First of all you will note that certain words commonly denote one thing, another thing in certain disciplines, and other different things in different disciplines. Thus numbering and measuring have one common denotation, another, and a more extensive one, in arithmetic and geometry, where they are defined as arts in numbering and measuring correctly. Thus many words taken at random sound more divinely in theology than when they are used of mundane matters, as faith, charity, grace, the church, feast, baptism, and so on. The predisposing cause and the primary cause indicate one thing in medicine, another thing in logic and ethics. Articles signify to grammarians prepositive or postpositive signs: to arithmeticians, units of tens: to anatomists, the joints of the fingers: to theologians also, ignorant of Latinity, the principal headings of the faith are called Articles of Faith. For, I may add, as the purity of the Latin tongue became impaired long ago, and barbarism invaded the Schools, a signification quite different from that given by the Latin writers was given to many words by theologians, philosophers, and others. For example: The word *unio*, which to the Romans signifies just a pearl, is now used far differently, when philosophers, theologians, and lawyers speak of the union of the soul and the body, of the hypostatic union of natures in Christ, of the union of offspring. And what were among the Romans in the vocabulary of the arts, are today called terms.

RENÉ DESCARTES
(1596-1650)

Most influential French philosopher. First educated mainly in mathematics at the Jesuit College, La Flèche, and later at the University of Poitiers. He served for years as a mercenary officer in foreign countries. Much of his life was spent in travel abroad. He lived in Holland from 1629 to 1649, forever changing his domicile. He died at the court of Queen Christina of Sweden. His quest for truth and profound rationalism revolutionized the thinking of Europe. His devoutness to Catholicism was more apparent than real. His use of the geometric method in philosophy and other fields of thought as well as the arts, his strong opposition to Aristotelian authorities as well as his radical method of doubt drew the open-minded of his century and later centuries to his works. He can rightly be called the father of modern philosophy. Somehow he managed all through his life to avoid a break with the Church.

Main Works:

> Discours de la méthode; Meditationes de prima philosophia; Le monde; Traité des passions de l'âme; Principia philosophiae; Regulae ad directionem ingenii.

Of the Nature of the Human Mind

The Meditation of yesterday has filled my mind with so many doubts, that it is no longer in my power to forget them. Nor do I see, meanwhile, any principle on which they can be resolved;

From: *Discours de la méthode.*

and, just as if I had fallen all of a sudden into very deep water, I am so greatly disconcerted as to be unable either to plant my feet firmly on the bottom or sustain myself by swimming on the surface. I will, nevertheless, make an effort, and try anew the same path on which I had entered yesterday, that is, proceed by casting aside all that admits of the slightest doubt, not less than if I had discovered it to be absolutely false; and I will continue always in this track until I shall find something that is certain, or at least, if I can do nothing more, until I shall know with certainty that there is nothing certain. Archimedes, that he might transport the entire globe from the place it occupied to another, demanded only a point that was firm and immoveable; so also, I shall be entitled to entertain the highest expectations, if I am fortunate enough to discover only one thing that is certain and indubitable.

I suppose, accordingly, that all the things which I see are false (fictitious); I believe that none of those objects which my fallacious memory represents ever existed; I suppose that I possess no senses; I believe that body, figure, extension, motion, and place are merely fictions of my mind. What is there, then, that can be esteemed true? Perhaps this only, that there is absolutely nothing certain.

But how do I know that there is not something different altogether from the objects I have now enumerated, of which it is impossible to entertain the slightest doubt? Is there not a God, or some being, by whatever name I may designate him, who causes these thoughts to arise in my mind? But why suppose such a being, for it may be I myself am capable of producing them? Am I, then, at least not something? But I before denied that I possessed senses or a body; I hesitate, however, for what follows from that? Am I so dependent on the body and the senses that without these I cannot exist? But I had the persuasion that there was absolutely nothing in the world, that there was no sky and no earth, neither minds nor bodies; was I not, therefore, at the same time, persuaded that I did not exist? Far from it; I assuredly existed, since I was persuaded. But there is I know not what being, who is possessed at once of the highest power and the deepest cunning, who is constantly employing all his ingenuity in deceiving me. Doubtless, then, I exist, since I am deceived; and, let him deceive me as he may, he can never bring it about that I am nothing, so long as I shall be conscious that I am something. So that it must, in fine, be maintained, all things being maturely and carefully considered, that this proposition (*pronunciation*) I am, I exist, is necessarily true each time it is expressed by me, or conceived in my mind.

But I do not yet know with sufficient clearness what I am, though assured that I am; and hence, in the next place, I must take care, lest perchance I inconsiderately substitute some other object in room of what is properly myself, and thus wander from truth, even in that knowledge (cognition) which I hold to be of all others the most certain and evident. For this reason, I will now consider anew that I formerly believed myself to be, before I entered on the present train of thought; and of my previous opinion I will retrench all that can in the least be invalidated by the grounds of doubt I have adduced, in order that there may at length remain nothing but what is certain and indubitable. What then did I formerly think I was? Undoubtedly I judged that I was a man. But what is a man? Shall I say a rational animal? Assuredly not; for it would be necessary forthwith to inquire into what is meant by animal, and what by rational, and thus, from a single question, I should insensibly glide into others and these more difficult than the first; nor do I now possess enough of leisure to warrant me in wasting my time amid subtleties of this sort. I prefer here to attend to the thoughts that sprung up of themselves in my mind, and were inspired by my own nature alone, when I applied myself to the consideration of what I was. In the first place, then I thought that I possessed a countenance, hands, arms, and all the fabric of members that appears in a corpse, and which I called by the name of body. It further occurred to me that I was nourished, that I walked, perceived, and thought, and all those actions I referred to the soul; but what the soul itself was I either did not stay to consider, or, if I did, I imagined that it was something extremely rare and subtile, like wind, or flame, or ether, spread through my grosser parts. As regarded the body, I did not even doubt of its nature, but thought I distinctly knew it, and if I had wished to describe it according to the notions I then entertained, I should have explained myself in this manner: By body I understand all that can be terminated by a certain figure; that can be comprised in a certain place, and so fill a certain space as therefrom to exclude every other body; that can be perceived either by touch, sight, hearing, taste, or smell; that can be moved in different ways, not indeed of itself, but by something foreign to it by which it is touched [and from which it receives the impression]; for the power of self-motion, as likewise that of perceiving and thinking, I held as by no means pertaining to the nature of body; on the contrary, I was somewhat astonished to find such faculties existing in some bodies.

But [as to myself, what can I now say that I am], since I suppose there exists an extremely powerful, and, if I may so speak, malignant being, whose whole endeavours are directed towards deceiving me? Can I affirm that I possess any one of all those attributes of which I have lately spoken as belonging to the nature of body? After attentively considering them in my own mind, I find none of them that can properly be said to belong to myself. To recount them were idle and tedious. Let us pass, then, to the attributes of the soul. The first mentioned were the powers of nutrition and walking; but, if it be true that I have no body, it is true likewise that I am capable neither of walking nor of being nourished. Perception is another attribute of the soul; but perception too is impossible without the body: besides, I have frequently, during sleep, believed that I perceived objects which I afterwards observed I did not in reality perceive. Thinking is another attribute of the soul; and here I discover what properly belongs to myself. This alone is inseparable from me. I am—I exist: this is certain; but how often? As often as I think; for perhaps it would even happen, if I should wholly cease to think, that I should at the same time altogether cease to be. I now admit nothing that is not necessarily true: I am therefore, precisely speaking, only a thinking thing, that is, a mind (*mens sive animus*), understanding, or reason,—terms whose signification was before unknown to me. I am, however, a real thing, and really existent; but what thing? The answer was, a thinking thing. The question arises, am I aught besides? I will stimulate my imagination with a view to discover whether I am not still something more than a thinking being. Now it is plain I am not the assemblage of members called the human body; I am not a thin and penetrating air diffused through all these members, or wind, or flame, or vapor, or breath, or any of all the things I can imagine; for I supposed that all these were not, and, without changing the supposition, I find that I still feel assured of my existence.

But it is true, perhaps, that those very things which I suppose to be non-existent, because they are unknown to me, are not in truth different from myself whom I know. This is a point I cannot determine, and do not now enter into any dispute regarding it. I can only judge of things that are known to me: I am conscious that I exist, and I who know that I exist inquire into what I am. It is, however, perfectly certain that the knowledge of my existence, thus precisely taken, is not dependent on things, the existence of which is as yet unknown to me: and consequently it is not dependent on any of the things I can feign in imagination. Moreover, the phrase itself, I frame an image (*effigio*), reminds me of my error; for I should in truth frame one if I were to imagine myself to be anything, since to imagine is nothing more than to contemplate the figure or image of a corporeal thing; but I already know that I exist, and that it is possible at the same time that all those images, and in general all that relates to the nature of body, are merely dreams [or chimeras]. From this I discover that it is not more reasonable to say, I will excite my imagination that I may know more distinctly what I am, than to express myself as follows: I am now awake, and perceive something real; but because my perception is not sufficiently clear, I will of express purpose go to sleep that my dreams may represent to me the object of my perception with more truth and clearness. And, therefore, I know that nothing of all that I can embrace in imagination belongs to the knowledge which I have of myself, and that there is need to recall with the utmost care the mind from this mode of thinking, that it may be able to know its own nature with perfect distinctness.

But what, then, am I? A thinking thing, it has been said. But what is a thinking thing? It is a thing that doubts, understands, [conceives], affirms, denies, wills, refuses, that imagines also, and perceives. Assuredly it is not little, if all these properties belong to my nature. But why should they not belong to it? Am I not that very being who now doubts of almost everything; who, for all that, understands and conceives certain things; who affirms one alone as true, and denies the others; who desires to know more of them, and does not wish to be deceived; who imagines many things, sometimes even despite his will; and is likewise percipient of many, as if through the medium of the senses. Is there nothing of all this as true as that I am, even although he who gave me being employed all his ingenuity to deceive me? Is there also any one of these attributes that can be properly distinguished from my thought, or that can be said to be separate from myself? For it is of itself so evident that it is I who doubt, I who understand, and I who desire, that it is here unnecessary to add anything by way of rendering it more clear. And I am as certainly the same being who imagines; for, although it may be (as I before supposed) that nothing I imagine is true, still the power of imagination does not cease really to exist in me and to form part of my thought. In fine, I am the same being who perceives, that is, who apprehends certain objects as by the organs of sense, since, in truth, I see light, hear a noise, and feel heat. But it will be said that these presentations are false, and that I am dreaming. Let it be so. At all events it is certain that I seem to see light, hear a noise, and feel heat; this cannot be false, and this is what in me is properly called perceiving (*sentire*), which is nothing else than thinking. From this I begin to know what I am with somewhat greater clearness and distinctness than heretofore.

But, nevertheless, it still seems to me, and I cannot help believing, that corporeal things, whose images are formed by thought, [which fall under the senses], and are examined by the same, are known with much greater distinctness than that I know not what part of myself which is not imaginable; although, in truth, it may seem strange to say that I know and comprehend with greater distinctness things whose existence appears to me doubtful, that are unknown, and do not belong to me, than others of whose reality I am persuaded, that are known to me, and appertain to my proper nature; in a word, than myself. But I see clearly what is the state of the case. My mind is apt to wander, and will not yet submit to be restrained within the limits of truth. Let us therefore leave the mind to itself once more, and, according to it every kind of liberty, [permit it to consider the objects that appear to it from without], in order that, having afterwards withdrawn it from these gently and opportunely, [and fixed it on the consideration of its being and the properties it finds in itself], it may then be the more easily controlled.

Let us now accordingly consider the objects that are commonly thought to be [the most easily, and likewise] the most distinctly known, viz., the bodies we touch and see; not, indeed, bodies in general, for these general notions are usually somewhat more confused, but one body in particular. Take, for example, this piece of wax; it is quite fresh, having been but recently taken from the bee-hive; it has not as yet lost the sweetness of the honey it contained; it still retains somewhat of the odour of the flowers from which it was gathered; its colour, figure, size, are apparent (to the sight); it is hard, cold, easily handled; and sounds when struck upon with the finger. In fine, all that contributes to make a body as distinctly known as possible, is found in the one before us. But, while I am speaking, let it be placed near the fire—what remained of the taste exhales, the smell evaporates, the colour changes, its figure is destroyed, its size increases, it becomes liquid, it grows hot, it can hardly be handled, and, although struck upon, it emits no sound. Does the same wax still remain after this change? It must be admitted that it does remain; no one doubts it, or judges otherwise. What, then, was it I knew with so much distinctness in the piece of wax? Assuredly, it could be nothing of all that I observed by means of the senses, since all the things that fell under taste, smell, sight, touch, and hearing are changed, and yet the same wax remains. It was perhaps what I now think, viz., that this wax was neither the sweetness of honey, the pleasant odour of flowers, the whiteness, the figure, nor the sound, but only a body that a little before appeared to me conspicuous under these forms, and which is now perceived under others. But, to speak precisely, what is it that I imagine when I think of it in this way? Let it be attentively considered, and, retrenching all that does not belong to the wax, let us see what remains. There remains nothing, except something extended, flexible, and movable. But what is meant by flexible and movable? Is it not that I imagine that the piece of wax, being round, is capable of becoming square, or of passing from a square into a triangular figure? Assuredly such is not the case, because I conceive that it admits of an infinity of similar changes; and I am, moreover, unable to compass this infinity by imagination, and consequently this conception which I have of the wax is not the product of the faculty of imagination. But what now is this extension? Is it not also unknown? for it becomes greater when the wax is melted, greater when it is boiled, and greater still when the heat increases; and I should not conceive [clearly and] according to truth, the wax as it is, if I did not suppose that the piece we are considering admitted even of a wider variety of extension than I ever imagined. I must, therefore, admit that I cannot even comprehend by imagination what the piece of wax is, and that it is the mind alone (*mens,* Lat., *entendement,* F.) which perceives it. I speak of one piece in particular; for, as to wax in general, this is still more evident. But what is the piece of wax that can be perceived only by the [understanding or] mind? It is certainly the same which I see, touch, imagine; and, in fine, it is the same which, from the beginning, I believed it to be. But (and this it is of moment to observe) the perception of it is neither an act of sight, of touch, nor of imagination, and never was either of these, though it might formerly seem so, but is simply an intuition (*inspectio*) of the mind, which may be imperfect and confused, as it formerly was, or very clear and distinct, as it is at present, according as the attention is more or less directed to the elements which it contains, and of which it is composed.

But, meanwhile, I feel greatly astonished when I observe [the weakness of mind, and] its proneness to error. For although, without at all giving expression to what I think, I consider all this in my own mind, words yet occasionally impede my progress, and I am almost led into error by the terms of ordinary language. We say, for example, that we see the same wax when it is before us, and not that we judge it to be the same from its retaining the same color and figure: whence I should forthwith be disposed to conclude that the wax is known by the act of sight, and not by the intuition of the mind alone, were it not for the analogous instance of human beings passing on in the street below, as observed from a window. In this case I do not fail to say that I see the men themselves, just as I say that I see the wax; and yet what do I see from the window beyond hats and cloaks that might cover artificial machines, whose motions might be determined by springs? But I judge that there are human beings from these appearances, and thus I comprehend, by the faculty of judgment alone which is in the mind, what I believed I saw with my eyes.

The man who makes it his aim to rise to knowledge superior to the common, ought to be ashamed to seek occasions of doubting from the vulgar forms of speech: instead, therefore, of doing this, I shall proceed with the matter in hand, and inquire whether I had a clearer and more perfect perception of the piece of wax when I first saw it, and when I thought I knew it by means of the external sense itself, or, at all events, by the common sense (*sensus communis*), as it is called, that is, by the imaginative faculty; or whether I rather apprehend it more clearly at present, after having examined with greater care, both what it is, and in what way it can be known. It would certainly be ridiculous to entertain any doubt on this point. For what, in that first perception, was there distinct? What did I perceive which any animal might not have perceived? But when I distinguish the wax from its exterior forms, and when, as if I had stripped it of its vestments, I consider it quite naked, it is certain, although some error may still be found in my judgment, that I cannot, nevertheless, thus apprehend it without possessing a human mind.

But, finally, what shall I say of the mind itself, that is, of myself? for as yet I do not admit that I am anything but mind. What, then! I who seem to possess so distinct an apprehension of the piece of wax,—do I not know myself, both with greater truth and certitude, and also much more distinctly and clearly? For if I judge that the wax exists because I see it, it assuredly follows, much more evidently, that I myself am or exist, for the same reason: for it is possible that what I see may not in truth be wax, and that I do not even possess eyes with which to see anything; but it cannot be that when I see, or, which comes to the same thing, when I think I see, I myself who think am nothing. So likewise, if I judge that the wax exists because I touch it, it will still also follow that I am; and if I determine that my imagination, or any other cause, whatever it be, persuades me of the existence of the wax, I still draw the same conclusion. And what is here remarked of the piece of wax, is applicable to all the other things that are external to me. And further, if the [notion or] perception of wax appeared to me more precise and distinct, after that not only sight and touch, but many other causes besides, rendered it manifest to my apprehension, with how much greater distinctness must I know myself since all the reasons that contribute to the knowledge of the nature of wax, or of any body whatever, manifest still better the nature of my mind? And there are besides so many other things in the mind itself that contribute to the illustration of its nature, that those dependent on the body, to which I have here referred, scarcely merit to be taken into account.

But, in conclusion, I find I have insensibly reverted to the point I desired; for, since it is now manifest to me that bodies themselves are not properly perceived by the senses nor by the faculty of imagination, but by the intellect alone; and since they are not perceived because they are seen and touched, but only because they are understood [or rightly comprehended by thought], I readily discover that there is nothing more easily or clearly apprehended than my own mind. But because it is difficult to rid one's self so promptly of an opinion to which one has been long accustomed, it will be desirable to tarry for some time at this stage, that, by long continued meditation, I may more deeply impress upon my memory this new knowledge.

JOHN DEWEY
(1859-1952)

Leading American philosopher, was a native of Vermont. He revolted against German idealistic philosophy and repudiated its separation of the individual and the social since both, according to him, are concrete traits and capacities of human beings. His outlook was empirical and pragmatic; his theory of instrumentalism embodied his attack on the traditional concepts of truth. Dewey taught philosophy at Columbia from 1905; he was, for many decades, a leading public figure. He was deeply concerned with democracy, both in attempting to lay its philosophical foundations, and in vigilantly guarding against its violations. He was one of the standard bearers of American progressive education.

Main Works:

Psychology; Outline of Ethics; Studies in Logical Theory; Ethics; How We Think; Influence of Darwin on Philosophy; Democracy and Education; Essays in Experimental Logic; Reconstruction in Philosophy; Human Nature and Conduct; Experience and Nature; The Quest for Certainty; Art as Experience; Logic: Problems of Men.

Truth and Reality

The whole agnostic, positivistic controversy, is flanked by a single move. The issue is not an ideally necessary but actually impossible copying, *versus* an improper but unavoidable mod-

---

From: *The Philosophy of John Dewey*, ed. J. Ratner.

ification of reality through organic inhibitions and stimulations: but it is the right, the economical, the effective, and, if one may venture, the useful and satisfactory reaction *versus* the wasteful, the enslaving, the misleading and the confusing reaction. The presence of organic responses, influencing and modifying every content, every subject-matter of awareness, is the undoubted fact. But the significant thing is the *way* organic behavior enters in—the *way* it influences and modifies.

We assign very different values to different types of "knowledge"—or subject-matters involving organic attitudes and operations. Some are only guesses, opinions, suspicious characters; others are "knowledge" in the honorific and eulogistic sense— science; some turn out mistakes, blunders, errors. Whence and how this discrimination of character in what is taken at its own time to be good knowledge? Why and how is the matter of some "knowledge" genuine-knowing and of other mis-knowing?

Awareness is itself a blanket term, covering, in the same bed, delusion, doubt, confusion, ambiguity, and definition, organization, logical conclusiveness assured by evidence and reason. Any naturalistic or realistic theory is committed to the idea that all of these terms bear impartially the same relation to things considered as sheer existences. What we must have in any case is the same existences—the same kind—only differently arranged or linked up. But why then the tremendous difference in value? And if the unnaturalist, the non-realist, says the difference is one of existential kind, made by the working here malign, there benign of "consciousness," "psychical" operations and states, upon the existences which are the direct subject-matter of knowledge, there is still the problem of discriminating the conditions and nature of the respective beneficent and malicious interventions of the peculiar "existence" labelled consciousness. Of course on the theory I am interested in expounding, the so-called action of "consciousness" means simply the organic releases in the way of behavior which are the conditions of awareness, and which also modify its content.

The realness of error, ambiguity, doubt and guess poses a

problem. It is a problem which has perplexed philosophy so long and has led to so many speculative adventures, that it would seem worth while, were it only for the sake of variety, to listen to the pragmatic solution. It is the business of that organic adaptation involved in all knowing to make a *certain* difference in reality, but *not* to make any old difference, any casual difference. The right, the true, and good difference is that which carries out satisfactorily the specific purpose for the sake of which knowing occurs. All manufactures are the product of an activity, but it does not follow that all manufactures are equally good. And so all "knowledges" are differences made in things by knowing, but some differences are not calculated or wanted in the knowing, and hence are disturbers and interlopers when they come—while others fulfil the intent of the knowing, being in such harmony with the consistent behavior of the organism as to reinforce and enlarge its functioning. A mistake is literally a mishandling; a doubt is temporary suspense and vacillation of reactions; an ambiguity is the tension of alternative but incompatible modes of responsive treatment; an inquiry is a tentative and retrievable (because intra-organic) mode of activity entered upon prior to launching upon a knowledge which is public, ineluctable—without anchors to windward—*because* it has taken physical effect through overt action.

It is practically all one to say that the norm of honorable knowing is to make no difference in *its* object, and that its aim is to attain and buttress a specific kind of difference in reality. Knowing fails in its business if it makes a change in its *own* object—that is a mistake; but its own object is none the less a prior existence changed in a certain way. Nor is this a play upon the two senses—end and subject-matter of "object." The organism has its appropriate functions. To maintain, to expand adequate functioning is its business. This functioning does not occur *in vacuo*. It involves cooperative and readjusted changes in the cosmic medium. Hence the appropriate subject-matter of awareness or consciousness is not reality at large, a metaphysical heaven to be mimeographed at many removes upon a badly constructed mental carbon paper which yields at best only fragmentary, blurred, and erroneous copies. Its proper and legitimate object is that relationship of organism and environment in which functioning is most amply and effectively attained; or by which, in case of obstruction and consequent needed experimentation, its later eventual free course is most facilitated. As for the other reality, metaphysical reality at large, it may, so far as awareness is concerned, go to its own place.

For ordinary purposes, that is, for practical purposes, the truth and the realness of things are synonyms. A reality which is so taken in organic response as to lead to subsequent reactions that are off the track and aside from the mark, while it is, existentially speaking, perfectly real, is not *good* reality. It lacks the hall-mark of value. Since it is a certain *kind* of object which we want, that which will be as favorable as possible to a consistent and liberal or growing functioning, it is this kind, the *true* kind, which for us monopolizes the title of reality. Pragmatically, teleologically, this identification of truth and "reality" is sound and reasonable: rationalistically, it leads to the notion of the duplicate versions of reality, one absolute and static because exhausted; the other phenomenal and kept continually on the jump because otherwise its own inherent nothingness would lead to its total annihilation. Since it is only genuine or sincere things, things which are good for what they pretend to in the way of consequences, that we want or are after, *morally* they alone are "real."

The Correspondence Theory of Truth Is Inadequate

That fruitful thinking—thought that terminates in valid knowledge—goes on in terms of the distinction of facts and judgment, and that valid knowledge is precisely genuine correspondence or agreement, *of some sort,* of fact and judgment, is the common and undeniable assumption. But the discussions are largely carried on in terms of an epistemological dualism, rendering the solution of the problem impossible in virtue of the very terms in which it is stated. The distinction is at once identified with that between mind and matter, consciousness and objects, the psychical and the physical, where each of these terms is supposed to refer to some fixed order of existence, a world in itself. Then, of course, there comes up the question of the nature of the agreement, and of the recognition of it. What is the experience in which the survey of both idea and existence is made and their agreement recognized? Is it an idea? Is the agreement ultimately a matter of self-consistency of ideas? Then what has become of the postulate that truth is agreement of idea with existence beyond idea? Is it an absolute which transcends and absorbs the difference? Then, once more, what is the test of any specific judgment? What has become of the correspondence of fact and thought? Or, more urgently, since the pressing problem of life, of practice and of science, is the discrimination of the *relative*, or *superior*, validity of this or that theory, plan, or interpretation, what is the criterion of truth within present nonabsolutistic experience, where the distinction between factual conditions and thoughts and the necessity of some working adjustment persist?

Putting the problem in yet another way, either both fact and idea are present all the time or else only one of them is present. But if the former, why should there be an idea at all, and why should it have to be tested by the fact? When we already have what we want, namely, existence, reality, why should we take up the wholly supernumerary task of forming more or less imperfect ideas of those facts, and then engage in the idle performance of testing them by what we already know to be? But if only ideas are present, it is idle to speak of comparing an idea with facts and testing its validity by its agreement. The elaboration and refinement of ideas to the uttermost still leaves us with an idea, and while a self-consistent idea stands a show of being true in a way in which an incoherent one does not, a self-consistent idea is still but a hypothesis, a candidate for truth. Ideas are not made true by getting bigger. But if only "facts" are present, the whole conception of agreement is once more given up—not to mention that such a situation is one in which there is by definition no thinking or reflective factor at all.

This suggests that a strictly monistic epistemology, whether idealistic or realistic, does not get rid of the problem. Suppose for example we take a sensationalistic idealism. It does away with the ontological gulf between ideas and facts, and by reducing both terms to a common denominator seems to facilitate fruitful discussion of the problem. But the problem of the distinction and reference (agreement, correspondence) of two types or sorts of sensations still persists. If I say the box there is square, and call "box" one of a group of ideas or sensations and "square" another sensation or "idea," the old question comes up: Is "square" already a part of the "facts" of the box, or is it not? If it is, it is a supernumerary, an idle thing, both as an idea and as an assertion of fact; if it is not, how can we compare the two ideas, and what on earth or in heaven does their agreement or correspondence mean? If it means simply that we experience the two "sensations" in juxtaposition, then the same is true, of course, of any casual association or hallucination. On the sensational basis, accordingly, there is still a distinction of something "given," "there," brutally factual, the box, and something else which stands on a different level, ideal, absent, intended, demanded, the "square," which is asserted to hold good or be true of the thing "box." The fact that both are sensations throws no light on the logical validity of any proposition or belief, because by theory a like statement holds of every possible proposition.

The same problem recurs on a realistic basis. For example, there has recently been propounded the doctrine of the distinction between relations of space and time and relations of meaning or significance, as a key to the problem of knowledge. Things exist in their own characters, in their temporal and spatial relations. When knowledge intervenes, there is nothing new of a subjective or psychical sort, but simply a new relation of the things—the suggesting or signifying of one thing by another. Now this seems to be an excellent way of stating the logical problem, but, I take it, it states and does not solve. For the characteristic of such situations, claiming to terminate in knowledge, is precisely that the meaning-relation is predicated *of* the other relations; it is referred to them; it is not simply a supervention existing side by side with them, like casual suggestions or the play of phantasy. It is something which the facts, the qualitative space and time things, must bear the burden of, must accept and take unto themselves as part of themselves. Until this happens, we have only "thinking," not accomplished knowledge. Hence, logically, the existential relations play the role of fact, and the relation of signification that of idea, distinguished from fact and yet, if valid, to hold *of* fact. In other words, "ideas" is a term capable of assuming any definition which is logically appropriate—say, meaning. It need not have anything to do with the conception of little subjective entities or psychical stuffs.

This appears quite clearly in the following quotation: "It is the ice which means that it will cool the water, just as much as it is the ice which does not cool the water when put into it." There is, however, a possible ambiguity in the statement. That the "ice" (the thing regarded as ice) *suggests* cooling is as real as is a case of actual cooling. But, of course, not every suggestion is valid. The "ice" may be a crystal, and it will not cool water at all. So far as it is already certain that this *is* ice, and also certain that ice, under all circumstances, cools water, the meaning-relation stands on the same level as the physical, being not merely suggested, but part of the facts ascertained. It is not a meaning-relation as such at all. We already have truth; the entire work of knowing as logical is done; we have no longer the relation characteristic of reflective situations. Here again the implication of the thinking situation is of some "correspondence" or "agreement" between two sets of distinguished relations; the problem of valid determination remains the central question of any theory of knowing in its relation to facts and truth.

John Dewey

The Instrumental Theory of Truth

I hope the above statement of the difficulty, however inadequate, will serve at least to indicate that a functional logic inherits the problem in question and does not create it; that it has never for a moment denied the *prima facie* working distinction between "ideas," "thoughts," and "facts," "existences," "the environment," nor the necessity of a control of meaning by facts. It is concerned not with denying, but with understanding. What is denied is not the genuineness of the problem of the terms in which it is stated, but the reality and value of the orthodox interpretation. What is insisted upon is the relative, instrumental, or working character of the distinction—that it *is a logical* distinction, instituted and maintained in the interests of intelligence, with all that intelligence imparts in the exercise of the life functions.

It may prove convenient to take an illustration of a man lost in the woods, taking this case as typical of any reflexive situation in so far as it involves perplexity—a problem to be solved. The problem is to find a correct idea of the way home a practical idea or plan of action which will lead to success, or the realization of the purpose to get home. Now the critics of the experimental theory of logic make the point that this practical idea, the truth of which is evidenced in the successful meeting of a need, is dependent for its success upon a purely presentative idea, that of the existent environment, whose validity has nothing to do with success but depends on agreement with the given state of affairs. It is said that what makes a man's idea of his environment true is its agreement with the actual environment, and "generally a true idea in any situation consists in its agreement with reality." I have already indicated my acceptance of this formula. But it was long my misfortune not to be possessed offhand of those perfectly clear notions of just what is meant in this formula by the terms "idea," "existence," and "agreement" which are possessed by other writers on epistemology; and when I analyzed these notions I found the distinction

301

between the practical idea and the theoretical not fixed nor final, and I found a somewhat startling similarity between the notions of "success" and "agreement."

Just what is the environment of which an idea is to be formed: *i.e.*, what is the intellectual content or objective detail to be assigned to the term "environment"? It can hardly mean the actual visible environment—the trees, rocks, etc., which a man is actually looking at. These things are there and it seems superfluous to form an idea of them; moreover, the wayfaring man, though lost, would have to be an unusually perverse fool if under such circumstances he were unable to form an idea (supposing he chose to engage in this luxury) in agreement with these facts. The environment must be a larger environment than the visible facts; it must include things not within the direct ken of the lost man; it must, for instance, extend from where he is now to his home, or to the point from which he started. It must include unperceived elements in their contrast with the perceived. Otherwise the man would not be lost. Now we are at once struck with the facts that the lost man has no alternative except either to wander aimlessly or else to *conceive* this inclusive environment; and that this conception is just what is meant by idea. It is not some little psychical entity or piece of consciousness-stuff, but is *the interpretation of the locally present environment in reference to its absent portion,* that part to which it is referred as another part so as to give a view of a whole. Just how such an idea would differ from one's plan of action in finding one's way, I do not know. For one's plan (if it really be a plan, a method) is a conception of what is given in its hypothetical relations to what is not given, employed as a guide to that act which results in the absent being also given. It is a map constructed with one's self lost and one's self found, whether at starting or at home again, as its two limits. If this map in its specific character is not also the only guide to the way home, one's only plan of action, then I hope I may never be lost. It is the *practical* facts of being lost and desiring to be found which constitute the limits and the content of the "environment."

Then comes the test of *agreement* of the idea and the environment. Supposing the individual stands still and attempts to compare his idea with the reality, with what reality is he to compare it? Not with the presented reality, for *that* reality is the reality of himself lost; not with the complete reality, for at this stage of proceedings he has only the idea to stand for the complete theory. What kind of comparison is possible or desirable then, save to treat the mental layout of the whole situation as a working hypothesis, as a plan of action, and proceed to *act* upon it, to use it as a director and controller of one's divagations instead of stumbling blindly around until one is either exhausted or accidentally gets out? Now suppose one uses the idea—that is to say, the present facts projected into a whole in the light of absent facts—as a guide of action. Suppose, by means of its specifications, one works one's way along until one comes upon familiar ground—finds one's self. *Now*, one may say, my idea was right, it was in accord with facts; it agrees with reality. That is, acted upon sincerely, it has led to the desired conclusion; it has, *through action,* worked out the state of things which it contemplated or intended. The agreement, correspondence, is between purpose, plan, and its own execution, fulfillment; between a map of a course constructed for the sake of guiding behavior and the result attained in acting upon the indications of the map. Just how does such agreement differ from success?

If we exclude acting upon the idea, no conceivable amount or kind of intellectualistic procedure can confirm or refute an idea, or throw any light upon its validity. How does the non-pragmatic view consider that verification takes place? Does it suppose that we first look a long while at the facts and then a long time at the idea, until by some magical process the degree and kind of their agreement becomes visible? Unless there is some such conception as this, what conception of agreement is possible except the experimental or practical one? And if it be admitted that verification involves action, how can that action be relevant to the truth of an idea, unless the idea is itself already relevant to action? If by acting in accordance with the experimental definition of facts (viz., as obstacles and conditions), and experimental definition of the end or intent (viz., as plan and method of action) a harmonized situation effectually presents itself, we have the adequate and the only conceivable verification of the intellectual factors. If the action indicated be carried out and the disordered or disturbed situation persists, then we have not merely confuted the tentative positions of intelligence, but we have in the very process of acting introduced new data and eliminated some of the old ones, and thus afforded an opportunity for the resurvey of the facts and the revision of the plan of action. By acting faithfully upon an inadequate reflective presentation, we have at least secured the elements for its improvement. This, of course, gives no absolute guaranty that the reflection will at any time be so performed as to prove its validity in fact. But the self-rectification of intellectual content through acting upon it in good faith is the "absolute" of knowledge, loyalty to which is the religion of intellect.

Not infrequently the intellectualist admits that the process of verification is experimental, consisting in setting on foot various activities that express the intent of the idea and confirm or refute it according to the changes effected. This seems to mean that truth is simply the tested or verified belief as such. But then a curious reservation is introduced; the experimental process *finds*, it is said, that an idea is true, while the error of the pragmatist is to take the process by which truth is *found* as one by which it is made. The claim of "making truth" is treated as blasphemy against the very notion of truth: such are the consequences of venturing to translate the Latin "verification" into the English "making true."

If we face the bogie thus called up, it will be found that the horror is largely sentimental. Suppose we stick to the notion that truth is a character which belongs to a meaning so far as tested through action that carries it to successful completion. In this case, to make an idea true is to modify and transform it until it reaches this successful outcome; until it initiates a mode of response which in its issue realizes its claim to be the method of harmonizing the discrepancies of a given situation. The meaning is remade by constantly acting upon it, and by introducing into its content such characters as are indicated by any resulting failures to secure harmony. From this point of view, verification and truth are two names for the same thing. We call it "verification" when we regard it as process; when the development of the idea is strung out and exposed to view in all that makes it true. We call it "truth" when we take it as product, as process telescoped and condensed.

Suppose the idea to be an invention, say of the telephone. In this case, is not the verification of the idea and construction of the device which carries out its intent one and the same? In this case, does the truth of the idea mean anything else than that the issue proves the idea can be carried into effect? There are certain intellectualists who are not of the absolutist type; who do not believe that all of men's aims, designs, projects, that have to do with action, whether industrial, social, or moral in scope, have been from all eternity registered as already accomplished in reality. How do such persons dispose of this problem of the truth of practical ideas?

Is not the truth of *such* ideas an affair of *making* them true by constructing, through appropriate behavior, a condition that satisfies the requirements of the case? If, in this case, truth means the effective capacity of the idea "to make good," what is there in the logic of the case to forbid the application of analogous considerations to any idea?

I hear a noise in the street. It suggests as its meaning a street-car. To test this idea I go to the window and through listening and looking intently—the listening and the looking being modes of behavior—organize into a single situation elements of existence and meaning which were previously disconnected. In this way an idea is made true; that which was a proposal or hypothesis is no longer merely propounding or a guess. If I had not reacted in a way appropriate to the idea it would have remained a mere idea; at most a candidate for truth that, unless acted upon, upon the spot, would always have remained a theory.

Now in such a case—where the end to be accomplished is the discovery of a certain order of facts—would the intellectualist claim that apart from the forming and entertaining of some interpretation, the category of truth has either existence or meaning? Will he claim that without an original practical uneasiness introducing a practical aim of inquiry there must have been, whether or no, an idea? Must the world for some purely intellectual reason be intellectually reduplicated? Could not that occurrence which I now identify as a noisy street-car have retained, so far as pure intelligence is concerned, its unidentified complex of matter-in-motion? Was there any *intellectual* necessity that compelled the event to arouse just this judgment, that it meant a street-car? Was there any physical or metaphysical necessity? Was there any necessity save a need of characterizing it for some purpose of our own? And why should we be mealy-mouthed about calling this need practical? If the necessity which led to the formation and development of an intellectual judgment was purely objective (whether physical or metaphysical) why should not the thing have also to be characterized in countless millions of other ways; for example, as to its distance from some crater in the moon, or its effect upon the circulation of my blood, or upon my irascible neighbor's temper, or bearing upon the Monroe Doctrine? In short, do not intellectual positions and statements mean new and significant events in the treatment of things?

EPICTETUS

(about 60-110 A.D.)

A Greek born in Asia Minor, the son of a slave. He was legally emancipated after being the slave, among others, of the Emperor Nero. Another brutal master crippled him. But he maintained, through all his misfortunes, an exemplary faith in humanity that made him become a model for free men. He taught philosophy in Rome and Greece. Epictetus' philosophy was Stoic and appealed to men suffering from the buffetings of fate. He strongly influenced Marcus Aurelius.

Main Works:

> Discourse; Encheiridion (compiled from his lectures by his disciple Arrian).

Hypothetical Arguments

Most men ignore the fact that the treatment of variable premisses and hypothetical arguments and again of syllogisms that conclude by way of question, and, in a word, of all such arguments is concerned with conduct. For really, whatever subject we are dealing with, our aim is to find how the good man may fitly deal with it and fitly behave towards it. It follows then that either they must say that the virtuous man will not condescend to question and answer, or that if he does he will take no care to avoid behaving lightly and at random in questioning and answering; or else, if they accept neither alternative, they must admit that we have to investigate those subjects round which

------

From: *Discourses of Epictetus.*

question and answer chiefly turn. For what do we promise in a discussion? To establish what is true, to remove what is false, to withhold assent in what is uncertain. Is it enough then merely to learn that this is so?

"It is enough."

Is it enough then for him who wishes not to go wrong in the use of coin merely to be told why you accept genuine drachmas and reject spurious ones?

"It is not enough."

What then must you acquire besides? Surely you must have a faculty to test and distinguish genuine drachmas from spurious. Is it not true then in regard to argument also that merely to hear what is said is not enough; a man must acquire the faculty to test and distinguish the true from the false and the uncertain?

"It must be so."

This being so, what is required in argument?

"Accept what follows from the premisses you have duly granted."

Here again, is it enough merely to know this? No, you must learn how a conclusion follows from the premisses, and how sometimes one proposition follows from one other, and sometimes from many together. May we say then that this faculty too must be acquired by him who is to behave with good sense in discussion, and who is himself to prove each point in his demonstrations of others, and to avoid being led astray by sophistical arguments, posing as demonstrations? Thus it comes about that we are led to think it really necessary to discuss and to practise the arguments and moods which are conclusive.

But note this: there are cases where we have granted the premisses properly, and such and such a conclusion follows which, though it follows, is none the less false. What then is it fitting for me to do? Must I accept the false conclusions? How can I do that? Must I say that I was wrong in granting the premisses?

"No, you may not do this either."

That it does not follow from the premisses granted?
"No, you may not do this."

What then is one to do in these circumstances? May we not
say that just as in order to be in debt it is not enough merely
to borrow, but one must remain a borrower and not have paid
off the loan, so in order to be bound to admit an inference it is
not enough to have granted the premisses, but one must abide
by having granted them?

In a word, if they remain to the end as we granted them, we
are absolutely bound to remain by our concessions and accept
what follows the premisses; if, on the other hand, they do not
remain as they were granted, we are also absolutely bound to
abandon the concession and no longer to accept what is inconsistent with the premisses; for since we have abandoned our
agreement as to the premisses, this inference which is drawn
no longer concerns us or touches us. We must then examine into
premisses of this sort and into such changes and alterations in
them, by which they are changed in the actual process of question or answer or syllogism or the like, and so afford occasion
to the foolish to be troubled because they do not see the sequence of the argument. Why must we do so? That in this
sphere we may do what is fitting by avoiding what is random
or confused in argument.

And we ought to do the same with hypotheses and hypothetical arguments. For it is necessary sometimes to assume a hypothesis as a step to the next argument. Must we then concede
every given hypothesis or not? And if not every one, which?
And, having conceded it, must we abide by it once for all and
maintain it, or are we sometimes to abandon it, and are we to
accept what follows from it and reject what conflicts with it?
"Yes."

But a man says, "If you accept a hypothesis of what is possible, I will reduce you in argument to what is impossible."

Will the prudent man refuse to meet him in argument, and
avoid examination and discussion with him? Nay, it is just the
prudent man who is capable of reasoning logically and who is

expert at questioning and answering, yes and who is proof against deception and sophistry. Will he then consent to argue, but take no pains to avoid being careless and casual in argument? If so, will he not cease to be the man we consider him to be? But without some such training and preparation as I suggest can he guard the sequence of his argument? Let them show that he can, and then all these speculations are idle; they were absurd and inconsistent with the conception we have formed of the good man.

Why do we persist in being lazy and indolent and sluggish, why do we seek excuses to enable us to avoid toiling early and late to perfect ourselves in logical theory?

"Do you call it parricide if I go wrong in logic?"

Slave, here is no father for you to kill. You ask what you have done; you have committed the one error which was possible in this field. Your answer is the very one I made myself to Rufus when he rebuked me because I could not find the one missing step in a syllogism. "Well," said I, "suppose I have not burnt the Capitol down"; and he answered, "Slave, the missing step here is the Capitol."

You are not going to tell me, are you, that setting fire to the Capitol and killing one's father are the only forms of wrongdoing? To deal with one's impressions without thought or method, to fail to follow argument or demonstration or sophism, in a word, to be unable to see what concerns himself and what does not in question and answer—is there no wrongdoing, I ask, in any of these?

EUCLID

(about 335-275 B.C.)

A Greek from Egypt who gave mathematics the form that it maintained until the 19th century, when "non-Euclidian" systems were first developed. He also established standards of scientific exactitude that are still valid. His chief interest lay in geometry.

Main Work:
    Stoicheia (Elements).

The First Elements

A point is that which has no part.
A line is breadthless length.
The extremities of a line are points.
A straight line is a line which lies evenly with the points on itself.
A surface is that which has length and breadth only.
The extremities of a surface are lines.
A plane surface is a surface which lies evenly with the straight lines on itself.
A plane angle is the inclination to one another of two lines in a plane which meet one another and do not lie in a straight line.
And when the lines containing the angle are straight, the angle is called rectilineal.

From: *Stoicheia.*

When a straight line set up on a straight line makes the adjacent angles to one another, each of the equal angles is right, and the straight line standing on the other is called a perpendicular to that on which it stands.

An obtuse angle is an angle greater than a right angle.

An acute angle is an angle less than a right angle.

A boundary is that which is an extremity of anything.

A figure is that which is contained by any boundary or boundaries.

A circle is a plane figure contained by one line such that all the straight lines falling upon it from one point among those lying within the figure are equal to one another.

And the point is called the center of the circle.

A diameter of the circle is any straight line drawn through the center and terminated in both directions by the circumference of the circle, and such a straight line also bisects the circle.

A semicircle is the figure contained by the diameter and circumference cut off by it. And the center of the semicircle is the same as that of the circle.

Rectilineal figures are those which are contained by straight lines, trilateral figures being those contained by three, quadrilateral those contained by four, and multilateral those contained by more than four straight lines.

Of trilateral figures, an equilateral triangle is that which has its three sides equal, an isosceles triangle that which has two of its sides alone equal, and a scalene triangle that which has its three sides unequal.

Further, of trilateral figures, a right-angled triangle is that which has a right angle, an obtuse-angled triangle that which has an obtuse angle, and an acute-angled triangle that which has its three angles acute.

Of quadrilateral figures, a square is that which is both equilateral and right-angled; an oblong that which is right-angled but not equilateral; a rhombus that which is equilateral but not right-angled; and a rhomboid that which has its opposite sides and angles equal to one another but is neither equilateral nor right-angled. And let quadrilaterals other than these be called trapezia.

Parallel straight lines are straight lines which, being in the same plane and being produced indefinitely in both directions, do not meet one another in either direction.

POSTULATES

Let the following be postulated:

To draw a straight line from any point to any point.

To produce a finite straight line continuously in a straight line.

To describe a circle with any center and distance.

That all right angles are equal to one another.

That, if a straight line falling on two straight lines make the interior angles on the same side less than two right angles, the two straight lines if produced indefinitely, meet on that side on which are the angles less than the two right angles.

COMMON NOTIONS

Things which are equal to the same thing are also equal to one another.

If equals be added to equals, the wholes are equal.

If equals be subtracted from equals, the remainders are equal.

Things which coincide with one another are equal to one another.

The whole is greater than the parts.

PEDRO FONSECA
(1528-1599)

Portuguese humanist, born at Cortizada and died in Lisbon. Taught philosophy at the University of Coimbra from 1552. Edited and commented on the works of Aristotle.

Main Works:
> Institutionum dialecticarum libri octo; Isagoge Philosophica.

Status, Time and Appellations

To begin with status, it should be observed: That the first four affections are affections of suppositions rather than of nouns. For we say with more truth that suppositions rather than nouns have status or are amplified, and so on. However, as affections of suppositions extend to nouns and either expression is used by logicians, which term we use in the course of our exposition is of slight importance.

With reference to status, it should be said that nouns acquire a status of their denotation when they are adequately understood to stand for those things that exist in a time signified through the principal copula of the proposition. For example: A man sitting is debating. Each term is taken as standing for present things only in respect of the difference of the copula. The same assertion must be made about the terms of this proposition: A sitting man debates, because it matters very little

---

From: *Institutionum dialecticarum libri.*

whether the copula is expressed explicitly, as in the former proposition, or implicitly, as in the latter proposition. I said: *Through* the *principal copula* (in as much as it connects the predicate of the proposition with the subject), because the principal copula, of whatever kind, that is included in the subject of the proposition: A sitting man is different from one standing, does not make the proposition affirmative or negative, nor should it be taken as a norm or a rule of this type of affirmation.

The status of nouns is triple, namely: the present, the past, and the future, with reference to the three distinctions in time, that can be signified by the principal verb in the proposition. The first status is observed in the terms of this proposition: A sitting man debates. The second status occurs in the terms of this proposition: The man who was sitting was debating. The third status occurs in the term of this one: The man who sits will debate. The evidences for discovering this kind of affection of nouns or categories can be posited as two in number. Let the first evidence be: Every verb that is neither restricted nor amplified, nor distributed, has a status according to the tense of the principal copula, as when one says: A man is sitting. A man sat. A man will sit. The verb *sits* will be adequately understood for those who are now sitting: *sat* for those who sat: *will sit,* for those who will sit. By the name of the verb we must here understand the verb properly so called, as distinguished from the noun. What is said of the verb must also be understood of those expressions that are attached to verbs, provided they signify a proper action, or the passivity of the verbs, or follow such action or passivity, as though one were to say: The grammarian talks in order to correct speech. Wood experiences heat, and such like expressions. There is alteration in regard to other additions, as when one says: The historian writes about the past. The philosopher discusses thunder. But this evidence, to be correctly judged, requires a knowledge of amplification, restriction, and distribution. The second evidence: Every subject of an affirmative proposition and in the present tense,

whose predicate cannot suit the subject unless the existence of
the subject is denoted, has a status in the present tense, as when
one says: Every man is white. The subject is adequately taken
for all men and men only, who now exist, since if only these
were white the proposition would unquestionably be granted:
which would be impossible, if the predicate did not denote the
existence as in these propositions: Every man is an animal. Every
man is, and the like: which must be explained a little later on.

For a further knowledge, however, of those matters that have
been stated and will be stated in due course, careful attention
must be paid to this point, that there must be one explanation
for the existence of status, amplification and the other two affections in absolute nouns, and another explanation in the case
of connected nouns. For consider the two following propositions: A man debates. A logician debates. Thus we shall explain
the status of the first subject: A man who exists, debates. Similarly with these two propositions: A man debated. A logician
debated. The amplification of the word *man* will have to be
explained as follows: A man who exists, or who existed, debated.
The logician explains it thus: The man who is, or was, a logician debated. And similarly in other cases. So, in making the
explanation, the absolute noun must become the subject of the
verb itself: *is* or *was*, etc., while the connotative noun is predicated by the interposition of the verb *is* or *was*, etc., of the relative pronoun of the connoted thing.

With regard to amplification it must be stated that the nouns
or categories are amplified when they are taken to denote other
things than are contained in the difference of time signified
through the principal copula of the proposition. On this account
we say that the subject of this proposition is amplified: The
sitting man stood up, because a distinction is understood in the
case of those who are now sitting, or sat, as Aristotle asserts.
For the meaning is: The man who is sitting or was sitting, stood
up. Now it seems that amplification is quadruple: First, with
reference to the present and the past, as appears in the example
given. Secondly, with reference to the present and the future,

as is seen in the subject of this proposition: The man who is living or will live, will die. Thirdly, with reference to the past and the future, as one may observe in the subjects of these propositions: A man who is born will die. A man will die who was born. The sense of the first proposition is: A man who was born or is now born or will still be born, will die. By reason of any one of these explanations the proposition could be true. The sense of the last one is this: The man who will die or is dying, now or will presently die, was born. Fourthly, with reference to the present, the past, the future, and those notions whose existence cannot be refuted, although they never were, nor are, nor will be, that are called possible, as terms of the following proposition are understood: Every man is an animal. The sense is: Every man who is, or was, or will be, or can otherwise be, is an animal that was, or is, or will be, or certainly can be. Certain other writers add to the past, the future possible and the imaginable present, that is, things that can exist only in the mind. In this sense, they say, is the noun Monster understood. Their proposition is: A man imaginatively is a Monster. But this does not seem to me necessary. For the term *Monster,* in the above proposition, is not understood as a fictitious monster, but as a real monster, that we yet so predicate of a man that we do not say a man is a real monster, which would be false, but a man is imagined as a real monster, or is imaginatively a real monster. Thus the names of real things that do not depend on the operation of the mind do not appear to be amplified in relation to fictitious things: which they do not really signify, but only to possible things. Now with respect to the names of fictitious things, and other things whose existence is nothing but what is presented mentally, our statement must be relative to our assertion regarding nouns signifying real things. For there is only this difference, that *being, to have been going to be,* and *to be able to be,* are not to be taken for *being, having been,* and other notions in the nature of things (that are called *a parte rei*), but for that which is presented to the understanding, has been so presented, will necessarily be presented, and can be presented. Again, in all amplifications it should be observed that the noun, which is amply understood, is always understood disjunctively with respect to those differences *being, having been, going to be,* and *can be,* whether the amplification extends to all things or to three or two, as one may deduce from the examples given. I say: *With respect to those differences,* because with respect to the things for which it is understood, it can be understood in a far different sense, as copulatively, disjunctively, and in other ways, as is evident from what has been said.

To understand which nouns are amplified and the manner, a great number of extremely useful evidences can be adduced. First: Every noun that gives denotation to an adjectival verb in the past tense is amply taken to stand for past nouns and present. Examples are: A temple was built. Adam died. Every old man was a boy. The sense of the first proposition is: A temple that was, or is, was built. The second: Adam, who perhaps is now (in as much as he was raised from the dead with Christ), or at least was at some time, died, or suffered burial. The third: Every man who is or was an old man was a boy. The elements of grammar teach that the noun adds a denotation to the verb. I said: To an adjectival *verb,* because for the verb *to be,* which is called a substantive, there is another explanation. If one were to say: Every man was, the noun *man* will not be understood only for past men and present men, as we shall state a little later. The same thing will be said of things denoted or subjects of predicates having the sense of the adjectival verb in the past tense, on account of the verb: because there is no difference between saying *The man was white* and *The man became white* and *The old man was young* and *The old man was a youth.* The fact is that the subjects are amplified correspondingly in the first propositions and in the second. By the same reasoning, if an adjectival verb is understood as a signification of a substantive, it will not be necessary for the subject to be understood for past things and present only. It is as if one said: Every man has lived, and so on. It is the same as with their denotations and the denotation of the adjectival verb. One point however must be added to this evidence. Those items must be eliminated that can be a hindrance, as status, distribution, restriction, and whatever else there may be. This moderation must be applied to other evidences as well.

Second: Every noun that gives denotation to an adjectival verb in the future tense is amply taken to denote the future and the present. Examples: A temple will be built. Walls will collapse. Every man will die. The sense of the first proposition is: A temple, which is, or will be, will be built, and so on. By means of these two evidences one will explain many true propositions that at first sight appear false, as: The boy grew old. The man will grow up. That these propositions are true you will understand from these propositions: The old man was a boy. The youth will be a man, that are converted into the former propositions. Then too if one infers in the subjects other nouns, as follows: The boy Isaac grew old. The wicked man, the Antichrist, will grow up; statements that contain a clear truth, there will then be no ambiguity, if, according to the first evidence, one explains the first proposition thus: The person who is or was a boy, grew old. The next proposition, according to the second evidence: The person who is or will be a man, will grow up. There are many other propositions, whose obscure and hidden truth is revealed by these evidences.

Thirdly: Every name of a thing that is said to begin to be is amply understood to stand for the present and the future, while the name of a thing that is said to cease being is amply understood to represent the present and the past. Examples are: This boy's soul is now beginning to be. The motion of this stone now begins. This man now ceases to be. The motion of this stone ceases. The first proposition is understood thus: This boy's soul, that is now for the first time and will be very presently, now begins to be. The second proposition: The motion of this stone, that is now first moved, or will be very shortly, now begins. The third proposition: This man, who is now at last, or

319

was just recently, now ceases to be. The fourth proposition: The motion of this stone, that has now finally been moved, or was a very short while ago, now ceases.

Fourthly: When a statement asserts that something is or was anteriorly to something else that is called the name of the thing posteriorly, it is amply understood for all the things that are or were in the temporal difference for significations by the verb, and in future instances. When it asserts that something is or will be posteriorly to something else that is called the name of the thing anteriorly, it is amply understood for all things that are or will be in a temporal difference for significations through the verb in previous instances. For example: Lutherans are anterior to Antichristians. By this name we must understand those who are or were followers of Antichrist. If one says: The Pelagians were anterior to the Lutherans, we must understand by this term those who were or are or will be Lutherans. But if one says: The Lutherans are posterior to the Pelagians, this word must be understood for those who are or were Pelagians. If one says: The Antichristians will be posterior to the Lutherans, this term must be understood for those who will be, or are, or were Lutherans.

Fifthly: The words of necessary propositions, unless there is some obstruction, are understood in the widest sense, that is, for all things, even possible things, that they signify. For instance: Man is an animal. Man is not a stone. The expression is usually the same in the case of terms of impossible propositions, as: Man is a stone. Man is not an animal. But if one says: A man, who is, is an animal, the noun *man* will be understood only for men who are. The addition *who is* does not prevent amplification. If one says: Man is a rational animal, the word *animal* is not extended to living beasts too, as it was in the proposition: Man is an animal (although it was extended disjunctively), because it is restricted by the word *rational*.

Sixthly: When the substantive verb or another that has the same value is predicated absolutely of the subject, then the subject is amplified to possibilities. For this reason the following propositions are rejected: Every man is. Every man was. Every man will be. This propostion too can be denied: Every man was, or is, or will be, since many men can be who have neither been, nor are, nor will ever be. This evidence however does not conflict with the latter evidence of status, because in it there was a statement about predicates that, to fit the subjects, do not denote the existence of the subjects, although they signify it.

In the seventh place: The subjects of negative propositions are amplified to possibilities also, as when one says: A certain man is not sitting. That the negative subject of this proposition is understood for the past also, and the future, and possibilities, I grant. I take the noun Nero, who was, and is no longer, and the noun *Antichrist*, who is still to be, and also the noun *a certain possible man*, who neither was, nor is, nor will be, because he is called, say, John. Will it not be false for you to affirm of any of them that he is sitting? Manifestly false. Therefore you will be correct in saying that he is not sitting. Since then a particular is validly inferred from any singular proposition, the proposition is true: A certain man is not sitting, even if there is none of the men among those now existing, who is not sitting. Its subject therefore is understood not only for those men now existing, but also for all who existed, will exist, and can exist even if they never will exist. But if any objection is raised that in this way there will be two contradictions true at the same time, namely: Every man is sitting, which (as is clear from the second evidence of status) is true if one posits that all men who exist now, are sitting, and similarly this proposition: A certain man is not sitting, as was proved, you will find, after assuming the hypothesis that we mentioned, that they are both true and that they are not contradictory. For the subject of the negative proposition is extended more widely than the subject of the affirmative proposition. Therefore, in order for them to be contradictory, the subject of the negative proposition must necessarily be restricted to all men who now exist, for whom the subject of the affirmative is adequately understood.

In regard to distraction, it should be stated that the noun or the categorema is distracted, when it is taken for those things only that are in some difference of time, different from that which is signified through the principal copula of the proposition, as when one says: The man who stood up, is standing. The subject of this proposition is understood for the man only, who stood up in the past tense, although the principal copula of the proposition signifies the present tense. For the postulated proposition is equally valid as if one says: The man who was getting up is standing.

Distraction can be divided into six species, so to speak. If the principal copula of the proposition signifies the present tense, distraction can occur either by reason of the past tense or by reason of the future tense, as though one were to say: He who has learned, teaches. He who will die is born. The subject of the first proposition is understood only for him who has learned: the subject of the second proposition, only for him who will die: since the principal copula of each proposition signifies the present tense.

But if the principal copula signifies the past tense, distraction can occur either by reason of the present or by reason of the future tense, as when one says: The man who teaches, has learned. The man who will die was born. If, lastly, it signifies the future tense, distraction can occur either by reason of the present or by reason of the past tense, as when one says: The man who is living will die. The man who was born will die. Hence there are as it were six species of distraction, as is evident in the subjects of the postulated propositions. Therefore this too must be observed, although no expression is usually distracted by the dialecticians, except by reason of some difference of tense included in the verb that is not the principal one, or in some participle, as may be learned from the examples given: however, in the Gospels the opposite occurs, as when the Lord says: The blind see: the lame walk: the deaf hear. The meaning is: Those who were blind, see. Those who were lame, walk. Those who were deaf, hear, although in these propositions there is no secondary verb or participle that makes the subjects understood for the past tense, nor are there predicates amplificative, as it were, to the past tense, as is evident. Therefore these locutions are used because they are connotative: *blind, lame, deaf* are taken as participles in the past tense, as though the expression were: Those who were previously deprived of the faculty of sight see, and so for the rest.

Restriction of nouns occurs when their status or amplification or distraction is contracted to a smaller compass by the addition of some word, as when one says: Sitting in a chair he talks. The expression *in a chair* restricts the status of the participle sitting to those only who are sitting in a chair. Now observe that restriction sometimes occurs by the addition of an oblique case or with a preposition, as in the example given, or without a preposition, as: The man's face watches the sky. Sometimes an adjectival noun is added, as: Aristotle was a very distinguished philosopher. Sometimes, the apposition of a substantive, as: The apostle Peter was the first vicar of Christ. Occasionally, an adverbial adjunct, as: Plato debated very cleverly. At times, an expression is interposed, as: All natural things, that are produced, perish. An expression interposed, consisting of a relative pronoun and the verb *to be*, is called by more recent authorities by a special name, a copula of implication, as: Every man who is, will die. Two points, however, should here be noted. The first is, that a word or an expression that is placed at one end, does not restrict the other end, but only the word that is at the same end. For example: this word *rational*, in this proposition: Man is a rational animal, does not restrict the word *man*, which is the subject, but the word *animal* that is contained in the same predicate along with it, and so with the rest. The second is, that no restriction occurs, when a word is added that makes the noun that was properly understood, understood improperly. For example: If one adds to the noun *man* in this proposition: A man is in the hall, then the word *depicted*, and says: A man is depicted in the hall. Or in the proposition: A man is lying in the street, one adds the word *dead* and says: A man is lying dead in the street, one does not restrict the denotation of the noun but changes it into an improper one. For what is completely removed is neither amplified nor restricted. Therefore by such addition denotation is not restricted but alienated, as more recent writers assert. These are simple illustrations that require no evidence. If anyone is inspired by a greater concern about the number of genera of restriction, and species, or quasi-species, he can be answered by an explanation of restriction itself. Restriction is three-fold in genus: one, of status, one of amplification, and the third of distraction. The species of restriction are as many as there are status, amplifications, and distractions, that is, thirteen. One may find examples of all these in the subjects of the following propositions: Sitting in a chair he talks. The man who was sitting in a chair was talking. The man who will sit in a chair will talk. These are examples of restriction of status. Examples of restriction of amplification are as follows: Sitting in a chair, he stood up. Living happily, he will die. He was born, destined to die in battle. A man who exists, is an animal. Lastly, examples of restrictions of distraction: The man who has learned diligently, teaches. The man who will die tomorrow, is born. The man who teaches philosophy, learned. The old man who will die, was born. The man who lives unconcernedly will sometime have fear. So much for restriction. It remains to speak of appellation.

The term *appellation* is variously used by dialecticians. Those who employ the term more properly and in a more acceptable sense understand by this term denomination, whereby one expression denominates another. For example, if one says: Socrates is a good lute-player, the term *good* is said to name the term *lute-player*, not the term *Socrates*, because it denominates the former, not the latter. For the sense is not: Socrates is good and a lute-player, but he is trained in playing the lute and singing. Aristotle frequently mentions this mutual affection of words as matters not to be ignored or disdained: for example, in his treatises *On Interpretation* and *Elenchi*, but he nowhere names them specifically, just as he does not name previous affections of nouns. Thus the thing itself is old, the word, new. Appellation then is the denomination whereby one word designates another, and denomination is appellation. A denominating word is called appellative. Two distinctions however should be noted between an appellative word and the word denominated. One is, an appellative word is always an adjective, or like an adjective. A denominated word is a substantive, or like a substantive. An example has been given of adjectives, or like substantives, here are examples: Socrates is remarkably learned. Socrates is moderately learned. If the adverbs *remarkably* and *moderately* are adjectival, the word *learned* is not adjectival but the first two words, because they denominate, are quasi-adjectives: but *learned,* being denominated, is a quasi-substantive. The other distinction is, that the appellative word must always be understood in accordance with the formally signified expression: while the denominated word is sometimes taken formally, as in the examples given, sometimes materially, as when one says: This lute-player is good. The sense is not that he is an expert in playing and singing but that he is a good man, or endowed with virtue. I know that among some writers denomination, whereby a word is denominated according to a material signification, is not called appellation. But there is no reason for such a rigid statement that a denomination of this kind should not be a nominating appellation. Another reason lies in the denominating word. For if it is taken according to the material signification, it will certainly take the place of denomination: a kind of trivial and petty repetition of the same thing, as when we say: Socrates is an honest man. The sense is: Socrates is a man. From these statements therefore a double appellation can be deduced: one, whereby a word is denominated according to its formal signification: the other according to the material signification.

Appellation is usually also divided into real and rational. Real appellation occurs, when a word that is appellative signifies a real being, as in the examples already given. Appellation is called rational, when an appellative word signifies a rational being, as when one says: Man is a species. Nor is it strange that in the example of the adjectival or quasi-adjectival word I mention the noun *species,* which is a substantive. For every connotative word, of the type whose name is a species, is called by comparison with the connoted noun or rather the connoted object, a quasi-adjective.

Finally, for the recognition of the appellation of nouns, consider these three types of evidence. First: The adjectival or the quasi-adjectival noun, that is predicated of some subject having a material signification, gives appellation to the material signification of the subject, unless it signifies an accident of reason. For example: This lute-player is good. A man is sitting. Christ always was. For the predicate of the first proposition gives appellation to the man who is a lute-player, not to the lute-player qua lute-player. The predicate of the second proposition gives appellation to some man among individual men, not to any man: individual men, although they are not properly called material significations of the word *man,* yet since they are mediate significations, can in some sense be called material significations. The predicate of the third proposition too gives appellation to the divine word, that is in some sense a material signification of the name *Christ,* and not to God incarnate, which is his formal signification. Hence it is that we deny the proposition *Christ was created,* because it signifies that the participle of appellation *created* is taken away and the divine word was created. I stated: Unless it signifies an accident of reason, because such predicates are called formal and immediate significations of the subjects, provided there is no obstruction. It is as if one said: Man is a species. Man is predicated of many. For by these predicates man in general and in the abstract, not some man among particular men, is called and denominated. Hence it is that we deny the propositions: Animal is the lowest species. Man is an individual Something, because the former signifies that animal is the lowest species common to man and beast, while the latter signifies it is something particular common to all particular men. I added: Provided there is no obstruction, because appellation of this kind can be obstructed in many ways. For example, if one says: This man is a species. Every animal is a genus, the words *This* and *Every* will make the nouns *man* and *animal* not denominated according to formal and immediate significations, but according to mediate significations, which are here considered to be material. Hence it is that the propositions are false.

Secondly: The adjective or quasi-adjective that is placed before the substantive or quasi-substantive at the same end of the proposition acquires its formal signification, as when one says: This man is a good lute-player. Christ was made man. The sense of the first proposition is: This man is good according to the art of playing on the lute and singing. The sense of the second proposition is: Christ was made according to the nature of man, that he assumed. It will therefore not be correct to conclude thus: This lute-player is good. Therefore he is a good lute-player. Nor the contrary: He is a good lute-player. Therefore he is good. Nor thus: He was not made. Therefore he was not made man: because the appellation is changed. I stated: Before its substantive, for if the substantive is placed before the adjective, often the adjective will not give formal but material signification of the substantive. For the proposition: Christ was made man, is denied according to the meaning of the words for no other reason than that the word *made* seems to give appellation to the material signification of the word *man*, which is a divine word, and that the word *made* is placed after the word *man*. But if anyone should object that the words according to the Nicene Creed: *Et homo factus est*, in which the word *made* is placed after the word *man*, one can reply: These words were not arranged in the form of a proposition but should be so arranged: *Et est factus homo*. Or: *Et factus est homo*. Although this may be said, that this rule, regarding the order of words, is not always but generally observed.

Thirdly: Words signifying a mental act of comprehension and acquisition give appellation to the formal signification of those things in which they are placed, as when one says: I know that he is coming. I want something sweet. The meaning is: I know that he is coming. I want something sweet, qua sweet, although the substance of the sweet object does not affect me: provided the word signifying a mental act of this kind precedes the one in which it is placed, as in the examples given. For if one says: I know that he is coming. I want something sweet, these words give appellation to the material signification of the preceding words. The sense will be: I know the man who is coming, even if I do not at all perceive his coming. I want a thing, which is sweet, although I do not want it for the reason of its sweetness. Hence they say that this form of argument is defective: I know his coming: therefore I know that he is coming. Similarly, I want sweetness: therefore I want a sweet thing, and vice versa. But this condition appears to be disregarded more often in this type of evidence than in the former type. Even the first condition is again and again ignored. This could easily be illustrated by examples, if I did not appear to expatiate too much on such points. However, the latter evidences are to a large extent true and far from useless, especially in theological disputations, and the former type should not be disdained by dialecticians.

Let this suffice for supposition and the other affections of nouns. How useful they are in solving sophistic problems and in understanding more clearly those contained in this treatise, will be realized by anyone who has studied them. Therefore, since all that was promised at the beginning has been elucidated, there is nothing more for me to say.

GOTTLOB FREGE
(1848-1925)

German mathematician. More than any one else he contributed to the interpretation of basic mathematical concepts in terms of the fundamental concepts of logic which operate with exact determinations right from the start. His influence on mathematical logic has been felt mainly through Bertrand Russell who extensively used Frege in his *Principia Mathematica.*

Main Works:

Die Grundlagen der Arithmetik; Grundgesetze der Arithmetik; Begriffsschrift.

Definitions

1

A definition of a concept (of a possible predicate) must be complete; it must unambiguously determine, as regards any object, whether or not it falls under the concept (whether or not the predicate is truly assertible of it). Thus there must not be any object as regards which the definition leaves in doubt whether it falls under the concept; though for us men, with our defective knowledge, the question may not always be decidable. We may express this metaphorically as follows; the concept must have a sharp boundary. If we represent concepts in extension by areas on a plane, this is admittedly a picture that may be used only with caution, but here it can do us good service. To

---

From: *Die Grundlagen der Arithmetik.*

a concept without a sharp boundary there would correspond an area that had not a sharp boundary-line all round, but in places just vaguely faded away in to the background. This would not really be an area at all; and likewise a concept that is not sharply defined is wrongly termed a concept. Such quasi-conceptual constructions cannot be recognized as concepts by logic; it is impossible to lay down precise laws for them. The law of excluded middle is really just another form of the requirement that the concept should have a sharp boundary. Any object Δ that you choose to take either falls under the concept φ or does not fall under it; *tertium non datur.* E.g. would the sentence "any square root of 9 is odd" have a comprehensible sense at all if *square root of 9* were not a concept with a sharp boundary? Has the question "Are we still Christians?" really got a sense, if it is indeterminate whom the predicate "Christian" can truly be asserted of, and who must be refused it?

2

Now from this it follows that the mathematicians' favorite procedure, piecemeal definition, is inadmissible. The procedure is this: First they give the definition for a particular case—e.g. for positive integers—and make use of it; then, many theorems later, there follows a second definition for another case—e.g. for negative integers and zero—; here they often commit the further mistake of making specifications all over again for the case they have already dealt with. Even if in fact they avoid contradictions, in principle their method does not rule them out. What is more, as a rule they do not attain to completeness, but leave over some cases, as to which they make no specification; and many are naive enough to employ the word or symbol for these cases too, as if they had given it something to stand for. Such piecemeal definition is a procedure comparable to drawing the boundary of a part of a surface in bits, perhaps without making them join up. But the chief mistake is that they are already using the symbol or word for theorems before it has been completely defined—often, indeed, with a view to further development of the definition itself. So long as it is not completely defined, or known in some other way, what a word or symbol stands for, it may not be used in an exact science—least of all with a view to further development of its own definition.

3

Now, of course, it must be admitted that scientific progress, which has been effected by conquering wider and wider domains of numbers, made such a procedure almost inevitably necessary; and this necessity might serve as an excuse. It would indeed have been possible to replace the old symbols and terms by new ones, and logic really demands this; but that is a hard decision to make. And this horror over the introduction of new symbols or words is the cause of many obscurities in mathematics. The old definitions likewise could have been rejected as invalid, and new ones used, in order to set up the science over again from the beginning; but such a clean cut was never made, because the old definitions were believed indispensable for the beginnings of the science. Didactic requirements may also have made themselves heard in this connection. In this way people have got used to piecemeal definition; and what was originally an awkward makeshift became customary, and was admitted as one of the legitimate methods of science. The result is that nowadays hardly anybody is shocked when a symbol is first defined for a limited domain and then used in order to define the same symbol once more for a wider domain; for general custom has a power of justifying what is done, just as fashion can give the cachet of beauty to the most detestable mode. It is all the more necessary to emphasize that logic cannot recognize as concepts quasi-conceptual constructions that are still fluid and have not yet been given definite and sharp boundaries, and that therefore logic must reject all piecemeal definition. For if the first definition is already complete and has drawn sharp boundaries, then either the second definition draws the same boundaries—

and then it must be rejected, because its content ought to be proved as a theorem—or it draws different ones—and then it contradicts the first one. For example, we may define a conic section as the intersection of a plane with a conical surface of rotation. When once we have done this, we may not define it over again, e.g. as a curve whose equation in Cartesian co-ordinates is of the second degree; for now that has to be proved. Likewise we cannot now define it as a plane figure whose equation in linear co-ordinates is of the second degree; for that would also include the point-pair, which cannot be regarded as the intersection of a plane and a conic surface. Here, then, the boundaries of the concept is not drawn in the same way, and it would be a mistake to use here the same term "conic section." If the second definition is not ruled out by the first one in either of these ways, that is possible only because the first one is incomplete and has left the concept unfinished, i.e. in a condition in which it may not be employed at all—in particular, not for definitions.

4

It will be not unprofitable to give an example, so as to counterbalance the abstractness of these remarks. E. Heine sets up the following definition.

"Number-signs are called equal or interchangeable when they belong to equal series of numbers, and unequal or non-interchangeable when they belong to unequal series.

What would people say to the following definition?

"Signs are called white when they belong to white objects." Now I may legitimately take, as a sign for the white sheet of paper that I have before me, a circular black patch, so long as I have not already employed this sign in some other way. And such a patch would now be white by definition. As against this, we must say: In using the expression "if they belong to white objects," the definition presupposes that we know what the word "white" stands for; for otherwise it would be wholly unspecified what signs belong to white objects. Very well! If the word "white" is known, we cannot want to define it over again. We ought to regard it as quite self-evident that a word may not be defined by means of itself; for if we do that we are in one breath treating the word as known and as unknown. If it is known, a definition is at least superfluous; if it is not known, it cannot serve for the purpose of definition. This is obvious, and yet people sin against it so often! We get the same case for Heine's definition. The use of the words "if they belong to equal series of numbers" presupposes that we know what the word "equal" stands for, and this is the very word that is to be defined.

5

Heine would probably remark in answer to this that he is not presupposing that we know what the word "equal" stands for in all cases; in his Def. 3, § 1, its reference is supposed already given only for unbracketed number-series, whereas here he is speaking of bracketed number-series and other symbols. Besides the reasons against this procedure given above, it may be added that double definition of a word is objectionable because then we are left in doubt whether the definitions do not contradict each other. People ought at least to ask for a proof that there is no contradiction; but this duty is regularly evaded, and indeed in Heine there is not to be found a trace of such a proof. In general, we must reject a way of defining that makes the correctness of a definition depend on our having first to carry out a proof; for this makes it extraordinarily difficult to check the rigor of the deduction, since it is necessary to inquire, as regards each definition, whether any propositions have to be proved before laying it down—an inquiry, however, that is almost always left undone. People are hardly ever conscious of this sort of gap, which is therefore specially dangerous as regards rigor. In arithmetic it just will not do to make any assertion you like without proof or with a sham proof, and then wait and see if anybody succeeds in proving its falsity; on the contrary, it must be demanded that every assertion that is not completely self-evident should have a real proof; and this involves that any expressions or symbols used in the proof, unless they may be regarded as generally known, must be introduced in an unexceptionable way.

And moreover it is so easy to avoid a plurality of definitions for one and the same symbol. Instead of first defining a symbol for a limited domain and then using it for the purpose of defining itself in regard to a wider domain, we need only choose different signs, confining the reference of the first, once for all, to the narrower domain; in this way the first definition is now complete and draws sharp boundary-lines. This in no way prejudges the relation between the reference of one sign and that of the other; we can investigate this without its being possible that the result of the investigation should make it questionable whether the definitions were justified.

It really is worth the trouble to invent a new symbol if we can thus remove not a few logical difficulties and ensure the rigor of the proofs. But many mathematicians seem to have so little feeling for logical purity and accuracy that they will use a word to stand for three or four different things, sooner than make the frightful decision to invent a new word.

6

Piecemeal definition likewise makes the status of theorems uncertain. If, e.g., the words "square root of 9" have been defined with a restriction to the domain of positive integers, then we can prove, e.g., the proposition that there is only one square root of 9; but this is at once overthrown when we extend our treatment to negative numbers and supplement the definition accordingly. But who can tell if we have now reached a definitive proposition? Who can tell but that we may see ourselves driven to recognize four square roots of 9? How are we really going to tell that there are no more than two square roots of -1? So long as we have no final and complete definitions, it is impossible. It may perhaps be objected that in that case some propositions would no longer hold good. The same reason would go against admitting a second square root of 9. In this way we never have really firm ground underfoot. We never emerge from incompleteness and vagueness.

7

We get the same case for a relation as for a concept: logic can recognize a relation only if it is determinate, as regards any one object and any other object, whether or not the one stands to the other in relation. Here too we have a *tertium non datur;* the case of its being undecided is ruled out. If there were a relation for which this requirement were not fulfilled, then the concepts that we can derive from it by partly filling it up likewise would not have completely sharp boundaries, and would thus, strictly speaking, not be concepts at all, but inadmissible sham concepts. If, e.g., the relation *greater than* is not completely defined, then it is likewise uncertain whether a quasi-conceptual construction obtained by partly filling it up, e.g. *greater than zero* or *positive,* is a proper concept. For it to be a proper concept, it would have to be determinate whether, e.g., the Moon is greater than zero. We may indeed specify that only numbers can stand in our relation, and infer from this that the Moon, not being a number, is also not greater than zero. But with that there would have to go a complete definition of the word "number," and that is just what is most lacking.

It is just as regards the relation *greater than* that piecemeal, and therefore incomplete, definition, is, so to say, good form in mathematics. The words "greater than" are first defined in the domain of positive integers, i.e., incompletely. The pseudo-relation thus obtained, which it is wrong to use at all, is then used in order to complete the first definition; and here, of course, one cannot always tell when the definition of the relation *greater than* is to count as complete. For the relation of equality the case is quite similar; here too piecemeal definition is absolutely a part of good form. Nevertheless we must stick to our point: without complete and final definitions, we have no firm ground underfoot, we are not sure about the validity of our theorems, and we cannot confidently apply the laws of logic, which certainly presuppose that concepts, and relations too, have sharp boundaries.

8

At this point it is easy to draw a conclusion in regard to functions that are neither concepts nor relations. Let us take as an example the expression "the half of something," which purports to be a name of such function. Here the word "something" is keeping a place open for the argument; it corresponds to the letter "ξ" in "$\frac{1}{2}\xi$." Such an expression can become part of a concept-name, e.g. "something the half of which is less than one."

Now if this last expression is actually to stand for a concept with sharp boundaries, then it must be determinate, e.g., as regards the Moon whether the half of it is less than one. But in order that this should happen, the expression "the half of the Moon" must have a reference; i.e. there must be one and only one object designated by this. Now according to common usage this is not the case, for nobody knows which half of the Moon is meant. So here, too, we must make a more precise specification, so that it is determined, as regards every object, which object is the half of it; otherwise it is wrong to use the expression "the half of x" with the definite article. Thus a first-level function of one argument must always be such as to yield an object as its value, whatever object we may take as its argument—whatever object we may use to "saturate" the function.

9

We must make the corresponding requirement as regards functions with two arguments. The expression

"the sum of one object and another object"

purports to be the name of such a function. Here too, then, it must be determinate, as regards any one object and any other object, which object is the sum of the one and the other; and there must always be such an object. If that is not the case, then it is likewise indeterminate which object gives the result one when added to itself. In that case, therefore, the words "something that gives the result one when added to itself" do not stand for any concept with sharp boundaries, i.e. for anything that can be used in logic. And the question how many objects there are that give the result one when added to themselves is unanswerable.

But can we not stipulate that the expression "the sum of one object and another object" is to have a reference only when both objects are numbers? In that case, you may well think, the concept *something that gives the result one when added to itself* is one with sharp boundaries; for now we know that no obect that is not a number falls under it. E.g. the Moon does not fall under it, since the sum of the Moon and the Moon is not one. This is wrong. On the present view, the sentence "the sum of the Moon and the Moon is one" is neither true nor false; for in either case the words "the sum of the Moon and the Moon" would have to stand for something, and this was expressly denied by the suggested stipulation. Our sentence would be comparable, say, to the sentence "Scylla had six dragon necks." This sentence likewise is neither true nor false, but fiction, for the proper name "Scylla" designates nothing. Such sentences can indeed be objects of a scientific treatment, e.g. of myth; but no scientific investigation can issue in them. If our sentence "the sum of the Moon and the Moon is not one" were a scientific one, then it would assert that the words "the sum of the Moon and the Moon" and the word "one" did not coincide in reference; but with the stipulation suggested above, the former words would not have any reference; accordingly we could not truly assert either that their reference did coincide with the reference of the word "one" or that it did not coincide with it. Thus it would be impossible to answer the question whether the sum of the Moon and the Moon is one, or whether the Moon falls under the concept *something that gives the result one when added to itself.* In other words, what we have just called a concept would not be a genuine concept at all, since it would lack sharp boundaries. But when once we have introduced the expression "a added to b gives the result c," we can no longer stop the construction of a concept-name like "something that gives the result one when added to itself." If people would actually try to lay down laws that stopped the formation of such concept-names as this, which, though linguistically possible, are inadmissible, they would soon find the task exceedingly difficult and probably impracticable. The only way left open is to give to the words "sum," "addition," etc., if one means to use them at all, such definitions that the concept-names constructed out of the words in a linguistically correct manner stand for concepts with sharp boundaries and are thus admissible.

Thus the requirement we have here set up—that every first-level function of two arguments must have an object as its value for any one object as its first argument and any other object as its second—is a consequence of the requirement that concepts must have sharp boundaries and that we may not tolerate expressions which seem by their structure to stand for a concept but only create an illusion of one, just as we may not admit proper names that do not actually designate an object.

10

What has been said about verbal expressions holds good also for arithmetical symbols. If the sign of addition has been completely defined, then

$$"\xi + \xi = \zeta"$$

gives us the name of a relation—the relation of single to double. If that is not the case, then we cannot say whether the equation

$$"x + x = 1"$$

has an unique solution or several solutions. Now anybody will answer: "I forbid anything but numbers to be taken into account at all." We dealt above with a similar objection; here we may throw light on the matter from other sides. If anybody wants to exclude from consideration all objects that are not numbers, he must first say what he takes "number" to mean, and then further extension of the term is inadmissible. Such a restriction would have to be incorporated in the definition, which would thus take some such form as: "If a and b are numbers, then $a + b$ stands for . . ." We should have a conditional definition. But the sign of addition has not been defined unless every possible complex symbol of the form "$a + b$" has a definite reference, whatever proper names with a reference may take the place of "a" and "b." If on the contrary such complex symbols are defined, e.g. only for the case when symbols for real integers are taken instead of "a" and "b," then what has really been defined is only the complex symbols, not the sign of addition: an offence against the second principle of definition, which we still have to discuss. And yet people cannot help imagining they know what the sign of addition stands for; and accordingly they employ it also in cases for which no definition has been given.

As soon as people aim at generality in propositions they will need in arithmetical formulae not only symbols for definite objects—e.g. the proper name "2"—but also letters that only indicate and do not designate; and this already leads them, quite unawares, beyond the domain within which they have defined their symbols. One may try to avoid the dangers thus arising by not making the letters indicate objects in general (as I did), but only those of a domain with fixed boundaries. Let us suppose for once that the concept *number* has been sharply defined; let it be laid down that italic letters are to indicate only numbers, and let the sign of addition be defined only for numbers. Then in the proposition "$a + b = b + a$" we must mentally add the conditions that a and b are numbers; and these conditions, not being expressed, are easily forgotten. But let us deliberately not forget them for once! By a well-known law of logic, the proposition

"if a is a number and b is a number then $a + b = b + a$"

can be transformed into the proposition

"if $a + b$ is not equal to $b + a$, and a is a number, then b is not a number"

and here it is impossible to maintain the restriction to the domain of numbers. The force of the situation works irresistibly towards the breaking down of such restrictions. But in this case our antecedent clause

"if $a + b$ is not equal to $b + a$"

is senseless, assuming that the sign of addition has not been completely defined.

Here again we likewise see that the laws of logic presuppose concepts with sharp boundaries, and therefore also complete definitions for names of functions, like the *plus* sign. In vol. i we expressed this as follows: every function-name must have a reference. Accordingly all conditional definitions, and any procedure of piecemeal definition, must be rejected. Every symbol must be completely defined at a stroke, so that, as we say, it acquires a reference.

All of this hangs very close together, and may be regarded as derived from the principle of completeness in definitions.

11

Given the reference of an expression and of a part of it, obviously the reference of the remaining part is not always determined. So we may not define a symbol or word by defining an expression in which it occurs, whose remaining parts are known. For it would first be necessary to investigate whether—to use a readily understandable metaphor from algebra—the equation can be solved for the unknown, and whether the unknown is unambiguously determined. But as I have already said above, it is not feasible to make the correctness of a definition depend on the outcome of such an investigation—one which, moreover, would perhaps have the character of an equation that is solved for the unknown, and on the other side of which nothing unknown occurs any longer.

Still less will it do to define two things with one definition; any definition must, on the contrary, contain a single sign, and fix the reference of this sign. One equation alone cannot be used to determine two unknowns.

Moreover, we sometimes find a whole system of definitions set up, each one containing several words that need definition, in such a way that each of these words occurs in several of the definitions. This is like a system of equations with several unknowns; and here again it remains completely doubtful whether the equations can be solved and whether the solution is unambiguously determined.

Any symbol or word can indeed be regarded as consisting of parts; but we do not deny its simplicity unless, given the general rules of grammar, or of the symbolism, the reference of the whole would follow from the reference of the parts, and these parts occur also in other combinations and are treated as independent signs with a reference of their own. In this sense, then, we may say: the word (symbol) that is defined must be simple. Otherwise it might come about that the parts were also defined separately and that these definitions contradicted the definition of the whole.

Of course names of functions, because of their characteristic "unsaturatedness," cannot stand alone on one side of a defining equation; their argument-places must always be filled up somehow or other. In my ideography, as we have seen, this is done by means of italic letters, which must then occur on the other side as well. In language, instead of these, there occur pronouns and particles ("something," "what," "it") which indicate indefinitely. This is no violation of our principle; for these letters, pronouns, particles do not stand for anything, but only indicate.

12

Often there is an offence against both principles of definition at once. E.g. the *equals* sign is defined along with what stands to the right and left of it. In this case the *equals* sign has already been defined previously, but only in an incomplete way. Thus there arises a queer twilight; the *equals* sign is treated in a half-and-half way, as known and again as unknown. On the one hand, it looks as though we were meant to recall the earlier definition and extract from it something to go towards determining what now appears on the right and left sides of the *equals* sign. On the other hand, however, this earlier definition will not do for our present case. A similar thing happens over other signs too. This twilight is needed by many mathematicians for the performing of their logical conjuring tricks. The ends that are meant to be achieved in this way are unexceptionably attained through our transformation of an equality that holds generally into an equality between ranges of values, by Axiom V.

It has not been my aim to give here a complete survey of all that has to be observed in giving definitions; I will content myself with stating these two principles, the ones against which mathematicians sin oftenest.

ARNOLD GEULINCX
(1624-1669)

Born in Antwerp, taught at the University of Louvain. He became a Calvinist in Holland and taught at the University of Leyden. His ethics is founded upon metaphysics; he summed up his doctrine *"Ita est, ergo ita sit."* (So it is, therefore be it so.) His philosophy is mainly Aristotelian. He became known for his Doctrine of Occasionalism by which men are considered mere onlookers and not actors of their lives.

Main Works:

Tractatus Ethicus primus; Metaphysica vera et ad mentem peripateticam; Methodus inveniendi argumenta, quae solertia quibusdam dicitur; De Virtute.

Instruments of Logic

The root of logic is affirmation. For what has been transmitted through logic is derived therefrom in a continuous and uninterrupted sequence as far as the attainment of the advances of our art, that are called the instruments of knowledge.

We have to explain what affirmation is. This is the primary principle in logic and the most widely known, and we perform this act, that we call affirmation, hundreds of times daily. At this point I shall present examples to eliminate any ambiguity

---

From: *Logica fundamentis suis, a quibus hactenus collapsa fuerat restituta.*

in the term *affirmation. I stand* then is an affirmation: similarly, *it is disputed,* and *Peter is learned,* and so on. Those who postulate such expressions are considered to affirm something and their utterances are called affirmations.

From this root there spring, first of all, two branches: subject and predicate. If I affirm, it is necessary for that about which I affirm to exist (and this is called the subject), and it is necessary that there should be something to affirm of it (this is called the predicate). Thus in *I stand* the subject is *I* (for I am making an affirmation about myself when I state that I am standing), and the predicate is *am standing* (for I likewise affirm of myself). To the grammarians the subject, it seems, is the person, but the predicate is nameless. The subject likewise and the predicate are called in common *terms* and *extremes* for they enclose an affirmation at either end, when the affirmation is arranged in the order that the sense demands.

Beyond these extremes there is in an affirmation something with a middle sense, that logicians call a copula and grammarians a verb. This is nothing but a sign of affirmation. Just as *whether* is a sign of interrogation, *here!* of invitation, *woe!* of threat, *O!* of exclamation, and so on, so the entire nature of the copula or the verb rests in this act of stamping an affirmation. What is attached to the verb apart from this sign does not refer to the verb but subsists apart from its nature. Hence grammarians are in error, when they classify with the genuine verb *to be* so many spurious verbs, active, passive, neuter deponents, and so on. These are not verbs, but verbs with their extremes, or with one of the extremes: for example, I stand is not a verb, for a verb enfolds in itself both the subject or the preceding person and the predicate following. If I say: *Peter stands,* the expression *stands* no longer contains in itself the person (for this precedes in the word *Peter*), but only the verb with the predicate.

Apart from this scoria of extremes there frequently develop with the verb certain modes: as the mode of the present tense, the mode of the past tense, and the mode of the future. And this first scoria eludes the grammarians, and the second is unknown to logicians. For they think that this scoria refers to the nature of the verb, although in defining the verb they include mention of the signification of time. They are inconsistent as well, sometimes saying that in propositions of eternal truth the verb is released from tense: for nothing can ever be released from its nature. For example: Two and three are five. The verb *are* is released, they say, from tense, that is, it signifies no time. For the meaning is not: Two and three are now five, or once, or recently, or tomorrow, but simply: Two and three are five: so that the verb *are* does nothing else in the proposition beyond giving the sign of affirmation. Thus it is a genuine verb, properly cleansed of all scoria. *Is* in the proposition: Charles is king, is not a pure verb. For although it is separated from its extremes, still the mode or adverb of time coalesces with it, whence this is to be inferred: Charles is now king. The word *is* that occurs here is an utterly pure verb, a bare sign of affirmation. For the words that are around it perform other functions that this expression is accustomed to encounter at times. The word itself stripped of all this, signifies neither time nor person, much less the predicate: only it retains for itself some grammatical privilege of assuming certain of these functions, at a given opportunity.

Thus we have presented the pure, proper verb, stripped of everything that is not germane to it: and it was worth while, because in our root (in affirmation) the verb is primary and as it were the soul: for the extremes supply affirmation with a kind of body only. For instance: King Charles is not an affirmation, but some kind of skeleton of an affirmation. As soon as a verb is added (thus: Charles is king), it now revives and breathes an affirmation.

Negation is opposed to affirmation. What it is can be explained only by an example: *It is not disputed: Peter is not learned,* etc., are negations. Why these terms and many similar ones are not to be defined, you will see later, when I treat of definition. For the present, observe that affirmation is always contained in negation, as *I stand* is contained in *I do not stand.* Affirmation, I assert, but not complete or undiminished, but corrupted and damaged through the adverb of negation *not,* which is itself sometimes specially called negation, but in another sense. As a shipwreck is impossible without a ship, so negation is impossible without affirmation: although in the shipwreck the ship, and in negation the affirmation somehow perish. Therefore as there is affirmation in negation, subject too and predicate are in negation, by the very fact that they are in affirmation. However, subject and predicate are not part of the negation itself (although the logicians usually consider it so, erroneously), but of the included affirmation.

The affirmation and negation are together called propositions. Thus when we state a proposition, one must understand by this term either affirmation or negation.

What the logical square is, and its purpose, I shall explain more conveniently later, when I present six similar squares and show the logical cube constructed therefrom. As a preliminary, it is sufficient to give this reminder, that, when four axioms are found in any square, there are as many lines encircling this square. Two of them, joined by an affinity of meaning, are affirmative and produce from themselves two negatives by a conversion of the sorites. But what this conversion is cannot be explained here, but in part three.

First axiom: What is stated of the predicate is also stated of the subject. For instance: If A is the predicate, and B its subject, and C is stated of A, it will be necessary for C to be stated of B as well. For since C is predicated of B, consequently A contains B. But since C is predicated of A, C consequently contains A. Therefore C contains B too, for what the container contains, contains also its content (as a cellar contains a cask, in which wine is contained: hence too the cellar contains wine). If then C contains B, in as much as it is an affirmation, as I understood it here, C will be affirmed of B.

Q.E.D.

Second axiom: What is not stated of the subject is equally not stated of the predicate. For if it were stated of the predicate, it would be stated of the subject too, according to the previous axiom. This is the negative axiom, corresponding to the previous affirmative axiom by conversion.

Third axiom: Of what the subject is stated, of that same thing is the predicate stated. For if something is contained in the contained (the subject) it will also be contained in the container (the predicate). This is another affirmative axiom, because by an affinity of meaning it is conjoined with the first axiom.

Fourth axiom: Of what the predicate is not stated, of that the subject too is not stated. For if the subject were stated of it, the predicate too would be stated of it, according to the third axiom. This is a negative axiom, corresponding by conversion to the third axiom.

As students scarcely perceive these bare, abstract demonstrations, we shall offer examples. Let these be the terms: *Gold, metal, body.* Since then *metal* is the predicate of *gold,* and *body* is said of *metal, body* will be said of *gold* too, by the First Axiom (what is said of the predicate is also said of the subject). Again, since *metal* is the subject of *body, metal* also may be said of *gold*: hence *body* too will be said of *gold,* by the Third Axiom (of what the subject is said, of that is the predicate too said). Now take the terms: *Gold, metal, stone.* As stone is not affirmed of the subject *gold,* it is not affirmed either of the predicate *metal,* by the Second Axiom. Again, as the predicate *metal* is not said of *stone,* the subject *gold* too is not said of *stone,* by the Fourth Axiom.

You will say: *Beast* is not said of the subject *man* and yet it is said of its predicate *animal*: for *a certain animal* is a beast. My reply is: *Beast* is not said of *animal* (for it is false that *an animal is a beast,* since an animal is not more a beast than a man), but *beast* is said only of *a certain animal.* Although *a certain animal* is the predicate of *man,* as: Man is a certain animal, it is however a different *certain animal,* that is affirmed of *man,* from that of which *beast* is affirmed.

Predicate is classified into potentiality and action. Potentiality is a predicate that is affirmed with respect to *power,* as *heating.* For this is *capable of producing heat.* And so it is affirmed of *fire, water,* and so on, with respect to *power.*

Action is a predicate that is affirmed with respect to *being,* and not with respect to *power,* as *man, heating,* and so on. Action is a true predicate, but potentiality is not a true predicate, but a predicate taken with a mode or an adverb of a copula. For when I say: Water is heat-producing, the proposition becomes modal, as follows: Water possibly heats: and so heat-producing is the same as possibly heat-producing. Thus it is not a mere predicate taken with the mode of a copula. For the modes *necessarily, not, possibly,* and so on cannot occur except in a copula, as will be clearer in part two, where the modal proposition will be discussed. Hence when these modes are withdrawn from a copula and are placed beside the predicated word, they still always adhere in sense and in a kind of affection to the copula.

Every potentiality whatsoever has action. And the predicate, that is included possibly beyond the mode in some potentiality, is called the action of potentiality. For instance, the action of *heating* is *heat-producing.* For *heating* is the same as *possibly heat-producing,* and so *heat-producing* is a predicate, that is found in the predicated potentiality apart from the mode *possibly.* Potentiality is considered to terminate with its own action: because in meaning the action follows the mode *possibly,* that formally represents potentiality: as in *heating* or *possibly heat-producing.* The action *heat-producing* in sense follows after the mode *possibly.* For this mode in sense adheres to the copula. *Heat-producing* stands in relation to the predicate. Now the copula in meaning precedes the predicate. Potentiality is also said to be reduced to action, and also to pass into action, when it is said not only of its subject, but its action: so *heating* is reduced *in water* to *action,* when the water boils, and so it is not only heating, but heat-producing as well.

Hence potentiality is divided into pure and impure. Impure potentiality is that which is reduced to action, as *heating* with respect to *boiling water* or *fires* for they can not only produce heat but actually do so. Pure potentiality is that which does not pass into action: as *heating* with respect to *cold water.* For it is said to be *heating* in regard to water that is now cold (for it can produce heat by the very fact of its power to be heated), but *heat-producing* is not asserted of it. Absolute potentiality (considering pure and impure potentiality) is either pure or impure potentiality. Pure potentiality can be removed from its subject and impure as well: but absolute potentiality cannot be removed from its subject. Thus *purely heating* is removed from water when it heats, and *impurely heating* is removed from it when it gets cold and does not heat any more. But *absolutely heating* cannot be removed from it: for it can always, speaking absolutely, produce heat, whether it produces heat or not, even whether it exists or not. For it can exist and become hot, and so can produce heat as well. Potentiality is also near and remote. It is remote when it is reduced to action only by a previous change of subject: so heating is a remote potentiality in *cold water,* for it is not reduced to action except by a change of subject, that is, by water turning from cold to hot. Near potentiality is that which is reduced to action without any other change of its subject, as *heating* with respect to *hot water.* Absolute potentiality (considering near and remote potentiality) is either near or remote potentiality. Near potentiality can be removed from its subject: as *ambulatory* from a sick person (when *ambulatory* is taken for near potentiality). Remote potentiality also can be removed from its subject: but absolute potentiality cannot.

From what has been said these axioms are easily understood. Potentiality is impossible, when it cannot be reduced to action: for potentiality is nothing but possible action. If then something cannot produce heat (that is, cannot be reduced to the action of *heat-producing*), it is impossible for it to be *possibly heat-producing*. Potentiality is useless, when it is always reduced to action: that is, we say *useless* is *able to be,* because *it is* always and perpetually. For example: We say inaccurately: Gold can be a metal, because gold perpetually and simply is a metal. It is a useless potentiality in relation to potentiality: that is, terminated potentiality is useless in relation to another potentiality. For potentiality (that is, absolute potentiality) always and simply is. In place of this axiom, some say: Potentiality is not given to potentiality. They are too impulsive. For since, for example, Peter can walk, it follows that he can be able to walk: and it follows from this, again, that he can be able to do this, and so on endlessly: nor in this progression to infinity does something impossible occur, but only something useless. Potentiality is useless, when it is never reduced to action: that is, it is not presumed to be potentiality, when no action from it produces it.

Potentiality is divided into positive and negative. Positive potentiality is true potentiality, already defined. Negative potentiality is non-conflicting (in relation to predication). Such potentiality is the predicate of this proposition: Metal can be gold. This is thus explained: Metal does not conflict with gold with respect to predication. The meaning is not that metal can properly be gold, because potentiality is impossible when it cannot be reduced to action. Now it is impossible that metal should ever be gold: but only a certain metal is gold, and that conjointly and perpetually.

The subect of potentiality is said to be in potentiality. Thus *water* is in the potentiality of heating, or, as the usual expression goes, in the power of heat: and if it is hot, and if it heats by action and in actuality, it is in a remote power, and likewise in a pure power to heat. *Animal* too is in a positive power to feel, suffer, become enraged, and so on: but it is only in a negative power to heat. Animal too is in a positive power to feel, suffer, become enraged, and so on: but it is only in a negative power to be a man, or to be a beast. For *animal* can feel, can suffer, can become enraged. It can be a man only in this sense, that it does not conflict with man, and only in a similar sense can it be a beast. But it cannot be either a man or a beast absolutely and properly speaking, because there is no moment in all Eternity and all possible time, when this is true: An animal is a man. Or this is true: An animal is a beast. And so any properly so called potentiality whatever is here impossible, in as much as it cannot be reduced to action. Negative potentiality however (that is, not conflicting with beast) is of course in animal, as will be made clearer later, when we speak of conflict.

The four predicates are: Superior, difference, property, and accidents. Logicians generally list five predicates, namely: genus, species, difference, property, and accident. But we included the first two, genus and species, under superior. The distinction between genus and species does not seem to me a matter for logical consideration. For I do not see what benefits redound to logic from this distinction. For this reason I have considered it sufficient to combine both under a common name. Furthermore, these four predicates are compared with subjects distinct from them, for when the substantive is affirmed of itself, it is neither a superior of itself, nor a difference, nor a property, nor an accident.

I have explained what form is. One form is through itself, another through accident. Form through accident is form, but accident of another thing, as white with respect to *white man.* For form belongs to *white man* but is an accident of another thing, for example, this paper. Form by itself: Form by itself is form and the accident of nothing, as *rational* with respect to *man.* For it is the form of *man* but the accident of nothing. Of that of which there is no form, (as, for example, there is no form of *wall or water,* and so on), there is not even a predicate, and consequently there is neither an accident. Thus extension is a from through itself with respect to body: for with whatever subject extension is compared, it is either the form of that subject, or it is not predicate of it, and so there can never be an accident. Conformably, mixed substantives are divided into mixed through themselves and mixed through accident. A substantive mixed through itself occurs, when its nearest form is a form through itself, as *body, man, stone,* etc. A substantive mixed through accident occurs, when its nearest form is a form through accident, as: *white man,* likewise *sphere,* because its nearest form is a solid globe, which is an accident of the wood shaped into a globe.

Form through itself is called *difference:* and thus one of the four predicates appears to be unearthed from its hiding place. From a disquisition of it we see that it is based not in a pure subject (for this has no form), not in a mixed subject mixed through accident (for this does have a form, but not a form through itself), but only in the subject mixed through itself. It is easy to designate it: for it is designated through the adjective *certain,* as when I say: A *certain stone,* thinking *flint,* the adjective *certain* designates the difference of *flint.* And when I say: A *certain tree,* thinking of the *laurel,* the adjective designates the difference of *laurel,* and so forth. To grasp and present this difference according to itself is very difficult. And hence the difficulty of definition: for difference enters into definition as a special part of it. From the difficulty of definition stems the difficulty in understanding: for understanding is knowing through definition.

The whole is many taken together. Part is one of many taken together. Thus a tree is a whole, for it is root, trunk, and branches taken together. But a *root* is a part, for it is one of these many. A part is usually compared with the whole: as *root* is said to be *part of the tree.* The whole too is compared with the part, but not so readily: hence *the tree is the whole of the root* is rather harsh and becomes acceptable only by some kind of circumlocution, as: A tree is a whole by comparison with its root. From this you also see that the whole and the part are not in the nature of things, but occur through the operation of our mind, when it takes them together. There are, I repeat, many things in nature and of these many there are individual things: but the particular things do not come under the concept of the part, nor do the many things come under the concept of the whole, unless our own mind adds a taking-together of the many items. In logic it is convenient to take the whole as a term meaning many things taken together: similarly, the part can be taken as a term.

As the whole is many, these many have to be enumerated. They may be enumerated in two ways: copulatively, as by *and*, and disjunctively, as by *or*. Hence the whole is also double: actual and potential. The actual whole is the copulative whole, that is, many taken together with the intervening particle *and*, as *tree*, in as much as it is *root, trunk, and branches*. The potential whole is a disjunctive whole, that is, many taken together with the intervening particle *or*, as *tree*, in as much as it is *laurel* or *oak* or *cherry*, and so on. The actual whole is called by one name *compound*, and is said to be composed of its parts. Thus *tree is* said to be composed of branches, root, and trunk. Tho potontial wholo io not oaid to bo oompocod of ito parto, but it is considered to comprehend them within itself. Thus *tree* is not said to be composed of oak, linden, ash, and so on, but we say that tree comprehends in itself laurel, oak, linden, and so on. And hence also the potential parts of the whole are called subjective parts.

Compound is divided into essential and integral. Essential is that in which the parts exist as matter and form, as: *white man*, and generally all mixed substantives, in so far as they are composed of their own matter and form. Integral compound is that in which the parts exist not as matter and form, as: *tree*, in so far as it is composed of branches, trunk, and root: similarly, table, in so far as it is composed of stakes and props. For none of these is either matter or a form of compound, since none of them is affirmed separately of the compound, for a tree is not a branch or root, nor is a table a stake or a prop. Form and matter must be affirmed separately of the compound, since they are predicated of it. But you will say: *Bronze* is the matter of a statue and a certain shape is its form: and yet none of these is affirmed of *statue*. My reply is: This is the general way of

expression: but I think it is an abuse of phraseology, and a figure stems therefrom, it seems to me, that substitutes the substantive in the place of the adjective. For, granting that bronze
is the matter of a certain statue (meaning that the statue is
merely bronze shaped in a certain way), yet *this certain shape*
cannot be called its form, properly speaking: but *shaped in a
certain way* either is its form, or denotes it. This mode that substitutes the substantive for the adjective is common. Refer to
the orators; compare too these current usages: *Your Lordship,
Your Reverence, Highness, Majesty,* and so on. You see substantives in the place of adjectives. However it may be, certainly
matter and form must not be reckoned to be a subject of logical consideration, unless predicated of the compound. For nothing must be accepted by logic that does not stem from the root
of affirmation.

Logical composition, then, or what is a subject of logical
consideration, is divided into compound through accident. They
coincide with mixed through themselves and through accident.
Potential whole too is divided into through itself and through
accident. Potential whole through itself is potential whole whose
subjective parts are inferior to it, as metal with respect to gold,
silver, and so on: likewise tree with respect to oak, linden, and
so on. Potential whole through accident is potential whole compared with its subjective parts, that are not its inferiors, but
are composed of themselves and diverse forms through accident, as: Man with respect to soldier, merchant, sailor, and so on.

Potential whole is predicated of any of its parts. For it contains its subjective parts with affirmation or disjunctively, and
so it is predicated of any of them, according to what was demonstrated in Section I, chapter 2, notes 7 and 8. Hence if the
subjective parts are in conflict, the potential whole too will be
subordinate to them: as is clear from the last demonstration of
the preceding chapter. And this potential whole is more in use:
for we are accustomed to compare it with the conflicting subjective parts. But every subordinating expression compared with
its many subordinate subjects (to which, as is demonstrated in

the preceding chapter, not II, it can always be compared) is also a potential whole with respect to them. For since they are its subjects, they are contained in it disjunctively, as is demonstrated in Section I, chapter 2, notes 7 and 8, and so the subordinating is the many expressions subordinated by the intervention of the particle *or*: and so the subordinating is the potential whole, and the subordinated subjects the subjective parts, according to the definition of the potential whole.

The grammatical copula is, so to speak, the very soul of the compound proposition: and it exists in the compound proposition as the verb exists in the proposition. The grammatical copula is a particle that is joined to the proposition, and affects its meaning that must be expanded by the apposition of another proposition: as the particle *and*. For example, taking the proposition *I stand*, you have perfect meaning. But if you add to it the particle just mentioned, thus: *I stand and*, the meaning is affected and rendered imperfect: but, when another proposition is added, for instance, *I speak*, the meaning is finally completed, thus: *I stand and I speak*. Similarly, as you will readily note, with the articles *or, therefore, if*, and so on.

I enumerate then six or seven grammatical copulas: copulative, *and*: disjunctive, *or*: conditional, *if*: illative, *therefore*: similar, *as*: temporal, *when*: although some of these are frequently equipollent. Hence just as many species occur with compound propositions rejoicing in the same names, namely: copulative proposition, whose copula is *and*, as *I stand and speak*: disjunctive proposition, whose copula is *or*, as *Either I stand or I speak*: conditional, whose copula is *if*, as *If I stand, I speak* (although this is false, because it is irrelevant to a proposition of this or that species): illative, whose copula is *therefore*, as *I stand, therefore I can stand*: causal, whose copula is *because*, as *Because I run, I am tired*: similar, whose copula is *as*, as *Affirmation is in negation as a ship is in a shipwreck*: finally, temporal, whose copula is *when*, as: *An eclipse takes place, when the earth is interposed between the sun and the moon*. A grammatical copula is considered to be a copula of this or that compound proposition, when it intervenes between its nearest parts: for the copula that intervenes between the remote parts only (and this occurs in the second kind of compounds) is not considered a copula of the proposition itself, but a part of it.

Among these copulas some are pure, others impure. A pure copula is one that is not different from an impure copula, that is, a copula that copulates so that implicitly it contains some proposition as well. The pure copulas are only *and* and *or*. All the rest are impure and implicitly contain some proposition, and so not only copulate, but do so as much as possible, as: *Therefore*. For example: *I stand, therefore I speak*. The meaning is: *I both stand and I speak*, and *from I stand rightly follows I speak*, which is the last proposition in the meaning and is implicitly contained in the copula *therefore* of the preceding proposition. The same thing appears here in the copula *because*: *Because I run, I am tired*. The meaning is: *I both run and I am tired*, and my running is the cause of my tiredness. Here again the final proposition is contained in *because* of the preceding causal. This is peculiar in a conditional copula, because it contains not so much some part, as the entire conditional proposition, so that it is determined only by the parts: as is sufficiently clear from what has been said previously.

Pure copulas have this peculiarity, that they are included in certain other signs accustomed to precede the subject, namely, in the signs: *all, none, someone*, because *all* and *none* include the copula *and*, while *someone* includes the copula *or*. And this is the difference between *all* and *none*, that *all* includes *and* simply: *none* includes *nor*, that is, *and not*. For example: Every man is learned: that is, Peter is learned and Paul is learned, and so on, where *and* expressly rendered in the meaning is implicitly contained in the sign *every*, prefixed to the subject of the preceding proposition. No man is learned: that is: Both Peter is not learned, and so on. This too is the peculiarity of pure copulas, that they are frequently accustomed to duplicate and to be prefixed to the extremes that they connect, and at the same time to be interposed between them, as: I both stand and I speak. Similarly: I either stand or I speak. This does not occur in other grammatical copulas, that are either prefixed only, or only intervene between their extremes, as: Because I run, I am tired. Or: I am tired, because I run.

The natural position of the copula is midway between the extremes: and that is why it is called a copula, because it intervenes like a kind of chain. Hence too all grammatical copulas occupy this position, even require it, if one considers the meaning. For example: The copula *and* occupies the midway position only here: I stand and I speak. Disjunctively: I stand or I speak. Conditional: I can stand, if I stand. Illative: I stand, therefore I can stand. Causal: I am tired, because I run, and so on. There are also three copulas, that are confined to a middle position: *and, or, therefore,* of which the first two can be distributed into the anterior part by their own duplication, while the last one stands only in the middle. The remaining copulas permit of being thrust to the front part, as: Conditional: If I stand, I can stand. Causal: Because I run, I am tired. Temporal: When I run, I am tired. Similarly, however, is not thrust out of its middle position, without leaving some trace of itself. For example: Just like a ship in a shipwreck, so affirmation is in negation. Here the trace *so* is left in the middle position. Furthermore, when the copulas are thus thrust forward into an anterior position, the order of the extremes must be changed: for what was last between the extremes, with the copula is occupying a middle position, becomes first, when the copula is brought forward: as is sufficiently clear in the examples given.

Certain violations of the copula occur, to make contradiction easier. If I say: Because I run, I am tired, the contradictory is easily formed: Not because I run, am I tired. But if I say: I am tired because I run, the contradictory will not be correspondingly easy. For: *I am tired not because I run* is not the contradictory, but much less so is this its contradictory: I am not tired because I run: unless perhaps you assume the adverb *not* to embrace the whole (as is customarily said), which, however, creates difficulty and obscurity in meaning. Hence in a rational proposition contradiction is difficult, and in denying it we proceed rather through the parts, as is evident in disputation.

GEORG WILHELM FRIEDRICH HEGEL
(1770-1831)

Studied at the University of Tübingen and earned his living as a
tutor until 1801, when he began to lecture at Jena. He lost his post,
worked as journalist and high school principal, until he was again
offered a university post, this time at Heidelberg, in 1816. From 1818,
he taught at Berlin, the place with which he is most identified. Hegel
is one of the chief philosophers of German idealism. But he was perhaps the last European philosopher who had something of Aristotle's
encyclopedic breadth of mind; he wrote both on natural sciences and
humanities. His dialectics have been attacked and defended with
equal fervor, and his political legacy is embodied in Prussianism,
Communism, Fascism and nationalism.

Main Works:

> Phaenomenologie des Geistes; Wissenschaft der Logik; Encyklo-
> paedie der philosophischen Wissenschaften im Grundrisse;
> Grundlinien der Philosophie des Rechts; Philosophie der Ge-
> schichte.

The Logic of Philosophy

Systematic Introduction

§12

Logic as logic of philosophy develops the Idea of the whole
of reality in the abstract medium of thought: This definition of
logic, in turn, is the result of logic itself. A prime example of
the fact that the determinations of logic grow out of and are
grounded in a whole, which is present in its entirety to the
logician.

From: *Encyclopedia of Philosophy.*

Usually, logic is said to be the science of thought—its determinations and laws. But to say this implies self-knowledge, an identity of knowledge with itself. Thus it is that dialectic is the all-pervasive method manifest in each function of Logic —even in formal logic. The Idea determines itself in a totality of functions in which it produces itself.

Logic, thus conceived, is both difficult and simple. Geometry can appeal to abstract intuitions, commonsense to sensuous perceptions; logic does not have this advantage. It requires at once the power to concentrate on thoughts as such—bracketing out experiential contents—and to integrate manifold thoughts into a whole and living movement.

On the other hand, logic is the easiest of the sciences. Its contents are determinations of the same thinking which reflects on them: They are as simple as they are familiar.

Logic has a utility value. It produces a cultivated mind. Man matures in his practice of thought, and in his reflection upon it. Utility, however, is not the highest value of logic. The term "logical" is equivalent to "trustful"; logic is truth in the form of truth.

§13

There are three aspects in every thought which is logically real or true: The abstract or rational form, which says what something is; the dialectical negation, which says what something is not; the speculative—concrete comprehension: A is also that which it is not, A is non-A. These three aspects do not constitute three parts of logic, but are moments of everything that is logically real or true. They belong to every philosophical Concept. Every Concept is rational, is abstractly opposed to another, and is united in comprehension together with its opposites. *This is the definition of dialectic.*

§14

Thinking as *reason* (Verstand) requires fixed or identical determinations in clear distinction from other identities. To reason, such limited abstractions are evident as valid and as real.

§15

The dialectical movement, in contrast to reason, cancels such one-sided determinations. Dialectically they are related to that which they are not. It is this negative relation which defines them. They themselves require their opposites, and are determined by them. When dialectic is exclusively rational, it leads to *skepticism*. Reason, as isolated aspect of dialectic, points to the untruth of every thought.

Historically, dialectic is considered a sophistic trick which arbitrarily and deliberately produces confusion in conception. This confusion, it is supposed, is destroyed by reason; and this formal destruction of illusions is proudly proclaimed as truth. Reason as the correction of all one-sided determinations and of historical misconceptions remains tied to their irrationality. In comprehending reason as such a struggle, dialectical reflection passes beyond or transcends reason.

While rational terms are preserved in their limited validity, they belong to complex relationships in which they constantly change their functions. Dialectic is not an external reflection, but belongs immanently to the transitoriness of all finite, one-sided, and merely rational positions. It is their own negation which they are, without knowing it. It is the moving soul of the world-as-process. It guarantees to philosophy the immanent connection or necessary consistency between its contrary and essential disciplines.

§16

Speculative comprehension grasps and is the unity of all essential opposites. It is the principle of systematic philosophizing. In realizing the limitation of every finite standpoint, it realizes the infinity of Being through the non-finality in all finite beings. The Absolute maintains itself in the transition of all its own non-absolute or partial manifestations.

The positive result of dialectic is not an abstract void, an abyss into which everything is thrown. Dialectic denies absolutely one thing alone: The claim that any particular thing of the finite world exists absolutely. The Absolute appears as "*nothing*" to those finite positions which want to cling to their pseudo-absolute claims. This does not mean that "nothing is." To suppose this is to confuse thoughtlessly the dialectical-ontological negation with a formal-logical self-contradiction, wherein reason isolates the negative function of comprehensiveness as if it were a simple identity beyond all definite contents. Rather, the identity of speculative comprehension is the concrete unity of all essential opposites in the world itself. This alone is the ultimate concern of philosophy. The abstractions of reason are pierced, so that reason may reach its own concrete thought.

The logic of philosophy retains and includes the formal logic of reason. Leave out dialectical comprehension and formal logic remains! Formal logic may unravel the tale of finite object-thinking in the sciences; if the story of the sciences is absolutized, science degenerates into scientism.

§17

Concepts of philosophy are concrete realities and values of Being, thought together with their opposites. Philosophy contemplates them as they are in themselves as well as what they are for those to which they are evident. Contents are thereby realized as manifestation of Being, which is both in and for itself; or which relates itself to itself in an eternal movement. The ontological categories are thus also the foundation for the self-comprehension of mind and spirit. Form and content of Concepts are not abstractly separated. As self-manifestations and self-determinations of the living whole, they are at once its forms as well as its value-contents.

The formal logic of reason, on the other hand, handles forms in abstraction from contents. Neither form nor content expresses self-knowledge. Since they are not true for themselves, they are not forms of living truth. It is even essential that material data of formal logic remain alien to their forms. The logic of speculative philosophy, in contrast, thinks that which is real in and for itself. The Absolute is present in the subject thinking it. The Concept is absolute in thinking subjects together in their unity, as well as in their difference. Concept (noesis noeseos) is what Aristotle called the principle of his First Philosophy or metaphysics.

As Concept (Begriff), reality becomes conscious of itself in the thinking mind. Herein philosophy seems to be occupied exclusively with the thinking mind and sundered from the richness of the sensuous world; and from the more concrete and intelligible historical world. But the dialectic of philosophy is not confined to the actual subject: It pertains equally to the structures of Being, to essential universals. Philosophy, in this enlarged sense, is cognition of reality as such.

The dialectic of philosophy also is present in the oppositeness of essential universal structures of Being (ontology); also the realistic treasures of the world presuppose onto-logic. These treasures also belong to the all-pervasive ultimacy of Truth. The concrete universals abstractly presented in logic prefigure all essential values of the spirit. The highest among them is religion.

On its highest plane philosophy contemplates the Concept of all Concepts, the eternal Absolute—the God who is worshipped in religion. Philosophy then culminates in speculative theology.

Historical Introduction

§18

Logic as the logic of speculative philosophy replaces what used to be called metaphysics. It evolved through the history and critique of metaphysics, maturing, as it were, in purgatory.

Matured, logic is Science. Because of the development in the advent of logic, we must acquaint ourselves with the problems of metaphysics and understand how their logical truths burst through their historical shells. Metaphysics is not a pastime for mere antiquarian curiosity. It was engrossed in persistent problems, which are the very problems of logic. Its main defect was that it approached them from a rationalistic point of view (Verstandes-Ansicht).

§19

Rationalism erred in identifying categories of thought with the principles of given things. Its assumption, Being can be truly thought or makes itself available in thought, is a high principle—higher than the negative or skeptical scientism of recent vintage. But it failed when the Absolute was thought as if it were a thing consisting of general rational predicates. Rationalism did not evaluate critically the categories of Reason (Verstandes-Bestimmungen); let alone their competence to determine the Absolute. External object—science and metaphysics—were tangled up in a knot. For example, existence (Dasein) is not a formal-logical predicate as it is used in the proposition "God has existence." Finite and infinite, simple and complex, one and many, are dialectical opposites: They must be viewed together. Therefore the questions of reason: Is the world finite or infinite? Is the soul simple or complex? Is the thing a one or a whole? are meaningless.

§20

The problems of metaphysics were comprehensive totalities, such as the soul, the world, God—but rationalism treated them as if they were object-images (Vorstellung) of given finished things. It applied categories of reason to them as object-sciences do to things, and in doing so demonstrated that object-thinking cannot furnish a sufficient standard of absolute problems.

Georg Wilhelm Friedrich Hegel

§21

Assuming that the formal-logical laws of contradiction and of the excluded middle were laws of Reality, metaphysics became *dogmatic*. Seeing that contradictory contentions cannot both be true—if the one is true, the other must be false—metaphysics failed to see that this law is valid only for finite situations. In no sense is it relevant when applied to absolute totalities.

§22

Ontology is one of the major parts of metaphysics: the study of the essence of Being. For *rationalism* the essence of Being is studied in abstraction from the manifold particulars of finite existence. The contents of the finite world were blindly accepted as empirical and contingent only. Thus rationalism lost itself in empty forms of reason. *Empiricism,* in turn, fell greedily on data; its goal was to get as many particulars together as possible. For *Nominalism* knowledge became nothing but a formally consistent use of language and correct definition of terms. Correct analysis was unconcerned with truth and its necessity. Universals are mere labels to be placed on particulars. In all these ventures, the lack of a dialectical principle, uniting the finite and the essence of Being, left the reality-value of both undetermined.

The formal-logical rule of consistency holds for ordinary propositions. The predicate must not be predicated of the subject of the proposition if this implies self-contradiction. But propositions of object-thinking are not ontological. The ontological Concept is a concrete unity of opposite distinctions. Truth, therefore, is not merely the absence of formal-logical contradictions. The necessary correlation of essential being and finite existence, of simplicity and complexity, etc., constitutes the dialectical Concept. Such ontological terms become contradictory only in formal-logical sentences. In their necessary correlation and in correlation with thought thinking them, they exemplify Being which is true both in and for itself.

§23

The second part of metaphysics was called *rational psychology*. Its fallacy consisted in treating the soul or spirit as a given thing or object—without reflection that the soul meets itself in its self-estrangement.

The problem of immortality was mixed up with temporal changes, quantitative compositions, and qualitative degrees. They have their legitimate place in a sphere where increases and decreases can be measured.

§24

The third part of metaphysics, *cosmology*, dealt with the world. Its over-all problems are: Eternity and spatial-temporal finitude; necessity and contingency; formal laws and irrational changes; freedom of man and the origin of evil; efficient and final cause or purpose; essence and appearance, substance and existence; form and matter; happiness and misery; good and evil.

In dealing with these dialectical relations, the opposites were either over-emphasized or falsely absolutized.

§25

The fourth part of metaphysics, *natural* or *rational theology*, contemplated the concept of God or the possibility thereof. In so doing, it developed proofs of his existence and theories of his attributes.

Rationalism erred in misunderstanding the speculative Concept. It either objectified the Absolute as if it were a person over against the subject; or emptied the Absolute so that it became a vague being-in-general or essence, devoid of all concrete determinations.

An absolute *dualism* is posited between the world, which is declared to be nothing or something positively evil; and God, who is to be considered to be all that the world is not, and absolutely good. This cleavage leaves nothing to be desired for either side. While the contradiction is perfect, it simply says the same thing twice. Thus the failure of all rational theology is clear: It is unable to see that a dialectical negation is also an affirmative relation. If infinity is thought by itself, apart from the finitude of the existing world, then infinity itself becomes something finite; it is limited by this otherness of the world.

A further error of rational theology lies in the perverse assumption that the existence of God depends upon, or is mediated by reasons—as if he were a conclusion in a syllogism (Verstandes-Identität der Bestimmtheiten).

The circular reasoning of *idealism* is no better. For it the name God simply describes a state of a subjective pious consciousness. It then asks how all other concepts of God agree with its own subjectivistic preconception.

A truly religious emancipation from the finite world cannot be achieved if the transition from the finite to the infinite is not an interacting process of both. As long as reason insists on splitting the Absolute into separate objects over against each other, it can never escape its own contradictions. The attributes of God are, on the one hand, exaggerations of moral values such as justice, kindness, power, wisdom; but on the other hand, they all denied him because none of them is infinite. They sink to the level of an edifying nebulous chatter.

§26

Rationalistic metaphysics succumbed to attacks which came from two opposite directions. The first was led by *empiricism*. It took its stand in immediate experience, which was either sensuous and external or psychic and internal. The empiricist believed he was able to derive all contents of thought from given facts of consciousness; at the same time, in contradistinction to this, he believed that formal-logical analysis of empirical facts—

formal abstraction and identities—is the source of truth. The supersensuous Absolute was either radically denied or agnostically doubted.

§27

Kant criticized both rationalistic and empiristic metaphysics. He questioned the validity of reason for metaphysics. Its categories, he asserted, were synthetic propositions a priori of rational content, valid only for scientific experience or object-thinking; they are not derivable from the senses, but from the spontaneity of thought, creating universal, necessary, objective relations.

§28

The transcendental unity of self-consciousness—I am identical in all my thinking—is the original derivation and justification of all categories; they all unify experience.

The manifold object-images, given to feeling and perception, are the empirical contents which are located by the forms of sensibility, space and time; they are thereby outside of one another. These contents are then thought by logical forms. Contents and forms are opposite in an original identity. Such is Kant's apperception of consciousness: I think and connect objects and also relate them to myself; the categories of reason are ways by which I unify the object in myself. (As Kant puts it: The conditions which make true judgments possible are the same conditions which make the objects of judgment real.)

§29

While immediate perception is elevated to the rank of scientific experience by the objectivity of rational categories, their use is nevertheless restricted to experience. Without the given materials they are empty.

Georg Wilhelm Friedrich Hegel

§30

On account of this finitude of reason, scientific object-knowledge is incapable of determining the Absolute, because it is given in no perception.

§31

Insight into the limited character or conditional nature of object-sciences rests on our ability to think the unconditional whole. In its light the scientific objects are known as appearance. This is comprehension (Vernunft).

Kant, however, underrates the impact of his own notion of comprehension. He refers to the Infinite as if it were a thing; and suggests that if reason is to know this thing-in-itself, as it knows other things, it produces necessary self-contradictions, antinomies. If it is to know the soul in the same manner as if it were a given object, the necessary self-contradiction involved is the fallacy of paralogism. Comprehension is thus reduced to reason (Verstand); and reason, which ought to unify experience, is unable to fulfill this demand. The difficulty is again clear: Reason can be critical only of object-metaphysics; it cannot be an organ of truth.

§32

In its critique of the finitude of the categories of reason, critical philosophy is right. But it is one-sided in that it fails to comprehend its own comprehensiveness. The dialectical tension between logical, organizing form and organized, irrational material is not understood as a concrete logical process. Kant does not realize that he is not practicing rational scientific logic when he comprehends it in its limited truth.

A further deficiency in Kant is his lack of a systematic-dialectical determination of the categories. He depends on empiricism and formal logic. If this were remedied, the transcendental unity of self-consciousness would cease to be a mere formal unity. There are many syntheses a priori or concrete unities of opposites in which the unity of self-consciousness manifests and determines itself; and its categories—the categories of comprehensions, including those of scientific reason—determine each other mutually and in the whole; each is that which it is, by being also that which it is not. This mutual dialectical relation justifies them systematically (deduziert).

Kant's mannerism and love of formalistic schemes must not let us overlook his merits. He has accomplished the profoundest and most decisive progress in the philosophy of recent times. He demonstrated that dialectical opposites are necessary and essential in and for the comprehensive whole. Reason makes them articulate, but it should not confuse its formal-logical contradictions with the ontological reality of the opposites. Equally important is Kant's emphasis of the ontological status and reality of the soul. He has rescued this problem from object-metaphysics and from an empiricistic meaningless question. The genuine and essential reality of the soul lies in its identity with its own self-experience; the "I am" is a being which knows and is the self-knowledge which exists. In grasping this appearance of *freedom* as the essence as well as the existence of the soul, the absolute first ground of philosophy has been reached.

§33

These objective values, however, are obscured by Kant's standpoint, which is subjective *idealism* or *criticalism*. It disagrees with empiricism as to what constitutes experience; but agrees with it that there can be no comprehension of the all-comprehensive Absolute, because knowledge is said to be restricted to sensuous stuff. It remains tied to the finite which is never ultimately real, and to an object-knowledge which wavers between the poles of subjectivity and externality.

§34

Further, Kant's criticism contradicts his own concept of knowledge. On the one hand, scientific reason alone furnishes objec-

370

tive knowledge, but on the other hand, it only furnishes knowledge of appearance to finite observers. In this self-limitation of objective reason, the comprehensive Idea or the Concept of absolute truth is lost when Comprehension is degraded to a regulative formal unity; and the absolute Being to an empty thing-in-itself.

It is of the uttermost inconsistency to admit that reason is confined to know appearances only, and at the same time to contend that this is the only true knowledge we have. A deficient, incomplete, limited mode of knowledge can only be known in comparison with the really-present Idea of a complete whole. It is sheer unconsciousness not to realize that by this dialectical negation of one side, which thereby is known to be finite and limited, a true knowledge is practiced. It proves the reality and the presence of an unlimited Infinite.

Also religious and moral life presuppose knowledge of the Absolute to be true; it is implied in them. Both have overcome the abstract separation of being in itself from being for itself. The Absolute is not merely a negative Beyond but it comprehends and dissolves the negativity of finite, fixed and subjective standpoints within itself.

This agreement between dialectical ontology and the practical spirit in ethics and religion also eliminates Kant's division of theoretical and practical reason. Likewise the atomistic division of the soul contradicts the complete unity of self-consciousness. The faculties of the soul do not dwell in separate compartments. What would practical reason be, if it were not a synthesis a priori, or manifestation of dialectical truth?

§35

When philosophy reaches logical maturity, it is *Science*. It requires abandoning all dogmatic assumptions, subjective presuppositions, and one-sided standpoints.

We have illustrated this self-criticism of philosophy in four standpoints; First, *rationalism* assumes the fixed validity of concepts of reason, even though they oppose and modify one another; second, *objectivism* assumes finished and given objects to function as a standard of thought, but when the two sides are compared the question of inadequate cognition cannot be answered; third, *formalism* treats knowledge as a relation of formally defined terms, and is *skepticism* in regard to an indefinite substratum; fourth, *dualism* assumes a subject of knowledge over against an object of knowledge. Both are independent of each other and both *shall* but never *can* meet.

§36

Philosophy as *Science* contains all such assumptions within itself but also shows why it cannot rest satisfied with any one of them. Every assumption is criticized by thinking through the consequences of its own contention. Seen as false in its exclusiveness, it is abandoned; seen as the criticism implicit in its own standpoint, it is transcended. The Logic of philosophy or philosophy as Science assumes nothing but itself as the critical movement of thought.

This self-critical movement appears in historical life. One-sided assumptions occurring in Logic as moments of pure thought are also found in immediate consciousness; it is engaged in belaboring a given world. Its object-images, representations, opinions, and presuppositions are the given problems of and for philosophical critique; it shows why they must be given up or why they are given as problems (Das Gegebene ist aufzugeben).

I have previously told this story in my *Phenomenology of Mind*. It was intended to be a first part or introduction to philosophy leading up to the logic or Science of philosophy and terminating in its Concept.

But further, the critical history of consciousness is also an organic member in the infinite circle of philosophy. Like every other philosophical discipline, it is not *the* beginning, but *a* beginning. The absolute beginning is the whole movement of comprehension.

This movement might also be presented as a total *skepticism* in which all finite forms of cognition meet their doom. But in its abstract isolation, this negative dialectic is just as unsatisfactory as any other abstract standpoint. It is, as mentioned before, an essential function within the speculative logic of philosophy. The decision to think radically, to call everything into question, to make everything problematic, and to be trapped by nothing, is both a complete doubt and desperation (Zweifel und Verzweiflung) as well as a complete freedom which grasps in the breakdown of all uncertainties, in the uncertainty of all things finite, the infinite certainty of itself which is one and the same as thought pure and simple.

The Logic of philosophy must fulfill Kant's demand of a total comprehension comprehending itself through the critique of all its essential manifestations of faculties.

§37

Pure Science or Logic is divided into four branches. Logic of Being qua Being or ontology; Logic of Essence, in which Being is understood to be essentially dialectical; Logic of the Concept, in which the dialectical nature of Being becomes intelligible for itself; Logic of the Idea, in which all opposites are actualized in a teleological process. All opposites in reality are also opposites in philosophical reflection. Reality is in thought, thought is in reality.

Logic includes *thought in so far as it is just as much world-itself as it is thought,* or *world-itself in so far as it is just as much concrete, universal thought.* World-conceptions unfold themselves in self-consciousness or in the form of self: This subject-object which exists and is intelligible in and for itself; and in the Idea, which is teleological movement or final cause, in which the Concept is a moment. These world-contents make it impossible for a logic of philosophy to be merely formal; if we wish still to employ the word *matter,* then the genuine matter of philosophy is at the same time formal self-differentiation of the Absolute. Logic is the realm of pure comprehension and truth as it is in and for itself. . . .

I could not, of course, imagine that the method I have followed would not be open to much improvement and elaboration; at the same time I know it is the only method which is not separable from its objective content: Dialectic is not an external reflection, but the movement of the content in itself. Thus it is that philosophical expositions may be regarded as Scientific only as they conform to the course and rhythm of world-itself.

In accord with this method I would observe further that the divisions and headings, sections, and chapters of the book, which are given in their work are made for the purposes of a preliminary survey; they have, in fact, only *historical* value. They do not belong to the content and body of the Science, but are compiled by external reflection, which, having already run through the whole of the scheme, knows and indicates the sequence in advance of its actual presentation.

§38

Only recently the difficulty in finding a beginning in philosophy has been stressed. The reason for this difficulty, as well as the possibility of solving it, has been much discussed. It is supposed that the beginning of philosophy must be either mediate or immediate; it is easy to show that it can be neither one nor the other, thus refuting either approach. True, the principle of any philosophy also expresses a beginning, but this beginning is objective and not subjective; it is the beginning of all things. The principle is a content somehow determined—water, the One, *nous,* idea, substance, monad, and so forth; or, where it relates to the nature of cognition—like thought, intuition, sensation, ego, or subjectivity itself—it still begins with content. A subjective beginning in the sense of some contingent way of introducing the exposition is unimportant. The only important consideration is only the *question* with which philosophy must begin: What is the truth and the absolute basis of all things?

The need of philosophy to begin with its own question is denied by dogmatists, who seek a demonstration of their principle; by skeptics, who seek a subjective criterion with which to meet dogmatic philosophy; and by those who begin with explosive abruptness from their inner revelation, faith, intellectual intuition, and the like, and desire to dispense with method and logic.

To begin the beginning with a chosen content is to begin with an abstraction. The difficulty in this approach is this: In its development thought is forced to regard itself, the behavior of cognition, every bit as much as the content on which it reflects. *Subjective activity is grasped as an essential moment of objective truth, necessitating the uniting method with content, and form with principle.* There is nothing in Heaven, Nature, Spirit, or anywhere else, which does not contain immediacy as well as mediacy, so that these two determinations are seen to be unseparated and inseparable.

Any and every immediacy is what it is in distinction from the mediated; it is always at every moment simply that which it is in opposition to all complexity. As such it is a Being pure and simple; it is Being and nothing else, without any further determination or filling. Being is here the beginning, represented as arising from the negation of mediation. To begin on the subjective side with pure being is to begin in abstraction from all specific and complex content of finite knowledge. Nothing is considered except the decision (which might appear arbitrary) to consider thought as such. Abstracted from all presuppositions and mediations, thought has no foundation except itself. Further, immediate being is thus also the *thought* of immediacy as it cannot hold in itself any such determination relative to another —the latter would be differentiation and mutual relation, and thus mediation. The beginning therefore is pure thought *and* Being.

Beginning is the beginning of something and not of nothing,

namely of that which begins in and with it; it cannot hold on to its immediacy. Thus consciousness is led back on its road from immediacy, with which it begins, to absolute knowledge as its inmost truth; and the first term, which entered the stage as the immediate, arises, precisely, from this last term, the foundation. What is essential is not so much that a pure immediate is the beginning, but that the Absolute in its totality, forms a cycle returning upon itself, wherein the first is also last, and the last first. This consideration is of essential importance, as will be more clearly evident in the logic itself.

In order to appease those who are dissatisfied with "being" as the beginning of logic, we could omit being as the beginning. Then the only requirement would be to make a pure beginning. Nothing but beginning is left and it would remain to be seen what that is, for, so far, there is nothing but an immediate beginning as something which is to begin. The beginning is not pure nothing; it is a nothing from which something is to proceed; being is already contained in the beginning. In other words, the beginning contains both, being and nothing; it is the unity of both—not-being which is being, and being which is also not-being.

Further, on the one hand being and nothing are present in the beginning as distinct from one another: The beginning points to something other; it is not-being related to being which is to be. That which is beginning, as yet is not, it is advancing toward being. The beginning therefore contains being as having this characteristic. It stems from and transcends not-being, as its opposite. On the other hand the beginning is the undifferentiated unity of that which is beginning to be and equally, as yet, is not. The opposites, being and not-being, are in immediate in the beginning. The analysis of the beginning thus yields the concept of the unity of being and not-being, or the unity of the state of being differentiated and of being un-differentiated, or the identity of identity and non-identity.

If anyone, impatient of the consideration of the abstract beginning, should demand that we begin, not with the beginning, but directly with the subject-matter itself, the answer is that the task is to discover what this subject-matter is. The Science must not presuppose this as known.

If any form is taken for the beginning in preference to empty being, then the beginning suffers from the flaws mentioned. Those who remain dissatisfied with this beginning are asked to set themselves the task of beginning differently and yet avoid these faults.

PETRUS HISPANUS
(1210/1220-1277)

Leading logician of the 13th century, was a Portuguese, born in Lisbon. He became a priest and rose quickly in the Church to become archdeacon of Braga, cardinal bishop of Tusculum and, after the death of Hadrian IV, pope. He took the name of John XXI, but his pontificate lasted only a few months.

Main Works:

Summulae Logicales; De Anima; Tractatus Majorum Fallacium; Syncategoremata.

_____

Suppositions and Distributions

Among linguistic statements some are complex, as: A man runs. A white man. Others are incomplex, as: Man, itself, which is an incomplex term. Now every simple incomplex term signifies either substance, or quality, or quantity, or something else, and similarly with the other ten categories. A term, as taken here, is a word signifying the universal or the particular, as: Man. Or Socrates. The signification of a term, as it is taken here, is the conventional representation of a thing by speech. But, since everything is either universal or particular, it is necessary that words not signifying a universal or a particular do not signify anything, as the signification of a term is here understood. And so it is not a term as the expression *term* is here understood: and hence the signs neither of universality nor of particularity are terms.

_____

From: *Summulae Logicales.*

Of signification one is substantive and this occurs through a substantive noun, as: Man. Another is adjectival and this occurs through an adjective or a verb, as: White. He runs. This is not, properly speaking, substantive or adjectival signification, but something is signified substantively or adjectivally, because adjectivity and substantivity are modes of the things that are signified, and not significations. Substantive nouns are said to stand for something, while adjectives and also verbs are said to coordinate.

Supposition is the acceptance of a substantive term for something. But supposition and signification differ, because signification occurs through the imposition of a word to signify a thing, while supposition is the acceptance of the term itself, already signifying a thing as something: as when we say: A man runs. The term *man* denotes Socrates or Plato and so, other men. Thus, signification is prior to supposition, and they are not identical because signification applies to the word, while supposition refers to the term already composed of the word and its signification. Therefore supposition is not signification. Moreover, signification applies to a sign in relation to the signified, while supposition is not the relation of a sign to the signified but of that which denotes to the thing denoted: therefore signification and supposition differ. Coordination is the acceptance of an adjectival term for something.

One kind of supposition is general: the other, discrete. General supposition is that which occurs through a general term, as: Man. Discrete supposition is that which occurs through a discrete term. Again, one kind of general supposition is natural: the other, accidental. Natural supposition is the acceptance of a general term for all the things of which, by its natural character, it can be predicated, as: Man, taken by itself, denotes by its nature all men who exist, and who have existed, and who will exist. Accidental supposition is the acceptance of a general term for all the things that the adjunct demands, as: Man is. The term man denotes all men existing at the present time. When we say: Man was, it denotes men who existed in the past. When we say: Man will be, it denotes men who will exist, and thus it has different suppositions according to the diversity of the terms that are added to it.

One type of accidental suppositions is simple: the other, personal. Simple supposition is the acceptance of a general term for a universal thing signified by the term itself, as when it is said: Man is a species. Or: Animal is a genus. The term *man* denotes man in general and not something under it: and similarly with any general term whatever, as: Risible is a property. Rational is a difference.

One kind of simple suppositions is that of a general term placed in the subject, as: Man is a species. Another type is that of a general term placed in the predicate, as: Every man is an animal. The term *animal* acting as the predicate has simple supposition, because it denotes only the nature of the genus. Another type is that of a general term placed after the exceptive expression, as: Every animal except man is irrational. The term *man* has a simple supposition. Hence it does not follow that: Every animal except man is irrational: therefore every animal except this man is irrational. There is a fallacy of figure of speech here, in proceeding from simple to personal supposition. Similarly: Man is a species: therefore some man is a species. And again: Every man is an animal: therefore every man is this animal. In all these instances the procedure is from simple supposition to personal supposition.

That a general term, placed in a predicate, is considered simply, is clear, because when we say: There is the same science for all contraries, unless the term *science* had simple supposition, there would be a fallacy. For there is no particular science of all contraries: for medicine is not a science of all contraries but only of health and sickness: and grammar, of what is suitable and unsuitable, and so on.

Personal supposition is the acceptance of a general term for its particulars, as when we say: Man runs. The term man denotes its particulars, namely Socrates and Plato and so on.

Moreover, one kind of personal supposition is determinate,

the other, indeterminate. Determinate supposition is the acceptance of a general term taken indefinitely or with a sign of particularity, as: A man runs. Or: Some man runs. In each case the supposition is called determinate, because although in each instance the term *man* denotes every man both running and not running, yet the suppositions are true of one man only who is running. For there is a difference between denotation and rendering a statement true of something in the above propositions. As has been stated, the term *man* denotes all men running and not running, but it produces a true statement only in respect of the man running. But it is evident that there is determinate supposition in both suppositions, because when we say: An animal is Socrates, an animal is Plato, and so forth: therefore every animal is every man: there is a fallacy of figure of speech here in proceeding from many determinates to one determinate. Thus the general term taken indefinitely has determinate supposition: and similarly with a sign of particularity.

Indeterminate supposition is the acceptance of a general term by many by means of a universal sign, as when we say: Every man is an animal: the term *man* denotes many men by means of the universal sign, because it refers to anything whatever denoted.

Again, one kind of indeterminate suppositions is indeterminate by necessity of the sign or mode: the other, by the necessity of the thing, as when we say: Every man is an animal: the term *man* becomes indeterminate or is distributed by the necessity of the sign for anything whatever denoted: and since every single man has his own essence, the verb *is* by the necessity of the thing denotes as many essences as *man* denotes men. And, since every single man has his own animality, *animal* in that case consequently by the necessity of the thing denotes as many animals as *man* denotes men and as the verb *is* denotes essences. Hence the term *man* is said to denote indeterminately and movably and distributively, but it denotes indeterminately and distributively because it denotes every man. It denotes movably because a valid inference can be drawn from it for any one whatever of its particulars, as: Every man is an animal: therefore Socrates or Plato is an animal. But the term animal is said to be immovably indeterminate because no valid inference can be made from it, as: Every man is an animal: therefore every man is this animal. In this case, the procedure is from a simple supposition to a personal supposition, just as in the following instance: Man is the noblest of creatures: therefore some man is the noblest of creatures. And: The rose is the most beautiful of flowers: therefore some rose is the most beautiful of flowers. But they differ because in the latter instance there is simple supposition on the part of the subject, while in the former there is simple supposition on the part of the predicate.

But let there not appear to be a contradiction to what was said previously, that in the proposition: Every man is an animal, the term *animal* placed in the predicate has simple supposition, although it was previously stated that it had indeterminate supposition immovably. To this the reply must be made, according to certain people, that this genus of animal is predicated of many species and the term *animal* is taken to denote the common character itself because it is a genus and has simple supposition. But according to the common nature of this genus that is multiplied by means of the suppositions of man, it is said to have indeterminate supposition not movably but immovably. For indeterminate supposition movably cannot occur along with simple supposition, not in the same sense or in different senses, but indeterminate supposition immovably can occur along with simple supposition not in the same sense but in different senses, as has been stated. And so it is necessary to resolve this contrariety that appeared to those who maintained that the term posited in the predicate had simple supposition and became indeterminate immovably by means of the affirmative universal sign in the subject, as: Every man is an animal.

But I believe that it is impossible for a general term placed in a predicate to be immovably or movably indeterminate when a universal affirmative sign is in the subject, as: Every man is an animal, and in other similar propositions. For, as Porphyry has it, everything that is predicated of something is either greater than or equal to that of which it is predicated: and he meant predicated essentially. But in this proposition: Every man is an animal, the predication is essential and not equally distributed: therefore the predication is greater, but not accidental: therefore it is substantial or essential: therefore it is a genus or a difference. But it is not a difference: therefore it is a genus. But the nature of a genus, multiplied movably or immovably, is not a genus. Therefore, when we say: Every man is an animal, since the genus is predicated there, it is impossible for the general term to be multiplied movably or immovably, because that signifies the nature of a genus; because it would no longer be a genus, just as if *man* were indeterminate movably or immovably.

Again, this same view appears evident in Aristotle's treatise on the *Topics*. He says that everything predicated of another thing is necessarily predicated of it either convertibly or not: if convertibly, it is a difference or a property. If it is not predicated convertibly of a thing, it either falls under the definition of the thing or not. If it does not, it is an accident. If it does fall under the definition, it is either a genus or a difference. And here Aristotle referred to direct predication and to the species as subject in itself or as distributed. But in this proposition: Every man is an animal, there is direct predication and *man* is the subject: the predication is not equally distributed and is not an accident: therefore the predication is a genus or a difference. But it is not a difference: therefore it is a genus. And so we are back to the same view as before, because it is not possible for a general term placed in a predicate to be indeterminate movably or immovably.

Again, the universal whole that is a genus and the quantitative whole are related in opposite senses. The universal whole is a general term taken without a universal sign, as: Animal. The quantitative whole on the other hand is a universal sign, as: Every man. But the quantitative whole is two-fold: because one kind is a kind of completion, as whenever a general term is indeterminate movably: the other kind of quantitative whole is incomplete or diminished, as whenever a general term is indeterminate movably, as: *Every man* is a quantitative whole, because if a general term is distributed it becomes a simple quantitative whole. So in a sense it is, and in another sense it is not: therefore it is impossible for a quantitative whole to be a genus, as such: therefore it is not possible for a general term placed in a predicate to be indeterminate, as was stated.

Again, that composition, according to which the more particular is reduced to the more general, is opposed to the composition according to which the more general is reduced to the more particular. But according to the first composition, general is taken in the sense of what is common, for thus what is general contains in itself all the particulars that are under it. But according to the second composition, general is taken as distributed or indeterminative for everything or for some things. If then the genus exists by itself in the sense of genus or in the sense of that which is common, it is not possible for it to be distributed as such. And all these views are granted.

Now the reason that suggested these views can be solved easily. For they say, when it is asserted: Every man is an animal, that, since each has his own essence and his animality, because it is not possible to be a man without being an animal: therefore the term *animal* is understood for as many animals as *man* is understood for men. Now it seems that in this argument there is no validity. For when I say: Every man is white. Every man is black, since it is impossible to be a man without being an animal, it is necessary that as many animals or animalities should be understood in the subject as there are men for whom the term *man* is understood.

However, it is stupid to declare that the number of animalities is here derived from the distribution of the predicate, since *white* is here predicated. Hence it must be said that man, speaking logically and not naturally, is constituted of rational animal and that is why man has animal in himself. Hence when man is distributed, he has in himself a multiplicity of these animalities, as when I say: Every man is white. Every man is black, man in no sense has these animalities from the predicate.

Similarly with the discussion in hand, when the genus is predicated, as: Every man is an animal. In this proposition *man* is the subject, in which is understood a multiplicity of these animalities, as was stated, and this genus, that is, animal, is predicated, that is in no sense indeterminate, either movably or immovably, but here represents its general essence of the genus predicable of many things. Hence animal is predicated and animal understood in the subject, thus: Every rational mortal animal is an animal.

Again, I assert that the verb *is* is not distributed movably or immovably, because the fact that an animal was or existed in this man meant the subject itself before it became a subject in a proposition with an essential or an accidental predicate. And on this account we dispense with a certain previous division of suppositions, namely, supposition of indeterminates. One kind is indeterminate by the necessity of the sign or mode: the other, by the necessity of the thing.

For we declare that every indeterminate occurs by the necessity of the mode, as: Every rational animal is *mortal:* the term animal is understood, by virtue of the sign, for every animal that is a man. Similarly: Every man is an animal: the term *man* is understood not only for every man but for every animal that is a man. And that is the reason why there are as many animalities as there are humanities, naturally speaking (because there is the same humanity, according to the manner of speaking logically, not naturally, in every individual man). Thus man in general is the same. Hence the fact that there is this or that animality is by reason of matter.

Now in the way that nature has, my humanity in itself is different from your humanity, just as my animality, through which my humanity is in me, is different from your animality, through which your humanity occurs in you. And on this account the sign or mode, making man indeterminate, does not make animal indeterminate, but animal stands generally in relation to man through his differences. Hence all indeterminateness arises by the necessity of the mode or sign. And this should be sufficient regarding suppositions.

Distribution is the diversity of a general term produced through a universal sign, as when one says: Every man runs. The term *man* is distributed or becomes indeterminate for anything whatever below it through the sign *all*, and thus there is diversity in this case. I say *of a general term*, because a singular term cannot be distributed. Hence these propositions are incongruous: Every Socrates. Every Plato, and so with other instances. And there is here a solecism.

Among universal signs, some are disruptive of substance, as: all, none, and the like. Others are distributive of accidents, as: of whatever kind, however large. A sign that is distributive of the substance is one that distributes things according to the mode *what*, or the mode of substance, as when one says: Every white man. Every black man. Hence *of the substance* is generally understood in relation to things of any kind, when it is called a distributive sign of substance. Now the sign *distributive of accident* is that which distributes things through the mode of accident, as through the mode *of what kind* or *how large*, as: of whatever kind, however large.

Again, some of the signs of the distributives of the substance are distributive of the integral parts, as: whole: Others are distributive of subjective parts, as: Every, none, each. Again, some of the signs of the distributives of the subjective parts are distributive of two, as: which of the two, neither, and similar expressions: others are distributive of many, as: all, none, and similar expressions.

In respect of all these, we must first speak of the signs distributive of substance, and among the first of the sign *every*. It should be understood that this sign *every* is taken in the plural number in a double sense: whenever it is taken collectively as here: All the apostles are twelve: then it does not follow: Therefore the apostles are twelve, some of them only being indicated.

Sometimes it is taken distributively, as: All men naturally want to know.

Further, it is asked what the sign *every* signifies, and it seems that it does not signify anything, for everything is either universal or particular, but the sign *every* does not signify anything. Similarly, *every* is not a predicable of one or many. Therefore it is not a universal or a particular and thus it signifies nothing. But on the other hand: From the fact that a thing either is or is not, a statement is said to be true or false. Therefore if *every* signifies nothing, by its opposition or remoteness truth or falsehood will not occur in a statement. But this statement is true: An animal is a man. Therefore this one also is true: Every animal is a man. Therefore the first instance, too, namely, *every*, signifies nothing.

Reply: To the first objection it must be stated that *every* does not signify a universal but signifies the extent of the universality, for it signifies that a general term is taken for something below it, as: every man: and so *every* signifies something. But a thing is duplex, for it is a certain thing that is the subject or that is predicated, as: man, or: animal, runs, or debates; and the previous objection is to this, that *every* signifies nothing in so far as such a thing is, because every thing is either universal or particular. There is another thing that is the disposition of a thing either as a subject or predicable: and the sign *every* signifies such a thing. And truth or falsehood in a statement is caused by this thing as well as by the other.

The objection is raised that *every* does not signify the disposition of the subject, because in every syllogism a middle must be repeated along with its disposition in the minor proposition. Therefore we must form a syllogism as follows: Every man is an animal. Socrates is every man. Therefore Socrates is an animal: because *every* is the disposition of the subject in the major proposition. Therefore it must be repeated in the minor, which is false. Therefore *every* is not the disposition of the subject.

Reply: Just as father implies two things: that which is a father, and father qua father, so *subject* implies two things: and accordingly we say that the disposition of the subject is duplex, for there is a certain disposition of that which is the subject, as: white, black, and so with other absolute dispositions. And they must be repeated in the minor proposition along with middle. There is another disposition of the subject qua subject, as: every, none and all signs, both universal and particular. And such dispositions do not have to be repeated in the minor proposition with the middle, because they are respective. For they dispose the subject in comparison with the predicate, as when we say: Every white man runs. The disposition *white* must be repeated, because it is absolute and so it is absolute of that which is the subject. But the disposition *every* is not to be repeated in relation to the predicate, and so it is respective of the subject qua subject. Hence we must form the following syllogism: Every white man runs. Socrates is every white man.

The signification of the sign *every* and the manner of its disposition having been considered, it is next asked whether it requires three appellations. And it appears that it does, for every perfection is in three, according to the view at the beginning of the *De Caelo et Mundo*. Therefore perfection is in three and everything perfect is in the same, according to the same reference. Therefore everything is in three. Therefore everything will have three appellations.

Again, in regard to the same point Aristotle says in the same passage that we do not say, of two men, *every man*: but at least of three. Therefore *every* will have three appellations. But on the other hand: In any demonstration there are all the universal propositions. But the demonstrations are formed from the sun and the moon. Therefore one must say: *Every* sun and *every* moon. But the sun has one denotation only: and likewise the moon. Therefore *every* does not require three appellations.

Another reply: Everything deprived of light by the opposition of the earth is defective. This proposition is granted by everyone, since it is held by Aristotle, and it is a universal. But *deprived of light by the opposition of the earth* has one denotation only, namely, the moon. Therefore *every* does not require the diversification of the subject. For example: If a man is simply, then he is risible too simply. And if a man is diminished, risible too is diminished. But the universal is sometimes preserved in many, as *man, horse, lion.* Therefore *every* does not always require three appellations but sometimes three, sometimes only one.

Still another refutation: Form is two-fold, for a certain form is the form of matter, as: my soul is the form of my body, and your soul is of yours, and this form is a part that is not predicated of that of which it is a form. There is another form that is predicable of many, and so all superior things, as genus and species, are called a form of the lower things, as *man, horse,* and *animal.* But the particulars of the predicable form are called its matter. Therefore since the form of the predicated modes neither exceeds its matter, nor is exceeded by it, then no universal will exceed its particulars nor be exceeded by them. Therefore since *every* means the perfect agreement of the universal with its particulars, as *every* man, then it is necessary that the *sun* and the *moon* should have only one denotation.

We grant then that the expressions previously mentioned are true and that *every* does not always require three appellations. But when it is conjoined to a universal term having many denotations, then *every* will have three or more appellations. But when it is conjoined to a universal term having one particular only, it requires one denotation only.

To the first objection that every perfection is in three, it must be replied that it is true and that these are the three: substance of the thing and its virtue and its function. And Aristotle refers to these three as follows: The harmony of nature acts thus. For in saying *nature* he refers to the substance of the thing. In saying *harmonious* he refers to its virtue. In saying *acts thus* he refers to its due function. Hence the sign *man* has the substance of man and his virtue and due function. And similarly the sign *every* has the substance of the universal sign and its virtue that is distributive and its function when it distributes. And thus its perfection is in three.

To the second objection it must be stated that there is a difference between *man* and *men*, because *man* means the species itself according to itself, that is predicable of man, but *men* in the plural does not mean the species according to itself, but the species distributed in action through the numerically diverse natures of the particulars. Hence *every* in the plural, by reason of the distribution made through diverse natures, will have at least three appellations. But *every* in the singular, because it refers to the species itself and not the matter of the particulars, requires only the essence naturally suitable for predication of many, or is shared in action by many or by one only, and for that reason sometimes requires three appellations, and sometimes one only, according to the nature of the universal to which it is joined.

Some writers say that *every* will have at least three appellations and they give the following reason: Whenever an affirmative universal sign is added to a general term not having a sufficiency of appellations, it always refers to non-being, as when one says: Every phoenix is, because the term *phoenix* has one denotation only, which is in action in it. On this account the sign *every* refers to non-existent phoenix. And for that reason when one says: Every phoenix is, the sense is: this phoenix and two more phoenix, that are not, are. And hence they say that the two propositions: Every phoenix is: a certain phoenix is not, are likewise false, and are not contradictory, because in the negative proposition a phoenix is denoted that is, and in the positive proposition two phoenix that are not denoted, and so there is not the same subject in each proposition.

This argument can be refuted in a number of ways. First, because disagreement follows from falsity in regard to denotation, namely, that *every* will have at least three appellations: which, as has already been shown, is false. Moreover, as Aristotle has it in his treatise *On Interpretation*, the proposition, in which the universal is universally taken as the subject of some predicate, contradicts the proposition in which the same universal is not universally taken as the subject of the same predicate. But these propositions are as follows: Every phoenix is. A certain phoenix is not. Therefore they are contradictory, because they deny each other, and so the rule in regard to them is false.

Again, another refutation: A general term is restricted to the denotation of things that are under the form of the denoting term. Therefore, when one says: A phoenix is, the term *phoenix* is restricted to denoting one phoenix only, since one thing only is denoted. Therefore by the other rule stated previously: If the universal sign applies to it, it distributes it for one denotation only. Therefore there will be no reference to non-existent phoenix. Thus the rule they propose is false and based on falsity.

According to what has already been said, it is asked, in respect of this sophism: Every man is and whatever differs from him is not a man.

Proof: This is a kind of copulative proposition, of which each part is true. Therefore the whole is true.

Refutation: Every man is, etc. Therefore Socrates is and whatever differs from him is not a man. Which is false. Therefore the proposition itself is false.

Elucidation: *Different from every man* is less than *different from Socrates,* because *different from every man* denotes only things other than man: but *different from Socrates* denotes the same things and also all men other than Socrates. Hence it follows: Different from every man: therefore different from Socrates. This is a topic from the species or from the subjective part. Hence if the universal sign is attached to both parts, there is a progression from the lower to the higher with distribution, and thus the sophism of the consequent falls under the refutation according to progression. Because in refutation the progression is two-fold: for it follows validly: Every man: therefore

Socrates, and this is a topic from the quantitative whole, but it does not follow: Whatever is different from every man is a non-man: therefore whatever is different from Socrates is a non-man. But the consequent here, as has been said, is as follows: Every man: therefore every animal.

DAVID HUME
(1711-1776)

A native of Scotland, never held an academic post and earned his living as a man of letters. The only post of importance he ever held was that of Secretary to the British Embassy in Paris. Hume was a sceptic and a hedonist who managed to shock, on occasions, even the tolerant 18th century. But "the Infidel", as he was called, powerfully influenced the development of such modern sciences as psychology and sociology.

Main Works:

Treatise of Human Nature; An Enquiry Concerning Human Understanding; Dialogue Condoning Natural Religion; History of England; Essays Moral and Political; Philosophical Essays.

Of the Association of Ideas

It is evident that there is a principle of connection between the different thoughts or ideas of the mind, and that, in their appearance to the memory or imagination, they introduce each other with a certain degree of method and regularity. In our more serious thinking or discourse this is so observable that any particular thought, which breaks in upon the regular tract or chain of ideas, is immediately remarked and rejected. And even in our wildest and most wandering reveries, nay in our very dreams, we shall find, if we reflect, that the imagination ran not altogether at adventures, but that there was still a connection

---

From: *An Enquiry Concerning Human Understanding.*

upheld among the different ideas, which succeeded each other. Were the loosest and freest conversation to be transcribed, there would immediately be observed something which connected it in all its transitions. Or where this is wanting, the person who broke the thread of discourse might still inform you, that there had secretly revolved in his mind a succession of thought, which had gradually led him from the subject of conversation. Among different languages, even where we cannot suspect the least connection or communication, it is found, that the words, expressive of ideas, the most compounded, do yet nearly correspond to each other: a certain proof that the simple ideas, comprehended in the compound ones, were bound together by some universal principle, which had an equal influence on all mankind.

Though it be too obvious to escape observation, that different ideas are connected together; I do not find that any philosopher has attempted to enumerate or class all the principles of association; a subject, however, that seems worthy of curiosity. To me, there appear to be only three principles of connection among ideas, namely, *Resemblance, Contiguity* in time or place, and *Cause* or *Effect*.

That these principles serve to connect ideas will not, I believe, be much doubted. A picture naturally leads our thoughts to the original: the mention of one apartment in a building naturally introduces an enquiry or discourse concerning the others: and if we think of a wound, we can scarcely forbear reflecting on the pain which follows it. But that this enumeration is complete, and that there are no principles of association except these, may be difficult to prove to the satisfaction of the reader, or even to a man's own satisfaction. All we can do, in such cases, is to run over several instances, and examine carefully the principle which binds the different thoughts to each other, never stopping till we render the principle as general as possible. The more instances we examine, and the more care we employ, the more assurance shall we require, that the enumeration, which we form from the whole, is complete and entire.

David Hume

SCEPTICAL DOUBTS CONCERNING THE
OPERATIONS OF THE UNDERSTANDING

Part I

All the objects of human reason or enquiry may naturally be divided into two kinds, to wit, *Relation of Ideas*, and *Matters of Fact*. Of the first kind are the sciences of Geometry, Algebra, and Arithmetic; and in short, every affirmation which is either intuitively or demonstratively certain. *That the square of the hypotenuse is equal to the squares of the two sides*, is a proposition which expresses a relation between these figures. *That three times five is equal to the half of thirty*, expresses a relation between these numbers. Propositions of this kind are discoverable by the mere operation of thought, without dependence on what is anywhere existent in the universe. Though there never were a circle or triangle in nature, the truths demonstrated by Euclid would for ever retain their certainty and evidence.

Matters of fact, which are the second objects of human reason, are not ascertained in the same manner; nor is our evidence of their truth, however great, of a like nature with the foregoing. The contrary of every matter of fact is still possible; because it can never imply a contradiction, and is conceived by the mind with the same facility and distinctness, as if ever so conformable to reality. *That the sun will not rise tomorrow* is no less intelligible a proposition, and implies no more contradiction than the affirmation, *that it will rise*. We should in vain, therefore, attempt to demonstrate its falsehood. Were it demonstratively false, it would imply a contradiction, and could never be distinctly conceived by the mind.

It may, therefore, be a subject worthy of curiosity, to enquire what is the nature of that evidence which assures us of any real existence and matter of fact, beyond the present testimony of our senses, or the records of our memory. This part of philosophy, it is observable, has been little cultivated, either by the ancients or moderns; and therefore our doubts and errors, in the prosecution of so important an enquiry, may be the more excusable; while we march through such difficult paths without any guide or direction. They may even prove useful, by exciting curiosity, and destroying that implicit faith and security, which is the bane of all reasoning and free enquiry. The discovery of defects in the common philosophy, if any such there be, will not, I presume, be a discouragement, but rather an incitement, as is usual, to attempt something more full and satisfactory than has yet been proposed to the public.

All reasoning concerning matters of fact seems to be founded on the relation of *Cause and Effect*. By means of that relation alone we can go beyond the evidence of our memory and senses. If you were to ask a man, why he believes any matter of fact, which is absent; for instance, that his friend is in the country, or in France; he would give you a reason; and this reason would be some other fact; as a letter received from him, or the knowledge of his former resolutions and promises. A man finding a watch or any other machine in a desert island, would conclude that there had once been men in that island. All our reasonings concerning fact are of the same nature. And here it is constantly supposed that there is a connection between the present fact and that which is inferred from it. Were there nothing to bind them together, the inference would be entirely precarious. The hearing of an articulate voice and rational discourse in the dark assures us of the presence of some person: Why? because these are the effects of the human make and fabric, and closely connected with it. If we anatomize all the other reasonings of this nature, we shall find that they are founded on the relation of cause and effect, and that this relation is either near or remote, direct or collateral. Heat and light are collateral effects of fire, and the one effect may justly be inferred from the other.

If we would satisfy ourselves, therefore, concerning the nature of that evidence, which assures us of matters of fact, we must enquire how we arrive at the knowledge of cause and effect.

I shall venture to affirm, as a general proposition, which admits of no exception, that the knowledge of this relation is not, in any instance, attained by reasonings *a priori;* but arises entirely from experience, when we find that any particular objects are constantly conjoined with each other. Let an object be presented to a man of ever so strong natural reason and abilities; if that object be entirely new to him, he will not be able, by the most accurate examination of its sensible qualities, to discover any of its causes or effects. Adam, though his rational faculties be supposed, at the very first, entirely perfect, could not have inferred from the fluidity and transparency of water that it would suffocate him, or from the light and warmth of fire that it would consume him. No object ever discovers, by the qualities which appear to the senses, either the causes which produced it, or the effects which will arise from it; nor can our reason, unassisted by experience, ever draw any inference concerning real existence and matter of fact.

This proposition, that *causes and effects are discoverable, not by reason but by experience,* will readily be admitted with regard to such objects as we remember to have once been altogether unknown to us; since we must be conscious of the utter inability, which we then lay under, of foretelling what would arise from them. Present two smooth pieces of marble to a man who has no tincture of natural philosophy; he will never discover that they will adhere together in such a manner as to require great force to separate them in a direct line, while they make so small resistance to a lateral pressure. Such events, as bear little analogy to the common course of nature, are also readily confessed to be known only by experience; nor does any man imagine that the explosion of gunpowder, or the attraction of a loadstone, could ever be discovered by arguments *a priori.* In like manner, when an effect is supposed to depend upon an intricate machinery or secret structure of parts, we make no difficulty in attributing all our knowledge of it to experience. Who will assert that he can give the ultimate reason, why milk or bread is proper nourishment for man, not for a lion or tiger?

But the same truth may not appear, at first sight, to have the same evidence with regard to events, which have become familiar to us from our first appearance in the world, which bear a close analogy to the whole course of nature, and which are supposed to depend on the simple qualities of objects, without any secret structure of parts. We are apt to imagine that we could discover these effects by the mere operation of our reason, without experience. We fancy, that were we brought on a sudden into this world, we could at first have inferred that one Billiard-ball would communicate motion to another upon impulse; and that we needed not to have waited for the event, in order to pronounce with certainty concerning it. Such is the influence of custom, that, where it is strongest, it not only covers our natural ignorance, but even conceals itself, and seems not to take place, merely because it is found in the highest degree.

But to convince us that all the laws of nature, and all the operations of bodies without exception, are known only by experience, the following reflections may, perhaps, suffice. Were any object presented to us, and were we required to pronounce concerning the effect, which will result from it, without consulting past observation; after what manner, I beseech you, must the mind proceed in this operation? It must invent or imagine some event, which it ascribes to the object as its effect; and it is plain that this invention must be entirely arbitrary. The mind can never possibly find the effect in the supposed cause, by the most accurate scrutiny and examination. For the effect is totally different from the cause, and consequently can never be discovered in it. Motion in the second Billiard-ball is a quite distinct event from motion in the first: nor is there anything in the one to suggest the smallest hint of the other. A stone or piece of metal raised in the air, and left without any support, immediately falls; but to consider the matter *a priori,* is there anything we discover in this situation which can beget the idea of a downward, rather than an upward, or any other motion, in the stone or metal?

And as the first imagination or invention of a particular effect, in all natural operations, is arbitrary, where we consult not experience; so must we also esteem the supposed tie or connection between the cause and effect, which binds them together, and renders it impossible that any other effect could result from the operation of that cause. When I see, for instance, a Billiard-ball moving in a straight line towards another; even suppose motion in the second ball should by accident be suggested to me, as the result of their contact or impulse; may I not conceive, that a hundred different events might as well follow from that cause? May not both these balls remain at absolute rest? May not the first ball return in a straight line, or leap off from the second in any line or direction? All these suppositions are consistent and conceivable. Why then should we give preference to one, which is no more consistent or conceivable than the rest? All our reasonings *a priori* will never be able to show us any foundation for this preference.

In a word, then, every effect is a distinct event from its cause. It could not, therefore, be discovered in the cause, and the first invention or conception of it, *a priori,* must be entirely arbitrary. And even after it is suggested, the conjunction of it with the cause must appear equally arbitrary; since there are always many other effects, which, to reason, must seem fully as consistent and natural. In vain, therefore, should we pretend to determine any single event, or infer any cause or effect, without the assistance of observation and experience.

Hence we may discover the reason why no philosopher, who is rational and modest, has ever pretended to assign the ultimate cause of any natural operation, or to show distinctly the action of that power, which produces any single effect in the universe. It is confessed, that the utmost effort of human reason is to reduce the principles, productive of natural phenomena, to a greater simplicity, and to resolve the many particular effects into a few general causes, by means of reasonings from analogy, experience, and observation. But as to the causes of these general causes, we should in vain attempt their discovery; nor shall we ever be able to satisfy ourselves, by any particular explication of them. These ultimate springs and principles are totally shut up from human curiosity and enquiry. Elasticity, gravity, cohesion of parts, communication of motion by impulse; these are probably the ultimate causes and principles which we ever discover in nature; and we may esteem ourselves sufficiently happy, if, by accurate inquiry and reasoning, we can trace up the particular phenomena to, or near to, these general principles. The most perfect philosophy of the natural kind only staves off our ignorance a little longer: as perhaps the most perfect philosophy of the moral or metaphysical kind serves only to discover larger portions of it. Thus the observation of human blindness and weakness is the result of all philosophy, and meets us at every turn, in spite of our endeavors to elude or avoid it.

Nor is geometry, when taken into the assistance of natural philosophy, ever able to remedy this defect, or lead us into knowledge of ultimate causes, by all that accuracy of reasoning for which it is so justly celebrated. Every part of mixed mathematics proceeds upon the supposition that certain laws are established by nature in her operations; and abstract reasonings are employed, either to assist experience in the discovery of these laws, or to determine their influence in particular instances, where it depends upon any precise degree of distance and quantity. Thus, it is a law of motion, discovered by experience, that the moment or force of any body in motion is in the compound ratio or proportion of its solid contents and its velocity; and consequently, that a small force may remove the greatest obstacle or raise the greatest weight, if, by any contrivance or machinery, we can increase the velocity of that force, so as to make it an overmatch for its antagonist. Geometry assists us in the application of this law, by giving us the just dimensions of all the parts and figures which can enter into any species of machine; but still the discovery of the law itself is owing merely to experience, and all the abstract reasonings in the world could never lead us one step towards the knowledge of it. When we reason *a priori,* and consider merely any object or cause, as it appears to the mind, independent of all observation, it never could suggest to us the notion of any distinct object, such as its effect; much less, show us the inseparable and inviolable connection between them. A man must be very sagacious who could discover by reasoning that crystal is the effect of heat, and ice of cold, without being previously acquainted with the operation of these qualities.

PART II

But we have not yet attained any tolerable satisfaction with regard to the question first proposed. Each solution still gives rise to a new question as difficult as the foregoing, and leads us on to farther enquiries. When it is asked, *What is the nature of all of our reasonings concerning matter of fact?* the proper answer seems to be, that they are founded on the relation of cause and effect. When again it is asked, *What is the foundation of all our reasonings and conclusions concerning that relation?* it may be replied in one word, Experience. But if we still carry on our sifting humor, and ask, *What is the foundation of all conclusions from experience?* this implies a new question, which may be of more difficult solution and explication. Philosophers, that give themselves airs of superior wisdom and sufficiency, have a hard task when they encounter persons of inquisitive dispositions, who push them from every corner to which they retreat, and who are sure at last to bring them to some dangerous dilemma. The best expedient to prevent this confusion, is to be modest in our pretensions; and even to discover the difficulty ourselves before it is objected to us. By this means, we may make a kind of merit of our very ignorance.

I shall content myself, in this section with an easy task, and shall pretend only to give a negative answer to the question here proposed. I say then, that, even after we have experience of the operations of cause and effect, our conclusions from that experience are *not* founded on reasoning, or any process of the understanding. This answer we must endeavor both to explain and to defend.

It must certainly be allowed, that nature has kept us at a great distance from all her secrets, and has afforded us only the knowledge of a few superficial qualities of objects; while she conceals from us those powers and principles on which the influence of those objects entirely depends. Our senses inform us of the color, weight, and consistence of bread; neither sense nor reason can ever inform us of those qualities which fit it for the nourishment and support of a human body. Sight or feeling conveys an idea of the actual motion of bodies; but as to what wonderful force or power, which would carry on a moving body for ever in a continued change of place, and which bodies never lose but by communicating to others; of this we cannot form the most conception. But notwithstanding this ignorance of natural powers and principles, we always presume, when we see like sensible qualities, that they have like secret powers, and expect that effects, similar to those which we have experienced, will follow from them. If a body of like color and consistence with that bread which we have formerly eaten, be presented to us, we make no scruple of repeating the experiment, and foresee, with certainty, like nourishment and support. Now this is a process of the mind or thought, of which I would willingly know the foundation. It is allowed on all hands that there is no known connection between the sensible qualities and the secret powers; and consequently, that the mind is not led to form such a conclusion concerning their constant and regular conjunction, by anything which it knows of their nature. As to past *Experience*, it can be allowed to give *direct* and *certain* information of those precise objects only, and that precise period of time, which fell under its cognizance: but why this experience should be extended to future times, and to other objects, which, for aught we know, may be only in appearance similar; this is the main question on which I would insist. The bread, which I formerly ate, nourished me; that is, a body of such sensible qualities was, at that time, endued with such secret powers: but does it follow, that other bread must also nourish me at another time, and that like sensible qualities must always be attended with like secret powers? The consequence seems nowise necessary. At least, it must be acknowledged that there is here a consequence drawn by the mind; that there is a certain step taken; a process of thought, and an inference, which wants to be explained. These two propositions are far from being the same, *I have found that such an object has always been attended with such an effect,* and *I foresee, that other objects, which are, in appearance, similar, will be attended with similar effects.* I shall allow, if you please, that the one proposition may justly be inferred from the other; I know, in fact, that it always is inferred. But if you insist that the inference is made by a chain of reasoning, I desire you to produce that reasoning. The connection between these propositions is not intuitive. There is required a medium, which may enable the mind to draw such an inference, if indeed it be drawn by reasoning and argument. What that medium is, I must confess, passes my comprehension; and it is incumbent on those to produce it, who assert that it really exists, and is the origin of all our conclusions concerning matter of fact.

This negative argument must certainly, in process of time, become altogether convincing, if many penetrating and able philosophers shall turn their enquiries this way and no one be ever able to discover any connecting proposition or intermediate step, which supports the understanding in this conclusion. But as the question is yet new, every reader may not trust so far to his own penetration, as to conclude, because an argument escapes his enquiry, that therefore it does not really exist. For this reason it may be requisite to venture upon a more difficult task; and enumerating all the branches of human knowledge, endeavor to show that none of them can afford such an argument.

All reasonings may be divided into two kinds, namely demonstrative reasoning, or that concerning relations of ideas, and moral reasoning, or that concerning matter of fact and existence. That there are no demonstrative arguments in the case seems evident; since it implies no contradiction that the course of nature may change, and that an object, seemingly like those which we have experienced, may be attended with different or contrary effects. May I not clearly and distinctly conceive that a body, falling from the clouds, and which, in all other respects, resembles snow, has yet the taste of salt or feeling of fire? Is there any more intelligible proposition than to affirm, that all the trees will flourish in December and January, and decay in May and June? Now whatever is intelligible, and can be distinctly conceived, implies no contradiction, and can never be proved false by any demonstrative argument or abstract reasoning *a priori*.

If we be, therefore, engaged by arguments to put trust in past experience, and make it the standard of our future judgment, these arguments must be probable only, or such as regard matter of fact and real existence, according to the division above mentioned. But that there is no argument of this kind, must appear, if our explication of that species of reasoning be admitted as solid and satisfactory. We have said that all arguments concerning existence are founded on the relation of cause and effect; that our knowledge of that relation is derived from experience; and that all our experimental conclusions proceed upon the supposition that the future will be conformable to the past. To endeavor, therefore, the proof of this last supposition by probable arguments, or arguments regarding existence, must be evidently going in a circle, and taking that for granted, which is the very point in question.

In reality, all arguments from experience are founded on the similarity which we discover among natural objects, and by which we are induced to expect effects similar to those which we have found to follow from such objects. And though none but a fool or madman will ever pretend to dispute the authority of experience, or to reject that great guide of human life, it may surely be allowed a philosopher to have so much curiosity at least as to examine the principle of human nature, which gives this mighty authority to experience, and makes us draw advantage from that similarity which nature has placed among different objects. From causes which appear *similar* we expect similar effects. This is the sum of all our experimental conclusions. Now it seems evident that, if this conclusion were formed by reason, it would be as perfect at first, and upon one instance, as after ever so long a course of experience. But the case is far otherwise. Nothing so like as eggs; yet no one, on account of this appearing similarity, expects the same taste and relish in all of them. It is only after a long course of uniform experiments in any kind, that we attain a firm reliance and security with regard to a particular event. Now where is that process of reasoning which, from one instance, draws a conclusion, so different from that which it infers from a hundred instances that are nowise different from that single one? This question I propose as much for the sake of information, as with an intention of raising difficulties. I cannot find, I cannot imagine any such reasoning. But I keep my mind still open to instruction, if any one will vouchsafe to bestow it on me.

Should it be said that, from a number of uniform experiments, we *infer* a connection between the sensible qualities and the secret powers; this, I must confess, seems the same difficulty, couched in different terms. The question still recurs, on what process of argument this *inference* is founded? Where is the medium, the interposing ideas, which join propositions so very wide of each other? It is confessed that the color, consistence, and other sensible qualities of bread appear not, of themselves, to have any connection with the secret powers of nourishment and support. For otherwise we could infer these powers from the first appearance of these sensible qualities, without the aid of experience; contrary to the sentiment of all philosophers and contrary to plain matter of fact. Here, then, is our natural state of ignorance with regard to the powers and influence of all objects. How is this remedied by experience? It only shows us a number of uniform effects, resulting from certain objects, and teaches us that those particular objects, at that particular time, were endowed with such powers and forces. When a new object, endowed with similar sensible qualities, is produced, we expect similar powers and forces, and look for a like effect. From a body of like color and consistence with bread we expect like nourishment and support. But this surely is a step or progress of the mind, which wants to be explained. When a man says, *I have found, in all past instances, such sensible qualities conjoined with such secret powers:* And when he says, *Similar sensible qualities will always be conjoined with similar secret powers,* he is not guilty of a tautology, nor are these propositions in any respect the same. You say that the one proposition is an inference from the other. But you must confess that the inference is not intuitive; neither is it demonstrative: Of what nature is it, then? To say it is experimental, is begging the question. For all inferences from experience suppose, as their foundation, that the future will resemble the past, and that similar powers will be conjoined with similar sensible qualities. If there be any suspicion that the course of nature may change, and that the past may be no rule for the future, all experience becomes useless, and can give rise to no inference or conclusion. It is impossible, therefore, that any arguments from experience can prove this resemblance of the past to the future; since all these arguments are founded on the supposition of that resemblance. Let the course of things be allowed hitherto ever so regular; that alone, without some new argument or inference, proves not that, for the future, it will continue so. In vain do you pretend to have learned the nature of bodies from your past experience. Their secret nature, and consequently all their effects and influence, may change, without any change in their sensible qualities. This happens sometimes, and with regard to some objects: Why may it not happen always, and with regard to all objects? What logic, what process of argument secures you against this supposition? My practice, you say, refutes my doubts. But you mistake the purport of my question. As an agent, I am quite satisfied in the point; but as a philosopher, who has some share of curiosity, I will not say scepticism, I want to learn the foundation of this inference. No reading, no enquiry has yet been able to remove my difficulty, or give me satisfaction in a matter of such importance. Can I do better than propose the difficulty to the public, even though, perhaps, I have small hopes of obtaining a solution? We shall, at least, by this means, be sensible of our ignorance, if we do not augment our knowledge.

I must confess that a man is guilty of unpardonable arrogance who concludes, because an argument has escaped his own investigation, that therefore it does not really exist. I must confess that, though all the learned, for several ages, should have employed themselves in fruitless search upon any subject, it may still, perhaps, be rash to conclude positively that the subject must, therefore, pass all human comprehension. Even though we examine all the sources of our knowledge, and conclude them unfit for such a subject, there may still remain a suspicion, that the enumeration is not complete, or the examination not accurate. But with regard to the present subject, there are some considerations which seem to remove all this accusation of arrogance or suspicion of mistake.

It is certain that the most ignorant and stupid peasants—nay infants, nay even brute beasts—improve by experience, and learn the qualities of natural objects, by observing the effects which result from them. When a child has felt the sensation of pain from touching the flame of a candle, he will be careful not to put his hand near any candle; but will expect a similar effect from a cause which is similar in its sensible qualities and appearance. If you assert, therefore, that the understanding of the child is led into this conclusion by any process of argument or ratiocination, I may justly require you to produce that argument; nor have you any pretense to refuse so equitable a demand. You cannot say that the argument is abstruse, and may possibly escape your enquiry; since you confess that it is obvious to the capacity of a mere infant. If you hesitate, therefore, a moment, or if, after reflection, you produce any intricate or profound argument, you, in a manner, give up the question, and confess that it is not reasoning which engages us to suppose the past resembling the future and to expect similar effects from causes which are, to appearance, similar. This is the proposition which I intended to enforce in the present section. If I be right, I pretend not to have made any mighty discovery. And if I be wrong, I must acknowledge myself to be indeed a very backward scholar; since I cannot now discover an argument which, it seems, was perfectly familiar to me long before I was out of my cradle.

EDMUND HUSSERL
(1859-1938)

Studied in Vienna, and taught philosophy at the Universities of Halle, Goettingen and Freiburg. Of Jewish origin, he fell victim to the Nazi academic purge. Husserl developed the movement called phenomenology, which strongly influenced the development of existentialism. Husserl opposed "psychologism" and taught the "autonomy of spiritual structures" which can be comprehended by specific essential insight. Heidegger was his best known pupil.

Main Works:

Formale und transzendentale Logik; Logische Untersuchungen; Ideen zu einer reinen Phänomenologie und phänomenologischen Philosophie. Philosophie der Arithmetik; Prolegomena zur reinen Logik; Untersüchüngen zur Phänomenologie und Theorie der Erkenntnis; Elemente einer phänomenologischen Aufklärung der Erkenntnis.

Consciousness and Natural Reality

All the essential characteristics of experience and consciousness which we have reached are for us necessary steps towards the attainment of the end which is unceasingly drawing us on, the discovery, namely, of the essence of that *"pure"* consciousness which is to fix the limits of the phenomenological field. Our inquiries were eidetic; but the individual instances of the essences we have referred to as experience, stream of experience, "consciousness" in all its senses, belonged as real events to the natural world. To that extent we have not abandoned the ground of the natural standpoint. Individual consciousness is interwoven with the *natural world* in a *twofold* way: it is some

------

From: *Ideen zu einer reinen Phänomenologie und phänomenologischen Philosophie.*

man's consciousness, or that of some *man* or *beast,* and in a large number at least of its particularizations it is a consciousness of this world. *In respect now of this intimate attachment with the real world, what is meant by saying that consciousness has an essence "of its own,"* that with other consciousness it constitutes a self-contained *connection determined purely through this, its own essence,* the connection, namely, of the stream of consciousness? Moreover, since we can interpret consciousness in the widest sense to cover eventually whatever the concept of experience includes, the question concerns the experience-stream's own essential nature and that of all its components. To what extent, in the first place, must the *material world* be fundamentally different in kind, *excluded from the experience's own essential nature?* And if it is this, if over against all consciousness and the essential being proper to it, it is that which is "foreign" and "other," how can consciousness be *interwoven* with it, and consequently with the whole world that is alien to consciousness? For it is easy to convince oneself that the material world is not just any portion of the natural world, but its fundamental stratum to which all other real being is *essentially* related. It still fails to include the souls of men and animals; and the new factor which these introduce is first and foremost their "experiencing" together with their conscious relationship to the world surrounding them. *But here consciousness and thinghood form a connected whole,* connected within the particular psychological unities which we call *animalia;* and in the last resort within the *real unity of the world as a whole.* Can the unity of a whole be other than made one through the essential proper nature of its parts, which must therefore have some *community of essence* instead of a fundamental heterogeneity?

To be clear, let us seek out the ultimate sources whence the general thesis of the world which I adopt when taking up the natural standpoint draws its nourishment, thereby enabling me as a conscious being to discover over against me an existing world of things, to ascribe to myself in this world a body, and to find for myself within this world a proper place. This ultimate source is obviously *sensory experience*. For our purpose, however, it is sufficient to consider *sensory perception*, which in a certain proper sense plays among experiencing acts the part of an original experience, whence all other experiencing acts draw a chief part of their power to serve as a ground. Every perceiving consciousness has this peculiarity, that it is the consciousness of *the embodied (leibhaftigen) self-presence of an individual object*, which on its own side and in a pure logical sense of the term is an individual or some logico-categorical modification of the same. In our own instance, that of sensory perception, or, in distincter terms, perception of a world of things, the logical individual is the Thing; and it is sufficient for us to treat the perception of things as representing all other perception (of properties, processes, and the like).

The natural wakeful life of our Ego is a continuous perceiving, actual or potential. The world of things and our body within it are continuously present to our perception. How then does and can *Consciousness itself* separate out as a *concrete thing in itself*, from that within it, of which we are conscious, namely, the *perceived being*, *"standing over against"* consciousness *"in and for itself"*?

I mediate first as would the man "in the street." I see and grasp the thing itself in its bodily reality. It is true that I sometimes deceive myself, and not only in respect of the perceived constitution of the thing, but also in respect of its being there at all. I am subject to an illusion or hallucination. The perception is not the "genuine." But if it is, if, that is, we can "confirm" its presence in the actual context of experience, eventually with the help of correct empirical thinking, then the perceived thing *is real* and itself really given, and that bodily in perception. Here perceiving considered simply as consciousness, and apart from the body and the bodily organs, appears as something in itself essenceless, an empty looking of an empty "Ego" towards the object which comes into contact with it in some astonishing way

WILLIAM JAMES
(1842-1910)

Son of the Swedenborgian theologian Henry James, enjoyed a cosmopolitan education both in Europe and America. He turned to philosophy only after trying anatomy and chemistry, and his interests always remained broad and included religion, psychology and parapsychological phenomena. Taught at Harvard from 1872. In this most influential of American philosophers we can discern three main directions: Voluntarism, radical empiricism and pragmatism. Will and interest dominate, true is what favors our manner of thinking, knowledge is instrumental.

Main Works:

> Principles of Psychology; The Varieties of Religious Experience; Pragmatism; A Pluralistic Universe; The Will to Believe; The Meaning of Truth; Essays in Radical Empiricism; Some Problems in Philosophy.

Pragmatism

Truth, as any dictionary will tell you, is a property of certain of our ideas. It means their "agreement," as falsity means their disagreement, with "reality." Pragmatists and intellectualists both accept this definition as a matter of course. They begin to quarrel only after the question is raised as to what may precisely be meant by the term "agreement" and what by the term "reality," when reality is taken as something for our ideas to agree with.

In answering these questions the pragmatists are more analytic and painstaking, the intellectualists more offhand and ir-

---

From: *Pragmatism.*

reflective. The popular notion is that a true idea must copy its reality. Like other popular views, this one follows the analogy of the most usual experience. Our true ideas of sensible things do indeed copy them. Shut your eyes and think of yonder clock on the wall, and you get just such a true picture or copy of its dial. But your idea of its "works" (unless you are a clockmaker) is much less of a copy, yet it passes muster, for it in no way clashes with the reality. Even though it should shrink to the mere word "works," that word still serves you truly; and when you speak of the "time-keeping function" of the clock, or of its spring's "elasticity," it is hard to see exactly what your ideas can copy.

You perceive that there is a problem here. Where our ideas cannot copy definitely their object, what does agreement with that object mean? Some idealists seem to say that they are true whenever they are what God means that we ought to think about that object. Others hold the copy-view all through, and speak as if our ideas possessed truth just in proportion as they approach to being copies of the Absolute's eternal way of thinking.

These views, you see, invite pragmatistic discussion. But the great assumption of the intellectualists is that truth means essentially an inert static relation. When you've got your true idea of anything, there's an end of the matter. You're in possession; you *know*; you have fulfilled your thinking destiny. You are where you ought to be mentally; you have obeyed your categorical imperative; and nothing more need follow on that climax of your rational destiny. Epistemologically you are in stable equilibrium.

Pragmatism, on the other hand, asks its usual question. "Grant an idea or belief to be true," it says, "what concrete difference will its being true make in any one's actual life? How will the truth be realized? What experiences will be different from those which would obtain if the belief were false? What, in short, is the truth's cash-value in experiential terms?"

The moment pragmatism asks this question, it sees the answer: *True ideas are those that we can assimilate, validate, corroborate and verify. False ideas are those that we can not.* That is the practical difference it makes to us to have true ideas; that, therefore, is the meaning of truth, for it is all that truth is known as.

This thesis is what I have to defend. The truth of an idea is not a stagnant property inherent in it. Truth *happens* to an idea. It *becomes* true, is *made* true by events. Its verity *is* in fact an event, a process: the process namely of its verifying itself, its veri-*fication*. Its validity is the process of its valid-*ation*.

But what do the words verification and validation themselves pragmatically mean? They again signify certain practical consequences of the verified and validated idea. It is hard to find any one phrase that characterizes these consequences better than the ordinary agreement-formula—just such consequences being what we have in mind whenever we say that our ideas "agree" with reality. They lead us, namely, through the acts and other ideas which they instigate, into or up to, or towards, other parts of experience with which we feel all the while—such feeling being among our potentialities—that the original ideas remain in agreement. The connections and transitions come to us from point to point as being progressive, harmonious, satisfactory. This function of agreeable leading is what we mean by an idea's verification. Such an account is vague and it sounds at first quite trivial, but it has results which it will take the rest of my hour to explain.

Let me begin by reminding you of the fact that the possession of true thoughts means everywhere the possession of invaluable instruments of action; and that our duty to gain truth, so far from being a blank command from out of the blue, or a "stunt" self-imposed by our intellect, can account for itself by excellent practical reasons.

The importance to human life of having true beliefs about matters of fact is a thing too notorious. We live in a world of realities that can be infinitely useful or infinitely harmful. Ideas that tell us which of them to expect count as the true ideas in all his primary sphere of verification, and the pursuit of such ideas is a primary human duty. The possession of truth, so far from being an end in itself, is only a preliminary means toward other vital satisfactions. If I am lost in the woods and starved, and find what looks like a cow path, it is of the utmost importance that I should think of a human habitation at the end of it, for if I do so and follow it, I save myself. The true thought is useful here because the house which is its object is useful. The practical value of true ideas is thus primarily derived from the practical importance of their objects to us. Their objects are, indeed, not important at all times. I may on another occasion have no use for the house; and then my idea of it, however verifiable, will be practically irrelevant, and had better remain latent. Yet since almost any object may someday become temporarily important, the advantage of having a general stock of *extra* truths, of ideas that shall be true of merely possible situations, is obvious. We store such extra truths away in our memories, and with the overflow we fill our books of reference. Whenever such an extra truth becomes practically relevant to one of our emergencies, it passes from cold storage to do work in the world and our belief in it grows active. You can say of it then either that "it is useful because it is true" or that "it is true because it is useful." Both these phrases mean exactly the same thing, namely that here is an idea that gets fulfilled and can be verified. True is the name for whatever idea starts the verification process, useful is the name for its completed function in experience. True ideas would never have been singled out as such, would never have acquired a class-name, least of all a name suggesting value, unless they had been useful from the outset in this way.

From this simple cue pragmatism gets her general notion of truth as something essentially bound up with the way in which one moment in our experience may lead us towards other moments which it will be worth while to have been led to. Primarily, and on the common sense level, the truth of a state of mind means this function of a *leading that is worth while*. When a moment in our experience, of any kind whatever, inspires us with a thought that is true, that means that sooner or later we

dip by that thought's guidance into the particulars of experience
again and make advantageous connection with them. This is a
vague enough statement, but I beg you to retain it, for it is
essential.

*"The true," to put it briefly, is only the expedient in the way
of our thinking, just as "the right" is only the expedient in the
way of our behaving.* Expedient in almost any fashion; and expedient in the long run and on the whole of course; for what
meets expediently all the experience insight won't necessarily
meet all farther experiences equally satisfactorily. Experience,
as we know, has ways of *boiling over,* and making us correct
our present formulas.

The "absolutely" true, meaning what no farther experience
will ever alter, is that ideal vanishing-point towards which we
imagine that all our temporary truths will some day converge.
It runs on all fours with the perfectly wise man, and with the
absolutely complete experience; and, if these ideals are ever
realized, they will all be realized together. Meanwhile we have
to live today by what truth we can get today, and be ready tomorrow to call it falsehood. Ptolemaic astronomy, euclidean
space, aristotelian logic, scholastic metaphysics, were expedient
for centuries, but human experience has boiled over those limits,
and we now call these things only relatively true, or true within
those borders of experience. "Absolutely" they are false; for we
know that those limits were casual, and might have been transcended by past theorists just as they are by present thinkers.

When new experiences lead to retrospective judgments, using
the past tense, what these judgments utter *was true,* even though
no past thinker had been led there. We live forwards, a Danish
thinker has said, but we understand backwards. The present
sheds a backward light on the world's previous processes. They
may have been truth-processes for the actors in them. They are
not so for one who knows the later revelations of the story.

This regulative notion of a potential better truth to be established some day absolutely, and having powers of retroactive
legislation, turns its face, like all pragmatist notions towards the

future. Like the half-truths, the absolute truth will have to be *made*, as a relation incidental to the growth of a mass of verification-experience, to which the half true ideas are all along contributing their quota.

I have already insisted on the fact that truth is made largely out of previous truths. Men's beliefs at any time are so much experience *funded*. But the beliefs are themselves parts of the sum total of the world's experience, and become matter, therefore, for the next day's funding operations. So far as reality means experienceable reality, both it and the truths men gain about it are everlastingly in process of mutation towards a definite goal—it may be—but still mutation.

Mathematicians can solve problems with two variables, with distance, but distance also varies with acceleration. In the realm of truth-processes facts come independently and determine our beliefs provisionally. But these beliefs make us act, and as fast as they do so, they bring into sight or into existence new facts which re-determine the beliefs accordingly. So the whole coil and ball of truth, as it rolls up, is the product of a double influence. Truths emerge from facts; but they dip forward into facts again and add to them; which facts again create or reveal new truth (the word is indifferent) and so on indefinitely. The "facts" themselves meanwhile are not *true*. They simply *are*. Truth is the function of the beliefs that start and terminate among them.

The case is like a snowball's growth, due as it is to the distribution of the snow on the one hand, and to the successive pushes of the boys on the other, with these factors co-determining each other incessantly.

JOACHIM JUNGIUS
(1587-1657)

A German mathematician and physicist, was an important precursor of the mechanistic conception of nature. He was Professor of mathematics (1609-1614) at Giessen and at Rostock, and from 1629 to 1640 was Rector of the Johanneum at Hamburg. Jung, or Jungius, considered that philosophy required a mathematical foundation. Leibniz places Jungius on a level with Galileo and Kepler.

Main Works:

Logica Hamburgensis; De Plantis doxocopiae physicae minores; Isagoge Phytoscopica.

Falsehood and Truth

Logic is an art that directs the operations of the mind to distinguish between truth and falsehood.

There are three mental operations: Notion or Concept, Proposition, and Dianoia or Disputation.

Notion is the first operation of the mind, whereby as in a picture we express something. Notion is an image, homoioma, whereby a thing is represented in the mind.

Hence we are said to conceive, apprehend, think of a thing, when we perceive or form its notion, as when we think of *man, horse, rose, oak tree, handsome man, swift horse, purple flower.*

Proposition is the second mental operation, so composed of

From: *Logica Hamburgensis.*

notions that what is true or false arises in it. For example, true propositions: The sun shines. Man is a biped. An oak is a tree. False propositions: The sun does not shine. Man is a quadruped. An oak is not a tree. An oak is a stone.

A notion is particularly adapted to the representation of things that actually exist. If however a thing in the nature of things does not respond to some notion, the notion itself is not consequently rendered false, as if one thinks of *Elysian Fields*, a *Centaur, Purgatory*. This thought of mine is not false. But if I should state: The Elysian Fields are somewhere. Achilles was trained by a Centaur. Purgatory exists. Or: Souls are tortured in Purgatory, then my thought is false. Dianoia is the third mental operation, so constituted from propositions that something true is inferred from some other truth, as: No tree is a stone. Therefore no stone is a tree. Similarly: Bread is moderately sweet. Therefore bread is nourishing. Similarly: Every miser is in need. Therefore no miser is rich.

The first operation is also called apprehension of simple things: the second, composition and division. By composition we understand an affirmative proposition: by division, a negative proposition.

Observe that notion is the same as formation of notion, proposition as the performance of a proposition, argumentation as the construction of argumentation. For they are immanent actions, and do not abandon their functions.

Logic, according to Zabarella and his followers, is defined as an organic or instrumental habit of mind that distinguishes truth from falsehood.

It is called an organic habit, because it supplies us with organs or instruments whereby we distinguish truth from falsehood.

Organs are called the second voices of notion, or second notions, as: genus, species, proposition, subject, predicate, ratiocination, middle term, and such like. For we are said to be and by them in cognition as by instruments.

The school of Peter Ramus defines logic that they also call

dialectics, as the art of effective speaking or using of reason, that is, of explaining and clarifying anything whatever, whether true or false, and reasoning about it and debating and discussing it.

The term logic has been widely accepted, and embraces three arts that involve the logos, that is, speech: logic properly so called, rhetoric, and grammar. However, logic properly so called derives its name from reason rather than speech: for logos signifies both.

The truth of a proposition is two-fold. One is truth properly so called or necessary truth: the other is probable, or likely.

Necessary truth is that which cannot be otherwise, as: Twice three are six. Fire burns. Wood floats in water. God is just.

Probable truth is that which is approved by many men or by the wiser ones, that is, it is considered as truth, as: It is right to repel force by force. Health is preferable to beauty. Truth produces hatred.

Hence arises the genuine part of logic. For logic is divided into a general part and a special part. The general part is that which aims at the truth in general, that is, which transmits the precepts that commonly serve the determinates of truth, both necessary and probable.

Furthermore, general logic is divided into three parts for the triple operation of the mind, of which the first considers notions, the second propositions, the third interpretations.

Special logic views the truth in the species, and is two-fold: apodeictic and dialectic. Apodeictic or demonstrative is that which is necessarily in truth: dialectic, which involves probable truth.

The necessary appendix of both is sophistic, which distinguishes the apparent truth from that which is really true. Petrus Ramus classifies logic into Invention and Judgment. He declares that Invention treats of inventing arguments: Judgment, of arranging these arguments for effective judgment.

He calls arguments single reasons or notions considered by themselves, in so far as they mutually prove themselves, that is, refer to themselves. He explains that arguments or notions are arranged partly in the second, and partly in the third operation.

What Ramus explains in the first part of his logic, that is, in Invention, should be found here partly in the predicables, partly in the category of relation, and partly in the fifth book, that deals with dialectics.

As we cannot converse with each other by means of notions, but explain to one another the perceptions of the mind by means of words and talk, logic never neglects, in any of the previously mentioned parts, either oral or written speech, but embraces it too under its consideration, in so far as it is a sign of mental operations, and thus in its own way capable of truth.

Hence it arises that that too which is composed of notions in the mind is called mental or inner speech, likewise the inner logos or the inner spoken word, whether the composition subsists within the first mental operation, as: Rational animal, a plane bounded by three straight lines, a brave man, hot water, a carnivorous bird: or whether it advances toward the second or third mental operation.

Speech itself, properly so called, is termed, for the purpose of distinction, external speech, or the outer logos.

The end of logic is the discovery and judgment of the truth of knowledge. The object or subject of logic is that to which something is near and something remote. Near, again, may be primary or secondary.

The near primary object is the mental operations, particularly the second one. The near secondary object is external speech in so far as it expresses a mental operation appositely in relation to the truth. The remote object is the universal thing with which both the mental operations and external speech are concerned.

Though dialectics has less prestige than epistemology, it transcends it in practice and facility. For by cognition of the probables it exercises and prepares the inexperienced mind for the perception of the things that are properly and basically true, by epistemological methods.

A dialectic or probable argument is an attempt to infer a conclusion from probable assumptions. From probabilities a probable conclusion only can be deduced.

A probable statement or proposition, a valid protasis, that is also termed plausible, is one that is approved by all or very many men, or certainly by the wiser, more intelligent, or more learned, that is, it is considered to be true. For example: It is permissible to repel force by force. Intellectual good is preferable to physical good. Intemperance is exposed to disease. Living bodies are composed of atoms.

A proposition of this kind must also be understood when the one word probable is used. An improbable proposition is one that is not probable, that is, is considered false by the majority of men. Among the Greeks it is termed adoxos or paradox, as: The earth moves. Only the wise man is rich. Sins are alike.

It may therefore happen that what is probable is false, and what is improbable is true.

Taken in a wider sense, dialectic argumentation also embraces the argument that is termed concession, since we make an inference from less probable assumptions that are yet conceded by the opponent and are acceptable. This is also called *argumentum ad hominem.*

Dialectic argument is various in relation to the variety of species into which dianoia is divided. It is called the immediate dialectic consequence, and the dialectic syllogism, and the dialectic sorites, and dialectic induction, and so on, if the form of the argument is applied to probable propositions or to matter.

Dialectic argument is used by us in the same sense as dialectic argumentation. The same expression is used by others sometimes for a primary assumption of a dialectic argument, sometimes for the middle term of a logical syllogism.

When it is used as a term, it is less properly called a probable invention: when the term is true or false, it cannot be called probable or improbable.

The scope of dialectics and the final end are opinion. But if it attempts persuasion, it is an abuse of the art of logic.

Opinion, *doxa*, is a probable proposition, accepted as probable, that is, opinion is a feeble assent whereby we assent to a probable proposition so that we establish it as being probable only.

Persuasion occurs when we assent to a probable proposition firmly, as though it were simply true and necessary, or demonstrated from necessary assumptions. Persuasion therefore is error. Opinion is an approach to knowledge.

On this account dialectics is also called an apodeictic instrument.

Persuasion is often also termed opinion and doxa. Persuasion involves difficulties for those who do not know the difference between apodeictic and dialectic argument.

The intermediate end of dialectics is the dialectic argument itself.

Its nearest object is probable propositions. Its remote object is things that are both necessary and contingent.

The question precedes dialectic argument. For no one seeks to confirm by argument what nobody doubts or questions. The question—in Greek, the zetsis, the zetema, the problem—is twofold. One type of question seeks the answer *yes* or *no*. The other type seeks some term in the reply or requires a part of the term to be added to the parts included in the question.

The Stoics, interested in distinctions of speech, called the first kind of question erotema, that is, interrogation: the second kind they called pusma, that is, inquiry or investigation.

An inquiry occurs, when I ask: How many elements are there in natural bodies? What is the genus of place? What is art?

Interrogation occurs, when I ask: Are there four elements? Is surface the genus of place? Is art a habit coordinate with true reason?

Interrogation may also be defined as a dubious proposition, whose truth or falsity is still undetermined.

Response is a proposition that determines the doubt of a question.

Proposition is usually distinguished as judicial and apprehensive. It is called judicial when it is really a second mental operation, sharing in truth or falsity, as: A son is like a father. It is apprehensive, when it is posited as a notion and part of another proposition, as: It is probable that a son is like his father.

A question is an apprehensive proposition: a reply is a judicial proposition. A question asked dialectically by itself is an interrogation, to which accordingly an inquiry, if feasible, must be applied for the terms used. For example, the inquiry: What is the genus of logic? is applied to these interrogations: Is the genus of logic an art or a science or an instrumental habit? Hence interrogation is generally called a dialectic question.

Not every interrogation, however, is dialectic, but only such about which men either do not think at all, or establish contradictories. An example of the first is the question: Is the number of stars odd or even? An example of the second: Is the sun much greater than the earth or not?

A question that is reprehensible or meaningless is not a dialectic question. For example: Should God be worshipped or not? Should parents be honored or not? are reprehensible. Anyone who is in doubt about the questions: Is snow white? Is fire hot? should be refuted by sense, not by dialectic arguments.

Interrogation is either simple or multiple. It is simple when it questions one contradiction, as: Is pleasure man's greatest good? At Christ's resurrection shall we too not be resurrected?

A simple interrogation is either of a simple mode or a double mode. It is of a simple mode, when it expresses at least one of two contradictories, as: Is virtue the greatest good?

A simple interrogation is of double mode, when it presents both parts of the contradiction by questioning or a two-fold token of interrogation is used, as: Is virtue the greatest good or not? Or: Is war permissible or not?

Interrogation of a simple mode generally shows which part of the contradiction the question approves, or at least toward which part it inclines. For example, when I ask: Do we not become just by just action? Will the universe not perish? Is not virtue a habit? Bees are not really intelligent, are they? All anger is not a desire for vengeance, is it? Similarly I grant: Just action makes us just. The universe will perish. Virtue is a habit. Bees are not really intelligent. Not all anger is a desire for vengeance. Or: A certain anger is not a desire for vengeance.

The two-fold mode of questioning involves the questioner's mind more, as when I propose the following questions: Do we become just by just action, or not? Will the universe perish, or not? Is all anger a desire for vengeance, or not? And so on.

Multiple interrogation occurs when it postulates several contradictions at once, and on this account it can be resolved into as many simple questions.

Multiple interrogation must be considered not so much interrogation as interrogations. It is explicitly multiple.

Explicit multiple interrogation questions many things conjunctively or disjunctively. Conjunctively, as: Is music useful and necessary for a well-born youth? Was not Cicero a just orator? Was Lucullus a voluptuous commander? Disjunctively, as: Is a hazel-tree a shrub or a tree? Is geometry an art or a science? Is pleasure the greatest good of man, or virtue, or a virtuous act? Is virtue acquired by learning, or by habit, or by either? Is Demosthenes the greater orator, or Cicero, or is neither greater than the other?

Implicit multiple interrogation is expressed in as many codes as a proposition itself, as: Ought man to want to consult man's interest because he is a man? Should only the apostles among all the saints be called upon? Is Homer greater than Hesiod? Is it true that Pyrrhus defeated the Romans?

There is furthermore another mode also of implicit multiple interrogation, that may be termed by presupposition, when the reply which is simply true hints at another false reply, or presupposes it. For instance, when I ask: Does not science confirm the inherent principles of theology more than metaphysics? Is any good work more deserving of the grace of conversion than charity? Similarly, if I ask about a temperate person: Has he stopped gormandizing? Or about a man who always pursues virtue: Has he begun to be honest? For although this interrogation is true simply: No philosophical science confirms the inherent principles of theology more than metaphysics, since its contradictory is false, namely: Some philosophical science confirms the inherent principles of theology more than metaphysics, because the postulated proposition presupposes, according to the common custom of speech, and hints that this proposition is false (metaphysics confirms the inherent principles of theology, and that equally with or more than any other science), the postulated question is multiple and deceptive. So this proposition is true simply: Socrates has not stopped gormandizing: for he cannot stop if he never began. Yet if one says: Socrates has not stopped gormandizing, he seems to suggest: Socrates is still accustomed to gormandize. So if I should ask: Was Socrates more handsome than Thersites?, I suggest that both were handsome, although neither was. So if I should ask: Was Cicero a greater orator than Pomponius Atticus?, the person who affirms asserts that Atticus was an orator: the person who denies this, suggests that Atticus was equal in eloquence to Cicero or even greater.

A multiple question should be handled with care, and a simple reply must not be used, but as many replies as may be necessary, and at the same time the ambiguity must be resolved.

Certain inquiries are deceptive, for they suppose a false proposition. For instance, when I ask: What is the beginning of Vergil's twelfth Eclogue? In what respect are homonyms different from equivocations? What are the species of man? By how many degrees is Hamburg more northern than Antwerp?

Further, interrogation receives all the numerous divisions that a proposition admits, as: Categorical, conjunctive, causal: affirmative negative: universal, particular: pure, modal, etc.

The divisions of a question so far postulated were derived from form: there now follows the distinction of questions derived from matter or the object.

By reason of matter, then, a question is real or conceptual. It is real, when it asks about things taken by themselves, not in so far as they have been denominated by our intelligence. A conceptual question, also termed notional, is one that asks about things in so far as they are apprehended.

A real inquiry occurs, when I ask: What is the cause of the downward motion of gravity? How many parts has a comedy? What is the ultimate end of human action? What is the relation of a Greek foot to a Roman foot? Of what notions does the idea of a triangle consist?

Real interrogation occurs, when I ask: Is the substantial form of heavy bodies the cause of their downward motion? Does every comedy consist of a protasis, epitasis, and a catastrophe? Is every triangle either equilateral or isosceles or scalene? Is there really an intellectual virtue and a moral virtue? Is every war unjust? Is every natural body in a place? Can a straight line, tangent to a circle, be drawn from any given point? Is a Greek foot longer than a Roman foot? Is every notion simple? Is a syllogism an immanent action?

A conceptual inquiry occurs, when I ask: What is the genus of a semi-tone? What is the nearest genus of opinion? What are the species of a triangle? How manifold is virtue? What are the demonstrable affections of being? What is the definition of animal?

A notional interrogation occurs, when I ask: Is an interval of sounds a genus of a semi-tone? Is a mental habit the nearest genus of opinion? Should an accident be predicated of quality as transcending genus? Is quality the highest genus? Is a sentient animate body a definition of animal? Is it a property of man to be capable of virtue? Is sickness a general accident of man? Is place a suitable affection of a natural body? Is the touch of a straight line a demonstrable affection of a circle?

A notional question always asks about some relationship based on reason that is such that it cannot be attributed to a particular or an individual, as when I erroneously assert: This animal is a genus. This man is a species. This rational animal is a definition.

A real dialectic question is also called a question of simple inherence, because it asks simply whether a predicate is in a subject: since a notional question asks about the mode and how it is in the subject.

A real dialectic question is either absolute or comparative. It is absolute, when it asks absolutely whether this is that, whether this is such, as: Is virtue to be pursued?

A comparative question, which is an *a fortiori* question, asks whether this is more than that, or—which amounts to the same thing—whether that is less than this. Should honor be pursued more than wealth? Should justice be preferred to courage? Is poetry or oratory more useful to the state? Is drunkenness less of a sin than wantonness? Was Aeneas or Turnus braver?

A real dialectic question is either categorical or transcendental. It is categorical, when each term of the question is in a definite category, either by itself, or reductively, as: Is there some physical virtue? Is a comedy a poem? A transcendental question occurs, when either one of the terms of a question is transcendent, as: Is being a true relation? Is that better which makes a thing, in which it is, better? Is that which is more simple more perfect?

A transcendentally relative question occurs, when the principal part of a predicate is a transcendental relation. A transcendental relation is here so called, when it transcends all the highest genera, when it is taken from an inherent relation, or a contingent one, or from both.

Examples of a transcendentally relative question are as follows: Is hair a part of the body? Is a body a part of man? Is fire the efficient cause of salt arising from combustion? Is interposition an efficient cause of an eclipse? Are a dancer and an actor equal in prestige? Is the knowledge of the angels greater or more perfect than that of man? Is sacrilege a greater sin than peculation? Does an egg naturally come before the hen? Is there anything brighter than the sun? Do heat and cold coexist in the same subject?

From these examples it is established that a comparative question is comprehended in a transcendentally relative question, or is reduced to it.

In geometry, when it is asked: Is there any square greater than a triangle?, the question is neither transcendentally relative nor dialectic, because the word *greater* is understood not in a transcendental sense, but in a more limited and geometric signification, on account of the postulated definitions.

In either of the two contradictory propositions, arguments must be sought whereby to confirm the question. Arguments are drawn partly from topics, partly from dialectic instruments.

A dialectic topic or a topic of a dialectic argument is a name taken from some very general relation, in which are included many major propositions containing this relation, as: Topic of genus, topic of cause, topic of the greater.

Dialectic topic is commonly defined as the basis of argument. The major proposition is a very probable universal statement, connecting, by the inclusion of some very general relation, the consequent of an argument with the antecedent, as: What is suitable for the genus, is suitable for the species too. If the necessarily acting cause is posited, the effect is posited. What cannot be exceeded by the greater, cannot be exceeded by a lesser either. The major proposition is also termed major absolutely, and also dialectic axiom.

A dialectic argument is said to be derived, elicited, drawn from the topic whose relation is included in the major proposition, on which the argument particularly depends, and in that part of the major that concerns the antecedent of the argument, as when I argue as follows:

> Every animal feels.
> Every fish is an animal.
> Therefore every fish feels.

The argument is said to be drawn from the topic of genus, because it depends on this major proposition: What is suitable for the genus, is suitable for the species also, and this part of the major proposition: What is suitable for the genus, refers to the antecedent of the argument, that is, to this major: Every animal feels. The remaining part of the major: it is suitable for

429

the species also, refers to the conclusion: Every fish feels. Similarly when I deduce as follows: The sun has risen. Therefore it is day, is called an argument drawn from the topic of cause, because part of the major proposition, that mentions the cause, refers to the antecedent of the argument, for: the sun has risen, is the cause of day.

We are said to argue from the genus to the species, when the argument is drawn from the topic of the genus, and on the other hand to infer from the species to the genus when the argument is drawn from the topic of species.

Topics of arguments are called opposed, when they are denominated by relations mutually opposed, as: The topic of genus is said to be opposed to the topic of species: the topic of the efficient to the topic of the effected.

Relation denominating a topic or *topos* is called a topical relation. Argument too is called topical, for it is drawn from a dialectic topic. Even dialectics itself is called a topical art or faculty from these topics.

At this point a caution must be entered on homonyms of a dialectic topic: for topic is understood by logicians in three modes.

First comes the Greatest, or the Dialectic Axiom, and so Aristotle almost invariably uses the term. Next, difference of the Greatest, or the title and sign whereby one Greatest is distinguished from another, as Cicero and more recent authorities understand topic; and in this sense we too consistently use the dialectic topic just as we defined it.

Thirdly, it is understood as a *canon* or *precept*. For example, if I were to assert: Inquiry must be converted into interrogations. Aristotle occasionally combines canons of this type in his topics, and calls them topics.

A dialectic topic is either technical or non-technical. A technical topic, *topos entechnos*, is one whose relation refers to the parts of a question, that is, the subject or the predicate, if the question is a categorical one: or the antecedent or consequent, if the question is compound.

430

Argument is also called either technical or non-technical, *epicherema entechnon* or *atechnon*, according as it is taken from a technical or non-technical topic. Arguments are called technical and technical of topic, because the excogitation of arguments of this kind requires more skill.

A technical argument consists of one categorical syllogism, for another reason apart from the reason that was indicated in the last chapter and that permits the topic of the argument to be designated. For an argument can be said to be taken from the topic that is denominated by relation, whereby the middle term or part of the middle term refers to the end term or part of the end term, as in the previous syllogism:

> Every animal feels.
> Every fish is an animal.
> Therefore every fish feels,

because the middle term with respect to the last minor is a genus; hence the argument is said to be drawn from the topic of genus. Similarly, as the middle term of the last major is the nearest adequate subject, we consequently say that the argument is drawn from the topic of an adequate subject.

So in another argument: wherever the sun has risen, it is day: The sun has risen in Hamburg. Therefore it is day in Hamburg, the consequent of the middle term in relation to the cause refers to the major term: hence we say that the argument is drawn from the topic of cause. Furthermore, as the sun stands in relation to the area illuminated by its rising as an adjunct possessed in relation to an object, this argument can be said to be derived from the topic of possessed adjunct as well.

Thus when I assert: A tyrant is not happy because of his fear, with respect to the end minor I am arguing from a necessary adjunct, and with respect to the major, from an opposition.

Consider this other triterminal argument. A person who studies science needs a knowledge of demonstration. A person who studies geometry studies science. Therefore a person who studies geometry needs a knowledge of demonstration.

Here the consequent or the dependent part or the posterior of the middle term stands in relation to the posterior part of the end minor as genus to species, or the whole middle term to the whole end minor, as universal to particular. Similarly, the posterior part of the end major, as end to the thing aimed at. So the argument can be shown to be derived either from the genus or from the universal or from the end.

Sometimes the safe form of an argument designating topic is observed, when the argument has a syllogism involving respects and so apparently is contained in one syllogism, as: A person on whom a greater favor is bestowed has more affection. A person for whom a great debt is remitted receives a great favor. Therefore a person for whom a great debt is remitted has more affection.

Here the consequent part of the middle term refers to the consequent part of the term as genus to species, and to the major term as efficient to that which is effected. Therefore we say that the argument is derived from the topic either of genus or of efficient cause.

The more syllogisms an argument consists of, the more topical relations it contains in itself, according to which it refers to diverse topics, as: The miser covets: therefore he fears, and consequently he is not free. Horace is now an old man, and so love does not suit him: therefore lyric poems too do not suit him, for they usually deal with love.

Now the use of technical topics is quite different from the diversity of questions: hence it must be explained first in a real absolute question, then in a comparative question, and lastly in a conceptual question.

IMMANUEL KANT
(1724-1804)

Born and died in the East Prussian city of Koenigsberg. He hardly ever left his native town, whose citizens used to set their watches by his regular walks. He studied and taught at the University of Koenigsberg, refusing flattering outside offers. Kant advanced political ideals which make him a forerunner of the United Nations concept. He founded the transcendental Idealism, trying to offer solutions to problems raised by Hume and Leibniz. His philosophy is a synthesis of empiricism and critical rationalism investigating the limits and possibilities of human cognition, to which the essence of being, the "Ding an sich" forever escapes.

Main Works:

Kritik der reinen Vernunft; Kritik der praktischen Vernunft; Kritik der Urteilskraft; Logik; Zum Ewigen Frieden; Grundlegung zur Metaphysik der Sitten; Religion innerhalb der Grenzen der blossen Vernunft.

The Analytic of Judgments

TRANSCENDENTAL JUDGMENT

If understanding is called the faculty of rules, judgment will be the faculty of *subsumption* under rules, that is the faculty of deciding whether something stands under a given rule or not (*casus datae legis*). Now pure general logic does not, and indeed cannot, lay down rules for the application of judgment.

From: *Kritik der reinen Vernunft.*

For, as it abstracts from all the *content* of knowledge, its sole business is to analyze the pure form of knowledge, as expressed in conceptions, judgments, and inferences, and from this analysis to derive formal rules for the general use of understanding. The business of transcendental logic, on the other hand, is to lay down definite rules which may enable judgment to make a correct and certain use of the conceptions of understanding. For transcendental philosophy has the peculiarity that it not only brings to light the rules, or rather the universal condition of rules, implied in the pure conceptions of understanding, but it is able also to indicate *a priori* the case to which each rule should be applied. The reason of its superiority in this respect over all other theoretical sciences, except mathematics, is that the conceptions with which it deals relate to objects *a priori*.

The transcendental doctrine of judgment consists of two chapters. The first treats of the sensuous condition without which no pure conceptions of understanding can be used. This is called the schematism of understanding. The second deals with the synthetic judgments, which arise *a priori* when the pure conceptions of understanding are brought into use under that condition, and which underlie all other *a priori* knowledge. It treats, in other words, of the principles of pure understanding.

Chapter I.—The Schematism of the Categories

In all subsumption, the object of which we are conscious must be *homogeneous* with the conception under which it is brought; in other words, the conception must contain some determination that is also present in the object subsumed under it. This in fact is what we mean when we say that an object is contained under a conception. The empirical conception of a *plate,* for instance, is homogeneous with the pure geometrical conception of a *circle,* because the roundness which is thought as a determination of the plate is presented as a perception in the circle.

Now, a pure conception, or category, is quite heterogeneous

from an empirical perception, or indeed from any sensuous perception, and hence no pure conception can ever be found realized in a perception. No one will say that the category of cause can be made visible to sense, or can be presented in a particular perception as a property of it. How then can a perception be subsumed under a pure conception? How can a category be applied in determination of an object of sense? It is because this very natural and very important question demands an answer that a transcendental doctrine of judgment is necessary. It must be shown how *pure conceptions* of understanding can possibly be applied to phenomena. In other sciences it is not necessary to show that conceptions are applicable to objects, because the general conception of the object is not in the same way distinct and heterogeneous from the object as presented *in concreto.*

Manifestly there must be some third thing, which is homogeneous on the one hand with the category, and on the other hand with the object of sense, and which thus makes the application of the one to the other possible. This mediating idea must be *pure,* or free from any empirical element, and yet it must be at once *intellectual* and *sensuous.* Such an idea is the *transcendental schema.*

The category contains the pure synthetic unity of any elements of which we can be conscious as different. Time, as the formal condition of the various determinations of inner sense, and therefore of the connections of all our ideas, contains *a priori* in pure perception a variety of differences. Now, a transcendental determination of time is so far homogeneous with the category which gives unity to it, that it is *universal,* and rests upon an *a priori* rule. But, on its other side, that determination is to a certain extent homogeneous with the *object of sense,* since time is present in every object of which we can be empirically conscious. By means of the transcendental determination of time or schema, the category may therefore be applied to phenomena, or, what is the same thing, the phenomenon may be subsumed under the category.

In itself a schema is merely a product of imagination; but, as in producing it imagination does not seek to set before itself an individual object of perception, but to produce unity in the general determination of sensibility, we must distinguish between the schema and the image. If I set down five points one after the other, thus . . . . . I have before me an image of the number five. But if I think simply of number—of any number at all, be it five or a hundred—my thought is rather of the method by which a certain sum, say a thousand, may be presented in an image, in conformity with a certain conception, than itself an image. It would, in fact, be very hard to compare the image of so large a number as a thousand with the conception of it. Now, the consciousness of a universal process of imagination, by which an image is provided for conception, is what I call the schema of a conception.

In point of fact, schemata, and not images, lie at the foundation of our pure sensuous conceptions. No image of a triangle can ever be adequate to the general conception of triangle. The conception includes all triangles—right-angled, obtuse-angled, etc.; and, hence, the image which I can set before myself can never reach to the universality of the conception, but occupies only a part of its sphere. The schema of the triangle can exist nowhere but in thought: it is simply a rule for the synthesis of imagination, in the determination of pure figures in space. Much less can a single object of experience, or an image of a single object, reach to the universality of an empirical conception. The direct relation of an empirical conception is to the schema of imagination, or the rule by which a perception is determined in conformity with that conception. The conception of a dog, for instance, is a rule for the guidance of imagination in tracing out the figure of a certain four-footed animal; but it cannot be restricted to any single determinate figure that experience can supply, nor can it even be presented *in concreto* in any possible image that I am capable of imagining. This schematism of our understanding, in its application to phenomena and to their pure form, is an art hidden away in the depths of the human soul, the secret of which we need not hope to drag forth to the light of day. This much may be said: that the *image* is a product of the empirical faculty of productive imagination; while the *schema* of sensuous conceptions, as, for instance, of figures in space, is a product, and as it were a monogram, of pure *a priori* imagination, which makes the consciousness of an image possible at all. An image is necessarily connected with a conception through the schema, and is in no case quite congruent with the conception. But what distinguishes the schema of a pure conception of understanding as such, is that it cannot be presented in an image at all, but is simply the pure synthesis, which conforms to a rule of unity expressed in the category. Such a schema is a transcendental product of imagination. It is a determination of the inner sense according to conditions of its form of time in view of all Ideas, a determination which is necessary, if ideas are to be brought together *a priori* in one conception, in conformity with the unity of apperception.

The pure image of all magnitudes (*quanta*) that are presented in outer sense is space; the pure image of all objects of sense, inner as well as outer, is time. But quantity (*quantitas*), as a conception of understanding, has as its schema *number*, or the idea of the successive addition of homogeneous unit to homogeneous unit. Number is, therefore, the unity of synthesis implied in putting together any homogeneous units of perception whatever, a unity which results from the generation of time itself in the apprehension of the perception.

The category of *reality* is the conception of that which corresponds to any sensation whatever, and therefore of that, the very idea of which is that it has being in time; the category of *negation* is the conception of that, the very idea of which is that it has no being in time. The opposition of reality and negation therefore rests upon the distinction between a time as filled and the same time as empty. And, as time is merely the form of perception, that which in the phenomenon corresponds to sensation is the transcendental matter, or reality, of all objects as actual things. Now, every sensation has a degree or magnitude by which it is capable of filling the same time more or less, or, in other words, of occupying the inner sense, with more or less completeness, down to the vanishing point (=o=*negatio*). Hence, there is a relation and connection, or rather a transition from reality to negation, which makes us capable of setting every reality before ourselves as a quantum. The schema of reality, as the quantity of something so far as it fills a time, is just this continuous and uniform generation of reality in time, by the gradual descent from a sensation that has a certain degree in time to its disappearance, or, what is the same thing, the gradual ascent from the negation of sensation to its definite degree.

The schema of substance is the permanence of the real in time, or the idea of the real as presupposed in the empirical determination of time, and as persisting while all else changes. Time does not itself pass away, but the changeable in time passes away in its particular being. What corresponds in the phenomenon to time, which is in itself unchangeable and permanent, is the unchangeable in existence, or substance; and only in reference to substance can the succession and the co-existence of phenomena be determined in time.

The schema of cause, and of the causality of a thing in general, is the real which is supposed never to exist without being followed by something else. It consists, therefore, in the succession of various determinations, in so far as that succession is subject to a rule.

The schema of community (reciprocal action), or of the reciprocal causality of substances as regards their accidents, is the co-existence in conformity with a universal rule of the determinations of one substance with those of another.

The schema of possibility is the harmony of the synthesis of different ideas with conditions of time in general. Opposites, for instance, cannot exist in the same thing at the same time, but only one after the other. The schema of possibility therefore determines how a thing is capable of being known at any time.

The schema of actuality is existence in a determinate time.

The schema of necessity is the existence of an object at all times.

From all this it is plain that the schema of every one of the categories is in some way relative to time. The schema of quantity is the generation or synthesis of time itself in the successive apprehension of an object; the schema of quality, the synthesis of sensation, as implied in observation, with the consciousness of time, or, in other words, it is the filling up of time; the schema relation, the relation of different perceptions to one another at all times, or in conformity with a rule for the determination of time; lastly, the schema of modality, in its three forms, time itself as the correlative of the determination whether and how an object belongs to time. The schemata are, therefore, just *a priori* determinations of time in conformity with rules. Following the order of the categories, we find that these rules, which apply to all possible objects of experience, relate to the *series of time*, the *content of time*, the *order of time*, and the *comprehension of time*.

We thus see that the schematism of understanding, through the transcendental synthesis of imagination, is neither more nor less than the way in which the various determinations of perception are reduced to unity in the inner sense, and so indirectly to the unity of apperception, the function that corresponds to the receptivity of inner sense. The schemata are, therefore, the true and only conditions under which the categories obtain *significance*, by being brought into relation with objects. In the end, therefore, the categories have no other application than to objects of a possible experience. They merely serve to bind phenomena together under universal rules of synthesis, by means of a necessary *a priori* unity that has its source in the necessary combination of all consciousness in the original unity of apperception. Thus it is that the categories make phenomena fit for a thoroughgoing connection in one experience.

Within this whole of possible experience all our knowledge

lies, and in the universal relation to possible experience consists that transcendental truth which precedes empirical truth and makes it possible.

But no one can fail to see that, although only the schemata of sensibility can realize the categories, they none the less *restrict* them. For the schemata limit the categories by conditions that lie outside of understanding and in sensibility. The schema is in harmony with the category, but it is properly merely the sensuous appearance or sensuous conception of an object. Now, it is naturally supposed that the sphere of a conception previously restricted is enlarged when the restriction is taken away. Hence it may be thought that the categories in their purity, or apart from all conditions of sensibility, hold true of things *as they really are;* while the schemata present them only *as they appear.* On this view the categories will have a much wider meaning than the schemata, and will be quite independent of them. And this is so far true that, even apart from all sensuous conditions the categories are not meaningless, for they still have the logical meaning of the unity of our ideas of objects. But no conception has in itself objective meaning, because, apart from the conditions of sensibility, there is no object to which it can be applied. Substance, for instance, viewed apart from the sensuous determination of permanence, simply means, that which can be thought only as subject, never as the predicate of anything else. But such an idea has no meaning for us, because it tells us nothing whatever about the actual nature of the thing that is thought to be an ultimate subject. Without schemata, therefore, the categories are only functions of understanding for conceptions, and give no knowledge of objects. Meaning comes to them from sensibility, and sensibility realizes understanding only by restricting it.

Chapter II.—Principles of Pure Understanding

In the preceding chapter, we have considered the transcendental faculty of judgment with reference only to the universal conditions, under which it is justified in employing the categories for the production of synthetic judgments. We have now set forth, in systematic order, the judgments which understanding, under that critical provision, actually produces *a priori*. The table of categories will no doubt be a safe and natural guide. Accordingly we find that all the principles of pure understanding are—

1. Axioms of Perception.

<table>
<tr><td>2. Anticipations of Observation.</td><td>3. Analogies of Experience.</td></tr>
</table>

4. Postulates of Empirical Thought.

1. *Axioms of Perception*

The principle of these is: All perceptions are extensive magnitudes.

Proof.

By an extensive magnitude, I mean a magnitude in which the idea of the parts necessarily precedes and makes possible the idea of the whole. I cannot have the idea of a line, however small it may be, without drawing it in thought; only by producing its parts one after the other, beginning from a certain point, do I mark out the line as a perception. Similarly with every portion of time, even the smallest. I am conscious of time only in the successive advance from one moment to another, and it is by the addition of all the parts that a definite quantity of time is at last generated. Now, either space or time is present in every phenomenon as its pure element; and as this pure element can be known in apprehension only by a successive synthesis of part with part, every perception is an extensive magnitude. No phenomenon, therefore, can be perceived at all without being perceived as an aggregate or collection of previously given parts, a characteristic which does not hold good of every sort of magnitude, but only of those magnitudes, which from their very nature, are apprehended and presented in consciousness as extensive.

On this successive synthesis of productive imagination in the generation of figures, Geometry, as the mathematics of extension, is based. The axioms of geometry express the conditions of sensuous perception *a priori* without which no schema of any pure conception of an external object is possible; as, for instance, that between any two points only one straight line can be drawn; that two straight lines cannot enclose a space, etc. Such axioms as these properly apply only to magnitudes (*quanta*) as such.

As to quantity (*quantitas*), that is, the answer to the question how large a thing is, there are, strictly speaking, no axioms, although several of the propositions referring to it are synthetic and immediately certain (*indemonstrabilia*). The propositions, that if equals be added to equals the wholes are equal, and that if equals be taken from equals the remainders are equal, are analytic propositions; for I am directly conscious that the quantity generated in the one case is identical with the quantity generated in the other; these propositions, therefore, have no title to be called axioms, which must needs be *a priori* synthetic propositions. There are, indeed, simple numerical propositions which are synthetic; but, unlike the synthetic propositions of geometry, they are not universal, and therefore even they cannot be called axioms, but only numerical formulae. That $7 + 5 = 12$ is not an analytical proposition. For neither the idea of 7, nor that of 5, nor the idea of the combination of the two, yields the number 12. But while it is synthetic, the proposition $7 + 5 = 12$ is merely individual. The synthesis of the homogeneous can here take place only in one way, although no doubt the numbers may afterwards be *employed* universally. If I say that a triangle may be constructed out of three lines, any two of which are together greater than the third, I have before my mind the mere function of productive imagination, which may draw the lines greater or smaller, and bring them together in all sorts of angles at will. On the other hand, the number 7 is possible only in one way, and the number 12 can be produced only by the synthesis of 5 with it. If mere formulae like this are to be called axioms the number of axioms will be infinite.

This transcendental principle of the mathematics of nature greatly enlarges our *a priori* knowledge. It shows, as nothing else can show, that mathematics in all its precision is applicable to objects of experience; and this, so far from being self-evident, has been the occasion of much controversy. Phenomena are not things in themselves. Empirical perception is possible only through the pure perception of space and of time; and, therefore, whatever geometry says of pure perception is beyond dispute true also of empirical perception. All attempts to evade this conclusion, by showing that objects of sense need not conform to the rules of geometrical construction—for instance, the rule of the infinite divisibility of lines and angles—must be at once set aside. Were such a contention true, the objective truth of geometry, and therefore of all mathematics, would be overthrown, and it would be impossible to say why and how far mathematics should be applied to phenomena at all. The synthesis of spaces and times, as the essential forms of all perception, is that which makes the apprehension of a phenomenon even possible, and hence it is the condition of all external experience, and so of all knowledge of external objects. Whatever pure mathematics proves to be true of space and time must necessarily hold good of all external objects. All objections to the truth of applied mathematics are but the chicanery of an ill-advised reason, which wrongly seeks to free objects of sense from the formal condition of our sensibility, and to treat them as if they were things in themselves apprehended by understanding. If phenomena were really things in themselves, we could know nothing whatever of them *a priori;* and as no synthetic judgments can be based upon pure conceptions of space, geometry, as the science of the properties of space, would itself be impossible.

2. *Anticipations of Observation.*

The principle of these is: In all phenomena the real, which is an object of sensation, has intensive magnitude or degree.

Proof.

If it should turn out that in all sensations as such, however they may differ from one another, there is something that can be known *a priori;* this would, in a very special sense, deserve to be called an anticipation. For by this name we should call attention to the remarkable fact that it is possible to say something *a priori* about the nature of empirical objects, that is, about that very element in them which is due to experience.

If no heed is paid to the succession of different sensations, apprehension by means of mere sensation is found to occupy only a moment. Here there is no successive synthesis, advancing from the consciousness of the parts to the consciousness of the whole, and therefore that in the phenomenon which is called sensation has no extensive magnitude. The absence of sensation from the moment that it fills would therefore carry with it the consciousness of that moment as empty = 0. Now that which in empirical perception corresponds to sensation is reality (*realitas phaenomenon*); that which corresponds to the absence of sensation is negation = 0. But every sensation is capable of diminution, so that it can decrease and gradually disappear. Between reality in the phenomenon and negation, there is, therefore, a continuous series of many possible intermediate sensations, the difference between any two of which is always less than the difference between the given sensation and zero or complete negation. That is to say, the real in the phenomenon always has a quantity, but of this quantity there is no consciousness in apprehension, because apprehension, so far as it is due to the inner sensation, takes place in one moment, and does not consist in a successive synthesis of different sensations, and therefore does not advance from the parts to the whole. Hence the real has magnitude, but not extensive magnitude.

Now, a magnitude that is apprehended only as unity, plurality being conceived in it as simply approximation to negation = 0, I call an *intensive magnitude*. Every reality in a phenomenon has therefore intensive magnitude or degree. This reality may be regarded as a cause, either of sensation or of some other reality in the phenomenon, for instance, a change. The degree of reality is then called *momentum*, as when we speak of the momentum of gravity, to indicate a quantity, the apprehension of which is not successive but instantaneous. I make this remark merely in passing, for this is not the place to treat of causality.

Every sensation, then, and consequently every reality in a phenomenon, however small it may be, has an intensive magnitude or degree that can always become less, and between reality and negation there is a continuous series of possible realities, and of possible smaller perceptions. The color red, for instance, has a degree which, however small it may be, is never the smallest possible; and so with heat, the momentum of gravity, etc.

The property of magnitudes, by which no part in them is the smallest possible, or no part is simple, is called their *continuity*. Space and time are *quanta continua*, because no part of them can be presented that is not enclosed between limits (points or moments), and therefore each part of space is itself a space, each part of time is itself a time. Space consists only of spaces, time of times. Points and moments are but limits, that is, mere places of limitation in space and time, and as such always presuppose the perceptions which they are to limit or determine. Mere places are not constituent parts, which can be given prior to space or time, and out of which space and time can be made up. Such magnitudes may also be called *fluent*, because the synthesis of productive imagination, by which they are generated, is a progression in time, the continuity of which is usually designated by the term *flux* or *flowing*.

All phenomena are continuous magnitudes, and that in two

445

ways: as pure perceptions, they are continuous extensive magnitudes, and as perceptions of sense containing sensation, and therefore reality, they are continuous intensive magnitudes. When the synthesis of determinations is interrupted, we have an aggregate of various objects of sense, not a single phenomenon as a quantum. Such an aggregate is produced, not by continuing without a break the productive synthesis with which we begin, but by continually renewing a synthesis that is continually coming to an end.

As all phenomena, whether they are viewed extensively or intensively, are continuous magnitudes, the continuity of all change, or transition of a thing from one state into another, might readily be proved here, and indeed proved mathematically. But the causality of a change, as presupposing empirical principles, does not come within the province of transcendental philosophy. Understanding can give us no hint *a priori* that there can be a cause, which is capable of changing the state of things, that is, determining them to the opposite of a given state. It is not simply that we cannot understand *a priori* how this can take place—for there are many other instances of a similar failure in *a priori* knowledge,—but that only certain determinations of objects are capable of change at all, and what these determinations are we can learn only from experience, although no doubt the cause must lie in that which is unchangeable. The only data that we have here before us, are the pure conceptions implied in all possible experience, which contain nothing empirical; nor can we avail ourselves of the primary facts of experience which lie at the foundation of pure physics without destroying the unity of our system.

At the same time, there is no difficulty in showing that the principle of understanding now under consideration is of great value in enabling us to anticipate perceptions of sense, and even to some extent to supply their place, by guarding us against all false inferences that might be drawn from their absence.

If all reality in perception has a degree, between which and negation there is an infinite series of ever smaller degrees, and if each sense must have a definite degree of receptivity for sensations, it is evident that no perception, and therefore no experience, can prove, directly or indirectly, by any possible ingenuity of reasoning, that a phenomenon is absolutely destitute of reality. That is to say, there is no way of proving from experience that there is empty space or empty time. For in the first place, the complete absence of reality from a perception of sense can never be observed; and, in the second place, the absence of all reality can never be inferred from any variation in the degree of reality of a phenomenon, nor ought it ever to be brought forward in explanation of that variation. For, although the whole perception of a certain definite space or time is real through and through, so that no part of it is empty; yet, as every reality has a degree, which may diminish by infinite degrees down to nothing (the void), while the extensive magnitude of the phenomenon remains unchanged, there must be an infinity of degrees with which space or time may be filled; hence the intensive magnitude may be greater or less in different phenomena, although the extensive magnitude of the perception remains the same.

The *quality* of sensation—color, taste, etc.,—is always merely empirical, and cannot be known *a priori*. But the real that corresponds to sensations in general, and is opposed to negation = 0, stands merely for that the very conception of which implies being, and it has, therefore, no other meaning than the synthesis in empirical consciousness generally. In the inner sense, that empirical consciousness can be raised from 0 to any higher degree, so that the extensive magnitude of a perception may be greater or less, even when the intensive magnitude remains the same. Thus, the degree of sensation excited by an illuminated surface, may be as great as that produced by a number of less illuminated surfaces, the aggregate extent of which is twice as large. In considering the intensive magnitude of a phenomenon, we may, therefore, abstract entirely from its extensive magnitude, and think only of the sensation, filling a single moment, as generated by a synthesis that advances uniformly from 0 to the given empirical consciousness. Thus, while all sensations as such are given *a posteriori*, it can be known *a priori* that to all belongs the property of having a degree. It is remarkable that of quantity in general only a single *quality*—the quality of continuity, can be known *a priori*, but that of quality, or the reality of phenomena, nothing more than the intensive *quantity*, or the possession of degree, can be known *a priori*, while all else has to be learned from experience.

3. *Analogies of Experience.*

The principle of these is: Experience is possible only through the consciousness of a necessary connection of perception of sense.

Proof.

The three *modi* of time are *permanence, succession,* and *co-existence*. All the relations of phenomena in time will therefore be expressed in three rules, which precede all experience and make it possible at all. These rules state all the conditions under which phenomena can possibly exist, in conformity with their unity in time.

The principle of all three analogies rests upon the necessary *unity* of apperception in all empirical consciousness, or perceptions of sense, *at every moment of time*. And as the unity of apperception is the *a priori* condition of all perception, that principle is based upon the synthetic unity of all phenomena as regards their relation in time. The original apperception is related to the inner sense, which contains all possible objects of consciousness, or, more exactly, it is related *a priori* to the form of inner sense, as the manner in which the manifold determinations of empirical consciousness are ordered in time. Now, in original apperception all those determinations are to be united, as regards their relation in time; for nothing can enter into my knowledge, or be mine, nothing can be for me an object, that does not stand under the *a priori* transcendental unity of apperception. This *synthetic unity* in the temporal relation of all perceptions is, therefore, *determined a priori,* and is expressed in the law, that all empirical determinations in time must stand under universal rules of determination in time. The Analogies of Experience must therefore be rules of this kind.

These Analogies have the peculiarity, that they are not concerned with the synthesis of empirical perception implied in the consciousness of objects of sense, but only with the *existence* of such objects, and the *relations* to one another by which their existence is determined. Now, a phenomenon may be so determined *a priori,* that the rule of its synthesis yields at once the perception which is presented to us in every empirical instance of it; or, in other words, the rule may not only tell us the character of the synthesis, but may set the object before us as a perception. But the *existence* of phenomena cannot thus be known *a priori.* We may indeed in this way come to know that something exists, but we cannot definitely know what it is, nor can we anticipate how it will differ from other objects, when it is empirically perceived.

The two principles already discussed, which I called mathematical, to indicate that they justify the application of mathematics to objects of sense, showed merely how phenomena were possible, and how their perceptive form, as well as the real sense perception, could be generated in conformity with rules of a mathematical synthesis. Both principles, therefore, entitle us to estimate phenomena numerically and quantitatively. The degree of sensation of sunlight, for instance, may be determined *a priori,* or constructed, by putting together, say, 200,000 illuminations of the moon. Those principles may therefore be called constitutive.

It is quite different with the principles that show how the existence of phenomena comes under *a priori* rules. Existence cannot be constructed; all that can be done is to state the rules that determine the relations of existence, and these rules yield

only *regulative* principles. Here, therefore, there can be neither axioms nor anticipations. If in observation something is presented as related in time to something else, as yet unknown, it is impossible to tell *what* that something else may be, or what may be its *magnitude;* all that we can tell is how the two perceptions, to exist at all, must be connected with each other. .
. . . . . An analogy of experience is, therefore, merely a rule which states the conditions under which observations of sense may be reduced to the unity of experience. Incompetent to tell us the conditions of observation, so far as its empirical element is concerned, it is not a principle *constitutive* of objects of sense or phenomena, but is merely *regulative.* In like manner, the postulates of empirical thought are regulative principles. The certitude is as great for the regulative as for the mathematical or constitutive principles, for both are *a priori,* but the kind of evidence is different.

In regard to the general method of proof in philosophy, it must be observed that a *demonstration* is an apodictic case of discursive knowledge, even those judgments which are based upon *a priori* conceptions, and are therefore apodictic, cannot be proved by a direct appeal to perception. It is only mathematics that admits of demonstrative evidence, for mathematics alone derives its knowledge, not from conceptions, but from the construction of conceptions—that is, from the perception which corresponds to certain conceptions and can be presented a *priori.* Even the solution of an algebraic equation is a process of construction, though not of geometrical construction; for, it consists in presenting conceptions in perception by means of symbols, and especially conceptions of the relation of quantities. Although, therefore, in its methods algebra is not heuristic, it is able to guard against error in its results by placing all the conceptions that it employs directly before the eyes. But, while mathematics views the universal *in concreto*—that is, in pure perception, where every error becomes immediately visible—philosophical knowledge has to dispense with this advantage, and to consider the universal *in abstracto,* or through the medium of conceptions.

It is therefore contrary to the true spirit of philosophy, and especially of pure philosophy, to boast of its dogmatic procedure, and to bedeck itself with the orders and the titles of mathematics. Such empty boasts can only retard the progress of philosophy, and prevent it from detecting the illusion into which reason falls when it is unaware of its true limits.

Apodictic propositions may be distinguished as either *dogmata* or *mathemata.* By a *dogma* is meant a synthetic proposition which is directly derived from conceptions; by a *mathema,* one that is obtained by the construction of a conception. Of these two classes of *a priori* synthetic propositions, popular language permits us to apply the term dogma only to philosophical knowledge, for we should hardly call a proposition in arithmetic or geometry a dogma. The ordinary use of words thus confirms the distinction we have drawn between judgments that are derived from conceptions, and judgments that rest upon the construction of conceptions.

Now, it is impossible to find in the whole domain of pure speculative reason a single synthetic judgment that is directly derived from conceptions. For, reason is unable to obtain from its pure ideas any synthetic judgment which holds true objectively. It is true that, by means of the conceptions of understanding, reason is able to show that there are certain principles which rest upon a solid foundation; but these principles it does not directly derive from conceptions, but only indirectly, by showing the relation of the conceptions in question to something that is perfectly contingent—namely, *possible experience.* If something is presupposed as an object of possible experience, no doubt those principles are apodictically certain; but, in themselves, or directly, they can never be known *a priori.* Thus, no one, simply from the conceptions contained in it, can see what is the foundation of the proposition, that whatever happens has its cause. Such a proposition can certainly be shown readily

451

enough to be apodictic, if it applied only within the field of experience; but it cannot be a dogma. It must be called a *principle*, and not a *theorem*, because it has the peculiar property, that it is the condition of that by which it is proved—namely, experience, and must always be presupposed as essential to experience.

Now, if in the speculative use of pure reason there are no dogmata, all dogmatic methods, whether they are borrowed from the mathematician or are peculiar to the individual thinker, are self-condemned. For they only serve to conceal defects and errors, and to give rise to philosophical illusion, instead of securing the true aim of philosophy, which is to exhibit every step of reason in the clearest possible light. Yet the method of philosophy, though it is not dogmatic, may be *systematic*. For our reason is itself subjectively a system, though, if we regard it merely as a source of pure conceptions, it is not a system of knowledge, but only a system by which our investigations may be carried on: in other words, it supplies the principles of unity for knowledge, and must look to *experience* to supply the materials to be determined in accordance with these principles.

JOHN NEVILLE KEYNES
(1852-1949)

Professor of Moral Science and Metaphysics at Cambridge and University College, London. Keynes taught ethics and political philosophy. His "Studies and Exercises in Formal Logic" is perhaps the most perfect presentation of classical formal logic. It had a wide and beneficial influence upon the training in that field.

Main Works:

Studies and Exercises in Formal Logic; Scope and Method of Political Economy.

Propositions

CHAPTER I

Kinds of Propositions. The Quantity and Quality of Propositions.

Categorical, Hypothetical and Disjunctive Propositions.

For logical purposes, a *Proposition* may be defined as "a sentence indicative or assertory," (as distinguished, for example, from sentences imperative or exclamatory); in other words, a proposition is a sentence making an affirmation or denial, as—All *S* is *P*, No vicious man is happy.

From: *Formal Logic.*

A proposition is *Categorical* if the affirmation or denial is absolute, as in the above examples. It is *Hypothetical* if made under a condition, as—If *A* is *B*, *C* is *D*; Where ignorance is bliss, 'tis folly to be wise. It is *Disjunctive* if made with an alternative, as—Either *P* is *Q*, or *X* is *Y*; He is either a knave or a fool.[1]

[The above threefold division is adopted by Mansel. It is perhaps more usual to commence with a twofold division, the second member of which is again subdivided, the term Hypothetical being employed sometimes in a wider and sometimes in a narrower sense. To prevent confusion, it may be helpful to give the following table of the usage of one or two modern logicians with regard to this division.

Whately, Mill and Bain:—

    1. Categorical.
    2. Hypothetical, or Compound, or Complex. $\begin{cases} (1) & \text{Conditional} \\ (2) & \text{Disjunctive.} \end{cases}$

Hamilton and Thomson:—

    1. Categorical.
    2. Conditional. $\begin{cases} (1) & \text{Hypothetical.} \\ (2) & \text{Disjunctive.} \end{cases}$

Fowler (following Boëthius):—

    1. Categorical.
    2. Conditional. or Hypothetical. $\begin{cases} (1) & \text{Conjunctive.} \\ (2) & \text{Disjunctive.} \end{cases}$

Mansel, as I have already remarked, gives at once a threefold division.

---

[1] It should be observed that in a disjunctive proposition there may be two distinct subjects as in the first of the above examples, or only one as in the second. Disjunctive propositions in which there is only one distinct subject are the more amenable to logical treatment.

1. Categorical.
2. Hypothetical or Conditional.
3. Disjunctive.

He states his reasons for his own choice of terms as follows:—
"Nothing can be more clumsy than the employment of the word
conditional in a specific sense, while its Greek equivalent, *hypothetical,* is used generically. In Boëthius, both terms are properly
used as synonymous, and generic; the two species being called
conjunctivi, conjuncti, or *connexi,* and *disjunctivi* or *disjuncti.*
With reference to modern usage, however, it will be better to
contract the Greek word than to extend the Latin one. *Hypothetical* in the following notes, will be used as synonymous with
conditional" (Mansel's edition of *Aldrich,* p. 103).]

A logical analysis of the Categorical Proposition.

In logical analysis, the categorical proposition always consists
of three parts, namely, two terms which are united by means
of a copula.

The *subject* is that term about which affirmation or denial is
made; it represents some notion already partially determined in
our mind, and which it is our aim further to determine.

The *predicate* is that term which is affirmed or denied of the
subject; it enables us further to determine the subject, *i.e.,* to
enlarge our knowledge with regard to it.

The *copula* is the link of connection between the subject and
the predicate, and consists of the words *is* or *is not* according as
we affirm or deny the latter of the former.

In attempting to apply the above analysis to such a proposition as "All that love virtue love angling," we find that, as it
stands, the copula is not separately expressed. It may however
be written,—

| subj. | cop. | pred. |
| All lovers of virtue | are | lovers of angling; |

and in this form the three different elements of the logical proposition are made distinct. This analysis should always be performed in the case of any proposition that may at first present itself in an abnormal form. A difficulty that may sometimes arise in discriminating the subject and the predicate is dealt with subsequently.

The older logicians distinguished propositions *secundi adjacentis,* and propositions *tertii adjacentis.* In the former, the copula and the predicate are not separated; *e.g.,* The man runs, All that love virtue love angling. In the latter, the copula and the predicate are made distinct; *e.g.,* The man is running, All lovers of virtue are lovers of angling. A categorical proposition, therefore, when expressed in exact logical form, is *tertii adjacentis.*

Exponible, copulative, exclusive, exceptive propositions.

Propositions that are resolvable into more propositions than one have been called *exponible,* in consequence of their susceptibility of analysis. *Copulative* propositions are formed by a direct combination of simple propositions, *e.g.,* P is both Q and R (*i.e.,* P is Q, P is R), A is neither B nor C (*i.e.,* A is not B, A is not C); they form one class of exponibles. *Exclusive* propositions contain some such word as "only," thereby limiting the predicate to the subject; *e.g.,* Only S is P. This may be resolved into S is P, and P is S. Propositions of this kind also are therefore exponibles. *Exceptive* propositions limit the subject by such a word as "unless" or "except"; *e.g.* A is X, unless it happens to be B. These too may perhaps be regarded as exponible propositions.

The Quantity and Quality of Propositions.

The *Quality* of a proposition is determined by the copula, being *affirmative* or *negative* according as the copula is of the form "is" or "is not."

456

Propositions are also divided into *universal* and *particular,* according as the affirmation or denial is made of the whole or only of a part of the subject. This division of Propositions is said to be according to their *Quantity.*

Combining the two principles of division, we get four fundamental forms of propositions:—

(1) the *universal affirmative,* All S is P, usually denoted by the symbol A;

(2) the *particular affirmative,* Some S is P, usually denoted by the symbol I;

(3) the *universal negative,* No S is P, usually denoted by the symbol E;

(4) the *particular negative,* Some S is not P, usually denoted by the symbol O.

These symbols A, I and E, O are taken from the Latin words *affirmo* and *nego,* the affirmative symbols being the first two vowels of the former, and the negative symbols the two vowels of the latter.

Besides these symbols, it will also be found convenient sometimes to use the following,—

$$SaP = \text{All } S \text{ is } P;$$
$$SiP = \text{Some } S \text{ is } P;$$
$$SeP = \text{No } S \text{ is } P;$$
$$SoP = \text{Some } S \text{ is not } P$$

The above are useful when we wish that the symbol which is used to denote the proposition as a whole should also indicate what symbols have been chosen for the subject and the predicate respectively. Thus,

$$MaP = \text{All } M \text{ is } P;$$
$$PoQ = \text{Some } P \text{ is not } Q.$$

The universal negative should be written in the form *No S is P*, not *All S is not P*; for the latter would usually be understood to be merely particular. Thus, All that glitters is not gold is really an O proposition, and is equivalent to—Some things that glitter | are not | gold.

Indefinite Propositions.

According to Quantity, Propositions have sometimes been divided into (1) Universal, (2) Particular, (3) Singular, (4) Indefinite. Singular propositions are discussed in the following section.

By an *Indefinite* Proposition is meant one "in which the Quantity is not explicitly declared by one of the designatory terms *all, every, some, many*, &c." We may perhaps say with Hamilton that *indesignate* or *preindesignate* would be a better term to employ. There can be no doubt that, as Mansel remarks, "The true indefinite proposition is in fact the particular; the statement 'some *A* is *B*' being applicable to an uncertain number of instances, from the whole class down to any portion of it. For this reason particular propositions were called indefinite by Theophrastus" (*Aldrich*, p. 49).

Some indesignate propositions are no doubt intended to be understood as universals, *e.g.*, Comets are subject to the law of gravitation; but in such cases before we deal with the proposition logically it is better that the word *all* should be explicitly prefixed to it. If we are really in doubt with regard to the quantity of the proposition it must logically be regarded as particular.

Other designations of quantity besides *all* and *some, e.g., most*, are discussed later.

The term *indefinite* has also been applied to propositions in another sense. According to Quality, instead of the two-fold division given in the preceding example, a threefold division is sometimes adopted, namely into affirmative, negative, and infinite or *indefinite*. For further explanation, see section Infinite or Indefinite Terms and Propositions.

John Neville Keynes

Singular Propositions.

By a *Singular* or *Individual* Proposition is meant a proposition of which the subject is a singular term, one therefore in which the affirmation or denial is made but of a single specified individual; *e.g.*, Brutus is an honorable man; Much Ado about Nothing is a play of Shakespeare's; My boat is on the shore.

Singular propositions may usually be regarded as forming a sub-class of Universal propositions, since in every singular proposition the affirmation or denial is of the *whole* of the subject. Such propositions have however certain peculiarities of their own, as we shall note subsequently, *e.g.*, they have not like other universal propositions a contrary distinct from their contradictory.

Hamilton distinguishes between Universal and Singular Propositions, the predication being in the former case of a *Whole Undivided,* and in the latter case of a *Unit Indivisible.* This separation is sometimes useful; but I think it better not to make it absolute. A singular proposition may without risk of confusion be denoted by one of the symbols A or E; and in syllogistic inferences, a singular may always be regarded as equivalent to a universal proposition. The use of independent symbols for affirmative and negative singular propositions would introduce considerable additional complexity into the treatment of the Syllogism; and for this reason alone it seems desirable as a rule to include particulars under universals. We may however divide universal proposition into *General* and *Singular,* and we shall then have terms whereby to call attention to the distinction wherever it may be necessary or useful to do so.

There is a certain class of propositions with regard to which there is some difference of opinion as to whether they should be regarded as singular or particular; for example, such as the following: A certain man had two sons; A great statesman was present. Mansel (*Aldrich,* p. 49) decides that they should be dealt with as particulars, and I think rightly, on the ground that if we have two such propositions, "a certain man" or "a great statesman" being the subject of each, we cannot be sure that the

459

same individual is referred to in both cases. Sometimes however the context may enable us to decide the case differently.

There are propositions of another kind with a singular term for subject about which a few words may be said; namely, such propositions as—Browning is sometimes obscure; That boy is sometimes first in his class. These propositions may be treated as universal with a somewhat complex predicate, (and it should be noted that in bringing propositions into logical forms we are frequently compelled to use very complex predicates); thus:—

Browning | is | a poet who is sometimes obscure.
That boy | is | a boy who is sometimes first in his class.

By a certain transformation however these propositions may be dealt with as particulars, and such transformation may sometimes be convenient; thus, Some of Browning's writings are obscure, Some of the boy's places in his class are the first places. But when the proposition is thus modified, the subject is no longer a singular term.

The logical signification of the words *some, most, few, all, any*.

Some may mean merely "some at least," *i.e.*, not none, or it may carry the further implication, "some at most," *i.e.*, not all. Professor Bain is probably right in saying (*Logic, Deduction*, p. 81) that in ordinary speech the latter meaning is the more usual. With most modern logicians, however, the logical implication of some is limited to some at least, not exclusive of all. Using the word in this sense, if we want to express "some, but not all, S is P," we must make use of two propositions,

Some S is P,
Some S is not P.

The particular then is not exclusive of the universal. As already suggested, it is indefinite, though with a certain limit; that is, it is indefinite so far that it may apply to any number from a single one up to all, but on the other hand it is definite so far as it excludes "none."

It may be added that in regarding "some" as implying no more than *at least one*, we are probably again departing from the ordinary usage of language, which would regard it as implying *at least two*.

[It should perhaps be noted that on rare occasions "some" may have a slightly different implication. For example, the proposition "Some truth is better kept to oneself" may be so emphasized as to make it perfectly clear to what particular kind of truth reference is made. This is however extra-logical. Logically the proposition must be treated as particular, or it must be written in another form, "All truth of a certain specified kind is better kept to oneself." Thus, Spalding remarks (*Logic*, p. 63), "The logical 'some' is totally indeterminate in its reference to the constitutive objects. It is always *aliqui*, never *quidam*; is designates some objects or other of the class, not some certain objects definitely pointed out."]

Most is to be interpreted "at least one more than half." *Few* has a negative force, "Few S is P" being equivalent to "Most S is not P"; (with perhaps the further implication "although *some* S is P"; thus Few S is P is given by Kant as an example of the *exponible* proposition, on the ground that it contains both an affirmation and a negation, though one of them in a concealed way). Formal logicians (excepting De Morgan and Hamilton) have not as a rule recognized these additional signs of quantity; and it is true that in many logical combinations we are unable to regard them as more than particular propositions, Most S is P being reduced to Some S is P, and Few S is P to Some S is not P. Sometimes however we are able to make use of the extra knowledge given us; *e.g.*, from Most M is P, Most M is S we can infer Some S is P, although from Some M is P, Some M is S we can infer nothing.

It should be observed that *A few* has not the same signification as *Few*, but must be regarded as affirmative, and, generally, as simply equivalent to *some; e.g.*, A few S is P=Some S is P. Sometimes, however, it means "a small number," and in this case the proposition is perhaps best regarded as singular, the subject being collective. Thus "a few peasants successfully defended the citadel" may be rendered "a small band of peasants successfully defended the citadel," rather than "some peasants successfully defended the citadel," since the stress is intended to be laid at least as much on the paucity of their numbers as on the fact that they were peasants. In this case, the proposition would be A, not I.

It may here be remarked that in all cases, where we are dealing with propositions which as originally stated are not in a logical form, the first problem in reducing them to logical form is one of interpretation, and we must not be surprised to find that in many cases different methods of interpretation lead to different results. No confusion will ensue if we make it perfectly clear what we do regard as the logical form of the proposition, and also how we have arrived at our result.

All is ambiguous, so far as it may be used either distributively or collectively. In the proposition "All the angles of a triangle are less than two right angles" it is used distributively, the predicate applying to each and every angle of triangle taken separately. In the proposition "All the angles of a triangle are equal to two right angles" it is used collectively, the predicate applying to all the angles taken together, and not to each separately.

Any as the sign of quantity of the subject of a categorical proposition, (*e.g.*, any S is P), is logically equivalent to "all" in its distributive sense. Whatever is true of the whole class taken at random is necessarily true of the whole of that class. When not the subject of a categorical proposition, *any* may have a different signification. For example, in the hypothetical proposition, If any A is B, C is D, it has the same indefinite character which we logically ascribe to "some"; since the antecedent condition is satisfied if a single A is B. The proposition might indeed be written—If one or more A *is* B, C *is* D.

Examine the logical signification of the italicized words in the following propositions:—

Some are born great.
Few are chosen.
All is not lost.
All men are created equal.
All that a man hath will he give for his life.
If *some* is *B*, *some C* is *D*.
If *any A* is *B*, *any C* is *D*.
If *all A* is *B*, *all C* is *D*.

Distinguish the collective and distributive use of the word *all* in the following propositions:

(1) All Albinos are pink-eyed people;
(2) Omnes apostoli sunt duodecim;
(3) Non omnis moriar;
(4) Non omnia possumus omnes;
(5) All men find their own in all men's good,
 And all men join in noble brotherhood.
(6) Not all the gallant efforts of the officers and escort of the British Embassy at Cabul were able to save them.

[Jevons, *Elementary Lessons in Logic*, p. 297. *Studies in Deductive Logic*, pp. 19, 28.]

Infinite or *indefinite* terms and propositions.

Infinite and *indefinite* are designations applied to terms having a thoroughgoing negative character; to such a term for example as "not-white," understood as denoting not merely colored things other than white, but the whole infinite or indefinite class of things of which "white" cannot be truly affirmed, including such entities as Mill's *Logic*, a dream, Time, a soliloquy, New Guinea, the Seven Ages of Man.

It is however to be observed that if symbols are used, it is impossible to say which of the terms S or not-S really partakes of this indefinite character, since, for example, there is nothing to prevent our having originally written S for "non-white," in which case "white" becomes not-S, and S is the really *indefinite* or *infinite* term.

Following out the above idea, propositions were divided by Kant into three classes in respect of Quality, namely, affirmative —A is B, negative—A is not B, and *infinite* (*or indefinite*)—A is not-B. Logically however the last proposition (which is equivalent to the second in meaning) must be regarded as simply affirmative. As just shewn, it is impossible to say which of the terms B or not-B is really infinite or indefinite; and it is therefore also impossible to say which of the propositions "A is B" or "A is not-B" is really infinite or indefinite. Logically then they must be regarded as belonging to the same type of proposition, and we have to fall back upon the two-fold division into affirmative and negative.

Can distinctions of Quality and Quantity be applied to Hypothetical and Disjunctive Propositions?

The parts of the *Hypothetical* Proposition are called the Antecedent and the Consequent. Thus, in the proposition, "If A is B, C is D," the Antecedent is "A is B," the Consequent is "C is D." The Quality of the Hypothetical Proposition depends upon the Quality of the Consequent. Thus the proposition If A is B, C is not D, is to be considered negative. Hypothetical propositions may also be regarded as Universal or Particular, according as the consequent is affirmed to follow from the antecedent in all or only in some cases. We have then the four fundamental types of proposition:—

(1) If A is B, C is D.   A.
(2) In some cases in which A is B, C is D.   I.
(3) If A is B, C is not D.   E.
(4) In some cases in which A is B, C is not D.   O.

John Neville Keynes

The student must be warned against treating such a proposition as "If any *A* is *B*, some *C* is *D*" as particular. Regarded separately the antecedent and the consequent in this example are both particular; but the connection between them is affirmed universally, the proposition asserting that "*in all cases* in which any *A* is *B*, some *C* is *D*."

It should be observed that in a considerable number of cases, the hypothetical is of the nature of a singular proposition, the event referred to in the antecedent being in the nature of things one which can happen but once; *e.g.*, If I perish in the attempt, I shall not die unavenged.

To the *Disjunctive* Proposition we are unable to apply distinctions of Quality. The proposition, Neither *P* is *Q* nor *X* is *Y* states no alternative, and is therefore not disjunctive at all. Distinctions of Quantity are however still applicable. Thus,

Universal,—Either *P* is *Q* or *X* is *Y*.
Particular,—In some cases either *P* is *Q* or *X* is *Y*.

It is again to be observed that frequently the disjunctive proposition is of the nature of a singular proposition, the reference being but to a single occasion on which it is asserted that one of the alternatives will hold good.

Determine the Quantity and Quality of the following propositions, stating precisely what you regard as the subject and predicate, or in the case of hypothetical propositions, the antecedent and consequent of each:—

(1) All men think all men mortal but themselves.
(2) Not to know me argues thyself unknown.
(3) To bear is to conquer our fate.
(4) Berkeley, a great philosopher, denied the existence of Matter.
(5) A great philosopher has denied the existence of Matter.
(6) The virtuous alone are happy.

465

(7) None but Irish were in the artillery
(8) Not every tale we hear is to be believed.
(9) Great is Diana of the Ephesians!
(10) All sentences are not propositions.
(11) Where there's a will there's a way.
(12) Some men are always in the wrong.
(13) Facts are stubborn things.
(14) He that increaseth knowledge increaseth sorrow.
(15) None think the great unhappy, but the great.
(16) He can't be wrong, whose life is in the right.
(17) Nothing is expedient which is unjust.
(18) Mercy but murders, pardoning those that kill.
(19) If virtue is involuntary, so is vice.
(20) Who spareth the rod, hateth his child.

Analyze the following propositions, *i.e.*, express them in one or more of the strict categorical forms admitted in Logic:—

(i) No one can be rich and happy unless he is also temperate and prudent, and not always then.

(ii) No child ever fails to be troublesome if ill taught and spoilt.

(iii) It would be equally false to assert that the rich alone are happy, or that they alone are not. [v].

(i) contains *two* statements which may be reduced to the following forms,—

All who are rich and happy | are | temperate and prudent.   A.

Some who are temperate and prudent | are not | rich and happy.   O.

(ii) may be written, All ill-taught and spoilt children are troublesome.   A.

(iii) Here two statements are given *false*, namely, the rich alone are happy; the rich alone are not happy.

We may reduce these false statements to the following,—all

who are happy are rich; all who are not happy are rich. And this gives us these true statements,—

Some who are happy are not rich.   O.
Some who are not happy are not rich.   O.

The original proposition is expressed therefore by means of these two particular negative propositions.

The Distribution of Terms in a Proposition.

A term is said to be distributed when reference is made to *all* the individuals denoted by it; it is said to be undistributed when they are only referred to *partially, i.e.,* information is given with regard to a portion of the class denoted by the term, but we are left in ignorance with regard to the remainder of the class. It follows immediately from this definition that the subject is distributed in a universal, and undistributed in a particular, proposition. It can further be shewn that the predicate is distributed in a negative, and undistributed in an affirmative proposition. Thus, if I say, All S is P, I imply that at any rate *some* P is S, but I make no implication with regard to the whole of P. I leave it an open question as to whether there is or is not any P outside the class S. Similarly if I say, Some S is P. But if I say, No S is P, in excluding the whole of S from P, I am also excluding the whole of P from S, and therefore P as well as S is distributed. Again, if I say, Some S is not P, although I make an assertion with regard to a part only of S, I exclude this part from the whole of P, and therefore the whole of P from it. In this case, then, the predicate is distributed, although the subject is not.

Summing up our results we find that

A distributes its subject only,
I distributes neither its subject nor its predicate,
E distributes both its subject and its predicate,
O distributes its predicate only.

467

How does the Quality of a Proposition affect its Quantity? Is the relation a necessary one? [L].

By the Quantity of a Proposition must here be meant the Quantity of its Predicate, and we have shewn in the preceding section that this is determined by its Quality. The predicate is distributed in negative, undistributed in affirmative, propositions.

The latter part of the above question refers to Hamilton's doctrine of the Quantification of the Predicate. According to this doctrine, the predicate of an affirmative proposition is sometimes expressly distributed, while the predicate of a negative proposition is sometimes given undistributed. For example, the following forms are introduced:—

Some S is all P,
No S is some P.

This doctrine is discussed and illustrated in Part III. chapter 9.

In doubtful cases how should you decide which is the subject and which the predicate of a proposition? [v.]

The nature of the distinction between the subject and the predicate of a proposition may be expressed by saying that the subject is that of which something is affirmed or denied, the predicate is that which is affirmed or denied of the subject; or perhaps still better, the subject is that which we think of as the determined or qualified notion, the predicate that which we think of as the determining or qualifying notion.

Now, can we say that the subject always precedes the copula, and that the predicate always follows it? In other words, can we consider the order of the terms to suffice as a criterion? If the proposition is reduced to an equation, as in the doctrine of the quantification of the predicate, I do not see what other criterion we can take; or we might rather say that in this case the distinction between subject and predicate itself fails to hold good. The two are placed on an equality, and we have nothing left by which to distinguish them except the order in which they are stated. This view is indicated by Professor Baynes in his *Essay on the New Analytic of Logical Forms*. In such a proposition, for example, as "Great is Diana of the Ephesians," he would call "great" the subject, reading the proposition, however, "(Some) great is (all) Diana of the Ephesians."

But leaving this view on one side, we cannot say that the order of terms is always a sufficient criterion. In the proposition just quoted, "Diana of the Ephesians" would generally be accepted as the subject. What further criterion then can be given? In the case of E and I propositions, (propositions, as will be shewn, which can be simply converted), we must appeal to the context or to the question to which the proposition is an answer. If one term clearly conveys information regarding the other term, it is the predicate. It is also more usual that the subject should be read in extension and the predicate in intension. If none of these considerations are decisive, then I should admit that the order of the terms must suffice. In the case of A and O propositions, (propositions, as will be shewn, which cannot be simply converted), a further criterion may be added. From the rules relating to the distribution of terms in a proposition it follows that in affirmative propositions the distributed term, (if either term is distributed), is the subject; whilst in negative propositions, if only one term is distributed, it is the predicate. I am not sure that the inversion of terms ever occurs in the case of an O proposition; but in A propositions it is not infrequent. Applying the above to such a proposition as "Workers of miracles were the apostles," it is clear that the latter term is distributed while the former is not. The latter term is therefore the subject. A corollary from the rule is that in an affirmative proposition if one and only one term is singular that is the subject, since a singular is equivalent to a distributed term. This decides such a case as "Great is Diana of the Ephesians."

What do you consider to be respectively the subject and the predicate of the following sentences, and why?

(1) Few men attain celebrity.
(2) Blessed are the peacemakers.
(3) It is mostly the boastful who fail.
(4) Clematis is Traveller's Joy.   [v.]

What do you consider to be the essential distinction between the Subject and Predicate of a proposition? Apply your answer to the following:—

(1) From thence thy warrant is thy sword.
(2) That is exactly what I wanted.   [v.]

SOEREN KIERKEGAARD
(1813-1855)

Remained relatively unknown outside his native Denmark, during his brief and uneventful lifetime. It was only in our own day that his German and French disciples gave him world fame as the father of modern existentialism. Kierkegaard was a typical romantic: his philosophy prompted by religious doubts, is essentially subjective and individualist. He viewed man in general and himself in particular, as living in a state of loneliness face to face with God. This view of man has obvious attractions in any age of great stress. The real and for a hundred years almost forgotten founder of Existentialist philosophy. His existentialism was born out of revolt against the abstract idealism of Hegel, out of protest against metaphysical detachment and estranging of man from himself by generalities. The religious existence of man is placed in the center of his thinking. Man's absolute self shall be realized in the unity between finite and infinite with spontaneity and passion of thought. In such union the paradox against reason and objective order is realized and the inner self comes out of despair of the unreal being and knowing.

Main Works:

Either-Or; Philosophical Fragments; Concluding Unscientific Postscript; The Gospel of Suffering; Fear and Trembling; Sickness Unto Death; Diaries.

Essential Knowledge

All essential knowledge relates to existence, or only such knowledge as has an essential relationship to existence is essen-

---

From: *Concluding Unscientific Postscript.*

tial knowledge. All knowledge which does not inwardly relate itself to existence, in the reflection of inwardness, is, essentially viewed, accidental knowledge; its degree and scope is essentially indifferent. That essential knowledge is essentially related to existence does not mean the above-mentioned identity which abstract thought postulates between thought and being; nor does it signify, objectively, that knowledge corresponds to something existent as its object. But it means that knowledge has a relationship to the knower, who is essentially an existing individual, and that for this reason all essential knowledge is essentially related to existence. Only ethical and ethico-religious knowledge has an essential relationship to the existence of the knower.

Mediation is a mirage, like the I-am-I. From the abstract point of view everything is and nothing comes into being. Mediation can therefore have no place in abstract thought because it presupposes *movement*. Objective knowledge may indeed have the existent for its object; but since the knowing subject is an existing individual, and through the fact of his existence in process of becoming, philosophy must first explain how a particular existing subject is related to a knowledge of mediation. It must explain what he is in such a moment, if not pretty nearly *distrait*; where he is, if not in the moon? There is constant talk of mediation and mediation; is mediation then a man, as Peter Deacon believes that *Imprimatur* is a man? How does a human being manage to become something of this kind? Is dignity, this great *philosophicum*, the fruit of study, or does the magistrate give it away, like the office of deacon or gravedigger? Try merely to enter into these and other such plain questions of a plain man, who would gladly become mediation if it could be done in some lawful and honest manner, and not either by saying *ein zwei drei kokolorum*, or by forgetting that he is himself an existing human being, for whom existence is therefore something essential, and an ethico-religious existence a suitable *quantum satis*. A speculative philosopher may perhaps find it in bad taste to ask such question. But it is important not to direct the polemic to the wrong point, and hence not to begin in a fantastic objective manner to discuss *pro* and *contra* whether there is a mediation or not, but to hold fast what it means to be a human being.

In an attempt to make clear the difference of way that exists between an objective and a subjective reflection, I shall now proceed to show how a subjective reflection makes its way inwardly in inwardness. Inwardness in an existing subject culminates in passion; corresponding to passion in the subject the truth becomes a paradox; and the fact that the truth becomes a paradox is rooted precisely in its having a relationship to an existing subject. Thus the one corresponds to the other. By forgetting that one is an existing subject, passion goes by the board and the truth is no longer a paradox; the knowing subject becomes a fantastic entity rather than a human being, and the truth becomes a fantastic object for the knowledge of this fantastic entity.

When a question of truth is raised in an objective manner, reflection is directed objectively to the truth, as an object to which the knower is related. Reflection is not focussed upon the relationship, however, but upon the question of whether it is the truth to which the knower is related. If only the object to which he is related is the truth, the subject is accounted to be in the truth. When the question of the truth is raised subjectively, reflection is directed subjectively to the nature of the individual's relationship; if only the mode of this relationship is in the truth, the individual is in the truth even if he should happen to be thus related to what is not true.* Let us take as an example the knowledge of God. Objectively, reflection is directed to the problem of whether this object is the true God; subjectively, reflection is directed to the question whether the individual is related to a something *in such a manner* that his relationship is in truth a God-relationship. On which side is the truth now to be found? Ah, may we not here resort to a mediation, and say: It is on neither side, but in the mediation of both? Excellently well said, provided we might have it explained how an existing individual manages to be in a state of mediation.

For to be in a state of mediation is to be finished, while to exist is to become. Nor can an existing individual be in two places at the same time—he cannot be an identity of subject and object. When he is nearest to being in two places at the same time he is in passion; but passion is momentary, and passion is also the highest expression of subjectivity.

The existing individual who chooses to pursue the objective way enters upon the entire approximation-process by which it is proposed to bring God to light objectively. But this is in all eternity impossible, because God is a subject, and therefore exists only for subjectivity in inwardness. The existing individual who chooses the subjective way apprehends instantly the entire dialectical difficulty involved in having to use some time, perhaps a long time, in finding God objectively; and he feels this dialectical difficulty in all its painfulness, because every moment is wasted in which he does not have God.* That very instant he has God, but not by virtue of any objective deliberation, but by virtue of the infinite passion of inwardness. The objective inquirer, on the other hand, is not embarrassed by such dialectical difficulties as are involved in devoting an entire period of investigation to finding God—since it is possible that the inquirer may die tomorrow; and if he lives he can scarcely regard God as something to be taken along if convenient, since God is precisely that which one takes *a tout prix*, which in the understanding of passion constitutes the true inward relationship to God.

It is at this point, so difficult dialectically, that the way swings off for everyone who knows what it means to think, and to think existentially; which is something very different from sitting at a desk and writing about what one has never done, something very different from writing *de omnibus dubitandum* and at the same time being as credulous existentially as the most sensuous of men. Here is where the way swings off, and the change is marked by the fact that while objective knowledge rambles comfortably on by way of the long road of approximation without being impelled by the urge of passion, subjective knowledge counts every delay a deadly peril, and the decision so infinitely important and so instantly pressing that it is as if the opportunity had already passed.

Now when the problem is to reckon up on which side there is most truth, whether on the side of one who seeks the true God objectively, and pursues the approximate truth of the God-idea; or on the side of one who, driven by the infinite passion of his need of God, feels an infinite concern for his own relationship to God in truth (and to be at one and the same time on both sides equally, is as we noted not possible for an existing individual, but is merely the happy delusion of an imaginary I-am-I): the answer cannot be in doubt for anyone who has not been demoralized with the aid of science. If one who lives in the midst of Christendom goes up to the house of God, the house of the true God, with the true conception of God in his knowledge, and prays, but prays in a false spirit; and one who lives in an idolatrous community prays with the entire passion of the infinite, although his eyes rest upon the image of an idol: where is there most truth? The one prays in truth to God though he worships an idol; the other prays falsely to the true God, and hence worships in fact an idol.

*   *   *   *   *

The objective accent falls on WHAT is said, the subjective accent on HOW it is said. This distinction holds even in the aesthetic realm, and receives definite expression in the principle that what is in itself true may in the mouth of such and such a person become untrue. In these times this distinction is particularly worthy of notice, for if we wish to express in a single sentence the difference between ancient times and our own, we should doubtless have to say: "In ancient times only an individual here and there knew the truth; now all know it, except that the inwardness of its appropriation stands in an inverse relationship to the extent of its dissemination."* Aesthetically the contradiction that truth becomes untruth in this or that person's mouth, is best construed comically: In the ethico-religious sphere, accent is again on the "how." But this is not to be understood as referring to demeanor, expression, or the like; rather it refers to the relationship sustained by the existing individual, in his own existence, to the content of his utterance. Objectively the interest is focussed merely on the thought-content, subjectively on the inwardness. At its maximum this inward "how" is the passion of the infinite, and the passion of the infinite is the truth. But the passion of the infinite is precisely subjectivity, and thus subjectivity becomes the truth. Objectively there is no infinite decisiveness, and hence it is objectively in order to annul the difference between good and evil, together with the principle of contradiction, and therewith also the infinite difference between the true and the false. Only in subjectivity is there decisiveness, to seek objectivity is to be in error. It is the passion of the infinite that is the decisive factor and not its content, for its content is precisely itself. In this manner subjectivity and the subjective "how" constitute the truth.

But the "how" which is thus subjectively accentuated precisely because the subject is an existing individual, is also subject to a dialectic with respect to time. In the passionate moment of decision, where the road swings away from objective knowledge, it seems as if the infinite decision were thereby realized. But in the same moment the existing individual finds himself in the temporal order, and the subjective "how" is transformed into a striving, a striving which receives indeed its impulse and a repeated renewal from the passion of the infinite, but is nevertheless a striving.

When subjectivity is the truth, the conceptual determination of the truth must include an expression for the antithesis to objectivity, a memento of the fork in the road where the way swings off; this expression will at the same time serve as an indication of the tension of the subjective inwardness. Here is such a definition of truth: *An objective uncertainty held fast in an appropriation-process of the most passionate inwardness is the truth,* the highest truth attainable for an *existing* individual. At the

476

point where the way swings off (and where this is cannot be specified objectively, since it is a matter of subjectivity), there objective knowledge is placed in abeyance. Thus the subject merely has, objectively, the uncertainty; but it is this which precisely increases the tension of that infinite passion which constitutes his inwardness. The truth is precisely the venture which chooses an objective uncertainty with the passion of the infinite. I contemplate the order of nature in the hope of finding God, and I see omnipotence and wisdom; but I also see much else that disturbs my mind and excites anxiety. The sum of all this is an objective uncertainty. But it is for this very reason that the inwardness becomes as intense as it is, for it embraces this objective uncertainty with the entire passion of the infinite. In the case of a mathematical proposition the objectivity is given, but for this reason the truth of such a proposition is also an indifferent truth.

But the above definition of truth is an equivalent expression for faith. Without risk there is no faith. Faith is precisely the contradiction between the infinite passion of the individual's inwardness and the objective uncertainty. If I am capable of grasping God objectively, I do not believe, but precisely because I cannot do this I must believe. If I wish to preserve myself in faith I must constantly be intent upon holding fast the objective uncertainty, so as to remain out upon the deep, over seventy thousand fathoms of water, still preserving my faith.

*   *   *   *   *

The Subjective Thinker—His Task, His Form, His Style

If an excursion into the realm of pure thought is to determine whether a man is a thinker or not, the subjective thinker is *ipso facto* excluded from consideration. But in and with his exclusion every existential problem also goes by the board; and the melancholy consequences are audible as an undertone of warning accompanying the jubilant cries with which modern speculative thought has hailed the System.

There is an old saying that *oratio, tentatio, meditatio faciunt theologum*. Similarly there is required for a subjective thinker imagination and feeling, dialectics in existential inwardness, together with passion. But passion first and last; for it is impossible to think about existence in existence without passion. Existence involves a tremendous contradiction, from which the subjective thinker does not have to abstract, though he can if he will, but in which it is his business to remain. For a dialectic of world-history the individuals vanish in humanity; you and I, any particular existing individual, cannot become visible to such a dialectic, even by the invention of new and more powerful magnifying instruments for the concrete.

The subjective thinker is a dialectician dealing with the existential, and he has the passion of thought requisite for holding fast to the qualitative disjunction. But on the other hand, if the qualitative disjunction is applied in empty isolation, if it is applied to the individual in an altogether abstract fashion, one may risk saying something infinitely decisive and be quite correct in what one says, and yet, ludicrously enough, say nothing at all. Hence it is a psychologically noteworthy phenomenon that the absolute disjunction may be used quite disingenuously, precisely for the purpose of evasion. When the death-penalty is affixed to every crime, it ends in no crime being punished at all. So also in the case of the absolute disjunction. Applied abstractly it becomes an unpronounceable mute letter, or if pronounced, it says nothing. The subjective thinker has the absolute disjunction ready to hand; therefore, as an essential existential moment he holds it as a last decisive resort, to prevent everything from being reduced to merely quantitative differences. He holds it in reserve, but does not apply it so as by recurring to it abstractly to inhibit existence. Hence the subjective thinker adds to his equipment aesthetic and ethical passion, which gives him the necessary concreteness.

All existential problems are passionate problems, for when

existence is interpenetrated with reflection it generates passion. To think about existential problems in such a way as to leave out the passion, is tantamount to not thinking about them at all, since it is to forget the point, which is that the thinker is himself an existing individual. But the subjective thinker is not a poet, though he may also be a poet; he is not an ethicist, though he may also be an ethicist; he is not a dialectician though he may also be a dialectician. He is essentially an existing individual, while the existence of the poet is non-essential in relation to the poem, the existence of the ethicist, in relation to his doctrine, the existence of the dialectician, in relation to his thought. The subjective thinker is not a man of science, but an artist. Existing is an art. The subjective thinker is aesthetic enough to give his life aesthetic content, ethical enough to regulate it, and dialectical enough to interpenetrate it with thought.

The subjective thinker has the task of understanding himself in his existence. Abstract thought is wont to speak of contradiction, and of its immanent propulsive power, although by abstracting from existence and from existing it removes the difficulty and the contradiction. The subjective thinker is an existing individual and a thinker at one and the same time; he does not abstract from the contradiction and from existence, but lives in it while at the same time thinking. In all his thinking he therefore has to think the fact that he is an existing individual. For this reason he always has enough to think about. Humanity in the abstract is a subject soon disposed of, and likewise world-history; even such tremendous portions as China, Persia, and so forth, are as nothing to the hungry monster of the historical process. The abstract concept of faith is soon disposed of; but the subjective thinker who in all his thinking remains at home in his existence, will find an inexhaustible subject for thought in his faith, when he seeks to follow its declension in all the manifold *casibus* of life. Such subjective reflection is by no means a light matter; for existence is the most difficult of all subjects to penetrate when the thinker has to remain in it, because the moment is commensurable for the highest decision, and yet again a vanishing instant in the possible seventy years of a human life.

While abstract thought seeks to understand the concrete abstractly, the subjective thinker has conversely to understand the abstract concretely. Abstract thought turns from concrete men to consider man in general; the subjective thinker seeks to understand the abstract determination of being human in terms of this particular existing human being.

PIERRE SIMON DE LAPLACE
(1749-1827)

A French mathematician and astronomer, developed, together with Kant, the theory of heavens that bears their joint name. His place in the history of philosophy is assured by his studies on probability. Laplace taught mathematics in the Ecole Militaire of Paris; he became vice president of the Senate and in 1803 chancellor. In 1816 he was elected to the French Academy. He was the originator of "Laplace's coefficients" and introduced potential function. These are two basic means of analytical approach to physical problems.

Main Works:

Mécanique céleste; Essai philosophique sur les probabilités; Exposition du système du monde.

The Calculus of Probabilities

First Principle.—The first of these principles is the definition itself of probability, which as has been seen, is the ratio of the number of favorable cases to that of all the cases possible.

Second Principle.—But that supposes the various cases equally possible. If they are not so, we will determine first their respective possibilities, whose exact appreciation is one of the most delicate points of the theory of chance. Then the probability will be the sum of the possibilities of each favorable case. Let us illustrate this principle by an example.

Let us suppose that we throw into the air a large and very thin

---

From: *Essai philosophique sur les probabilités.*

coin whose two large opposite faces, which we will call heads and tails, are perfectly similar. Let us find the probability of throwing heads at least one time in two throws. It is clear that four equally possible cases may arise, namely, heads at the first throw and tails at the second; tails at the first throw and heads at the second; finally, tails at both throws. The first three cases are favorable to the event whose probability is sought; consequently this probability is equal to $^3/_4$; so that it is a bet of three to one that heads will be thrown at least once in two throws.

We can count at this game only three different cases, namely, heads at the first throw, which dispenses with throwing a second time; tails at the first throw and heads at the second; finally, tails at the first and at the second throw. This would reduce the probability to $^2/_3$ if we should consider with d'Alembert these three cases as equally possible. But it is apparent that the probability of throwing heads at the first throw is $^1/_2$, while that of the two other cases is $^1/_4$, the first case being a simple event which corresponds to two events combined: heads at the first and at the second throw, and heads at the first throw, tails at the second. If we then, conforming to the second principle, add the possibility $^1/_2$ of heads at the first throw to the possibility $^1/_4$ of tails at the first throw and heads at the second, we shall have $^3/_4$ for the probability sought, which agrees with what is found in the supposition when we play the two throws. This supposition does not change at all the chance of that one who bets on this event; it simply serves to reduce the various cases to the cases equally possible.

Third Principle.—One of the most important points of the theory of probabilities and that which lends the most to illusions is the manner in which these probabilities increase or diminish by their mutual combination. If the events are independent of one another, the probability of their combined existence is the product of their respective probabilities. Thus the probability of throwing one ace with a single die is $^1/_6$; that of throwing two aces in throwing two dice at the same time is $^1/_{36}$. Each face of the one being able to combine with the six faces of the other, there are in fact thirty-six equally possible cases, among which one single case gives two aces. Generally the probability that a simple event in the same circumstances will occur consecutively a given number of times is equal to the probability of this simple event raised to the power indicated by this number. Having thus the successive powers of a fraction less than unity diminishing without ceasing, an event which depends upon a series of very great probabilities may become extremely improbable. Suppose then an incident be transmitted to us by twenty witnesses in such manner that the first has transmitted it to the second, the second to the third, and so on. Suppose again that the probability of each testimony be equal to the fraction $^9/_{10}$; that of the incident resulting from the testimonies will be less than $^1/_8$. We cannot better compare this diminution of the probability than with the extinction of the light of objects by the interposition of several pieces of glass. A relatively small number of pieces suffices to take away the view of an object that a single piece allows us to perceive in a distinct manner. The historians do not appear to have paid sufficient attention to this degradation of the probability of events when seen across a great number of successive generations; many historical events reputed as certain would be at least doubtful if they were submitted to this test.

In the purely mathematical sciences the most distant consequences participate in the certainty of the principle from which they are derived. In the applications of analysis to physics the results have all the certainty of facts or experiences. But in the moral sciences, where each inference is deduced from that which precedes it only in a probable manner, however probable these deductions may be, the chance of error increases with their number and ultimately surpasses the chance of truth in the consequences very remote from the principle.

Fourth Principle.—When two events depend upon each other, the probability of the compound event is the product of the probability of the first event and the probability that, this event having occurred, the second will occur. Thus in the preceding case of the three urns A, B, C, of which two contain only white balls and one contains only black balls, the probability of drawing a white ball from the urn C is $^2/_3$, since of the three urns only two contain balls of that color. But when a white ball has been drawn from the urn C, the indecision relative to that one of the urns which contains only black balls extends only to the urns A and B; the probability of drawing a white ball from the urn B is $^1/_2$; the product of $^2/_3$ by $^1/_2$, or $^1/_3$, is then the probability of drawing two white balls at one time from the urns B and C.

We see by this example the influence of past events upon the probability of future events. For the probability of drawing a white ball from the urn B, which primarily is $^2/_3$, becomes $^1/_2$ when a white ball has been drawn from the urn C; it would change to certainty if a black ball had been drawn from the same urn. We will determine this influence by means of the following principle, which is a corollary of the preceding one.

Fifth Principle.—If we calculate *a priori* the probability of the occurred event and the probability of an event composed of that one and a second one which is expected, the second probability divided by the first will be the probability of the event expected, drawn from the observed event.

Here is presented the question raised by some philosophers touching the influence of the past upon the probability of the future. Let us suppose at the play of heads and tails that heads has occurred oftener than tails. By this alone we shall be led to believe that in the constitution of the coin there is a secret cause which favors it. Thus in the conduct of life constant happiness is a proof of competency which should induce us to employ preferably happy persons. But if by the unreliability of circumstances we are constantly brought back to a state of absolute indecision, if, for example, we change the coin at each throw at the play of heads and tails, the past can shed no light upon the future and it would be absurd to take account of it.

Sixth Principle.—Each of the causes to which an observed event may be attributed is indicated with just as much likelihood as there is probability that the event will take place, supposing the event to be constant. The probability of the existence of any one of these causes is then a fraction whose numerator is the probability of the event resulting from this cause and whose denominator is the sum of the similar probabilities relative to all the causes; if these various causes, considered *a priori,* are unequally probable, it is necessary, in place of the probability of the event resulting from each cause, to employ the product of this probability by the possibility of the cause itself. This is the fundamental principle of this branch of the analysis of chances which consists in passing from events to causes.

This principle gives the reason why we attribute regular events to a particular cause. Some philosophers have thought that these events are less possible than others and that at the play of heads and tails, for example, the combination in which heads occurs twenty successive times is less easy in its nature than those where heads and tails are mixed in an irregular manner. But this opinion supposes that past events have an influence on the possibility of future events, which is not at all admissible. The regular combinations occur more rarely only because they are less numerous. If we seek a cause wherever we perceive symmetry, it is not that we regard a symmetrical event as less possible than the others, but, since this event ought to be the effect of a regular cause or that of chance, the first of these suppositions is more probable than the second. On a table we see letters arranged in this order, *C o n s t a n t i n o p l e,* and we judge that this arrangement is not the result of chance, not because it is less possible than the others, for if this word were not employed in any language we should not suspect it came from any particular cause, but this word being in use among us, it is incomparably more probable that some person has thus arranged the aforesaid letters than that this arrangement is due to chance.

This is the place to define the word *extraordinary*. We arrange in our thought all possible events in various classes; and we regard as *extraordinary* those classes which include a very small number. Thus at the play of heads and tails the occurrence of heads a hundred successive times appears to us extraordinary because of the almost infinite number of combinations which may occur in a hundred throws; and if we divide the combinations into regular series containing an order easy to comprehend, and into irregular series, the latter are incomparably more numerous. The drawing of a white ball from an urn which among a million balls contains only one of this color, the others being black, would appear to us likewise extraordinary, because we form only two classes of events relative to the two colors. But the drawing of the number 475813, for example, from an urn that contains a million numbers seems to us an ordinary event; because, comparing individually the numbers with one another without dividing them into classes, we have no reason to believe that one of them will appear sooner than the others.

From what precedes, we ought generally to conclude that the more extraordinary the event, the greater the need of its being supported by strong proofs. For those who attest it, being able to deceive or to have been deceived, these two causes are as much more probable as the reality of the event is less. We shall see this particularly when we come to speak of the probability of testimony.

Seventh Principle.—The probability of a future event is the sum of the products of the probability of each cause, drawn from the event observed, by the probability that, this cause existing, the future event will occur. The following example will illustrate this principle.

Let us imagine an urn which contains only two balls, each of which may be either white or black. One of these balls is drawn and put into the urn before proceeding to a new draw.

486

Suppose that in the first two draws white balls have been drawn; the probability of again drawing a white ball at the third draw is required.

Only two hypotheses can be made here: either one of the balls is white and the other black, or both are white. In the first hypothesis the probability of the event observed is $^1/_4$; it is unity or certainty in the second. Thus in regarding these hypotheses as so many causes, we shall have for the sixth principle $^1/_5$ and $^4/_5$ for their respective probabilities. But if the first hypothesis occurs, the probability of drawing a white ball at the third draw is $^1/_2$; it is equal to certainty in the second hypothesis; multiplying then the last probabilities by those of the corresponding hypotheses, the sum of the products, or $^9/_{10}$, will be the probability of drawing a white ball at the third draw.

When the probability of a single event is unknown we may suppose it equal to any value from zero to unity. The probability of each of these hypotheses, drawn from the event observed, is, by the sixth principle, a fraction whose numerator is the probability of the event in this hypothesis and whose denominator is the sum of the similar probabilities relative to all the hypotheses. Thus the probability that the possibility of the event is comprised within given limits is the sum of the fractions comprised within these limits. Now if we multiply each fraction by the probability of the future event, determined in the corresponding hypothesis, the sum of the products relative to all the hypotheses will be, by the seventh principle, the probability of the future event drawn from the event observed. Thus we find that an event having occurred successively any number of times, the probability that it will happen again the next time is equal to this number increased by unity divided by the same number, increased by two units. Placing the most ancient epoch of history at five thousand years ago, or at 182623 days, and the sun having risen constantly in the interval at each revolution of twenty-four hours, it is a bet of 1826214 to one that it will rise again tomorrow. But this number is incomparably greater for him who, recognizing in the totality of phenomena the principal regulator of days and seasons, sees that nothing at the present moment can arrest the course of it.

Buffon in his *Political Arithmetic* calculates differently the preceding probability. He supposes that it differs from unity only by a fraction whose numerator is unity and whose denominator is the number 2 raised to a power equal to the number of days which have elapsed since the epoch. But the true manner of relating past events with the probability of causes and of future events was unknown to this illustrious writer.

GOTTFRIED WILHELM VON LEIBNIZ
(1646-1716)

Studied at Leipzig and Jena and spent most of his life in the service of various German princes. He was a man of universal interests who dabbled in politics, economics, theology, linguistics, statistics etc., in addition to his solid achievements in mathematics and philosophy which made him the first great figure of Germany's classical age. His main aim was to achieve harmony between discordant elements, be it in diplomacy, religion or philosophy. He coined the concept of *monad* or "true atom" and considered there was order of monads, which, together, compose this best of all possible worlds. His greatest mathematical achievement is the development of the infinitesimal, which he shares with Newton.

Main Works:

De arte combinatoria; Theoria motus concreti et abstracti; Discours de la métaphysique; Système nouveau de la nature; Nouveaux Essais sur l'entendement humain; Théodicée; Monadoligie.

First Truths

First truths are those which predicate something of themselves or deny the opposite of their opposites. For example, A is A, or A is not non-A; if it is true that A is B, it is false that A is not B or that A is non-B. Likewise, everything is what it is; everything is similar or equal to itself; nothing is greater or less than itself. These and other truths of this kind, though they may have various degrees of priority, can nevertheless all be grouped under the one name of *identities*.

From: *Kleinere Philosophische Schriften.*

All other truths are reduced to first truths with the aid of definitions or by the analysis of concepts; in this consists *proof* a priori, which is independent of experience. I shall give as example this proposition which is accepted as an axiom by mathematicians and all other people alike: the whole is greater than its part, or the part is less than the whole. This is very easily demonstrated from the definition of less or greater, with the addition of a primitive axiom or identity. For that is *less* which is equal to a part of another thing (*the greater*). This definition is very easily understood and is consistent with the general practice of men, when they compare things with each other and measure the excess by subtracting an amount equal to the smaller from the greater. Hence one may reason as follows. A part is equal to a part of the whole (namely, to itself, by the axiom of identity, according to which each thing is equal to itself). But what is equal to a part of a whole is less than the whole (by definition of less). Therefore the part is less than the whole.

The predicate or consequent therefore always inheres in the subject or antecedent. And as Aristotle, too, observed, the nature of truth in general or the connection between the terms of a proposition consists in this fact. In identities this connection and the inclusion of the predicate in the subject are explicit; in all other propositions they are implied and must be revealed through the analysis of the concepts, which constitutes a demonstration a priori.

This is true, moreover, in every affirmative truth, universal or singular, necessary or contingent, whether its terms are intrinsic or extrinsic denominations. Here lies hidden a wonderful secret which contains the nature of contingency or the essential distinction between necessary and contingent truths and which removes the difficulty involved in a fatal necessity determining even free things.

These matters have not been adequately considered because they are too easy, but there follow from them many things of great importance. At once they give rise to the accepted axiom that *there is nothing without a reason, or no effect without a cause.* Otherwise there would be truth which could not be proved a priori or resolved into identities—contrary to the nature of truth, which is always either expressly or implicitly identical. It follows also that, if there is a correspondence between two data in a determining series, then there will also be a correspondence of the same kind in the series sought for and determined by the former. For no difference can be accounted for unless its reason is found in the data. A corollary, or, better, an example, of this is the postulate of Archimedes stated at the beginning of his book on the balance—that if the arms of a balance and its weights are supposed equal, everything will be in equilibrium. This also gives a *reason for eternal things.* If it be assumed that the world has existed from eternity and has contained only spheres, a reason should have to be given why it contains spheres rather than cubes.

It follows also that *there are no two individual things in nature which differ only numerically.* For surely it must be possible to give a reason why they are different, and this must be sought in some differences within themselves. Thus the observation of Thomas Aquinas about separate intelligences, which he declared never differ in number alone, must be applied to other things also. Never are two eggs, two leaves, or two blades of grass in a garden to be found exactly similar to each other. So perfect similarity occurs only in incomplete and abstract concepts, where matters are conceived, not in their totality but according to a certain single viewpoint, as when we consider only figures and neglect the figured matter. So geometry is right in studying similar triangles, even though two perfectly similar material triangles are never found. And, although gold or some other metal, or salt, and many liquids, may be taken for homogeneous bodies, this can be admitted only as concerns the senses and not as if it were true in an exact sense.

It follows further that *there are no purely extrinsic denomina-*

tions which have no basis at all in the denominated thing itself. For the concept of the denominated subject necessarily involves the concept of the predicate. Likewise, whenever the denomination of a thing is changed, some variation has to occur in the thing itself.

The complete or perfect concept of an individual substance involves all its predicates, past, present, and future. For certainly it is already true now that a future predicate will be a predicate in the future, and so it is contained in the concept of the thing. Therefore there is contained in the perfect individual concepts of Peter or Judas, considered as merely possible concepts and setting aside the divine decree to create them, everything that will happen to them, whether necessarily or freely. And all this is known by God. Thus it is obvious that God elects from an infinity of possible individuals those whom he judges best suited to the supreme and secret ends of his wisdom. In an exact sense, he does not decree that Peter should sin or Judas be damned but only that, in preference to other possible individuals, Peter, who will sin—certainly, indeed, yet not necessarily but freely—and Judas, who will suffer damnation—under the same condition—shall come into existence, or that the possible concept shall become actual. And although the eternal possible concept of Peter also contains his future salvation, the cooperation of grace is not yet absent from it, for this same perfect concept of this possible Peter also contains as a possibility the help of divine grace which will be granted to him.

Every individual substance involves the whole universe in its perfect concept, and all that exists in the universe has existed or will exist. For there is no thing upon which some true denomination, at least of comparison or relation, cannot be imposed by another thing. Yet there is no purely extrinsic denomination. I have shown the same thing in many other ways which are in harmony with each other.

All individual created substances, indeed, are different expressions of the same universe and of the same universal cause, God. But these expressions vary in perfection as do different representations or perspectives of the same city seen from different points.

Every created individual substance exerts physical action and passion on all others. For if a change occurs in one, some corresponding change results in all others, because their denomination is changed. This is confirmed by our experience of nature, for we observe that in a vessel full of liquid (the whole universe is such a vessel) a motion made in the middle is propagated to the edges, though it may become more and more insensible as it recedes farther from its origin.

It can be said that, speaking with metaphysical rigor, *no created substance exerts a metaphysical action or influence upon another.* For to say nothing of the fact that it cannot be explained how anything can pass over from one thing into the substance of another, it has already been shown that all the future states of each thing follow from its own concept. What we call causes are in metaphysical rigor only concomitant requisites. This is illustrated by our experiences of nature, for bodies in fact recede from other bodies by force of their own elasticity and not by any alien force, although another body has been required to set the elasticity (which arises from something intrinsic to the body itself) working.

If the diversity of soul and body be assumed, their union can be explained from this without the common hypothesis of an *influx,* which is unintelligible, and without the hypothesis of occasional causes, which calls upon a God *ex machina.* For God has equipped both soul and body from the beginning with such great wisdom and workmanship that, through the original constitution and essence of each, everything which happens in one corresponds perfectly and automatically to whatever happens in the other, just as if something had passed over from the one into the other. I call this the *hypothesis of concomitance.* This is true of all the substances in the whole universe but is not perceptible in all as it is in the soul and body.

There is no vacuum. For the different parts of empty space would be perfectly similar and congruent with each other and

493

could not by themselves be distinguished. So they would differ in number alone, which is absurd. Time too may be proved not to be a thing, in the same way as space.

There is no corporeal substance in which there is nothing but extension, or magnitude, figure, and their variations. For otherwise there could exist two corporeal substances perfectly similar to each other, which is absurd. Hence it follows that there is something in corporeal substances analogous to the soul, which is commonly called form.

There are no atoms; indeed, there is no body so small that it is not actually subdivided. By this very fact, since it is affected by all other things in the entire world, and receives some effect from all which must cause a change in the body, it has even preserved all past impressions and anticipates the future ones. If anyone says that this effect is contained in the motions impressed on the atom, which receives the effect *in toto* without any division in it, it can be replied that not only must an effect in the atom result from all the impressions of the universe but, conversely, the entire state of the universe can be gathered from the atom. Thus the cause can be inferred from the effect. But, from the figure and motion of the atom alone, we cannot by regression infer what impressions have produced the given effect on it, since the same motion can be caused by different impressions, not to mention the fact that we cannot explain why bodies of a definite smallness should not be further divisible.

Hence it follows that *every small part of the universe contains a world with an infinite number of creatures.* But a continuum is not divisible into points, nor is it divisible in all possible ways. It is not divisible into points, because points are not parts but limits. It is not divisible in all possible ways, because not all creatures are in the same part; yet it is certain that the parts are infinitely divisible. Thus, if you bisect a straight line and then any part of it, you will set up different divisions than if you trisect it.

There is no actual determinate figure in things, for none can satisfy the infinity of impressions. So neither a circle nor an ellipse nor any other line is definable by us except in our intellect, or, if you prefer, before the lines are drawn or their parts distinguished.

Space, time, extension, and motion are not things but well-founded modes of our consideration.

Extension, motion, and bodies themselves, insofar as they consist in extension and motion alone, are not substances but true phenomena, like rainbows and parhelia. For figures do not define things, and, if only their extension is considered, bodies are not one substance but many.

For the substance of bodies there is required something which lacks extension; otherwise there would be no principle to account for the reality of the phenomena or for true unity. There would always be a plurality of bodies, never one body alone; and therefore there could not, in truth, be many. By a similar argument Cordemoi proved the existence of atoms. But, since these have been excluded, there remains only something that lacks extension, something like the soul, which was once called a form or species.

Corporeal substance can neither come into being nor perish except through creation or annihilation. For, once it does last, it will last always, for there is no reason for a change. Nor does the dissolution of a body have anything in common with its destruction. *Therefore ensouled beings neither begin nor perish; they are only transformed.*

JOHN LOCKE
(1632-1704)

Studied at Oxford and, after a journey to the Continent, became physician to Lord Anthony Ashley, later Lord Shaftesbury, and tutor to his son and grandson. He became a prominent public figure after the Glorious Revolution of 1688 which brought into power men who favored his political and religious principles. Locke's philosophy is one of rational empiricism, opposing all concepts of innate ideas. His medical training made him interested in the psychological roots of human behavior. He preached toleration in religion and democracy in politics. Politically he exercised a great influence on America's Founding Fathers.

Main Works:

Essay Concerning Human Understanding; Two Treatises of Government; Letters on Toleration; Some Thoughts concerning Education; Reasonableness of Christianity.

Ideas in General

1. *Idea is the object of thinking.*—Every man being conscious to himself, that he thinks, and that which his mind is applied about, whilst thinking, being the ideas that are there, it is past doubt that men have in their mind several ideas, such as are those expressed by the words, "whiteness, hardness, sweetness, thinking, motion, man, elephant, army, drunkenness," and others: it is in the first place then to be inquired, How he comes

---

From: *Essay Concerning Human Understanding.*

by them? I know it is a received doctrine, that men have native ideas and original characters stamped upon their minds in their very first being. This opinion I have at large examined already; and, I suppose, what I have said in the foregoing book will be much more easily admitted, when I have shown whence the understanding may get all the ideas it has, and by what ways and degrees they may come into the mind; for which I shall appeal to every one's own observation and experience.

2. *All ideas come from sensation or reflection.*—Let us then suppose the mind to be, as we say, white paper, void of all characters, without any ideas; how comes it to be furnished? Whence comes it by that vast store, which the busy and boundless fancy of man has painted on it with an almost endless variety? Whence has it all the materials of reason and knowledge? To this I answer, in one word, From experience; in that all our knowledge is founded, and from that it ultimately derives itself. Our observation, employed either about external sensible objects, or about the internal operations of our minds, perceived and reflected on by ourselves, is that which supplies our understandings with all the materials of thinking. These two are the fountains of knowledge, from whence all the ideas we have, or can naturally have, do spring.

3. *The object of sensation one source of ideas.*—First. Our senses, conversant about particular sensible objects, do convey into the mind several distinct perceptions of things, according to those various ways wherein those objects do affect them; and thus we come by those ideas we have of yellow, white, heat, cold, soft, hard, bitter, sweet, and all those which we call sensible qualities; which when I say the senses convey into the mind, I mean, they from external objects convey into the mind what produces there those perceptions. This great source of most of the ideas we have, depending wholly upon our senses, and derived by them to the understanding, I call, "sensation."

4. *The operations of our minds the other sources of them.*—
Secondly. The other fountain, from which experience furnisheth
the understanding with ideas, is the perception of the operations
of our own minds within us, as it is employed about the ideas
it has got; which operations when the soul comes to reflect on
and consider, do furnish the understanding with another set of
ideas which could not be had from things without; and such are
perception, thinking, doubting, believing, reasoning, knowing,
willing, and all the different actings of our minds; which we,
being consciousness of, and observing in ourselves, do from
these receive into our understandings as distinct ideas, as we
do from bodies affecting our senses. This source of ideas every
man has wholly in himself; and though it be not sense as having
nothing to do with external objects, yet it is very like it, and
might properly enough be called "internal sense." But as I call
the other "sensation," so I call this "reflection," the ideas it af-
fords being such only as the mind gets by reflecting on its own
operations within itself. By reflection, then, in the following
part of this discourse, I would be understood to mean that notice which the mind takes of its own operations, and the manner
of them, by reason whereof there come to be ideas of these
operations in the understanding. These two, I say, viz., external
material things as the objects of sensation, and the operations
of our own minds within as the objects of reflection, are, to me,
the only originals from whence all our ideas take their beginnings. The term "operations" here, I use in a large sense, as
comprehending not barely the actions of the mind about its
ideas, but some sort of passions arising sometimes from them,
such as is the satisfaction or uneasiness arising from any thought.

5. *All our ideas are of the one or the other of these.*—The understanding seems to me not to have the least glimmering of
any ideas which doth not receive from one of these two. External objects furnish the mind with the ideas of sensible qualities,
which are all those different perceptions they produce in us;

and the mind furnishes the understanding with ideas of its own operations.

These, when we have taken a full survey of them, and their several modes, [combinations, and relations,] we shall find to contain all our whole stock of ideas; and that we have nothing in our minds which did not come in one of these two ways. Let any one examine his own thoughts, and thoroughly search into his understanding, and then let him tell me, whether all the original ideas he has there, are any other than of the objects of his senses, or of the operations of his mind considered as objects of his reflection; and how great a mass of knowledge soever he imagines to be lodged there, he will, upon taking a strict view, see that he has not any idea in his mind but what one of these two have imprinted, though perhaps with infinite variety compounded and enlarged by the understanding, as we shall see hereafter.

6. *Observable in children.*—He that attentively considers the state of a child at his first coming into the world, will have little reason to think him stored with plenty of ideas that are to be the matter of his future knowledge. It is by degrees he comes to be furnished with them; and though the ideas of obvious and familiar qualities imprint themselves before the memory begins to keep a register of time or order, yet it is often so late before some unusual qualities come in the way, that there are few men that cannot recollect the beginning of their acquaintance with them: and, if it were worth while, no doubt a child might be so ordered as to have but a very few even of the ordinary ideas till he were grown up to a man. But all that are born into the world being surrounded with bodies that perpetually and diversely affect them, variety of ideas, whether care be taken about it or not, are imprinted on the minds of children. Light and colors are busy at hand every where when the eye is but open; sounds and some tangible qualities fail not to solicit their proper senses, and force an entrance to the mind; but yet I think

it will be granted easily, that if a child were kept in a place where he never saw any other but black and white till he were a man, he would have no more ideas of scarlet or green than he that from his childhood never tasted an oyster or a pineapple has of those particular relishes.

7. *Men are differently furnished with these according to the different objects they converse with.*—Men then come to be furnished with fewer or more simple ideas from without, according as the objects they converse with afford greater or less variety; and from the operations of their minds within, according as they more or less reflect on them. For, though he that contemplates the operations of his mind cannot but have plain and clear ideas of them; yet, unless he turns his thoughts that way, and considers them attentively, he will have no more clear and distinct ideas of all that may be observed therein, than he will have all the particular ideas of any landscape, or of the parts and motions of a clock, who will not turn his eyes to it, and with attention heed all the parts of it. The picture or clock may be so placed, that they may come in his way every day; but yet he will have but a confused idea of all the parts they are made of, till he applies himself with attention to consider them each in particular.

8. *Ideas of reflection later, because they need attention.*—And hence we see the reason why it is pretty late before most children get ideas of the operations of their own minds; and some have not any very clear or perfect ideas of the greatest part of them all their lives:—because, though they pass there continually, yet like floating visions, they make not deep impressions enough to leave in the mind, clear, distinct, lasting ideas, till the understanding turns inwards upon itself, reflects on its own operations, and makes them the objects of its own contemplation. Children, when they come first into it, are surrounded with a world of new things, which, by a constant solicitation of their senses, draw the mind constantly to them, forward to take no-

tice of new, and apt to be delighted with the variety of changing objects. Thus the first years are usually employed and diverted in looking abroad. Men's business in them is to acquaint themselves with what is to be found without; and so, growing up in a constant attention to outward sensations, seldom make any considerable reflection on what passes within them till they come to be of riper years; and some scarce ever at all.

9. *The soul begins to have ideas when it begins to perceive.* —To ask, at what time a man has first any ideas, is to ask when he begins to perceive; having ideas, and perception, being the same thing. I know it is an opinion, that the soul always thinks; and that it has the actual perception of ideas in itself constantly, as long as it exists; and that actual thinking is as inseparable from the soul, as actual extension is from the body; which if true, to inquire after the beginning of a man's ideas is the same as to inquire after the beginning of his soul. For by this account, soul and its ideas, as body and its extension, will begin to exist both at the same time.

10. *The soul thinks not always; for this wants proofs.*—But whether the soul be supposed to exist antecedent to, or coeval with, or some time after, the first rudiments or organization, or the beginnings of life in the body, I leave to be disputed by those who have better thought of that matter. I confess myself to have one of those dull souls that doth not perceive itself always to contemplate ideas; nor can conceive it any more necessary for the soul always to think, than for the body always to move; the perception of ideas being, as I conceive, to the soul, what motion is to the body: not its essence, but one of its operations; and, therefore, though thinking be supposed never so much the proper action of the soul, yet it is not necessary to suppose that it should be always thinking, always in action: that, perhaps, is the privilege of the infinite Author and Preserver of things, "who never slumbers nor sleeps;" but it is not competent to any finite being, at least not to the soul of man. We know

certainly, by experience, that we sometimes think; and thence draw this infallible consequence,—that there is something in us that has a power to think; but whether that substance perpetually thinks, or no, we can be no farther assured than experience informs us. For to say, that actual thinking is essential to the soul and inseparable from it, is to beg what is in question, and not to prove it by reason; which is necessary to be done, if it be not a self-evident proposition. But whether this—that "the soul always thinks," be a self-evident proposition, that everybody assents to on first thinking, I appeal to mankind. [It is doubted whether I thought all last night or no; the question being about a matter of fact, it is begging it to bring as a proof for it an hypothesis which is the very thing in dispute; by which way one may prove any thing; and it is but supposing that all watches, whilst the balance beats, think, and it is sufficiently proved, and past doubt, that my watch thought all last night. But he that would not deceive himself ought to build his hypothesis on matter of fact, and make it out by sensible experience, and not presume on matter of fact because of his hypothesis; that is, because he supposes it to be so; which way of proving amounts to this,—that I must necessarily think all last night, because another supposes I always think, though I myself cannot perceive that I always do so.

But men in love with their opinions may not only suppose what is in question, but allege wrong matter of fact. How else could any one make it an inference of mine, that a thing is not, because we are not sensible of it in our sleep? I do not say, there is no soul in a man because he is not sensible of it in his sleep; but I do say, he cannot think at any time, waking or sleeping, without being sensible of it. Our being sensible of it is not necessary to any thing but to our thoughts; and to them it is, and to them it will always be, necessary, till we can think without being conscious of it.]

11. *It is not always conscious of it.*—I grant that the soul in a waking man is never without thought, because it is the con-

dition of being awake; but whether sleeping without dreaming be not an affection of the whole man, mind as well as body, may be worth a waking man's consideration; it being hard to conceive that any thing should think and not be conscious of it. If the soul doth think in a sleeping man without being conscious of it, I ask, whether, during such thinking, it has any pleasure or pain, or be capable of happiness or misery? I am sure the man is not, no more than the bed or earth he lies on. For to be happy or miserable without being conscious of it, seems to me utterly inconsistent and impossible. Or if it be possible that the soul can, whilst the body is sleeping, have its thinking, enjoyments, and concerns, its pleasure or pain, apart, which the man is not conscious of, nor partakes in, it is certain that Socrates asleep and Socrates awake is not the same person; but his soul when he sleeps, and Socrates the man, consisting of body and soul, when he is waking, are two persons; since waking Socrates has no knowledge of, or concernment for that happiness or misery of his soul, which it enjoys alone by itself whilst he sleeps, without perceiving any thing of it, no more than he has for the happiness or misery of a man in the Indies, whom he knows not. For if we take wholly away all consciousness of our actions and sensations, especially of pleasure and pain, and the concernment that accompanies it, it will be hard to know wherein to place personal identity.

OF SIMPLE IDEAS

1. *Uncompounded appearances.*—The better to understand the nature, manner, and extent of our knowledge, one thing is carefully to be observed concerning the ideas we have; and that is, that some of them are simple, and some complex.

Though the qualities that affect our senses are, in the things themselves, so united and blended that there is no separation, no distance between them; yet it is plain the ideas they produce in the mind enter by the senses simple and unmixed. For though

the sight and touch often take in from the same object, at the
same time, different ideas—as a man sees at once motion and
color, the hand feels softness and warmth in the same piece of
wax—yet the simple ideas thus united in the same subject are
as perfectly distinct as those that come in by different senses;
the coldness and hardness which a man feels in a piece of ice
being as distinct ideas in the mind as the smell and whiteness
of a lily, or as the taste of sugar and smell of a rose: and there
is nothing can be plainer to a man than the clear and distinct
perception he has of those simple ideas; which, being each in
itself uncompounded, contains in it nothing but one uniform
appearance or conception in the mind, and is not distinguishable into different ideas.

2. *The mind can neither make nor destroy them.*—These simple ideas, the materials of all our knowledge, are suggested and
furnished to the mind only by those two ways above mentioned,
viz., sensation and reflection. When the understanding is once
stored with these simple ideas, it has the power to repeat, compare, and unite them, even to an almost infinite variety, and so
can make at pleasure new complex ideas. But it is not in the
power of the most exalted wit or enlarged understanding, by
any quickness or variety of thought, to invent or frame one new
simple idea in the mind, not taken in by the ways before mentioned; nor can any force of the understanding destroy those
that are there: the dominion of man in this little world of his
own understanding, being much-what the same as it is in the
great world of visible things, wherein his power, however managed by art and skill, reaches no farther than to compound and
divide the materials that are made to his hand but can do nothing towards the making the least particle of new matter, or destroying one atom of what is already in being. The same inability
will everyone find in himself, who shall go about to fashion in
his understanding any simple idea not received in by his senses
from external objects, or by reflection from the operations of
his own mind about them. I would have any one try to fancy

any taste which had never affected his palate, or frame the idea of a scent he had never smelt; and when he can do this, I will also conclude, that a blind man hath *ideas* of colors, and a deaf man true, distinct notions of sounds.

3. This is the reason why, though we cannot believe it impossible to God to make a creature with other organs, and more ways to convey into the understanding the notice of corporeal things than those five as they are usually counted, which he has given to man; yet I think it is not possible for any one to imagine any other qualities in bodies, howsoever constituted, whereby they can be taken notice of, besides sounds, tastes, smells, visible and tangible qualities. And had mankind been made with but four senses, the qualities then which are the objects of the fifth sense had been as far from our notice, imagination, and conception, as now any belonging to a sixth, seventh, or eighth sense can possibly be; which, whether yet some other creatures, in some parts of this vast and stupendous universe, may not have, will be a great presumption to deny. He that will not set himself proudly at the top of all things, but will consider the immensity of this fabric, and the great variety that is to be found in this little and inconsiderable part of it which he has to do with, may be apt to think, that in other mansions of it there may be other and different intelligible beings, of whose faculties he has as little knowledge or apprehension, as a worm shut up in one drawer of a cabinet hath of the senses or understanding of a man; such variety and excellency being suitable to the wisdom and power of the Maker. I have here followed the common opinion of man's having five senses, though perhaps there may be justly counted more; but either supposition serves equally to my present purpose.

RAIMUNDUS LULLUS
(1235-1315)

A fervent apologist of Christianity until he found martyrdom in Tunis at the age of 80. He aimed at creating a general or universal science through the "combinatory method", later admired by Giordano Bruno and Leibniz. His mysticism pervades not only his philosophy but also his poetry, written in Catalan. He maintained that every article of faith could be logically proven.

Main Work:

    Ars major.

The Terminology, Materials, and Procedures of Logic

Logic is an art by means of which truth and falsehood are discovered through reasoning and are distinguished by argumentation. Among other considerations, there are three factors in logic: the term, proposition, and the argument. The term is the significative expression from which the proposition is or can be established: as goodness, size, etc., or God, angel, and justice, wisdom, avarice, gluttony, and so on. The term is two-fold, namely, common and distinctive. It is common when it signifies or can signify many things under one heading: as, man, animal, and similar concepts. It is distinctive when it signifies or can signify one thing under one heading: as, Jesus Christ, Mary, etc.

From: *Dialectica, sec. Logica Nova.*

Certain terms are called universal signs, and certain others, particular signs. The universals are affirmative: as, all, anyone, each, whithersoever, wherever, always. Negative signs are: nobody, no one, neither, never, nowhere, etc. Particular signs are: some one, a certain one, one of them, sometimes, somewhere, etc. In the proposition one term is the subject, another is the predicate, another the copula. The copula is the first, second, or third person, singular or plural, explicit or implicit of the verb *to be*. The subject is the term that is before the copula: as, goodness is being, goodness is the subject, etc. The predicate is the term that stands after the copula, and is so called from the term standing before the copula, that is, from the subject: as, goodness is great. The term *great* is the predicate. The universal and the particular signs, previously mentioned, are never subject or predicate.

THE PROPOSITION

The proposition is a statement composed of terms, signifying that something is or is not: as, goodness is great, avarice is not good. The proposition is two-fold, namely: true and false. A true proposition is that which signifies that which is so: as, justice is virtue. A false proposition is that which signifies what is not so: as, goodness is bad, a man is not a being, etc. A proposition is to be of two modes: one is categorical, the other is hypothetical. A categorical proposition is a statement in which there are a subject and a predicate and a copula: as, goodness is lovable, God is eternal, faith is a great virtue, avarice is evil. A categorical proposition is four-fold, namely: universal, particular, indefinite, and singular. A universal proposition is one whose subject is a common term, added to the universal sign: as, every stone is sensible, all power is good, etc. A particular proposition is one whose subject is a common term added to the particular sign: as, a certain goodness is greatness, some virtue is sensible. An indefinite proposition is one whose subject

507

is a common term without a sign: as, goodness is powerful, man is created, etc. A singular proposition is one whose subject is a distinctive term, or a term that is joined to a demonstrative pronoun. An example of the first type: Jesus Christ is God, and the man Bernard is a scholar. An example of the second type: That man is a theologian. A categorical proposition is two-fold, namely: affirmative and negative. It is affirmative when the predicate is attributed to the subject or seems to be attributed: as, man is created, man is rational. It is negative when the predicate is withdrawn from the subject or seems to be withdrawn: as, man is not a stone, man is not a plant, etc. The logician uses three forms of the *petitio* in a proposition, namely: which, what kind, how big. By which he seeks to find whether the proposition is categorical or hypothetical. By *how big* he asks whether it is universal, particular, indefinite, or singular. By *what kind*, whether it is affirmative or negative. Certain propositions agree with others in three modes: one mode, when they are of the same quantity and quality: as, one is universal, because the other is universal, etc. Or, one is affirmative because the other is affirmative: and so with the negative. The second mode, when they have the same subject or predicate: as, goodness is enduring, greatness is enduring, etc. The third mode, when they are similar in subject and predicate: as, goodness is great, goodness is not great: and so with the rest.

CONVERSION

Conversion is the change of the subject into the predicate and vice versa. The logician makes two conversions: one is called simple, the other by accident. Simple conversion is the change of the subject into the predicate, and vice versa, the same quantity remaining in each proposition: as, no goodness is hateful. The conversion is: nothing hateful is goodness. Similarly, a certain goodness is greatness. The conversion is: A certain greatness is goodness. By this conversion the negative universal and the affirmative particular are converted. Conversion by accident is the change of the subject into the predicate and vice versa, the same quality and a different quantity remaining in each proposition: as, everything sensual is different. The conversion is: a certain different thing is sensual. Similarly, no animal is a stone. The conversion is: a certain stone is not an animal, etc. By this conversion the affirmative universal and the negative universal are converted. And thus the affirmative particular is converted. Similarly with the indefinite and the singular according to their mode. No conversion properly so-called occurs in the negative particular, because a true proposition can be converted into a false one: as, a certain animal is not a man. The conversion would be: a certain man is not an animal. This would be false. And in the same mode the same assertion cannot be made of other similar propositions.

PROPOSITIONS

In the propositions, that agree in similar subject and predicate, four oppositions take place, namely: the contrary, the contradictory, the subcontrary, and the subalternate. Contrary oppositions are affirmative and negative universals, agreeing in subject and predicate: as, all goodness is great, no goodness is great, and so with the rest. Contradictory oppositions are negative universals and affirmative particulars: or affirmative universals and negative particulars, etc. Of the first type: no goodness is great, a certain goodness is great. Of the second type: no goodness is great, a certain goodness is not great, and so with the rest. Subcontrary oppositions are affirmative particulars and negative particulars agreeing in subject and predicate: as, a certain goodness is great, a certain goodness is not great, and so with the rest: as is clear in the following figure, and whatever is stated of the particular can be stated of the indefinite and the singular.

509

Every man is an animal   Contrary   No man is an animal

Subalternates   Contradictory / Contradictory   Subalternates

Subcontrary

A certain man is an animal   A certain man is not an animal

The extremes of the categorical proposition are the subject and the predicate. The categorical proposition is two-fold: one has a disjunctive extreme: the other a conjunctive extreme. It is a categorical proposition with a disjunctive extreme when in the subject or predicate there is a disjunctive conjunction: as, goodness or greatness is great in itself: or, a man is an animal or a stone. It is a categorical proposition with a conjunctive extreme when in its subject or predicate there is a copulative conjunction: as, goodness and greatness are lovable: or, goodness is great and powerful. And sometimes a categorical proposition may have either extreme disjunctive or conjunctive: and sometimes one extreme disjunctive and the other conjunctive. A contradiction is an affirmation, and its contradictory is a negation.

THE MATTER OF THE PROPOSITION

Matter is three-fold: natural, contingent, and discrete. It is natural, when the essence of the subject or its property is predicated: as, man is an animal, man is risible. It is contingent, when the predicate can exist or not apart from the corruption of the subject: as, man is white. It is discrete when the predicate is inconsistent with the subject: as, man is a donkey.

THE HYPOTHETICAL PROPOSITION

The hypothetical proposition is a statement in which two categorical propositions are conjunctively united: as, goodness is

510

great and greatness is good, etc. A hypothetical proposition is six-fold: conjunctive, disjunctive, conditional, rational, temporal, and local. A conjunctive proposition is a hypothetical proposition in which there are two categorical propositions joined by a copulative conjunction: as, goodness is great and difference is agreement, etc. A disjunctive hypothetical proposition is one in which there are two categorical propositions joined by a disjunctive conjunction: as, man is an animal, or a lion is sensible, etc. A conditional hypothetical proposition is one in which there are two categorical propositions joined by the term *if*: as, if duration is powerful, power is enduring, etc. A rational hypothetical proposition is one in which there are two categorical propositions joined by the conjunctions *therefore* or *hence*: as, wisdom is appealing, therefore goodness is powerful, etc. A temporal hypothetical proposition is one in which there are two categorical propositions joined by a temporal adverb: as, goodness is great, when greatness is good, etc. A local hypothetical proposition is one in which there are two categorical propositions joined by some adverb of place: as, virtue is where justice is, etc.

In regard to the conjunctive proposition being true, its two categorical terms must be true, but when one part of the categorical proposition is false, then the categorical proposition is false: as, a man is an animal and a man is a she-goat, and hence the conjunctive proposition is said to be wholly false, if it is partly false. In regard to the disjunctive proposition being true, it is sufficient for some part of its terms to be true: as, goodness is virtuous, or a man is not an animal, etc. And hence it is said, if a disjunctive proposition is partly true, that it is all true. But in regard to a disjunctive proposition being false, it is necessary for both its categorical terms to be false: as, man is irrational, or a stone is an animal, etc. For the truth of a conditional proposition it is required that the antecedent cannot stand without a consequence: as, you are a man, therefore you are a being. To discover this, it should be considered whether the opposition of the consequence contradicts the antecedent. To discover the falsity, it is necessary for the antecedent to be able to stand without the consequence, which it will appear to do, considering that the opposition of the consequence is not inconsistent with the antecedent, etc.

Every proposition is necessary, possible, impossible, or contingent. It is necessary, when it is so true that it can in no way whatever be false: as, God is good, great, and eternal: man is an animal, etc. It is possible, when it can be or not: as, a man will be a scholar, a man will not be a laborer, etc. But when a thing could be or not, it is contingent: as, he is a gamester, etc. It is impossible when it signifies a thing that can in no manner whatever exist: as, man is irrational, man is not an animal, etc.

SUPPOSITIONS

A supposition is the taking of a term for a universal or singular thing: and it is three-fold, namely: simple, personal, and material. A simple supposition is the taking of a term for a universal thing: as, man is a species. A personal supposition is the taking of a term for a singular thing: as, man runs. A material supposition is the taking of a term for a thing considered materially: as, a man is a disyllabic expression.

AMPLIFICATIONS

Amplification is the standing of a common term for different tenses, about which rules are laid down. The first is, that in every proposition in which there is a verb in the perfect tense or a participle, the preceding term is amplified for that in which is or was: as, the girl was a prostitute. The second rule is, that in every proposition in which there is a verb or a participle in the future tense, the preceding term stands for that which is or will be: as, the boy will be an old man. The third rule is, that every term in a proposition in respect of the verb *to be able* or

its participle stands for that which is or can be: as, white can
be black.

RESTRICTION

Restriction is the standing of a term in a proposition for fewer
meanings than is required by its nature: as, every white man
runs: every devout man is pleasing to God.

PREDICABLES AND CATEGORIES

There are five predicables, namely: genus, species, difference,
property, and accident. Genus is that which is predicated about
many things different in species. Species is the being that is
predicated about many things different in number. Difference
is the being by which certain things differ from others. Property
is that which is proper to one thing and not another: as, it is
proper for man to be risible, for a dog to bark, etc. Accident is
being that can exist neither by itself nor in itself.

There are ten categories, namely: substance, quantity, quality,
relation, action, passion, position, when, where, possession. Substance is that for which it is properly fitting to be and to exist
by itself. Quantity is the mensurable being of substance. Quality is that according to which we are said to be of a particular
kind. Action is the act according to which we are said to act.
Passion is that according to which we are said to suffer. Relation
is that by means of which one thing is related to another. Position is the habit of placing a thing in relation to a thing in position. When is duration, according to the permanence of a
thing. Where is the habit of placing a thing in relation to a
thing already placed. Possession is the habit of possessing a
thing in relation to a thing possessed. Category is the arrangement of terms according to above and below, as is evident in
the following figure:

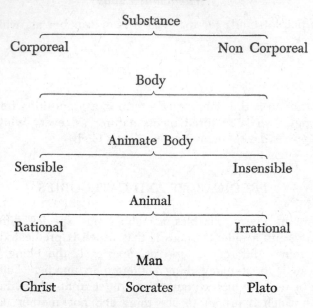

As in the case of this tree illustrating the category of the substance, the same thing may be done with the other categories: so that what is superior and inferior in any category is manifest to the sense. Hence by such knowledge a person can all the better investigate the varieties of things and discover them more readily.

ARGUMENT

The argument is the sum of the statements from which other statements follow: as, it is good, therefore it is something. An argument is a statement composed of the antecedent and the consequence.

An argument has four species, namely: syllogism, induction, enthymeme, and example.

Proof is argument in which there is evident truth, and it can assume three modes, namely: authority, necessary reason, and demonstration.

Demonstration is the manifestation of something unknown through something known, or less known through more known. And this can occur in three modes, namely: by what, by cause, by equalization.

Demonstration by what occurs when the effect is demonstrated by a cause, either inferior or posterior, or superior or anterior. Demonstration by cause occurs when a cause is demonstrated through the effect, or when the superior or the anterior is demonstrated by the inferior or the posterior. Demonstration by equalization occurs when something equally unknown or equally less known is demonstrated through the equally more known, and this is a better and more necessary proof than the previously mentioned, since through it greater matters are demonstrated.

THE SYLLOGISM

The syllogism is an argument in which, from two premises arranged in due mode and figure, a conclusion follows. A syllogism in itself must have two premises and one conclusion: as, everything good is lovable: every virtue is good: every virtue is lovable. And of these two premises, the first is called the major, the second the minor, and the one that follows from these is called the conclusion. Three terms are necessary to make a syllogism, one of which is called the middle, another the major extreme, the third the minor extreme. The middle is the term that is stated twice before the conclusion, namely, once in the major premise, and once in the minor premise. The major extreme is the term which together with the middle makes the first proposition. The minor extreme is the term that with the middle makes the second proposition. The middle must never be placed in the conclusion, but must result from the major extreme and the minor. And all these statements are clear in the above mentioned syllogism. And it should be observed that a particular conclusion may be direct, and another one indirect. A direct conclusion is one in which the major extreme is predicated of the minor.

An indirect conclusion is one in which the minor extreme is predicated of the major.

It should also be observed that every proper syllogism must be in a figure and a mode. The figure is the correct arrangement of terms in respect of subject and predicate. The figures of the syllogisms are three in number, and each one has its modes. A mode is the proper arrangement of propositions in quantity and quality. In the modes of the figures these vowels appear: a, e, i, o. A is a universal affirmative. E is a universal negative. I is a particular affirmative. O is a particular negative. Hence the mnemonic lines:

> A affirms, E denies: universally both.
> I affirms, O denies: particularly both.

The general conditions for all figures are five. The first, that in every syllogism one of the premises is a universal. The second, that in every syllogism one of the premises is affirmative. The third, that if one of the premises is a particular, the conclusion is particular, but not the converse. The fourth, that if the conclusion is negative, one of the premises is negative, and conversely: for it should be noted that in the syllogism from simple negatives and simple particulars nothing follows. The fifth, that in no figure is a middle placed in the conclusion.

FIRST FIGURE

The first figure is one in which a term, that is the subject in the major premise, is the predicate in the minor: as, everything good is true, duration is good, therefore duration is true. It has four modes with direct conclusions and sometimes with indirect conclusions. The first four are those that are indicated by these expressions: Barbara, Celarent, Darii, Ferio. The first mode consists of the premises in A, with conclusion in A: as, everything good is enduring, all greatness is good, therefore all greatness is enduring, etc. The second mode consists of the major premise in E and the minor in A, with conclusion in E: as, no evil is lovable, every vice is evil, therefore no vice is lovable.

The third mode consists of the major in A and the minor in I, with conclusion in I: as, all power is intelligible, God is power, therefore God is intelligible.

The fourth mode consists of the major in E and the minor in I, with conclusion in O: as, nothing spiritual is visible, a certain angel is spiritual, therefore a certain angel is not visible.

The five modes with indirect conclusions are those that are indicated by these expressions: Baralipton, Celantes, Dabitis, Fapesmo, Frisesomorum. Baralipton consists of the major in A and the minor in A, with conclusion in I: as, everything good is positive, whatever God makes is good, therefore God makes the positive. Celantes consists of a major in E and a minor in A, with conclusion in E: as, nothing virtuous is vicious, all glory is virtuous, therefore nothing vicious is glory. Dabitis consists of a major in A and a minor in I, with conclusion in I: as, every being is intelligible, a certain particular is a being, therefore a certain intelligible is a particular. Fapesmo consists of a major in A and a minor in E, with conclusion in O: as, all new things please, no old thing is new, therefore a certain pleasing thing is not old. Frisesomorum consists of a major in I and a minor in E, with conclusion in O: as, a certain man is a servant of the Lord, no donkey is a man, therefore a certain servant of the Lord is not a donkey. The conditions of a proper figure are two. The first, that in it every kind of conclusion is included, namely, the universal affirmative and negative, and the particular affirmative and negative. The second is that the middle is the subject in the major premise and the predicate in the minor premise.

THE SECOND FIGURE

The second figure is one in which the term that is the predicate in the major premise is the predicate in the minor premise:

as, no animal is a plant, all grass is a plant, therefore no grass is an animal. And it has four modes that are indicated by these expressions: Cesare, Camestres, Festino, Baroco. The first mode consists of the major in E and the minor in A, with conclusion in E: as in the preceding syllogism. The second mode consists of the major in A and the minor in E, with conclusion in E: as, every man is an animal, no stone is an animal, therefore no stone is a man. The third mode consists of the major in E and the minor in I, with conclusion in O: as, no virtue is hateful, a certain vice is hateful, therefore a certain vice is not a virtue. The fourth mode consists of a major in A and a minor in O, with conclusion in O: as, everything created is good, a sin is not good, therefore a sin is not created. The conditions of the second figure are two. The first, that the middle in each premise is a predicate. The second, that the major premise is a universal in any syllogism.

THE THIRD FIGURE

The third figure is the one in which the term that is the subject in the major premise is the subject in the minor premise. It has six modes that are represented by these expressions: Darapti, Felapton, Disamis, Datisi, Bocardo, Ferison. The first mode consists of the premises in A, with conclusion in I: as, all goodness is enduring, therefore a certain enduring thing is great. The second mode consists of the major premise in A, with conclusion in O: as, nothing good is vicious, everything good is lovable, therefore a certain lovable thing is not vicious. The third mode consists of a major premise in I and a minor in A, with conclusion in I: as, a certain goodness is eternity, all goodness is great, therefore a certain greatness is eternity. The fourth mode consists of the major premise in A and the minor in I, with conclusion in I: as, every man is rational, a certain man is a laborer, therefore a certain laborer is rational. The fifth mode consists of a major premise in O and a minor in A with conclusion in O: as, a certain sensible thing is not mortal, every sensible thing is visible, therefore a certain visible thing is not mortal. The sixth mode consists of a major premise in E and a minor premise in I, with conclusion in O: as, nothing intellectual is colored, a certain intellectual thing is spirit, therefore a certain spirit is not colored, etc. The conditions of the third figure are three: The first, that the middle in each premise is a subject. The second, that the major premise is affirmative. The third, that there is no conclusion, except a particular one.

ERNST MACH
(1838-1916)

Physicist and philosopher, taught at the Universities of Graz, Prague and Vienna. His achievements as physicist lie in the areas of mechanics, theory of heat, optics and acoustics. His name was given to the standard unit of supersonic speed. He refused to be called a philosopher, but did pioneering work in the methodology of science and the psychology of knowledge, which he attempted to free from metaphysics and anthropomorphy.

Main Works:
Analyse der Empfindungen; Erkenntnis und Irrtum.

Antimetaphysical Observations

1. The great results achieved by physical science in modern times—results not restricted to its own sphere but embracing that of other sciences which employ its help—have brought it about that physical ways of thinking and physical modes of procedure enjoy on all hands unwonted prominence, and that the greatest expectations are associated with their application. In keeping with this drift of modern inquiry, the physiology of the senses, gradually abandoning the method of investigating sensations in themselves followed by men like Goethe, Schopenhauer, and others, but with greatest success by Johannes Müller, has also assumed an almost exclusively physical character. This tendency must appear to us as not altogether appropriate, when we reflect that physics, despite its considerable development,

---

From: *Analyse der Empfindungen.*

nevertheless constitutes but a portion of a *larger* collective body of knowledge, and that it is unable, with its limited intellectual implements, created for limited and special purposes, to exhaust all the subject-matter in question. Without renouncing the support of physics, it is possible for the physiology of the senses, not only to pursue its own course of development, but also to afford to physical science itself powerful assistance. The following simple considerations will serve to illustrate this relation between the two.

2. Colors, sounds, temperatures, pressures, spaces, times and so forth, are connected with one another in manifold ways; and with them are associated dispositions of mind, feelings, and volitions. Out of this fabric, that which is relatively more fixed and permanent stands prominently forth, engraves itself on the memory, and expresses itself in language. Relatively greater permanency is exhibited, first, by certain complexes of colors, sounds, pressures, and so forth, functionally connected in time and space, which therefore receive special names, and are called bodies. Absolutely permanent such complexes are not.

My table is now brightly, now dimly lighted. Its temperature varies. It may receive an ink stain. One of its legs may be broken. It may be repaired, polished, and replaced part by part. But, for me, it remains the table at which I daily write.

My friend may put on a different coat. His countenance may assume a serious or a cheerful expression. His complexion, under the effects of light or emotion, may change. His shape may be altered by motion, or be definitely changed. Yet the number of the permanent features presented, compared with the number of the gradual alterations, is always so great, that the latter may be overlooked. It is the same friend with whom I take my daily walk.

My coat may receive a stain, a tear. My very manner of expressing this shows that we are concerned here with a sum-total of permanency, to which the new element is added and from which that which is lacking is subsequently taken away.

Our greater intimacy with this sum-total of permanency, and the preponderance of its importance for me as contrasted with the changeable element, impel us to the partly instinctive, partly voluntary and conscious economy of mental presentation and designation, as expressed in ordinary thought and speech. That which is presented in a single image receives a single designation, a single name.

Further, that complex of memories, moods, and feelings, joined to a particular body (the human body), which is called the "I" or "Ego," manifests itself as relatively permanent. I may be engaged upon this or that subject, I may be quiet and cheerful, excited and ill-humored. Yet, pathological cases apart, enough durable features remain to identify the ego. Of course, the ego also is only of relative permanency.

The apparent permanency of the ego consists of its changes. The many thoughts and plans of yesterday that are continued today, and of which our environment in waking hours incessantly reminds us (whence in dreams the ego can be very indistinct, doubled, or entirely wanting), and the little habits that are unconsciously and involuntarily kept up for long periods of time, constitute the groundwork of the ego. There can hardly be greater differences in the egos of different people, than occur in the course of years in one person. When I recall my early youth, I should take the boy that I then was, with the exception of a few individual features, for a different person, were it not for the existence of the chain of memories. Many an article that I myself penned twenty years ago impresses me now as something quite foreign to myself. The very gradual character of the changes of the body also contributes to the instability of the ego, but in a much less degree than people imagine. Such things are much less analyzed and noticed than the intellectual and the moral ego. Personally, people know themselves very poorly. When I wrote these lines in 1886, Ribot's admirable little book, *The Diseases of Personality,* was unknown to me. Ribot ascribes the principal role in preserving the continuity of the ego to the general sensibility. Generally, I am in perfect accord with his views.

The ego is as little absolutely permanent as are bodies. That which we so much dread in death, the annihilation of our permanency, actually occurs in life in abundant measure. That which is most valued by us, remains preserved in countless copies, or, in cases of exceptional excellence, is even preserved of itself. In the best human being, however, there are individual traits, the loss of which neither he himself nor others need regret. Indeed, at times, death, viewed as a liberation from individuality, may even become a pleasant thought. Such reflections of course do not make physiological death any the easier to bear.

After a first survey has been obtained, by the formation of the substance-concepts "body" and "ego" (matter and soul), the will is impelled to a more exact examination of the changes that take place in these relatively permanent existences. The element of change in bodies and the ego, is in fact, exactly what moves the will to this examination. Here the component parts of the complex are first exhibited as its properties. A fruit is sweet; but it can also be bitter. Also, other fruits may be sweet. The red color we are seeking is found in many bodies. The neighborhood of some bodies is pleasant; that of others, unpleasant. Thus, gradually, different complexes are found to be made up of common elements. The visible, the audible, the tangible, are separated from bodies. The visible is analyzed into colors and into form. In the manifoldness of the colors, again, though here fewer in number, other component parts are discerned—such as primary colors, and so forth. The complexes are disintegrated into elements, that is to say, into their ultimate component parts, which hitherto we have been unable to subdivide any further. The nature of these elements need not be discussed at present; it is possible that future investigations may throw light on it. We need not here be disturbed by the fact that it is easier for the scientist to study relations of these elements than the direct relations between them.

3. The useful habit of designating such relatively permanent compounds by single names, and of apprehending them by single thoughts, without going to the trouble each time of an analysis of their component parts, is apt to come into strange conflict with the tendency to isolate the component parts. The vague image which we have of a given permanent complex, being an image which does not perceptibly change when one or another of the component parts is taken away, seems to be something which exists in itself. Inasmuch as it is possible to take away singly every constituent part without destroying the capacity of the image to stand for the totality and to be recognized again, it is imagined that it is possible to subtract all the parts and to have something still remaining. Thus naturally arises the philosophical notion, at first impressive, but subsequently recognized as monstrous, of a "thing-in-itself," different from its "appearance," and unknowable.

Thing, body, matter, are nothing apart from the combinations of the elements—the colors, sounds, and so forth—nothing apart from their so-called attributes. That protean pseudo-philosophical problem of the single thing with its many attributes, arises wholly from a misinterpretation of the fact that summary comprehension and precise analysis, although both are provisionally justifiable and for many purposes profitable, cannot be carried on simultaneously. A body is one and unchangeable only so long as it is unnecessary to consider its details. Thus both the earth and a billiard-ball are spheres, if we are willing to neglect all deviations from the spherical form, and if greater precision is not necessary. But when we are obliged to carry on investigations in orography or microscopy, both bodies cease to be spheres.

4. Man is pre-eminently endowed with the power of voluntarily and consciously determining his own point of view. He can at one time disregard the most salient features of an object, and immediately thereafter give attention to its smallest details; now consider a stationary current, without a thought of its con-

tents (whether heat, electricity, or fluidity), and then measure the width of a Fraunhofer line in the spectrum; he can rise at will to the most general abstractions or bury himself in the minutest particulars. Animals possess this capacity in a far less degree. They do not assume a point of view, but are usually forced to it by their sense-impressions. The baby that does not know its father with his hat on, the dog that is perplexed at the new coat of its master, have both succumbed in this conflict of points of view. Who has not been worsted in similar plights? Even the man of philosophy at times succumbs, as the grotesque problem, above referred to, shows.

In this last case, the circumstances appear to furnish a real ground of justification. Colors, sounds, and the odors of bodies are evanescent. But their tangibility, as a sort of constant nucleus, not readily susceptible of annihilation, remains behind, appearing as the vehicle of the more fugitive properties attached to it. Habit thus keeps our thought firmly attached to this central nucleus, even when we have begun to recognize that seeing, hearing, smelling, and touching are intimately akin in character. A further consideration is that, owing to the singularly extensive development of mechanical physics, a kind of higher reality is ascribed to the spatial and to the temporal than to colors, sounds, and odors; agreeably to which, the temporal and spatial links of colors, sounds, and odors appear to be more real than the colors, sounds, and odors themselves. The physiology of the senses, however, demonstrates that spaces and times may just as appropriately be called sensations as colors and sounds. But of this later.

5. Not only the relation of bodies to the ego, but the ego itself also, gives rise to similar pseudo-problems, the character of which may be briefly indicated as follows:

Let us denote the above-mentioned elements by the letters $A \, B \, C \ldots, K \, L \, M \ldots, \alpha \, \beta \, \gamma \ldots$ Let those complexes of colors, sounds, and so forth, commonly called bodies, be denoted, for the sake of clearness, by $A \, B \, C \ldots$; the complex, known as our own body, which is a part of the former complexes distinguished by certain peculiarities, may be called $K\ L\ M$ . . . ; the complex composed of volitions, memory-images, and the rest, we shall represent by $\alpha\ \beta\ \gamma$ . . . . Usually, now, the complex $\alpha\ \beta\ \gamma$ . . . $K\ L\ M$ . . . , as making up the ego, is opposed to the complex $A\ B\ C$ . . . , as making up the world of physical objects; sometimes also, $\alpha\ \beta\ \gamma$ . . . is viewed as ego, and $K\ L\ M$ . . . $A\ B\ C$ . . . as world of physical objects. Now, at first blush, $A\ B\ C$ . . . appears independent of the ego, and opposed to it as a separate existence. But this independence is only relative, and gives way upon closer inspection. Much, it is true, *may* change in the complex $\alpha\ \beta\ \gamma$ . . . without much perceptible change being induced in $A\ B\ C$ . . . ; and vice versa. But many changes in $\alpha\ \beta\ \gamma$ . . . do pass, by way of changes in $K\ L\ M$ . . . , to $A\ B\ C$ . . . ; and vice versa. (As, for example, when powerful ideas burst forth into acts, or when our environment induces noticeable changes in our body.) At the same time the group $K\ L\ M$ . . . appears to be more intimately connected with $\alpha\ \beta\ \gamma$ . . . and with $A\ B\ C$ . . . , than the latter with one another; and their relations find their expression in common thought and speech.

Precisely viewed, however, it appears that the group $A\ B\ C$ . . . is always codetermined by $K\ L\ M$ . . . . A cube when seen close at hand, looks large; when seen at a distance, small; its appearance to the right eye differs from its appearance to the left; sometimes it appears double; with closed eyes it is invisible. The properties of one and the same body, therefore, appear modified by our own body; they appear conditioned by it. But where, now, is that *same body*, which appears so *different?* All that can be said is, that with different $K\ L\ M$ . . . different $A\ B\ C$ . . . are associated.

A common and popular way of thinking and speaking is to contrast "appearance" with "reality." A pencil held in front of us in the air is seen by us as straight; dip it into the water, and we see it crooked. In the latter case we say that the pencil *appears* crooked, but is in *reality* straight. But what justifies us in declaring one fact rather than another to be the reality, and degrading the other to the level of appearance? In both cases we have to do with facts which present us with different combinations of the elements, combinations which in the two cases are differently conditioned. Precisely because of its environment, the pencil dipped in water is optically crooked; but it is tactually and metrically straight. An image in a concave or flat mirror is *only* visible, whereas under other and ordinary circumstances a tangible body as well corresponds to the visible image. A bright surface is brighter beside a dark surface than beside one brighter than itself. To be sure, our expectation is deceived when, not paying sufficient attention to the conditions, and substituting for one another different cases of the combination, we fall into the natural error of expecting what we are accustomed to, although the case may be an unusual one. The facts are not to blame for that. In these cases, to speak of "appearance" may have a practical meaning, but cannot have a scientific meaning. Similarly, the question which is often asked, whether the world is real or whether we merely dream it, is devoid of all scientific meaning. Even the wildest dream is a fact as much as any other. If our dreams were more regular, more connected, more stable, they would also have more practical importance for us. In our waking hours the relations of the elements to one another are immensely amplified in comparison with what they were in our dreams. We recognize the dream for what it is. When the process is reversed, the field of psychic vision is narrowed; the contrast is almost entirely lacking. Where there is no contrast, the distinction between dream and waking, between appearance and reality, is quite otiose and worthless.

The popular notion of an antithesis between appearance and reality has exercised a very powerful influence on scientific and philosophical thought. We see this, for example, in Plato's pregnant and poetical fiction of the Cave, in which, with our backs turned towards the fire, we observe merely the shadows of what passes (*Republic,* Book VII). But this conception was not thought out to its final consequences, with the result that it has had an unfortunate influence on our ideas about the universe. The universe, of which nevertheless we are a part, became completely separated from us, and was removed an infinite distance away. Similarly, many a young man, hearing for the first time of the refraction of stellar light, has thought that doubt was cast on the whole of astronomy, whereas nothing is required but an easily effected and unimportant correction to put everything right again.

6. We see an object having a point S. If we touch S, that is, bring it into connection with our body, we receive a prick. We can see S, without feeling the prick. But as soon as we feel the prick we find S on the skin. The visible point, therefore, is a permanent nucleus, to which the prick is annexed, according to circumstances, as something accidental. From the frequency of analogous occurrences we ultimately accustom ourselves to regard all properties of bodies as "effects" proceeding from permanent nuclei and conveyed to the ego through the medium of the body; which effects we call sensations. By this operation, however, these nuclei are deprived of their entire sensory content, and converted into mere mental symbols. The assertion, then, is correct that the world consists only of our sensations. In which case we have knowledge *only* of sensations, and the assumption of the nuclei referred to, or of a reciprocal action between them, from which sensations proceed, turns out to be quite ideal and superfluous. Such a view can only suit with a half-hearted realism or a half-hearted philosophical criticism.

7. Ordinarily the complex $\alpha \beta \gamma \ldots K L M \ldots$ is contrasted as ego with the complex $A B C \ldots$. At first only those elements of $A B C \ldots$ that more strongly alter $\alpha \beta \gamma \ldots$, as a prick, a pain, are wont to be thought of as comprised in the ego. Afterwards, however, through observations of the kind just referred to, it appears that the right to annex $A B C \ldots$ to the ego nowhere ceases. In conformity with this view, the ego can be so

extended as ultimately to embrace the entire world. The ego is not sharply marked off, its limits are very indefinite and arbitrarily displaceable. Only by failing to observe this fact, and by unconsciously narrowing those limits, while at the same time we enlarge them, arise, in the conflict of points of view, the metaphysical difficulties met with in this connection.

As soon as we have perceived that the supposed unities "body" and "ego" are only makeshifts, designed for provisional orientation and for definite practical ends (so that we may take hold of bodies, protect ourselves against pain, and so forth), we find ourselves obliged, in many more advanced scientific investigations, to abandon them as insufficient and inappropriate. The antithesis between ego and world, between sensation (appearance) and thing, then vanishes, and we have simply to deal with the connection of the elements $\alpha \beta \gamma \ldots A B C \ldots K L M \ldots$, of which this antithesis was only a partially appropriate and imperfect expression. This connection is nothing more or less than the combination of the above-mentioned elements with other similar elements (time and space). Science has simply to accept this connection, and to get its bearings in it, without at once wanting to explain its existence.

On a superficial examination the complex $\alpha \beta \gamma \ldots$ appears to be made up of much more evanescent elements than $A B C \ldots$ and $K L M \ldots$, in which last the elements seem to be connected with greater stability and in a more permanent manner (being joined to solid nuclei as it were). Although on closer inspection the elements of all complexes prove to be homogeneous, yet even when this has been recognized, the earlier notion of an antithesis of body and spirit easily slips in again. The philosophical spiritualist is often sensible of the difficulty of imparting the needed solidity to his mind-created world of bodies; the materialist is at a loss when required to endow the world of matter with sensation. The monistic point of view, which reflection has evolved, is easily clouded by our older and more powerful instinctive notions.

8. The difficulty referred to is particularly felt when we consider the following case. In the complex $A \, B \, C \ldots$, which we have called the world of matter, we find as parts, not only our own body $K \, L \, M \ldots$, but also the bodies of other persons (or animals) $K' \, L' \, M' \ldots$, $K'' \, L'' \, M'' \ldots$, to which, by analogy, we imagine $\alpha' \, \beta' \, \gamma' \ldots$, $\alpha'' \, \beta'' \, \gamma'' \ldots$, annexed, similar to $\alpha \, \beta \, \gamma \ldots$ So long as we deal with $K' \, L' \, M' \ldots$, we find ourselves in a thoroughly familiar province which is at every point accessible to our senses. When, however, we inquire after the sensations or feelings belonging to the body $K' \, L' \, M' \ldots$, we no longer find these in the province of sense: we add them in thought. Not only is the domain which we now enter far less familiar to us, but the transition into it is also relatively unsafe. We have the feeling as if we were plunging into an abyss.[1] Persons who adopt this way of thinking only, will never thoroughly rid themselves of that sense of insecurity, which is a very fertile source of illusory problems.

But we are not restricted to this course. Let us consider, first, the reciprocal relations of the elements of the complex $A \, B \, C \ldots$, without regarding $K \, L \, M \ldots$ (our body). All physical investigations are of this sort. A white ball falls upon a bell; a sound is heard. The ball turns yellow before a sodium lamp, red before a lithium lamp. Here the elements ($A \, B \, C \ldots$) appear to be connected only with one another and to be independent of our body ($K \, L \, M \ldots$). But if we take santonine, the ball again turns yellow. If we press one eye to the side, we see two balls. If we close our eyes entirely, there is no ball there at all. If we sever the auditory nerve, no sound is heard. The elements $A \, B \, C \ldots$, therefore, are not only connected with one another, but also with $K \, L \, M \ldots$ To this extent, and to this extent only, do we call $A \, B \, C \ldots$ *sensations*, and regard $A \, B \, C \ldots$ as belonging to the ego. In what follows, wherever the reader finds the terms "sensation," "sensation-complex," used alongside of or instead of the expressions "element," "complex of elements," it must be borne in mind that it is *only* in the connection and relation in question, *only* in their functional dependence, that the elements are sensations. In another functional relation they are at the same time physical objects. We only use the additional term "sensations" to describe the elements, because most people are much more familiar with the elements in question *as* sensations (colors, sounds, pressures, spaces, times, etc.), while according to the popular conception it is particles of mass that are considered as physical elements, to which the elements, in the sense here used, are attached as "properties" or "effects."

In this way, accordingly, we do not find the gap between bodies and sensations above described, between what is without and what is within, between the material world and the spiritual world. All elements *A B C* . . . , *K L M* . . . , constitute a *single* coherent mass only, in which, when any one element is disturbed, *all* is put in motion; except that a disturbance in *K L M* . . . has a more extensive and profound action than one in *A B C* . . . . A magnet in our neighborhood disturbs the particles of iron near it; a falling boulder shakes the earth; but the severing of a nerve sets in motion the *whole* system of elements. Quite involuntarily does this relation of things suggest the picture of a viscous mass, at certain places (as in the ego) more firmly coherent than in others. I have often made use of this image in lectures.

9. Thus the great gulf between physical and psychological research persists only when we asquiesce in our habitual stereotyped conceptions. A color is a physical object as soon as we consider its dependence, for instance, upon its luminous source, upon other colors, upon temperatures, upon spaces, and so forth. When we consider, however, its dependence upon the retina (the elements *K L M* . . .), it is a psychological object, a sensation. Not the subject-matter, but the direction of our investigation, is different in the two domains.

Both in reasoning from the observation of the bodies of other men or animals, to the sensations which they possess, as well as in investigating the influence of our own body upon our own sensations, we have to complete observed facts by analogy. This is accomplished with much greater ease and certainty, when it relates, say, only to nervous processes, which cannot be fully observed in our own bodies—that is, when it is carried out in the more familiar physical domain—than when it is extended to the psychical domain, to the sensations and thoughts of other people. Otherwise there is no essential difference.

10. The considerations just advanced, expressed as they have been in an abstract form, will gain in strength and vividness if we consider the concrete facts from which they flow. Thus, I lie upon my sofa. If I close my right eye, the picture represented is presented to my left eye. In a frame formed by the ridge of my eyebrow, by my nose, and by my moustache, appears a part of my body, so far as visible, with its environment. My body differs from other human bodies—beyond the fact that every intense motor idea is immediately expressed by a movement of it, and that, if it is touched, more striking changes are determined than if other bodies are touched —by the circumstance that it is only seen piecemeal, and, especially, is seen without a head. If I observe an element A within my field of vision, and investigate its connection with another element B within the same field, I step out of the domain of physics into that of physiology or psychology, provided B, to use the apposite expression of a friend of mine made upon seeing this drawing, passes through my skin. Reflections like that for the field of vision may be made with regard to the province of touch and the perceptual domains of the other senses.

11. Reference has already been made to the different character of the groups of elements denoted by A B C . . . and α β γ . . . . As a matter of fact, when we see a green tree before us, or remember a green tree, that is, represent a green tree to ourselves, we are perfectly aware of the difference of the two cases. The represented tree has a much less determinate, a much more changeable form; its green is much paler and more evan-

escent; and, what is of especial note, it plainly appears in a different domain. A movement that we will execute is never more than a represented movement, and appears in a different domain from that of the executed movement, which always takes place when the image is vivid enough. Now the statement that the elements A and α appear in different domains, means, if we go to the bottom of it, simply this, that these elements are united with different other elements. Thus far, therefore, the fundamental constituents of $A\ B\ C\ \ldots$, $\alpha\ \beta\ \gamma\ \ldots$ would seem to be *the same* (colors, sounds, spaces, times, motor sensations . . .), and only the character of their connection different.

Ordinarily pleasure and pain are regarded as different from sensations. Yet not only tactual sensations, but all other kinds of sensations, may pass gradually into pleasure and pain. Pleasure and pain also may be justly termed sensations. Only they are not so well analyzed or so familiar, nor, perhaps, limited to so few organs as the common sensations. In fact, sensations of pleasure and pain, however faint they may be, really constitute an essential part of the content of all so-called emotions. Any additional element that emerges into consciousness when we are under the influence of emotions may be described as more or less diffused and not sharply localized sensations. William James, and after him Théodule Ribot, have investigated the physiological mechanism of the emotions: they hold that what is essential is purposive tendencies of the body to action—tendencies which correspond to circumstances and are expressed in the organism. Only a part of these emerges into consciousness. We are sad because we shed tears, and not vice versa, says James. And Ribot justly observes that a cause of the backward state of our knowledge of the emotions is that we have always confined our observation to so much of these physiological processes as emerges into consciousness. At the same time, he goes too far when he maintains that everything psychical is merely *"surajouté"* to the physical, and that it is only the physical that produces effects. For us this distinction is non-existent.

Thus, perceptions, presentations, volitions, and emotions, in short the whole inner and outer world, are put together, in combinations of varying evanescence and permanence, out of a small number of homogeneous elements. Usually, these elements are called sensations. But as vestiges of a one-sided theory inhere in that term, we prefer to speak simply of elements, as we have already done. The aim of all research is to ascertain the mode of connection of these elements. If it proves impossible to solve the problem by assuming *one* set of such elements, then more than one will have to be assumed. But for the questions under discussion it would be improper to begin by making complicated assumptions in advance.

12. That in this complex of elements, which fundamentally is only one, the boundaries of bodies and of the ego do not admit of being established in a manner definite and sufficient for all cases, has already been remarked. To bring together elements that are most intimately connected with pleasure and pain into one ideal mental-economical unity, the ego; this is a task of the highest importance for the intellect working in the service of the pain-avoiding, pleasure-seeking will. The delimitation of the ego, therefore, is instinctively effected, is rendered familiar, and possibly becomes fixed through heredity. Owing to their high practical importance, not only for the individual, but for the entire species, the composites "ego" and "body" instinctively make good their claims, and assert themselves with elementary force. In special cases, however, in which practical ends are not concerned, but where knowledge is an end in itself, the delimitation in question may prove to be insufficient, obstructive, and untenable.

The primary fact is not the ego, but the elements (sensations). What was said just above as to the term "sensation" must be borne in mind. The elements constitute the I. "*I* have the sensation green," signifies that the element green occurs in a given complex of other elements (sensations, memories). When *I* cease to have the sensation green, when *I* die, then the elements no longer occur in the ordinary, familiar association. That is all.

Only an ideal mental-economical unity, not a real unity, has ceased to exist. The ego is not a definite, unalterable, sharply-bounded unity. None of these attributes are important, for all vary even within the sphere of individual life; in fact their alteration is even sought after by the individual. *Continuity* alone is important. This view accords admirably with the position which Weismann has reached by biological investigations. But continuity is only a means of preparing and conserving what is contained in the ego. This content, and not the ego, is the principal thing. This content, however, is not confined to the individual. With the exception of some insignificant and valueless personal memories, it remains preserved in others even after the death of the individual. The elements that make up the consciousness of a given individual are firmly connected with one another, but with those of another individual they are only feebly connected, and the connection is only casually apparent. Contents of consciousness, however, that are of universal significance, break through these limits of the individual, and, attached of course to individuals again, can enjoy a continued existence of an impersonal, superpersonal kind, independently of the personality by means of which they were developed. To contribute to this is the greatest happiness of the artist, the scientist, the inventor, the social reformer, etc.

The ego must be given up. It is partly the perception of this fact, partly the fear of it, that has given rise to the many extravagances of pessimism and optimism, and to numerous religious, ascetic, and philosophical absurdities. In the long run we shall not be able to close our eyes to this simple truth, which is the immediate outcome of psychological analysis. We shall then no longer place so high a value upon the ego, which even during the individual life greatly changes, and which, in sleep or during absorption in some idea, just in our very happiest moments, may be partially or wholly absent. We shall then be willing to renounce individual immortality, and not place more value upon the subsidiary elements than upon the principal ones. In this way, we shall arrive at a freer and more enlightened view of life, which will preclude the disregard of other egos and the overestimation of our own. The ethical ideal founded on this view of life will be equally far removed from the ideal of the ascetic, which is not biologically tenable for whoever practises it, and vanishes at once with his disappearance, and from the ideal of an overweening Nietzschean "superman," who cannot, and I hope will not be tolerated by his fellow-men.

If a knowledge of the connection of the elements (sensations) does not suffice us, and we ask, "*Who* possesses this connection of sensations, *Who* experiences it?" then we have succumbed to the old habit of subsuming every element (every sensation) under some unanalyzed complex, and we are falling back imperceptibly upon an older, lower, and more limited point of view. It is often pointed out, that a psychical experience which is not the experience of a determinate subject is unthinkable, and it is held that in this way the essential part played by the unity of consciousness has been demonstrated. But the Ego-consciousness can be of many different degrees and composed of a multiplicity of chance memories. One might just as well say that a physical process which does not take place in some environment or other, or at least somewhere in the universe, is unthinkable. In both cases, in order to make a beginning with our investigation, we must be allowed to abstract from the environment, which, as regards its influence, may be very different in different cases, and in special cases may shrink to a minimum. Consider the sensations of the lower animals, to which a subject with definite features can hardly be ascribed. It is out of sensations that the subject is built up, and, once built up, no doubt the subject reacts in turn on the sensations.

The habit of treating the unanalyzed ego-complex as an indiscerptible unity frequently assumes in science remarkable forms. First, the nervous system is separated from the body as the seat of the sensations. In the nervous system again, the brain is selected as the organ best fitted for this end, and finally, to save the supposed psychical unity, a *point* is sought in the brain as the seat of the soul. But such crude conceptions are hardly fit even to foreshadow the roughest outlines of what future research will do for the connection of the physical and the psychical. The fact that the different organs and parts of the nervous system are physically connected with, and can be readily excited by, one another, is probably at the bottom of the notion of "psychical unity."

I once heard the question seriously discussed, how the perception of a large tree could find room in the little head of a man. Now, although this "problem" is no problem, yet it renders us vividly sensible of the absurdity that can be committed by thinking sensations spatially into the brain. When I speak of the sensations of another person, those sensations are, of course, not exhibited in any optical or physical space; they are mentally added, and I conceive them causally, not spatially, attached to the brain observed, or rather, functionally presented. When I speak of my own sensations, these sensations do not exist spatially in my head, but rather my "head" shares with them the spatial field, as was explained above.

The unity of consciousness is not an argument in point. Since the apparent antithesis between the real world and the world given through the senses lies entirely in our mode of view, and no actual gulf exists between them, a complicated and variously interconnected content of consciousness is no more difficult to understand than is the complicated interconnection of the world.

If we regard the ego as a real unity, we become involved in the following dilemma: either we must set over against the ego a world of unknowable entities (which would be quite idle and purposeless), or we must regard the whole world, the egos of other people included, as comprised in our own ego (a proposition to which it is difficult to yield serious assent).

But if we take the ego simply as a practical unity, put together for purposes of provisional survey, or as a more strongly cohering group of elements, less strongly connected with other groups of this kind, questions like those above discussed will not arise, and research will have an unobstructed future.

In his philosophical notes Lichtenberg says: "We become conscious of certain presentations that are dependent upon us; of others that we at least think are dependent upon us. Where is the border-line? We know only the existence of our sensations, presentations, and thoughts. We should say, *'It thinks,'* just as we say *'It lightens.'* It is going too far to say *Cogito,* if we translate *Cogito* by *'I think.'* The assumption, or postulation, of the ego is a mere practical necessity." Though the method by which Lichtenberg arrived at this result is somewhat different from ours, we must nevertheless give our full assent to his conclusion.

13. Bodies do not produce sensations, but complexes of elements (complexes of sensations) make up bodies. If, to the physicist, bodies appear the real, abiding existences, whilst the "elements" are regarded merely as their evanescent, transitory appearance, the physicist forgets, in the assumption of such a view, that all bodies are but thought-symbols for complexes of elements (complexes of sensations). Here, too, the elements in question form the real, immediate, and ultimate foundation, which it is the task of physiologico-physical research to investigate. By recognition of this fact, many points of physiology and physics assume more distinct and more economical forms, and many spurious problems are disposed of.

For us, therefore, the world does not consist of mysterious entities, which by their interaction with another, equally mysterious entity, the ego, produce sensations, which alone are accessible. For us, colors, sounds, spaces, times, . . . are provisionally the ultimate elements, whose given connection it is our business to investigate. It is precisely in this that the exploration of reality consists. In this investigation we must not allow ourselves to be impeded by such abridgments and delimitations as body, ego, matter, spirit, etc., which have been formed for special, practical purposes and with wholly provisional and limited ends in view. On the contrary, the fittest forms of thought must be created in and by that research itself, just as is done in every special science. In place of the traditional, instinctive ways of thought, a freer, fresher view, conforming to developed experience, and reaching out beyond the requirements of practical life, must be substituted throughout.

14. Science always has its origin in the adaptation of thought to some definite field of experience. The results of the adaptation are thought-elements, which are able to represent the whole field. The outcome, of course, is different, according to the character and extent of the field. If the field of experience is enlarged, or if several fields heretofore disconnected are united, the traditional, familiar thought-elements no longer suffice for the extended field. In the struggle of acquired habit with the effort after adaptation, problems arise, which disappear when the adaptation is perfected, to make room for others which have arisen meanwhile.

To the physicist, *qua* physicist, the idea of "body" is productive of a real facilitation of view, and is not the cause of disturbance. So also, the person with purely practical aims is materially supported by the idea of the *I* or ego. For, unquestionably, every form of thought that has been designedly or undesignedly constructed for a given purpose, possesses for that purpose a *permanent* value. When, however, physics and psychology meet, the ideas held in the one domain prove to be untenable in the other. From the attempt at mutual adaptation arise the various atomic and monadistic theories—which, however, never attain their end. If we regard sensations, in the sense above defined, as the elements of the world, the problems referred to appear to be disposed of in all essentials, and the first and most important adaptation to be consequently effected. This fundamental view (without any pretension to being a philosophy for all eternity) can at present be adhered to in all fields of experience; it is consequently the one that accommodates itself with the least expenditure of energy, that is, more economically than any other, to the present temporary collective state of knowledge. Furthermore, in the consciousness of its purely economical function, this fundamental view is eminently tolerant. It does not obtrude itself into fields in which the current conceptions are still adequate. It is also ever ready, upon subsequent extensions of the field of experience, to give way before a better conception.

The presentations and conceptions of the average man of the world are formed and dominated, not by the full and pure desire for knowledge as an end in itself, but by the struggle to adapt himself favorably to the conditions of life. Consequently they are less exact, but at the same time also they are preserved from the monstrosities which easily result from a one-sided and impassioned pursuit of a scientific or philosophical point of view. The unprejudiced man of normal psychological development takes the elements which we have called $A \, B \, C \, \ldots$ to be spatially contiguous and external to the elements $K \, L \, M \, \ldots$, and he holds this view *immediately,* and not by any process of psychological projection or logical inference or construction; even were such a process to exist, he would certainly not be conscious of it. He sees, then, an "external world" $A \, B \, C \, \ldots$ different from his body $K \, L \, M \, \ldots$ and existing outside of it. As he does not observe at first the dependence of the $A \, B \, C's \, \ldots$ on the $K \, L \, M's \, \ldots$ (which are always repeating themselves in the same way and consequently receive little attention), but is always dwelling upon the fixed connection of the $A \, B \, C's \, \ldots$ with one another, there appears to him a world of things independent of his Ego. This Ego is formed by the observation of the special properties of the particular thing $K \, L \, M \, \ldots$ with which pain, pleasure, feeling, will, etc., are intimately connected. Further, he notices things $K' \, L' \, M' \, \ldots$, $K'' \, L'' \, M''$ $\ldots$, which behave in a manner perfectly analogous to $K \, L \, M$ $\ldots$, and whose behavior he thoroughly understands as soon as he has thought of analogous feelings, sensations, etc., as attached to them in the same way as he observed these feelings, sensations, etc., to be attached to himself. The analogy impelling him to this result is the same as determines him, when he has observed that a wire possesses *all* the properties of a conductor charged with an electric current, except *one* which has not yet been directly demonstrated, to conclude that the wire possesses this one property as well. Thus, since he does not perceive the sensations of his fellow-men or of animals but only supplies them by analogy, while he infers from the behavior of his fellow-men that they are in the same position over against himself, he is led to ascribe to the sensations, memories, etc., a particular *A B C . . . K L M . . .* of a different nature, always differently conceived according to the degree of civilization he has reached; but this process, as was shown above, is unnecessary, and in science leads into a maze of error, although the falsification is of small significance for practical life.

These factors, determining as they do the intellectual outlook of the plain man, make their appearance alternately in him according to the requirements of practical life for the time being, and persist in a state of nearly stable equilibrium. The scientific conception of the world, however, puts the emphasis now upon one, now upon the other factor, makes sometimes one and sometimes the other its starting-point, and, in its struggle for greater precision, unity, and consistency, tries, so far as seems possible, to thrust into the background all but the most indispensable conceptions. In this way dualistic and monistic systems arise.

The plain man is familiar with blindness and deafness, and knows from his everyday experience that the look of things is influenced by his senses; but it never occurs to him to regard the whole world as the creation of his senses. He would find an idealistic system, or such a monstrosity as solipsism, intolerable in practice.

It may easily become a disturbing element in unprejudiced scientific theorizing when a conception which is adapted to a particular and strictly limited purpose is promoted in advance to be the foundation of *all* investigation. This happens, for example, when all experiences are regarded as "effects" of an external world extending into consciousness. This conception gives us a tangle of metaphysical difficulties which it seems impossible to unravel. But the specter vanishes at once when we look at the matter as it were in a mathematical light, and make it clear to ourselves that all that is valuable to us is the discovery of *functional relations,* and that what we want to know is merely the dependence of experiences on one another. It then becomes obvious that the reference to unknown fundamental variables which are not given (things-in-themselves) is purely fictitious and superfluous. But even when we allow this fiction, uneconomical though it be, to stand at first, we can still easily distinguish different classes of the mutual dependence of the elements of "the facts of consciousness"; and this alone is important for us.

$$
\begin{array}{|cc|}
\hline
\begin{array}{l} A\ B\ C\ .\ .\ .\ K\ L\ M\ .\ .\ . \\ \qquad\qquad K'\ L'\ M'\ .\ .\ . \\ \qquad\qquad K''\ L''\ M''\ .\ .\ . \end{array} &
\boxed{\begin{array}{l} \alpha\ \beta\ \gamma\ .\ .\ . \\ \alpha'\ \beta'\ \gamma'\ .\ .\ . \\ \alpha''\ \beta''\ \gamma''\ .\ .\ . \end{array}} \\
\hline
\end{array}
$$

The system of the elements is indicated in the above scheme. Within the space surrounded by a single line lie the elements which belong to the sensible world—the elements whose regular connection and peculiar dependence on one another represent both physical (lifeless) bodies and the bodies of men, animals, and plants. All these elements, again, stand in a relation of quite peculiar dependence to certain of the elements $K\ L\ M$ . . .—the nerves of our body, namely—by which the facts of sense-physiology are expressed. The space surrounded by a double line contains the elements belonging to the higher psychic life, memory-images and presentations, including those which we form of the psychic life of our fellow-men. These may be distinguished by accents. These presentations, again, are connected with one another in a different way (association, fancy) from the sensational elements $A\ B\ C$ . . . $K\ L\ M$ . . . , but it cannot be doubted that they are very closely allied to the latter, and that in the last resort their behavior is determined by $A\ B\ C$ . . . $K\ L\ M$ . . . (the totality of the physical world), and especially by our body and nervous system. The presentations $\alpha'\ \beta'\ \gamma'$ . . . of the contents of the consciousness of our fellow-

542

men play for us the part of *intermediate substitutions,* by means of which the behavior of our fellow-men—the functional relation of K' L' M' ... to A B C ...—becomes intelligible, in so far as in and for itself (physically) it would remain unexplained.

It is therefore important for us to recognize that in all questions in this connection that can be asked intelligibly and that can interest us, everything turns on taking into consideration different *ultimate variables* and different *relations of dependence.* That is the main point. Nothing will be changed in the actual facts or in the functional relations, whether we regard all the data as contents of consciousness, or as partially so, or as completely physical.

The biological task of science is to provide the fully developed human individual with as perfect a means of orientating himself as possible. No other scientific ideal can be realized, and any other must be meaning less.

The philosophical point of view of the average man—if that term may be applied to his naive realism—has a claim to the highest consideration. It has arisen in the process of immeasurable time without the intentional assistance of man. It is a product of nature, and is preserved by nature. Everything that philosophy has accomplished—though we may admit the biological justification of every advance, nay, of every error—is, as compared with it, but an insignificant and ephemeral product of art. The fact is, every thinker, every philosopher, the moment he is forced to abandon his one-sided intellectual occupation by practical necessity, immediately returns to the general point of view of mankind. Professor X., who theoretically believes himself to be a solipsist, is certainly not one in practice when he has to thank a Minister of State for a decoration conferred upon him, or when he lectures to an audience. The Pyrrhonist who is cudgeled in Molière's *Le Mariage Forcé* does not go on saying *"Il me semble que vous me battez,"* but takes his beating as really received.

JOHN STUART MILL

(1806-1873)

An infant prodigy whose education was forced at such a pace by his father, it is amazing that he emerged from it as unwarped a human as he was. Mill was a great Victorian liberal in both theory and practice: he not only advocated democracy but served a term in the House of Commons. A man of many-sided interests, he has solid achievements to his credit in economics, sociology and political science as well as in philosophy. There he continued the great English empirical and inductive tradition.

Main Works:

> System of Logic; Principles of Political Economy; Essay on Liberty; Auguste Comte and Positivism; Utilitarianism.

Of Propositions

§ 1. In treating of Propositions, as already in treating of Names, some considerations of a comparatively elementary nature respecting their form and varieties must be premised, before entering upon that analysis of the import conveyed by them, which is the real subject and purpose of this preliminary book.

A proposition, we have before said, is a portion of discourse in which a predicate is affirmed or denied of a subject. A predicate and a subject are all that is necessarily required to make up a proposition: but as we cannot conclude from merely seeing two names put together, that they are a predicate and a subject, that is, that one of them is intended to be affirmed or denied

---

From: *System of Logic.*

of the other, it is necessary that there should be some mode or form of indicating that such is the intention; some sign to distinguish a predication from any other kind of discourse. This is sometimes done by a slight alteration of one of the words, called an *inflection;* as when we say, Fire burns; the change of the second word from *burn* to *burns* showing that we mean to affirm the predicate burn of the subject fire. But this function is more commonly fulfilled by the word *is,* when an affirmation is intended, *is not,* when a negation; or by some other part of the verb *to be.* The word which thus serves the purpose of a sign of predication is called, as we formerly observed, the *copula.* It is important that there should be no indistinctness in our conception of the nature and office of the copula; for confused notions respecting it are among the causes which have spread mysticism over the field of logic, and perverted its speculations into logomachies.

It is apt to be supposed that the copula is something more than a mere sign of predication; that it also signifies existence. In the proposition, Socrates is just, it may seem to be implied not only that the quality *just* can be affirmed of Socrates, but moreover that Socrates *is,* that is to say, exists. This, however, only shows that there is an ambiguity in the word *is;* a word which not only performs the function of the copula in affirmations, but has also a meaning of its own, in virtue of which it may itself be made the predicate of a proposition. That the employment of it as a copula does not necessarily include the affirmation of existence, appears from such a proposition as this, A centaur is a fiction of the poets; where it cannot possibly be implied that a centaur exists, since the proposition itself expressly asserts that the thing has no real existence.

Many volumes might be filled with the frivolous speculations concerning the nature of Being, (το ὄν οὐσία, Ens, Entias, Essentia, and the like) which have arisen from overlooking this double meaning of the word *to be;* from supposing that when it signifies *to exist,* and when it signifies *to be* some specified thing, as to *be* a man, to *be* Socrates, to *be* seen or spoken of, to *be* a phantom, even to *be* a nonentity, it must still, at bottom, answer to the same idea; and that a meaning must be found for it which shall suit all these cases. The fog which rose from this narrow spot diffused itself at an early period over the whole surface of metaphysics. Yet it becomes us not to triumph over the great intellects of Plato and Aristotle because we are now able to preserve ourselves from many errors into which they, perhaps inevitably, fell. The fireteazer of a modern steam-engine produces by his exertions far greater effects than Milo of Crotona could, but he is not therefore a stronger man. The Greeks seldom knew any language but their own. This rendered it far more difficult for them than it is for us, to acquire a readiness in detecting ambiguities. One of the advantages of having accurately studied a plurality of languages, especially of those languages which eminent thinkers have used as the vehicle of their thoughts, is the practical lesson we learn respecting the ambiguities of words, by finding that the same word in one language corresponds, on different occasions, to different words in another. When not thus exercised, even the strongest understandings find it difficult to believe that things which have a common name, have not in some respect or other a common nature; and often expend much labor very unprofitably (as was frequently done by the two philosophers just mentioned) in vain attempts to discover in what this common nature consists. But, the habit once formed, intellects much inferior are capable of detecting even ambiguities which are common to many languages: and it is surprising that the one now under consideration, though it exists in the modern languages as well as in the ancient, should have been overlooked by almost all authors. The quantity of futile speculation which had been caused by a misapprehension of the nature of the copula, was hinted at by Hobbes; but Mr. James Mill was, I believe, the first who distinctly characterized the ambiguity, and pointed out how many errors in the received systems of philosophy it has had to answer for. It has indeed misled the moderns scarcely less than the ancients, though their mistakes, because our understandings are not yet so completely emancipated from their influence, do not appear equally irrational.

We shall now briefly review the principal distinctions which exist among propositions, and the technical terms most commonly in use to express those distinctions.

§2. A proposition being a portion of discourse in which something is affirmed or denied of something, the first division of propositions is into affirmative and negative. An affirmative proposition is that in which the predicate is *affirmed* of the subject; as, Caesar is dead. A negative proposition is that in which the predicate is *denied* of the subject; as, Caesar is not dead. The copula, in this last species of proposition, consists of the words *is not,* which are the sign of negation; *is* being the sign of affirmation.

Some logicians, among whom may be mentioned Hobbes, state this distinction differently; they recognize only one form of copula, *is,* and attach the negative sign to the predicate. "Caesar is dead," and "Caesar is not dead," according to these writers, are propositions agreeing not in the subject and predicate, but in the subject only. They do not consider "dead," but "not dead," to be the predicate of the second proposition, and they accordingly define a negative proposition to be one in which the predicate is a negative name. The point, though not of much practical moment, deserves notice as an example (not infrequent in logic) where by means of an apparent simplification, but which is merely verbal, matters are made more complex than before. The notion of these writers was, that they could get rid of the distinction between affirming and denying, by treating every case of denying as the affirming of a negative name. But what is meant by a negative name? A name expressive of the *absence* of an attribute. So that when we affirm a negative name, what we are really predicating is absence and not presence; we are asserting not that anything is, but that something is not; to express which operation no word seems so proper as the word denying. The fundamental distinction is between a fact and the non-existence of that fact; between seeing something and not seeing it, between Caesar's being dead and his not being dead; and if this were a merely verbal distinction, the generalization which brings both within the same form of assertion would be a real simplification: the distinction, however, being real, and in the facts, it is the generalization confounding the distinction that is merely verbal; and tends to obscure the subject, by treating the difference between two kinds of truths as if it were only a difference between two kinds of words. To put things together, and to put them or keep them asunder, will remain different operations, whatever tricks we may play with language.

A remark of a similar nature may be applied to most of those distinctions among propositions which are said to have reference to their *modality;* as, difference of tense or time; the sun *did* rise, the sun *is* rising, the sun *will* rise. These differences, like that between affirmation and negation, might be glossed over by considering the incident of time as a mere modification of the predicate: thus, The sun is *an object having risen*, The sun is *an object to rise hereafter.* But the simplification would be merely verbal. Past, present, and future, do not constitute so many different kinds of rising; they are designations belonging to the event asserted, to the *sun's* rising today. They affect, not the predicate, but the applicability of the predicate to the particular subject. That which we affirm to be past, present, or future, is not what the subject signifies, nor what the predicate signifies, but specifically and expressly what the predication signifies; what is expressed only by the proposition as such, and not by either or both of the terms. Therefore the circumstance of time is properly considered as attaching to the copula, which is the sign of predication, and not to the predicate. If the same cannot be said of such modifications as these, Caesar *may* be dead; Caesar is *perhaps* dead; it is *possible* that Caesar is dead; it is only because these fall altogether under another head, being properly assertions not of anything relating to the fact itself, but of the state of our own mind in regard to it; namely, our absence of disbelief of it. Thus "Caesar may be dead" means "I am not sure that Caesar is alive."

§3. The next division of propositions is into Simple and Complex; more aptly (by Professor Bain) termed Compound. A simple proposition is that in which one predicate is affirmed or denied of one subject. A compound proposition is that in which there is more than one predicate, or more than one subject, or both.

At first sight this division has the air of an absurdity; a solemn distinction of things into one and more than one; as if we were to divide horses into single horses and teams of horses. And it is true that what is called a complex (or compound) proposition is often not a proposition at all, but several propositions, held together by a conjunction. Such, for example, is this: Caesar is dead, and Brutus is alive: or even this, Caesar is dead, *but* Brutus is alive. There are here two distinct assertions; and we might as well call a street a complex house, as these two propositions a complex proposition. It is true that the syncategorematic words *and* and *but* have a meaning; but that meaning is so far from making the two propositions one, that it adds a third proposition to them. All particles are abbreviations, and generally abbreviations of propositions; a kind of shorthand, whereby something which, to be expressed fully, would have required a proposition or a series of propositions, is suggested to the mind at once. Thus the words, Caesar is dead and Brutus is alive, are equivalent to these: Caesar is dead; Brutus is alive; it is desired that the two preceding propositions should be thought of together. If the words were, Caesar is dead, *but* Brutus is alive, the sense would be equivalent to the same three propositions together with a fourth; "between the two preceding propositions there exists a contrast:" viz. either between the two facts themselves, or between the feelings with which it is desired that they should be regarded.

In the instances cited the two propositions are kept visibly distinct, each subject having its separate predicate, and each predicate its separate subject. For brevity, however, and to avoid repetition, the propositions are often blended together: as in this, "Peter and James preached at Jerusalem and in Galilee," which contains four propositions: Peter preached at Jerusalem, Peter preached in Galilee, James preached at Jerusalem, James preached at Galilee.

We have seen that when the two or more propositions comprised in what is called a complex proposition are stated absolutely and not under any condition or proviso, it is not a proposition at all, but a plurality of propositions; since what it expresses is not a single assertion, but several assertions, which, if true when joined, are true also when separated. But there is a kind of proposition which, though it contains a plurality of subjects and of predicates, and may be said in one sense of the word to consist of several propositions, contains but one assertion; and its truth does not at all imply that of the simple propositions which compose it. An example of this is, when the simple propositions are connected by the particle *or;* as, either A is B or C is D; or by the particle *if;* as, A is B if C is D. In the former case, the proposition is called *disjunctive,* in the latter, *conditional:* the name *hypothetical* was originally common to both. As has been well remarked by Archbishop Whately and others, the disjunctive form is resolvable into the conditional; every disjunctive proposition being equivalent to two or more conditional ones. "Either A is B or C is D," means "if A is not B, C is D; and if C is not D, A is B." All hypothetical propositions, therefore, though disjunctive in form, are conditional in meaning; and the words hypothetical and conditional may be, as indeed they generally are, used synonymously. Propositions in which the assertion is not dependent on a condition, are said, in the language of logicians, to be *categorical.*

An hypothetical proposition is not, like the pretended complex propositions which we previously considered, a mere aggregation of simple propositions. The simple propositions which form part of the words in which it is couched, form not part of the assertion which it conveys. When we say, If the Koran comes from God, Mahomet is the prophet of God, we do not intend to affirm either that the Koran does not come from God, or that Mahomet is really his prophet. Neither of these simple propositions may be true, and yet the truth of the hypothetical proposition may be indisputable. What is asserted is not the truth of either of the propositions, but the inferrability of the one from the other. What, then, is the subject, and what the predicate of the hypothetical proposition? "The Koran" is not the subject of it, nor is "Mahomet": for nothing is affirmed or denied either of the Koran or of Mahomet. The real subject of the predication is the entire proposition, "Mahomet is the prophet of God"; and the affirmation is, that this is a legitimate inference from the proposition, "the Koran comes from God." The subject and predicate, therefore, of an hypothetical proposition are names of propositions. The subject is some one proposition. The predicate is a general relative name applicable to propositions of this form —"an inference from so and so." A fresh instance is here afforded of the remark, that particles are abbreviations; since "If A is B, C is D," is found to be an abbreviation of the following: "The proposition C is D, is a legitimate inference from the proposition A is B."

The distinction, therefore, between hypothetical and categorical propositions, is not so great as it at first appears. In the conditional, as well as in the categorical form, one predicate is affirmed of one subject, and no more: but a conditional proposition is a proposition concerning a proposition; the subject of the assertion is itself an assertion. Nor is this a property peculiar to hypothetical propositions. There are other classes of assertions concerning propositions. Like other things, a proposition has attributes which may be predicated of it. The attribute predicated of it in an hypothetical proposition, is that of being an inference from a certain other proposition. But this is only one of many attributes that might be predicated. We may say, That the whole is greater than its part, is an axiom in mathematics: That the

Holy Ghost proceeds from the Father alone, is a tenet of the Greek Church: The doctrine of the divine right of kings was renounced by Parliament at the Revolution: The infallibility of the Pope has no countenance from Scripture. In all these cases the subject of the predication is an entire proposition. That which these different predicates are affirmed of, is *the proposition,* "the whole is greater than its part"; *the proposition,* "the Holy Ghost proceeds from the Father alone"; *the proposition,* "kings have a divine right"; *the proposition,* "the Pope is infallible."

Seeing, then, that there is much less difference between hypothetical propositions and any others, than one might be led to imagine from their form, we should be at a loss to account for the conspicuous position which they have been selected to fill in treatises on logic, if we did not remember that what they predicate of a proposition, namely, its being an inference from something else, is precisely that one of its attributes with which most of all a logician is concerned.

§ 4. The next of the common divisions of Propositions is into Universal, Particular, Indefinite, and Singular: a distinction founded on the degree of generality in which the name, which is the subject of the proposition, is to be understood. The following are examples:

All men are mortal— Universal.
Some men are mortal— Particular.
Man is mortal— Indefinite.
Julius Caesar is mortal— Singular.

The proposition is Singular, when the subject is an individual name. The individual name need not be a proper name. "The Founder of Christianity was crucified," is as much a singular proposition as "Christ was crucified."

When the name which is the subject of the proposition is a general name, we may intend to affirm or deny the predicate, either of all the things that the subject denotes, or only of some. When the predicate is affirmed or denied of all and each of the things denoted by the subject, the proposition is universal: when of some undefined portion of them only, it is particular. Thus, All men are mortal; Every man is mortal; are universal propositions. No man is immortal, is also an universal proposition, since the predicate immortal, is denied of each and every individual denoted by the term man; the negative proposition being exactly equivalent to the following, Every man is not-immortal. But "some men are wise," "some men are not wise," are particular propositions; the predicate *wise* being in the one case affirmed and in the other denied not of each and every individual denoted by the term man, but only of each and every one of some portion of those individuals, without specifying what portion; for if this were specified, the proposition would be changed either into a singular proposition, or into an universal proposition with a different subject; as, for instance, "all *properly instructed* men are wise." There are other forms of particular propositions; as, "*Most* men are imperfectly educated": it being immaterial how large a portion of the subject the predicate is asserted of, as long as it is left uncertain how that portion is to be distinguished from the rest.

When the form of expression does not clearly show whether the general name which is the subject of the proposition is meant to stand for all the individuals denoted by it, or only for some of them, the proposition is, by some logicians, called Indefinite; but this, as Archbishop Whately observes, is a solecism, of the same nature as that committed by some grammarians when in their list of genders they enumerate the *doubtful* gender. The speaker must mean to assert the proposition either as an universal or as a particular proposition, though he has failed to declare which: and it often happens that though the words do not show which of the two he intends, the context, or the custom of speech, supplies the deficiency. Thus, when it is affirmed that

"Man is mortal," nobody doubts that the assertion is intended of all human beings; and the word indicative of universality is commonly omitted, only because the meaning is evident without it. In the proposition, "Wine is good," it is understood with equal readiness, though for somewhat different reasons, that the assertion is not intended to be universal, but particular. As is observed by Professor Bain, the chief examples of Indefinite propositions occur "with names of material, which are the subjects sometimes of universal, and at other times of particular predication. 'Food is chemically constituted by carbon, oxygen, &c.' is a proposition of universal quantity; the meaning is all food—all kinds of food. 'Food is necessary to animal life' is a a case of particular quantity; the meaning is some sort of food, not necessarily all sorts. 'Metal is requisite in order to strength' does not mean all kinds of metal. 'Gold will make a way,' means a portion of gold."

When a general name stands for each and every individual which it is a name of, or in other words, which it denotes, it is said by logicians to be *distributed,* or taken distributively. Thus, in the proposition, All men are mortal, the subject, Man, is distributed, because mortality is affirmed of each and every man. The predicate, Mortal, is not distributed, because the only mortals who are spoken of in the proposition are those who happen to be men; while the word may, for aught that appears, and in fact does, comprehend within it an indefinite number of objects besides men. In the proposition, Some men are mortal, both the predicate and the subject are undistributed. In the following, No men have wings, both the predicate and the subject are distributed. Not only is the attribute of having wings denied of the entire class Man, but that class is severed and cast out from the whole of the class Winged, and not merely from some part of that class.

This phraseology, which is of great service in stating and demonstrating the rules of the syllogism, enables us to express very concisely the definitions of an universal and a particular proposition. An universal proposition is that of which the subject is distributed; a particular proposition is that of which the subject is undistributed.

There are many more distinctions among propositions than those we have here stated, some of them of considerable importance. But, for explaining and illustrating these, more suitable opportunities will occur in the sequel.

AUGUSTUS DE MORGAN
(1806-1871)

Brought up at Worcester and Taunton, educated at private schools, and "read algebra like a novel." Spent four years at Trinity, Cambridge. As a result of his revolt from early evangelical training he did not take orders; law proved distasteful; in 1828 he became first Professor of Mathematics in University College, London. He became secretary of the Royal Astronomical Society. A mathematician of the first order, he was minutely versed in the history of the mathematical and physical sciences; he also devoted himself to the development of the Aristotelian or "formal" logic. He never renounced his claim of promoting metaphysics in no lesser degree than he did mathematics and logic.

Main Works:

> Elements of Arithmetic; Algebra; Numbers and Magnitude; Trigonometry; Essay on Probabilities; Formal Logic; Arithmetical Books; Book of Almanacks; Budget of Paradoxes.

On the Syllogism

When the premises of a syllogism are true, the conclusion is also true, and when the conclusion is false, one or both of the premises are false. There are two kinds of modifications which it may be useful to consider: those which concern the entrance of the proposition into the argument; and those which affect the connection of the subject and predicate.

From: *Formal Logic.*

Augustus de Morgan

As to the proposition itself, it may be true or false absolutely, or it may have any degree of truth, credibility, or probability. This relation will be hereafter considered; and, according to the principles of Chapter IX. so far as the proposition is probable it is credible, and so far as it is credible, it is true. But as to other modes of looking at the syllogism, are we entitled to say that every thing which can be announced as to the premises may be announced in the same sense as to the conclusion? The answer is, that we cannot make such announcement absolutely; but of the premises *as derived from that conclusion* we can make it. In what manner soever two premises are applicable, their conclusion as from those premises is also applicable: because the conclusion is in the premises. For instance, in the syllogism "all men are trees, all trees are rational, therefore all men are rational," the premises are absurd and false, and the conclusion taken independently is rational and true: but that conclusion, as from those premises, is as absurd as the premises themselves. Again, in "all pirates are convicted, all convicts are punished, therefore all pirates are punished," the premises are *desirable,* and so is the conclusion with those premises. But the conclusion is not desirable in itself: as that pirates should be punished with or without trial. Neither may we say "X ought to be Y and Y ought to be Z, therefore X ought to be Z" except in this manner, that we affirm X ought to be Z in a particular way. We may not even say that when "X ought to be Y, and Y *is* Z" it follows that "X ought to be Z" for it may be that Y ought to be Z. Thus a royalist, in 1655, would say that the hundred excluded members of Cromwell's parliament ought to be allowed to take their seats, and also that all who took any seats in that parliament were rebels; but he would not infer that the hundred members ought to be rebels. There is nothing which, being the property of the premises, is necessarily the independent property of the conclusion, except *absolute truth.* It should be noted that in common language and writing, the usual meaning of conclusions is that they are stated as of their premises and to stand or fall with them, even as to truth. Though a conclusion may be true when its premises are false, the proponent does not mean, for the most part, to claim more than his premises will give, nor that any thing should stand longer than the premises stand.

Next, we are not to argue from what we may say of a proposition to what we may say of the instances it contains, except as to what concerns the truth of those instances, or else to what concerns the instances as parts of a whole. If I say "Every X is Y" I assert, no doubt, of each X independently of the rest: that is, the truth of "Every X is Y" involves the truth of "this X is Y." But if, to take something else, I maintain "Every X is Y" to be a desirable rule, I do not therefore assert "this X is Y" to be a desirable case, except upon an implied necessity that there should be a rule. And if I say that "every X is Y" is unintelligible, I do not say that "this X is Y" is unintelligible; and so on. Thus, where there must be a rule, as in law, "every man's house is his castle" is desirable, because there is but one alternative "no man's house, &c." But the proposition, by itself, may not be desirable as to the instance of a generally reputed thief or receiver.

There is one case, however, in which a term cannot be applied to the general proposition, unless it can be applied in a higher degree to the instances. The proposition "Every X is Y" cannot be announced as of any degree of probability, unless each instance has a much higher degree of probability. If μ, ν, ρ, etc. be the probabilities of the several instances, supposed independent, that of the proposition (Chapter IX.) is $\mu\nu\rho$ which product must be less than that of any one of the fractions of which it is formed.

I now come to the consideration of circumstances which modify the internal structure of the premises themselves. And first of conditions.

A *conditional* proposition is only a grammatical variation of the ordinary one; as in "If it be X, then it is Y." The common form of this, "Every X is Y," is called *categorical*, or *predicative*. Of the two forms, categorical and conditional, either may always be reduced to the other; as follows,

Augustus de Morgan

"Every X is Y" or "If X, then it is Y"

"No   X is Y" or "If X, then it is not Y"

The particular propositions might be given conditionally in various ways, but the transformation is not so common. Thus "some Xs are Ys" might be "if X, then it may be Y" or "if X, then Y must not therefore be denied of it, &c."

Of the two common subject-matters of names, ideas and propositions, it is most common to apply the categorical form to the first, and the conditional form to the second: in truth we might call the conditional form a grammatical convenience for the expression of dependence of propositions on one another, and of names which require complicated forms of expression.

A condition may be either *necessary,* or *sufficient,* or both. A necessary condition is that without which the thing cannot be; a sufficient condition is one with which the thing must be. I have sufficiently pointed out elsewhere the completeness of the connection between the conditional and the categorical forms. In any case the sufficient must contain all that is necessary, and may contain more.

After what is said previously it is not necessary to dwell on the reduction of a conditional syllogism to a categorical one. The premises contain the conclusion. But I think that the reduction of conditional to categorical forms, though just, and, for inference, complete, is not the representation of the whole of what passes in our minds.

Precedent to all propositions, there are the numerical conditions which prescribe the limits of the universe under consideration. Say there are 250 instances in that universe: this is the first condition. Of these 100 are Xs and 200 are Ys; giving a second and third condition. If we take a proposition, as 20XY, and ask whether it be spurious or not, we have reference to the three conditions understood. But this is not necessary: for it would be possible categorically to express these conditions by "20Xs out of 100 in a universe of 250 instances containing 200 Ys are to be found among those 200 Ys"? It is of course the rule of brevity not to drag about these conditions with every proposition which is employed, but rather to state them once for all. There is however something more. The conditions are a restriction throughout. The attachment of them to each individual proposition does not express this: if they be seen in twenty consecutive propositions, there is no more than a presumption that they are to be seen in the twenty-first. It is better that the limits allowed should each have a description of the boundary itself.

Just as a universe of names is defined by specifying one or more names to constitute collectively the *summum genus*, or *universe* so one of propositions may be defined by stating propositions which are to be true, or which are not to be contradicted, as the case may be. These propositions may be conditions preceding all, or some only, of the premises which are used in argument; or some may precede some, and others others. In analyzing arguments, it would be found that many propositions which enter as premises, enter each with a condition understood, and well understood, to be granted. Whatever the conditions may be, so long as the consequent propositions act logically together to produce the final result, then that same result depends at last only on the conditions, and must be affirmed when the conditions, and their connection with their consequents, are affirmed. But then it must be understood that the result also stands upon the conditions, and may fall with them. Let us now examine the common syllogism, and see whether there be any preceding conditions, on which the result depends.

On looking into any writer on logic, we shall see that *existence* is claimed for the significations of all names. Never, in the statement of a proposition, do we find any room left for the alternative, *suppose there should be no such things.* Existence as objects, or existence as ideas, is tacitly claimed for the terms of every syllogism. The existence of an idea we must grant whenever it is distinctly apprehended, and (therefore) not self-contradictory: we cannot for instance admit the notion of a lamp which is both metal and not metal; but, as an idea, we are at liberty to figure to ourselves such a lamp as that with which Aladdin made his fortune. An attempt at a self-contradicting idea is no idea; we have not that apprehension of it in which an idea conflicts: but in no other way can we say that the attempt to produce an idea fails. It may then be more convenient here to dwell on *objective* definition of terms, as more easily conceived with relation to existence and non-existence. Accordingly, let us take the propositions X)Y and X.Y, of the character of which the particulars must partake, as to the point before us. By the meaning of y, in relation to Y, it follows that every thing is either Y or y: if we say that Y does not exist, then every thing is y. If then X exist, and Y do not, the proposition X)Y, or X.y is false, and X)y or X.Y is true. If neither X nor Y exist, I will not so far imitate some of the questions of the schools as to attempt to settle what nonexisting things agree or disagree. If Y exist, but not X, then y)x is certainly true, but not thence X)Y, for when x is, as here, the whole universe, the proof of y)x= X)Y fails to present intelligible ideas, that is, fails to be a proof. But Y)x or Y.X is true.

If all my readers were mathematicians, I might pursue these extreme cases, as having interest on account of their analogy with the extreme cases which the entrance of zero and of infinite magnitude oblige him to consider. But as those who are not mathematicians would not be interested in the analogy, and those who are can pursue the subject for themselves, I will go on to say that the preceding order is not the natural one. We cannot, to useful purpose, laying down the truth of the proposition, *first,* then proceed to enquire how the non-existence of the terms must be first settled, and then the truth or falsehood of the proposition. The affirmative proposition requires the existence of both terms: the negative proposition, of one; being necessarily true if the other term do not exist, and depending upon the matter, as usual, if it do exist.

Let us make the existence of the terms to be preceding conditions of the propositions. The syllogism $A_1A_1A_1$ is then as follows,

If X and Y both exist,	Every X is Y
If Z also exist	Every Y is Z
Therefore If X, Y, Z all exist	Every X is Z.

As to the concluding terms, X and Z, they remain, as it were, to tell their own story. Whatever conditions accompany their introduction unto the premises, these same conditions may be conceived to accompany them in the conclusion. But the middle term disappears: and, not showing itself in the conclusion, the conditions which accompany it must be expressly preserved. The conclusion then is "every X is Z, if Y exist" which may be thrown into the form of a dilemma, "Either every X is Z, or Y does not exist."

But taking X and Z to exist, let us consider the following syllogism, *as it appears to be,*

Every X is (Y, if Y exist)
Every (Y, if Y exist) is Z
Therefore Every X is Z.

If this be not a valid syllogism, what *expressed* law of the ordinary treatises does it break? The middle term, a curious one, is strictly middle: but there is no rule for excluding middle terms of a certain degree of singularity. That it does break, and very obviously, an implied rule, I grant.

The two uses of the word *is* do not amount to one such use as is made in the conclusion. That X is (conditionally) Y which is (on the same condition) Z, gives that X is (on the same condition) Z. Accordingly, the absolute conclusion is only true upon such conditions as give the middle term absolute existence.

But it must be particularly noted that it is enough if this existence be given to the middle term by the fulfilment of the conditions which precede the entrance of one of the concluding terms. The condition of the act of inference is, that the comparison must be really made, if the terms to be compared with the middle term really exist, or, which is the same, if the conditions under which they are to enter be satisfied. The other terms being ready, there must *then* be a real middle term: and there will be, if the mere entrance of one of the concluding terms be proof of the existence of a middle term; while, if the other terms cannot be brought in, from nonexistence, there is no occasion to inquire about a middle term, for it is otherwise known that the comparison cannot be completed. I will take two concrete instances, in the first of which one of the concluding terms, if existing, is held to furnish a middle term as real as itself, and in the second of which no such supposition occurs. Of course I have nothing here to do with the truth of the premises.

Philip Francis, (if the author of Junius), was an accuser whose silence was simultaneous with a government appointment: an accuser &c. reflects disgrace upon the government (if they knew that their nominee was the accuser): therefore Francis (if &c.) reflects disgrace upon the government (if &c.).

Homer (if there were such a person) was a perfect poet (if ever there were one): a perfect poet (if &c.) is faultless in morals: therefore Homer (if &c.) was faultless in morals.

The first inference is good, even though we grant that our only possible mode of knowing of the existence of an accuser &c. is by establishing that Francis was Junius: it is even good against one who should assert the accuser &c. is a contradiction in terms in every actual and imaginable case except that of Junius.

In the second case, we put it that the man Homer (if he ever existed; some critics having contended for the contrary) was a perfect poet, if ever there were one. There may never have been one; and then Homer (existent or nonexistent) was not a perfect poet. There is no condition here, which being fulfilled, is held to amount to an assertion that the middle term must have existed: but the condition of the existence of the middle term is independent. Accordingly, the second inference is not good: it should be Homer (if &c.) was a perfect poet, if ever there were one: that is, or else there never was a perfect poet.

These points refer to the matter of a syllogism, and not to the form; or rather, perhaps, hold a kind of intermediate relation.

There is another process which is often necessary, in the formation of the premises of a syllogism, involving a transformation which is neither done by syllogism, nor immediately reducible to it. It is the substitution, in a compound phrase, of the name of the genus for that of the species, when the use of the name is particular. For example, "man is animal, therefore the head of a man is the head of an animal" is inference, but not syllogism. And it is not mere substitution of identity, as would be "the head of a man is the head of a *rational animal*" but a substitution of a larger term in a particular sense.

Perhaps some readers may think they can reduce the above to a syllogism. If *man* and *head* were connected in a manner which could be made subject and predicate, something of the sort might be done, but in appearance only. For example, "Every man is an animal, therefore he who kills a man kills an animal." It may be said that this is equivalent to a statement that in "Every man is an animal; some one kills a man; therefore some one kills an animal," the first premise, and the second premise *conditionally*, involve the conclusion as *conditionally*. This I admit: but the last is not a syllogism: and involves the very difficulty in question. "Every man *is* an animal; some one *is* the killer of a man": here is no middle term. To bring the first premise into "Every killer of a man is the killer of an animal" is just the thing wanted. By the earlier principles undoubtedly the copula *is* might in certain inferences be combined with the copula *kills,* or with any verb. But so simple a case as the preceding is not the whole difficulty. If any one should think he can syllogize as to the instances I have yet given, let him try the following. "Certain *men,* upon the report of certain other *men* to a third set of *men,* put a fourth set of *men* at variance with a fifth set of *men.*" Now every man is an animal: and therefore "Certain *animals,* upon the report of certain other *animals,* &c." Let the description be turned into the second, by any number of syllogisms, and by help of "Every man is an animal."

The truth is, that in the formation of premises, as well as in their use, there is a postulate which is constantly applied, and therefore of course constantly demanded. And it should be demanded openly. It contains the very important *dictum de omni et nullo* and it is as follows. For every term used universally *less* may be substituted, and for every term used particularly, *more.* The species may take the place of the genus, when all the genus is spoken of: the genus may take the place of the species when some of the species is mentioned, or the genus, used particularly, may take the place of the species universally. Not only syllogism, but in all the ramifications of the description of a complex term. Thus for "men who are not Europeans" may be substituted "animals who are not English." If this postulate be applied to the unstrengthened forms of the Aristotelian Syllogism, it will be seen that all which contain A are immediate applications of it, and all the others easily derived.

I now pass to the consideration of the invention of names, and of the distinctions which are made to exist for the want of it.

Any one may invent a name, that is, may choose a sound or symbol which is to apply to any class of ideas or objects. The class should, no doubt, be well defined: but small caution is here necessary, for invented words are generally much more definite than those which have undergone public usage. They come from the coiner's hand as sharp at the edges as a new halfpenny: and in process of time we look in vain for any edge at all. The right of invention being unlimited, and the actual stock having been got together without any uniform rule of formation, *there can be no reason why we should admit any distinction which can be abrogated by the invention of a name,* so far as inference is concerned. I do not dispute that the modes of supplying the want of names may be of importance in many points of view: what I deny is, that they create any peculiar modes of inference.

The invention of names must either be by actually pointing out objects named, or by description in terms of other names. With the former mode of invention, as "let this, that, &c (showing them) be called X" we can have nothing to do. As to the latter, we may make a symbolic description of the process by joining together the names to be used, with a symbol indicative of the mode of using them, in extension of the system. Thus, P, Q, R, being certain names, if we wish to give a name to everything which is all three, we may join them thus, PQR: if we wish to give a name to every thing which is either of the three (one or more of them) we may write P, Q, R: if we want to signify any thing that is either both P and Q, or R, we have PQR. The contrary of PQR is p,q,r; that of P, Q, R is pqr; that of P, Q, R is (p,q)r: in contraries, conjunction and disjunction change places. This notation would enable us to express any complication of the preceding conditions: thus, to name that which is one and one only of the three, we have Pqr, Qrp, Rpq; for that which is two and two only, PQr, QRp, RPq. Thus, XY includes the instances common to X and Y; but X,Y includes all X and all Y: accordingly X,Y is a wider term than XY, except when X and Y are identical. As XY, the term, supposed to exist, is XY, an earlier proposition, if we wish to distinguish, we may make X-Y the term, and XY the proposition, the hyphen having its common grammatical use. Thus, X-Y P-Q tells us the same as XYP-Q both meaning, *for inference*, no more than that there exist objects or ideas to which the four names are applicable. But the first tells it thus, some XYs are PQs; and the second thus, some things are Xs, Ys, and PQs.

With respect to this and other cases of notation, repulsive as they may appear, the reader who refuses them is in one of two circumstances. Either he wants to give his assent or dissent to what is said of the form by means of the matter, which is easing the difficulty by avoiding it, and stepping out of logic: or else he desires to have it in a shape in which he may get that most futile of all acquisitions, called a *general idea,* which is truly, to use the contrary adjective term as colloquially, *nothing particular,* a whole without parts.

If the difficulty of abstract assertion be to be got over, the easiest way is by first conquering that of abstract expression, to the extent of becoming able to make a little use of it.

Suppose we ask for the alternative of the following supposition, "Both X, and either P, or Q and one of the two R or S." This is no impossible complication: for instance, "He was rich, and if not absolutely mad, was weakness itself subjected either to bad advice or to most unfavorable circumstances." The representation of the complex term is X $\{P, Q(R,S)\}$; of the contrary, x, p(q,rs) or x,pq,prs. If not the above, he was either not rich, or both not mad and not very weak, or neither mad nor badly advised, nor unfavorably circumstanced.

When a name thus formed, whether conjunctively or disjunctively, enters a simple inference, it gives rise to what have been called the *copulative* syllogism, the *disjunctive* syllogism, and the *dilemma.* The two last are not well distinguished by their definitions as given: the disjunctive syllogism seems to be that in which *propositions* are so used. But a proposition entering as part of a proposition, enters merely as a name, the predicates being usually only *true* or *false,* or some equivalent terms. A proposition may only enter for its matter, or it may enter in such a way that its truth is the matter: in this last case it is only as a name that it is the subject of inference. Thus, "It is true that he was fired at" is "the assertion (that he was fired at) is a true assertion." I believe the best way would be to apply the term *disjunctive* argument so as to include the dilemma, marking by the latter word (as a term rather of rhetoric than of logic) every argument in which the disjunctive proposition is meant to be a difficulty for the opponent on every case, or *born,* of it.

Whatever has right to the name P, and also to the name Q, has right to the compound name PQ. This is an absolute identity, for by the name PQ we signify nothing but what has right to both names. Accordingly X)P+X)Q=X)PQ is not a syllogism, nor even an inference, but only the assertion of our right to use at our pleasure either one of two ways of saying the same thing instead of the other. But can we not effect the reduction syllogistically? Let Y be identical with PQ; we have then PQ)Y and Y)PQ, and also Y)P and Y)Q. Add to these X)P and X)Q, and we have all the propositions asserted. But we cannot deduce from them alone X)Y, the result wanted, by any syllogistic combination of the six. Nor must it be thought surprising that we cannot, by a train of argument, arrive at demonstration of it being allowable to give to anything which has right to two names, a third name invented expressly to signify that which has such right. We might as well attempt to syllogize into the result, that a person who fells the meat he has killed is a butcher.

I lay stress upon this, to an extent which may for a moment appear like diligently grinding nothing in a mill which might be better employed, for two reasons. First, the young mathematician is very apt to try, in algebra, to make one principle deduce another by mere force of symbols: and the above attempt may show him what he is liable to. Secondly, I am inclined to suppose that the distinction drawn between the classes of syllogisms to which I presently come, and the ordinary categorical ones, is due to what must be described in my language as a want of perception of the absolute, *less than inferential* (so to speak) identity of X)P+X)Q and X)PQ. But all other propositions of the kind, however simple, may be made deductions. For instance, "if X be both P and Q, and if P be R, and Q be S, then X is both Q and S" is thus deduced: X)P+P)R=X)R, and X)Q+Q)S=X)S, and X)R+X)S is X)RS. Even P)R+Q)R=P,Q)R is deducible; being P)R+Q)R=r)p+r)q=r)pq=P,Q)R. Thus it is seen that, as soon as the *conjunctive* postulate is laid down, the identity of the corresponding disjunctive postulate with it may be shown. Next, if X must be either P or Q, or X)P,Q, and if P be always R, and Q be always S, then X)R,S may be *deduced* from the preceding.

Augustus de Morgan

First, that X)P and Y)Q give XY)PQ can be deduced; evident as it may be, it is a succession of applications. XY)X+X)P gives XY)P, and XY)Y+Y)Q gives XY)Q, and XY)P+XY)Q is XY)PQ by the postulate. Next, X)P,Q is pq)x, and P)R is r)p, and Q)S is s)q, whence as just proved rs)pq. Now, rs)pq+pq)x =rs)x, which is X)R,S. It will be a good exercise for the reader to translate this proof into ordinary language.

I may now proceed to extend this idea and notation relative to propositions of complex terms. The complexity consists in the terms being conjunctively or disjunctively formed from other terms, as in PQ, that to which both the names P and Q belong conjunctively; and as in P,Q that to which one (or both) of the names P and Q belong disjunctively. The contrary of PQ is p,q; that of P,Q is pq. *Not both* is either not one or not the other, or not either. *Not either P or Q* (which we might denote by: P,Q or P,Q) is logically *"not P and not* Q" or pq: and this is then the contrary of P,Q.

The disjunctive name is of two very different characters, according as it appears in the universal or particular form: so very different that it has really different names in the two cases, *copulative* and *disjunctive*. This distinction I here throw away: opposing *disjunctive*, (having one or more of the names) to *conjunctive*, (having all the names). The disjunctive particle *or* has the same meaning with the distributive copulative *and*, when used in a universal. Thus, "Every thing which is P or Q is R or S" means "Every P *and* every Q is R *or* S." But PQ is always "both P and Q in one." Accordingly

Conjunctive PQR uses *and* collectively.

Disjunctive P,Q,R in a universal uses *and* distributively.
P,Q,R in a particular uses *or* disjunctively, in the common sense of that word.

"Either P or Q is true" is an ambiguous phrase, which is P,Q)T or T)P,Q according to the context.

The manner in which the component of a name enters, whether conjunctively or disjunctively, is to pass as it were for a part of the quality of the name itself. Thus the contrary of P (conjunctive, as indicated by the absence of the comma) is ,p (disjunctive, as indicated by the comma). To test this assertion about the mode of making contraries, let us ask what is that of "one only of the two P or Q?" We know it of course to be "both or neither." The name proposed is Pq,Qp and its contrary is (p,Q) (q,P), that is, one of the two p,Q, *and* one of the two q,P. It is then either pq, pP, qQ, or PQ: the second and third cannot exist, therefore it is pq, PQ, as already seen. I need hardly have remarked that (P,Q)(R,S) is PR, PS, QR, QS.

Observe that though X)PQ gives X)P, and that XPQ gives XP, we may not say that XY)P gives X)P, nor that X)P,Q gives X)P. But any disjunctive element may be rejected from a universal term, and any conjunctive element from a particular one. Thus P)QR gives P)Q and P,Q)R gives P)R. Also P.Q,R gives P.Q and PQ:R,S gives P:R. All these rules are really one, namely that PQ is of the same extent at least as PQR. This will appear from our rules of transposition presently given.

Let change from one member of the proposition to the other be called *transposition*. I proceed to inquire how many transpositions the various forms will bear, and what they are. It will however be necessary to complete our forms by the recognition, as a proposition, of the simple assertion of existence or non-existence. By XU we mean that there are in the universe things to which the name X applies, and we speak of such things under the name. Accordingly X)U and XU do not differ in meaning. By u, the contrary of U, we can only denote non-existence; thus X.U or X)u throws the name X out of consideration. Thus Y)X =U)X,y; Y.X=YX)u, &c. To signify, for instance, that X and Y are complements (contraries or subcontraries) we have U)X,Y, which our rules will transpose into xy)u, or x.y.

Having to consider subject and predicate, conjunctive and disjunctive, affirmative and negative, universal and particular, we must think of sixteen different forms. Thus the four forms of the universal affirmative are

$$XY)PQ; \quad X,Y)PQ; \quad XY)P,Q; \quad X,Y)P,Q$$

It will be best here to neglect the contranominal converses of A and O equally with the simple converses of E and I: thus XY)PQ may be read as identical with p,q)x,y. There is also one obvious transposition which we must not merely neglect but throw out; since it does not give a result identical with its predecessor. I mean the transposition of M)PQ into MP)Q: the second follows from the first but not the first from the second. Also the corresponding change of M.P,Q into Mp.Q, for the same reason.

This being premised, the following are the rules;—

Direct transposition is the change from one member to the other without alteration of name or junction: *contrary*, with alteration of both.

The convertibles (E,I) allow direct transposition of conjunctive elements either way, from subject to predicate, or from predicate to subject: and these are the only direct transpositions. Thus X.YZ=XY.Z, and X-YZ=XY-Z.

The inconvertibles (A,O) allow contrary transposition of conjunctive elements from subject to predicate, and of disjunctive elements from predicate to subject: best remembered by allowing SP to stand for *conjunctive* and PS for *disjunctive*. And these are the only contrary transpositions. Thus XY)M=X)M,y and M)X,Y=My)X.

An element that can be rejected cannot be transposed, and *vice versa*. Thus X,Y)M gives X)M, and Y cannot be transposed.

The following table exhibits the varieties of the forms A and E, equivalents being written under one another, and conversions, contranominal or simple, opposite.

XY)P,Q	pq)x,y	XY.PQ	PQ.XY
Xp)Q,y	Yq)P,x	XP.QY	QY.XP
Xq)P,y	Yp)Q,x	XQ.PY	PY.XQ
X)P,Q,y	pqY)x	X.PQY	PQY.X
Y)P,Q,x	pqX)y	Y.PQX	PQX.Y
p)Q,x,y	XYq)P	P.QXY	QXY.P
q)P,x,y	XYp)Q	Q.PXY	PXY.Q
XYpq)u	U)P,Q,x,y	XYPQ.U	U.XYPQ

XY)PQ	p,q)x,y	XY.P,Q	P,Q.XY
X)PQ,y	[p,q]Y)x	X.[P,Q]Y	[P,Q]Y X
Y)PQ,x	[p,q]X)y	Y.[P,Q]X	[P,Q]X,Y
XY[p;q])u	U)[x,y],PQ	XY[P,Q].U	U.XY[P,Q]

X,Y)P,Q	pq)xy	X,Y.PQ	PQ.X,Y
[X,Y]p)Q	q)xy,P	[X,Y]P.Q	Q.[X,Y]P
[X,Y]q)P	p)xy,Q	[X,Y]Q.P	P.[X,Y]Q
[X,Y]pq)u	U)xy,P,Q	[X,Y]PQ.U	U.[X,Y]PQ

X,Y)PQ	p,q)xy	X,Y.P,Q	P,Q.X,Y
[x,y][p,q])u	U)xy,PQ	[X,Y][P,Q].U U	U.[X,Y][P,Q]

If for) we write (:) in the left hand divisions, and erase the
(.) and use the hyphens on the right, we have the transpositions of O and I. And if we write p and q for P and Q
on the left, and change the form X)Y into X.y, we thereby
change the forms of A into those of E. If more than two elements
were used, the transpositions would now be perfectly easy.

It appears that there are no less than sixteen A forms into
which XY)P,Q may be varied: the reason is that both subject
and predicate are transposibly constructed. But XY)PQ shows
only a transposible subject; X,Y)P,Q only a transposible predicate: and these have only four forms each. Lastly, X,Y)PQ, having neither transposible, has only two forms. By transposibly
constructed, I mean capable of having the elements separated
by transposition. The whole term is always transposible: that is,

the complete subject, or the complete predicate, may be looked on as conjunctive or disjunctive, at pleasure. Thus in X)Y, if we consider this as XU)Y,u, we may make this yU)x,u or y)x. So that the ordinary contranominal conversion may be considered as a case of the more general rule. Just as, in arithmetic, a number, 5, may be made to obey the laws of $a+b$ as $0+5$, or of ab as 1×5.

Syllogisms of complex terms might be widely varied, even if we chose to consider only each first case of the preceding table as fundamental. Thus

$$XY)P, \quad Q+VW)P, \quad Q=(x,y)-(v,w) \quad A_,A'I'$$

would give sixty-four varieties of premises. I now proceed to show that the ordinary disjunctive and dilemmatic forms are really common syllogisms with complex terms, reducible to ordinary syllogisms by invention of names.

Example 1. Every S is either P, Q, R; no P is S; no Q is S; therefore every S is R. Let S represent "the true proposition" (singular), and let P, Q, R be names of propositions, and this then represents a very common form, which would be expressed thus "either A is B, or C is D, or E is F; but A is not B, C is not D; therefore E is F." I say that, where the necessary names exist, the final step of this could not be distinguished from a common syllogism; which accordingly it becomes by invention of names.

We have S)P,Q,R, whence Spq)R. But S.P and S.Q or S)p and S)q give S)pq, with which S)S combined gives S)pqS. And S)pqS +pqS)R = S)R. Let M be the name of what is S and not P and not Q, and the thing required is done. Here then is a syllogism of the ordinary kind, to one premise of which we are led by a use of the *conjunctive postulate*: the necessity for which is the distinction between the class we are considering and others. It happens here that two of the terms of our final syllogism are identical: for Spq is of no greater extent than S. But the use made of S)S is perfectly legitimate.

Example 2. "If A be B, E is F; and if C be D, E is F; but either A is B or C is D; therefore E is F." This can be reduced to

$$P)R + Q)R +S)P,Q = S)R$$

which is immediately made a common syllogism by changing $P)R + Q)R$ into $P,Q)R$.

Example 3. "From P follows Q; and from R follows S; but Q and S cannot both be true; therefore P and R cannot both be true." This may be reduced to

$$P)Q + R)S + T.QS = T.PR$$
$$\text{or } PR)QS \quad + T.QS = T.PR$$

Example 4. "Every X is either P, Q, or R; but every P is M, every Q is M, every R is M; therefore every X is M." This is a common form of the dilemma; it is obviously reducible to $P,Q,R)M + X)P,Q,R = X)M$.

Example 5. "Every X is either P or Q, and every Q is X." This is wholly inconclusive, and leads to an identical result, as follows; $X)P,Q$ gives $Xp)Q$, which with $Q)X$ gives $Xp)X$, a necessary proposition.

Example 6. If we throw $X)R$ into the form $X)R,R$, we have $Xr)R$, or "Every X which *is not* R *is* R," a contradiction in terms. But it evidently implies that there can be no Xs which are not Rs; and thus also we return to $X)R$. Take "every X is either P, Q, or R." Here $X)P,Q,R =Xr)P,Q$, which with $P,Q)M$ gives $Xr)M$, which with $M)R$ gives $Xr)R$ or $X)R$.

Example 7. "Every X is either P or Q, and only one." This gives two propositions, $X)P,Q + X.PQ$. Now $X)XP,XQ$ is identical with $X)P,Q$, and this may be looked on as an extreme case of

$$X)P,Q + X)Y = X)PY,QY$$

but X.PQ gives $XP)q$ and $XQ)p$, from which we can obtain
$$X)XP,XQ + XP)q + XQ)p = X)p,q$$
Hence $X)P,Q + X)p,q = X)[P,Q,][p,q.]$
$$= X)Pp,Pq,Qp,Qq = X)Pq,Qp$$

since Pp and Qq are subject to X.Pp and X.Qq. All this being worked out in syllogistic detail, shows us that the transition from "Every X is P or Q, and no X is both" to " Every X is either P and not Q, or Q and not P" is capable of being made syllogistically. The student of logic may thus acquire the idea, which so soon becomes familiar to the student of mathematics, of perfectly self-evident propositions which are deducible from those which are not.

Example 8. "Every X is one only of the two, P or Q; every Y is both P and Q, except when P is M, and then it is neither; therefore no X is Y." Here is a case in which it is the fact of the exception and not its nature which determines the inference: M may be anything. This ought to appear in our reduction: and it does appear in this way. From X)P,Q it is obvious that X)P,Q,R,S, is syllogistically demonstrable from X)P,Q, and Xrs)X. Now in the second premise we have

$$Y)PQm,pqM, \text{ or } [p,q,M][P,Q,m])y$$
$$\text{or } pQ,Pq,PM,QM,pm,qm)y$$

from which, by rejection, follows pQ,Pq)y. And the first premise is X)Pq,Qp. Whence X)y or X.Y.

It is not necessary to multiply examples: I will conclude this part of the subject by pointing out that the ordinary propositions X)Y, &c. are, with reference to their instances, disjunctively composed: the difference between the universal and particular lying in the latter being indefinite in the number of its instances. Thus, if there be three Xs and four Ys, the four propositions are, applying the name to each instance, as seen written at length in X,X,X)Y,Y,Y,Y; X,X,X.Y,Y,Y,Y; (X,X,X)(Y,Y,Y,Y); and (X,X,X): Y,Y,Y,Y.

I now come to the *sorites*, the *heap* or chain of syllogisms, in which the conclusion of the first is a premise of the second, and so on. Take a set of terms, P, Q, R, S, &c. and let the order of reference be PQ, QR, &c. Then, A,A,A,A, &c. is a sorites, and the only one usually considered: thus,

$$P)Q+Q)R+R)S+S)T=P)T$$

The first two links give P)R, which with the third gives P)S, which with the fourth gives P)T. Thus we have *links, intermediate conclusions,* and a *final conclusion.*

A great number of different sorites may be formed, under the following conditions.

The first particular proposition which occurs, be it link or conclusion, prevents any future link from being particular: for all the conclusions thence become particular.

Examine the cases of syllogism which proceed by the first rule of accentuation that is, which have beginning and ending both universal, or both particular: these only can occur in a sorites, except at the end, or in the place where a particular proposition first enters. It will be found that the conclusion, when the argument goes on, must come after something connected with that which comes after it by the first rule of accentuation: except at the place where a particular conclusion comes in for the first time. For instance, E,E' gives $A,$, which, still keeping conclusions universal, must be followed by $A,$ or $E,$, which follow E' by the first rule. Again, take O,E', which gives $I,$; this must be followed either by $A,$ or $E,$, which follow E' by the same rule: and so on. Accordingly,

Any chain of universals, in which affirmation is followed by a like proposition, and negation by a different one, as A,A,E,A' $E'A,E,E'$, &c., may be part of the chain of a sorites. And the chain must be either of this kind wholly, or once only broken in one of two ways: either by the direct entrance of a particular proposition, or by a breach of the rule. In a chain of this kind, unbroken, the conclusions are affirmative or negative, according as an even or odd number of negatives goes to the formation of them. All the conclusions have the same accent as the first link.

Let a particular premise be introduced, as in $A,E,E'I'$ &c. The accent of the particular introduced must be the same as or contrary to that of the first link, according as the preceding number of negatives is odd or even. For the accent of the first link remains as long as the conclusion is universal, and a syllogism with the second premise particular follows the second rule. Thus, inserting the intermediate conclusions, the above is $A_,E_,(E_,)E'(A_,)I'(I')$. And after (I') must come A' or E', so that the first rule still continues. But the accent of the conclusions changes.

Now let the rule of accentuation be broken. The *accent* of the conclusion still requires the first rule to be resumed. Thus, $E_,E'$ (rule unbroken) gives $A_,$, and $E_, E_,$ (rule broken) gives I', and $A_,$ requires $A_,$ or $E_,$ to follow E', while I' requires A' or E' to follow $E_,$. This one breach of rule only changes the conclusion from universal to particular. The accent of the conclusion changes as before.

The links of a sorites, then, are either a chain of universals following the first rule of accentuation, or such a chain with *one* breach of the rule, or such a chain with one particular inserted, of the same or contrary accent to the first link, according as the preceding negatives are odd or even, and made the commencement of the resumption of the rule (if broken). In all these cases the conclusion is affirmative or negative according as the preceding negatives are even or odd in number: the unbroken chain has a universal conclusion with the accent of the first link, and the broken one a particular with the contrary accent.

A'E'E,A'E'	$E_,A'A_,E_,E'A_,$	$A_,E_,A'O_,A'E'$
E'A'A'E'	$E_,O'I'O'O'$	$E_,E_,I'I'O'$

Here are examples of the three kinds. The chain is in the first row, the intermediate and final conclusions in the second. Thus the second example presents the syllogisms $E_,A'E_,$, $E_,A_,O'$, $O'E_,I'$, $I'E'O'$, $O'A_,O'$; and at length is

$$P.Q+R)Q+R)S+S.T+t.u+U(V=V:P$$

The sorites usually considered are only $A_,A_,A_,$ . . . . and A'A'A' . . . . To these might be added without abandoning the Aristotelian syllogism, such as $A_,E_,A'A'A'$ . . . ., $A_,E_,A'A_,A_,$ . . . . But it would not be very easy to follow the chain in thought without introducing the intermediate conclusions, and thus destroying the specific character of the process.

And just as the ordinary universal syllogism can be reduced to $A_,A_,A_,$, so the universal sorites can always be reduced to a chain of $A_,$. Thus A'E'E$_,$A'E' or

$$Q)P+q.r+R.S+T)S+t.u=p.u$$
$$\text{is} \quad u)T+T)S+S)r+r)Q+Q)P=u)P$$

WILLIAM OF OCKHAM
(1290-1349)

An English Franciscan, studied at Oxford and taught there for several years. He was jailed at Avignon following an accusation of heresy in 1324 but escaped from jail four years later and took refuge with the Emperor. He died while attempting a reconciliation with the Pope. Ockham was primarily a logician. The sharpness of his thought process is commemorated by the name of "Ockham's razor", a device for pruning unnecessary concepts. His philosophy was "terminalist" conccptualism. According to Ockham only individual things and not universals have reality. Universals are mere signs or abstractions of the mind. Logic therefore is concerned with signs not realities. Intuition is our immediate experience of the individual and thus real knowledge.

Main Works:

> Quodlibeta septem; Quaestiones in octo libros Physicorum; Summulae in libros Physicorum; Tractatus logicae or Summa Totius Logicae; Super Quattuor Libros Sententiarum; De Sacramento Altaris; Opus nonaginta dierum; Dialogus.

Problems of Epistemology

Since a general knowledge of terms is not sufficient for the logician, it is necessary for him to know terms in greater detail. Therefore, after the treatment of the general divisions of terms, we must proceed to certain questions involved in some of those divisions.

From: *Summa Totius Logicae.*

First of all we must discuss terms of second intention: secondly, terms of first intention. Now it has been stated that terms of second intention are such as *universal, genus, species,* and so on. On this account we must speak about those that are posited as the five universals. First, however, we must speak of the general term *universal,* which is predicated of every universal, and of the expression *singular,* opposed to it.

First we must understand that *singular* is taken in two senses. In one sense, the term *singular* denotes all that is one thing and not many things. And in that sense those who maintain that a universal is a certain mental quality predicable of many things; not, however, representing itself but those many things, must say that every universal is truly and really singular: because just as every word, however general it may be conventionally, is truly and really singular and numerically one, since it is one and not many, so the mental purpose signifying many things externally is truly and really singular and numerically one, since it is one thing and not many, although it signifies many things.

In another way the name *singular* is taken for that which is one and not many, nor is it by nature a sign of plurality. And with this acceptance of *singular,* no universal is singular, because every universal is by nature predicated of many things. Hence, calling universal something that is not numerically one, an acceptation that many attribute to universal, I assert that nothing is universal, unless perhaps you misuse this expression by saying that people are one universal, because they are not one but many: but that would be puerile.

It must therefore be asserted that every universal is one singular thing, and hence there is no universal except through signification, because it is a sign of many things. And it is this that Avicenna asserts in the fifth book of the *Metaphysics:* One form in the intellect refers to a multitude, and in this respect is universal, since the universal is an intention in the intellect, whose relationship does not vary, whatever you take. And he proceeds: Although this form is universal in relation to individuals, it is yet singular in relation to the mind in which it is impressed: for it is one of the forms that are in the intellect. He means that the universal is one singular intention of the mind itself, naturally predicated of many things. Thus, because of this fact, that it is naturally predicated of many things representing not itself but those many things, it is termed a universal. But on account of the fact that it is a form existing really in the intellect, it is said to be singular. And this singular taken in the first sense is predicated of the universal, but not, however, when taken in the second sense. Just as we say that the sun is a universal cause, and yet it is truly a particular and singular thing, and consequently it is truly a singular and particular cause. For the sun is said to be a universal cause, because it is a cause of many things, namely, of all those generative and corruptible things below. But it is termed a particular cause, because it is one cause and not many causes. Thus the intention of the mind is called universal, because it is a sign predicable of many things: but it is also termed singular, because it is one thing and not many things.

However, it must be realized that the universal is two-fold. One kind is naturally universal, being a sign naturally predicable of many things: just as, comparatively speaking, smoke naturally signifies fire, and a groan a sick man's pain, and laughter an inner joy. And such a universal is nothing but the intention of the mind. Thus no substance outside the mind and no accident outside the mind is such a universal. And of such a universal I shall speak in the following chapters.

There is another universal by convention. And thus the utterance of a word, which is truly a single quality, is universal: for it is a conventional sign established to signify many things. Hence, just as a word is called common, so it can be called universal. But it does not have this character from its nature, but only from established convention.

And as it is not sufficient to state this proof without evident reasoning, I shall on this account adduce some reasons for what has previously been said, and I shall confirm them by authoritative demonstration.

For, that no universal is a substance existing outside the mind, can be proved by evidence.

First of all, as follows: No universal is a substance singular and numerically one. For if it were said to be so, it would follow that Socrates is a universal, because there is no greater reason why one universal should be a singular substance rather than another universal. Therefore no singular substance is a universal, but every substance is numerically one and singular. Because every substance is either one thing and not many things, or it is many things. If it is one thing and not many things, it is numerically one: for this is generally called numerically one. But if a substance is many things, it is either many singular things or many universal things. If the first hypothesis is granted, it follows that a substance would be many singular substances, and consequently, by the same reasoning, some substance would be many men: and then, although a universal would be distinguished from one particular, it would not however be distinguished from a number of particulars. But if a substance were many universal things, I take one of these universal things and I ask: Is it many things or one thing and not many things? If the second view is accepted, it follows that it is singular. If the first view is conceded, I ask: Is it many singular things or many universal things? And so there will be a continuity to infinity, or it will be decided that no substance is universal in such a manner as not to be singular. From this argument the conclusion remains that no substance is universal.

Similarly, if a universal were one substance existing in singular substances and distinct from them, it would follow that it could exist without them, because everything naturally anterior to another thing can exist without it by the divine power: but this is an absurd conclusion.

Again, if that opinion were true, no individual could be created, but something of the individual would pre-exist, because it would not receive its entirety from nothing, if the universal, that is in it, existed anteriorly in another thing. For the same reason, it would follow that God could not destroy one individual of a substance without destroying the other individuals. Because if he annihilated an individual, he would destroy the entirety that is the essence of the individual, and consequently he would destroy that universal that is in it and in others: and consequently the other individuals would not remain, since they could not remain without a part of themselves, such as the universal is assumed to be.

Further, such a universal could not be assumed as something totally outside the essence of an individual: therefore it would be of the essence of the individual, and consequently the individual would be composed of universals and so the individual would not be more singular than universal.

Likewise, it follows that something of the essence of Christ would be miserable and damned, because that common nature existing really in Christ and in the damned would be damned, because it exists in Judas. But this is absurd.

Many other reasons could be adduced that I omit for the sake of brevity. And I confirm the same conclusion by authorities.

First, by Aristotle in Book I of the *Metaphysics,* where he raises a question drawn from his text, whether the universal is a substance, and demonstrates that no universal is a substance. Hence he asserts: It is impossible for anything predicated universally to be a substance.

Again, in Book 10 of the *Metaphysics* he declares: So, if it is possible for no universal to be a substance, as has been stated in our discussions on substance and being, this universal itself cannot be a substance in so far as some singular thing apart from many things.

From these statements it is clear that according to Aristotle's intention no universal is a substance, although it represents substances.

Again, the Commentator of Book 7 of the *Metaphysics,* comment 44, says: In the individual there is no other substance but the matter and particular form of which it is composed.

Further, in the same writer, comment 45: Let us say, then, that it is impossible that any of those things that are called universals should be a substance of some thing, although they clarify the substance of things.

Again, similarly in comment 47: It is impossible that they are parts of substances that exist through themselves.

Further, in Book 8 of the *Metaphysics*, comment 2: The universal is not a substance or a genus.

Again, in Book 10 of the *Metaphysics*, comment 6: Since the universals are not substances, it is manifest that the common being is not a substance extrinsic to the mind.

From the above quoted authorities and many others it can be deduced that no universal is a substance, in whatever way it is considered. Hence consideration of the intellect does not make something into a substance or not, although the signification of the term makes the name substance predicated or not of itself, not for itself. Just as, if the term dog in the proposition: A dog is an animal, should stand for a barking animal, the proposition is true: if it stands for a star in the heavens, it is false. But that the same thing should be a substance on account of one consideration, and not a substance on account of another consideration, is impossible.

And hence it must be granted simply that no universal is a substance, in whatever way it is considered. But every universal is an intention of the mind, that according to one probable opinion does not differ from the act of understanding. Hence they say that the intellect, whereby I understand a man, is a natural sign of man, as natural as a groan is a sign of sickness or sadness or pain, and it is such a sign as may stand for men in mental propositions, just as a word can stand for things in vocal propositions.

For, that the universal is an intention of the mind is sufficiently expressed by Avicenna, in Book 5 of the *Metaphysics*, where he says: I assert therefore that the universal is so termed in three ways. It is called universal according to what is predicated in act of many, as, man; and a universal is called an intention that it is possible to predicate of many. And he proceeds:

A universal is also called an intention when there is nothing to prevent its being thought as predicated of many things.

From these and many other arguments it is evident that the universal is an intention of the mind, naturally predicated of many things. This may also be confirmed by reason. For every universal by general consensus is predicable of many things, but only a mental intention or a conventional sign, not a substance, is naturally predicated. Therefore only a mental intention or a conventional sign is universal. But now I do not use *universal* as a conventional sign, but as that which is naturally universal. For it is evident that a substance is not naturally predicated. Because if it were so, it would follow that a proposition would be composed of particular substances and consequently the subject would be in Rome and the predicate in England: which is absurd.

Again, there is no proposition except in the mind or in speech or in writing. Therefore its parts exist only in the mind or in speech or in writing. But there are no particular substances of this kind. It is therefore an established fact that no proposition can be composed of substances. But a proposition is composed of universals. Therefore universals are not substances in any sense.

Although it is evident to many that a universal is not a substance existing outside the mind in individuals and really distinct from them, still it seems to some that a universal is in some sense outside the mind in individuals, not indeed really distinct from them, but only formally so. Hence they say that in Socrates there is human nature, which is contracted to Socrates by an individual differentia that is distinct from that nature not really but formally. Hence they are not two things, yet one is not formally the other.

But this opinion seems to me altogether improbable.

In the first place, because in creatures there can never be any distinction whatever outside the mind, except where there are distinct things. If therefore between this nature and this differentia there is any distinction whatever, it is necessary that they should be really distinct things. I prove this assumption in a syllogistic form, as follows: This nature is not formally distinct from its own nature. This individual differentia is formally distinct from this nature. Therefore this individual is not this nature.

Again, the same thing is not common and proper. But according to them the individual differentia is proper, while the universal is common. Therefore universals and individual differentiae are not the same things.

Again, opposites cannot harmonize with the same created thing. But common and proper are opposites. Therefore the same thing is not common and proper: but this would follow, if the individual differentia and common nature were the same thing.

Further, if common nature were really the same as an individual differentia, then there would be as many common natures really as there are individual differentiae, and consequently none of them would be common, but anyone whatever would be the property of a differentia with which it is really identical.

Furthermore, whatever thing is distinguished from anything else is distinguished of itself or by something intrinsic to itself. But the humanity of Socrates is one thing, and the humanity of Plato another thing. Therefore they are of themselves distinguished, and not, therefore, through the addition of differences.

Again, according to Aristotle's opinion, whatever things differ in species, differ in number. But a man's nature and a donkey's nature are specifically distinguished of themselves. Therefore they are of themselves numerically distinguished. Therefore each nature is of itself numerically one.

Further, that which through no power can coexist with many things, is through no power predicable of many things. But such a nature, if it is really the same as the individual differentia, can through no power belong to many things: because it can in no way belong to another individual. Therefore through no power can it be predicable of many things, and consequently through no power can it be universal.

Again, I take this individual differentia and the nature that it contracts, and I ask: Is the distinction between them greater than between two individuals, or smaller? Not greater, because they do not really differ, while individuals do really differ. Nor smaller, because then they would be of the same concept, just as two individuals are of the same concept: and consequently, if one is of itself numerically one, the other one will be of itself also numerically one.

Further, I ask: Is the nature the individual difference, or not? If it is so, I argue syllogistically as follows: This individual differentia is nature. Therefore the nature is proper and not common: which was the object of proof. Similarly, I argue syllogistically as follows: This individual differentia is proper and not common. This individual differentia is the nature. Therefore the nature is proper and not common: which was the object of proof. Similarly, I argue syllogistically as follows: This individual differentia is not formally distinct from the individual differentia. This individual differentia is the nature. Therefore the nature is not distinct formally from the individual differentia. But if it is posited that this individual differentia is not the nature, the object of proof is attained, for it follows: The individual differentia is not the nature: therefore the individual differentia is not really the nature, because from the opposite of the consequent the opposite of the antecedent follows by this argument: The individual differentia is really the nature. Therefore the individual is the nature. The deduction is clear, because from a determinable taken with a determination that does not remove or diminish it to a determinable taken by itself, the conclusion is valid. But *really* is not a removing or diminishing determination. It follows therefore: The individual differentia is really the nature: therefore the individual differentia is the nature.

It must therefore be asserted that in creatures there is no such formal distinction. But whatever elements in creatures are distinct, are really distinct and are distinct things, if each of two things is a true thing. Hence, just as in creatures such modes of argument as the following must never be denied: This is A, this is B: therefore B is A. Or: This is not A, this is B: therefore B is not A, so in the case of creatures it must never be denied that, whenever contradictions are true of some things, they are distinct things, unless some determination or some syncategorematic expression is the cause of such a verification: which must not be assumed in our proposed argument.

And so we must say with the philosophers that in a particular substance nothing is totally substantial except the particular form and the particular matter or some composite of these. And hence it must not be imagined that in Socrates there is humanity or human nature distinct from Socrates in any way, to which is added an individual differentia contracting this nature. But whatever imaginable substantial element exists in Socrates is either a particular matter or a particular form or something compounded of both. And thus every essence and quiddity and whatever is substance, if it is really extrinsic to the mind, is either simply and absolutely matter or form or a composition of both, or a separate immaterial substance, according to the doctrine of the Peripatetics.

PARMENIDES

(6th century B.C.)

Born at Elea in southern Italy. He taught the unity and indivisibility of being. "Only being is, nonbeing is not; all becoming is unreal, creating opinions but not truth."

Main Works:
Nature; On Truth.

————

The Two Ways of Search

Thou shalt inquire into everything: both the motionless heart of well-rounded Truth, and also the opinions of mortals, in which there is no true reliability. But nevertheless thou shalt learn these things (*opinions*) also—how one should go through all the things-that-seem, without exception, and test them.

Come, I will tell you—and you must accept my word when you have heard it—the ways of inquiry which alone are to be thought: the one that IT IS, and it is not possible for IT NOT TO BE, is the way of credibility, for it follows Truth; the other, that IT IS NOT TO BE: this I tell you is a path that cannot be explored; for you could neither recognize that which is NOT, nor express it.

For it is the same thing to think and to be.

Observe nevertheless how things absent are securely present to the mind; for it will not sever Being from its connection with

————

From: *On Truth.*

Being, whether it is scattered everywhere utterly throughout the universe, or whether it is collected together.

It is all the same to me from what point I begin, for I shall return again to this same point.

One should both say and think that Being Is; for To Be is possible, and Nothingness is not possible. This I command you to consider; for from the latter way of search first of all I debar you. But next I debar you from that way along which wander mortals knowing nothing, two-headed, for perplexity in their bosoms steers their intelligence astray, and they are carried along as deaf as they are blind, amazed, uncritical hordes, by whom To Be and Not To Be are regarded as the same and not the same, and (*for whom*) in everything there is a way of opposing stress.

For this (*view*) can never predominate, that That Which Is Not exists. You must debar your thought from this way of search, nor let ordinary experience in its variety force you along this way (*namely, that of allowing*) the eye, sightless as it is, and the ear, full of sound, and the tongue, to rule; but (*you must*) judge by means of the Reason (*Logos*) the much contested proof which is expounded by me.

There is only one other description of the way remaining, (*namely*), that (*What Is*) Is. To this way there are very many signposts: that Being has no coming-into-being and no destruction, for it is whole of limb, without motion, and without end. And it never Was, nor Will Be, because it Is now, a Whole all together, One, continuous; for what creation of it will you look for? How, whence (*could it have*) sprung? Nor shall I allow you to speak or think of it as springing from Not-Being; for it is neither expressible nor thinkable that What-Is-Not Is. Also, what necessity impelled it, if it did spring from Nothing, to be produced later or earlier? Thus it must Be absolutely, or not at all. Nor will the force of credibility ever admit that anything should come into being, beside Being itself, out of Not-Being. So far as that is concerned, Justice has never released (*Being*) in its fetters and set it free either to come into being or to perish, but holds it fast. The decision on these matters depends on the following: IT IS, OR IT IS NOT. It is therefore decided—as is inevitable—(*that one must*) ignore the way as unthinkable and inexpressible (for it is no true way) and take the other as the way of Being and Reality. How could Being perish? How could it come into being? If it came into being, it Is Not; and so too if it is about-to-be at some future time. Thus Coming-into-Being is quenched, and Destruction also into the unseen.

Nor is Being divisible, since it is all alike. Nor is there anything (*here or*) there which could prevent it from holding together, nor any lesser thing, but all is full of Being. Therefore it is altogether continuous; for Being is close to Being.

But it is motionless in the limits of mighty bonds, without beginning, without cease, since Becoming and Destruction have been driven very far away, and true conviction has rejected them. And remaining the same in the same place, it rests by itself and thus remains there fixed; for powerful Necessity holds it in the bonds of a Limit, which constrains it round about, because it is decreed by divine law that Being shall not be without boundary. For it is not lacking; but if it were (*spatially infinite*), it would lack everything.

To think is the same as the thought that It Is; for you will not find thinking without Being, in (*regard to*) which there is an expression. For nothing else either is or shall be except Being, since Fate has tied it down to be a whole and motionless; therefore all things that mortals have established, believing in their truth, are just a name: Becoming and Perishing, Being and Not-Being, and Change of position, and alteration of bright color.

But since there is a (*spatial*) Limit, it is complete on every side, like the mass of a well-rounded sphere, equally balanced from its center in every direction; for it is not bound to be at all either greater or less in this direction or that; nor is there Not-Being which could check it from reaching to the same point, nor is it possible for Being to be more in this direction, less in that, than Being, because it is an inviolate whole. For, in all directions equal to itself, it reaches its limits uniformly.

At this point I cease my reliable theory (*Logos*) and thought, concerning Truth; from here onwards you must learn the opinions of mortals, listening to the deceptive order of my words.

They have established (*the custom of*) naming two forms, one of which ought not to be (*mentioned*): that is where they have gone astray. They have distinguished them as opposite in form, and have marked them off from another by giving them different signs: on one side the flaming fire in the heavens, mild, very light (*in weight*), the same as itself in every direction, and not the same as the other. This (*other*) also is by itself and opposite: dark Night, a dense and heavy body. This world-order I describe to you with all its phenomena, in order that no intellect of mortal men may outstrip you.

But since all things are named Light and Night, and names have been given to each class of things according to the power of one or the other (*Light or Night*), everything is full equally of Light and invisible Night, as both are equal, because to neither of them belongs any share (of the other).

You shall know the nature of the heavens, and all the signs in the heavens, and the destructive works of the pure bright torch of the sun, and whence they came into being. And you shall learn of the wandering works of the round-faced moon, and its nature; and you shall know also the surrounding heaven, whence it sprang and how Necessity brought and constrained it to hold the limits of the stars.

BLAISE PASCAL
(1623-1662)

A philosopher and mathematician who, with Descartes, inaugurated
the modern period of French thought. Pascal started as a rationalist.
He astonished his contemporaries by his geometric and algebraic
discoveries. He early underwent a crisis which turned him towards
Jansenism, of which his beloved sister was an ardent adherent. This
got him into trouble with the Jesuits, whom he attacked in turn. Pascal
became more and more theological in his interests, outlined "the logic
of the human heart" and stressed "the spirit of subtlety" against
Descartes' "spirit of geometry." He maintained throughout his interest
in the mechanics of thought.

Main Works:
   Lettres provinciales; L'art de penser; Pensées sur la religion.

Disproportions

This is where our intuitive knowledge leads us. If it be not
true, there is no truth in man; and if it be, he finds therein a
great reason for humiliation, because he must abase himself in
one way or another. And since he cannot exist without such
knowledge, I wish that before entering on deeper researches
into nature he would consider her seriously and at leisure, that
he would examine himself also, and knowing what proportion
there is . . . Let man then contemplate the whole realm of nature in her full and exalted majesty, and turn his eyes from the

---

From: *Les Pensées.*

low objects which hem him round; let him observe that brilliant light set like an eternal lamp to illumine the universe, let the earth appear to him a point in comparison with the vast circle described by the sun, and let him see with amazement that even this vast circle is itself but a fine point in regard to that described by the stars revolving in the firmament. If our view be arrested there, let imagination pass beyond, and it will sooner exhaust the power of thinking than nature that of giving scope for thought. The whole visible world is but an imperceptible speck in the ample bosom of nature. No idea approaches it. We may swell our conceptions beyond all imaginable space, yet bring forth only atoms in comparison with the reality of things. It is an infinite sphere, the center of which is everywhere, the circumference nowhere. It is, in short, the greatest sensible mark of the almighty power of God, that imagination loses itself in that thought.

Then, returning to himself, let man consider his own being compared with all that is; let him regard himself as wandering in this remote province of nature; and from the little dungeon in which he finds himself lodged, I mean the universe, let him learn to set a true value on the earth, on its kingdoms, its cities, and on himself.

What is a man in the infinite? But to show him another prodigy no less astonishing, let him examine the most delicate things he knows. Let him take a mite which in its minute body presents him with parts incomparably more minute; limbs with their joints, veins in the limbs, blood in the veins, humors in the blood, drops in the humors, vapors in the drops; let him, again, dividing these last, exhaust his power of thought; let the last point at which he arrives be that of which we speak, and he will perhaps think that here is the extremest diminutive in nature. Then I will open before him therein a new abyss. I will paint for him not only the visible universe, but all that he can conceive of nature's immensity in the enclosure of this diminished atom. Let him therein see an infinity of universes of which each has its firmament, its planets, its earth, in the same proportion as in the visible world; in each earth animals, and at the last the mites, in which he will come upon all that was in the first, and still find in these other the same without end and without cessation; let him lose himself in wonders as astonishing in their minuteness as the others in their immensity; for who will not be amazed at seeing that our body, which before was imperceptible in the universe, itself imperceptible in the bosom of the whole, is now a colossus, a world, a whole, in regard to the nothingness to which we cannot attain.

Whoso takes this survey of himself will be terrified at the thought that he is upheld in the material being, given him by nature, between these two abysses of the infinite and nothing, he will tremble at the sight of these marvels; and I think that as his curiosity changes into wonder, he will be more disposed to contemplate them in silence than to search into them with presumption.

For after all what is man in nature? A nothing in regard to the infinite, a whole in regard to nothing, a mean between nothing and the whole; infinitely removed from understanding either extreme. The end of things and their beginnings are invincibly hidden from him in impenetrable secrecy, he is equally incapable of seeing the nothing whence he was taken, and the infinite in which he is engulfed.

What shall he do then, but discern somewhat of the middle of things in an eternal despair of knowing either their beginning or their end? All things arise from nothing, and tend towards the infinite. Who can follow their marvellous course? The author of these wonders can understand them, and none but he.

Of these two infinites in nature, the infinitely great and the infinitely little, man can more easily conceive the great.

Because they have not considered these infinites, men have rashly plunged into the research of nature, as though they bore some proportion to her.

It is strange that they have wished to understand the origin of all that is, and thence to attain to the knowledge of the whole, with a presumption as infinite as their object. For there is no doubt that such a design cannot be formed without presumption or without a capacity as infinite as nature.

If we are well informed, we understand that nature having graven her own image and that of her author on all things, they are almost all partakers of her double infinity. Thus we see that all the sciences are infinite in the extent of their researches, for none can doubt that geometry, for instance, has an infinite infinity of problems to propose. They are also infinite in the number and in the nicety of their premises, for it is evident that those which are finally proposed are not self-supporting, but are based on others, which again having others as their support have no finality.

But we make some apparently final to the reason, just as in regard to material things we call that an indivisible point beyond which our senses can no longer perceive anything, though by its nature this also is infinitely divisible.

Of these two scientific infinities, that of greatness is the most obvious to the senses, and therefore a few persons have made pretensions to universal knowledge. "I will discourse of the all," said Democritus.

But beyond the fact that it is a small thing to speak of it simply, without proving and knowing, it is nevertheless impossible to do so, the infinite multitude of things being so hidden, that all we can express by word or thought is but an invisible trace of them. Hence it is plain how foolish, vain, and ignorant is that title of some books: *De omni scibili.*

But the infinitely little is far less evident. Philosophers have much more frequently asserted they have attained it, yet in that very point they have all stumbled. This has given occasion to such common titles as *The Origin of Creation, The Principles of Philosophy,* and the like, as presumptuous in fact, though not in appearance as that dazzling one, *De omni scibili.*

We naturally think that we can more easily reach the center of things than embrace their circumference. The visible bulk of the world visibly exceeds us, but as we exceed little things, we think ourselves more capable of possessing them. Yet we need no less capacity to attain the nothing than the whole. Infinite capacity is needed for both, and it seems to me that whoever shall have understood the ultimate principles of existence might also attain to the knowledge of the infinite. The one depends on the other, and leads to the other. Extremes meet and reunite by virtue of their distance, to find each other in God, and in God alone.

Let us then know our limits; we are something, but we are not all. What existence we have conceals from us the knowledge of first principles which spring from the nothing, while the pettiness of that existence hides from us the sight of the infinite.

In the order of intelligible things our intelligence holds the same position as our body in the vast extent of nature.

Restricted in every way, this middle state between two extremes is common to all our weaknesses.

Our senses can perceive no extreme. Too much noise deafens us, excess of light blinds us, too great distance or nearness equally interferes with our vision, prolixity or brevity equally obscures a discourse, too much truth overwhelms us. I know even those who cannot understand that if four be taken from nothing nothing remains. First principles are too plain for us, superfluous pleasure troubles us. Too many concords are unpleasing in music, and too many benefits annoy, we wish to have wherewithal to overpay our debt. Beneficia eo usque laeta sunt dum videntur exsolvi posse; ubi multum antevenere pro gratia odium redditur.

We feel neither extreme heat nor extreme cold. Qualities in excess are inimical to us and not apparent to the senses, we do not feel but are passive under them. The weakness of youth and age equally hinders the mind, as also too much and too little teaching.

In a word, all extremes are for us as though they were not; and we are not, in regard to them; they escape us, or we them.

This is our true state; this is what renders us incapable both of certain knowledge and of absolute ignorance. We sail on a vast expanse, ever uncertain, ever drifting, hurried from one to the other goal. If we think to attach ourselves firmly to any point, it totters and fails us; if we follow, it eludes our grasp, and flies us, vanishing for ever. Nothing stays for us. This is our natural condition, yet always the most contrary to our inclination; we burn with desire to find a steadfast place and an ultimate fixed basis whereon we may build a tower to reach the infinite. But our whole foundation breaks up, and earth opens to the abysses.

We may not then look for certainty or stability. Our reason is always deceived by changing shows, nothing can fix the finite between the two infinites, which at once enclose and fly from it.

If this be once well understood I think that we shall rest, each in the state wherein nature has placed him. This element which falls to us as our lot being always distant from either extreme, it matters not that a man should have a trifle more knowledge of the universe. If he has it, he but begins a little higher. He is always infinitely distant from the end, and the duration of our life is infinitely removed from eternity, even if it lasts ten years longer.

In regard to these infinities all finites are equal, and I see not why we should fix our imagination on one more than on another. The only comparison which we can make of ourselves to the finite troubles us.

Were man to begin with the study of himself, he would see how incapable he is of proceeding further. How can a part know the whole? But he may perhaps aspire to know at least the parts with which he has proportionate relation. But the parts of the world are so linked and related, that I think it impossible to know one without another, or without the whole.

Man, for instance, is related to all that he knows. He needs place therein to abide, time through which to exist, motion in order to live; he needs constituent elements, warmth and food to nourish him, air to breathe. He sees light, he feels bodies, he contracts an alliance with all that is.

To know man then it is necessary to understand how it comes that he needs air to breathe, and to know the air we must understand how it has relation to the life of man, etc.

Flame cannot exist without air, therefore to know one we must know the other.

All that exists then is both cause and effect, dependent and supporting, mediate and immediate, and all is held together by a natural though imperceptible bond, which unites things most distant and most different. I hold it impossible to know the parts without knowing the whole, or to know the whole without knowing the parts in detail.

I hold it impossible to know one alone without all the others, that is to say impossible purely and absolutely.

The eternity of things in themselves or in God must also confound our brief duration. The fixed and constant immobility of Nature in comparison with the continual changes which take place in us must have the same effect.

And what completes our inability to know things is that they are in their essence simple, whereas we are composed of two opposite natures differing in kind, soul and body. For it is impossible that our reasoning part should be other than spiritual; and should any allege that we are simply material, this would far more exclude us from the knowledge of things, since it is an inconceivable paradox to affirm that matter can know itself, and it is not possible for us to know how it should know itself.

So, were we simply material, we could know nothing whatever, and if we are composed of spirit and matter we cannot perfectly know what is simple, whether it be spiritual or material. For how should we know matter distinctly, since our being, which acts on this knowledge, is partly spiritual, and how should we know spiritual substances clearly since we have a body which weights us, and drags us down to earth.

Moreover what completes our inability is the simplicity of things compared with our double and complex nature. To dispute this point were an invincible absurdity, for it is as absurd as impious to deny that man is composed of two parts, differing in their nature, soul and body. This renders us unable to know all things; for if this complexity be denied, and it be asserted that we are entirely material, it is plain that matter is incapable of knowing matter. Nothing is more impossible than this.

Let us conceive that almost all philosophers have confounded us out of proportion.

Hence it comes that almost all philosophers have confounded different ideas, and speak of material things in spiritual phrase, and of spiritual things in material phrase. For they say boldly that bodies have a tendency to fall, that they seek after their center, that they fly from destruction, that they fear a void, that they have inclinations, sympathies, antipathies; and all of these are spiritual qualities. Again, in speaking of spirits, they conceive of them as in a given spot, or as moving from place to place; qualities which belong to matter alone.

Instead of receiving the ideas of these things simply, we color them with our own qualities, and stamp with our complex being all the simple things which we contemplate.

Who would not think, when we declare that all that is consists of mind and matter, that we really understand this combination? Yet it is the one thing we least understand. Man is to himself the most marvelous object in Nature, for he cannot conceive what matter is, still less what is mind, and less than all how a material body should be united to a mind. This is the crown of all his difficulties, yet it is his very being: Modus quo corporibus adhaeret spiritus comprehendi ab homine non potest et hoc tamen homo est.

These are some of the causes which render man so totally unable to know nature. For nature has a two-fold infinity, he is finite and limited. Nature is permanent, and continues in one stay; he is fleeting and mortal. All things fail and change each instant, he sees them only as they pass, they have their beginning and end, he conceives neither the one nor the other. They are simple, he is composed of two different natures. And to complete the proof of our weakness, I will finish by this reflection on our natural condition. In a word, to complete the proof of our weakness, I will end with these two considerations.

The nature of man may be considered in two ways, one according to its end, and then it is great and incomparable; the other according to popular opinion, as we judge of the nature of a horse or a dog, by popular opinion which discerns in it the power of speed, et animum arcendi; and then man is abject and vile. These are the two ways which make us judge of it so differently and which cause such disputes among philosophers.

For one denies the supposition of the other; one says. *He was not born for such an end, for all his actions are repugnant to it;* the other says, *He cannot gain his end when he commits base deeds.*

Two things instruct man about his whole nature, instinct and experience.

CHARLES SANDERS PEIRCE
(1839-1914)

Lecturing occasionally at Harvard and other universities, Peirce preferred government service. He first employed the term Pragmatism in a paper on logic, the gateway to philosophy. Peirce was first to propose that meaning as well as verity of an idea must be determined by its pragmatic consequences. His many philosophical papers and fragments have greatly influenced William James, Josiah Royce, John Dewey and others.

Main Works:

> Studies in Logic; Philosophical Lectures; Chance, Love and Logic.

Abduction and Induction

I

All our knowledge may be said to rest upon *observed facts*. It is true that there are psychological states which antecede our observing facts as such. Thus, it is a fact that I see an inkstand before me; but before I can say that I am obliged to have impressions of sense into which no idea of an inkstand, or of any separate object, or of an "I," or of seeing, enter at all; and it is true that my judging that I see an inkstand before me is the product of mental operations upon these impressions of sense. But it is only when the cognition has become worked up into a proposition, or judgment of a fact, that I can exercise any direct control over the process; and it is idle to discuss the "le-

---

From: *Philosophical Lectures.*

gitimacy" of that which cannot be controlled. Observations of fact have, therefore, too be accepted as they occur.

But observed facts relate exclusively to the particular circumstances that happened to exist when they were observed. They do not relate to any future occasions upon which we may be in doubt how we ought to act. They, therefore, do not, in themselves, contain any practical knowledge.

Such knowledge must involve additions to the facts observed. The making of those additions is an operation which we can control; and it is evidently a process during which error is liable to creep in.

Any proposition added to observed facts, tending to make them applicable in any way to other circumstances than those under which they were observed, may be called a hypothesis. A hypothesis ought, at first, to be entertained interrogatively. Thereupon, it ought to be tested by experiment so far as practicable. There are two distinct processes, both of which may be performed rightly or wrongly. We may go wrong and be wasting time in so much as entertaining a hypothesis, even as a question. That is a subject for criticism in every case. There are some hypotheses which are of such a nature that they never can be tested at all. Whether such hypotheses ought to be entertained at all, and if so in what sense, is a serious question; but it hardly concerns our present inquiry. The hypotheses with which we shall have in this paper to deal are capable of being put to the test. How this is to be done is a question of extreme importance; but my intention is to consider it only in a very cursory manner, at present. There are, moreover, many hypotheses in regard to which knowledge already in our possession may, at once, quite justifiably either raise them to the rank of opinions, or even positive beliefs, or cause their immediate rejection. This also is a matter to be considered. But it is the first process, that of entertaining the question, which will here be of foremost importance.

Before we go further, let us get the points stated above quite clear. By a *hypothesis*, I mean, not merely a supposition about an observed object, as when I suppose that a man is a Catholic priest because that would explain his dress, expression of countenance, and bearing, but also any other supposed truth from which would result such facts as have been observed, as when van't Hoff, having remarked that the osmotic pressure of one per cent solutions of a number of chemical substances was inversely proportional to their atomic weights, thought that perhaps the same relation would be found to exist between the same properties of any other chemical substance. The first starting of a hypothesis and the entertaining of it, whether as a simple interrogation or with any degree of confidence, is an inferential step which I propose to call *abduction* [or *retroduction*]. This will include a preference for any one hypothesis over others which would equally explain the facts, so long as this preference is not based upon any previous knowledge bearing upon the truth of the hypotheses, nor on any testing of any of the hypotheses, after having admitted them on probation. I call all such inference by the peculiar name, *abduction,* because its legitimacy depends upon altogether different principles from those of other kinds of inference.

Long before I first classed abduction as an inference it was recognized by logicians that the operation of adopting an explanatory hypothesis—which is just what abduction is—was subject to certain conditions. Namely, the hypothesis cannot be admitted, even as a hypothesis, unless it be supposed that it would account for the facts or some of them. The form of inference, therefore, is this:

The surprising fact, C, is observed;
But if A were true, C would be a matter of course,
Hence, there is reason to suspect that A is true.

Thus, A cannot be abductively inferred, or if you prefer the expression, cannot be abductively conjectured until its entire content is already present in the premiss, "If A were true, C would be a matter of course."

The operation of testing a hypothesis by experiment, which consists in remarking that, if it is true, observations made under certain conditions ought to have certain results, and then causing those conditions to be fulfilled, and noting the results, and, if they are favorable, extending a certain confidence to the hypothesis, I call *induction*. For example, suppose that I have been led to surmise that among our colored population there is a greater tendency to female births than among our whites. I say, if that be so, the last census must show it. I examine the last census report and find that, sure enough, there was a somewhat greater proportion of female births among colored births than among white births in that census year. To accord a certain faith to my hypothesis on that account is legitimate. It is a strong induction. I have taken all the births of that year as a sample of all the births of years in general, so long as general conditions remain as they were then. It is a very large sample, quite unnecessarily so, were it not that the excess of the one ratio over the other is quite small. All induction whatever may be regarded as the inference that throughout a whole class a ratio will have about the same value that it has in a random sample of that class, provided the nature of the ratio for which the sample is to be examined is specified (or virtually specified) in advance of the examination. So long as the class consists of units, and the ratio in question is a ratio between counts of occurrences, induction is a comparatively simple affair. But suppose we wish to test the hypothesis that a man is a Catholic priest, that is, has all the characters that are common to Catholic priests and peculiar to them. Now characters are not units, nor do they consist of units, nor can they be counted, in such a sense that one count is right and every other wrong. Characters have to be estimated according to their significance. The consequence is that there will be a certain element of guess-work in such an induction; so that I call it an *abductory induction*. I might say to myself, let me think of some other character that belongs to Catholic priests, beside those that I have remarked in this man, a character which I can ascertain whether he possesses or not.

All Catholic priests are more or less familiar with Latin pronounced in the Italian manner. If, then, this man is a Catholic priest, and I make some remark in Latin which a person not accustomed to the Italian pronunciation would not at once understand, and I pronounce it in that way, then if that man is a Catholic priest he will be so surprised that he cannot but betray his understanding of it. I make such a remark; and I notice that he does understand it. Bu how much weight am I to attach to that test? After all, it does not touch an essential characteristic of a priest or even of a Catholic. It must be acknowledged that it is but a weak confirmation, and all the more so, because it is quite uncertain how much weight should be attached to it. Nevertheless, it does and ought to incline me to believe that the man is a Catholic priest. It is an induction, because it is a test of the hypothesis by means of a prediction, which has been verified. But it is only an abductory induction, because it was a sampling of the characters of priests to see what proportion of them this man possessed, when characters cannot be counted, nor even weighed, except by guess-work. It also partakes of the nature of abduction in involving an original suggestion; while typical induction has no originality in it, but only tests a suggestion already made.

In induction, it is not the fact predicated that in any degree necessitates the truth of the hypothesis or even renders it probable. It is the fact that it has been predicted successfully and that it is a haphazard specimen of all the predictions which might be based on the hypothesis and which constitutes its practical truth. But it frequently happens that there are facts which, merely as facts, apart from the manner in which they have presented themselves, necessitate the truth, or the falsity, or the probability in some definite degree, of the hypothesis. For example, suppose the hypothesis to be that a man believes in the infallibility of the Pope. Then, if we ascertain in any way that he believes in the immaculate conception, in the confessional, and in the prayers for the dead, or on the other hand that he disbelieves all or some of these things, either fact will be almost decisive of the truth or falsity of the proposition. Such inference is *deduction*. So if we ascertain that the man in question is a violent partisan in politics and in many other subjects. If, then, we find that he has given money toward a Catholic institution, we may fairly reason that such a man would not do that unless he believed in the Pope's infallibility. Or again, we might learn that he is one of five brothers whose opinions are identical on almost all subjects. If, then, we find that the other four all believe in the Pope's infallibility or all disbelieve it, this will affect our confidence in the hypothesis. This consideration will be strengthened by our general experience that while different members of a large family usually differ about most subjects, yet it mostly happens that they are either all Catholics or all Protestants. Those are four different varieties of deductive considerations which may legitimately influence our belief in a hypothesis.

These distinctions are perfectly clear in principle, which is all that is necessary, although it might sometimes be a nice question to say to which class a given inference belongs. It is to be remarked that, in pure abduction, it can never be justifiable to accept the hypothesis otherwise than as an interrogation. But as long as that condition is observed, no positive falsity is to be feared; and therefore the whole question of what one out of a number of possible hypotheses ought to be entertained becomes purely a question of economy.

II

Mill denies that there was any reasoning in Kepler's procedure. He says it is merely a description of the facts. He seems to imagine that Kepler had all the places of Mars in space given him by Tycho's observations; and that all he did was to generalize and so obtain a general expression for them. Even had that been all, it would certainly have been inference. Had Mill had even so much practical acquaintance with astronomy as to have practised discussions of the motions of the double stars, he would have seen that. But so to characterize Kepler's work is to betray total ignorance of it. Mill certainly never read the *De Motu* [*Motibus*] *Stellae Martis*, which is not easy reading. The reason it is not easy is that it calls for the most vigorous exercise of all the powers of reasoning from beginning to end.

What Kepler had given was a large collection of observations of the apparent places of Mars at different times. He also knew that, in a general way, the Ptolemaic theory agrees with the appearances, although there were various difficulties in making it fit exactly. He was furthermore convinced that the hypothesis of Copernicus ought to be accepted. Now this hypothesis, as Copernicus himself understood its first outline, merely modifies the theory of Ptolemy so far as [to] impart to all the bodies of the solar system one common motion, just what is required to annul the mean motion of the sun. It would seem, therefore, at first sight, that it ought not to affect the appearances at all. If Mill had called the work of Copernicus mere description he would not have been *so very far* from the truth as he was. But Kepler did not understand the matter quite as Copernicus did. Because the sun was so near the center of the system, and was of vast size (even Kepler knew its diameter must be at least fifteen times that of the earth), Kepler, looking at the matter dynamically, thought it must have something to do with causing the planets to move in their orbits. This retroduction, vague as it was, cost great intellectual labor, and was most important in its bearings upon all Kepler's work. Now Kepler remarked that the lines of apsides of the orbits of Mars and of the earth are not parallel; and he utilized various observations most ingeniously to infer that they probably intersected in the sun. Consequently, it must be supposed that a general description of the motion would be simpler when referred to the sun as a fixed point of reference than when referred to any other point. Thence it followed that the proper times at which to take the observations of Mars for determining its orbit were when it appeared just opposite the sun—the true sun—instead of when it was opposite the *mean* sun, as had been the practice. Carrying out this idea, he obtained a theory of Mars which satisfied the longitudes at all the oppositions observed by Tycho and himself, thirteen in number, to perfection. But unfortunately, it did not satisfy the latitudes at all and was totally irreconcilable with observations of Mars when far from opposition.

At each stage of his long investigation, Kepler has a theory which is approximately true, since it approximately satisfies the observations (that is, within 8', which is less than any but Tycho's observations could decisively pronounce an error), and he proceeds to modify this theory, after the most careful and judicious reflection, in such a way as to render it more rational or closer to the observed fact. Thus, having found that the center of the orbit bisects the eccentricity, he finds in this an indication of the falsity of the theory of the equant and substitutes, for this artificial device, the principle of the equable description of areas. Subsequently, finding that the planet moves faster at ninety degrees from its apsides than it ought to do, the question is whether this is owing to an error in the law of areas or to a compression of the orbit. He ingeniously proves that the latter is the case.

Thus, never modifying his theory capriciously, but always with a sound and rational motive for just the modification he makes, it follows that when he finally reaches a modification—of most striking simplicity and rationality—which exactly satisfies the observations, it stands upon a totally different logical footing from what it would if it had been struck out at random, or the reader knows not how, and had been found to satisfy the observation. Kepler shows his keen logical sense in detailing the whole process by which he finally arrived at the true orbit. This is the greatest piece of Retroductive reasoning ever performed.

III

Modern science has been builded after the model of Galileo, who founded it, on *il lume naturale*. That truly inspired prophet had said that, of two hypotheses, the *simpler* is to be preferred; but I was formerly one of those who, in our dull self-conceit fancying ourselves more sly than he, twisted the maxim to mean the *logically* simpler, the one that adds the least to what has been observed, in spite of three obvious objections; first, that so there was no support for any hypothesis; secondly, that by the same token we ought to content ourselves with simply formulating the special observations actually made; and thirdly, that every advance of science that further opens the truth to our view discloses a world of unexpected complications. It was not until long experience forced me to realize that subsequent discoveries were every time showing I had been wrong, while those who understood the maxim as Galileo had done, early unlocked the secret, that the scales fell from my eyes and my mind awoke to the broad and flaming daylight that it is the simpler Hypothesis in the sense of the more facile and natural, the one that instinct suggests, that must be preferred; for the reason that, unless man have a natural bent in accordance with nature's, he has no chance of understanding nature at all.

PLATO

(427-347 B.C.)

An Athenian from a noble family, was a student of Socrates and never forgave Athenian democracy the execution of his master. It was he who systematized Socrates' thoughts and used them to develop his own philosophical system which he embodied in dialogues, whose very form recalls the master's conversational method. Plato and his disciple Aristotle have been, for over two thousand years, the two poles towards which Western philosophers have tended. Only of Ideas can man have knowledge, Plato reasons, of phenomena only opinion. The Just and the Beautiful are highest forms of reality giving meaning to man's life. In spite of this emphasis upon goodness and inner beauty in life and society, Plato's political precepts favor intellectual aristocracy with little regard for the masses and slaves.

Main Works:

> Gorgias; Protagoras; Meno; Apology; Crito; Phaedo; Phaedrus; Republic; Theaetetus; Timaeus; Sophistes; Critias; Cratylus.

On Truth

Socrates. Have you never heard, simpleton, that I am the son of a midwife, brave and burly, whose name was Phaenarete?
Theaetetus. Yes, I have.
Soc. And that I myself practise midwifery?
Theaet. No, never.
Soc. Let me tell you that I do though, my friend: but you must not reveal the secret, as the world in general has not

From: *Theaetetus.*

found me out; and therefore they only say of me, that I am the strangest of mortals and drive men to wits' end. Did you ever hear that too?

Theaet. Yes.

Soc. Shall I tell you the reason?

Theaet. By all means.

Soc. Bear in mind the whole business of the midwives, and then you will see my meaning better:—No woman, as you are probably aware, who is still able to conceive and bear, attends other women, but only those who are past bearing.

Theaet. Yes, I know.

Soc. The reason of this is said to be that Artemis—the goddess of childbirth—is not a mother, and she honors those who are like herself; but she could not allow the barren to be midwives, because human nature cannot know the mystery of an art without experience; and therefore she assigned this office to those who are too old to bear.

Theaet. I dare say.

Soc. And I dare say too, or rather I am absolutely certain, that the midwives know better than others who is pregnant and who is not?

Theaet. Very true.

Soc. And by the use of potions and incantations they are able to arouse the pangs and to soothe them at will; they can make those who have a difficulty in bearing, and if they think fit they can smother the embryo in the womb.

Theaet. They can.

Soc. Did you ever remark that they are also most cunning matchmakers, and have a thorough knowledge of what unions are likely to produce a brave brood?

Theaet. No, never.

Soc. Then let me tell you that this is their greatest pride, more than cutting the umbilical cord. And if you reflect, you will see that the same art which cultivates and gathers in the fruits of the earth, will be most likely to know in what soils the several plants or seeds should be deposited.

Theaet. Yes, the same art.

Soc. And do you suppose that with women the case is otherwise?

Theaet. I should think not.

Soc. Certainly not; but midwives are respectable women who have a character to lose, and they avoid this department of their profession, because they are afraid of being called procuresses, which is a name given to those who join together man and woman in unlawful and unscientific way; and yet the true midwife is also the true and only matchmaker.

Theaet. Clearly.

Soc. Such are the midwives, whose task is a very important one, but not so important as mine; for women do not bring into the world at one time real children, and at another time counterfeits which are with difficulty distinguished from them; if they did, then the discernment of the true and false birth would be the crowning achievement of the art of midwifery—you would think so?

Theaet. Indeed I should.

Soc. Well, my art of midwifery is in most respects like theirs; but differs, in that I attend men and not women, and I look after their souls when they are in labor, and not after their bodies: and the triumph of my art is in thoroughly examining whether the thought which the mind of the young man brings forth is a false idol or a noble and true birth. And like the midwives, I am barren, and the reproach which is often made against me, that I ask questions of others and have not the wit to answer them myself, is very just—the reason is, that the god compels me to be a midwife, but does not allow me to bring forth. And therefore I am not myself at all wise, nor have I anything to show which is the invention or birth of my own soul, but those who converse with me profit. Some of them appear dull enough at first, but afterwards, as our acquaintance ripens, if the god is gracious to them, they all make astonishing progress; and this in the opinion of others as well as in their own. It is quite clear that they never learned anything from me; the many fine discoveries to which they cling are of their own making. But to me and the god they owe their delivery. And the proof of my words is, that many of them in their ignorance, either in their self-conceit despising me, or falling under the influence of others, have gone away too soon; and have not only lost the children of whom I had previously delivered them by an ill bringing up, but have stifled whatever else they had in them by evil communications, being fonder of lies and shams than of the truth; and they have at last ended by seeing themselves, as others see them, to be great fools. Aristeides, the son of Lysimachus, is one of them, and there are many others. The truants often return to me, and beg that I would consort with them again—they are ready to go to me on their knees—and then, if my familiar allows, which is not always the case, I receive them, and they begin to grow again. Dire are the pangs which my art is able to arouse and to allay in those who consort with me, just like the pangs of women in childbirth; night and day they are full of perplexity and travail which is even worse than that of the women. So much for them. And there are others, Theaetetus, who come to me apparently having nothing in them; and as I know that they have no need of my art, I coax them into marrying some one, and by the grace of God I can generally tell who is likely to do them good. Many of them I have given away to Prodicus, and many to other inspired sages. I tell you this long story, friend Theaetetus, because I suspect, as indeed you seem to think yourself, that you are in labor—great with some conception. Come then to me, who am a midwife's son and myself a midwife, and do your best to answer the question which I will ask you. And if I abstract and expose your first-born, because I discover upon inspection that the conception department which you have formed is a vain shadow, do not quarrel with me on that account, as the manner of women is when their first children are taken from them. For I have actually known some who were ready to bite me when I deprived them of a darling folly; they did not perceive that I acted from goodwill, not knowing that no god is the enemy of man—that was not within the range of their ideas; neither am I their enemy in all this, but it would be wrong for me to admit falsehood, or to stifle the truth. Once more, then, Theaetetus, I repeat my old question. "What is knowledge?"—and do not say that you cannot tell; but quit yourself like a man, and by the help of God you will be able to tell.

Theaet. At any rate, Socrates, after such an exhortation I should be ashamed of not trying to do my best. Now he who knows perceives what he knows, and, as far as I can see at present, knowledge is perception.

Soc. Bravely said, boy; that is the way in which you should express your opinion. And now, let us examine together this conception of yours, and see whether it is a true birth or a mere wind-egg:—You say that knowledge is perception?

Theaet. Yes.

Soc. Well, you have delivered yourself of a very important doctrine about knowledge; it is indeed the opinion of Protagoras, who has another way of expressing it. Man, he says, is the measure of all things, of the existence of things that are, and of the non-existence of things that are not:—You have read him?

Theaet. O yes, again and again.

Soc. Does he not say that things are to you such as they appear to you, and to me such as they appear to me, and that you and I are men?

Theaet. Yes, he says so.

Soc. A wise man is not likely to talk nonsense. Let us try to understand him: the same wind is blowing, and yet one of us may be cold and the other not, or one may be slightly and the other very cold?

Theaet. Quite true.

Soc. Now is the wind, regarded not in relation to us but absolutely, cold or not; or are we to say, with Protagoras, that the wind is cold to him who is cold, and not to him who is not?

Theaet. I suppose the last.

Soc. Then it must appear so to each of them?

Theaet. Yes.

Soc. And "appears to him" means the same as "he perceives."

Theaet. True.

Soc. Then appearing and perceiving coincide in the case of hot and cold, and in similar instances; for things appear, or may be supposed to be, to each one such as he perceives them?

Theaet. Yes.

Soc. Then perception is always of existence, and being the same as knowledge is unerring?

Theaet. Clearly.

Soc. In the name of the Graces, what an almighty wise man Protagoras must have been! He spoke these things in a parable to the common herd, like you and me, but told the truth, "his Truth," in secret to his own disciples.

Theaet. What do you mean, Socrates?

Soc. I am about to speak of a high argument, in which all things are said to be relative; you cannot rightly call anything by any name, such as great or small, heavy or light, for the great will be the small and the heavy light—there is no single thing or quality, but out of motion and change and admixture all things are becoming relatively to one another, which "becoming" is by us incorrectly called being, but is really becoming, for nothing ever is, but all things are becoming. Summon all philosophers —Protagoras, Heracleitus, Empedocles, and the rest of them, one after another, and with exception of Parmenides they will agree with you in this. Summon the great masters of either kind of poetry—Epicharmus, the prince of Comedy, and Homer of Tragedy; when the latter sings of

"Ocean whence sprang the gods, and mother Tethys,"
does not he mean that all things are the offspring of flux and motion?

Theaet. I think so.

Soc. And who could take up arms against such a great army having Homer for its general, and not appear ridiculous?

Theaet. Who, indeed, Socrates?

Soc. Yes, Theaetetus; and there are plenty of other proofs which will show that motion is the source of what is called being and becoming, and inactivity of not-being and destruction; for fire and warmth, which are supposed to be the parent and guardian of all other things, are born of movement and of friction, which is a kind of motion; —is not this the origin of fire?

Theaet. It is.

Soc. And the race of animals is generated in the same way?

Theaet. Certainly.

Soc. And is not the bodily habit spoiled by rest and idleness, but preserved for a long time by motion and exercise?

Theaet. True.

Soc. And what of the mental habit? Is not the soul informed, and improved, and preserved by study and attention, which are motions; but when at rest, which in the soul only means want of attention and study, is uninformed, and speedily forgets whatever she has learned?

Theaet. True.

Soc. Then motion is a good, and rest an evil, to the soul as well as to the body?

Theaet. Clearly.

Soc. I may add, that breathless calm, stillness and the like waste and impair, while wind and storm preserve; and the palmary argument of all, which I strongly urge, is the golden chain in Homer, by which he means the sun, thereby indicating that so long as the sun and the heavens go round in their orbits, all things human and divine are and are preserved, but if they were chained up and their motion ceased, then all things would be destroyed, and, as the saying is, turned upside down.

Theaet. I believe, Socrates, that you have truly explained his meaning.

Soc. Then now apply his doctrine to perception, my good friend, and first of all to vision; that which you call white color is not in your eyes, and is not a distinct-thing which exists out of them. And you must not assign any place to it: for if it had position it would be, and be at rest, and there would be no process of becoming.

Theaet. Then what is color?

Soc. Let us carry out the principle which has just been affirmed, that nothing is self-existent, and then we shall see that white, black, and every other color, arises out of the eye meeting the appropriate motion, and that what we call a color is in each case neither the active nor the passive element, but something which passes between them, and is peculiar to each percipient; are you quite certain that the several colors appear to a dog or to any animal whatever as they appear to you?

Theaet. Far from it.

Soc. Or that anything appears the same to you as to another man? Are you so profoundly convinced of this? Rather would it not be true that it never appears exactly the same to you, because you are never exactly the same?

Theaet. The latter.

Soc. And if that with which I compare myself in size, or which I apprehended by touch, were great or white or hot, it could not become different by mere contact with another unless it actually changed; nor again, if the comparing or apprehending subject were great or white or hot, could this, when unchanged from within, become changed by any approximation or affection of any other thing. The fact is that in our ordinary way of speaking we allow ourselves to be driven into most ridiculous and wonderful contradictions, as Protagoras and all who take his line of argument would remark.

Theaet. How? and of what sort do you mean?

Soc. A little instance will sufficiently explain my meaning: Here are six dice, which are more by a half when compared with four, and fewer by a half than twelve—they are more and also fewer. How can you or any one maintain the contrary?

Theaet. Very true.

Soc. Well, then, suppose that Protagoras or some one asks whether anything can become greater or more if not by increasing, how would you answer him, Theaetetus?

Theaet. I should say "No," Socrates, if I were to speak my mind in reference to this last question, and if I were not afraid of contradicting my former answer.

Soc. Capital! excellent! spoken like an oracle, my boy! And if you reply "Yes," there will be a case for Euripides; for our tongue will be unconvinced, but not our mind.

Theaet. Very true.

Soc. The thoroughbred Sophists, who know all that can be known about the mind, and argue only out of the superfluity of their wits, would have had a regular sparring-match over this, and would have knocked their arguments together finely. But you and I, who have no professional aims, only desire to see what is the mutual relation of these principles,—whether they are consistent with each other or not.

Theaet. Yes, that would be my desire.

Soc. And mine too. But since this is our feeling, and there is plenty of time, why should we not calmly and patiently review our own thoughts, and thoroughly examine and see what these appearances in us really are? If I am mistaken, they will be described by us as follows:—first, that nothing can become greater or less, either in number or magnitude, while remaining equal to itself—you would agree?

Theaet. Yes.

Soc. Secondly, that without addition or subtraction there is no increase or diminution of anything, but only equality.

Theaet. Quite true.

Soc. Thirdly, that which was not before cannot be afterwards, without becoming and having become.

Theaet. Yes, truly.

Soc. These three axioms, if I am not mistaken, are fighting with one another in our minds in the case of the dice, or, again, in such a case as this—if I were to say that I, who am of a certain height and taller than you, may within a year, without gaining or losing in height, be not so tall—not that I should have lost, but that you would have increased. In such a case, I am afterwards what I once was not, and yet I have not become; for I could not have become; for I could not have become without becoming, neither could I have become less without losing somewhat of my height; and I could give you ten thousand examples of similar contradictions, if we admit them at all. I believe that you follow me, Theaetetus; for I suspect that you have thought of these questions before now.

Theaet. Yes, Socrates, and I am amazed when I think of them; by the Gods I am! and I want to know what on earth they mean; and there are times when my head quite swims with the contemplation of them.

Soc. I see, my dear Theaetetus, that Theodorus had a true insight into your nature when he said that you were a philosopher, for wonder is the feeling of a philosopher, and philosophy begins in wonder. He was not a bad genealogist who said that Iris (the messenger of heaven) is the child of Thaumas (wonder). But do you begin to see what is the explanation of this perplexity on the hypothesis which we attribute to Protagoras?

Theaet. Not as yet.

Soc. Then you will be obliged to me if I help you to unearth the hidden "truth" of a famous man or school.

Theaet. To be sure, I shall be very much obliged.

Soc. Take a look round, then, and see that none of the uninitiated are listening. Now by the uninitiated I mean the people who believe in nothing but what they can grasp in their hands, and who will not allow that action or generation or anything invisible can have real existence.

Theaet. Yes, indeed, Socrates, they are very hard and impenetrable mortals.

Soc. Yes, my boy, outer barbarians. Far more ingenious are the brethren whose mysteries I am about to reveal to you. Their first principle is, that all is motion, and upon this all the affections of which we were just now speaking are supposed to depend: there is nothing but motion, which has two forms, one active and the other passive, both in endless number; and out of the union and friction of them there is generated a progeny endless in number, having two forms, sense and the object of sense, which are ever breaking forth and coming to the birth at the same moment. The senses are variously named hearing,

Plato

seeing, smelling; there is the sense of heat, cold, pleasure, pain, desire, fear, and many more which have names, as well as innumerable others which are without them; each has its kindred object,—each variety of color has a corresponding variety of sight, and so with sound and hearing, and with the rest of the senses and the objects akin to them. Do you see, Theaetetus, the bearings of this tale on the preceding argument?

Theaet. Indeed I do not.

Soc. Then attend, and I will try to finish the story. The purport is that all these things are in motion, as I was saying, and that this motion is of two kinds, a slower and a quicker; and the slower elements have their motions in the same place and with reference to things near them, and so they beget; but what is begotten is swifter, for it is carried to and fro, and moves from place to place: Apply this to sense:—When the eye and the appropriate object meet together and give birth to whiteness and the sensation connatural with it, which could not have been given by either of them going elsewhere, then, while the sight is flowing from the eye whiteness proceeds from the object which combines in producing the color; and so the eye is fulfilled with sight, and really sees, and becomes, not sight, but a seeing eye; and the object which combined to form the color is fulfilled with whiteness, and becomes not whiteness but a white thing, whether wood or stone or whatever the object may be which happens to be colored white. And this is true of all sensible objects, hard, warm, and the like, which are similarly to be regarded, as I was saying before, not as having any absolute existence, but as being all of them of whatever kind generated by motion in their intercourse with one another; for the agent and patient, as existing in separation, no trustworthy conception, as they say, can be formed, for the agent has no existence until united with the patient, and the patient has no existence until united with the agent; and that which by uniting with something becomes an agent, by meeting with some other thing is converted into a patient. And from all these considerations, as I said at first, there arises a general reflection, that there is no one self-existent

621

thing, but everything is becoming and in relation; and being must be altogether abolished, although from habit and ignorance we are compelled even in this discussion to retain the use of the term. But great philosophers tell us that we are not to allow either the word "something," or "belonging to something," or "to me," or "this" or "that," or any other detaining name to be used; in the language of nature all things are being created and destroyed, coming into being and passing into new forms; nor can any name fix or detain them; he who attempts to fix them is easily refuted. And this should be the way of speaking, not only of particulars but of aggregates; such aggregates as are expressed in the word "man," or "stone," or any name of an animal or of a class. Theaetetus, are not these speculations sweet as honey? And do you not like the taste of them in the mouth?

Theaet. I do not know what to say, Socrates; for, indeed, I cannot make out whether you are giving your own opinion or only wanting to draw me out.

Soc. You forget, my friend, that I neither know, nor profess to know, anything of these matters; you are the person who is in labor, I am the barren midwife; and this is why I soothe you, and offer you one good thing after another, that you may taste them. And I hope that I may at last help to bring your own opinion into the light of day: when this has been accomplished, then we will determine whether what you have brought forth is only a wind-egg or a real and genuine birth. Therefore, keep up your spirits, and answer like a man what you think.

Theaet. Ask me.

Soc. Then once more: Is it your opinion that nothing is but what becomes?—the good and the noble, as well as all the other things which we were just now mentioning?

Theaet. When I hear you discoursing in this style, I think that there is a great deal in what you say, and I am very ready to assent.

Soc. Let us not leave the argument unfinished, then; for there still remains to be considered an objection which may be raised

622

about dreams and diseases, in particular about madness, and the various illusions of hearing and sight, or of other senses. For you know that in all these cases the *esse-percipi* theory appears to be unmistakably refuted, since in dreams and illusions we certainly have false perceptions; and far from saying that everything is which appears, we should rather say that nothing is which appears.

Theaet. Very true, Socrates.

Soc. But then, my boy, how can any one contend that knowledge is perception, or that to every man what appears is?

Theaet. I am afraid to say, Socrates, that I have nothing to answer, because you rebuked me just now for making this excuse; but I certainly cannot undertake to argue that madmen or dreamers think truly, when they imagine, some of them that they are gods, and others that they can fly, and are flying in their sleep.

Soc. Do you see another question which can be raised about these phenomena, notably about dreaming and waking?

Theaet. What question?

Soc. A question which I think that you must often have heard persons ask:—How can you determine whether at this moment we are sleeping, and all our thoughts are a dream: or whether we are awake, and talking to one another in the waking state?

Theaet. Indeed, Socrates, I do not know how to prove the one any more than the other, for in both cases the facts precisely correspond; and there is no difficulty in supposing that during all this discussion we have been talking to one another in a dream; and when in a dream we seem to be narrating dreams, the resemblance of the two states is quite astonishing.

Soc. You see, then, that a doubt about the reality of sense is easily raised, since there may even be a doubt whether we are awake or in a dream. And as our time is equally divided between sleeping and waking, in either sphere of existence the soul contends that the thoughts which are present to our minds at the time are true; and during one half of our lives we affirm the truth of the one, and, during the other half, of the other; and are equally confident of both.

Theaet. Most true.

Soc. And may not the same be said of madness and other disorders? the difference is only that the times are not equal.

Theaet. Certainly.

Soc. And is truth or falsehood to be determined by duration of time?

Theaet. That would be in many ways ridiculous.

Soc. But can you certainly determine by any other means which of these opinions is true?

Theaet. I do not think that I can.

Soc. Listen, then, to a statement of the other side of the argument, which is made by the champions of appearance. They would say, as I imagine—Can that which is wholly other than something, have the same quality as that from which it differs? and observe, Theaetetus, that the word "other" means not "partially," but "wholly other."

Theaet. Certainly, putting the question as you do, that which is wholly other cannot either potentially or in other way be the same.

Soc. And must therefore be admitted to be unlike?

Theaet. True.

Soc. If, then, anything happens to become like or unlike itself or another, when it becomes like we call it the same—when unlike, other?

Theaet. Certainly.

Soc. Were we not saying that there are agents many and infinite, and patients many and infinite?

Theaet. Yes.

Soc. And also that different combinations will produce results which are not the same, but different?

Theaet. Certainly.

Soc. Let us take you and me, or anything as an example:—

There is Socrates in health, and Socrates sick—Are they like or unlike?

Theaet. You mean to compare Socrates in health as a whole, and Socrates in sickness as a whole?

Soc. Exactly; that is my meaning.

Theaet. I answer, they are unlike.

Soc. And if unlike, they are other?

Theaet. Certainly.

Soc. And would you not say the same of Socrates sleeping and waking, or in any of the states which we were mentioning?

Theaet. I should.

Soc. All agents have a different patient in Socrates, accordingly as he is well or ill.

Theaet. Of course.

Soc. And I who am the patient, and that which is the agent, will produce something different in each of the two cases?

Theaet. Certainly.

Soc. The wine which I drink when I am in health, appears sweet and pleasant to me?

Theaet. True.

Soc. For, as has been already acknowledged, the patient and agent meet together and produce sweetness and a perception of sweetness, which are in simultaneous motion, and the perception which comes from the patient makes the tongue percipient, and the quality of sweetness which arises out of and is moving about the wine, makes the wine both to be and to appear sweet to the healthy tongue.

Theaet. Certainly; that has been already acknowledged.

Soc. But when I am sick, the wine really acts upon another and a different person?

Theaet. Yes.

Soc. The combination of the draught of wine, and the Socrates who is sick, produces quite another result; which is the sensation of bitterness in the tongue, and the motion and creation of bitterness in and about the wine, which becomes not bitterness but something bitter; as I myself become not perception but percipient?

Theaet. True.

Soc. There is no other object of which I shall ever have the same perception, for another object would give another perception, and would make the percipient other and different; nor can that object which affects me, meeting another subject, produce the same, or become similar, for that too will produce another result from another subject, and become different.

Theaet. True.

Soc. Neither can I by myself, have this sensation, nor the object of itself, this quality.

Theaet. Certainly not.

Soc. When I perceive I must become percipient of something —there can be no such thing as perceiving and perceiving nothing; the object, whether it become sweet, bitter, or of any other quality, must have relation to a percipient; nothing can become sweet which is sweet to no one.

Theaet. Certainly not.

Soc. Then the inference is, that we [the agent and patient] are or become in relation to one another; there is a law which binds us one to the other, but not to any other existence, nor each of us to himself; and therefore we can only be bound to one another; so that whether a person says that a thing is or becomes, he must say that it is or becomes to or of or in relation to something else; but he must not say or allow any one else to say that anything is or becomes absolutely:—such is our conclusion.

Theaet. Very true, Socrates.

Soc. Then, if that which acts upon me has relation to me and to no other, I and no other am the percipient of it?

Theaet. Of course.

Soc. Then my perception is true to me, being inseparable from my own being; and, as Protagoras says, to myself I am judge of what is and what is not to me.

Theaet. I suppose so.

Soc. How then, if I never err, and if my mind never trips in the conception of being or becoming, can I fail of knowing that which I perceive?

Theaet. You cannot.

Soc. Then you were quite right in affirming that knowledge is only perception; and the meaning turns out to be the same, whether with Homer and Heracleitus, and all that company, you say that all is motion and flux, or with great sage Protagoras, that man is the measure of all things; or with Theaetetus, that, given these premises, perception is knowledge. Am I not right, Theaetetus, and is not this your new-born child, of which I have delivered you? What say you?

Theaet. I cannot but agree, Socrates.

Soc. Then this is the child, however he may turn out, which you and I have with difficulty brought into the world. And now that he is born, we must run round the hearth with him, and see whether he is worth rearing, or is only a wind-egg and a sham. Is he to be reared in any case, and not exposed? or will you bear to see him rejected, and not get into a passion if I take away your first-born?

Theod. Theaetetus will not be angry, for he is very good-natured. But tell me, Socrates, in heaven's name, is this, after all, not the truth?

Soc. You, Theodorus, are a lover of theories, and now you innocently fancy that I am a bag full of them, and can easily pull one out which will overthrow its predecessor. But you do not see that in reality none of these theories come from me; they all come from him who talks with me. I only know just enough to extract them from the wisdom of another, and to receive them in a spirit of fairness. And now I shall say nothing myself, but shall endeavor to elicit something from our young friend.

Theod. Do as you say, Socrates; you are quite right.

Soc. Shall I tell you, Theodorus, what amazes me in your acquaintance Protagoras.

Theod. What is it?

Soc. I am charmed with his doctrine, that what appears is to each one, but I wonder that he did not begin his book on Truth with a declaration that a pig or a dog-faced baboon, or some other yet stranger monster which has sensation, is the measure of all things; then he might have shown a magnificent contempt for our opinion of him by informing us at the outset that while we were reverencing him like a God for his wisdom he was no better than a tadpole, not to speak of his fellow-men—would not this have produced an overpowering effect? For if truth is only sensation, and no man can discern another's feelings better than he, or has any superior right to determine whether his opinion is true or false, but each, as we have several times repeated, is to himself the sole judge, and everything that he judges is true and right, why, my friend, should Protagoras be preferred to the place of wisdom and instruction, and deserve to be well paid, and we poor ignoramuses have to go to him, if each one is the measure of his own wisdom? Must he not be talking "ad captandum" in all this? I say nothing of the ridiculous predicament in which my own midwifery and the whole art of dialectic is placed; for the attempt to supervise or refute the notions or opinions of others would be a tedious and enormous piece of folly, if to each man his own are right; and this must be the case if Protagoras' Truth is the real truth, and the philosopher is not merely amusing himself by giving oracles out of the shrine of his book.

Theod. He was a friend of mine, Socrates, as you were saying, and therefore I cannot have him refuted by my lips, nor can I oppose you when I agree with you; please, then, to take Theaetetus again; he seemed to answer very nicely.

Soc. If you were to go into a Lacedaemonian palestra, Theodorus, would you have a right to look on at the naked wrestlers, some of them making a poor figure, if you did not strip and give them an opportunity of judging of your own person?

Theod. Why not, Socrates, if they would allow me, as I think you will, in consideration of my age and stiffness; let some more supple youth try a fall with you, and do not drag me into the gymnasium.

Soc. Your will is my will, Theodorus, as the proverbial philosophers say, and therefore I will return to the sage Theaetetus: Tell me, Theaetetus, in reference to what I was saying, are you not lost in wonder, like myself, when you find that all of a sudden you are raised to the level of the wisest of men, or indeed of the gods?—for you would assume the measure of Protagoras to apply to the gods as well as men?

Theaet. Certainly I should, and I confess to you that I am lost in wonder. At first hearing, I was quite satisfied with the doctrine, that whatever appears is to each one, but now the face of things has changed.

Soc. Why, my dear boy, you are young, and therefore your ear is quickly caught and your mind influenced by popular arguments. Protagoras, or some one speaking on his behalf, will doubtless say in reply,—Good people, young and old, you meet and harangue, and bring in the gods, whose existence or non-existence I banish from writing and speech, or you talk about the reason of man being degraded to the level of the brutes, which is a telling argument with the multitude, but not one word of proof or demonstration do you offer. All is probability with you, and yet surely you and Theodorus had better reflect whether you are disposed to admit of probability and figures of speech in matters of such importance. He or any other mathematician who argued from probabilities and likelihoods in geometry, would not be worth an ace.

Theaet. But neither you nor we, Socrates, would be satisfied with such arguments.

Soc. Then you and Theodorus mean to say that we must look at the matter in some other way?

Theaet. Yes, in quite another way.

Soc. And the way will be to ask whether perception is or is not the same as knowledge; for this was the real point of our argument, and with a view to this we raised (did we not?) those many strange questions.

Theaet. Certainly.

Soc. Shall we say that we know every thing which we see

and hear? for example, shall we say that not having learned, we do not hear the language of foreigners when they speak to us? or shall we say that we not only hear, but know what they are saying? Or again, if we see letters which we do not understand, shall we say that we do not see them? or shall we aver that, seeing them, we must know them?

Theaet. We shall say, Socrates, that we know what we actually see and hear of them—that is to say, we see and know the figure and color of the letters, and we hear and know the elevation or depression of the sound of them; but we do not perceive by sight and hearing, or know, that which grammarians and interpreters teach about them.

Soc. Capital, Theaetetus; and about this there shall be no dispute, because I want you to grow; but there is another difficulty coming, which you will also have to repulse.

Theaet. What is it?

Soc. Some one will say, Can a man who has ever known anything, and still has and preserves a memory of that which he knows, not know that which he remembers at the time when he remembers? I have, I fear, a tedious way of putting a simple question, which is only, whether a man who has learned, and remembers, can fail to know?

Theaet. Impossible, Socrates; the supposition is monstrous.

Soc. Am I talking nonsense, then? Think: is not seeing perceiving, and is not sight perception?

Theaet. True.

Soc. And if our recent definition holds, every man knows that which he has seen?

Theaet. Yes.

Soc. And you would admit that there is such a thing as memory?

Theaet. Yes.

Soc. And is memory of something or of nothing?

Theaet. Of something, surely.

Soc. Of things learned and perceived, that is?

Theaet. Certainly.

Soc. Often a man remembers that which he has seen?

Theaet. True.

Soc. And if he closed his eyes, would he forget?

Theaet. Who, Socrates, would dare to say so?

Soc. But we must say so, if the previous argument is to be maintained.

Theaet. What do you mean? I am not quite sure that I understand you, though I have a strong suspicion that you are right.

Soc. As thus: he who sees knows, as we say, that which he sees; for perception and sight and knowledge are admitted to be the same.

Theaet. Certainly.

Soc. But he who saw, and has knowledge of that which he saw, remembers, when he closes his eyes, that which he no longer sees.

Theaet. True.

Soc. And seeing is knowing, and therefore not-seeing is not-knowing.

Theaet. Very true.

Soc. Then the inference is, that a man may have attained the knowledge of something, which he may remember and yet not know, because he does not see; and this has been affirmed by us to be a monstrous supposition.

Theaet. Most true.

Soc. Thus, then, the assertion that knowledge and perception are one, involves a manifest impossibility?

Theaet. Yes.

Soc. Then they must be distinguished?

Theaet. I suppose that they must.

Soc. Once more we shall have to begin, and ask, "What is knowledge" and yet, Theaetetus, what are we going to do?

Theaet. About what?

Soc. Like a good-for-nothing cock, without having won the victory, we walk away from the argument and crow.

Theaet. How do you mean?

Soc. After the manner of disputers, we were satisfied with mere verbal consistency, and were well pleased if in this way we could gain an advantage. Although professing not to be mere Eristics, but philosophers, I suspect that we have unconsciously fallen into the error of that ingenious class of persons.

Theaet. I do not as yet understand you.

Soc. Then I will try to explain myself: just now we asked the question, whether a man who had learned and remembered could fail to know, and we showed that a person who had seen might remember when he had his eyes shut and could not see, and then he would at the same time remember and not know. But this was an impossibility. And so the Protagorean fable came to naught, and yours also, who maintained that knowledge is the same as perception.

FRANK PLUMPTON RAMSEY
(1903-1930)

An Englishman who taught at the University of Cambridge. His premature death was felt to be a heavy loss by leading thinkers in the fields of philosophy, mathematical logic and theory of economics. Ramsey started where Russell and Wittgenstein left off. His fundamental distinction is between *human logic*, which deals with useful mental habits, and *formal logic*, which is concerned with the rules of consistent thought. In his work on probability he influenced Keynes who partly yielded to his theories.

Main Work:
> The Foundations of Mathematics.

On Philosophy

Philosophy must be of some use and we must take it seriously; it must clear our thoughts and so our actions. Or else it is a disposition we have to check, and an inquiry to see that this is so; i.e. the chief proposition of philosophy is that philosophy is nonsense. And again we must then take seriously that it is nonsense, and not pretend, as Wittgenstein does, that it is important nonsense!

In philosophy we take the propositions we make in science and everyday life, and try to exhibit them in a logical system with primitive terms and definitions, etc. Essentially a philoso-

---

From: *The Foundations of Mathematics.*

phy is a system of definitions or, only too often, a system of descriptions of how definitions might be given.

I do not think it is necessary to say with Moore that the definitions explain what we have hitherto meant by our propositions, but rather that they show how we intend to use them in future. Moore would say they were the same, that philosophy does not change what anyone meant by "This is a table." It seems to me that it might; for meaning is mainly potential, and a change might therefore only be manifested on rare and critical occasions. Also sometimes philosophy should clarify and distinguish notions previously vague and confused, and clearly this is meant to fix our future meaning only. But this is clear, that the definitions are to give at least our future meaning, and not merely to give any pretty way of obtaining a certain structure.

I used to worry myself about the nature of philosophy through excessive scholasticism. I could not see how we could understand a word and not be able to recognize whether a proposed definition of it was or was not correct. I did not realize the vagueness of the whole idea of understanding, the reference it involves to a multitude of performances any of which may fail and require to be restored. Logic issues in tautologies, mathematics in identities, philosophy in definitions; all trivial but all part of the vital work of clarifying and organizing our thought.

If we regard philosophy as a system of definitions (and elucidations of the use of words which cannot be nominally defined), the things that seem to me problems about it are these:

(1) What definitions do we feel it up to *philosophy* to provide, and what do we leave to the sciences or feel it unnecessary to give at all?

(2) When and how can we be content without a definition but merely with a description of how a definition might be given? [This point is mentioned above.]

(3) How can philosophical enquiry be conducted without a perpetual *petitio principii*?

(1) Philosophy is not concerned with special problems of definition but only with general ones: it does not propose to

define particular terms of art or science, but to settle e.g. problems which arise in the definition of any such term or in the relation of any term in the physical world to the terms of experience.

Terms of art and science, however, must be defined, but not necessarily nominally; e.g. we define mass by explaining how to measure it, but this is not a nominal definition; it merely gives the term "mass" in a theoretical structure a clear relation to certain experimental facts. The terms we do not need to define are those which we know we could define if need arose, like "chair," or those which like "clubs" (the suit of cards) we can translate easily into visual or some other language, but cannot conveniently expand in words.

(2) The solution to what we called in (1) a "general problem of definition" is naturally a description of definitions, from which we learn how to form the actual definition in any particular case. That we so often seem to get no actual *definitions,* is because the solution of the problem is often that nominal definition is inappropriate, and that what is wanted is an explanation of the use of the symbol.

But this does not touch what may be supposed to be the real difficulty under this head (2); for what we have said applies only to the case in which the word to be defined being merely described (because treated as one of a class), its definition or explanation is also, of course, merely described, but described in such a way that when the actual word is given its actual definition can be derived. But there are other cases in which the word to be defined being given, we are given in return no definition of it but a statement that its meaning involves entities of such-and-such sorts in such-and-such ways, i.e. a statement which *would* give us a definition if we had names for these entities.

As to the use of this, it is plainly to fit the term in connection with variables, to put it as a value of the right complex variable; and it presupposes that we can have variables without names for all their values. Difficult questions arise as to whether we must always be *able* to name all the values, and if so what kind of ability this means, but clearly the phenomenon is in some way possible in connection with sensations for which our language is so fragmentary. For instance, "Jane's voice" is a description of a characteristic of sensations for which we have no name. We could perhaps name it, but can we identify and name the different inflections of which it consists?

An objection often made to these definitions of sensory characteristics is that they express what we should find on analysis, but that this kind of analysis changes the sensation analyzed by developing the complexity which it pretends merely to discover. That attention can change our experience is indubitable, but it seems to me possible that sometimes it reveals a pre-existing complexity (i.e. enables us to symbolize this adequately), for this is compatible with any change in incidental facts, anything even except a creation of the complexity.

Another difficulty with regard to descriptions of definitions is that if we content ourselves with them we may get simply nonsense by introducing nonsensical variables, e.g. described variables such as "particular" or theoretical ideas such as "point." We might for instance say that by "patch" we mean an infinite class of points; if so we should be giving up philosophy for theoretical psychology. For in philosophy we analyze *our* thought, in which patch could not be replaced by infinite class of points: we could not determine a particular infinite class extensionally; "This patch is red" is not short for "a is red and b is red etc. . . ." where a, b, etc., are points. (How would it be if just a were not red?) Infinite classes of points could only come in when we look at the mind from outside and construct a theory of it, in which its sensory field consists of classes of colored points about which it thinks.

Now if we made this theory about our own mind we should have to regard it as accounting for certain *facts*, e.g. that this patch is red; but when we are thinking of other people's minds we have no facts, but are altogether in the realm of theory, and can persuade ourselves that these theoretical constructions exhaust the field. We can turn back on our own minds, and say that what are really happening there are simply these theoretical processes. The clearest instance of this is, of course, materialism. But many other philosophics, e.g. Carnap's, make just the same mistake.

(3) Our third question was how we could avoid *petitio principii*, the danger of which arises somewhat as follows:—

In order to clarify my thought the proper method seems to be simply to think out with myself "What do I mean by that?" "What are the separate notions involved in this term?" "Does this really follow from that?" etc., and to test identity of meaning of a proposed definiens and the definiendum by real and hypothetical examples. This we can often do without thinking about the nature of meaning itself; we can tell whether we mean the same or different things by "horse" and "pig" without thinking at all about meaning in general. But in order to settle more complicated questions of the sort we obviously need a logical structure, a system of logic, into which to bring them. These we may hope to obtain by a relatively easy previous application of the same methods; for instance, it should not be difficult to see that for either not-*p* or not-*q* to be true is just the same thing as for not both *p* and *q* to be true. In this case we construct a logic, and do all our philosophical analysis entirely *unselfconsciously*, thinking all the time of the facts and not about our thinking about them, deciding what we mean without any reference to the nature of meanings. [Of course we could also think about the nature of meaning in an unselfconscious way, i.e. think of a case of meaning before us without reference to our meaning *it*.] This is one method and it may be the right one; but I think it is wrong and leads to an impasse, and I part company from it in the following way.

It seems to me that in the process of clarifying our thought we come to terms and sentences which we cannot elucidate in the obvious manner by defining their meaning. For instance, variable hypotheticals and theoretical terms we cannot define, but we can explain the way in which they are used, and in this explanation we are forced to look not only at the objects which we are talking about, but at our own mental states. As Johnson would say, in this part of logic we cannot neglect the epistemic or subjective side.

Now this means that we cannot get clear about these terms and sentences without getting clear about meaning, and we seem to get into the situation that we cannot understand e.g. what we say about time and the external world without first understanding meaning and yet we cannot understand meaning without first understanding certainly time and probably the external world which are involved in it. So we cannot make our philosophy into an ordered progress to a goal, but have to take our problem as a whole and jump to a simultaneous solution; which will have something of the nature of a hypothesis, for we shall accept it not as the consequence of direct argument, but as the only one we can think of which satisfies our several requirements.

Of course, we should not strictly speak of argument, but there is in philosophy a process analogous to "linear inference" in which things become successively clear; and since, for the above reason, we cannot carry this through to the end, we are in the ordinary position of scientists of having to be content with piecemeal improvements: we cannot make anything clear.

I find this self-consciousness inevitable in philosophy except in a very limited field. We are driven to philosophize because we do not know clearly what we mean; the question is always "What do I mean by x?" And only very occasionally can we settle this without reflecting on meaning. But it is not only an obstacle, this necessity of dealing with meaning; it is doubtless an essential clue to the truth. If we neglect it I feel we may get into the absurd position of the child in the following dialogue: "Say breakfast." "Can't." "What can't you say?" "Can't say breakfast."

But the necessity of self-consciousness must not be used as a justification for nonsensical hypotheses; we are doing philosophy not theoretical psychology, and our analyses of our statements, whether about meaning or anything else, must be such as we can understand.

The chief danger to our philosophy, apart from laziness and wooliness is *scholasticism,* the essence of which is treating what is vague as if it were precise and trying to fit it into an exact logical category. A typical piece of scholasticism is Wittgenstein's view that all our everyday propositions are completely in order and that it is impossible to think illogically. (This last is like saying that it is impossible to break the rules of bridge because if you break them you are not playing bridge but, as Mrs. C. says, not-bridge.) Another is the argumentation about acquaintance with before leading to the conclusion that we perceive the past. A simple consideration of the automatic telephone shows that we could react differently to *AB* and *BA* without perceiving the past, so that the argument is substantially unsound. It turns on a play with "acquaintance" which means, first, capacity to symbolize and, secondly, sensory perception. Wittgenstein seems to equivocate in just the same way with his notion of "given."

PETRUS RAMUS
(PIERRE DE LA RAMÉE, 1515-1572)

Petrus Ramus was the Latinized name of Pierre de la Ramée, a French humanist who became a Calvinist and was murdered in the massacre of Saint Bartholomew's Day. He wanted to unite logic and rhetoric and to create a natural system of logic through a study of the processes of human thought. He opposed Aristotelianism.

Main Works:

Institutionum dialecticarum libri tres; Aristotelicae animadversiones.

The Meaning of Dialectics

Dialectics, also called Logic, is the art of speaking well. These two terms, dialectics and logic, are not different in meaning, but have the same force and significance. If one is of a general nature, and designates the common faculty of reasoning, it is called the dialectic art, because it submits principles, organized for the use of human life, to a most orderly and skilful system. For you see in logic the inclusion of numberless rules for inventing and judging an argument, everlastingly true, and peculiar to the art of logic, and reciprocal from the conjunction of equal things. Also, these rules are not confused with others by a disarrangement in their orderliness, but are measured by the excellence of the method. Lastly, these rules have not been established for vain and subtle ostentatious purposes, but de-

----

From: *Dialecticae Libri.*

scribed as an aid to the life of man. Dialectics then is an art. But actually an art of what? What is that which is comprehended by the principles of the discipline of logic? We shall readily understand this, if we know the origin of the principles. For the principles interpret and explain the things from the observation and induction of which the principles arise: just as the rules of grammatical syntax discuss the appropriateness of words and their correctness because they arise both from the observation of the appropriateness of words that produce agreement sometimes in case, gender, and number, and sometimes in number and person, and from the observation of their correctness, whereby some words are governed by others by a change in ending. Now from the observation of what have the rules of logic developed? Surely from the observation of natural reason, comprehended and expressed both by the sayings and writings of other distinguished men in the state, and also by the opinions and comments of poets, orators, philosophers, and theologians. For all of them have made use of divinely given natural reason, that is, they have revealed the causes and effects of things. They have observed what is the basis of things and what is added to them. They have noted how some things differ from others. On occasion they have made comparisons between things different from each other in different ways. Often they have considered terms derived from the same origin yet distinct in their various ends. They have also investigated the origin of terms. From their causes and other proofs they have expounded the nature of things, and to the extent of their ability they have also split nature into parts. When it was necessary, too, they produced evidences to corroborate their statements. After expressing the force of their natural inventiveness in these multiple ways, they applied themselves to the orderly classification and evaluation of things to the extent of their inherent talent. Hence it was that by affirmation or negation in simple or compound sentences they postulated things for the glorification of truth. If there was any obscurity, they referred it, as it were, to the light, meanwhile carefully noting how one thing followed from another. Whatever was confused and puzzling, they eagerly reduced to order. And these are acts of natural reason, that is, reason divinely inspired in the minds of men from the very beginning: acts that poets, orators, philosophers, politicians, theologians have expressed in their sayings or writings, whenever they undertook any thing that required explanation or discussion. These individual acts of natural reason learned men have observed. They have also noted how they occurred, and of what kind each was, and how numerous they were. Hence it happened that, according to my previous observation on the acts of the human mind, which I have already explained, they wrote down certain lines of counsel and outlined a method of imitating and expressing technically those acts that others achieved solely through the guidance of nature. Therefore the principles of the art of logic sprang from the observation of natural reason. It may be asked now: What is it the art of that dialectics expounds and professes? For one sees that it arose from the observation of acts of natural reason. Accordingly it expounds not the discipline of word building, or embellishing speech with metaphors and allegories, or mensuration, but the art of moulding and training the reason.

But if dialectics is the art of teaching natural reason effectively by a popular method, all the rules of dialectics will be directed toward effective speaking. For whatever is achieved by the faculty of natural reason will be submitted to the entire art of logic: will be completely under its observation, and will be its purpose. But those acts of finding and judging an argument, that I have examined individually, are produced by the strength of natural reason. So all the rules of the art of logic are invariably and exclusively associated with the acts of thinking and of arranging an argument, that is, with effective speaking. For what else is effective speaking but finding causes, effects, subjects, adjuncts, and other arguments, and when found applying them to judgment, that is, predicating them by axiom, classifying them syllogistically, arranging them methodically? Thus effective speech is the purpose of dialectics: not to which only other rules of the art refer, but the entire art and every rule of the art: just like the purpose of constructing a building, that considers not only the hall, but every part of the building. But how is this purpose of dialectics attained? Surely by practice in the rules, that is, under the guidance of logical principles, and by the invention of arguments and their disposition once they are invented: so that any one who has examined one by one all the precepts of logical invention and has made use of every principle of judgment has attained the purpose of the art of logic. It must not therefore be thought that the purpose of trained reasoning lies in a contingent result: it is, rather, so devised that there are as many steps, so to speak, that reach to this end, as there are rules in the art of logic. Anyone who wanted to reach the height passed through intermediate degrees before achieving the summit. Thus anyone who wishes to aspire to the ultimate end of logic must pass through every single rule step by step. On the completion of this course, he has attained the end of dialectics.

You now see that dialectics is the art of effective speaking, that is, presenting rules and method, finding good arguments, and good judgment. But in discussing and treating what subjects are the rules of dialectics exercised? This I have already explained. Are not arguments found by the rule of invention? Are not arguments, once invented, arranged according to the rules of judgment? The argument then is that which is subjected to the rules of the logical discipline in speaking and in exposition. Under the name of argument I include all things, whether they exist in themselves or in imaginative creations: or are probable, or necessary. The causes, effects, subjects, adjuncts of all things can thereby be discovered: even the difference between one thing and another can be indicated and a comparison drawn between different things. Similarly the same assertion may be made in regard to the other arguments. Whatever can be thought can likewise be methodically predicated and syllogistically deduced, if there is any dubiety: and can be systematically arranged, if there is any confusion. It is the function of natural reason, that God has inspired in men's minds, to discuss all matters that are in the nature of things: also all imaginative subjects: because imaginary things have causes, but imaginary ones. They also have imaginary actions, adjuncts, and subjects, imaginary differences and comparisons. But technical reason, that we call dialectics, is a kind of elaborated image of natural reason: and hence whatever things can be understood and known by the light of natural reason also dispute through the faculty of technical reason, that is, can be found and judged.

But some Aristotelians suggest that the art of dialectics is the art of speaking with probability. The expression *with probability* either refers to the system of rules under whose guidance the speaking is carried on, or it denotes the subjects, in which the rules of dialectics are exemplified. But if the expression applies to the rules and it is considered that dialectics uses only probable rules in speaking, a sophism is at once apparent. For all the rules of dialectics are, and must be, constant and necessarily veracious: otherwise falsity would be admitted in this art. Whatever is contingent and only probable has a nature of such a composition that today it may be true, and tomorrow false: and in one direction it embraces the truth, and in another, falsity. And so those who declare that dialectics is built on probable theorems which are applied by the logician for the purpose of explaining things, stigmatize a most excellent art and reveal their amazing ignorance.

But if the definition means that dialectics is the art of speaking of only probabilities, then dialectics is deprived of the greatest share of its patrimony. For through the faculty of natural reason, whose image dialectics reflects, all things, both necessary and probable, both imaginary and actually existent, can be understood and discussed and explained. What then is to prevent all things, whether probable or necessary, whether true or imaginary, from being treated and expounded by the faculty of the dialectic art, in which all the power of human reason is represented as though in a picture? Without question logic embraces the faculty generally relating to the discussion of everything, and accordingly to associate dialectics with the treatment of probabilities is like limiting arithmetic, whereby everything can be reckoned, to the reckoning of maritime things only.

Even if speaking with probability is identical with drawing a conclusion with probable reason, as many writers consider, it is certainly a definition of dialectics, in one of its parts. Of all the parts of dialectics the syllogism alone makes a conclusion, and that not always with probable reason, but frequently with necessary and often also with sophistic reason. Even the consequent inferred from the antecedent is always a necessary one.

Besides, if dialectics is defined as the art of judging probability, that is assigned to the whole of dialectics which applies to one phase of dialectics. For the judgment of probability is effected by the rules of the proposition: invention adds nothing in regard to judging probability, nor does the syllogism, nor the method. Even the definition of dialectics, proposed by Cicero, offends by its monstrous sophism. Dialectics, he declares, is the art of distinguishing truth from falsity. Cicero did not include by such a definition the entire essence and faculty of dialectics. For to what purpose have the rules of invention been described? Or the rules of the syllogism? Or of method? Invention interprets and explains the rule for inventing an argument: the syllogism interprets and explains the system for judging an inference; method interprets and explains the organizing procedure. There is no rule among them in regard to judging truth and falsity. Only the axiom establishes rules on such judgment. Therefore Cicero was mistaken in his definition of dialectics. For what applies to one phase only of dialectics must in no sense be attributed to dialectics as a whole. The first general law does not permit the conjunction of the special with the general, to prevent a charge of falsity as a consequence of such a conjunction. But Cicero in his definition of dialectics joins the special with the general. For the term dialectics comprehends a certain common force, and a faculty diffused among various things in general: but the judgment of truth and falsity is something special and peculiar to axioms: whence it follows that it is utterly false to say that the entire art of dialectics is defined in relation to the judgment of truth and falsity. Cicero would ridicule a man who defined the Capitol of the city of Rome by one house or one column on the Capitol. He would say that a man who defined the platane grove of Licinius Crassus by one branch should be shouted down with contempt. For this reason Cicero and others who subscribed to Cicero's definition of dialectics must in no instance be accepted. For the definition of dialectics is of such a character that it interprets not some phase of dialectics only, but scrupulously embraces its entire effectiveness, all its essence, and its faculty.

The distinction between art and science, whereby dialectics is said to be an art in respect of probable things that are under discussion, but a science in respect of its rules, that are necessary, is too subtle and ridiculous. For all the rules of any art have a necessary truth, and can be both in necessary and in probable things. There is no difference whatever between the art and the science, but the significance and meaning of both terms is identical.

Furthermore, the difference between rhetoric and dialectics, which other logicians strangely accept, smacks of the subtlety of the scholastic mind, without understanding the truth of its proper use. Dialectics is like a fist, with the fingers clasped together. Rhetoric is like the palm, with the fingers individually extended. The former follows the concise, contracted style of speaking: the latter pursues the entire subject more ornately and richly. But we are talking about the men who profess these arts, while nothing is said about the arts themselves. Those who formerly discussed a thesis in the schools, concluded their entire presentation with brief points in their arguments. But those who delivered speeches in court eloquently discussed a current controversy in lucid, fluent talk, using the rules of both phases of dialectics, the former very concisely and briefly, the latter eloquently and ornately. For no speech in court can be considered to be delivered with fluent richness of detail without the invention of arguments and without their systematic presentation in

the form of axioms. In fact, many arguments are concluded syllogistically in forensic speeches: almost everything is sifted
through a methodical order. If then in every speech that is re-
plete with the elegant figures of amplifications, dialectics is presented in arguments designed to dispute a proposed controversy
in the arrangement of these arguments axiomatically, in concluding the question by the third argument according to syllogistic
rules, in the harmonious method of dealing with the facts: what
is this egregious ignorance that says the art of logic is fettered
to concise, mutilated disputations, while rhetoric alone expounds
everything more eloquently and more copiously? Let them say
that Cicero, when speaking fluently in the forum, exhibited no
shrewdness in argumentation, that he affirmed or denied nothing by simple or compound axiom, produced no apothegm either
generally or specially, that he made no confirmation syllogistically during the sequence of his arguments. Let them say that
he confused everything by chaotic disarrangement of his material. Let them say, I repeat, that Cicero, in order to prove his
case, brought rhetoric only to bear in his metaphors and figures
and delivery, and that all his achievements lacked truth and reason. Would Cicero not bring against such men the most serious
charge of insanity? Would he not convince them that he had
made no magnificent amplifications, had treated no theme eloquently without the argument of logical invention and the aid
of his judgment? He would teach those who prefer knowledge
to ignorance that in brilliant rhetoric there is a great power in
metaphors and figures, in rhythmic harmony, in dignified decla-
mation, directed to pleasure and persuasion: but there is a
greater power in the weight of convincing reasons and in the
commendable wisdom of accurate judgment. He would passion-
ately contend that rhetoric lacks nothing for the instruction of
the audience, but that the entire method of elucidating and explaining a subject lies in arguments and in the judgment of such
arguments systematically propounded. Therefore a speech delivered in the forum with the most ornate elegance will be said
to be as much dialectical as rhetorical. At least the ornamenta-

tion of phraseology by metaphor and figure and harmonious rhythms produces a charming effect: then there is the delivery of a speech so embellished. These two factors only, I assert, belong to the art of rhetoric. But the exposition of the proposed disputation through causes, effects, subjects, adjuncts, differences, comparisons, and similar techniques, whether those arguments are linked together by a proposition, or whether they are arranged syllogistically, or whether, finally, they are reduced to orderly elegance, whatever, I say, is expounded and treated in this manner is achieved through the faculty and the aid of dialectics. The extent of dialectics then is as comprehensive as that of rhetoric, even more so. For a speech may be built up of the simplest words and without rhetoric. But no speech can be expounded and concluded without arguments, properly arranged. Dialectics may even be practiced in thought, mentally, when we utter nothing that is pure in diction, or brilliant with the spoken embellishment of words. Therefore it is very stupid to transfer the distinction that men speaking in the schools or in public made formerly, to these arts themselves. This ridiculous distinction, devised by others in the schools, seeped into many minds, inducing them to believe that the whole usefulness of dialectics lies in scholastic wrangling. For it is not circumscribed within scholastic limits, and generously pervades every phase throughout the entire span of life. It did not arise in order to lie obscurely hidden in shadow and in the treatises of philosophers, but to be brought forth into the sunlight.

Dialectics is the mistress of counsels and wisdom in the court of princes. It is an associate in deciding verdicts on the benches of magistrates. On the battlefield it is the leader in strategy and planning. Moreover, whether we deliberate in private, or discuss any matter publicly with others, the remarkable use of dialectics shines out.

There are two parts to dialectics: invention and judgment. There are as many parts to the art of dialectics as there are acts of the human mind involving the use of reason. But in reasoning the human mind performs two functions only; for it is directed either to invention or to correct judgment. Consider all the orators and poets, and all the historians; read their famous works: carefully peruse every single philosopher; even examine all the speeches of all the great orators. You will at once discover that nothing is contained in them that is not subject to the method either of finding or of judging an argument. There, every mental act, every deliberation, every thought, every digression must be related to either invention or judgment. For whatever refers to memory is as it were a reflection of judgment and springs from it. And so since there are in general two functions only of natural reason, there must be at least two phases of trained reasoning, that is, of the art of logic. But if there is any thing in logic that does not apply to invention, nor to judgment, it must be eliminated from dialectics.

Invention is the part of dialectics dealing with the inventing of arguments. That is, invention is a division of dialectics that presents the rules for finding causes, effects, subjects, adjuncts, and other arguments.

Argument is that which tends to produce a feeling toward something. Argument is defined by a certain faculty suitable and applicable to the exposition of a topic: If any argument contains the force that makes it adequate for the illustration and confirmation of another argument. As the cause is apt and fit to clarify and prove an effect, so in general there is in argument a certain aptness so to speak for demonstrating and proving the nature of a species. The same view must be held in regard to other arguments. But the force of such arguments, by which arguments are suited for the exposition of a subject, arises from the relations or affection and a kind of respect of one argument to another. For all arguments have an affection and relationship to each other. Thus a certain relationship intervenes between cause and effect. In the subject there is a mutual relationship to the adjunct. The genus has a mutual relationship with the species: and the definition with the thing defined. The same principle holds good with the other arguments. Thus the argument from the relationship of one thing to another is adapted for the clarification and demonstration of that thing, with which it is joined by mutual affection. In this regard it should be observed that some arguments at least are mutually explained and proved by others, among which affections and relationship of this kind exist. Hence it is that the whole only is proved by the parts: and the thing defined is at least explained by definition: and one thing which disagrees is made explicit by means of the other object of disagreement: and the compared thing is demonstrated by the thing with which it is compared: because it has an unimpaired relationship and affection only in regard to the parts; and because the entire relationship of the thing defined is with the definition alone: and difference with difference, and comparison with comparison. As to which arguments have this mutual affection and relationship, that is deduced from the definition of every argument. For every argument is defined by that argument with which it has a mutual relationship. For example: Cause is defined by effect, and similarly effect by cause. It must also not be forgotten that the name and the nature of the argument change in accordance with a different reason for its affection. A man compared with different things has a different relationship and affection, and if one regards his effects, man will be the cause. If his adjuncts are considered, he will be the subject. If his definition is considered, he will be the thing defined. You see now the power and meaning comprehended by the definition of an argument. The argument is that which is adapted to prove a point from its own relationship to relationship to another, that is, to judge, expound, illustrate, prove. To this it must be added that arguments are things themselves, feelings of the mind, and concepts of spirit and inner reason, not of language or external speech. Furthermore, these arguments themselves are considered in invention, according as some are disconnected and separated from others, not as joined together. For invention performs enough for its own function if it finds arguments and lays them bare: by the rules of judgment we are taught how arguments, once found and set down separately, should be joined and connected into one decision.

An argument is technical or non-technical. A technical argument is one that proves itself. The faculty of arguments in proving and expounding a question is not a faculty of the same reason. For most arguments have an inherent faculty for conviction native to themselves, in fact almost all of them except the one argument of testimony. For testimony does not have the power of explanation lodged and innate in itself, but borrows and acquires it from another source, that is, from the technical arguments.

Technical argument is first, or arises from the first. It is first, because it has an origin of its own. Not all arguments experience the same form of origin. Some are as it were first principles and spring from themselves, as: causes, effects, subjects, adjuncts, differences, comparisons: for their nature and explanation depend on themselves, and are not acquired elsewhere. But there are other arguments that issue from those first principles, as: conjugations, etymology, the whole and the part, genus, species, definition, and so on. The nature and the explanation of these are derived from the first arguments: genus and definition, from causes: species, from effects: etymology, occasionally from differences. Hence it is impossible to understand the nature of genus, species, definition, etymology, what power and affection they have as proofs, before first explaining and understanding what cause is and effect, and difference. On this account the first arguments are said to be of their own origin, because consideration of them is the first step, and because they contain the first principle of the nature and the affection that exist in the other arguments.

The first argument is simple or compound. Simple is that which is considered simply and absolutely. Arguments are considered either simply and absolutely and without comparison: or some arguments are compared with others. For example: Cicero argues. In this statement there are two arguments, but considered simply, that is, without comparison. Cicero is not compared with the discussion, nor the discussion with Cicero: hence each is a simple argument. But if I say: Cicero is more distinguished than Lentulus. Here Cicero is compared with Lentulus: and hence in this proposition Cicero and Lentulus will be comparative arguments.

A simple argument is suitable or unsuitable. Suitable, when it fits the subject under discussion. Whatever is considered simply without comparison either agrees with another argument or differs from it. Whatever things have some inner harmony must all be considered as suitable arguments. Socrates and the Scholar agree with each other: thus they are suitable arguments. Socrates and a Tree disagree with and oppose each other: they are therefore unsuitable.

An argument is suitable either absolutely or in some particular manner. Absolutely suitable arguments are cause and effect. Agreement among things is not well-matched and equal: some things agree in a narrower sense: others in a slighter sense, in some manner or other. Things between which there is a very close and as it were essential agreement are called absolutely suitable arguments: these are two-fold, cause and effect.

Cause is that whose strength it is. Cause is an absolutely suitable argument, by whose force the effect ensues. This is the general definition of cause, and it signifies the nature common to each cause. The expression *by whose force* denotes the *cause* by which, through which, on account of which the effect is produced. The term *things* in the definition is generally taken for the effect of any cause. The great importance of this argument is deduced from the fact that causes are, as it were, the sources of all cognition and knowledge. For once the causes are found and thoroughly understood, the thing itself is understood. For example: The one who has a spiritual and intellectual comprehension and knowledge of the causes of man, comprehends and understands man's entire nature.

Cause is efficient, material, formal, and final. There are two kinds of causes, but they lack names: thus, instead of the genus, two species are postulated. The first kind includes the efficient and the material cause: the second includes the formal and the final cause. No cause can be conceived that does not fall into this division: and it is either efficient, or material, or formal, or final.

The efficient cause is that whereby the thing is. It is so called because the effect comes from the power of the efficient cause. The expression *whereby* refers to the essential nature of the efficient cause and distinguishes the efficient from the other causes. For in order to produce an effect from an efficient cause, the effect is related and particular to the efficient. So a house comes from the architect: a picture is painted by Apelles. The architect therefore is the efficient cause of the house, as Apelles is of the painting.

JOSIAH ROYCE
(1855-1916)

Taught at Harvard from 1882, an outstanding protagonist of American idealism who maintained that only as far as man is knowing, this knowable world exists. Man's mind is part of Logos, the world soul, and only because of this participation can man think truth beyond his own self. Also ethically man must think in terms of the greater community and not narrowly of himself. He was influenced by Hegel, Peirce and James. Idealistic metaphysics was to him a guarantee not only for absolute certainty, but for a rule over the whole life by right judgment, directed by the impact of absolute truth.

Main Works:

Religious Aspect of Philosophy; The World and the Individual; The Problem of Christianity; Lectures on Modern Idealism; The Spirit of Modern Philosophy.

———

The Principles of Logic

§ 1. A very frequent account of the office of Logic runs substantially as follows: "Logic is a Normative Science. It deals, namely, with the Norms whereby sound or correct thinking is distinguished from incorrect thinking. It consists of two parts,— a general part, called Formal Logic, which defines the universal or formal normative principles to which all correct thinking must conform, and a special and very extended part called Applied Logic, or Methodology, which deals with the norms of thought

———

From: *The Encyclopedia of the Philosophical Sciences.*

in their application to the methods used in various special sciences."

From this conventional account the present sketch will deliberately depart. A discussion of some of the more important problems of Methodology will be comprised in our first section. The remaining paragraphs of this paper will be devoted to indicating, very summarily, the nature of a doctrine of which the traditional General or Formal Logic is but a part, and in fact, a very subordinate part. To this doctrine the name "The Science of Order" may be given. It is a science which is indeed incidentally concerned with the norms of the thinking process. But its character as a normative doctrine is wholly subordinate to other features which make it of the most fundamental importance for philosophy. It is today in a very progressive condition. It is in some notable respects new. It offers inexhaustible opportunities for future progress.

§ 2. Everyone will agree that throughout its history Logic has been concerned with the conduct and with the results of the thinking process. Now the thinking process is indeed, from its very nature, *methodical*. In every human science, and in every human art that is teachable at all, the thinking process appears either as the creator and the guide, or else as the formulator and the analyzer, of the methods which characterize this science or art. If an art grows up instinctively, as the product of social need and of individual talent, the efforts to teach this art, so that it may pass from master to apprentice, lead sooner or later to an analysis and thoughtful formulation of the methods employed by the skilful workman. And when an art or a science is deliberately invented or advanced by the conscious skill of the individual inquirer or discoverer, the procedure used either includes a purposeful application of already known methods to new undertakings, or else involves an effort to create methods. Everywhere, then, the consciousness of method grows in proportion as thought comes to play a successful part in the organization of human life.

Since, however, the methods used vary with the different arts and sciences, and yet have certain important features that are common to all or to many of the undertakings of these arts and sciences, it is natural that a comparative study of methods should form the topic of a more or less independent body of doctrine. And, as a fact, such a Methodology, such a "Normative doctrine," such an effort to survey and to systematize the methods used by all or by one or another great body of thoughtful workers, has repeatedly constituted the principal task assigned to Logic, whether the distinction between General or Formal Logic and Applied Logic has been emphasized or not. Logic as a branch of philosophy began, as is well known, when the differences of opinion amongst the various philosophers, when the dialectical problems brought to notice by the Eleatic school, and when the more or less practical inquiries of the Sophists into the arts of disputation and of persuasion, had led to a conscious need for a general study of the methods of right thinking. In Aristotle's case the task of surveying, and in part of creating, a systematic body of sciences constituted an additional ground for undertaking a general methodology of the thinking process. And ever since Aristotle the view that one main purpose of Logic is to expound the "Art of Thinking," or the definition of Logic in some more or less exclusively methodological fashion, has played a large part in the history of our science. And this is why the definition of Logic as a Normative Science is still so common, and in its place useful.

As a fact, however, Methodology, taken in its usual sense as a study of the norms and methods of thought used in the various arts and sciences, is the mother of Logic taken in the other sense hereafter to be expounded. For the undertakings of Methodology lead to certain special problems, such as Plato and Aristotle already began to study, and such as recent inquiry makes more and more manifold and important. These problems, when considered for their own sake, assume an aspect that pretty sharply differentiates them from the problems of Methodology proper. They are problems regarding, *not* the methods by which the thinker succeeds, nor yet the norms of correct thinking viewed as norms, but rather the *Forms,* the *Categories,* the *Types of Order,* which characterize any realm of objects which a thinker has actually succeeded in mastering, or can possibly succeed in mastering by his methods. Taken in this sense, *Logic is the General Science of Order,* the *Theory of the Forms of any Orderly Realm of Objects,* real or ideal.

Just because Logic, viewed as such a doctrine, has resulted from the efforts to formulate the norms and methods of thinking, the question how Logic as Methodology differs from and yet gives birth to Logic conceived as the Science of Order, must be summarily indicated in the rest of our opening section. To this end, we must consider some of the principal problems of Methodology.

§ 3. Let us then first return to a brief mention of some of the problems of method which characterize the well known early stages of logical inquiry, as they are represented, for instance, in remarks that frequently recur in the Platonic dialogues.

The "plastic youth" of the Platonic dialogues, is to be instructed by Socrates in the right method of thinking, and is to be warned against the false arts of the Sophists. The instruction that he most frequently receives relates: (1) To the proper method of definition; (2) To the task of systematic classification, with the prevailing use of dichotomy for the sake of dividing a wider class into its constituent species; (3) To a careful study of the evidence which attaches to certain notable propositions; (4) To a watchful examination of modes of inference. The special considerations which are so frequently repeated in the Platonic dialogues in regard to each of these matters, do not here, in any detail, concern us. It is enough to recall a few facts only. Definition, for instance, according to the Socratic and Platonic methodology, depends indeed upon a collection of special instances of the concept that is to be defined. But, as Socrates often points out, instances, taken merely as such, constitute no definition. For we do not learn what clay is merely by remembering or by naming several different sorts of clay. One must conceive, in universal terms, what is common to these sorts of clay. And so too it is if we want to define justice, or virtue, or knowledge. Definition gets at the essence, at the "Idea," at the type, which special instances exemplify, and depends upon taking the universal as such, and upon bringing it to our knowledge with clearness. But a definition, once thus formulated upon the basis of the instances first chosen, needs to be further tested. One tests it according to this methodological doctrine, by applying it to new instances, and by a deliberate search for possible inconsistencies. For a truly universal account of a concept must provide for all the cases that rightfully fall under the concept which is to be defined, and must exclude all instances which do not belong to the type in question. In case inconsistencies are discovered, by finding that the definition includes too much or too little, the definition first attempted must be amended. But in such consideration of right definitions, one is greatly aided by remembering that no universal types exist in isolation. And here a very important feature of Plato's methodology appears. *The universals, the "Ideas," form a system.* There are the more and the less inclusive universals. Instances, or classes of instances, which appear to possess mutually inconsistent characters, may still be conceived as members of the same larger class and in so far as illustrating the same universal, if only they can be shown to be determined to be thus distinct through a process of classification, whereby the essence of the more inclusive universal is in fact more clearly portrayed than it could be through a merely abstract definition. One knows number, in its universal essence, all the better, when one learns to classify the numbers as even and odd, as perfect squares or as not perfect squares, and so on. Such classifications are very commonly best made in the form of dichotomies.

The class A may be divided into A that is *b*, and the A that is not *b*. Arrays of classes and sub-classes may be arranged by repeating such a process. And then a sub-class whose traits are very highly specific, may be defined in universal terms by considering, first A (some "highest genus," as, in terms of the later logic, we may already name it); then B, which comprises whatever A possesses the character *b*; then C, which comprises whatever B possesses the differential mark *c*, and so on. Thus definitions may be rendered both consistent and systematic, and the system or true Order of the universals may be at least approached, if not fully grasped.

As for evidence which attaches to single propositions, that also must be considered in the light of special test-cases, must be subjected to the criterion of consistency, and must be made familiar by repeated examination. In the course of such examination and re-examination of the convictions which most interest the philosopher, the importance of a clear consciousness regarding the nature of correct inference often comes to light. One is clear that one infers rightly, not when one is carried away by the Sophist's torrent of persuasive oratory, but when one observes the necessity of each individual transition from thought to thought. If one believes that "All A is B," a closer examination readily shows the general truth that one may not thence infer that "All B is A." Yet in hasty discourse, or under the influence of a Sophist's oratory, one might let such a false inference pass unheeded.

§ 4. So much may here suffice as a mere hint and reminder of thoughts which now seem methodological commonplaces, but which, at that early stage of the history of Logic, were momentous for the whole future of the subject. The elementary textbooks still repeat the substance of these observations, even if their context is no longer that which appears in Plato's dialogues. It will be noted at once that such a methodology naturally leads to a view of the nature and constitution of the world of truth, whose significance, at least as Plato conceived it, goes far beyond the value of these precepts as guides for the learner of the art of thinking. If, namely, these things are so, then, in Plato's opinion: (1) *The realm of Universals or "Ideas" is essentially a System,* whose unity and order are of the first importance for the philosopher; (2) *Inference is possible because truths have momentous objective Relations,* definable precisely in so far as the process of inference is definable; (3) *The "Order and Connection" of our rational processes,* when we follow right methods, *is a sort of copy of an order and connection which the individual thinker finds, but does not make.* One thus sets out to formulate the right method. One discovers, through this very effort, a new realm—*a realm of types, of forms, of relations.* All these appear to be at least as real as the facts of the physical world. And in Plato's individual opinion they are far more real than the latter. Thus Methodology leads Plato to a new Ontology. The world of the Forms becomes the world of the Platonic Ideas; and Dialectic, with its methods, becomes for Plato the gateway of Metaphysics. Here he finds the key to unlock the mystery of Being.

We are not in the least concerned to estimate in this discussion the correctness or even the historical significance of the Platonic Metaphysic,—a doctrine thus merely suggested. It is enough to note, however, that even if one sets aside as false or as irrelevant all the principal metaphysical conclusions of Plato, one sees that in any case the Methodology of the logician, even in this early stage of the doctrine, inevitably gives rise to the problem as to the relatively objective order and system of those objects of thought to which the methodologist appeals when he formulates his procedure. The Platonic theory of Ideas, Aristotle's later theory of Forms, the innumerable variations of the Platonic tradition which the subsequent history of thought contains,—all these may or may not be of use in formulating a sound metaphysic. But in any case this comes to light: If a logician can indeed formulate any sound method at all, in any generally valid way, he can do so only because certain objects which he considers when he thinks,—be these objects definitions, classes, types, relations, propositions, inferences, numbers, or other "principles,"—form a more or less orderly system, or group of systems, whose constitution predetermines the methods that he must use when he thinks. This system, or these systems, and their constitution, are in some sense more or less objective. That is: What constitutes order, and what makes orderly method possible, is not the product of the thinker's personal and private caprice. Nor can he "by taking thought" wilfully alter the most essential facts and relations upon which his methods depend. If an orderly classification of a general class of objects is possible, then, however subjective the choice of one's principles of classification may be, there is *something* about the general nature of any such order and system of genera and species,—something which is the same for all thinkers, and which outlasts private caprices and changing selections of objects and of modes of classification.

Meanwhile (as we may here add by way of general comment), orderliness and system are much the same in their most general characters, whether they appear in a Platonic dialogue, or in a modern text-book of botany, or in the commercial conduct of a business firm, or in the arrangement and discipline of an army, or in a legal code, or in a work of art, or even in a dance, or in the planning of a dinner. Order is order. System is system. Amidst all the variations of systems and of orders, certain general types and characteristic relations can be traced. If then the methodologist attempts to conduct thinking processes in any orderly way, he inevitably depends upon finding in the objects about which he thinks those features, relations, orderly characters, upon which the very possibility of definite methods depends. Whatever one's metaphysic may be, one must therefore recognize that there is something objective about the Order both of our thoughts, and of the things concerning which we think; and one must admit that every successful Methodology depends upon grasping and following some of the traits of this orderly constitution of a realm that is certainly a realm of facts.

§ 5. This brief reference to the consequences to which the Socratic and Platonic Methodology so early led, may suffice to suggest a deep connection between Methodology proper, and what we have called the Science of Order. This connection becomes only the more impressive if we pass from those elementary and now commonplace considerations which play their part in the methodological passages of the Platonic dialogues, to a few observations that a brief review of contemporary scientific thinking will readily bring to the mind of any fairly well informed student.

Let us then at once turn from the earliest stages of Logic to its latest phases. Let us here omit any attempt to expound the Aristotelian Logic, or to estimate its methodological value, or to tell its later history. Let us pass over the often repeated story of the Baconian reform of scientific methods and of the vastly more important consequences of the experimental methods which Galileo and his contemporaries introduced into modern science. Let us come directly to the present day; let us remind ourselves of some of the most familiar of the doctrines of modern scientific Methodology; and then let us see how these doctrines lead us to problems which demand their own special treatment, and which again force us to define a Science of Order,—a science distinct from Methodology proper, but necessary to a true understanding of the latter.

It is a commonplace of modern Methodology that our knowledge of nature is gained through induction, and upon the basis of experience. It is equally a commonplace that scientific induction does not consist merely of the heaping up of the records of the facts of crude experience. Science is never merely knowledge; it is orderly knowledge. It aims at controlling systems of facts. Amongst the vastly numerous methods which various sciences employ in our day, there are some which stand out as especially universal and characteristic means of accomplishing the aim just emphasized. Let us mention the most prominent of these methods. Such mention will at once bring us again into contact with the fundamental problems whose nature we are here attempting to illustrate.

And so, first, every science, in dealing with the facts of experience, employs *Methods of Classification,* and is so far still making its own use of the lessons that Socrates taught. There is, in the development of every new science of nature, a stage in which, in the absence of more advanced insight into the laws to which the facts are subject, classification is the most prominent feature of the science. Botany and Zoology, in their earlier stages of growth, were, for a considerable time, sciences in which classification predominated. Anthropology, in its treatment of the problems presented by the racial distinctions of mankind, is still very largely in the stage of classification; while in other of its fields of work, as, for instance, in its comparative study of the forms and results of human culture, Anthropology now pursues methods which subordinate classification to the higher types of methodical procedure. Amongst the medical sciences, Psychiatry is just emerging from the stage where the classification of cases, of symptoms, and of disorders made up the bulk of the science; and has begun to live upon a higher plane of methods. In the Organic Sciences the stage of classification (as such instances remind us) very generally endures long, and is with difficulty transcended. And the more complex the facts to be understood, the harder it is for any science, organic or inorganic, to get beyond this first stage. In the case of Chemistry we have a notable instance of a science where the complexity of the facts long forced the science to consist in large part of the enumeration and classification of elements, compounds, properties, and reactions, despite the fact that the experimental methods used were especially well adapted to lead to knowledge of very general and exact laws. Recent Chemistry, however, has grown far beyond the stage of mere classification.

Where a science passes from this early stage to one of higher insight, *two* more or less sharply distinct types of methods, either separately or (as oftener happens) in combination, frequently play a large part in determining the transition. These are (1) The type of the methods that involve *comparing the corresponding stages* in the various *processes or products of natural Evolution* with which the science has to deal; and (2) The Statistical Method proper, that is the method *which uses exact enumerations as the bases of inductions.*

§ 6. In the wholly or partly organic sciences, the Comparative methods just mentioned play a very large part. How they lead beyond the stage of classification to higher sorts of knowledge, is well exemplified by the case of Geology. That science began with classifications of rocks and of formations. But almost from the outset of the science it became evident that these formations were not sudden creations, but had been the results of processes that had required long periods of time. The earlier efforts of "Vulcanists" and "Plutonists" to furnish adequate universal theories of these processes in more or less simple terms, showed that other methods must be used. The key to unlock *one* portion of the mysteries which the new science was to explore, was furnished by the comparative study of the geological formations found in various regions of the earth's crust. When this comparison showed, for instance, corresponding series of fossil-bearing strata, a new light was thrown upon the history of the earth. To be sure, such comparative study of geological series of formations and of fossils, constitutes but one portion of the resources of Geology. Other methods, and very different ones, play their part in Dynamical Geology. But the importance of the comparative study of corresponding geological formations for Historical Geology, serves as one example of what makes the comparative method, in its various analogous forms, significant in great numbers of scientific investigations.

Suppose, namely, that what is to be studied consists of the stages or of the results of any evolutionary process whatever. Something has grown, or has resulted from the aging or from the "weathering" of the crust of a planet, or from the slow accretion of the results of a civilization. Rock formations or the anatomical constitution of various organisms, or social systems such as those of law, or such as customs, or folklore, or language, are to be understood. One begins with classification. But herewith science is only initiated, not matured. For it is the evolutionary process itself, or the system of such processes, which is to be comprehended. The comparative procedure it is which first *correlates the corresponding stages of many analogous or "homologous" evolutionary processes and products,* and thus enables us not merely to classify but to unify our facts, by seeing how the most various phenomena may turn out to be stages in the expression of some one great process.

§ 7. Side by side with the Comparative Methods stand the Statistical Methods. These two sorts of methods are, in fact, by no means always very sharply to be distinguished. There are various transitions from one to the other. Every comparison of numerous evolutionary processes, or of the results of such processes, involves of course some more or less exact enumeration of the cases compared.

But such enumeration may not be the main object of consideration. Very many statistical enumerations are guided by the definite purpose to carry out with precision the comparative methods just exemplified. But, as the well known applications of statistical methods to insurance, and to other highly practical undertakings show us, the most characteristic features of the statistical procedure are independent of any such interest as leads the geologist to his correlations of corresponding formations, or the comparative philologist to his analysis of corresponding grammatical forms in different related languages. The Statistical Methods are often used as a short road to a knowledge of uniformities of nature whose true basis and deeper laws escape our knowledge. Mortality tables are good guides to the insurance companies, even when medical knowledge of many of the causes of death remains in a very elementary stage. The statistics of marriage and divorce, of suicide and of crime, or of commerce and of industry, furnish bases for sociological research, even when there is no present hope of reducing the science in question to any exact form.

But whatever their uses, the Statistical Methods involve us in certain problems which have to do with the *correlation of series of phenomena*. A glance at any considerable array of statistical results serves to show us how the mere heaping up of enumerations of classes of facts would be almost as useless as the mere collection of disordered facts without any enumeration. Statistical results, in fact, when they are properly treated, serve to describe for us the constitution of objects whose general type Fechner had in mind when he defined his *Collectivgegenstände*. Such a *Collectivgegenstand* is a conceptual object which results when we conceive a great number of individual facts of experience subjected to a process of thought whereof the following stages may here be mentioned:—

(a) These individual facts are classified with reference to certain of the features with respect to which they vary. Such features are exemplified by the varying sizes of organisms and of their organs, by various numbers of members which different interesting parts of the individual objects in question possess, by the extent to which certain recorded observations of a physical quantity differ from another, and so on.

(b) This classification of the facts with reference to their variations having been in general accomplished, the Statistical Method enumerates the members of each of the classes, in so far as such enumeration is possible or useful.

(c) The various enumerations, once made, are arranged in orderly series, with reference to questions that are to be answered regarding the laws to which the variations in question are subject. Such series, in case they are sufficiently definite and precise in their character, tend to show us *how two or more aspects of the phenomena in question tend to vary together,*—as, for instance, how human mortality varies with age; how the mean temperature of a place on the earth's surface varies with its latitude or with the season of the year; how the size of an organ or an organism varies with conditions that are known to be determined by heredity or by environment; and so on.

(d) *Various series,* when once defined with reference to such features, *are correlated with one another,* by means which the Methodology of the various Statistical Sciences has further to consider.

(e) And, as a result of such processes, the statistician comes to deal with "aggregates" or "blocks" of facts which, taken as *units,* so to speak, *of a higher order,* appear as possessing a structure in which laws of nature are exemplified and revealed. Such *ordered aggregates treated as units of a higher order are Collectivgegenstände.*

Now it is obvious that every step of such a methodical procedure presupposes and uses the concepts of *number*, of *series*, and of the *correlation of series;* and that the whole process, when successful, leads to the establishment of *an orderly array of objects of thought,* and to the revelation of the laws of nature through the establishment and the description of this order. *The concept of Order is thus a fundamental one both for the Comparative and for the Statistical Methods.*

§ 8. Both the Comparative Methods and the Statistical Methods are used, in the more developed sciences that employ them, in as close a relation as possible to a method which, in the most highly developed regions of physical science, tends to supersede them altogether. This Method consists in *The Organized Combination of Theory and Experience.* This combination reaches its highest levels in the best known regions of physical science. Its various stages are familiar, at least in their most general features. But the methodological problems involved are of great complexity, and the effort to understand them leads with peculiar directness to the definition of the task of the general Science of Order. Let us briefly show how this is the case. In order to do so we must call attention to a familiar general problem of method which has so far been omitted from this sketch.

By the Statistical and by the Comparative methods, laws of nature can be discovered, not with any absolute certainty, but only with a certain degree of *probability.* The degree of probability in question depends (1) upon the number of instances that have been empirically observed in applying these methods, and that have been compared, or statistically arrayed, and (2) upon the fairness with which these facts have been chosen. Since every induction has as its basis a finite number of empirical data, and in general a number that is very small in comparison with the whole wealth of the natural facts that are under investigation, any result of the comparative or of the statistical methods is subject to correction as human experience enlarges. A question that has always been prominent in the discussion of the general methodology of the empirical sciences, is the question as to our right *to generalize from a limited set of data,* so as to make assertions about a larger, or about an unlimited set of facts, in which our data are included. By the Comparative Method, one learns that such and such sets or series of facts are thus and thus correlated,—as for instance that the geological strata so far observed in a given region of the earth's surface show signs of having been laid down in a certain order, with these and these conformities and non-conformities, faultings, foldings, and so on. How far and in what sense has one a right, by what has been called "extrapolation," to extend the order-system thus defined to more or less nearly adjacent regions, and to hold that any still unobserved geological features of those regions will be, in their character and order, of the type that one has already observed? Or again, by the Statistical Method, one learns that certain facts enable one to define a *Collectiv-gegenstand* of a certain type. How far can one rightly "extrapolate," and extend one's statistical curves or other statistical order-types, to regions of fact that have not yet been subject to enumeration? For instance, how far can one make use of mortality tables, framed upon the basis of previous records of death, for the purpose of insuring lives in a population which inevitably differs, in at least some respects, from the population that has already met with its fate, and that has had its deaths recorded in the mortality tables?

The general answer to this question has often been attempted by methodologists, and has usually taken the form of asserting that such "extrapolation" logically depends, either upon the principle, *"That nature is uniform,"* or upon the still more general principle: "That *every event*" (or, as one sometimes asserts, *"every individual fact"*) *"has its sufficient reason."* It is commonly supposed, then, that the basis of our right to generalize from a limited set of data to a wider range of natural facts, some of which have not yet been observed, may be stated in either one of two ways:—(I.) "These and these facts have been observed to exemplify a certain order-system. But nature is uniform. That is, nature's various order-systems are all of them such as to exemplify either one invariant type, or a certain number of definable and invariant types. Hence the type of the observed facts can be, with due generalization, extended to the unobserved facts." Or again, using the so-called "Principle of Sufficient Reason," one has often stated the warrant for extrapolation substantially thus: (II.) "The facts observed are such as they are, and conform to their own order-system, not by chance, but for some Sufficient Reason. But a sufficient reason is something that, from its nature, is general, and capable of being formulated as a law of nature. The facts still unobserved will therefore conform to this same order type (will exemplify this same law), *unless there is some sufficient reason why they should not conform to this type.* This reason, if it exists, can also be stated in general terms, as another law of nature, and must in any case be *consistent* with the reason and the law that the observed facts have exemplified. Since law thus universally reigns in the natural world, since all is necessary, and since the observed facts not merely are what they are, but, for sufficient reason, *must be* what they are, we ought to regard the laws in terms of which the observed facts have been formulated as applicable to unobserved facts, unless there is a known and probable reason why they should not so conform. To be sure, our conclusion in any one case of such extrapolation is only probable, because it must be admitted, as a possibility, that there may be a sufficient reason why at least some of the unobserved facts should conform to laws now unknown. But the presumption is in favor of extrapolations unless sufficient reason is known why they should not be attempted.

§ 9. Familiar as such modes of stating the warrant for generalizations and extrapolations are, it requires but little reflection to see that the formulations just stated *leave untouched the most important features of the very problem that they propose to solve.* Let us suppose that one who is, in regard to a given scientific field of investigation, a layman, hears the expert give an account of certain uniformities of the data that have been observed in the field in question. So far, of course, the layman is dependent upon the expert for the correctness of the report. If the question then arises, "What right is there to generalize from these observed uniformities, so as to apply them to unobserved facts that belong to this same general field?" is the layman now able to use a general principle "That Nature is uniform," to decide this matter? No! The layman, if properly critical, usually knows that this latter question is quite as much one for the expert to decide, as it is the expert's business to observe or to estimate the uniformities that have already come under observation in his own realm. In the geological case, for instance, the question whether or not certain special features of formations that have already been explored are likely to be repeated in regions not yet subject to geological study, is itself a question for the geologist. It cannot be settled by any appeal to the supposed general principle of the "Uniformity of Nature." That principle, in its abstract formulation, fails to help us precisely when and where we most need help.

Nature, in fact, is indeed full of uniformities. But what these uniformities are is itself a matter of observation. And only the very sort of experience that assures us of certain observed uniformities, can be our guide whenever we attempt to generalize from the observed uniformities to the unobserved ones. Sometimes the fact that certain uniformities have been observed, gives us very good warrant for expecting them to be repeated, in definite ways, in other regions of experience. Sometimes this is not the case, beyond some very limited range. Thus, the fact that a given man has lived ninety years, gives no presumption, based upon the general "uniformity of nature," that he will continue to live long in future. On the contrary, we are accustomed to say that, just because of "the uniformity of nature," as we now know it, he is likely to die soon; because, at his age, whenever an exceptional man chances to reach it, the general death rate is presumably high in proportion to the number of men of ninety years of age.

It follows that, if one uses the principle of the "Uniformity of Nature" as the basis for his extrapolations and generalizations, he has at once to face the question: "What uniformities are of importance in the field in question?" And to this question the *general principle of uniformity gives no answer.* This answer can only come from an empirical study of the uniformities that each region of nature presents.

Equally useless, in aiding us with reference to any one decision regarding our right to generalization and extrapolation, is the direct application of the "Principle of Sufficient Reason." How can we judge, in advance of experience, whether or no there is a "sufficient reason" why the facts not yet observed in a given field should agree in their order-system with the facts that have already been observed? Surely by itself, the abstract "Principle of Sufficient Reason," even if fully granted, only assures us that every fact, and so, of course, every order-system of facts, is what it is by virtue of *some* sufficient reason, which is of course stateable in general terms as some sort of a law. But, the very question at issue is whether the still unobserved facts of any given field of inquiry conform to the *same* laws, and so have the *same* "sufficient reasons," as the thus far observed data. This question can admittedly be answered with certainty only when the now unobserved facts have come to be observed. Till then all remains, at best, only "probable." Now the "Principle of Sufficient Reason" does not by itself state any reason why only a *few* laws, or a *few* sorts of sufficient reasons should with probability be viewed as governing nature. It does not, therefore, of itself establish *any* definable probability why there should not actually be a sufficient reason why the unobserved facts should conform to new laws.

Thus neither the abstract principle of the "Uniformity of Nature" nor the still more abstract principle of "Sufficient Reason" serves to assure us of any definite probability that observed uniformities warrant a given generalization or extrapolation into regions not as yet subjected to observation. The question "What observed uniformities are such as to warrant a probable generalization in a given field?" is a question whose answer depends not upon any general application of either of the foregoing principles. They could both hold true in a world whose facts were such as defied our efforts to find out *what* the uniform types in question were, and *what* sufficient reasons there were for any fact that took place.

§ 10. What consideration is it, then, which makes generalizations and extrapolations, upon the basis of already observed uniformities, probable? To this question the American logician, Mr. Charles S. Peirce, has given the answer that is here to be summarized.

This answer will especially aid us in understanding why the methods of comparison, and the statistical methods, inevitably lead, whenever they succeed, to a stage of science wherein the method which organically unites Theory and Observation, becomes the paramount method. And hereby we shall also be helped to see why the types of Order whose methodical employment characterizes the highest stages of the natural sciences, are the proper topic of a special science that shall deal with their logical origin and with their forms.

Suppose that there exists any finite set of facts such as are *possible objects of human experience,* that is, suppose that there exists a finite set of facts belonging to what Kant calls the realm of *mögliche Erfahrung. One* presupposition regarding these facts we may here make, for the sake of argument, without at this point attempting to criticize that presupposition. It is the simple presupposition that these facts, and so the whole aggregate of them, whatever they are, have *some definite constitution.* That is, according to our presupposition, there are possible assertions to be made about these facts which are *either true or false* of each individual fact in the set in question. And, within some range of possible assertions which we here need not attempt further to define, it may be presupposed that: "Every such assertion, if made about any one of those individual facts, and if so defined as to have a precise meaning, either is true or is not true of that fact." Thus, if our realm of "objects of possible experience" is a realm wherein men may be conceived to be present, and if the term *man* has a precise meaning, then the assertion, made of any object A in that realm, "A is a man," either is true or is not true of A. And if our realm of objects is supposed to be one which consists of black and white balls deposited in an urn, the assertion, "A is a white ball," made about one of the balls in the urn, either is true or is false.

This presupposition of the *determinate constitution* of any set of facts such as are subject to inductive investigation, is by no means a simple, not even a "self-evident" presupposition. This, indeed, we shall later have occasion to see. But this presupposition, as Peirce has shown, is the one *natural and indispensable presupposition in all inductive inquiries.* And it is further Peirce's merit, as an inductive methodologist, to have made explicit a consideration which is implicitly employed by commonsense in the ordinary inductive reasonings used in the market place, or in any other region of our practical life. This consideration is that, *if we once grant the single principle of the determinate constitution of any finite set of facts of possible experience, we can draw probable conclusions regarding the constitution of such a set of facts, in case we choose "fair samples" of this collection,* and observe their constitution, and then generalize with due precautions. And in order thus to generalize from the sample to the whole collection, *we do not need any presupposition that the collection of facts which we judge by the samples has a constitution determined by any further principle of "uniformity" than is at once involved in the assertion that the collection sampled has in the sense just illustrated, some determinate constitution.* In other words, given a finite collection of facts which has *any* determinate constitution more or less "uniform," be the "sufficient reason" for this constitution some one law, or any possible aggregate of heterogeneous "reasons" whatever—it remains true that we can, *with probability,* although, of course, *only* with probability, judge the constitution of the whole collection by the constitution of the parts which are "fair samples" of that whole even when the collection is very large and the samples are comparatively small.

That we all of us make inductions, in our daily business, which employ the principle of "fair sampling" is easy to see. Peirce has emphasized the fact that the concept of the "fair sample" is not a concept which requires any special presupposition about the uniform constitution of the collection from which we take our samples. It is possible to judge by samples the probable constitution of otherwise unknown cargoes of wheat or of coal, the general characteristics of soils, of forests, of crowds of people, of ores, of rubbish heaps, of clusters of stars, or of collections of the most varied constitution. A mob or a rubbish heap can be judged by "samples" almost as successfully as an organized army or an orderly array of objects, if only we choose from the large collection that is to be sampled a sufficient number of representative instances. And the commercially useful samples employed when cargoes, or other large collections are to be judged, are frequently surprisingly small in proportion to the size of the whole collection that is to be judged by means of them.

§ 11. The reason why such a procedure gives good results can readily be illustrated. Let us take one of the simplest possible instances. Suppose that a certain collection consists of *four* objects, which we will designate by the letters *a, b, c, d*. And to make our instance still more concrete, suppose that our collection consists in fact of four wooden blocks, which are marked, respectively, by the letters (*a, b, c, d*). Suppose that these blocks are precisely alike, except that they are painted either *red* or *white*. Let us hereupon suppose that somebody is required to judge how *all* the four blocks are colored, by drawing *two* of them at random from a bag in which they are concealed, and by then forming the hypothesis that, just as the colors *white* and *red* are present in the pair that he draws, precisely so these colors will be present and distributed in the whole set of four. In other words, if he draws two white blocks he shall be required to generalize and say: "All four of the blocks are white." If he draws one white and one red block, he shall be required to say: "Half of the blocks (that is, two of them) are red, and the others white."

Suppose next that, as a fact, the blocks *a* and *b* are red, while

the blocks *c* and *d* are white. Let us consider what results of
such a process of judging the four objects by a sample composed
of two of them, are now, under the agreed conditions, *possible.*
Of the four blocks (*a, b, c, d*), there are six pairs:—

$$(a, b) \; (a, c) \; (a, d) \; (b, c) \; (b, d) \; (c, d).$$

Six different samples, then, could be made from the collection
of blocks under the supposed conditions. Of these six possible
samples, One, namely, the sample (*a, b*) would consist, by
hypothesis, of two red blocks. Whoever chanced to draw that
sample, so that he was consequently required, by the agreement,
to judge the whole set by that pair, would judge erroneously;
for he would say: "All the four blocks are red." Whoever chanced
to draw the pair (*c, d*), would have to say: "All the blocks
are white." And he too would be wrong. But whoever drew any
one of the *four samples,* (*a, c*) (*a, d*) (*b, c*) (*b, d*), would
by agreement be obliged to say: "Two of the blocks are red
and two are white," since he would be obliged, by the agreement, to judge that the whole collection of four showed the
same distribution of white and red as was shown in the pair
that he had drawn. Thus, if all the possible pairs were independently drawn by successive judges, each one drawing one
of the possible pairs from the bag in which the four blocks
were hidden then, under the supposed agreement, *two* of the
judges would be wrong, and *four* of them right in their judgments.

This simple case illustrates the principle which Peirce uses
in his theory of the inductive procedure. In general, if we choose
partial collections from a larger collection, and judge the constitution of the whole collection from that of the parts chosen,
fixing our attention upon definable characters present or absent,
in the partial collections, we are aided towards probable inferences by the fact that there are now *more* possible "samples,"
or partial collections, that at least approximately *agree* in their
constitution with the constitution of the whole, than there are

samples that widely disagree. Two of the possible samples in the foregoing simple case disagree, four agree, in the character in question, with the collection which is, by the supposed agreement, to be judged by the samples. That is, the possible ways of successful sampling are in this case twice as numerous as the possible unsuccessful ways.

What holds in this simple case holds in a vastly more impressive way when the collections sampled are large. Only then, to be sure, the probable inferences are, in general, only approximations. Suppose a large collection containing m objects. Suppose that a proportion or per cent. of these objects actually have some character q, while the rest lack this character. Suppose that the whole large collection of m objects is to be judged, with reference to the presence or absence of q, by some comparatively small sample containing n of these objects. The success of the judgment will depend upon how far the sample of n objects that happens to be chosen differs from or agrees with the whole collection, with reference to the proportion r' per cent. of the n objects which possess the character q. Of course it is possible that $r=r'$.

In case of large collections and fairly large samples, this will not often be exactly true. But if we consider *all possible selections* of n objects from the collection of m objects, even if n is a comparatively small number, while m is a very large number, a direct calculation will readily show that decidedly *more* of the *possible* sets of "samples" containing n objects will somewhat closely resemble in their constitution the whole collection in respect of the presence or absence of q than will very widely differ in their constitution from that collection. The matter will here in general be one of approximation, not of exact results. If, once more, r' per cent. represents the proportion of the members of a given sample of n objects that possess the character q, while r per cent. is the proportion of the numbers of the whole collection that possess this same character q, it is possible to compute the number of *possible* samples consisting of n objects each, in which r' will differ from r by not less than or by not more than a determinate amount, x. The computation will show that, as this amount of difference increases, the number of possible samples in question will rapidly decrease.

In consequence, as Peirce points out, our inductive inferences can generally be stated thus, in so far as they involve the direct processes of sampling collections:—

> "A proportion r' per cent. of the P's have the character q.
> The P's are a "fair sample" of the large collection M.
> "Hence, *probably and approximately*, a proportion r' per cent. of the large collection M have the character q."

The ground for this probability thus rests, not upon the uniformity of the collection M, but upon the fact that more of the possible "fair samples" agree approximately with the whole than widely disagree therewith.

Now a "fair sample" of the large collection M is a sample concerning which we have *no reason to suppose that it has been chosen otherwise than "at random,"* or in a representative way, from among the objects of the large collection that we judge.

Thus the methodology of inductive generalization, so far as the statistical and the comparative methods are concerned, rests simply upon the principle that the facts which we study have a determinate constitution, to which we can approximate, with probability, by fairly sampling the whole through a selection of parts. From its very nature the procedure in question in all such cases is therefore essentially *tentative,* is subject to correction as comparison and statistical enumeration advance from earlier to later stages, and is productive of approximately accurate results, and, in general, of approximations only.

From this point of view we see why it is that experience may be said to teach an expert in a given field, not only what uniformities have been observed in that field, but what approximate and probable right one has to generalize from the observed to still unobserved uniformities in precisely that region of experience. For the process of sampling tends, in the long run, to correct and to improve itself, so as to show to the expert, although generally not to the layman, what ways of sampling are "fair" in their application to a given region of facts. For the expert is one who has had experience of many samples of different *ways of sampling* in his own field.

§ 12. Herewith we are prepared to understand a step forward in methodical procedure which took place early in the history of physics, and which has since become possible in very various regions of science. It is obvious that such a step might be expected to consist in some improvement in the choice and in the definition of the regions within which the selection of "fair samples" should be made possible. As Peirce has pointed out, it is just such improvement that takes place when induction assumes the form of *sampling the possible consequences of given hypotheses* concerning the constitution or the laws of some realm of natural phenomena, *or of sampling facts viewed with reference to their relation to such hypotheses.*

The reasoning which is used when hypotheses are tested, is of a fairly well known type. The instance furnished by Newton's hypothesis that a falling body near the earth's surface and the moon in its orbit were alike subject to a force that followed the law of the "inverse squares," has been repeatedly used as an illustration in the text-books of the Logic of Induction. We need not here dwell upon the familiar aspects of the method of the "working hypothesis" and of its successful verification, or of its correction in the light of observation. Our interest lies in the bearing of the whole matter upon the Theory of Order. This bearing is neither familiar to most minds, nor immediately obvious.

We must therefore sketch the general way in which the union of Theory and Observation is accomplished in the more exact natural sciences, and must then try to show that *what makes this union most effective, depends upon the possibility of defining hypotheses in terms of certain conceptual order-systems whose exactness of structure far transcends, in ideal, the grade of exactness that can ever be given to our physical observations themselves.*

In its simplest form, the method of induction here in question appears as a discovery of natural processes, structures, or laws, through an imaginative anticipation of what they *may be,* and through a testing of the anticipation by subsequent experience. The first and most directly obvious use of an *Hypothesis,* which thus anticipates an observable fact, lies of course in its *heuristic* value. It leads an observer to look for what he otherwise might not have sought. It directs his attention.

But this, after all, is the least of the services which a good hypothesis renders to science. Its higher service is that, when it is indeed a good type of hypothesis for the field in which it is used, it may be made the starting point of a more or less extended *Deductive Theory,* which enables the investigator to discover indirect means of testing the hypothesis, in cases, where direct means fail. One often meets with the remark that a scientific hypothesis must be such as to be more or less completely capable of verification or of refutation by experience. The remark is sound. But equally sound it is to say that a hypothesis which, just as it is made, is, without further deductive reasoning, capable of receiving direct refutation or verification, *is not nearly as valuable to any science as is a hypothesis whose verifications, so far as they occur at all, are only possible indirectly, and through the mediation of a considerable deductive theory,* whereby the consequences of the hypothesis are first worked out, and then submitted to test. If Thales successfully predicted an eclipse, he made and verified a hypothesis. But if this hypothesis was solely founded upon an empirical knowledge of the cycle of former eclipses, his astronomy had not yet passed beyond the statistical stage, and could not pass beyond that stage through even a large number of such verifications. But when a modern astronomer deals with lunar theory, and uses the comparison between theory and observation as, in this case, a very accurate means of testing the degree of accuracy of the Newtonian hy-

pothesis of the law of inverse squares, as the law to which a
field of gravitative force is subject, the value of the work done
depends upon the vast range of deductive theory which here
separates the original Newtonian statement from the observed
facts. The recorded positions and movements of the moon, when
supplemented by the records of the known eclipses that were
recorded by the ancients, constitute a very vast "sample" of
the physical facts about the moon's motion. The computations
which lunar theory makes possible constitute a still vaster "sample" of special results of the Newtonian theory, as applied to
the moon. Now if the Newtonian theory of gravitation had only
a chance, or a temporary, or a superficial relation to the observable motions of the moon the chances are extremely small
that a very large sample of the results of the theory should
agree as nearly as they do with so large a sample of the results
of observation. For in such a case *two* samples of facts, the one
selected from a realm of *observed physical phenomena,* the other
selected from the realm of *the ideal consequences of the Newtonian theory of gravitation,* are compared, not merely in general, but in detail; so that the correspondence of theory with
observation is a correspondence of the two samples, so to speak,
member by member, each element of each of the two samples
approximately agreeing with some element of the other with
which, in case Newton's original hypothesis is true, it ought
to agree.

§ 13. What here takes place is, *mutatis mutandis,* identical
with what constitutes the most important feature in any successful and highly organized combination of Hypothesis, Theory
and Observation. The stages of the process are these.

(1) A Hypothesis is suggested regarding the constitution or
the laws of some region of physical fact.

(2) This hypothesis is *such as to permit an extensive and
exact Deductive Theory* as to what ought to be present in the
region in question, *in case* the hypothesis is true. *The more
extensive, exact and systematic the theory thus made possible
proves to be, the larger are the possible samples of the "conse-*

quences of the hypothesis" *which are available,* whenever they are needed for comparison with the physical facts.

(3) Samples of facts are chosen from a field open to observation and experiment, and are then compared with the results of theory. The more complete the theory, the larger the range of facts that can be called for to meet the need for comparison.

(4) This comparison no longer is confined (as is the case when the statistical and the comparative methods in their similar forms are used) to noting what proportion, r' per cent., of the members of a sample have a certain relatively simple character q. On the contrary, in case the deductive theory in question is highly developed and systematic, the sample of the results of theory which is accessible for comparison is not only complex, but *has a precise order-system of its own* (is, for instance, a system of ideally exact physical quantities) *which must be approximately verifiable in detail in case the original hypothesis is true.* The comparison of theory and fact is therefore here possible with a minuteness of individual detail which, in case of successful verification, may make it very highly probable that if the system of real physical facts under investigation has any determinate constitution whatever, its constitution very closely agrees with that which the hypothesis under investigation requires.

It thus becomes obvious that the value of the method here in question very greatly *depends upon the exactness, the order, and the systematic character of the concepts in terms of which the hypotheses thus indirectly tested are defined.* If these concepts are thus exact and systematic, they may permit extended and precise deductions, and the result will be that large samples of the exact consequences of a hypothesis, will be such that they can be compared with correspondingly large samples of the facts of observation and experiment. The comparison of two such samples can then be made, not merely in general, but element by element, minutely, with reference to the Order presented and conceived, and in such wise as to make a chance agreement of theory and fact extremely improbable.

The result will be that the truth of the hypothesis that is tested will still be at best only *probable and approximate,* but the probability will tend to become as great as possible, while the approximation will grow closer and closer as the theory reaches more and more exactness and fulness of deductive development, and as it confirmed by larger and larger ranges of observations.

An almost ideal union of deductive theory with a vast range of observations is found in the modern doctrine of Energy.

§ 14. In view of the foregoing considerations, we can now readily see that this, the most perfect of the scientific methods, namely *the organized union of Theory with Observation requires for its perfection concepts and systems of concepts which permit of precise and extended deductive reasonings,* such as the Newtonian theory of Gravitation and the modern theory of Energy exemplify. It is a commonplace of Methodology that hypotheses which are stated in *quantitatively precise terms,* especially meet, *at present,* this requirement, and lead to physical theories of the desired type. Our account, following Peirce's view of induction, shows *why,* in general, such theories are so important for the study of nature. The "samples of possible consequences" which they furnish are especially adapted to meet the requirements of a minute comparison, element by element, with the samples of observed facts in terms of which the theories in question are to be tested.

Meanwhile our sketch of the general Theory of Order will hereafter show us that quantitative concepts get their importance for deductive theoretical purposes *simply from the fact that the Order-System of the quantities is so precise and controllable a system. Herein, to be sure, the quantities are not alone amongst conceptual objects,* and it will be part of the business of our later sketch to show that *the two concepts, Exact Deductive Theory and Quantitative Theory, are by no means coextensive.* The prominence of quantitative concepts in our present physical theories is nothing that we can regard as absolutely necessary. There may be, in future, physical sciences that will be highly theoretical, and that will not use quantitative concepts as their principal ones. Yet it is certain that they will use *some exact conceptual Order-System.*

But, however this may be, our result so far is the following one:—

A sketch of Methodology has shown, in the case of the Comparative, and the Statistical Methods, and of the Method which unites Observation and Theory, that all these methods use and depend upon the general concept of the *Orderly Array* of objects of thought, with its subordinate concepts of *Series,* of the *Correlation of Series,* and of special *Order-Systems* such as that of the *Quantities.* All these concepts are essential to the understanding of the methods that thought employs in dealing with its objects. And thus a general view of Methodology leads us to the problems of the Science of Order.

BERTRAND RUSSELL
(born 1872)

Fellow, Trinity College, Cambridge, 1895; lecturer in philosophy, University of Cambridge, 1910-1916. Two aspects of his work are likely to remain of permanent importance: his major part in the twentieth century renaissance of logic, and his reiterated attempts to identify the methods of philosophy with those of the sciences. He is one of the chief representatives of Neo-positivism and Mathematical Logic. In questions of general philosophical character, he is an agnostic and sceptic.

Main Works:

The Philosophy of Leibniz; The Principles of Mathematics; Principia Mathematica (in collaboration with A. N. Whitehead); The Problems of Philosophy; Our Knowledge of the External World; Introduction to Mathematical Philosophy; The Analysis of Mind; The Analysis of Matter; An Outline of Philosophy; An Inquiry into Meaning and Truth; Philosophical Essays; Mysticism and Logic; A History of Western Philosophy.

Definition of Pure Mathematics

1. Pure Mathematics is the class of all propositions of the form "*p* implies *q*," where *p* and *q* are propositions containing one or more variables, the same in the two propositions, and neither *p* nor *q* contains any constants except logical constants. And logical constants are all notions definable in terms of the

----

From: *Principles of Mathematics.*

following: Implication, the relation of a term to a class of which it is a member, the notion of *such that*, the notion of relation, and such further notions as may be involved in the general notion of propositions of the above form. In addition to these, mathematics *uses* a notion which is not a constituent of the propositions which it considers, namely the notion of truth.

2. The above definition of pure mathematics is, no doubt, somewhat unusual. Its various parts, nevertheless, appear to be capable of exact justification—a justification which it will be the object of the present work to provide. It will be shown that whatever has, in the past been regarded as pure mathematics, is included in our definition, and that whatever else is included possesses those marks by which mathematics is commonly though vaguely distinguished from other studies. The definition professes to be, not an arbitrary decision to use a common word in an uncommon signification, but rather a precise analysis of the ideas which, more or less unconsciously, are implied in the ordinary employment of the term. Our method will therefore be one of analysis, and our problem may be called philosophical —in the sense, that is to say, that we seek to pass from the complex to the simple, from the demonstrable to its indemonstrable premises. But in one respect not a few of our discussions will differ from those that are usually called philosophical. We shall be able, thanks to the labors of the mathematicians themselves, to arrive at certainty in regard to most of the questions with which we shall be concerned; and among those capable of an exact solution we shall find many of the problems which, in the past, have been involved in all the traditional uncertainty of philosophical strife. The nature of number, of infinity, of space, time and motion, and of mathematical inference itself, are all questions to which, in the present work, an answer professing itself demonstrable with mathematical certainty will be given—an answer which, however, consists in reducing the above problems to problems in pure logic, which last will not be found satisfactorily solved in what follows.

3. The Philosophy of Mathematics has been hitherto as con-

troversial, obscure and unprogressive as the other branches of philosophy. Although it was generally agreed that mathematics is in some sense true, philosophers disputed as to what mathematical propositions really meant: although something was true, no two people were agreed as to what it was that was true, and if something was known, no one knew what it was that was known. So long, however, as this was doubtful, it could hardly be said that any certain and exact knowledge was to be obtained in mathematics. We find, accordingly, that idealists have tended more and more to regard all mathematics as dealing with mere appearance, while empiricists have held everything mathematical to be approximation to some exact truth about which they had nothing to tell us. This state of things, it must be confessed, was thoroughly unsatisfactory. Philosophy asks of Mathematics: What does it mean? Mathematics in the past was unable to answer, and Philosophy answered by introducing the totally irrelevant notion of mind. But now Mathematics is able to answer, so far at least as to reduce the whole of its propositions to certain fundamental notions of logic. At this point, the discussion must be resumed by Philosophy. I shall endeavour to indicate what are the fundamental notions involved, to prove at length that no others occur in mathematics, and to point out briefly the philosophical difficulties involved in the analysis of these notions. A complete treatment of these difficulties would involve a treatise on Logic, which will not be found in the following pages.

4. There was, until very lately, a special difficulty in the principles of mathematics. It seemed plain that mathematics consists of deductions, and yet the orthodox accounts of deduction were largely or wholly inapplicable to existing mathematics. Not only the Aristotelian syllogistic theory, but also the modern doctrines of Symbolic Logic, were either theoretically inadequate to mathematical reasoning, or at any rate required such artificial forms of statement that they could not be practically applied. In this fact lay the strength of the Kantian view, which asserted that mathematical reasoning is not strictly formal, but always uses

intuition, *i.e.*, the *a priori* knowledge of space and time. Thanks to the progress of Symbolic Logic, especially as treated by Professor Peano, this part of the Kantian philosophy is now capable of a final and irrevocable refutation. By the help of ten principles of deduction and ten other premises of a general logical nature (*e.g.* "implication is a relation"), all mathematics can be strictly and formally deducted; and all the entities that occur in mathematics can be defined in terms of those that occur in the above twenty premises. In this statement, Mathematics includes not only Arithmetic and Analysis, but also Geometry, Euclidean and non-Euclidean, rational Dynamics, and an indefinite number of other studies still unborn or in their infancy. The fact that all Mathematics is Symbolic Logic is one of the greatest discoveries of our age; and when this fact has been established, the remainder of the principles of mathematics consists in the analysis of Symbolic Logic itself.

5. The general doctrine that all mathematics is deduction by logical principles from logical principles was strongly advocated by Leibniz, who urged constantly that axioms ought to be proved and that all except a few fundamental notions ought to be defined. But owing partly to a faulty logic, partly to belief in the logical necessity of Euclidean Geometry, he was led into hopeless errors in the endeavour to carry out in detail a view which, in its general outline, is now known to be correct. The actual propositions of Euclid, for example, do not follow from the principles of logic alone; and the perception of this fact led Kant to his innovations in the theory of knowledge. But since the growth of non-Euclidean Geometry, it has appeared that pure mathematics has no concern with the question whether the axioms and propositions of Euclid hold of actual space or not: this is a question for applied mathematics, to be decided, so far as any decision is possible, by experiment and observation. What pure mathematics asserts is merely that the Euclidean propositions follow from the Euclidean axioms—*i.e.* it asserts an implication: any space which has such and such properties has also such and such other properties. Thus, as dealt with in pure

687

mathematics, the Euclidean and non-Euclidean Geometrics are equally true: in each nothing is affirmed except implications. All propositions as to what actually exists, like the space we live in, belong to experimental or empirical science, not to mathematics; when they belong to applied mathematics, they arise from giving to one or more of the variables in a proposition of pure mathematics some constant value satisfying the hypothesis, and thus enabling us, for that value of the variable, actually to assert both hypothesis and consequent instead of asserting merely the implication. We assert always in mathematics that if a certain assertion p is true of any entity x, or of any set of entities x, y, z, . . . , then some other assertion q is true of those entities; but we do not assert either p or q separately of our entities. We assert a relation between the assertion p and q, which I shall call *formal implications*.

6. Mathematical propositions are not only characterized by the fact that they assert implications, but also by the fact that they contain *variables*. The notion of the variable is one of the most difficult with which Logic has to deal, and in the present work a satisfactory theory as to its nature, in spite of much discussion, will hardly be found. For the present, I only wish to make it plain that there are variables in all mathematical propositions, even where at first sight they might seem to be absent. Elementary Arithmetic might be thought to form an exception: $1 + 1 = 2$ appears neither to contain variables nor to assert an implication. But as a matter of fact, as will be shown in Part II, the true meaning of this proposition is: "If x is one and y is one, and x differs from y, then x and y are two." And this proposition both contains variables and asserts an implication. We shall find always, in all mathematical propositions, that the words *any* or *some* occur; and these words are the marks of a variable and a formal implication. Thus the above proposition may be expressed in the form: "Any unit and any other unit are two units." The typical proposition of mathematics is of the form "$\phi(x, y, z, \ldots)$ implies $\psi(x, y, z, \ldots)$, whatever values x, y, z, . . . may have"; where $\phi(x, y, z, \ldots)$ and $\psi(x, y, z, \ldots)$, for every set of values

of $x, y, z, \ldots$, are propositions. It is not asserted that ϕ is always true, not yet that ψ is always true, but merely that, in all cases, when ϕ is false as much as when ϕ is true, ψ follows from it.

The distinction between a variable and a constant is somewhat obscured by mathematical usage. It is customary, for example, to speak of parameters as in some sense constants, but this is a usage which we shall have to reject. A constant is to be something absolutely definite, concerning which there is no ambiguity whatever. Thus 1, 2, 3, e, π, Socrates, are constants; and so are *man*, and the human race, past, present and future, considered collectively. Proposition, implication, class, etc. are constants; but a proposition, any proposition, some proposition, are not constants, for these phrases do not denote one definite object. And thus what are called parameters are simply variables. Take, for example, the equation $ax + by + c = 0$, considered as the equation to a straight line in a plane. Here we say that x and y are variables, while a, b, c are constants. But unless we are dealing with one absolutely particular line, say the line from a particular point in London to a particular point in Cambridge, our a, b, c are not definite numbers, but stand for any numbers, and are thus also variables. And in Geometry nobody does deal with actual particular lines; we always discuss *any* line. The point is that we collect the various couples x, y into classes of classes, each class being defined as those couples that have a certain fixed relation to one triad (a, b, c). But from class to class, a, b, c also vary, and are therefore properly variables.

7. It is customary in mathematics to regard our variables as restricted to certain classes: in Arithmetic, for instance, they are supposed to stand for numbers. But this only means that *if* they stand for numbers, they satisfy some formula, *i.e.* the hypothesis that they are numbers implies the formula. This, then, is what is really asserted, and in this proposition it is no longer that our variables should be numbers: the implication holds equally when they are not so. Thus, for example, the proposition "x and y are numbers implies $(x+y)^2 = x^2 + 2xy + y^2$" holds equally if for x and y we substitute Socrates and Plato: both hypothesis

and consequent, in this case, will be false, but the implication will still be true. Thus in every proposition of pure mathematics, when fully stated, the variables have an absolutely unrestricted field: any conceivable entity may be substituted for any one of our variables without impairing the truth of our proposition.

8. We can now understand why the constants in mathematics are to be restricted to logical constants in the sense defined above. The process of transforming constants in a proposition into variables leads to what is called generalization, and gives us, as it were, the formal essence of a proposition. Mathematics is interested exclusively in *types* of propositions; if a proposition *p* containing only constants be proposed, and for a certain one of its terms we imagine others to be successively substituted, the result will in general be sometimes true and sometimes false. Thus, for example, we have "Socrates is a man"; here we turn Socrates into a variable, and consider "*x* is a man." Some hypotheses as to *x*, for example, "*x* is a Greek," insure the truth of "*x* is a man"; thus "*x* is a Greek" implies "*x* is a man," and this holds for all values of *x*. But the statement is not one of pure mathematics, because it depends upon the particular nature of *Greek* and *man*. We may, however, vary these too, and obtain: If *a* and *b* are classes, and *a* is contained in *b*, then "*x* is an *a*" implies "*x* is a *b*." Here at last we have a proposition of pure mathematics, containing three variables and the constants *class*, *contained in*, and those involved in the notion of formal implications with variables. So long as any term in our proposition can be turned into a variable, our proposition can be generalized; and so long as this is possible, it is the business of mathematics to do it. If there are several chains of deduction which differ only as to the meaning of the symbols, so that propositions symbolically identical become capable of several interpretations, the proper course, mathematically, is to form the class of meanings which may attach to the symbols, and to assert that the formula in question follows from the hypothesis that the symbols belong to the class in question. In this way, symbols which stood for constants become transformed into variables, and new con-

stants are substituted, consisting of classes to which the old constants belong. Cases of such generalization are so frequent that many will occur at once to every mathematician, and innumerable instances will be given in the present work. Whenever two sets of terms have mutual relations of the same type, the same form of deduction will apply to both. For example, the mutual relations of points in a Euclidean plane are of the same type as those of the complex numbers; hence plane geometry, considered as a branch of pure mathematics, ought not to decide whether its variables are points or complex numbers or some other set of entities having the same type of mutual relations. Speaking generally, we ought to deal, in every branch of mathematics, with any class of entities whose mutual relations are of a specified type; thus the class, as well as the particular term considered, becomes a variable, and the only true constants are the types of relations and what they involve. Now a *type* of relation is to mean, in this discussion, a class of relations characterized by the above formal identity of the deductions possible in regard to the various members of the class; and hence a type of relations, as will appear more fully hereafter, if not already evident, is always a class definable in terms of logical constants. We may therefore define a type of relations as a class of relations defined by some property definable in terms of logical constants alone.

9. Thus pure mathematics must contain no indefinables except logical constants, and consequently no premisses, or indemonstrable propositions, but such as are concerned exclusively with logical constants and with variables. It is precisely this that distinguishes pure from applied mathematics. In applied mathematics, results which have been shown by pure mathematics to follow from some hypothesis as to the variable are actually asserted of some constant satisfying the hypothesis in question. Thus for example Euclidean Geometry, as a branch of pure mathematics, consists wholly of propositions having the hypothesis "S is a Euclidean space." If we go on to: "The space that exists is Euclidean," this enables us to assert of the space that

exists the consequents of all the hypotheticals constituting Euclidean Geometry, where now the variable S is replaced by the constant *actual space*. But by this step we pass from pure to applied mathematics.

10. The connection of mathematics with logic, according to the above account, is exceedingly close. The fact that all mathematical constants are logical constants, and that all the premisses of mathematics are concerned with these, gives, I believe, the precise statement of what philosophers have meant in asserting that mathematics is *a priori*. The fact is that, when once the apparatus of logic has been accepted, all mathematics necessarily follows. The logical constants themselves are to be defined only by enumeration, for they are so fundamental that all the properties by which the class of them might be defined presuppose some terms of the class. But practically, the method of discovering the logical constants is the analysis of symbolic logic, which will be the business of the following chapters. The distinction of mathematics from logic is very arbitrary, but if a distinction is desired, it may be made as follows. Logic consists of the premisses of mathematics, together with all other propositions which are concerned exclusively with logical constants and with variables but do not fulfil the above definition of mathematics (§ 1). Mathematics consists of all the consequences of the above premisses which assert formal implications containing variables, together with such of the premisses themselves as have these marks. Thus some of the premisses of mathematics, *e.g.* the principle of the syllogism, "if p implies q and q implies r, then p implies r," will belong to logic but not to mathematics. But for the desire to adhere to usage, we might identify mathematics and logic, and define either as the class of propositions containing only variables and logical constants; but respect for tradition leads me rather to adhere to the above distinction, while recognizing that certain propositions belong to both sciences.

JEAN-PAUL SARTRE
(born 1905)

Philosopher and playwright. Leader of the French school of existentialism. Agnostic with strong communist leanings. In his philosophy he shares with Kierkegaard vehement opposition to traditional generalities and calls for "existence before essence." Transcendence is rejected and man's relative existence takes the dominant position over systematic abstractions. Existence precedes essence and between "Being and Nothingness" man is condemned to freedom, anguish and loneliness.

Main Works:

L'Etre et le Néant; L'existentialisme est un humanisme.

––––––––––

Intuition

There is only intuitive knowledge. Deduction and discursive argument, incorrectly called examples of knowing, are only instruments which lead to intuition. When intuition is reached, methods utilized to attain it are effaced before it; in cases where it is not attained, reason and argument remain as indicating signs which point toward an intuition beyond reach; finally if it has been attained but is not a present mode of my consciousness, the precepts which I use remain as the results of operations formerly effected, like what Descartes called the "memories of ideas." If someone asks for a definition of intuition, Husserl will reply, in agreement with the majority of philosophers, that it is the presence of the thing (*Sache*) "in person" to consciousness.

––––––––––

From: *L'Etre et le Néant.*

Knowledge therefore is of the type of being which we described in the preceding chapter under the title of "presence to ——." But we have established that the in-itself can never by itself be presence. Being-present, in fact, is an ecstatic mode of being of the for-itself. We are then compelled to reverse the terms of our definition: intuition is the presence of consciousness to the thing. Therefore we must return now to the problem of the nature and the meaning of this presence of the for-itself to being.

While using the still not elucidated concept of "consciousness," we establish the necessity for consciousness to be consciousness *of* something. In fact it is by means of that of which it is conscious that consciousness distinguishes itself in its own eyes and that it can be self-consciousness; a consciousness which would not be consciousness (of) something would be consciousness (of) nothing. But at present we have elucidated the ontological meaning of consciousness or the for-itself. We can therefore pose the problem in more precise terms and ask: What do we mean when we say that it is necessary for consciousness to-be-consciousness *of* something—considered on the ontological level; *i.e.*, in the perspective of being-for-itself?

We know that the for-itself is the foundation of its own nothingness in the form of the phantom dyad—the reflection-reflecting. The reflecting exists only in order to reflect the reflection, and the reflection is a reflection only in so far as it refers to the reflecting. Thus the two terms outlined in the dyad point to each other, and each engages its being in the being of the other. But if the reflection is nothing other than the reflecting of *this* reflection, and if the reflection can be characterized only by its "being-in-order-to-be reflected in *this* reflecting," then the two terms of the quasi-dyad support their two nothingnesses on each other, conjointly annihilating themselves. It is necessary that the reflecting reflect *something* in order that the ensemble should not dissolve into nothing. But if the reflection, on the other hand, were *something*, independent of its being-in-order-to-be-reflected, then it would necessarily be qualified not as reflection but as an in-itself. This would be to introduce opacity into the system "the-reflection-reflecting" and, even more, to complete the suggested scissiparity. For in the for-itself the reflection is *also* the reflecting. But if the reflection is qualified, it is separated from the reflecting and its appearance is separated from its reality; the *cogito* becomes impossible. The reflection can be simultaneously "something to be reflected" and *nothing*, but only if it makes itself qualified by something other than itself or, if you prefer, if it is reflected as a relation to an outside which it is not.

What defines the reflection for the reflecting is always *that to which it is presence*. Even a joy, apprehended on the unreflective level, is only the "reflected" presence to a laughing and open world full of happy perspectives. But the few preceding comments have already informed us that non-being is an essential structure of presence. Presence incloses a radical negation as presence to that which one is not. What is present to me is what is not me. We should note furthermore that this "non-being" is implied *a priori* in every theory of knowledge. It is impossible to construct the notion of an object if we do not have originally a negative relation designating the object as that which *is* not consciousness. This is what made it quite easy to use the expression "non-ego," which was the fashion for a time, although one could not detect on the part of those who employed it the slightest concern to found this "not" which originally qualified the external world. Actually neither the connection of representation, nor the necessity of certain subjective ensembles, nor temporal irreversibility, nor an appeal to infinity could serve to constitute the object as such (that is, to serve as foundation for a further negation which would separate out the non-ego and oppose it to me as such) if this negation were not given first and if it were not the *a priori* foundation of all experience.

The thing, before all comparison, before all construction, is that which is present to consciousness as not being consciousness. The original relation of presence as the foundation of knowledge is negative. But as negation comes to the world by means of the for-itself, and as the thing is what it is in the absolute indifference of identity, it can not be the thing which is posited as not being the for-itself. Negation comes from the for-itself. We should not conceive this negation as a type of judgment which would bear on the thing itself and deny concerning it that it is the for-itself; this type of negation could be conceived only if the for-itself were a substance already fully formed, and even in that case it could emanate only as a third being established from outside a negative relation between two beings. But by the original negation the for-itself constitutes itself as not *being* the thing. Consequently the definition of consciousness which we gave earlier can be formulated in the perspective of the for-itself as follows: "The for-itself is a being such that in its being, its being is in question in so far as this being is essentially a certain way of *not being* a being which it posits simultaneously as other than itself."

Knowledge appears then as a mode of being. Knowing is neither a relation established after the event between two beings, nor is it an activity of one of these two beings, nor is it a quality of a property or a virtue. It is the very being of the for-itself in so far as this is presence to——; that is, in so far as the for-itself has to be its being by making itself not to be a certain being to which it is present. This means that the for-itself can be only in the mode of a reflection (reflet) causing itself to be reflected as not being a certain being. The "something" which must qualify the reflected in order that the dyad "the-reflection-reflecting" may not dissolve in nothingness is pure negation. The reflected causes itself to be qualified *outside* next to a certain being as *not being* that being. This is precisely what we mean by "to be consciousness *of* something."

But we must define more precisely what we understand by this original negation. Actually we should distinguish two types of negation and internal negation. The first appears as a purely external bond established between two beings by a witness. When I say, for example, "A cup is not an inkwell," it is very evident that the foundation of this negation is neither in the cup nor in the inkwell.[1] Both of these objects are what they are, and that is all. The negation stands as a categorical and ideal connection which I establish between them without modifying them in any way whatsoever, without enriching them or impoverishing them with the slightest quality; they are not even ever so slightly grazed by this negative synthesis. As it serves neither to enrich them nor to constitute them, it remains strictly external. But we can already guess the meaning of the other type of negation if we consider such expressions as "I am not rich" or "I am not handsome." Pronounced with a certain melancholy, they do not mean only that the speaker is denied a certain quality but that the denial itself comes to influence the inner structure of the positive being who has been denied the qualiy. When I say, "I am not handsome," I do not limit myself to denying with respect to myself as wholly concrete, a certain virtue which due to this fact passes into nothingness while I keep intact the positive totality of my being (as when I say, "The vase is not white, it is gray"—"The inkwell is not on the table, it is on the mantelpiece"). I intend to indicate that "not being handsome" is a certain negative virtue of my being. It characterizes me within; as negative it is a real quality of myself—that of not being handsome—and this negative quality will explain my melancholy as well as, for example, my failures in the world.

By an internal negation we understand such a relation between two beings that the one which is denied to the other qualifies the other at the heart of its essence—by absence. The negation becomes then a bond of essential being since at least one of the beings on which it depends is such that it points toward the other, that it carries the other in its heart as an absence. Nevertheless it is clear that this type of negation can not be applied to being-in-itself. By nature it belongs to the for-itself. Only the for-itself can be determined in its being which it is not. And if the internal negation can appear in the world —as when we say of a pearl that it is false, of a fruit that it is not ripe, of an egg that it is not fresh, *etc.*—it is by the for-itself that it comes into the world—like negation in general. Knowing belongs to the for-itself alone, for the reason that only the for-itself can appear to itself as not being what it knows. And as here appearance and being are one—since the for-itself has to be its appearance—we must conclude that the for-itself includes within its being the being of the object which it is inasmuch as the for-itself puts its own being into question as not being the being of the object.

Here we must rid ourselves of an illusion which may be formulated as follows: in order to constitute myself as *not being* a particular being, I must have ahead of time in some manner or other a knowledge of this being; for I can not judge the differences between myself and a being of which I know nothing. It is true, of course, that in our empirical existence we can not know how we differ from a Japanese or an Englishman, from a worker or an employer until we have some notion of these different beings. But these empirical distinctions can not serve as a basis for us here, for we are undertaking the study of an ontological relation which must render all experience possible and which aims at establishing how in general an object can exist for consciousness. It is not possible then for me to have any experience of an object as an object which is not me until I constitute it as an object. On the contrary, what makes all experience possible is an *a priori* upsurge of the object for the subject—or since the upsurge is the original fact of the for-itself, an original upsurge of the for-itself as presence to the object which it is not. What we should do then is to invert the terms of the preceding formula and formulate it thus: the fundamental relation by which the for-itself has to be as not being *this* particular object to which it is present is the foundation of all knowledge of this being. But we must describe this primary relation more exactly if we want to make it understandable.

The germ of truth remaining in the statement of the intellectualist illusion denounced in the preceding paragraph is the observation that can not determine myself not to be an object which is originally severed from all connection with me. I can not deny that I am a particular being if I am *at a distance* from that being. If I conceive of a being entirely closed in on itself, this being in itself will be solely that which it is, and due to this fact there will be no room in it for either negation or knowledge. It is in fact in terms of the being which it is not that a being can make *known to itself* what it is not. This means in the case of an internal negation that it is within and upon the being which it is not that the for-itself appears as not being what it is not. In this sense the internal negation is a concrete ontological bond. We are not dealing here with one of those empirical negations in which the qualities denied are distinguished first by their absence or even by their non-being. In the internal negation the for-itself collapses on what it denies. The qualities denied are precisely those to which the for-itself is most present; it is from them that it derives its negative force and perpetually renews it. In this sense it is necessary to see the denied qualities as a constitutive factor of the being of the for-itself, for the for-itself must be there outside itself upon them; it must be *they* in order to deny that it is they. In short the term-of-origin of the internal negation is the in-itself, the thing which *is there,* and outside of it there is nothing except an emptiness, a nothingness which is distinguished from the thing by a pure negation for which *this* thing furnishes the very content. The difficulty encountered by materialism in deriving knowledge from the object stems from the fact that materialism wants to produce a substance in terms of another substance. But this difficulty can not hinder us, for we affirm that there is *nothing* outside the in-itself except a reflection (reflet) of that nothing which is itself polarized and defined by the in-itself inasmuch as it is precisely the nothingness of *this* in-itself, the individualized nothing which is nothing only because it *is not* the in-itself. Thus in this ecstatic relation which is constitutive of the internal negation and of knowledge, it is the in-itself "in person" which is the concrete pole in its plenitude, and the for-itself is nothing other than the emptiness in which the in-itself is detached.

The for-itself is outside itself in the in-itself since it causes itself to be defined by what it is not; the first bond between the in-itself and the for-itself is therefore a bond of being. But this bond is neither a *lack* nor an *absence*. In the case of absence indeed I make myself determined by a being which I am not and which does not exist or which is not there; that is, what determines me is like a hollow in the middle of what I shall call my empirical plenitude. On the other hand, in knowledge, taken as a bond of ontological being, the being which I am not represents the absolute plenitude of the in-itself. And I, on the contrary, am the nothingness, the absence which determines itself in existence from the standpoint of this fullness. This means that in that type of being which we call knowing, the only being which can be encountered and which is perpetually *there* is the *known*. The knower is not; he is not apprehensible. He is nothing other than that which brings it about that there is a *being-there* on the part of the known, a presence—for by itself the known is neither present not absent, it simply is. But this presence of the known is the presence to *nothing*, since the knower is the pure reflection of a non-being; the presence appears then across the total translucency of the knower known, an *absolute* presence.

A psychological and empirical exemplification of this original relation is furnished us in the case of *fascination*. In fascination, which represents the immediate fact of *knowing*, the knower is absolutely nothing but a pure negation; he does not find or recover himself anywhere—he *is not*. The only qualification which he can support is that he *is not* precisely this particular fascinating object. In fascination there is nothing more than a gigantic object in a desert world. Yet the fascinated intuition is in no way a *fusion* with the object. In fact the condition necessary for the existence of fascination is that the object be raised in absolute relief on a background of emptiness; that is, I am precisely the immediate negation of the object and nothing but that.

We find this same pure negation at the basis of those pantheistic intuitions which Rousseau has several times described as concrete psychic events in his history. He claims that on those occasions he *melted* into the universe, that the world alone was suddenly found present as an absolute presence and unconditioned totality. And certainly we can understand this total, isolated presence of the world, its pure "being-there"; certainly we admit freely that at this privileged moment there was nothing else but the world. But this does not mean, as Rousseau claims, that there was a fusion of consciousness with the world. Such a fusion would signify the solidification of the for-itself in in-itself, and at the same stroke, the disappearance of the world and of the in-itself as presence. It is true that in the pantheistic intention there is no longer anything but the world—save for that which causes the in-itself to be present as the world; that is, a pure negation which is a non-thetic self-consciousness as negation. Precisely because knowledge is not *absence* but *presence*, there is *nothing* which separates the knower from the known.

Intuition has often been defined as the immediate presence of the known to the knower, but it is seldom that anyone has reflected on the requirements of the notion of the *immediate*. Immediacy is the absence of any mediator; that is obvious, for otherwise the mediator alone would be known and not what is mediated. But if we can not posit any intermediary, we must at the same time reject both continuity and discontinuity as a type of presence of the knower to the known. In fact we shall not admit that there is any continuity of the knower with the known, for it supposes an intermediary term which would be at once knower and known, which suppresses the autonomy of the knower in the face of the known while engaging the being of the knower in the being of the known. Then the structure of the object disappears since the object must be absolutely denied by the for-itself as the being of the for-itself. But neither can we consider the original relation of the for-itself to the in-itself as a relation of *discontinuity*. To be sure, the separation between two discontinuous elements is an emptiness—*i.e.*, in-itself. This substantialized nothing is as such a non-conductive density; it destroys the immediacy of presence, for it has qua nothing become *something*. The presence of the for-itself to the in-itself can be expressed neither in terms of continuity nor in terms of discontinuity, for it is pure *denied identity*.

To make this clearer, let us employ a comparison. When two

curves are tangential to one another, they offer a type of presence without intermediaries. Nevertheless the eye grasps only *a single line* for the length of their tangency. Moreover if the two curves were hidden so that one could see only the length A B where they are tangential to each other, it would be impossible to distinguish them. Actually what separates them is *nothing;* there is neither continuity nor discontinuity but pure identity. Now suddenly uncover the two figures and we apprehend them at once again as being two throughout all their length. This situation derives not from an abrupt factual separation which would suddenly be realized between them but from the fact that the two movements by which we *draw* the two curves so as to perceive them include each one a negation as a constituting act. Thus what separates the two curves at the very spot of their tangency is *nothing*, not even a distance; it is a pure negativity as the counterpart of a constituting synthesis. Such an image will enable us to understand better the relation of immediacy which originally unites the knower to the known.

Ordinarily indeed it happens that a negation depends on a "something" which exists before the negation and constitutes its matter. For example, if I say that the inkwell is not on the table, then table and inkwell are objects already constituted whose being in-itself will be the support of the negative judgment. But in the case of the relation "knower-known," there is nothing on the side of the knower which can provide a support for the negation; no difference, no principle of distinction "is there" to separate *in-itself* the knower from the known. But in the total indistinction of being, there is nothing but a negation which does not even exist but which *has to be,* which does not even posit itself as a negation. Consequently knowledge and finally the knower himself are nothing except the fact "that there is" being, that being in-itself *gives* and raises itself in relief on the ground of this nothing. In this sense we can call knowledge *the pure solitude of the known.* It is enough to say that the original phenomenon of knowledge *adds* nothing to being and creates nothing. It does not enrich being, for knowledge is pure negativity. It only brings it about that *there is* being. But this fact "that there is" being is not an inner determination of being—which is what it is—but of negativity. In this sense every revelation of a positive characteristic of being is the counterpart of an ontological determination as pure negativity in the being of the for-itself.

For example, as we shall see later, the revelation of the spatiality of being is one with the non-positional apprehension by the for-itself of itself as *unextended.* And the unextended character of the for-itself is not a positive mysterious virtue of spirituality which is hiding under a negative denomination; it is a natural ecstatic relation, for it is by and in the extension of the transcendent in-itself that the for-itself makes itself known to itself and realizes its own non-extension. The for-itself can not be first unextended in order later to enter into relation with an extended being, for no matter how we consider it, the concept of the unextended makes no sense by itself; it is nothing but the negation of the extended. If we could suppress—to imagine an impossibility—the extension of the revealed determinations of the in-itself, then the for-itself would remain *aspatial*; it would be neither extended nor unextended, and it could not possibly be characterized in any way whatsoever so far as extension is concerned. In this sense extension is a transcendent determination which the for-itself has to apprehend to the exact degree that it denies to itself as extended. That is why the term which seems best to indicate this inner relation between knowing and being is the word *realize,* which we used earlier in its double ontological and gnostic meaning. I realize a project in so far as I give it being, but I also *realize my situation in so far as I live it and* make it be with my being. I "realize" the scope of a catastrophe, the difficulty of an undertaking. To know is to realize in both senses of the term. It is to cause being "to be there" while having to be the reflected negation of this being. *The real is realization.* We shall define transcendence as that inner and realizing negation which reveals the in-itself while determining the being of the for-itself.

CHRISTOPHER SCHEIBLER

(1589-1653)

Referred to by admiring contemporaries as the Protestant Suarez, because of his ardent revival of Aristotelianism. He was one of the first to use logic in place of dialectics in his *opus logicum*. He taught at the Universities of Halle and of Giessen.

Main Work:
> Philosophia Compendiosa.

Logical Terminology

This equivocity, which communicates its name only, but not its nature, as: Dog to the constellation, to the sea creature, and to the domestic animal, is not properly a genus.

Species is predicated in *what* of its individuals, as: Man of Socrates, etc.

Difference (essential) is predicated in *what kind*, either of one genus and its species, as: sensible, when it is called generic. Or of one species and its individuals, as: rational, when it is called specific.

So there is exclusion of accidental difference (commonly called common or proper) arising from a common accident, or proper, because they refer to consequents.

Proper is predicated denominatively and convertibly of the generic subject, as: color of the body, when it is called generic.

From: *Philosophia Compendiosa.*

Or of the specific subject, as: risible of man, when it is called specific.

Accident is predicated denominatively and inconvertibly of the subject, as: whiteness of a wall.

Categories are the chief genera, or general classes: in which, according to *below* and *above*, genus and species are indicated; collaterally, the difference is posited:

Being

1. Simple: stone	Complex: proposition
2. Unit per se: man	Aggregate: army
3. Positive: sight	Deprivation: blindness
4. Real: gold	{ Skill: syllogism { Imaginary: Gold Mountain
5. Finite: angel	Infinite: God

Negative

6. Limited: body	Exceeding or transcendent: being, one, good, etc.
7. Complete: whole	Incomplete: parts, except by reduction
8. Universal: Man	Particular: Socrates
9. Univocal: brute	Equivocal: dog, before a continued distinction

There are ten categories, namely: one of substance, nine of accidents.

The category of substance is an orderly series of all the substances predicable, according to the predicated conditions.

The categories of accidents form an orderly series of homogeneous accidents, as: quantity, of quantities, etc.

The kinds of accidents are:

Quantity	Quality	Relation
Action	Passion	Place
Time	Position	Habit

They are distinguished by various ways of denominating the subject, thus:

1. Quantity		How big, as: surface, width, etc.
2. Quality		What kind, as: whiteness, white, etc.
3. Relation		Related, as: parenthood, father, etc.
4. Action	Denominates	Agents, as: branding, burning, etc.
5. Passion	the subject	Suffering, as: being burned, burned, etc.
6. Place		Being in a place, as: in a corner, etc.
7. Time		Being in time, as: in the present year, etc.
8. Position		Placed in a particular position, as: seated, sitting, etc.
9. Habit		Clothed, as: robe, robed, etc.

So much for the invention of words. Now comes the invention of arguments.

Invention of arguments is the part of logic that deals with inventing arguments.

Argument is that which refers to proving some effect: such are single notions, and those considered by themselves.

Argument is either technical (having within itself the power of proof) or non-technical, that does not have the power of proof within itself, but in some other technical argument.

A technical argument is either primary, because it stems from its own origin: or derived, because it depends on it; retaining, however, the same power of proof in itself as the technical argument.

A primary argument is either suitable, because it is considered simply and absolutely: or comparative, whereby a thing is considered by comparison of its quantity or its quality.

A simple argument is either suitable, agreeing with the thing that it discusses: or different, because it disagrees.

A suitable argument is either absolutely or in some other way.

Absolutely, as: cause and effect.

Cause and the object caused take first place among technical arguments.

Causes are four in number: efficient, material, formal, and final: not more or fewer.

The efficient cause is that by means of which a thing is.

It is divided into 1. creative, as: parents, and conserving, as: nurse: and into 2. unique cause, as: God in creation, or an associative cause, as: building together: and 3, that which acts by itself (by its nature, as fire: by intelligence, as man or angel) or by accident or chance, as: a stone falling from a roof: or by luck, as: a man who finds a treasure.

To the efficient (aiding) cause are also added instruments.

An instrument is that which is presented by a previous cause and moves to produce an effect greater than itself. It is either remote and substantial, as: a knife. Or near and accidental, as: shrewdness: thus, quality alone acts.

Matter and form are internal causes. They are called internal or essential, because they are within the essence of the thing that they constitute.

Material is the cause from which a thing is, as: a body in respect of a man: three propositions in respect of a syllogism. Formal is the cause through which a thing is that which it is, as: soul.

Substantial form has three functions: to grant being: to distinguish one thing from another: to be the origin of a series of operations.

The final cause is that for the purpose of which a thing is.

Related to the end are middles or objectives, which refer to the acquisition of the end.

After the enumeration of all these causes comes the effect.

That is the effect or the thing caused which exists from the causes.

As an example of effect may be cited motion, and the thing not produced by motion: similarly, sayings, writings, etc.

The primary topic for suitable arguments is in cause and in the thing caused. Now comes the second topic, on the subject and the adjunct.

The subject is that to which something is joined.

They are of this type: inherent existence in a subject, as: the soul in respect of doctrine: adherence in the subject, as: a man, in respect of clothing: occupying subject, as: a man is sick in respect of the physician. The locating subject, as: air in respect of man, who is in it.

The adjunct is that to which something is subjoined.

Its distribution is known as common and proper. Common is that which is in two or more subjects equally, as: whiteness in a swan and in a wall.

Proper is that which fits one subject only, primarily and by itself, as: risibility to man.

The third is that of suitable arguments in accidents and consequents.

Antecedents are what precede a thing, but are not its cause or the subject.

Consequents are what follow a thing, but are not its effects or adjuncts.

Such is the relationship of the *terminus a quo* to the *terminus ad quem*: of the necessary condition to the thing itself: of the required distance of fire to heat: of youth to old age: of Tuesday to Wednesday, and so on.

The consequent being necessarily posited, the antecedent was necessarily posited, as, for example: Once old age was posited, youth was posited.

The fourth topic is that of connections or concomitants. Connections are such that one is joined to the other, either by dependence, or by succession: such is the arsis between the adjuncts proper considered among themselves: in contingents, as in learning and probity. In necessary things it is sometimes otherwise, as in heat and lightness, and so on.

From this topic come these propositions: Honey is sweet. What is risible is capable of learning. Similarly: the body is united to the soul. The soul is united to the body. The generation of one thing is the corruption of another, and so on.

The fifth topic is that of relations. These are such as regard each other with mutual affection, as: father and son.

Relations present themselves reciprocally, as: If father is posited, son is posited: and vice versa.

Hitherto there were arguments in agreement. Now dissentient arguments follow.

Dissentient arguments are such as differ from the matter that they are disputing.

Dissentient arguments are equally manifest among themselves, and one is equally revealed by the other although they become much clearer by their own difference.

Dissentient arguments are either diverse only, or opposites too.

Diverse are those that dissent in reasoning only, as: Ulysses was not handsome but he was eloquent. Peter is not learned but he is wealthy.

After diverse, come opposites, that differ in reason or fact.

Hence the deduction: Opposition cannot be attributed to the same thing nor, again, in accordance with the same thing, in relation to the same thing, at the same time.

Opposites are either disparates improperly, or contraries properly opposed.

Disparates are such that one of them is equally opposed to many, as: Man is opposed to tree, stone, and horse.

Contraries are commonly called opposites one of which is opposed to one only, as: Father to son: sight to blindness.

They are distinguished in the affirmative, when each term is affirmative, or a positive being, as in adversatives and relations; and negative, when each term is negative, as in contradictions and deprivations.

Of contraries there are four kinds: relative, adversative, contradictory, and deprivative.

Relative contraries are affirmative, one of which depends on the mutual affection of the other, as: Father and son: master and servant: the same, diversely.

Adversative, commonly called contraries, are affirmative contraries that are opposed to each other perpetually in regard to place, or absolutely, as color and cold.

Contradictory are negative contraries, one of which denies everywhere, as: People, not people.

Deprivatives are negative contraries, one of which (that is, the deprivation) denies, only in the subject in which there is an affirmation according to its own nature, as: Blindness and sight.

Simple arguments have been discussed: now come comparisons.

Comparisons are such as are compared with each other. Comparisons are either complete or abbreviated.

An abbreviated comparison is that which is designated briefly by certain signs, as: Man is like a bubble. A complete comparison is one that is extended through the protasis and the apodosis. For example: As a bubble vanishes swiftly, so does man vanish swiftly.

In another sense: A comparison is in respect of quantity or quality.

In regard to quantity, comparisons are either equal, when the quantity is the same: or unequal, when the quantities are different.

Unequal comparisons are either greater, or smaller. The greater is that whose quantity exceeds. The smaller is that whose quantity is exceeded.

In syllogistic usage, the argument is from the greater, when it proceed from the greater thing to the smaller thing, as: God gave us life: he will therefore give us a cloak too. Argument from the smaller: An infant cannot speak: therefore it cannot argue.

Comparisons in respect of quality are similar or dissimilar. Similar comparisons are those whose quality is the same.

Similarity is either simple or compound. Simple is nudity of things coming together in the same quality: and this is the case with two terms only.

Compound is the comparison of the habit of things, and is called a kind of proportion.

This is either continuous, consisting of three terms, and in which the first term is to the second as the second to the third, as: As two is to four, so four is to eight. Or disjunctive, when four terms are disjunctive, as: As two is to four, so six is to twelve.

Dissimilars are those whose quality is different. Examples of such are: Dissimilar, unequal, different, other, unlike, and so on.

After the primary arguments reviewed so far, derived arguments follow.

Derived arguments are those that depend on others and are in relation to that which they dispute like the primary arguments from which they spring. Such arguments are either nominal, as: Conjugations, definitions of a term, distinction of a term. Or real, as: distribution and definition.

Conjugations are terms variously derived from the same origin, as: justice, just, justly.

Definition of a term is that whereby the meaning of a term is explained. This occurs either through notation or through transference. Notation is the first interpretation of a term from some argument, as: *Homo* is said to be derived from *humus*, the name being taken from the matter.

Allusion is related to notation, and it explains the word from a similar origin in relation to the meaning of the term. For example: City is said to be derived as if from the union of citizens.

Transference occurs, when a word is explained by another of equal value, as: Logic is the same as dialectics. Entelechy is the same as form.

Distinction of a word is that whereby various ambiguous meanings of a word are enumerated, as: Cancer sometimes designates a disease, and sometimes a creature living in streams and having a backward motion.

Distribution is the resolution of the whole into parts. The whole is therefore that which is distributed. The parts are what distribute.

Distribution is therefore of the integral whole, when resolution occurs into integral parts or members, as: Man into head, feet, arms. This distribution is based on matter. Or distribution of the essential whole, when resolution occurs into essential parts, as: Man into soul and body. This distribution is based on form and matter and on those things that are analogous to them. These two distributions are properly called partitions.

Or distribution of the universal whole or genus, when resolution occurs into species, as: animal into man and beast: or distribution of species, when resolution occurs into individuals, as: man into Socrates, Plato, and so on. This is properly called Division.

Or from external causes, that is, from the efficient cause and the end, as: Some men are from God by creation, others from men by generation. Some study for honors, others from necessity to earn a living.

Or from the effects of these causes, as: In the case of men, some write, others read.

Or from the subjects, when resolution occurs through the subjects, as: In the case of men, some are Europeans, others Asiatics, and so on.

Or from adjuncts, when resolution of the subjects occurs according to accidents, as: In the case of man, into giants and pygmies. In the case of animals, into male and female.

After distribution comes definition, whereby what a thing is is explained. The thing that is explained by definition is called the defined.

The parts of which the definition consists are the genus and the difference. The former contains the concept of community, or agreement: the latter, the concept of property and distinction.

Definition is either perfect or imperfect.

Perfect definition is that which explains a thing by its essential causes, or their symbols, that is, the genus and the substantial difference, as: man is a rational animal.

Imperfect definition is that which arises from an aggregate of attributes, or from another definition, or from non essentials, as: man is an animal capable of discipline, risible, and mortal.

So far, technical arguments have been discussed: now non technical arguments follow, which argue not by their own power but by an adopted power.

Such arguments are testimonies, that assume the force of argument from the authority of the witness, that is, from its adjuncts, effects, and so on.

Testimony is either divine or human. Divine testimony is that which has divine authority.

Related to this are testimonies not only derived immediately from God but also from the angels, prophets, and apostles: and among the pagans, from oracles, priests, and evil devils.

Human testimony is that which has human authority. It is either general, because it is used by many and it issues from many: or proper, because it arises from one. An example of the former is: A famous saying, a law, and so on. An example of the latter is: Cicero's testimony, and so on.

So far the first part of logic has dealt with simple terms, and arguments taken up individually. The second part that follows deals with the conjunctives called judgment.

Judgment then is the second part of logic, treating the arrangement of arguments for the purpose of good judgment.

Judgment is either axiomatic or dianoëtic. An axiomatic judgment deals with axioms.

An axiom is the disposition of one argument with another, whereby it is judged that something is, or is not. It is otherwise called a proposition or an assertion.

The parts of an axiom are two: The antecedent and the consequent. The former in a simple axiom is called the subject, and the latter, the predicate.

The antecedent is that of which something is postulated. The consequent is that which is postulated of another thing.

These parts are connected by a copula, which in the simple axiom is a verb, and in the compound axiom a conjunction.

So much for the axiom in the genus. Now come species and affections.

In regard to species, the axiom is either simple or compound. This is commonly called the division of a proposition according to substance.

A simple axiom is that which is contained in the copulative verb, as: Peter is an apostle. This is commonly called a categorical proposition.

Sometimes however the copulative verb is merely implicit, as: It is a rose. Peter runs. That is: A rose is a being. Peter is a running being. This is also called an implicit proposition.

All arguments (except complete comparisons and distributions) can be arranged in a simple axiom. Suitable arguments are arranged by affirmation: opposing arguments, by negation.

A simple axiom is either general, or special. This distribution of axioms is commonly called division of the proposition according to quantity.

A general axiom occurs, when the predicate is so postulated of the subject that nothing is contained below the subject that does not have this predicate, as: Every man is rational. This is commonly called a universal proposition.

A special axiom occurs, when the consequent is not attributed to the whole antecedent. This is either a particular axiom or a proper one.

A particular axiom occurs, when the consequent is attributed in part to the antecedent, that is, so that the term *certain* can be posited, or its equivalent, as: A certain man is learned. This is commonly called a particular proposition.

A proper axiom occurs, when the consequent is attributed to the individual antecedent, as: Cicero is learned. This is called a singular proposition.

The simple axiom has been treated: now comes the compound axiom.

A compound axiom is one that is joined together by a conjunction. This is commonly called a hypothetical proposition.

There are four kinds: copulative and conjunctive, which are cumulative: likewise adversative and disjunctive, that are called segregative.

The copulative is that which is joined together by a copulative, as: Body is size and place.

The conjunctive is that which is joined together by a conjunction, as: If a donkey flies, it has wings.

The adversative is that which is joined together by a separative conjunction, as: Although Peter is rich, yet he is not learned.

The disjunctive is that which is joined together by a disjunctive conjunction, as: It is either day, or it is night.

So much for the species of axioms: now we consider the affections, that are either absolute, or relative.

Absolute affections are those that agree by themselves with the axioms, or are considered in themselves: such are: Affirmation, negation, truth, falsity, and so on.

In this respect an axiom is either affirmative or negative. This is commonly called Division of the Proposition according to Quality.

An axiom is affirmative when its connective is affirmative, as: Man is an animal.

It is negative, when its connective is negated, as: Man is not a stone. Both types of axioms are either true, or false.

It is a true axiom, when it states the case as it is: false, when it states the contrary, as: Man is an animal. Man is not an animal.

A true axiom is either contingent, or necessary. It is contingent, when it is so true that it may also be false, as: It will rain tomorrow. It is necessary, when it is always true, and cannot be false, as: Man is an animal.

There are three degrees of demonstrative necessity: In relation to the whole, in relation to the thing itself, and in relation to first propositions.

In relation to the whole requires that the predicate should be in every subject: should always be in it, that is, at all times. For example: Every animal is sensible: should be affirmative.

In relation to the thing itself requires, in addition, that the predicate should be essential to the subject, and homogeneous, as: Every man is an animal.

In relation to first propositions requires, in addition, that 1. the predicate should be reciprocal with the subject 2. that it should fit the subject in respect of the subject's being what it is, as: Man is rational.

We have spoken of absolute affections of axioms: now come related affections. They agree with the axioms considered among themselves. Such are: Equipollence, conversion, opposition, and axiomatic sequence.

Equipollence is the agreement in sense of propositions verbally different. Such are: *Not all men are chosen and Certain men are chosen.*

Conversion is the transposition of the terms of a proposition, with the retention of the quality and the truth.

Conversion is three-fold: Simple, by accident, and by contraposition.

Simple conversion occurs simply, with the retention of the same quantity and quality, as: No man is a stone. No stone is a man.

Conversion by accident changes the quantity, as: Every man is an animal. A certain animal is a man.

Conversion by contraposition is made by changing the finite

terms into infinite ones, with the retention of the same quality and quantity, as: Every man is an animal. Every non animal is not a man. Or (which is the same thing), what is not an animal is not a man.

Opposition is the affirmation and negation of the same axiom. Opposition is either contrary, or contradictory.

It becomes contrary by retaining the same quantity, as: All men are good. It becomes contradictory by varying the quantity, as: No men are good. Some men are good.

Subcontraries are contained in contraries. Subordinates, since they do not affirm and deny at the same time, are not really opposites.

The sequence of propositions is that whereby one proposition follows another without a middle. For example, in a simple conversion a certain pleasure is good. Therefore a certain good is a pleasure.

We have discussed axiomatic judgment. Now comes dianoëtic judgment, which is a movement from one thing to another. This occurs both in the syllogism and in the method.

A syllogism is a *notion* whereby the question is so arranged with the argument that, positing the antecedent, it is necessarily deduced.

The parts of a syllogism are three propositions (the proposition called the major, the assumption, called the minor: and the conclusion, called the inference): or three terms: major, minor and middle term. The propositions are called immediate: the terms, the remote parts.

Syllogisms are considered in respect either of form or of matter.

In respect of form a syllogism is either imperfect, or implied and cryptic: or perfect or explicit.

An implied syllogism is one in which something is lacking, (that is, the major or the minor) or is excessive or redundant.

When a major or a minor is lacking, it is called an enthymeme, as: Man is rational. Therefore he is risible.

Induction and example are related to enthymeme. Induction

occurs, when the universal is inferred from the aggregate of particulars, as: Peter is risible, and John, and Christopher, and so on. Therefore all, and so on.

An example occurs, when another particular is inferred from a particular, as: The Israelites were punished for their sins. Therefore we too, and so on. This kind of argument is valid, when the parts and the circumstances are similar.

But when some part is excessive, as when it is proved or illustrated, it is a prosyllogism, in which something is added to the propositions.

The sorites and the dilemma are pertinent at this point. A sorites is a syllogism in which the predicate of the first proposition becomes the subject of the following proposition, until from the predicate of the last proposition and the subject of the first proposition a conclusion is inferred, as: Man is an animal. An animal is a body. A body is substance. Therefore man is substance.

A dilemma is a syllogism proceeding from contraries and striking its adversative on either side. Thus Bias proposed to draw the conclusion that one must not marry a wife: If she must be married, marry either a beautiful woman, or an ugly one. If she is beautiful, she will become a prostitute. If she is ugly, she will become a shrew.

To this a violence is usually added: A method of argumentation whereby the reasoning of the opponent is turned back upon himself, as: *I do not want to study literature, because I don't understand anything about it* is turned into: *All the more should the study of literature be pursued.*

So far we have treated imperfect or implied syllogisms. Now we discuss explicit or perfect syllogisms.

A perfect syllogism is either simple or compound. A syllogism is simple, in which the consequent part of the question is arranged in a proposition: the antecedent part is an assumption. This is commonly called a categorical syllogism.

This syllogism is distributed either through adjoined modes, or through figures.

In that mode a syllogism is either affirmative or negative: general, particular, or proper.

An affirmative syllogism is one that has all the propositions affirmative: a negative syllogism, either proposition negative.

A general syllogism is one that consists of a general proposition and a general assumption. A particular syllogism is one that consists of one of them being only a particular. A proper syllogism is one that consists of either proposition, a proper one, and it is called expository.

In the posterior mode, the syllogism is commonly distinguished by three figures: the first, second, and third.

The first figure of a simple syllogism occurs when an argument precedes in the proposition, and the affirmation follows in the assumption.

In this figure 1. The proposition always becomes either general, or proper. 2. The assumption always becomes affirmative.

The second figure occurs, when an argument always follows a negation in the other part.

In this figure 1. The proposition always becomes either universal, or proper. 2. The conclusion always becomes negative.

The third figure occurs when an argument always precedes, both in the proposition and in the assumption.

In this figure 1. The assumption always becomes affirmative. 2. The conclusion always becomes particular.

The fourth figure (that is posited by Galen), occurs when the argument is predicated in the proposition and is the subject in the assumption, as: Every man is an animal. Every animal is a substance. Therefore a certain substance is a man. This is rejected as an indirect conclusion.

A compound syllogism is one in which the entire question is arranged in an affirmative compound proposition. The argument is the remaining part. This is commonly called a hypothetical syllogism.

The hypothetical syllogism is two-fold: either conjunctive, or disjunctive.

A compound syllogism is conjunctive when it has a conjunctive proposition. Disjunctive, when it has a disjunctive proposition.

Each has two modes.

The conjunctive syllogism just posits the antecedent: and the consequent concludes. But the first is true: therefore the second is also true, as: If a man is alive, he has a body. But he is alive. Therefore, and so on. Here the conclusion is valid from the position of the antecedent to the position of the consequent: but not the contrary, except in reciprocal terms, as: If man is rational, he is also risible. Here the conclusion is valid either from rational to risible or vice versa.

A conjunctive syllogism of the second mode is one that negates the consequent in order to negate the antecedent. But the consequent is absurd: therefore the antecedent is also. For example: If a man is a stone, he is inanimate. But he is not inanimate. Therefore he is not a stone. Here the inference is valid from the remoteness of the consequent to the remoteness of the antecedent: but not the contrary, except in reciprocal terms. For example: If it is day, the sun has risen. This conclusion is valid either way.

The first mode of a disjunctive syllogism is one that destroys one thing and infers the remaining one. For example: It is either day, or it is night. But it is not day. Therefore it is night.

The second mode of a disjunctive syllogism is one that assumes one thing and negates the other. For example: But it is day. Therefore it is not night.

So much for the syllogism in respect of form. The next topic is the syllogism in respect of matter. The syllogism in respect of matter is either apodeictic or demonstrative, or topical or probable: or sophistic or fallacious.

A demonstrative syllogism is one that proves its validity from such premises as are primary propositions, and true. They are primary and true, when they have reliability not from others, but in themselves.

A syllogism is specially demonstrative in which affection is proved about the subject through the efficient cause, or the end (in a demonstrative *why*); or the effect (in a demonstrative *that*).

A topical syllogism is one that is from probable propositions. Things are probable that appear so to all or many men, or philosophers: such statements being completely acceptable either to all or to very many people, as: A mother loves her son.

A sophistic syllogism is one that has a wrong arrangement, or false matter, obscured by specious truth.

A sophism then is either in the form of a syllogism, or in matter. It is in the form, when it is defective in some rule of a syllogistic conclusion. For example, when in the second figure it becomes an affirmative syllogism.

It is a sophism in matter, when the propositions are sophistic. A sophism of matter occurs either in diction, or in actuality.

There is a fallacy in speech either in a homonym or equivocation, when the middle term is equivocal, as *canis*:or a fallacy in composition and division, when disjunctives are conjoined, or vice versa.

Ambiguities, accents, and figures of fallacious speech are included in equivocation, because some of them are equivocations.

A sophism in fact is a fallacy, either of ignoratio elenchi, or elenchus polyuzeteseos, or petitio principii, or a secundum quid a dicto, or ad dictum simply.

Here too belongs the elenchus of cause, subject, accident, disparates, similars, conjunctions, testimony, and so on.

For a more thorough understanding let them repeatedly learn how to oppose and solve various kinds of sophisms.

We spoke of notions in the syllogism. Now follows the purpose in method. Method is the purpose of various homogeneous axioms, posited in accordance with the nature of their clarity, by which the mutual agreement of all of them is judged and comprehended by the memory.

Method is also defined as a legitimate disposition of the doctrine of parts. Method is either of some theme, or of an entire science. The former is particular, the latter universal. In regard to the theme, if it is simple, the method has a means of 1. considering the noun; 2. finding the genus and causes; 3. determining the definition; 4. subjoining the accidents and effects; 5. dividing; and so on.

If the theme is compound or a problem, then the treatment consists of exposition of the terms, refutation, and confirmation.

The scientific method is either analytical, or synthetic. The analytical method is that whereby we proceed from the end to the middle, as in ethics from happiness to virtue.

The synthetic method is that whereby we proceed from causes to effects, as from matter to the thing created of matter.

The analytical method is adapted for practical matters: the synthetic for speculative discipline.

In both methods there is one method only, or the same general procedure: from what is primary and better known to what is later and less known.

MORITZ SCHLICK

(1882-1936)

Studied at the University of Rostock and taught at Rostock, Kiel, Vienna, Berkeley and Stanford. Founder of the Vienna Circle. Schlick did not aim at creating a system but wanted to find a way of philosophizing that would satisfy the demands of a most scrupulous scientific conscience. He was also concerned with the boundaries between the humanities and natural science. He was the spiritual rector of Logical Empiricism.

Main Works:

Allgemeine Erkenntnislehre; Naturphilosophie; Erkenntnistheorie und moderne Physik; Gesammelte Aufsaetze.

Causality

There is an old rule, formulated long ago in scholastic philosophy, that warns us against confusing the "post hoc" and the "propter hoc." This means that from the fact that an event E happened after another event C we must not infer that E happened "because of" C. In other words, the rule maintains that the meaning of the proposition "E follows C" is entirely different from the meaning of the proposition "E is the effect of the cause C." But what *is* the difference between the two meanings? This question, it seems to me, is the philosophical problem of Causality.

I call it philosophical, because it is a question of meaning

From: *"Causality in Everyday Life and in Recent Science."*

only, not of truth. It deals with the signification of the word "propter" or "because of"; we have to know what these words signify in order to understand the mere meaning of the principle of causality; the question whether this principle (if we can discover any meaning in it) is true or false would be a scientific problem, i.e., it could be decided only by observation and experience.

Our rule seems to presuppose that we are already acquainted with the signification of the words *post* and *propter*, for if we were not, there would be no possibility of ever applying the rule to any particular case. At best it would yield us an information of an entirely negative nature: it would tell us that the causal relation is *not* merely the relation of temporal succession, but something more; yet it would not give the slightest hint as to the positive essence of the causal relation.

Now there is no doubt that we do apply the rule continually and that it is a perfectly good and sound rule which people ought to follow even much more frequently than they do. If we take a certain medicine and get well after it, it would be very rash to assert that the medicine was the *cause* of our getting well. Or if we try to discover the causes of the depression, we know we are looking for much more than merely for events which *preceded* the depression. It is evident, therefore, that we actually are in possession of some kind of criterion which enables us to distinguish between events that merely follow each other and events that cause each other; for we do make this distinction every day, and we make it with a sufficient accuracy to have nearly all our behavior guided by it.

We simply have to observe how this distinction is actually made in order to find out the meaning of the concept of causality as it is used in our daily experience. This simple proceeding will surely not be difficult, and yet it is the general method —and I am convinced the only method—of philosophy: it discovers the meaning of propositions by finding out just how they are verified, i.e., how their truth or falsity is tested.

This is what I propose to do with propositions in which the

concept of causality is used. I shall certainly not propose any "theory of causality"; I believe there can be no such thing. There are no theories and hypotheses in philosophy; hypotheses are the material out of which the sciences are constructed, and I believe that philosophy is something different from the sciences.

How, then, do we verify the statement that the taking of some medicine was not only the antecedent but also the *cause* of the recovery of the patient?

At first glance there seem to be two different ways of such a verification (remember, we do not ask how it *should* be done, but how it is really done in practice):

1. We try the medicine many times and perhaps on many different patients. If we find that in every single case a person suffering from a particular complaint is cured, we shall say: the recovery after the use of the medicine was not a mere *chance*, but was *caused* by it. In other words: if the event E *always* occurs after the event C has occurred before, if C never occurs without being followed by E, then we do not hesitate to call C the cause and E the effect. It is important to notice that we do this whether we are able to "explain" the cure or not; there are cases in which we just know that a medicine is good without knowing how it works.

This is a fact; and I should like to express it, as it has often been expressed by thinkers of the positivist school, by saying that the difference between a mere temporal sequence and a causal sequence is the regularity, the uniformity of the latter. If C is *regularly* followed by E, then C is the cause of E; if E only "happens" to follow C now and then, the sequence is called a mere chance. And since (as we just saw) the observation of the regularity was, in this case, the *only* thing that was done, it was necessarily the *only* reason for speaking of cause and effect, it was the sufficient reason. The word cause, as used in everyday life, implies *nothing but* regularity of sequence, because *nothing else* is used to verify the propositions in which it occurs.

I am sure the reader must feel very much disappointed to have me repeat these old "positivistic" statements which have been discussed and, some believe, refuted so many times. I appeal to his patience and hope he will presently see the import of these remarks for the higher aspects of the problem of causality as they are presented by recent science.

Metaphysicians will, of course, find fault with our representation of the facts. Although they will admit, I think, that in the above example the verification consisted entirely in the observation of uniformity and nothing else, they will probably maintain that even the most unprejudiced observer never thinks that the regularity sequence constitutes the whole of causality, but regards it only as a sign or as the consequence of something else of some "real connection" or some peculiar "intimacy" between the cause and effect, or by whatever name he may call the unobservable "tie" which he believes to be present in causation.

I do not deny that this may be so, but I answer: we are not concerned with what any observer thinks or says; our investigation of meaning is concerned only with what he *does* and can show us. Speaking, thinking, believing implies interpretation; we must not discuss interpretations or the results of philosophical analysis, we have to do with verification only, which is always an act or an activity. With regard to meaning we have to be pragmatists, whatever we may be with regard to the conception of truth. If the existence of that mysterious "tie" is verified *only* by the observation of regular sequence, then this regularity will be all the meaning the word "tie" actually has, and no thinking, believing, or speaking can add anything to it.

Perhaps the best known objection against the identification of causality and regularity is the remark that nothing is more regular than the succession of day and night, and yet we do not call the one the cause of the other. But this is simply accounted for by the fact that "day" and "night" are really not names for "events" at all in the sense in which this word is used in science. And as soon as we analyze day and night into the series of natural events for which these names stand, we find that the sequence of those events must be regarded as a very good example of "causal connection."

The real difficulties involved in the notion of uniformity are of a different nature and much more serious. We said that E was called the effect of a cause C, if in many cases it was observed to follow C each time without exception. Should we not ask: *how many* times? A physician who has tried a medicine in six cases and has seen the patient get better six times may feel pretty confident that his remedy was the cause of the recovery of his patients (provided, of course, that in his former experience they did not get well without the medicine), but undoubtedly it is possible that in all future cases the remedy will fail to have the desired result; and then we shall say: those first six times were nothing but a chance, the word "chance" meaning simply the negation of causality. If instead of six times the experiment were repeated successfully a hundred times, surely everybody would believe in the beneficial effect of the medicine; nevertheless it must be admitted that the future may bring exceptions and destroy the regularity. A hundred will be considered absolutely satisfactory; for if in one single case only C were not followed by E, one would feel no longer justified to call C the cause of E, and for all we know such a crucial case might always occur in the future.

So this is the state of affairs: the proposition "C is the cause of E" seemed to mean nothing but "C is always followed by E"; but this latter proposition can unfortunately never be verified on account of the unfortunate "always" it contains. Verification would be possible only if a finite number is substituted for "always," but no finite number is satisfactory, because it does not exclude the possibility of exceptions.

This difficulty has been pointed out about as many times as the problem of induction has been discussed, and the conclusion has usually been that causality cannot be explained as meaning simply uniformity, but that it must mean something else. Perhaps so. But we must insist: it *can* mean something else only if there is a way of verifying causal judgments different from the one we have described. What shall we do if no such way is discovered?

We can do nothing but stick to the facts with absolute frankness. Since the meaning of a proposition lies entirely in its verification, it will have meaning only *in so far* as it is verified. And if the verification is never considered complete and final, if we never declare a certain C to be the cause of a certain E without reserving the right of revocation (and this, it is important to notice, not on account of any incorrect observation or similar "mistake"), then we shall have to admit that we simply have no clear concept of causality. Where there is no definite verification, there can be no definite meaning. The function of the word "cause" will be vague. A sentence containing this word may serve a very good purpose in the practice of everyday life as well as of science, but it will have no theoretical meaning.

There is a very curious way in which the difficulty hidden in the word "always" is sometimes apparently overcome. It consists in saying: if it cannot be verified that E *always* follows C, it can also never be falsified, for the cases in which it does not seem to be the case can be explained as mere appearances, and so our belief in the causal relation between C and E can never be proved to be false. A physician, for instance, who has had complete success with a cure in ninety-nine cases but finds it to fail in the hundredth case, will by no means give up his belief that his treatment has been the "cause" of the ninety-nine recoveries, but will explain that in the negative case there must have been a circumstance which intervened and prevented the effect. And we shall very likely accept this explanation as very natural, just as we would not blame a medicine for not making a patient well, if five minutes after taking it he were killed by an automobile accident. Theoretically, and in a very crude symbolism, we might say that in the negative case the cause is not any more C at all, but C + C′, where C′ is the intervening circumstance, and C + C′ does *not* have the effect E, which C alone would have had. This statement must, of course, be capable of being verified by really observing C′; if we were to admit unobservable C's we could consider *any* event to be the cause of any other event by merely assuming the existence of convenient C's, and then surely our judgments about causal relations would lose all meaning. There are certain philosophers, those who advocate the doctrine of "conventionalism," who believe that this is really the nature of all our causal judgments; in their opinion all these judgments—which would include all laws of nature—have no real meaning, they do not say anything about the world, but only indicate the way in which we select, or even arbitrarily invent, events in order to make them fit into a preconceived scheme, which we have decided to use as our most convenient means of describing nature. Among famous scientists the astronomer A. S. Eddington may be mentioned as holding similar views.

We must note here that the interpretation of negative cases by means of disturbing influences—intervening C's—does *not* offer any criterion of causality other than uniformity of sequence; on the contrary, it saves causality only by substituting a hidden regularity for an apparent irregularity.

The regularity may at first be hidden, but it must be discoverable, if we are not to fall into snares of conventionalism; that is, we must be able to find a C′ such that C and C′ will always be followed by an E′ which is different from E. And if there should be cases in which C + C′ is not followed by E′, we have to find a new event C″, and so on. Evidently it would be a great advantage and would help to elucidate special cases of causality, if there were a way of making sure that no further C's could possibly intervene. There would be no hope of doing this, if *any* event in the world could eventually play the role of the C′ for which we are looking. But if these events were restricted in a certain way so that it would be possible to examine *all* of them, then we would know that no other disturbing element could come into question, and verification would become more satisfactory.

Now it has usually been assumed by science that the possible causes were indeed very definitely restricted. In looking for the cause of a given event E it was thought that we could exclude all events happening *long before* E, and all events happening *at a great distance* from E (events occurring *after* E had, of course, been already ruled out by pre-scientific thinking). Assuming these conditions in their most rigorous and consistent form one arrived at the idea that no event could be regarded as the proper cause of E unless it occurred in the immediate spatial and temporal vicinity of E. So the causal relation between two events C and E was thought to imply their contiguity in space and time. Action-at-a-distance (temporal as well as spatial distance) was considered impossible. If this were so, one would have to look for the causes of any event only in its immediate neighborhood, there would indeed be no time and no room for any other event to interfere. It is irrelevant that this view was supported by *a priori* arguments such as "an event can act only at the place where it occurs, and nowhere else"; nevertheless such arguments show that one believed one could *understand* the causal relation better if there was contiguity; if cause and effect were separated from each other, their relation appeared to be more mysterious. This brings us to the consideration of the second way in which the existence of a causal relation seems to be established (the first one being observation of uniformity of sequence).

2. Supposing there were a case in which we believed we really and completely "understood" the working of a certain treatment or medicine in the human body: in such a case we should not have to wait for any repetition of the sequence treatment-recovery in order to assert a causal relation between these two events; we could assert it even before it occurred a single time, because our "understanding" of this particular causation would imply our conviction that the first event would entail the second one, or, as it is often put, C would *necessarily* be followed by E. If a surgeon amputates a man's leg, he will know beforehand that the man will be one-legged afterwards. Nobody thinks that we must wait for a long series of experiences in order to know that amputation results in the loss of a limb. We feel we "understand"

the whole process and therefore know its result without having experienced it.

So there seems to be a second way of verifying judgment independent of observation of regularity: it consists in simply pointing to the "understanding" of the particular causal relation. And those who believe in this second way will immediately add that it is the only real way, the only legitimate method, and that our first criterion—uniformity of occurrence—with nothing but an untrustworthy symptom, which might be good enough for an empiricist scientist, but could never satisfy the philosopher.

But let us examine what exactly is meant by "understanding" as the word is used here.

It is usually supposed to be a matter of "pure reason." Now, the only sense I can find for this term is the purely logical, which would mean the same as the purely deductive, the merely analytical. And there is indeed a purely logical element in the case we have just been examining. That amputation of a leg causes a man to be one-legged is an identical inference; it is, like all logical inferences, a mere tautology. But it is easy to see, unfortunately, that this has nothing to do with causation. The causal connection is hidden in the word "amputation." We usually believe we understand this connection, because we think we comprehend the process, say, of a saw cutting through a bone: the hard particles of steel are in immediate contact with the soft particles of the bone, and the latter somehow must give way to the former. Here again we have contiguity in space and time, which appears to flatter our imagination, but apart from that we have again nothing but a sequence of events which we have often observed to happen in a similar way and which we therefore expect to happen again. For aught we know we might some day come across a bone that would resist any saw and that no human power would be able to cut in two.

So we see that, at least in our example, we were led to think we understood or comprehended the causal nexus: partly by a misinterpretation of the way in which logical inference entered into our thought, and partly by analyzing the causal process into

731

a spatial and temporal continuity of events. This means that our second criterion is really only a hidden application of the first one; it is not different, and consequently not any better.

The examination of any other example leads to the same result. What, for instance, is the difference between a case in which we *understand* that a certain medicine must have a certain effect, and another case in which we just know by experience that it does have that effect? It is evidently this: in the second case we observe only two events, the application of the drug and, after a reasonable lapse of time, the recovery of the patient; in the first case we know how the gap between cause and effect is filled by an unbroken chain of events which are contiguous in space and time. The drug, e.g., is injected into the veins, we know it comes into immediate contact with the blood particles, we know that these will then undergo a certain chemical change, they will travel through the body, they will come in contact with a certain organ, this organ will be changed in a particular way, and so on. In this way we infer that in the end the patient *must* be healed, *if* all the other events follow each other in the way we have assumed. And how do we know that they do follow each other so? All we know is that in former experiences in the laboratory this has always been the regular course of things.

From all this we must draw negative conclusion that it is impossible—at least in so far as the judgments of everyday life and of qualitative science are concerned—to find any meaning for the word causation, except that it implies regularity of sequence. And this is rather vague, because there is no rule as to how many instances have to be observed in order to justify our speaking of regularity.

But the two chief things we can learn from the foregoing considerations seem to me to be these:

1. The "understanding" of a causal relation is not a process of logical reasoning; what is called causal necessity is absolutely different from logical necessity (which is nothing but identity). But at the same time we see why former philosophers so frequently made the mistake of confusing the two and believing

that the effect could be logically inferred from the cause. The only serious philosopher of our present time who still believes that there must be some kind of identity between them to be in some way rational or logical, is (so far as I know) E. Meyerson. He tries to prove this historically by analyzing the statements of famous philosophers and scientists; but the psychological explanation of his views lies in the fact that he started as a chemist, who is used to thinking in terms of identical substances, whereas the physicist, who goes more deeply into the explanation of nature, has to think in terms of events.

2. We learn that the causal relation between two separate events is actually explained or understood when we can conceive the two as being connected by a chain of intermediate events. If some of these are still separated, we have to look for new events between them, and so on, until all the gaps are filled out and the chain has become perfectly continuous in space and time. But evidently *we can go no further*, and it would be nonsense to expect more of us. If we look for the causal link that links two events together, we cannot find anything but another event (or perhaps several). Whatever can be observed and shown in the causal chain will be the links, but it would be nonsense to look for the linkage.

This shows that we are perfectly right when we think of cause and effect as *connected* by a causal chain, but that we are perfectly wrong when we think that this chain could consist of anything but events, that it could be a kind of mysterious tie called "causality." The conception of such a "tie," which is really not a concept but a mere word, is due to a faulty process of thinking that is very common in the history of philosophy: the continuation of a thought beyond its logical limit; we transcend the region in which a word makes sense and necessarily find ourselves in the region of nonsense. After the scientist has successfully filled up all the gaps in his causal chains by continually interpolating new events, the philosopher wants to go on with this pleasant game after all the gaps are filled. So he invents a kind of glue and assures us that in reality it is only his glue that holds events together at all. But we can never find the glue; there is no room for it, as the world is already completely filled by events which leave no chinks between them. Even in our times there are some philosophers who say that we directly experience causation, e.g., in the act of volition, or even in the feeling of muscular effort. But whatever such feelings of willing or of effort may be, they are certainly events in the world; they can be glued to other events, but they cannot be the glue.

All this has of course been seen very clearly by Hume when he said that it was impossible to discover any "impression" for the idea of causal nexus. Only we can express this even more strongly by saying that we are already committing a kind of nonsense when we try to *look* for such an impression. At this point we find complete agreement between Hume and Kant. Kant applauded Hume for seeing that when we speak of causation we cannot possibly mean a sort of tie which connects the events or establishes a kind of intimacy between them, and he conceived causality as something entirely different, namely as a Principle of Order. He believed that the human mind imposed a certain order on the events of its experience, and that causality was one of the principles according to which this was done. And according to him, the human mind did this because it could not help doing it; the Principle was simply part of its metaphysical nature.

Although we must of course reject the latter part of Kant's view, we can most heartily consent to his opinion that if caus- ality is anything at all it can be nothing but a Principle of Order.

ARTHUR SCHOPENHAUER
(1788-1860)

Son of a Danzig banker, studied at Goettingen and Jena. After teaching for twelve years at the University of Berlin, he withdrew into private life in 1831 and spent the rest of his life in Frankfurt. Schopenhauer founded a pessimistic system of mechanistic voluntarism which was deeply original, for all his indebtedness to Plato, Kant and the Indian Vedantic philosophy. A misanthrope and misogynist, his life was marked by a succession of petty hatreds for his fellow men and women. Profound and highly literate, he was one of the most influential thinkers of the 19th century. He considered the universe purely as man's imagination and one without sense or meaning at that. Will is the driving power of the world; morality lies in negation of the will.

Main Works:

Die Welt als Wille und Vorstellung; Die beiden Grundprobleme der Ethik; Ueber die vierfache Wurzel des Satzes vom zureichendem Grunde; Ueber den Willen in der Natur; Parerga und Paralipomena.

The Object of Experience and Science

§ 1. "The world is my idea": this is a truth which holds good for everything that lives and knows, though man alone can bring it into reflective and abstract consciousness. If he really does this, he has attained to philosophical wisdom. It then becomes clear and certain to him that what he knows is not a sun and an earth, but only an eye that sees a sun, a hand that feels

----

From: *Die Welt als Wille und Vorstellung.*

an earth; that the world which surrounds him is there only as idea, *i.e.*, only in relation to something else, the consciousness, which is himself. If any truth can be asserted *a priori*, it is this, for it is the expression of the most general form of all possible and thinkable experience: a form which is more general than time, or space, or causality, for they all presuppose it; and each of these, which we have seen to be just so many modes of the principle of sufficient reason, is valid only for a particular class of ideas; whereas the antithesis of object and subject is the common form of all these classes, is that form under which alone any idea of whatever kind it may be, abstract or intuitive, pure or empirical, is possible and thinkable. No truth therefore is more certain, more independent of all others, and less in need of proof than this, that all that exists for knowledge, and therefore this whole world, is only object in relation to subject, perception of a perceiver, in a word, idea. This is obviously true of the past and the future, as well as of the present, of what is farthest off, as of what is near; for it is true of time and space themselves, in which alone these distinctions arise. All that in any way belongs or can belong to the world is inevitably thus conditioned through the subject, and exists only for the subject. The world is idea.

This truth is by no means new. It was implicitly involved in the skeptical reflections from which Descartes started. Berkeley, however, was the first who distinctly enunciated it, and by this he has rendered a permanent service to philosophy, even though the rest of his teaching should not endure. Kant's primary mistake was the neglect of this principle, as is shown in the appendix. How early again this truth was recognized by the wise men of India, appearing indeed as the fundamental tenet of the Vedânta philosophy ascribed to Vyasa, is pointed out by Sir William Jones in the last of his essays: "On the philosophy of the Asiatics" (*Asiatic Researches,* Vol. IV., p. 164), where he says, "The fundamental tenet of the Vedânta school consisted not in denying the existence of matter, that is, of solidity, impenetrability, and extended figure (to deny which would be lunacy), but in correcting the popular notion of it, and in contending that it has no essence independent of mental perception; that existence and perceptibility are convertible terms." These words adequately express the compatibility of empirical reality and transcendental ideality.

In this first book, then, we consider the world only from this side, only so far as it is idea. The inward reluctance with which any one accepts the world as merely his idea, warns him that this view of it, however true it may be, is nevertheless one-sided, adopted in consequence of some arbitrary abstraction. And yet it is a conception from which he can never free himself. The defectiveness of this view will be corrected in the next book by means of a truth which is not so immediately certain as that from which we start here; a truth at which we can arrive only by deeper research and more severe abstraction, by the separation of what is different and the union of what is identical. This truth, which must be very serious and impressive if not awful to everyone, is that a man can also say and must say, "the world is my will.". . .

§ 2. That which knows all things and is known by none is the subject. Thus it is the supporter of the world, that condition of all phenomena, of all objects, which is always presupposed throughout experience; for all that exists, exists only for the subject. Every one finds himself to be subject, yet only in so far as he knows, not in so far as he is an object of knowledge. But his body is object, and therefore from this point of view we call it idea. For the body is an object among objects, and is conditioned by the laws of objects, although it is an immediate object. Like all objects of perception, it lies within the universal forms of knowledge, time and space, which are the conditions of multiplicity. The subject, on the contrary, which is always the knower, never the known, does not come under these forms, but is presupposed by them; it has therefore neither multiplicity nor its opposite unity. We never know it, but it is always the knower wherever there is knowledge.

So then the world as idea, the only aspect in which we consider it at present, has two fundamental, necessary, and inseparable halves. The one half is the object, the forms of which are space and time, and through these multiplicity. The other half is the subject, which is not in space and time, for it is present, entire and undivided, in every percipient being. So that any one percipient being, with the object, constitutes the whole world as idea just as fully as the existing millions could do; but if this one were to disappear, then the whole world as idea would cease to be. These halves are therefore inseparable even for thought, for each of the two has meaning and existence only through and for the other, each appears with the other and vanishes with it. They limit each other immediately; where the object begins the subject ends. The universality of this limitation is shown by the fact that the essential and hence universal forms of all objects, space, time, and causality, may, without knowledge of the object, be discovered and fully known from a consideration of the subject, *i.e.*, in Kantian language, they lie *a priori* in our consciousness. That he discovered this, is one of Kant's principal merits, and it is a great one. I however go beyond this, and maintain that the principle of sufficient reason is the general expression for all these forms of the object of which we are *a priori* conscious; and that therefore all that we know purely *a priori* is merely the content of that principle and what follows from it; in it all our certain *a priori* knowledge is expressed. . . .

§ 3. The chief distinction among our ideas is that between ideas of perception and abstract ideas. The latter form just one class of ideas, namely concepts, and these are the possession of man alone of all creatures upon earth. The capacity for these, which distinguishes him from all the lower animals, has always been called reason. We shall consider these abstract ideas by themselves later, but, in the first place, we shall speak exclusively of the *ideas of perception*. These comprehend the whole visible world, or the sum total of experience, with the conditions of its possibility. . . .

This quality of the universal forms of intuition, which was discovered by Kant, that they may be perceived in themselves and apart from experience, and that they may be known as exhibiting those laws on which is founded the infallible science of mathematics, is certainly very important. Not less worthy of remark, however, is this other quality of time and space, that the principle of sufficient reason, which conditions experience as the law of causation and of motive, and thought as the law of the basis of judgment, appears here in quite a special form, to which I have given the name of the ground of being. In time, this is the succession of its moments, and in space the position of its parts, which reciprocally determine each other *ad infinitum*.

Anyone who has fully understood from the introductory essay (*On the Fourfold Root of the Principle of Sufficient Reason*) the complete identity of the content of the principle of sufficient reason in all its different forms, must also be convinced of the importance of the knowledge of the simplest of these forms, as affording him insight into his own inmost nature. This simplest form of the principle we have found to be time. In it each instant is, only in so far as it has effaced the preceding one, its generator, to be itself in turn as quickly effaced. The past and the future (considered apart from the consequences of their content) are empty as a dream, and the present is only the indivisible and unenduring boundary between them. And in all the other forms of the principle of sufficient reason, we shall find the same emptiness, and shall see that not time only but also space, and the whole content of both of them, *i.e.*, all that proceeds from causes and motives, has a merely relative existence, is only through and for another like to itself, *i.e.*, not more enduring. The substance of this doctrine is old: it appears in Heraclitus when he laments the eternal flux of things; in Plato when he degrades the object to that which is ever becoming, but never being; in Spinoza as the doctrine of the mere accidents of the one substance which is and endures. Kant opposes what is thus known as the mere phenomenon to the thing in itself. Lastly, the ancient wisdom of the Indian philosophers declares, "It is

Mâyâ, the veil of deception, which blinds the eyes of mortals, and makes them behold a world of which they cannot say either that it is or that it is not: for it is like a dream; it is like the sunshine on the sand which the traveller takes from afar for water, or the stray piece of rope he mistakes for a snake." (These similes are repeated in innumerable passages of the Vedas and the Puranas.) But what all these mean, and that of which they all speak, is nothing more than what we have just considered— the world as idea subject to the principle of sufficient reason.

§ 4. Whoever has recognized the form of the principle of sufficient reason, which appears in pure time as such, and on which all counting and arithmetical calculation rests, has completely mastered the nature of time. Time is nothing more than that form of the principle of sufficient reason, and has no further significance. Succession is the form of the principle of sufficient reason in time, and succession is the whole nature of time. Further, whoever has recognized the principle of sufficient reason as it appears in the presentation of pure space, has exhausted the whole nature of space, which is absolutely nothing more than that possibility of the reciprocal determination of its parts by each other, which is called position. The detailed treatment of this, and the formulation in abstract conceptions of the results which flow from it, so that they may be more conveniently used, is the subject of the science of geometry. Thus also, whoever has recognized the law of causation, the aspect of the principle of sufficient reason which appears in what fills these forms (space and time) as objects of perception, that is to say, matter, has completely mastered the nature of matter as such, for matter is nothing more than causation, as any one will see at once if he reflects. Its true being is its action, nor can we possibly conceive it as having any other meaning. Only as active does it fill space and time; its action upon the immediate object (which is itself matter) determines that perception in which alone it exists. The consequence of the action of any material object upon any other, is known only in so far as the latter acts upon the immediate object in a different way from that in which it acted before; it consists only of this. Cause and effect thus constitute the whole nature of matter; its true being is its action. (A fuller treatment of this will be found in the essay on the Principle of Sufficient Reason, § 21.) The nature of all material things is therefore very appropriately called in German, *"Wirklichkeit,"* a word which is far more expressive than *"Realität."* Again, that which is acted upon is always matter, and thus the whole being and essence of matter consists in the orderly change which one part of it brings about in another part. The existance of matter is therefore entirely relative, according to a relation which is valid only within its limits, as in the case of time and space. . . .

§ 5. It is needful to guard against the grave error of supposing that because perception arises through the knowledge of causality, the relation of subject and object is that of cause and effect. For this relation subsists only between the immediate object and objects known indirectly, thus always between objects alone. It is this false supposition that has given rise to the foolish controversy about the reality of the outer world; a controversy in which dogmatism and skepticism oppose each other, and the former appears, now as realism, now as idealism. Realism treats the object as cause, and the subject as its effect. The idealism of Fichte reduces the object to the effect of the subject. Since however, and this cannot be too much emphasized, there is absolutely no relation according to the principle of sufficient reason between subject and object, neither of these views could be proved, and therefore skepticism attacked them both with success. Now, just as the law of causality precedes perception and experience as their condition, and therefore cannot (as Hume thought) be derived from them, so object and subject precede all knowledge, and hence the principle of sufficient reason in general, as its first condition; for this principle is merely the form of all objects, the whole nature and possibility of their existence as phenomena: but the object always presupposes the subject; and therefore between these two there can be no relation of reason and consequent. My essay on the principle of sufficient reason accomplishes just this: it explains the content of that principle as the essential form of every object—that is to say, as the universal nature of all objective existence, as something which pertains to the object as such; but the object as such always presupposes the subject as its necessary correlative; and therefore the subject remains always outside the province in which the principle of sufficient reason is valid. The controversy as to the reality of the outer world rests upon this false extension of the validity of the principle of sufficient reason to the subject also, and starting with this mistake it can never understand itself. On the one side realistic dogmatism, looking upon the idea as the effect of the object, desires to separate these two, idea and object, which are really one, and to assume a cause quite different from the idea, an object in itself, independent of the subject, a thing which is quite inconceivable; for even as object it presupposes subject, and so remains its idea. Opposed to this doctrine is skepticism, which makes the same false presupposition that in the idea we have only the effect, never the cause, therefore never real being; that we always know merely the action of the object. But this object, it supposes, may perhaps have no resemblance whatever to its effect, may indeed have been quite erroneously received as the cause, for the law of causality is first to be gathered from experience, and the reality of experience is then made to rest upon it. Thus both of these views are open to the correction, firstly, that object and idea are the same; secondly, that the true being of the object of perception is its action, that the reality of the thing consists in this, and the demand for an existence of the object outside the idea of the subject, and also for an essence of the actual thing different from its action, has absolutely no meaning, and is a contradiction: and that the knowledge of the nature of the effect of any perceived object, exhausts such an object itself, so far as it is object, *i.e.*, idea, for beyond this there is nothing more to be known. So far then, the perceived world in space and time, which makes itself known as causation alone, is entirely real, and is throughout simply what it appears to be, and it appears wholly and without reserve as idea, bound together according to the law of causality. This is its empirical reality. On the other hand, all causality is in the understanding alone, and for the understanding. The whole actual, that is, active world is determined as such through the understanding, and apart from it is nothing. This, however, is not the only reason for altogether denying such a reality of the outer world as is taught by the dogmatist, who explains its reality as its independence of the subject. We also deny it, because no object apart from a subject can be conceived without contradiction. The whole world of objects is and remains idea, and therefore wholly and for ever determined by the subject; that is to say, it has transcendental ideality. But it is not therefore illusion or mere appearance; it presents itself as that which it is, idea, and indeed as a series of ideas of which the common bond is the principle of sufficient reason. . . .

JOHN DUNS SCOTUS
(1266-1308)

Scot who became professor at Oxford, has been much maligned by later generations: his name, distorted into "dunce", became a synonym for blockhead. In his lifetime, however, he was an extremely popular teacher who attracted students from many countries by his daring attacks on Aquinas and Augustine. It was when the Church finally decided in favor of Aquinas that his reputation suffered a decrease of popularity. Duns Scotus was a pioneer of nominalistic criticism, with strong sceptic tendencies. He held that every individual thing is given individual form which can only directly be comprehended (Haecceitas).

Main Works:

> Opus oxoniense; Reportata parisiensia; Tractatus de primo principio; Quaestiones Quodlibetales; Quaestiones subtilissimae in Metaphysicam.

Cognition

Practical understanding is something in us that is not perpetual but has existence after non-existence, as we learn by experience.

Hence it is necessary to postulate an active cause for this and in some fashion one that subsists in us: otherwise it would not be in our power to understand when we wish to do so. This is in opposition to Aristotle. It is also evident here that the mind and the object present concur, and this in an intelligible species: because otherwise it is not present as being intelligible in action, with reference to a sensible and material object.

From: *De Ratione Cognitionis Humanae.*

I assert then that the entire active cause of this understanding is not the object, neither in itself, nor in its species. In that case the image could not be preserved in the mind as the mind is, because nothing in the mind itself would have the status of the originator.

Nor is the entire cause of understanding the intellective mind, or some part of it formally: because then the similarity of the object would have been produced.

The first view assigns all activity to the mind.

In question there is one view that assigns all activity with respect to the understanding to the mind itself. It is attributed to St. Augustine, who says that: Because the image of the body is in the spirit that is nobler than the body, for that reason the image of the body is nobler in the spirit than the body itself in its substance. And he continues: We must not think that the body acts in any way on the spirit, as though the spirit is substituted in the active body in place of matter. For in every sense the thing that acts is greater than the thing that is the object of action, nor is the body in any way greater than the spirit, but rather the spirit is greater than the body. Therefore although the image of the body begins to be in the spirit, yet by means of the same image, it is not the body in the spirit, but the spirit in itself that acts with remarkable swiftness.

And he goes on: The image of this, as it is seen in the spirit when a man sees with his eyes, is quickly formed without the lapse of the slightest fraction of time.

Again: The mind gathers up and carries along the images of bodies made in itself and about itself. For it gives to their formation something of its own substance, but it retains something whereby it is more mind, that is, rational intelligence, that is preserved for judgment. For we believe that we have in common with animals too those parts of the mind that are formed by corporeal similarities.

Therefore the mind forms in itself images of known bodies themselves, as this authoritatively and lucidly expressed statement asserts.

In favor of this view he argues rationally as follows: The effect does not exceed the cause in perfection. Now everything living is better than non-living, according to Augustine. Therefore there cannot be a living operation except by a vital or living principle of action. These operations of knowledge are vital operations. Therefore they come from the mind itself, just as from the principle of generation.

Proof that this is not Augustine's notion.

Against this view, it is evident that it is not Augustine's notion: It must clearly be maintained that every thing that we learn generates in us a knowledge of itself. For knowledge is produced in two ways, namely, by the learner, and by the thing learned.

Again: From the visible and the seeing, vision is produced.

Again: As has previously been stated, the thought formed by the thing itself that we know, is the word.

Therefore he proposes to attribute some degree of causality to the object. This too is argued rationally, as follows: There are only four kinds of causes in themselves. Therefore as they exist perfect in themselves and unhampered, and sufficiently proximate, the effect will follow from them if they are natural causes, or at least it will be potentially if they are causes acting freely. And as form has in some way *being* through production, and the end follows the production of the thing in *being*, or, if it precedes—that is, in so far as the efficient cause moves it to action—for this reason, since two causes prior to the thing itself, namely, the efficient cause and the material cause, are perfect in themselves, and approximate, and unhampered the effect follows, or at least follows potentially. Therefore, if the mind is the total active cause of generated knowledge, and is itself a material cause, whether a receptive subject, or a susceptive subject with respect to the same thing, and is always present in action since it is a natural cause: then there will always be practical understanding in that understanding of which it is itself the cause and of which it is itself the cause in regard to itself: or at least there will be some understanding into which it can preferably be placed. For imperfection of any cause cannot be assumed in itself if we maintain the first hypothesis, nor can non-approximation, nor obstruction, because nothing then appears obstructive.

Now we turn to the cause *sine qua non* which is required for the purpose of producing knowledge, that is, we say that all causes *per se* are not sufficient causes, but that something else is required on which the thing that is to be must depend essentially. Therefore there will not be four causes only, or four kinds of causes, but many. Or something will depend essentially on something which is not its cause.

To Augustine's views I reply that the image that is assumed by him to be in the spirit must be understood to be in the mind, or in some part of the mind as in the subject, and not precisely in the body so mixed. Otherwise it would not be concluded that this image is nobler than every body. What is in the mind, or in some part of the mind, as in the subject, is not the species that is commonly called *species,* but the species that is received in the part of the organ which is the body so mixed. But that which is received in the soul or in the power of the soul is the act of knowing. Therefore by *image* he understands such an act. He means that the training of the sense that occurs solely by means of the body is called vision. Therefore, just as that, which is properly an image, is called vision, so conversely vision can be called an image, and much more truly, because it is a certain quality related to truth. And such a quality is a certain similarity of the object.

With this understanding, it is readily evident what his views are. For I grant that this image, which is sensation, does not cause the body in the spirit as a total cause, but the mind causes in itself, with remarkable swiftness, yet not as a total cause, but as an object. Hence Augustine asserts that as soon as it is seen, and so on, implying that the presence of the object is required to be visible in the reason, so that the mind produces vision in itself. And it is not required except as in some sort a partial cause, as he expresses it: from seeing and from the visible, vision is produced.

The opinion denies all activity to the intellect.

Another opinion that is completely contrary asserts:
The intellective mind, in so far as it is intellective, has not activity or causality with respect to the intellect.

For the possible intellect does not have such causality, whether it is informed by an intelligible species, which they deny, or whether it is bare, because, according to them, the same thing cannot act in itself. They assent to this, because when an agent in action is such as was passive in power, it follows that it was the same in potentiality and in action. According to these propositions they say that the agent and the passive object are distinct in subject. They also say that, whatever difficulties occur in any matter, those principles should not be refuted on their account, because then all inquiry into the truth is destroyed through the denial of such principles. For in this way they are denied in one matter and in another. For the same reason they say that the intellect as agent cannot cause something effectively in the potential intellect, because it is not distinguished from the subject.

A refutation of this view.

The intellect as agent, according to him, causes nothing that is formally in the imagination: but only a removal occurs of prohibitive objects through a certain spiritual contact of this light within the imagination, and when this removal takes place, by virtue of the intellect as agent, information of the potential intellect occurs. From this it follows that nothing that is in the intellective part—which includes the intellect both as agent and as potential—will have any way of being active or an agent, or

748

being the subject of action with respect to any intelligence whatever. And so only the imagination effectively stands in relation to the intellect.

If there is here any efficiency through which irradiation or illumination takes place in imagination, that efficiency will be precisely that of God himself, who created such a light in the potential intellect. Therefore God either acts immediately on any intellect whatsoever, or the imagination will merely be the cause of all actions of the intellective parts, both of the intellect and of volition. Therefore there is nothing else that comes actively from God with respect to any perception, unless it is the imagination alone.

This appears very inconsistent, because it decidedly impairs the nature of the mind. For the imagination seems incapable of causing in the intellect any perfection that exceeds its nobility, because the equivocal effect cannot exceed its own cause, but falls off. Therefore nothing caused precisely by the imagination as by the entire active cause—as the view on the intellect posits —can be more perfect than the imagination, but must necessarily be more imperfect. And so no operation or perception will be more perfect in man than the imagination: which is absurd.

Refutation of Goffred's view

Converse: Habit is not posited precisely with passivity and especially in a passive effect greatly disposed to form. For it is not necessary that what is greatly disposed in itself to receive should be rendered easy for reception. But the intellect is greatly disposed to any perception whatever, because it has no contrary. Therefore it would not be necessary to posit any habit in the intellect, if it were precisely passive with respect to perception. The first proposition is proved, because *habit is that which we use when we wish: and habit causes the possessor of habit, and makes his task good.* All these factors contribute some activity to habit.

Similarly: How will the intellect run around forming syllogisms, or arguments, if imagination causes all perception? For it does not seem comprehensible how discursive acts of the imagination cause every discursive movement. Again: How will imagination cause logical notions, or rational relationships? For if imagination causes every perception, whatever is caused by it will be real, because that is said to be real perception which is caused immediately by the thing, or by the species representing the thing itself. Therefore no perception will cause logical notions or rational relationships, because the intellect can by no act of its own compare one object with another, for this comparison causes a rational relationship or a second notion in the object. Again: How will the intellect reflect upon its own action, and how will this be in the power of the reflective force? For if imagination causing perception has naturally to cause reflection toward this action, by the same reasoning it causes reflection of the reflective force too, and so on to infinity, as Augustine declares. But if it does not have to cause reflection, but only absolute action, and afterward another imagination occurs, it does not seem possible to indicate how there would be any reflection on any action.

Reply in Refutation.

The intellect is sometimes in near and accidental power to understand, although previously it was in essential and remote power. This however does not occur in the intellect except through some mutation. Not of the object, it is evident, because in the object there is only a rational relationship. Therefore a mutation of the intellect itself. Hence this mutation that takes place in relation to such an immediate power seems to be related to some form through which the intelligible object is present to the intellect. This form will be anterior naturally to the act of understanding, because the immediate power, whereby one is able to understand, is naturally prior to the act of understanding. Now this form, through which the object is so present, is called the species. Therefore it is possible to place the intelligible species in the intellect.

The third opinion rejects every intelligible species.

In this question it is denied that every intelligible species precedes naturally the act of understanding. This is the way it is postulated. As the impression of the sensible species lies in the organ of sense, and this entire progression proceeds toward the imaginative virtue, the intellect as agent withdraws from the object in the imagination and changes the potential intellect to the simple apprehension of the essence, with the restriction however that the potential intellect receives from the imagination no impression of the species. Nor is the object present to the intellect, unless the species is present in the imagination.

This is proved from this deduction. The sense receives another species from the action, because the organ is of the same kind as the middle, or because the species is received as an immediate disposition for receiving the act of feeling. Neither of these meets in the intellect. For the intellect is a non-organic virtue, and is highly disposed to the act of understanding. Therefore the intellect receives no species anterior to the act of understanding. This is also inferred from the assertion that *we speculate about quid est in the imagination and that imaginative occurrences stand in relation to the intellect as sensible things to sense, and that we understand nothing without imagination.* There are many more such statements that Aristotle makes. From them, Henry concludes that Aristotle postulates no intelligible species, because, if a species were postulated, the intellect would not speculate about *quid est* in imagination, but in the intelligible species. Similarly, it would not be necessary for the intellect to be converted to acts of imagination, but the intelligible species would suffice, in which it would have a present object into which to be converted.

The third opinion postulates that the intelligible is simply present to the intellect, not through the intelligible species, but

751

through the imagination, as is made clear by the intellect as agent. But the intellect, formed in the first act, can by its natural shrewdness move hither and thither and underneath in every single thing: by composing the *quid est,* dividing the differences that agree with the thing divided, and reasoning. And so it is possible to investigate the *quid* with respect to the simple intellect, and the *propter quid* with respect to the complex, as with respect to the knowable conclusion. And in this discursive course the intellect, in so far as it is discursive, is active; in so far, however, as it conceives, it is passive.

This same philosopher seems to retract and correct elsewhere this position regarding passivity, with respect to the first simple and confused knowledge, and regarding action, with respect to distinct and examined knowledge, and when he inquires about the active principle of vital action, namely, sensation and perception, he postulates that this principle is something in the animate object itself, and not only outside the object, just as he postulates in a sense that the species, impressed in the organ, only inclines, and, in so doing, arouses the power and, as it were, evokes it to its proper operation. Thus imagination in imaginative virtue inclines the intellect so that the intellect, thus inclined, is the final disposition to entice the perception.

BENEDICTUS DE SPINOZA
(1632-1677)

One of the very great in philosophy, was the son of a Sephardic refugee from the Portuguese terror of the Inquisition. A graduate rabbi in the city of Amsterdam, he saw his calling not as a clergyman, but as a free-lance teacher and writer. A student of Cartesianism, he fought to liberate religion from doctrinism, and philosophy from theological entanglement. He lived in quiet retirement the life of serenity which he considered the goal of all metaphysics, attacked by Christian and Jewish dogmatists alike.

In his works he endeavored to prove that the intuitive, or highest form of thinking *sub specie aeternitatis*, could be acquired by searching assiduously for the essence of creative nature, and that one could learn to uncover inadequate ideas and discard them, and, in doing so, reach not only almost perfect clarity of the mind, but also freedom over disconcerting passions. Confused ideas are only the other side of confusing emotions, as wisdom is only the other side of virtue.

Main Works:

Tractatus theologico-politicus; Tractatus de Deo et homine ejusque felicitate; Ethica; De intellectus emendatione.

Ways of Knowing

By body I mean a mode or created form which expresses in a certain determinate manner the essence of God, insofar as He is considered as an extended thing. I consider as belonging to the essence of a thing that which, being given, the thing is necessarily given also, and which, being removed, the thing is necessarily removed also; in other words, that without which the thing, and which itself without the thing, can neither be nor be conceived.

From: *Ethica.*

By idea, I mean the mental conception which is formed by the mind as a thinking thing. I say conception rather than perception, because the word perception seems to imply that the mind is passive in respect to the object; whereas conception seems to express an activity of the mind.

By an adequate idea, I mean an idea which, insofar as it is considered in itself, without relation to the object, has all the properties or intrinsic marks of a true idea. I say intrinsic, in order to exclude that mark which is extrinsic, namely, the agreement between the idea and its object.

Duration is the indefinite continuance of existing. I say indefinite, because it cannot be determined through the existence itself of the existing thing, or by its efficient cause, which necessarily gives the existence of the thing, but does not take it away. Reality and perfection I use as synonymous terms.

By particular things, I mean things which are finite and have a conditioned existence; but if several individual things concur in one action, so as to be all simultaneously the effect of one cause, I consider them all, so far, as one particular thing.

Thought is an attribute of God, or God is a thinking thing.

Extension is an attribute of God, or God is an extended thing.

The idea of God, from which an infinite number of things follow in infinite ways, can only be one.

Infinite intellect comprehends nothing save the attributes of God and his modifications. Now God is one. Therefore the idea of God, wherefrom an infinite number of things follow in infinite ways, can only be one.

The order and connection of ideas is the same as the order and connection of things.

Whatsoever can be perceived by the infinite intellect as constituting the essence of substance, belongs altogether only to one substance: consequently, substance *thinking* and substance *extended* are one and the same substance, comprehended now through one attribute, now through the other. So, also, a mode of extension and the idea of that mode are one and the same thing, though expressed in two ways. This truth seems to have been dimly recognized by those Jews who maintained that God, God's intellect, and the things understood by God are identical.

For instance, a circle existing in nature, and the idea of a circle existing, which is also in God, are one and the same thing displayed through different attributes. Thus, whether we conceive nature under the attribute of extension, or under the attribute of thought, or under any other attribute, we shall find the same order, or one and the same chain of causes—that is, the same things following in either case.

I said that God is the cause of an idea—for instance, of the idea of a circle—insofar as he is a thinking thing; and of a circle, insofar as he is an extended thing, simply because the actual being of the idea of a circle can only be perceived as a proximate cause through another mode of thinking, and that again through another, and so on to infinity. So long as we consider things as modes of thinking, we must explain the order of the whole of nature, or the whole chain of causes, through the attribute of thought only. And insofar as we consider things as modes of extension, we must explain the order of the whole of nature through the attribute of extension only; and so on, in the case of other attributes.

Wherefore of things as they are in themselves God is really the cause, inasmuch as he consists of infinite attributes.

The first element, which constitutes the actual being of the human mind, is the idea of some particular thing actually existing.

The human mind is part of the infinite intellect of God; thus when we say that the human mind perceives this or that, we make the assertion that God has this or that idea, not insofar as He is infinite, but insofar as He is displayed through the nature of the human mind, or insofar as He constitutes the essence of the human mind; and when we say that God has this or that idea, not only insofar as He constitutes the essences of the human mind, but also insofar as He, simultaneously with the human mind, has the further idea of another thing, we assert that the human mind perceives a thing in part or inadequately.

The object of the idea constituting the human mind is the body, in other words a certain mode of extension which actually exists, and nothing else.

We comprehend, not only that the human mind is united to the body, but also the nature of the union between mind and body. However, no one will be able to grasp this adequately or distinctly unless he first has adequate knowledge of the nature of our body. The propositions we have advanced hitherto have been entirely general, applying not more to men than to other individual things, all of which, though in different degrees, are animated. For of everything there is necessarily an idea in God, of which God is the cause, in the same way as there is an idea of the human body; thus whatever we have asserted of the idea of the human body must necessarily also be asserted of the idea of everything else. Still, on the other hand, we cannot deny that ideas, like objects, differ one from the other, one being more excellent than another and containing more reality, just as the object of one idea is more excellent than the object of another idea, and contains more reality.

Wherefore, in order to determine wherein the human differs from other things, and wherein it surpasses them, it is necessary for us to know the nature of its object, that is, of the human body. What this nature is, I am not able here to explain, nor is it necessary for the proof of what I advance, that I should do so. I will only say generally, that in proportion as any given body is more fitted than others for doing many actions or receiving many impressions at once, so also is the mind, of which it is the object, more fitted than others for forming many simultaneous perceptions; and the more the actions of one body depend on itself alone, and the fewer other bodies concur with it in action, the more fitted is the mind of which it is the object for distinct comprehension.

We may thus recognize the superiority of one mind over others, and may further see the cause, why we have only a very confused knowledge of our body, and also many kindred questions.

All bodies are either in motion or at rest.
Every body is moved sometimes more slowly, sometimes more quickly.
Bodies are distinguished from one another in respect of motion and rest, quickness and slowness, and not in respect of substance.

A body in motion or at rest must be determined to motion or rest by another body, which other body has been determined to motion or rest by a third body, and that third again by a fourth, and so on to infinity.

A body in motion keeps in motion, until it is determined to a state of rest by some other body; and a body at rest remains so, until it is determined to a state of motion by some other body. This is indeed self-evident. For when I suppose, for instance, that a given body, A, is at rest, and do not take into consideration other bodies in motion, I cannot affirm anything concerning the body A, except that it is at rest. If it afterwards comes to pass that A is in motion, this cannot have resulted from its having been at rest, for no other consequence could have been involved than its remaining at rest. If, on the other hand, A be given in motion, we shall, so long as we only consider A, be unable to affirm anything concerning it, except that it is in motion. If A is subsequently found to be at rest, this rest cannot be the result of A's previous motion, for such motion can only have led to continued motion; the state of rest therefore must have resulted from something, which was not in A, namely, from an external cause determining A to a state of rest.

All modes wherein one body is affected by another body follow simultaneously from the nature of the body affected and the body affecting; so that one and the same body may be moved in different modes, according to the difference in the nature of the bodies moving it; on the other hand, different bodies may be moved in different modes by one and the same body.

When a body in motion impinges on another body at rest, which it is unable to move, it recoils, in order to continue its motion, and the angle made by the line of motion in the recoil and the plane of the body at rest, whereon the moving body has impinged, will be equal to the angle formed by the line of motion of incidence and the same plane.

When any given bodies of the same or different magnitude are compelled by other bodies to remain in contact, or if they be moved at the same or different rates of speed, so that their mutual movements should preserve among themselves a certain fixed relation, we say that such bodies are in union, and that altogether they compose one body or individual, which is distinguished from other bodies by this fact of union.

In proportion as the parts of an individual, or a compound body, are in contact over a greater or less superficies, they will with greater or less difficulty admit of being moved from their position; consequently the individual will, with greater or less difficulty, be brought to assume another form. Those bodies, whose parts are in contact over large superficies, are called *hard;* those, whose parts are in contact over small superficies, are called *soft;* those, whose parts are in motion among one another, are called *fluid.*

If certain bodies composing an individual be compelled to change the motion which they have in one direction for motion in another direction, but in such a manner that they be able to continue their motions and their mutual communication in the same relations as before, the individual will retain its own nature without any changes of its actuality.

Furthermore, the individual thus composed preserves its nature, whether it be, as a whole, in motion or at rest, whether it be moved in this or that direction; so long as each part retains its motion, and preserves its communication with other parts as before.

A composite individual may be affected in many different ways, and preserve its nature notwithstanding. Thus far we have conceived an individual as composed of several individuals of diverse natures, other in respect of motion and rest, speed and slowness; that is, of bodies of the most simple character. If, however, we now conceive another individual composed of several individuals of diverse natures, we shall find that the number of ways in which it can be affected, without losing its nature, will be greatly multiplied. Each of its parts would consist of several bodies, and therefore each part would admit, without change to its nature, of quicker or slower motion, and would consequently be able to transmit its motions more quickly or more slowly to the remaining parts. If we further conceive a third kind of individual composed of individuals of this second kind, we shall find that they may be affected in a still greater number of ways without changing their actuality.

We may easily proceed thus to infinity, and conceive the whole of nature as one individual, whose parts, that is, all bodies, vary in infinite ways, without any change in the individual as a whole.

The human mind is capable of perceiving a great number of things, and is so in proportion as its body is capable of receiving a great number of impressions.

The idea which constitutes the actual being of the human mind, is not simple, but compounded of a great number of ideas.

The idea of every mode, in which the human body is affected by external bodies, must involve the nature of the human body, and is also the nature of the external body.

The human mind perceives the nature of a variety of bodies, together with the nature of its own.

The ideas which we have of external bodies indicate rather

the constitution of our own body than the nature of external bodies.

If the human body is affected in a manner which involves the nature of any external body, the human mind will regard the said external body as actually existing, or as present to itself, until the human body be affected in such a way as to exclude the existence or the presence of the said external body.

The human mind does not perceive any external body as actually existing, except through the ideas of the modifications of its own body.

The human mind has no knowledge of the body, and does not know it to exist, save through the ideas of the modifications through which the body is affected.

The mind does not know itself, except insofar as it perceives the ideas of the modifications of the body.

The human mind does not involve an adequate knowledge of the parts composing the human body.

We can only have a very inadequate knowledge of the duration of our body.

All ideas, insofar as they are referred to God, are true.

All ideas which are in God agree in every respect with their objects; therefore they are all true.

Every idea, which in us is absolute or adequate and perfect, is true.

When we say that an idea in us is adequate and perfect, we say, in other words, that the idea is adequate and perfect in God, insofar as He constitutes the essence of our mind; consequently, we say that such an idea is true.

Falsity consists in the privation of knowledge, which inadequate, fragmentary, or confused ideas involve.

Inadequate and confused ideas follow by the same necessity, and adequate or clear and distinct ideas.

All ideas are in God, and insofar as they are referred to God are true and adequate; therefore there are no ideas confused or inadequate, except in respect to a particular mind; therefore all ideas, whether adequate or inadequate, follow by the same necessity.

Whatsoever ideas in the mind follow from ideas which are therein adequate, are also themselves adequate.

For when we say that an idea in the human mind follows from ideas which are therein adequate, we say, in other words, that an idea is in the divine intellect, whereof God is the cause, not insofar as He is infinite, nor insofar as He is affected by the ideas of very many particular things, but only insofar as He constitutes the essence of the human mind.

* * *

I will briefly set down the causes whence are derived the terms styled *transcendental,* such as Being, Thing, Something. These terms arose from the fact that the human body, being limited, is only capable of distinctly forming a certain number of images within itself at the same time; if this number be exceeded, the images will begin to be confused; if this number of images, which the body is capable of forming distinctly within itself, be largely exceeded, all will become entirely confused one with another.

This being so, it is evident that the human mind can distinctly imagine as many things simultaneously as its body can form images simultaneously. When the images become quite confused in the body, the mind also imagines all bodies confusedly without any distinction, and will comprehend them, as it were, under one attribute, namely, under the attribute of Being, Thing, etc. The same conclusion can be drawn from the fact that images are not always equally vivid, and from other analogous causes, which there is no need to explain here; for the purpose which we have in view it is sufficient for us to consider one only.

All may be reduced to this, that these terms represent ideas in the highest degree confused. From similar causes arise those notions, which we call *general*, such as man, horse, dog, etc. They arise, to wit, from the fact that so many images, for instance, of men, are formed simultaneously in the human mind that the powers of imagination break down, not indeed utterly, but to the extent of the mind losing count of small differences between individuals (*e.g.* color, size, etc.) and their definite number, and only distinctly imagining that in which all the individuals, insofar as the body is affected by them, agree; for that is the point in which each of the said individuals chiefly affected the body; this the mind expresses by the name man, and this it predicates of an infinite number of particular individuals.

For, as we have said, it is unable to imagine the definite number of individuals. We must, however, bear in mind that these general notions are not formed by all men in the same way, but vary in each individual according as the point varies, whereby the body has been most often affected and which the mind most easily imagines or remembers. For instance, those who have most often regarded with admiration the stature of man, will by the name of man understand an animal of erect stature; those who have been accustomed to regard some other attribute, will form a different general image of man, for instance, that man is a laughing animal, a two-footed animal without feathers, a rational animal, and thus in other cases, everyone will form general images of things according to the habit of his body.

It is thus not to be wondered at, that among philosophers, who seek to explain things in nature merely by the images formed of them, so many controversies should have arisen.

From all that has been said above it is clear that we, in many cases, perceive and form our general notions:—(1.) From particular things represented to our intellect fragmentarily, confusedly, and without order through our senses; I have settled to call such perceptions by the name of knowledge from the mere suggestions of experience. (2.) From symbols, *e. g.*, from the fact of having read or heard certain words, we remember things and form certain ideas concerning them, similar to those through which we imagine things. I shall call both these ways of regarding things *knowledge of the first kind, opinion,* or *imagination.* (3.) From the fact that we have notions common to all men, and adequate ideas of the properties of things; this I call *reason* and *knowledge of the second kind.* Besides these two kinds of knowledge, there is a third kind of knowledge, which we call *intuition.* This kind of knowledge proceeds from an adequate idea of the absolute essence of certain attributes of God to the adequate knowledge of the essence of things.

Knowledge of the first kind is the only source of falsity, knowledge of the second and third kinds is necessarily true.

He who has a true idea simultaneously knows that he has a true idea, and cannot doubt of the truth of the thing perceived.

It is not in the nature of reason to regard things as contingent, but as necessary.

It is in the nature of reason to perceive things under a certain form of eternity.

Although each particular thing be conditioned by another particular thing to exist in a given way, yet the force whereby each particular thing perseveres in existing follows from the eternal necessity of God's nature.

The knowledge of the eternal and infinite essence of God which every idea involves is adequate and perfect.

We see that the infinite essence and the eternity of God are known to all. Now as all things are in God, and are conceived through God, we can from this knowledge infer many things which we may adequately know, and we may form that third kind of knowledge of which we spoke, and of the excellence and use of which we shall have occasion to speak again.

Men have not so clear a knowledge of God as they have of general notions, because they are unable to imagine God as they do bodies, and also because they associated the name of God with images of things that they are in the habit of seeing, as indeed they can hardly avoid doing, being, as they are, men, and continually affected by external bodies.

Many errors, in truth, can be traced to this head, namely, that we do not apply names to things rightly. For instance, when a man says that the lines drawn from the center of a circle to its circumference are not equal, he then, at all events, assuredly attaches a meaning to the word circle different from that assigned by mathematicians. So again, when men make mistakes in calculation, they have one set of figures in their mind, and another on the paper.

If we could see into their minds, they do not make a mistake; they seem to do so, because we think that they have the same numbers in their minds as they have on the paper. If this were not so, we should not believe them to be in error, any more than I thought that a man was in error whom I lately heard exclaiming that his entrance hall had flown into a neighbor's hen, for his meaning seemed to me sufficiently clear. *Very many controversies have arisen from the fact that men do not rightly explain their meaning,* or *do not rightly interpret the meaning of others.* For, as a matter of fact, as they flatly contradict themselves, they assume now one side, now another, of the argument, so as to oppose the opinions which they consider mistaken and absurd in their opponents.

In the mind there is no absolute or free will; but the mind is determined to wish this or that by a cause, which has also been determined by another cause, and this last by another cause, and so on to infinity.

Will and understanding are one and the same.

JAKOB THOMASIUS
(1622-1684)

Philosopher, philologist and mathematician, taught at Leipzig from 1643. He was basically an Aristotelian. Leibniz studied under him.

Main Works:
    Pro Aristotele; Philosophia practica.

The Nature of Logic

1. What is Logic? It is the art of disputation or of constructing a valid syllogism and of refuting an invalid one, in order to discover the truth.

2. How multiple is the end of Logic? It is two-fold: internal and external.

3. What is the internal end? A valid syllogism.

4. What is the external? Truth.

5. Give an example of a syllogism. Every man is an animal. Peter is a man. Therefore Peter is an animal.

6. Into what is the syllogism immediately resolved? Into three propositions.

7. How are they called? The major premise, the minor premise, and the conclusion.

From: *Erotemata Logica.*

8. Into what is the proposition immediately resolved? Into two terms, that are called subject and predicate.

9. Give an example. In the proposition: Every man is an animal, man stands for the subject, and animal for the predicate.

10. How many parts of Logic are there? Two, namely: the common or general part, and the particular or special part.

11. What is the theme of the general or common part? The syllogism in general, and the parts into which it is resolved.

12. What is the theme of the special or particular part? The three kinds of syllogism, considered from the viewpoint of matter.

13. Into how many parts can the general part be divided? Into three: The first of which treats of the term: the second, of propositions: the third, of the syllogism in general.

14. Into how many sections is the special part divided? Similarly, into three: The first of which treats of the demonstrative syllogism: the second, of the topical syllogism: the third, of the sophistic. These are the three types of syllogism considered materially.

CHAPTER 2

First Part of the General Section: the term, in general.

1. What is the term? A word into which the proposition is resolved, as, into subject or predicate.

2. Are all the words that are in the proposition called terms? No: unless we wish to take the expression *term* in a wider sense.

3. What words then are taken as terms? 1. The copula. 2. Negation. 3. Syncategorematic words.

4. What do you call copula? The verb *is*, when placed between the subject and the predicate, as you see in the proposition: Man is an animal.

5. What do you call negation? The negative adverb *not*, and

those that are similar. Take for example, this proposition: Man is not a stone.

6. What do you call a syncategorematic word? One that is neither the subject, nor the predicate, nor the copula, nor the negative, yet added to the proposition it gives it a certain mode of signification.

7. Which terms are included in this? 1. The signs in the universal or particular propositions: e.g. the word *every* in the proposition: Every man is an animal. 2. The modes in the modal proposition: It is necessary that a man is an animal.

8. How is the term called, to distinguish it better from the word syncategorematic? Categorematic, or even a categorematic term.

9. Is there not also a common word that includes both categorem and syncategorem? There is.

10. Give an example. No one. This is the same as if one said: No man, where *no* is a syncategorem, and *man* is a categorem.

11. What should be noted in regard to the term? The term, that is, the subject or the predicate, sometimes consists of one word, as: Man is an animal. Sometimes, of two or three words, as: A good man should be praised. Man is a creature of God. Of all visible creatures of God man is by far the noblest.

12. What else should be noted in the term? The various divisions and affections.

CHAPTER 3

The Divisions of Terms

1. How many special divisions of terms are there? Six.

2. What is the first division? The term is either finite or infinite.

3. What is a finite term? One that does not have prefixed to it the negative particle, as: Man.

4. What is an infinite term? One that has prefixed to it a negative, as: Not-man.

5. What is the second division? The term is either abstract or concrete.

6. What is an abstract term, or abstraction? It is a word involving one concept only, namely, the concept of form, without simultaneously denoting any subject: e.g. whiteness, paternity, animality.

7. What is a concrete term, or concreteness? It is a word involving two concepts, one of form, the other of subject: e.g. white, father, animal.

8. How do I know that those two concepts are involved in the concrete? From the resolution of the concrete.

9. How then is the concrete resolved? In the following, or in a similar manner: White, that is, a being having whiteness. Father, that is, a being having fatherhood. Animal, that is, a being having animality.

10. Clarify. In these resolutions the subject is expressed by the word *being* in the nominative case, while the form is abstract through the oblique case.

11. How multiple is the concrete? Two-fold: substantive, which is in the category of the substance. For example: Animal. And accidental, whose abstract form is in the category of an accident. For example: White, father.

12. What do the Scholastics call the ultimate abstract? That which is formed from another abstract through a new abstraction. For example: Whiteness.

13. Are adjectival words abstract or concrete? They are concrete. For example: White, brave, great, wise, and so on.

14. How should we consider substantive words? Some are abstract. For example: Whiteness, paternity. Others are concrete. For example: Father, Lord.

15. Of what type are participles? They are concrete. For example: Loving, beloved, and so on.

16. What should we know about verbs? Infinities are considered as abstract. For example: To love, to be loved, and so on. But the finite moods are considered as concrete. For example: I love, you love, he loves: I am loved, you are loved, he is loved.

17. What is the third division of terms? The term that is either denominating, or denominative.

18. What are the denominatives called in Greek by Aristotle? Paronyms.

19. What is a denominating term? Any abstract form. For example: Whiteness, paternity.

20. What is a denominated term? Any subject, of which the form can be predicated. For example: A wall (in which there is whiteness): Abraham (in whom there is paternity).

21. What is denominative? A concrete term. For example: White, father.

22. How multiple is denomination? Two-fold, internal and external.

23. When is denomination said to be internal? When the denominating form is in the subject denominated.

24. Give an example. When I say: The wall is white, that is internal denomination, because whiteness is a kind of denominating form in the wall itself.

25. When is denomination said to be external? When the denominating form is not in the denominated form, but is outside it.

26. Give an example: When I say: The wall is seen, or: The wall was seen, that is external denomination, because sight is a kind of denominating form in the wall, but outside the wall, in some creature that sees the wall.

27. What is the fourth division of the term? The term is either univocal or equivocal.

28. What does Aristotle call univocal in Greek? Synonyms.

29. What does he call equivocal? Homonyms.

30. In how many ways is the term univocal taken? In two: either for univocal univocating, or for univocal univocated.

31. What is univocal univocating? The univocal term itself.

32. What is univocal univocated? The thing that is signified by the univocal term.

33. In how many ways is the word *equivocal* taken? Similarly, in two: either for the equivocal equivocating, or for the equivocal equivocated.

34. What is equivocal equivocating? The equivocal term itself.

35. What is the equivocal equivocated? The thing that is signified by the equivocal term.

36. What is a univocal term? A word that signifies many things so that the same definition can be applied equally, in regard to this word, to those things individually.

37. Give an example. *Man* is a univocal term with respect to John, Peter, Paul, and so on, because the definition of man (that is a rational animal) can be applied equally to both John and to Peter or Paul, and so on.

38. What is an equivocal term? A word that signifies many things so that the same definition, in regard to this word, can not be applied to those things individually.

39. Give an example. Man is an equivocal term, with respect to a living man and a depicted man, because the definition of man (that is a rational animal) may be applied to a living man, but not to a depicted man.

40. How does Aristotle define univocated univocal, or things signified by a univocal name? Things that have a common name, and that have the same definition in respect of that name. For example: John, Peter, Paul with respect to the word man.

41. How does he define equivocated equivocal? Things that have a name only in common but whose definition is different in respect of that name. For example: A living man and a depicted man with respect to the word man.

Jakob Thomasius

42. How multiple are equivocals generally said to be? Twofold, produced intentionally, or by accident.

43. What is equivocal produced intentionally? A term whose denotations have reciprocally a valid similarity or relationship. For example: Man, when it signifies 1. a living being 2. a depicted man. Similarly: fox, when it signifies 1. a cunning four-footed animal 2. a cunning man.

44. What is equivocal produced by accident? A term whose denotations do not have any proper similarity or relationship. For example: Jus, which signifies 1. law 2. sauce.

45. What is cognate to univocal? Analogy.

46. What is analogous, or an analogous term? A word signifying many things, so that the same definition is applied to those things individually, not however equally, but unequally, namely: primary in one case, secondary in the other.

47. Give an example. A being analogous with respect to substance, to which the definition of being is applied primarily, and to accidents, to which it is applied in a secondary degree.

48. What is the name given to a thing signified, with which this definition agrees primarily? A more noble analogy, as in the above mentioned example *substance*.

49. What is the name given to a thing signified, with which this definition agrees in a secondary sense? A more ignoble analogy: e.g. accident.

50. Tell me the rule for analogy. Analogy by itself stands for nobler signification.

51. What is the fifth division of the term? The term is either singular, as Peter, or universal, as man.

52. How else is the singular called? Particular.

53. How else is the universal called? Predicable.

54. What else must be known about the particular and the universals? This will be explained in the succeeding chapters.

55. What is the sixth division of the term? The term is either categorical or transcendental.

56. What is a categorical term? One that signifies a thing residing in a category. For example: Man, animal, whiteness, paternity, and so on.

57. What is a transcendental term? One that signifies a thing or a concept transcending the categories. For example: A being with its affections, such as unity, truth, goodness, cause, effect, subject, adjunct, and such like.

58. Where are transcendental terms usually explained? In the general part of the metaphysics.

59. Where are the categorical terms usually explained? In logic, where the categories are discussed.

CHAPTER 4

The Particular

1. In how many ways is the particular taken? In two: Either for the name of the particular or for the thing of the particular.

2. What is the name of the particular? The name that signifies a singular thing: e.g. the name Peter.

3. What is the thing of the particular? The singular thing itself: e.g. Peter himself.

4. How else is a singular or a particular thing defined? A particular is that which consists of properties, the totality of which can never be the same in anything else.

5. In how many ways can a singular thing be stated or designated? In five ways.

6. What is the first way? By a proper noun: e.g. Virgil.

7. What is the second way? By a demonstrative pronoun: e.g. If, pointing with a finger to Virgil, as it were, I should say: This man.

8. What is the third way? By a periphrasis: e.g. The greatest of Roman poets, or: The poet of Mantua: that is, Virgil.

9. What is the fourth way? By antonomasia. For example. *Poet* for *Virgil*.

10. What is the fifth way? By a particular sign. For example: A certain man. A certain poet.

11. What is the name given to the individual that is thus expressed by a particular sign? The vague individual.

12. Why? Because when anyone hears of such an individual, his thoughts readily wander and he is not immediately certain what individual is indicated. For example: If I say to you that I met a certain man in the street, you would not know whether I meant Peter, or Paul, or some other man.

13. How multiple is the individual, or the thing of the individual? Two-fold: substantial and accidental.

14. What is a substantial individual? That which is in the category of the substance. For example: Peter, the angel Gabriel.

15. What is accidental? That which is in the category of any accident. For example: Peter's whiteness. Peter's justice.

16. Is there still another individual distinction? There is: the distinction lies in the insensible and the sensible.

17. What is the insensible individual? That which cannot be perceived by the senses. For example: The angel Gabriel: Peter's justice.

18. What is the sensible individual? That which can be perceived by the senses. For example: Peter, Peter's whiteness.

CHAPTER 5

Predicables in General

1. Are predicables and universals one and the same thing? They are the same in substance: but they differ in the manner of conceiving them.

2. Clarify this. I conceive the universal as being capable of existing in many things: the predicable, as being capable of being predicated of many things. For example: Man's nature is in many men, as in Peter, Paul, and so on.

3. How then is the predicable defined? That which is by nature apt to be predicated of many things.

4. How many predicables are there? Five: Species, as: man. Genus, as: animal. Differentia, as: rational. Property, as: risible, and Accident, as: biped.

5. Into how many classes can the predicables be divided? Into two: Some are essential, as: Species, Genus, Differentia. Others are extra-essential, as: Property and Accident.

6. What do you call essential? Those things that constitute the essence of the subject.

7. What do you call the extra-essential? Those things that do not constitute the essence of the subject, but follow it when it is so constituted.

8. Is there not another method also of dividing the predicables into classes? There is. Something is predicated into what, as species and genus. Or into what kind: and this in turn into what of what kind, as differentia. Or into what kind simply: that is, without apposition, as property and accident.

9. What is the meaning of being predicated into what? Predication in such a manner that a reply is given to the question: What is it? For example: To the question: What is Peter? I correctly answer: He is an animal.

10. What is predication into what kind? Predication in such a manner that a reply is given to the question: What is it? For example: To the question: What kind of animal is man? I correctly answer: a rational, risible biped.

11. Why is the differentia said to be predicated in what kind of what? Because it is so predicated into what kind, that at the same time it refers to the essence of the subject, just as that which is predicated into what refers to it.

12. Why are the property and the accident said to be predicated into what kind? Because they do not together refer to the essence of the subject, but finally follow it when it is so constituted.

CHAPTER 6

Species and Genus

1. How can the nature of species and of genus best be explained? From the categorical scale, that is, from the division of a category, as: substance.

2. How then is substance divided? Into spiritual substance, as angel, and corporeal substance.

3. How is corporeal substance or the material body subdivided? Into simple body and compound body.

4. How is the simple body subdivided? Into the firmament and the elements.

5. What is meant by the noun *firmament?* Not only the ethereal air, but also the heavenly bodies, that is, the stars.

6. How many elements are there? Four: Fire, air, water, earth.

7. How is a compound body subdivided? Into inanimate and animate.

8. How is the inanimate subdivided? Into stone (as, flint), metal (as, silver), and a mineral mean (as, sulphur).

9. How is animate or living subdivided? Into plant and animal.

10. How is animal subdivided? Into beast and man.

11. How is man subdivided? Into his particulars, as: Peter, Paul, John, etc., as you may see in the following diagram or rather in part of the scale:

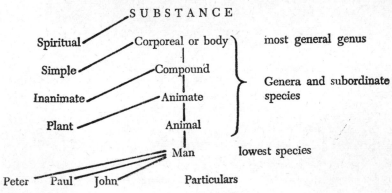

12. How may I know, from such a division or scale, the nature of species and genus? What in a scale of this type is the first of everything (as substance, in this case) is the most general genus. That which has the lowest position (as Peter, Paul, John, in this case) is the particular. What is immediately above the particular (as man, in this case) is called the lowest species. What is placed between the lowest species and the most general genus (as animal, animate body, etc., in this case), is the subordinate species, or, which is the same thing, the subordinate genus.

ALFRED NORTH WHITEHEAD
(1861-1947)

Studied mathematics at Cambridge, England, and taught at University College, London, until he moved to Harvard in 1924. While his main field lay in the relations between mathematics and philosophy, he had strong moral and ethical convictions and was widely influential both in his native land and the country of his adoption. The aim of his speculative philosophy was to frame a coherent, logical, necessary system of general ideas in terms of which every item of our experience can be interpreted. He taught a form of metaphysical evolutionism, searching for definite concepts of unified scientifically based relation. In his philosophy of organism he conceives the world as a process of interrelated organisms grasping for adjustment. God, Impersonal, is the Alpha and Omega of this cosmic rationale as well as that of ethics and religious experience.

Main Works:

> Principia Mathematicia (with Bertrand Russell); The Organization of Thought, Science and the Modern World; Modes of Thought; Adventures of Ideas; Process and Reality; An Inquiry Concerning the Principles of Natural Knowledge; Symbolism; The Concept of Nature; Religion in the Making; Essays in Science and Philosophy.

Philosophy of Life

The status of life in Nature is the problem of philosophy and of science. Indeed, it is the central meeting point of all the strains of systematic thought, humanistic, naturalistic, philo-

------

From: *Nature and Life.*

sophic. The very meaning of life is in doubt. When we understand it, we shall also understand its status in the world. But its essence and its status are alike baffling.

Of course, it is always possible to work one's self into a state of complete contentment with an ultimate irrationality. The popular positivistic philosophy adopts this attitude. The weakness of this positivism is the way in which we all welcome the detached fragments of explanation attained in our present stage of civilization. Suppose that a hundred thousand years ago our ancestors had been wise positivists. They sought for no reasons. What they had observed was sheer matter of fact. It was the development of no necessity. They would have searched for no reasons underlying facts immediately observed. Civilization would never have developed. Our varied powers of detailed observation of the world would have remained dormant. For the peculiarity of a reason is that the intellectual development of its consequences suggests consequences beyond the topics already observed. The extension of observation waits upon some dim apprehension of reasonable connection. For example, the observation of insects on flowers dimly suggests some congruity between the natures of insects and of flowers, and thus leads to a wealth of observation from which whole branches of science have developed. But a consistent positivist should be content with the observed facts —namely, insects visiting flowers. It is a fact of charming simplicity. There is nothing further to be said upon the matter, according to the doctrine of a positivist. At present the scientific world is suffering from a bad attack of muddle-headed positivism, which arbitrarily applies its doctrine and arbitrarily escapes from it. The whole doctrine of life in Nature has suffered from this positivist taint. We are told that there is the routine described in physical and chemical formulae, and that in the process of Nature there is nothing else.

The origin of this persuasion is the dualism which gradually developed in European thought in respect to mind and Nature. At the beginning of the modern period Descartes expressed this dualism with the utmost distinctness. For him, there are material substances with spatial relations, and mental substances. The mental substances are external to the material substances. Neither type requires the other type for the completion of its essence. Their unexplained interrelations are unnecessary for their respective existences. In truth, this formulation of the problem in terms of minds and matter is unfortunate. It omits the lower forms of life, such as vegetation and the lower animal types. These forms touch upon human mentality at their highest, and upon inorganic Nature at their lowest.

The effect of this sharp division between Nature and life has poisoned all subsequent philosophy. Even when the co-ordinate existence of the two types of actualities is abandoned, there is no proper fusion of the two in most modern schools of thought. For some, Nature is mere appearance and mind is the sole reality. For others, physical Nature is the sole reality and mind is an epiphenomenon. Here the phrases "mere appearance" and "epiphenomenon" obviously carry the implication of slight importance for the understanding of the final nature of things.

The doctrine that I am maintaining is that neither physical Nature nor life can be understood unless we fuse them together as essential factors in the composition of "really real" things whose inter-connections and individual characters constitute the universe.

The first step in the argument must be to form some concept of what life can mean. Also, we require that the deficiencies in our concept of physical Nature should be supplied by its fusion with life. And we require that, on the other hand, the notion of life should involve the notion of physical Nature.

Now as a first approximation the notion of life implies a certain absoluteness of self-enjoyment. This must mean a certain immediate individuality, which is a complex process of appropriating into a unity of existence the many data presented as relevant by the physical processes of Nature. Life implies the absolute, individual self-enjoyment arising out of this process of appropriation.

This concept of self-enjoyment does not exhaust that aspect of process here termed "life." Process for its intelligibility involves the notion of a creative activity belonging to the very essence of each occasion. It is the process of eliciting into actual being factors in the universe which antecedently to that process exist only in the mode of unrealized potentialities. The process of self-creation is the transformation of the potential into the actual, and the fact of such transformation includes the immediacy of self-enjoyment.

Thus, in conceiving the function of life in an occasion of experience, we must discriminate the actualized data presented by the antecedent world, the non-actualized potentialities which lie ready to promote their fusion into a new unity of experience, and the immediacy of self-enjoyment which belongs to the creative advance whereby it belongs to the essence of the universe, that it passes into a future. It is nonsense to conceive of Nature as a static fact, even for an instant devoid of duration. There is no Nature apart from transition, and there is no transition apart from temporal duration. This is the reason why the notion of an instant of time, conceived as a primary simple fact, is nonsense.

But even yet we have not exhausted the notion of creation which is essential to the understanding of Nature. We must add yet another character to our description of life. This missing characteristic is "aim." By this term "aim" is meant the exclusion of the boundless wealth of alternative potentiality, and the inclusion of that definite factor of novelty which constitutes the selected way of entertaining those data in that process of unification. The aim is at that complex of feeling which is the enjoyment of those data in that way. "That way of enjoyment" is selected from the boundless wealth of alternatives. It has been aimed at for actualization in that process.

Thus, the characteristics of life are absolutely self-enjoyment, creative activity, aim. Here "aim" evidently involves the entertainment of the purely ideal so as to be directive of the creative process. Also, the enjoyment belongs to the process and is not a characteristic of any static result. The aim is at the enjoyment belonging to the process.

The question at once arises as to whether this factor of life in Nature, as thus interpreted, corresponds to anything that we observe in Nature. All philosophy is an endeavor to obtain a self-consistent understanding of things observed. Thus, its development is guided in two ways—one is the demand for a coherent self-consistency, and the other is the elucidation of things observed. It is, therefore, our first task to compare the foregoing doctrine of life in Nature with our direct observations.

Without doubt the sort of observations most prominent in our conscious experience are the sense-impressions. Sight, hearing, taste, smell, touch constitute a rough list of our major modes of perception through the senses. But there are an indefinite set of obscure bodily feelings which form a background of feeling with items occasionally flashing into prominence. The peculiarity of sense-perception is its dual character, partly irrelevant to the body and partly referent to the body. In the case of sight, the irrelevance to the body is at its maximum. We look at the scenery, at a picture, or at an approaching car on the road, as an external presentation given for our mental entertainment or mental anxiety. There it is, exposed to view. But, on reflection, we elicit the underlying experience that we were seeing with our eyes. Usually this fact is not in explicit consciousness at the moment of perception. The bodily reference is recessive, the visible presentation is dominant. In the other modes of sensation the body is more prominent. There is great variation in this respect between the different modes. In any doctrine as to the information derived from sense-perception this dual reference— external reference and bodily reference—should be kept in mind. The current philosophic doctrines, mostly derived from Hume, are defective by reason of their neglect of bodily reference. Their vice is the deduction of a sharp-cut doctrine from an assumed sharp-cut mode of perception. The truth is that our sense-perceptions are extraordinarily vague and confused modes of experience. Also, there is every evidence that their prominent side of external reference is very superficial in its disclosure of the universe. It is important. For example, pragmatically a paving stone is a hard, solid, static, irremovable fact. This is what sense-perception, on its sharp-cut side, discloses. But if physical science be correct, this is a very superficial account of that portion of the universe which we call the paving stone. Modern physical science is the issue of a coordinated effort, sustained for more than three centuries, to understand those activities of Nature by reason of which the transitions of sense-perception occur.

Two conclusions are now abundantly clear. One is that sense-perception omits any discrimination of the fundamental activities within Nature. For example, consider the difference between the paving stone as perceived visually, or by falling upon it, and the molecular activities of the paving stone as described by the physicist. The second conclusion is the failure of science to endow its formulae for activity with any meaning. The divergence of the formulae about Nature from the appearance of Nature has robbed the formulae of any explanatory character. It has even robbed us of reason for believing that the past gives any ground for expectation of the future. In fact, science conceived as resting on mere sense-perception, with no other source of observation, is bankrupt, so far as concerns its claim to self-sufficiency.

Science can find no individual enjoyment in Nature; science can find no aim in Nature; science can find no negations are true of nature science. They are inherent in its methodology. The reason for this blindness of physical science lies in the fact that such science only deals with half the evidence provided by human experience. It divides the seamless coat—or, to change the metaphor into a happier form, it examines the coat, which is superficial, and neglects the body, which is fundamental.

The disastrous separation of body and mind which has been fixed on European thought by Descartes is responsible for this blindness of science. In one sense the abstraction has been a happy one, in that it has allowed the simplest things to be considered first, for about ten generations.

Yet is it untrue to state that the general observation of mankind, in which sense-perception is only one factor, discloses no aim. The exact contrary is the case. All explanations of the sociological functionings of mankind include "aim" as an essential factor in explanation. For example, in a criminal trial where the evidence is circumstantial the demonstration of motive is one chief reliance of the prosecution. In such a trial would the defense plead the doctrine that purpose could not direct the motions of the body, and that to indict the thief for stealing was analogous to indicting the sun for rising? Again no statesman can conduct international relations without some estimate—implicit or explicit in his consciousness—of the types of patriotism respectively prevalent in various nations and in the statesmen of these nations. A lost dog can be seen trying to find his master or trying find his way home. In fact we are *directly* conscious of our porposes as *directive* of our actions. Apart from such direction no doctrine could in any sense be acted upon. The notions entertained mentally would have no effect upon bodily actions. Thus, what happens would happen in complete indifference to the entertainment of such notions.

Scientific research is completely dominated by the presupposition that mental functionings are not properly part of Nature. Accordingly it disregards all those mental antecedents which mankind habitually presupposes as effective in guiding cosmological functionings. As a method this procedure is entirely justifiable, provided that we recognize the limitations involved. These limitations are both obvious and undefined. The gradual eliciting of their definition is the hope of philosophy.

The points that I would emphasize are: First, that this sharp division between mentality and Nature has no grounds in our fundamental observation. We find ourselves living within Nature. Second, I conclude that we should conceive mental operations as among the factors which make up the constitution of Nature.

783

Third, that we should reject the notion of idle wheels in the process of Nature. Every factor which emerges makes a difference, and that difference can only be expressed in terms of the individual character of that factor. Fourth, that we have now the task of defining natural facts, so as to understand how mental occurrences are operative in conditioning the subsequent course of Nature.

All sense-perception is merely one outcome of the dependence upon bodily functionings. Thus, if we wish to understand the relation of our personal experience to the activities of Nature, the proper procedure is to examine the dependence of our personal experiences upon our personal bodies.

Let us ask about our overwhelming persuasions as to our own personal body-mind relation. In the first place, there is the claim to unity. The human individual is one fact, body and mind. This claim to unity is the fundamental fact, always presupposed, rarely explicitly formulated. I am experiencing and my body is mine. In the second place, the functioning of our body has a much wider influence than the mere production of sense-experience. We find ourselves in a healthy enjoyment of life by reason of the healthy functionings of our internal organs—heart, lungs, bowels, kidneys; etc. The emotional state arises just because they are not providing any sense directly associated with themselves. Even in sight, we enjoy our vision because there is no eye-strain. Also, we enjoy our general state of life because we have no stomach-ache. I am insisting that the enjoyment of health, good or bad, is a positive feeling only casually associated with particular sensa. For example, you can enjoy the ease with which your eyes are functioning even when you are looking at a bad picture or a vulgar building. This direct feeling of the derivation of emotion from the body is among our fundamental experiences. There are emotions of various types—but every type of emotion is at least modified by derivation from the body. It is for physiologists to analyse in detail the modes of bodily functioning. For philosophy, the one fundamental fact is that the whole complexity of mental experience is either derived or modified by such functioning. Also, our basic feeling is this sense of derivation, which leads to our claim for unity, body and mind.

But our immediate experience also claims derivation from another source, and equally claims a unity founded upon this alternative source of derivation. This second source is our own state of mind directly preceding the immediate present of our conscious experience. A quarter of a second ago we were entertaining such and such ideas, we were enjoying such and such emotions, and we were making such and such observations of external fact. In our present state of mind we are continuing that previous state. The word "continuing" states only half the truth. In one sense it is too weak, and in another sense it overstates. It is too weak because we not only continue, but we claim absolute identity with, our previous state. It was our very identical self in that state of mind, which is, of course, the basis of our present experience a quarter of a second later. In another sense the word "continuing" overstates. For we do not quite continue in our preceding state of experience. New elements have intervened. All of these new elements are provided by our bodily functionings. We fuse these new elements with the basic stuff of experience provided by our state of mind a quarter of a second ago. Also, as we have already agreed, we claim an identification with our body. Thus, our experience in the present discloses its own nature in two sources of derivation, namely, the body and the antecedent experimental functionings. Also, there is a claim for identification with each of these sources. The body is mine, and the antecedent experience is mine. Still more, there is only one ego, to claim the body and to claim the stream of experience. I submit that we have here the fundamental basic persuasion on which we found the whole practice of our existence. While we exist, body and soul are inescapable elements in our being, each with the full reality of our own immediate self. But neither body nor soul possess the sharp observational definition which at first sight we attribute to them. Our knowledge of the body places it as a complex unity of happenings within the larger field of Nature. But its demarcation from the rest of Nature is vague in the extreme. The body consists of the co-ordinated functioning of billions of molecules. It belongs to the structural essence of the body that, in an indefinite number of ways, it is always losing molecules and gaining molecules. When we consider the question with microscopic accuracy, there is no definite boundary to determine where the body begins and external Nature ends. Again, the body can lose whole limbs, and yet we claim identity with the same body. Also, the vital functions of the cells in the amputated limb ebb slowly. Indeed, the limb survives in separation from the body for an immense time compared to the internal vibratory periods of its molecules. Also, apart from such catastrophes, the body requires the environment in order to exist. Thus, there is a unity of the body with the environment, as well as a unity of body and soul into one person.

But in conceiving our personal identity we are apt to emphasize rather the soul than the body. The one individual is that co-ordinated stream of personal experiences which is my thread of life or your thread of life. It is that succession of self-realization, each occasion with its direct memory of its past and with its anticipation of the future. That claim to enduring self-identity is our self-assertion of personal identity.

Yet, when we examine this notion of the soul, it discloses itself as even vaguer than our definition of the body. First, the continuity of the Soul—so far as concerns consciousness—has to leap gaps in time. We sleep or we are stunned. And yet it is the memory, and we ground our trust on the continuity of our body. Thus, Nature in general and the body in particular provide the stuff for the personal endurance of the soul. Again, there is a curious variation in the vividness of the successive occasions of the soul's existence. We are living at full stretch with a keen observation of external occurrence; then external attention dies away and we are lost in meditation; the meditation gradually weakens in vivid presentation—we doze; we dream; we sleep with a total lapse of the stream of consciousness. These functionings of the soul are diverse, variable, and discontinuous. The claim to the unity of the soul is analogous to the claim to the unity of the body, and is analogous to the claim to the unity of body and soul, and is analogous to the claim to the community of the body with an external Nature. It is the task of philosophic speculation to conceive the happenings of the universe so as to render understandable the outlook of physical science and to combine this outlook with these direct persuasions representing the basic facts upon which epistemology must build. The weakness of the epistemology of the eighteenth and nineteenth centuries was that it based itself purely upon a narrow formulation of sense-perception. Also, among the various modes of sensation, visual experience was picked out as the typical example. The result was to exclude all the really fundamental factors constituting our experience.

In such an epistemology we are far from the complex data which philosophic speculation has to account for in a system rendering the whole understandable. Consider the types of community of body and soul, of body and Nature, or successive occasions of bodily existence, or the soul's existence. These fundamental interconnections have one very remarkable characteristic. Let us ask what is the function of the external world for the stream of experience which constitutes the soul. This world, thus experienced, is the basic fact within those experiences. All the emotions, and purposes, and enjoyments, proper to the individual existence of the soul, are nothing other than the soul's reactions to this experienced world which lies at the base of the soul's existence. Thus, in a sense, the experienced world is one complex factor in the composition of many factors constituting the essence of the soul. We can phrase this shortly by saying that in one sense the world is in the soul.

But there is an antithetical doctrine balancing this primary truth. Namely, our experience of the world involves the exhibition of the soul itself as one of the components within the world. Thus, there is a dual aspect to the relationship of an occasion of experience as one relatum and the experienced world as another relatum. The world is included within the occasion in one sense, and the occasion is included in the world in another sense.

For example, I am in the room, and the room is an item in my present experience. But my present experience is what I now am. In this survey of the observational data in terms of which our philosophic cosmology must be founded, we have brought together the conclusions of physical science, and those habitual persuasions dominating the sociological functionings of mankind. These persuasions also guide the humanism of literature, of art, and of religion. Mere existence has never entered into the consciousness of man, except as the remote terminus of an abstraction in thought. Descartes' "Cogito, ergo sum" is wrongly translated, "I *think* therefore I am." It is never bare thought or bare existence that we are aware of. I find myself as essentially a unity of emotions, enjoyments, hopes, fears, regrets, valuations of alternatives, decisions—all of them subjective reactions to the environment as active in my nature. My unity—which is Descartes' "I am"—is my process of shaping this welter of material into a consistent pattern of feelings. The individual enjoyment is what I am in my role of a natural activity, as I shape the activities of the environment into a new creation, which is myself at this moment; and yet, as being myself it is a continuation of the antecedent world. If we stress the role of the environment, this process is causation. If we stress the role of my immediate pattern of active enjoyment, this process is self-creation. If we stress the role of the conceptual anticipation of future whose existence is a necessity in the Nature of the present, this process is the teleological aim at some ideal in the future. This aim, however, is not really beyond the present process. For the aim at the future is an enjoyment in the present. It thus effectively conditions the immediate self-creation of the new creature.

Physical science has reduced Nature to activity, and has discovered abstract mathematical formulae which are illustrated in these activities of Nature. But the fundamental question remains: How do we add content to the notion of bare activity? This question can only be answered by fusing life with Nature.

In the first place, we must distinguish life from mentality. Mentality involves conceptual experience, and is only one variable ingredient in life. The sort of functioning here termed "conceptual experience" is the entertainment of possibilities for ideal realization. The most obvious example of conceptual experience is the entertainment of alternatives. Life lies below this grade of mentality. Life is the enjoyment of emotion, derived from the past and aimed at the future. It is the enjoyment of emotion which was then, which is now, and which will be then. This vector character is of the essence of such entertainment. The emotion transcends the present in two ways. It issues from, and it issues toward. It is received, it is enjoyed, and it is passed along, from moment to moment. Each occasion is an activity of concern, in the Quaker sense of that term. It is the conjunction of transcendence and immanence. The occasion is concerned, in the way of feeling and aim, with things that in their own essence lie beyond it; although these things in their present functions are factors in the concern of that occasion. Thus, each occasion, although engaged in its own immediate self-realization, is concerned with the universe.

The process is always a process of modification by reason of the numberless avenues of supply, and by reason of the numberless modes of qualitative texture. The unity of emotion, which is the unity of the present occasion, is a patterned texture of qualities, always shifting as it is passed into the future. The creative activity aims at preservation of the components and at preservation of intensity. The modifications of pattern, the dismissal into elimination, are in obedience to this aim.

In so far as conceptual mentality does not intervene, the grand patterns pervading the environment are passed on with the inherited modes of adjustment. Here we find the patterns of activity studied by the physicists and chemists. Mentality is merely latent in all these occasions as thus studied. In the case of inorganic Nature any sporadic flashes are inoperative so far as our powers of discernment are concerned. The lowest stages of effective mentality, controlled by the inheritance of physical pattern, involve the faint direction of emphasis by unconscious ideal aim. The various examples of the higher forms of life exhibit the variety of grades of effectiveness of mentality. In the social habits of animals there is evidence of flashes of mentality in the past which have degenerated into physical habits. Finally, in the higher mammals and more particularly in mankind, we have clear evidence of mentality habitually effective. In our own experience, our knowledge consciously entertained and systematized can only mean such mentality, directly observed.

The qualities entertained as objects in conceptual activity are of catalytic agents, in the sense in which that phase is used in chemistry. They modify the aesthetic process by which the occasion constitutes itself out of the many streams of feeling received from the past. It is not necessary to assume that conceptions introduce additional sources of measurable energy. They may do so; for the doctrine of the conservation of energy is not based upon exhaustive measurements. But the operation of mentality is primarily to be conceived as a diversion of the flow of energy.

Philosophy begins in wonder. And, at the end, when philosophic thought has done its best, the wonder remains. There have been added, however, some grasp of the immensity of things, some purification of emotion by understanding. Yet there is a danger in such reflections. An immediate good is apt to be thought of in the degenerate form of a passive enjoyment. Existence is activity ever merging into the future. The aim at philosophic understanding is the aim at piercing the blindness of activity in respect to its transcendent functions.

LUDWIG WITTGENSTEIN
(1889-1951)

An Austrian of Jewish origin, studied engineering and was at first primarily concerned with architecture. A stay at Cambridge, England, before World War I led to a meeting with Russell and interest in philosophy. He became a leading figure of the "Vienna Circle" and one of the founders of logical positivism. He offered a general way of removing philosophical difficulties by investigating the logical structure of language.

Main Work:
    Tractatus Logico-Philosophicus.

_____

Facts

1   The world is everything that is the case.*

1.1   The world is the totality of facts, not of things.

1.11   The world is determined by the facts, and by these being *all the facts.*

1.12   For the totality of facts determines both what is the case, and also all that is not the case.

_____

From: *Tractatus Logico-Philosophicus.*

* The decimal figures as numbers of the separate propositions indicate the logical importance of the propositions, the emphasis laid upon them in my exposition. The propositions $n.1$, $n.2$, $n.3$, etc., are comments on proposition No. n; the propositions $n.m1$, $n.m2$, etc., are comments on the proposition No. $n.m$; and so on.

1.13   The facts in logical space are the world.

1.2   The world divides into facts.

1.21   Any one can either be the case or not be the case, and everything else remain the same.

2   What is the case, the fact, is the existence of atomic facts.

2.01   An atomic fact is a combination of objects (entities, things).

2.011   It is essential to a thing that it can be a constituent part of an atomic fact.

2.012   In logic nothing is accidental: if a thing *can* occur in an atomic fact the possibility of that atomic fact must already be prejudged in the thing.

2.0121   It would, so to speak, appear as an accident, when to a thing that could exist alone on its own account, subsequently a state of affairs could be made to fit.

If things can occur in atomic facts, this possibility must already lie in them.

(A logical entity cannot be merely possible. Logic treats of every possibility, and all possibilities are its facts.)

Just as we cannot think of spatial objects at all apart from space, or temporal objects apart from time, so we cannot think of *any* object apart from the possibility of its connection with other things.

If I can think of an object in the context of an atomic fact, I cannot think of it apart from the *possibility* of this context.

2.0122   The thing is independent, in so far as it can occur in all *possible* circumstances, but this form of independence is a form of connection with the atomic fact, a form of dependence. (It is impossible for words to occur in two different ways, alone and in the proposition.)

2.0123   If I know an object, then I also know the possibilities of its occurrence in atomic facts.

(Every such possibility must lie in the nature of the object.)

A new possibility cannot subsequently be found.

2.01231   In order to know an object, I must know not its external but all its internal qualities.

2.0124   If all objects are given, then thereby are all *possible* atomic facts also given.

2.013   Every thing is, as it were, in a space of possible atomic facts. I can think of this space as empty, but not of the thing without the space.

2.0131   A spatial object must lie in infinite space. (A point in space is a place for an argument.)

JACOB ZABARELLA
(1533-1589)

An almost forgotten logician of the 16th century. His interpretation of
Aristotelian logic is on a considerably higher level than of most of his
contemporaries. He taught philosophy at his native city of Padua, in
northern Italy.

Main Works:
   De rebus naturalibus; Opera logica.

Characteristics of Logic

In understanding the nature of the art of logic there is a far
greater difficulty than many think. For although the definition
of the word usually eludes practically no one, if by logic all men,
even the illiterate, understand that a certain training in argument, or a kind of skill in argumentation is denoted: yet the
definition of the term, that reveals the inner nature and character of its discipline, is so obscure that very many scholars and
professors of logic and philosophy, both in former times and in
our own day, are ignorant of it.

The reason for this difficulty, I believe, was that nobody can
comprehend clearly what logic is who does not know its nearest
genus, and subject, and end from which the differences are derived. The subject however of logic no one has so far understood
except Averroës alone. The end we cannot know perfectly as

From: *Opera logica.*

long as we do not know the subject. As for the genus of logic, that must be learned before all else, there is great dispute among philosophers. For some have considered logic an art, others neither a science nor an art, but a faculty: others, accepting none of these definitions, have thought it nothing but an instrument. We have therefore considered it worth while to write on this topic and state our view, especially since it differs very widely from other opinions, by first investigating the nearest genus of logic: then its end, and subject, and finally dividing logic as a whole into parts and treating the purpose and basis of each part.

In our investigation into the nature of logic it is necessary for us to begin with the division of things, if the diversity of disciplines too, and the nature of particular things, are derived therefrom. All things are divided into two classes by Aristotle in section three, chapter six of the *Nicomachean Ethics*. He asserts that some are necessary and eternal, others, contingent, that may be or not. Necessary he terms all those things that exist always through themselves and never become, and those that do become but not by our will but by nature operating through certain causes. For these latter things, although in as much as they are particulars are not always, yet are reduced to universality, and are considered to depend necessarily on certain causes so that their existence, or non-existence, their becoming or non-becoming, is not within the determination of our will, and to that extent can be called necessary and eternal. It is evident that all natural things are of this kind.

It remains for the other parts of the division to contain the things that depend on man's will, since to perform them or not rests with our discretion: therefore they have no necessity, but are called contingent and can then exist or not exist at our will. Since then it is necessary to treat every discipline that is informative as some thing, two kinds of disciplines arise, one of which deals with the things that are not performed by us, but either exist always, or follow certain other causes placed beyond our will. Any other kind of discipline I myself cannot conceive. For if any other one is established beyond these two, it will certainly be nothing, since it treats of nothing. And so some disciplines treat of necessary things, that cannot be accomplished by us, while others treat of the things that are performed by us. This two-fold treatment must necessarily have a two-fold end, and a two-fold purpose. For we are mentally considering something in order to get to know it, or to effect it, or to learn how to effect it. If anyone can think of any other purpose, let him acknowledge it openly. For I can conceive or imagine no other.

These two different ends are deduced from the very nature of things. For the things that we cannot effect, we contemplate only in order to get to know them, not to effect them. For it would be stupid for a man to want to do what can in no manner whatever be done by him. But the things that we can do, we consider with the intention of effecting them. But if we appear to be in quest of a knowledge of these things too, the main purpose however is not knowledge, but the operation. For we mentally search for those things, in order to be able to perform something through our knowledge that we either could not accomplish without knowledge or with difficulty and inferiorly. For this reason, speaking of moral discipline, Aristotle rightly said in section three, chapter three of his *Ethics*, that the end of moral discipline was not knowledge but action. Under these circumstances, the disciplines that involve necessary things for the sole purpose of a knowledge of them are properly called contemplative sciences. For they are in search of science as a contemplation only, not an operation: and an elaborate classification is made of all things that are in the universe. But we must dispense with an exposition of this, as it is not germane to our purpose. For the present, let it suffice to say that there are, in short, three contemplative sciences: divine science, that is called metaphysics, mathematics, and natural science.

Divine science considers subjects totally removed from matter. Natural science treats of material things, in so far as they are material. Mathematics treats of subjects that are material, because without matter they would not exist. However, since the essence of these things does not depend on sensible matter, they are separated from it by intellectual consideration. If no other kind of things that do not depend on our will, except these three, is granted, it follows that no other science exists except these three that we have just named. All the other disciplines involving those things that can be performed and not performed equally by the human will are called contingent by Aristotle, if we wish to use the proper term, but should not be called sciences, because they do not have knowledge as an end, as we stated; and also because that knowledge, not being of necessary things, cannot be called a science. For a science is a sure and enduring knowledge of things simply necessary and everlasting: as Aristotle declares in the memorable sixth section of his *Ethics*, where he defines it as a demonstrative habit. In the first book of his *Posterior Analytics* he says that science is a knowledge of a thing through its own cause together with intellectual certainty, that otherwise cannot be that thing on account of that cause. Aristotle also explains in that passage that a two-fold necessity is required in science: one in the known thing itself, which is simply necessary, and cannot be otherwise: the other, in the mind of the person knowing, who must be quite sure that the thing cannot be otherwise. If one of these two conditions is removed, we have no knowledge, as though our knowledge were of contingent things or necessary even, but with intellectual uncertainty and hesitation.

Of contingent things, depending on our will, there are two kinds, as Aristotle shows in section four, chapter six of his *Ethics*, from which two classes also of disciplines associated with them, arise. Of those that are performed by us, some are properly said to be done, others to be caused. Action of those things occurs, when they refer to virtue and vice, whose intellective habit is called prudence, and moral discipline is entirely involved in them. Efficient cause occurs, when things refer to material operations, whose intellective habit is called art. Because Aristotle, defining prudence and art, says that prudence is an active habit with true reason, while art is an efficient habit with true reason: between action and efficient cause there is the distinction, that is between the end, and those things that are before the end, or, as it were, between master and servant. For all the arts that deal with some matter are directed to the happiness of the citizenry, as though they were handmaidens, if the amenities of civil life are furnished by all of them: hence they effect nothing on their own account, but in the cause of happiness. But action is not directed to happiness, but it is happiness itself, according to Aristotle, who declares that happiness is not virtue itself, but action proceeding from the habit of virtue. Therefore action of this kind is dominant, and the end of all causes: all efficient causes on account of their action as though on account of their end are both its servants and its handmaidens.

But a detailed exposition of all these matters is for others to present. For us, let it suffice for the present occasion if we discover the number and differences of the intellective habits. We infer three intellective habits from what has been said, namely: science, prudence, and art. But Aristotle in Book six of the *Ethics* adds two more: understanding and wisdom. Understanding is called a knowledge of principles, whence we derive a knowledge of conclusions. Therefore it has greater certitude and necessity than science, as Aristotle demonstrates in chapter two, Book one of the *Posterior Analytics* and in the last chapter of Book two. Wisdom is a most excellent habit, uniting science with understanding, and, like science, has a beginning, as Aristotle expounds in Book six of the *Ethics*. Since therefore there are five intellective habits, it is quite evident that three are of necessary and eternal things simply, so that they have no place outside them, namely: science, understanding, and wisdom: and that two habits are of contingent things that are based on the decision of our will, namely: prudence and art. Apart from these, Aristotle posited no other intellective habit. On these points we have considered it incumbent to say a few words: because we cannot clearly understand the nature of logical habit without some knowledge of the habits themselves.

Since we are going to speak particularly of two habits, science and art, wherein practically the entire difficulty lies, it should not be forgotten what Aristotle says of science and art in the last chapter of Book two of the *Posterior Analytics*. He says that science comes from being, and art from generation: whereby he wants to indicate what we said a moment ago, that science involves the things that are now, while art regards their cause and generation, that do not yet exist and can be made by us. For the contemplative philosopher wants to produce nothing, but to learn the things that are now. Because in chapter four of Book six of the *Ethics* Aristotle says: All art rests in generation, by which he understands not natural generation, but generation that is created by us through habit of art, as the generation of a couch, a ship, a house, and such like. For these and similar things, that do not yet exist, art, with true reason, shows how to generate and produce.

That the logical habit is intellective we must have no doubt whatever. Knowing then the number of such habits, we have to see on which of them discipline is founded. First of all, there is much doubt whether it is a science. For although almost the entire school of Aristotelians has consistently denied it, yet there were some, both in ancient and in later times, who ventured to assert that logic is a science, even according to Aristotle's views. Now since we think that logic is not a science, we shall try to prove this first of all: not indeed by a multiplicity of arguments, but by reasoning drawn from the nature of the subject itself. If we have undertaken this task in order to instruct and aid, not to dispute, we shall presently find out the truth and bring forward certain important arguments of earlier authorities who asserted that logic is a science, and we shall resolve these arguments.

Since the nature of every discipline depends on the things that are considered in it, if we carefully weigh the subjects treated logically, we shall clearly perceive that it cannot be called a science. The general consensus of opinion is that only the second notions, as they are called, or the secondly understood ideas are treated by the logician, since it seems to be the function of the philosopher rather than the logician to consider the first notions. The first notions are nouns immediately signifying things through the intermediate concepts of the mind, as: animal and man. Or the concepts themselves, of which these names are signs. The second notions are other names imposed on these names, as: genus, species, noun, verb, proposition, syllogism, and other expressions of this kind, or the concepts themselves that are signified through these nouns. By means of the nouns of the first notion a thing immediately signified responds outside the mind, and for this reason they are not considered our task. For no one would assert that heaven, the elements, animals, and plants are a human operation: for though all names were invented by man, and were imposed on things by their own will, yet when we regard that which is signified by such a name, it is not said to be done by us, as we do not assert that an animal was made by man, although men were the inventors of this word. But no one would deny that the second notions are our work and that they are figments of our mind. A man and a horse exist, even when we do not think about them: but genus and proposition and syllogism, wherever they are, do not exist at all, if we do not think of them, except when they are made by us. The reason for this difference is that the nouns of the first notion signify things as they exist. For this reason that which is signified by them, even when we do not think of it, is said to exist, as without any thinking on our part, we see an animal, plants, and the elements existing. But the nouns of the second notions signify things as they are mentally conceived by us, not as they are outside the mind. Hence they are rather concepts of concepts, that signify the concepts of things: whence they are known as second concepts and second notions. Therefore they are rightly called the operations and the figments of our mind. All these explanations will become clearer by means of examples. When we consider that Socrates and Plato and Callias are similar in this respect, that they are men, we mentally form a common concept of man, that is called a concept of the thing, hence the first concept and the first notion. Later, when we consider that this concept is something common that is predicated of many not naturally different but merely numerically, and that for this reason we call the concept of man and every other similar concept a species, then we imagine a second notion. For we impose a second noun on the first noun and in the concept of the thing we form another second concept.

In the same way, when we consider that a man, an ox, and a horse are different in nature yet similar in the fact of being animals, we form a general concept of animal, that immediately signifies things and is called the first concept. Then, when we regard this concept and say that it is predicated of many things different in species in each single case and we call all such a genus, we form a second concept in the first, and a second notion in the first one, that is, in the concept of the thing. On this account it should be carefully observed, in order to understand properly what is usually asserted by everyone, that the logician considers these three operations of the mind: apprehension of simple things, composition and division, and ratiocination. For if we understand simply, that the logician considers these operations of our mind, we are led astray: because this treatment is quite remote from the logical faculty, since it refers only to treatises on the mind, where the discussion revolves around the nature of the human mind and its operations. But it should be realized that the logician considers three degrees of second notions, that are generated and produced from the triple operation of the mind by our own mind. For, as we just said, these second notions do not signify things as they are, but as they are mentally conceived by us.

Now our conception is three-fold, for we either apprehend a thing simply, from which apprehension the formation of the notions of genus, species, noun, verb, and similar ideas arises. Or we compare the concept of one thing with the concept of another thing by combining them, or separating them, an operation that we call a proposition, that is divided into affirmation and negation. Therefore a proposition is a second notion, that begins with the second operation of the mind. Or finally we proceed from this to that, and deduce one thing from another, an operation that we call ratiocination, as though we were generating this second notion in the third operation of the mind.

Having cleared up these points, let us argue as follows: The entire treatment of logic deals with second notions and those notions are our concern, and they can be, or not be, at our discretion. They are therefore not necessary things, but contingent, and so do not come under science, since science is a question of necessary things only, as was said. The assertion of the Romans that logic is a science, because it is the rational science, is ridiculous, since by this very argument it is proved that it is not a science: as when a person who wanted to deduce from the fact that some man was dead, that he was a man, demonstrated by cogent reasoning that he was not a man. For just as in the adjective *dead* there is contrariety that destroys the entire nature of the man and makes only the name *man* equivocal, so too the same argument holds good for the adjective rational: since those things that the Romans call beings of reason, do not come under science, as they are not necessary. Therefore to call a science rational is just like calling science moral, or medical, or constructive: and whoever should attempt to show that there is thus some new kind of science, would really prove by the most convincing argument that it is not a science. Hence in this respect there is no distinction between logical things and things produced by art. For if Aristotle calls things fashioned by art contingent, since they are made by us, why should we deny that logical things are contingent, which are similarly made by us, operating with free intellectual discretion? For though they are not material nor produced through corporeal instruments, like things fashioned by art, but constructed by mere mental cogitation, they cannot on that account be called necessary: since to be necessary either there is no contingent in that which is material, or not material: or in that which can, or cannot, be produced by us operating freely, as we have explained. Hence it is evident that logic is more like the arts than the sciences in respect of considered things: for the sciences deal simply with necessary things: while logic and all the arts deal with contingencies, that are produced by us. On this account too, by reason of its purpose, the end of logic is like the arts, and unlike the sciences. For the end of the sciences is solely a knowledge of considered things, while the end of the arts is not knowledge, but practice. For if they have any knowledge, they direct it to practice. It would be a stupid and puerile attitude for anyone to believe that a knowledge of those things that can be done by us is ever sought by us to the extent of our wishing to rest contented solely with it. For there would thus develop an almost infinite number of useless disciplines, although we can master very many that have no prestige in themselves nor have any other use. A knowledge of such things then is not sought by us for their own sake: but in order to find out some method or a proper method, and using this method to better advantage. It is clear that all the arts are of this kind: for they teach how many instruments are made by us that we may use afterward for the benefit of human lives. That logic then is not a science, and the reason therefor, is evident.

We are forced to grant and maintain these arguments, deduced from the nature of the subject itself: and they can be confirmed too by the very clear testimony of Aristotle. For Aristotle, in Book I of the *Prior Analytics,* at the beginning of Sections 2 and 3, asserts that he is expounding the origin of syllogisms, that is, how they are to be produced and how easily they can be made by us, with a view to our becoming adept in their production. But who could not see that all expository art is such? For if anyone wrote that art was edifying, he would be merely explaining how a house should be built well and easily, and similarly with other arts. There is another very convincing topic in Aristotle for the confirmation of this view, in chapter 9, Book I of the *Topics,* where Aristotle offers a definition of the dialectic problem, drawn from various sources, and lists three kinds of problems: active, contemplative, and logical. An active problem is: Is pleasure good? A contemplative problem: Is the world eternal? A logical problem: Does there exist a fourth figure of syllogisms?

Is the middle of a demonstration a definition of the subject or of affection? And similar questions. The arts too have their own problems, questions about doubtful points that are proposed for discussion. However, Aristotle mentions none of these in the passage, since he wants to dwell solely on the types of problems that can come under the consideration of philosophers.

Philosophers are wont to discuss and write about active matters, which are called the active part of philosophy, and about topics relating to contemplative philosophy: and also about questions on logic. For logic is an operation and invention of the philosophers. But respecting the themes that concern the productive arts, philosophers do not debate qua philosophers. These three kinds of problems, then, Aristotle is prepared to accept. He does not use their specific names, however, but writes about them through their specific characteristics, namely: through the purposes of the three different disciplines. For he declares that other problems in themselves regard choice and avoidance, which are problems concerning choice: for their purpose is not knowledge, but choice, or avoidance, that is, action or non-action. Other problems, he asserts, tend through themselves toward truth and knowledge, meaning speculative problems, whose sole purpose is a knowledge of the truth. Finally he says that others are an end to both parts of philosophy, that is, dialectic problems. For they are instruments, used by both active and contemplative philosophy. And so Aristotle's view is that there is no science of dialectic things, since by assuming this position he separates speculative problems from active and dialectic problems, and only speculative problems have knowledge for their purpose. But if some opponent should say that it can happen that the same thing should refer to other things and should be desirable for itself, just as we desire health both for itself and as helpful in the challenging activities of life. For this reason it appears that the same statement can be made of logic, that it merits recognition for itself, because it transmits a knowledge of dialectic matters, and also that it is an instrument useful for both parts of philosophy. Since then these two definitions do not mutually conflict, Aristotle says that logic is an instrument of philosophy, but does not on that account deny that it is a science in itself and worthy of recognition. This reply and Aristotle's words that we have just expounded, they do not accept, and far less so the other statements that here follow: Some problems it is expedient to know only in order to choose, or to avoid, as: Whether pleasure should be chosen or not. Other problems are for knowledge only, as: Is the world eternal or not? Some by themselves are for neither of these purposes, but are supports for some of them. For generally we do not want to know them for themselves but for the sake of others, in order to learn something particular through them.

Certainly Aristotle could not enunciate this truth more clearly and refute the error of his opponents: for he declares that dialectic matters are not worthy of recognition by themselves, but on account of other subjects: because they lead to the attainment of knowledge of those things that are worthy of recognition. This view is excellently expressed by Alexander in his preface to the first book of the *Topics*. He was quite well aware that it was Aristotle's opinion that logic is not a science, because it does not transmit a knowledge of anything.

From the same passage in Aristotle it is assumed that the Greek view is the best, while that of the Romans is the least acceptable. For although both admit that logic is duplex: one kind called by the Romans apodeictic, by the Greeks, divorced from things: the other kind termed by the Romans pragmatic or involving usage, and by the Greeks applied to things or to philosophy, still the Greeks deny that logic is a didactic science or a part of philosophy, but say it is only an instrument of philosophy: but they admit that it is an applied science belonging to philosophy. The Romans on the other hand say that what is instructional is a science, what is applied is not, but is an instrument. Nothing is more false than this view, as our reasoning has clearly shown and as Aristotle's memorable words demonstrate. For it is certain that logic is a science only in so far as it produces a science, while in so far as it does not produce a science, to that extent it is not a science. In the passage cited Aristotle partly asserts that logic produces a science, and partly denies it. He denies it *per se,* and asserts it on account of other things that are known through logic: as if to say that it produces a science remotely, not immediately. In his dialectic treatises that are a didactic logic, nothing worthy of recognition in itself is treated: hence, expository logic produces no science by itself and immediately: but it does so remotely, for it can be applied to philosophy and to things that should be known and it produces a knowledge of those things. Who then is so blind as not to see that Aristotle here manifestly says that logic taken by itself, and detached from things, and called didactic, is not a science? But applied to the sciences, and put to use, it really is a science? If an applied science produces a science, one that is detached presents no science of anything. But we want to know how to interpret the fact that logic applied to philosophy is a part of philosophy and a science: but it is not such a science as to be established as a certain science beyond other sciences, that is called logic, if another science does not exist except for these three contemplative sciences: but is is called a science in so far as it is such a science to which it is applied: for what else is natural philosophy but logic applied to natural subjects? The whole of natural philosophy is an accumulation of many propositions, inductions, and syllogisms formed in natural things. So we speak of geometry, arithmetic, and other sciences. For this reason applied logic does not retain the name of logic but is termed a science and takes its name from the things to which it is applied and is called a natural science, or arithmetic, or some other name. It seems to philosophers that what happened is what usually happens to many persons going on a long journey. Before they proceed on a journey, they plan their future trip, considering by what means they can reach more conveniently and more expeditiously their proposed destination. Presently they find a way, discover the means, and proceed on their journey, carrying out their original plan and putting it to use. In a similar sense the philosopher, eager to attain a knowledge of things, first plans the method that can direct him to it. On finding the method, he proceeds thereby to contemplation and is said to put to use his original plan. Speculation about a journey is the logic that is called instructional: its execution and practice is philosophy itself: and just as a person plans a future journey, without starting out, so when the philosopher transmits a knowledge of logic, he still does not present any science of anything, but expounds only precepts and a method for the acquisition of science. He then begins to know, or to transmit knowledge, when he begins to use it, and to philosophize according to the habit of logic. So the traveler too begins to travel, when he begins to carry out the plan he conceived and to use it. From what we have just said we may deduce that logic, simply so called, is not a science. For although science is said to be founded in practice, it is still not called logic any longer, but natural philosophy, or mathematics. But logic properly so termed is that which expounds and transmits precepts, and plans a future procedure, but it is not a science.

Having discovered the truth, it is appropriate for us to solve the arguments of others, that appear to conflict with this view: this will not be difficult. Two arguments are brought forward by Duns Scotus in the first question of the universals. In one argument he demonstrates that didactic logic is a science, as follows: The logician is knowledgeable. Therefore logic is a science. He proves his assumption thus: The logician demonstrates. Therefore he is knowledgeable. He demonstrates this assumption too: therefore logic has all the elements that are required for presenting a proof: for it has its own subject, namely, the syllogism: it has its affections that are demonstrated of it: it has principles through which they are demonstrated, for by the definition of syllogism many factors are shown to be in it. And so to the logician there is nothing to prevent him from being able to construct demonstrations in logical subjects.

In another argument he proves that logic based on practice is not a science: logic applied to philosophy proceeds through the general channels: but science springs from its own, not from general sources. Therefore this logic is not a science. He proves the minor proposition by the authority of Aristotle, who in many passages of natural philosophy, when using probable and general reasons that do not produce a science, calls them dialectic and distinguishes them from demonstrative reasons as though they were opposites: because they stem from general reasons, while demonstrative reasons stem from their own.

These are Duns Scotus' arguments, whose fatuity is easily demonstrated. The first argument, if it were valid, would have a place in all the practical arts no less than in logic: for if we assert that art teaches something, as medicine, or is edifying, it too would have its own subject in regard to which it would demonstrate many things through the particular principles of that art. For every discipline occurs through preconceived things, and through discussion from the known to the unknown. What happens then? Will an informative art that teaches be a speculative science? Scotus' first argument therefore must be refuted. For the logician is neither knowledgeable nor does he demonstrate, nor does he possess all the requirements for a true practical demonstration of true science: for he does not have a subject such as is required for a contemplative science. Science demands an eternal, not a contingent subject, that can be and not be, at our will. But a syllogism is an operation and an invention of ours: therefore it is not a suitable subject for a science, nor would it be worth while to make an effort to discover it in logic, if it were not a useful instrument for the acquisition of knowledge in philosophy. Moreover, it is far from true that the syllogism is propounded to the logician as a subject is postulated that has to be known, or rather that has to be originated and effected, as we have already shown: for we are seeking to find out the origin of the syllogism in order to make us capable of originating it and then using it, not merely find out what it is.

What we say of the syllogism must be said too of demonstration and of the other topics of logic. But if Duns Scotus should propose this objection: Does not the logician infer many necessary conclusions from necessary principles? He is then concerned about necessary, not contingent things. This objection has a place in the practical arts as well as in logic. For any instructional art, as building and medicine, takes certain necessary propositions from which it deduces necessary inferences. But if we consider properly, this is not necessity simply so called, but only an established end. For when an end is set, all other inferences are deduced therefrom, as: when a house is to be constructed for habitable purposes and for protection against cold and heat, it must be built of such and such material. So in the case of logic we say that, if an affirmative universal is to be inferred, it is necessary for a syllogism to be formed in the first mode of the first figure. If a perfect knowledge of the conclusion is to be produced through the syllogism, it is necessary for the syllogism to be formed from necessary propositions, and primary ones, and the causes of the conclusions. This entire necessity therefore comes from the constitution of the end, or, as they say, from the denotation: for, speaking simply, no necessity compels us to form a syllogism, or to acquire a knowledge of anything through a demonstration. However, when we have decided that knowledge must be pursued from this point of decision, it follows that it is necessary to assume such propositions, but it is not necessary for us simply to pursue knowledge: as it is not simply necessary for us to build, but once we have decided that a house should be constructed, it follows that it is necessary to secure such material for the construction.

The second argument, in which Duns Scotus proves that logic applied to things is not a science, is so foolish that I cannot cease wondering how a scholar is either so confused or wants to confuse others by the most fallacious reasoning through the ambiguity of words. For when Aristotle calls the arts that employ slight general reasons in philosophy, logical arts, he understands by this, probable arguments, that he usually distinguishes from analytical reasons and those derived from their own principles of science. For he takes logic not for the entire discipline of logic, but merely for its topical faculty. The reason why he calls this logic, when it is the general name for the art of logic, must be investigated, since I have observed that it has never been clarified by anyone.

There are two parts of logic among others, as we shall show later on. The demonstrative part, that is expounded in the *Posterior Analytics*: and the dialectic part, that is discussed in the *Topics*. There is this distinction between them, that while the demonstrative part teaches precepts and rules, it is not a science but an instrument of the sciences: but as it is applied to things, it is really a science, not indeed the science called logic, but it becomes a natural science, like geometry or any other: Since a natural science is merely that part of logic that is called demonstrative, applied for the contemplation of natural things and for securing a knowledge of those things from their own principles. But if this is true, as it certainly is completely so, I do not see, if we turn Scotus' argument against himself, what rebuttal Scotus can make to this. For he declares that logic applied to philosophy is not a science, since it does not produce knowledge, as it proceeds through generalities, not through properties. But let us take the logic treated in the *Posterior Analytics,* and let us posit the latter type in use in natural things. Shall we not discover, through the former, natural things from their own principles? Then this latter kind of logic will furnish a knowledge of those things. For to offer a knowledge of a thing through its own principles is to produce a science of it: therefore it will be a science: because science produces.

The topical faculty is not a science not only because it does not expound, but it is not based on use either. For when it is applied to any science, it does not assume the mediate properties of that science, but the general ones, that do not produce a science. From this distinction too arises the distinction of name. For the art of demonstration, when applied to any science, proceeds from the ultimate and particular principles of that science to a demonstration of things that are unknown: and mixes with these things or this science and is thrust into it so that it passes into its nature, and, losing its name of logic, takes on the name of a certain other science that prescribes for it the consideration of a certain nature of the subject, and is no longer called logic, but geometry, or arithmetic, or natural science.

The topical art, if applied to natural things, does not penetrate them intimately, or take its principles from their own nature. Hence it is not said to be intruded into natural things or natural science, nor does it take the name of that science: because it uses the middle generalities, which have no essential connection with the nature of these things, and can be applied to other things also no less than to natural things. Hence it is that they cannot be called natural principles, for every argument is named from the middle: therefore when a middle is common to many sciences, it is called the common principle, and takes its name from no certain science. Therefore since principles of this type do not assume a new name, they retain their own name, and are called logical principles. From these facts we deduce that it is the same, in natural things, whether we say analytical or demonstrative principles. For natural principles are so called when they are drawn from the specific nature of natural things: but it is not the same in the case of natural things as saying topical or logical principles and natural principles. For they are common to other sciences also, and cannot be termed natural. For this reason, care should be taken that no one, on account of what we have previously said, should fall into error: for when we said that expository logic, detached from things, is not a science but an instrument of philosophy, we understood this of all logic and all its parts. But when we said that logic applied to things is a science, this assertion was not intended to be accepted of all parts of logic, but only of the principal part, that is contained in the *Posterior Analytics* and other earlier treatises that were written for that particular purpose. For dialectics can never be called a science, neither when it is detached from things, nor when applied. But some one might doubt what we said, that logic detached from things is an instrument, but applied to them, is no longer an instrument but a science: for the nature of every instrument consists in its purpose and use; hence every instrument must be properly termed so, when based on use, as a sword should most properly be called an instrument, when it cuts something by its action. It therefore appears absurd and foreign to the nature of the instrument that, as we said, logic should be an instrument of philosophy, but based on use and applied to philosophy, it is no longer an instrument.

To this objection the reply must be that there is one nature for corporeal things, and another for spiritual things. A corporeal instrument cannot become that of which it is the instrument, as, for example: If a sword is used to cut bread, the sword cannot become the act of cutting itself, since a body cannot pass into a non-body and into an accident, nor can it happen that the bread cuts itself: because there is neither penetration of bodies, nor can one body change into another body without alteration. But spiritual things, by application and mutual conjunction, usually become one and the same thing, as we infer from Aristotle in Book 3, *De Anima*. Here he states that our intellective mind becomes the thing itself that is understood: because the understanding is the reception of the non-corporeal and spiritual species: accordingly that which understands and that which is understood and the understanding itself are the same. It is therefore not surprising if the habit of logic, when communicated to the spiritual concepts of things and applied to their contemplation, which is philosophy itself, becomes itself philosophy and that becomes an instrument of which it was said to be an instrument. In these cases then the nature of the instrument cannot be seen distinctly from that of which it is the instrument, unless it is separated from it and its use. Hence when logic is detached from things and withdrawn from use, it is found to be an instrument of philosophy. But when it is put to use, it is immediately a philosophy. However, corporeal instruments, both detached from use and applied to use, are called instruments for the reasons stated by us.

So far we have shown that instructional logic is not a science: for all that we have said up to this point was directed solely to this demonstration. In the same way it is shown that logic is necessary for the things that come under the heading of science and those whose understanding it is to be of the same genus and character: for science is a habit of conclusions, while understanding is a habit of principles from which the conclusions themselves are drawn: since then it is a science of simply necessary things, it follows that it is an understanding too no less of necessary things. For a necessary conclusion cannot be known to us through a syllogism, unless it is deduced from necessary principles, as Aristotle shows in Book I of the *Posterior Analytics*. Hence if logical things are not necessary simply, it follows that the habits of logic as it is not a science, so it is not understanding. Similarly it is shown that it is not philosophy, since philosophy is nothing but science along with understanding. But neither can it be called prudence, for Aristotle defines prudence as a habit with correct reasoning, if it concerns action, not knowledge, and no one ever asserted that logic is of this type: since it rather concerns knowledge and supplies the instruments of knowledge. Since all these explanations are sufficiently clear in themselves, they must now be concluded and we must pass on to other matters.

It follows that we must consider whether logic is an art, for someone might question this because of what has been said previously. For although we showed that it was not a science, we seemed to call it an art and to reduce it to the habit of an art. However, if we consider the definition of an art as presented by Aristotle in chapter 4, Book 6 of the *Ethics*, we shall see that logic is an effective habit with correct reasoning: now we are properly said to effect those things that we produce externally. Aristotle therefore in Book 2 declares that an art is the principle of operation in some other thing: by this distinction he separates art from nature, because nature is the principle of an operation received in that in which nature is inherent, that our writers term immanent operation: art on the other hand is the principle of an operation in something else, that is called transient, because in the operation of art itself there is no inherent art, but it is external, namely in the mind of the craftsman. This view we find also in Book 6 Aristotle's *Ethics*. Hence it is that every artifact is corporeal and material: for an operation produced in something else must be received in it as if in the subject matter. For an operation in another thing signifies this, while being received in another thing cannot be an operation of art, except in a natural body. Hence every operation of art is corporeal: and this operation is material too, by reason of the parts of our body, as the hands, or feet, with which we operate as with instruments. By virtue of all such distinctions art and logic are different and separate: for logic is a habit of the mind: not, however, effective of any operation external to the mind, but in the mind itself. Therefore its operation is immanent, and completely so, and truly immanent: because in the mind itself in which the habit of logic indwells, the operation remains without any communication with the body. There is also operation without any maker: for it is received in the understanding itself, that employs no corporeal organ, as Aristotle explains in section 6, Book 3 of his *De Anima.* He asserts that the intellective soul alone is the locale of the species, because there is sense through the reception of the species and its endurance. However, the species is not received in the sensible soul itself, but in an animate organ, as color is received not in vision, but in the eye: but the intellective soul uses no corporeal organ in receiving the species, but receives them itself: accordingly of all parts of the soul it alone is called the place for all species. For such is the only meaning of Aristotle's words in section 6, Book 3 of the *De Anima.*

Logic then is a habit that without any matter whatever operates both by reason of the organ and by reason of the recipient. So it cannot be called an art, in the true acceptance of the term. We should not deny, however, that in a broad sense it can be called not only an art, but a science too: for the term *science* is taken in a wide sense, for every type of knowledge whatsoever, not only logic, but active philosophy too and every instructional art can be termed a science: because it supplies some knowledge. For this reason medicine is frequently called a science. Similarly, if the term *art* is taken in a wide sense for any technical cogitation or operation of our mind (it is called technical when it is arranged in order and proceeds toward its determined purpose through convenient and suitable media), not only logic, but both active and contemplative philosophy as well can be termed an art, as Averroës is occasionally wont to call the speculative arts. These are however improperly called arts, since they refer to no production of any purpose, and involve contemplation only. On this account the significance of this term is very wide, since it extends to the contemplative sciences as well. It is more restricted, and more properly so called, when, with the sole exception of the contemplative sciences, it comprehends all the other disciplines, but particularly the properties, when it is taken solely for the effective arts, as Aristotle, in chapter 4, Book 6 of the *Ethics,* interpreted and defined the term art.

Logic then in this third mode cannot be called an art: in the first place however and secondly the name of *art* suits it, but by this name its nearest genus is not expressed, but its remote and very general genus: nor do we yet know under what intellective habit the habit of logic should be established: since art, which is placed by Aristotle among the intellective habits, does not embrace logic, as we have shown.

Acknowledgments

Abailard, Peter. Tr. by H. E. Wedeck from *Sic et Non*.

Albertus Magnus. Tr. & edited by Richard McKeon from *Parva Naturalia, De Intellectu et Intelligibili*; in "Selections from Medieval Philosophers" Volume I, copyright Charles Scribner's Sons, New York.

Al-Farabi. From "The Main Problems of Abu Nasr Al-Farabi."

Anselm of Canterbury. Tr. & edited by Richard McKeon from *Dialogus de Veritate*; in "Selections from Medieval Philosophers" Volume I, copyright Charles Scribner's Sons, New York.

Aquinas, Saint Thomas. From "Truth," Volume I; tr. by R. W. Mulligan; copyright, the Henry Regnery Company, Chicago.

Aristotle. Tr. by W. D. Ross from "Metaphysics"; The Clarendon Press, Oxford.

Arnauld, Antoine. Tr. by H. E. Wedeck from *Logique de Port-Royal*.

Bacon, Francis. From *Novum Organum*.

Bergson, Henri. Tr. by M. L. Andison; "Introduction to Metaphysics," Philosophical Library, New York.

Berkeley, George. From "Principles of Human Knowledge."

Bernouilli, Jacob. Tr. by H. E. Wedeck from *Ars Conjectandi*.

Boethius. Tr. by H. E. Wedeck from *De Syllogismo Hypothetico*.

Bolzano, Bernard. *Paradoxes of the Infinite*. Yale University Press, New Haven, Tr. by Donald A. Steele.

Boole, George. From *The Mathematical Analysis of Logic*, Philosophical Library, New York, and Basil Blackwell Ltd., Oxford.

Bosanquet, Bernard. *Logic*. Clarendon Press, Oxford, 1888.

Buridanus. *Dialectic Elements*, tr. by H. E. Wedeck from *Summula de Dialectica.*.

Capella, Martianus. Tr. by H. E. Wedeck from *De Nuptiis Philologiae et Mercurii*.

Carnap, Rudolf. Reprinted from "International Encyclopedia of Unified Science," edited by Neurath; by permission of University of Chicago Press. Copyright 1937.

Carroll, Lewis. *Symbolic Logic*.

Cassiodorus, Magnus Aurelius. Tr. by H. E. Wedeck from *De institutione devinarum et humanarum litterarum*.

Clauberg, Johannes. Tr. by H. E. Wedeck from *Logica Vetus et Nova*.

Descartes, René. From "The Meditations and Selections from the Principles of René Descartes," The Open Court Publishing Company, La Salle, Illinois.

Dewey, John. From "Essays in Honor of William James"; Longmans Green & Co., New York, 1908; "Essays in Experimental Logic," University of Chicago Press, Chicago, 1916; "Influence of

816

Darwin on Philosophy," Holt & Co., New York, 1910, reprinted by permission of Holt, Rinehart and Winston, Inc.

Epictetus. From "Epictetus, The Discourses and Manual," tr. by P. E. Metheson; The Clarendon Press, Oxford.

Euclid. From *Stoicheia.*

Fonseca, Pedro. Tr. by H. E. Wedeck from *Institutionum dialecticarum libri.*

Frege, Gottlob, "Translations from the Writings of Gottlob Frege," tr. by Peter Geach & Max Black; Philosophical Library, New York, and Basil Blackwell Ltd., Oxford.

Geulincx, Arnold. Tr. by H. E. Wedeck from *Logica fundamentis suis, a quibus hactenus collapsa fuerat restituta.*

Hegel, Georg Wilhelm Friedrich. From "Encyclopedia of Philosophy," tr. by Gustav Emil Mueller; Philosophical Library, New York.

Hispanus, Petrus. Tr. by H. E. Wedeck from *Summulae logicales.*

Hume, David. From "An Enquiry Concerning Human Understanding."

Husserl, Edmund. Tr. by W. R. B. Gibson from *Ideen zu einer reinen Phänomenologie und phänomenologischen Philosophie;* "Ideas," Reprinted with permission of The Macmillan Company, New York. First published in English by Allen & Unwin.

James, William. From "Pragmatism," Longmans, Green & Co., New York, 1907; and David McKay Co.; reprinted by permission of Paul R. Reynolds & Son, 599 Fifth Avenue, New York 17, N. Y.

Jungius, Joachim. Tr. by H. E. Wedeck from *Logica Hamburgensis.*

Kant, Immanuel. From *Kritik der reinen Vernunft.*

Keynes, John Neville. *Studies and Exercises in Formal Logic,* Macmillan & Co., London, 1884.

Kierkegaard, Soeren. From "Concluding Un-Scientific Postscript," tr. by David F. Swenson and Walter Lowrie; Princeton University Press, Princeton, N.J., for the American-Scandinavian Foundation, 1944.

Laplace, Pierre Simon de. From "Essai philosophique sur les probabilités," tr. by Frederick Wilson Truscott and Frederick Lincoln Emory.

Leibniz, Gottfried Wilhelm Von. Reprinted from "Gottfried Wilhelm Leibniz: Philosophical Papers and Letters," tr. by Leroy E. Loemker, 2 vols., 1956; University of Chicago Press. Copyright 1956 by University of Chicago.

Locke, John. "Essay Concerning Human Understanding."

Lullus, Raimundus. Tr. by H. E. Wedeck from *Dialectica, seu Logica Nova.*

Mach, Ernst. Tr. by C. M. Williams, and revised by Sidney Waterlow, from *Die Analyse der Empfindungen;* The Open Court Publishing Company, La Salle, Illinois, 1914.

817

Mill, John Stuart. From "A System of Logic," Longmans, Green & Co., London, 1879.

de Morgan, Augustus. From "Formal Logic," Taylor and Walton, London, 1847.

Ockham, William of. Tr. by H. E. Wedeck from *Summa Totius Logicae.*

Parmenides. "Ancilla to the Pre-Socratic Philosophers," ed. and tr. by Kathleen Freeman; Basil Blackwell Ltd., Oxford, 1948, and Harvard University Press, Cambridge, Mass.

Pascal, Blaise. Tr. by H. E. Wedeck from *Les Pensées.*

Peirce, Charles Sanders. From "The Philosophy of Peirce: Selected Writings," ed. Justus Buchler, Routledge & Kegan Paul Ltd., London, 1940; and "Philosophical Writings of Peirce," ed. Justus Buchler, Dover Publications, Inc., New York. From "A Neglected Argument for the Reality of God"; Hibbert Journal, 1908. George Allen & Unwin Ltd.

Plato. *Theaetetus,* tr. by Jowett, The Clarendon Press, Oxford, 1872.

Ramsey, Frank Pumpton. "The Foundations of Mathematics," ed. by R. B. Braithwaite, Routledge & Kegan Paul Ltd., London, 1931.

Ramus, Petrus. Tr. by H. E. Wedeck from *Dialecticae Libri Duo.*

Royce, Josiah. From "Encyclopedia of the Philosophical Sciences," Vol. I, Logic, ed. by Arnold Ruge; The Macmillan Company, London, 1914.

Russell, Bertrand. From "Principles of Mathematics"; W. W. Norton & Company, Inc., New York.

Sartre, Jean-Paul. From "Being and Nothingness," *L'Etre et le Néant;* tr. by Hazel Barnes; Philosophical Library, New York.

Scheibler, Christopher. Tr. by H. E. Wedeck from *Philosophia Compendiosa.*

Schlick, Moritz. From "Causality in Everyday Life and in Recent Science," Section I, in University of California Publications in Philosophy, Vol. 15, 1932; University of California Press.

Schopenhauer, Arthur. *"The World as Will and Idea,"* from "The Philosophy of Schopenhauer," ed. by Irwin Edman, was translated by R. B. Haldane and J. Kemp from *Die Welt als Wille und Vorstellung;* Random House, New York.

Scotus, John Duns. Tr. by H. E. Wedeck from *De Ratione Cognitionis Humanae.*

Spinoza, Benedictus de. Tr. by R. H. M. Elwes from *Ethica.*

Thomasius, Jakob. Tr. by H. E. Wedeck from *Erotemata Logica.*

Whitehead, Alfred North. From "Nature and Life," by permission of the University of Chicago Press, Chicago.

Wittgenstein, Ludwig. From "Tractatus Logico-Philosophicus," Routledge & Kegan Paul Ltd., London.

Zabarella, Jacob. Tr. by H. E. Wedeck from *Opera Logica.*